THE GREATEST WORKS OF RABINDRANATH TAGORE

THE HOME AND THE WORLD

SELECTED SHORT STORIES

SELECTED SHORT STORIES

MY REMINISCENCES

GITANJALI

FP

CLASSICS

Published 2024 by

FiNGERPRINT! CLASSICS
An imprint of Prakash Books India Pvt. Ltd

113/A, Darya Ganj,
New Delhi-110 002
Email: info@prakashbooks.com/sales@prakashbooks.com

 Fingerprint Publishing
 @FingerprintP
 @fingerprintpublishingbooks
www.fingerprintpublishing.com

ISBN: 978 93 8905 336 4

Who are you, reader, reading my poems an hundred years hence?
I cannot send you one single flower from this wealth of the spring, one single streak of gold from yonder clouds.
Open your doors and look abroad.
From your blossoming garden gather fragrant memories of the vanished flowers of an hundred years before.
In the joy of your heart may you feel the living joy that sang one spring morning, sending its glad voice across an hundred years.

—THE GARDENER

Born on May 7, 1861, to Sarada Devi and Debendranath Tagore, a Hindu philosopher and head of the Brahmo Samaj, Rabindranath Tagore was brought up in a literary, intellectual, and social household. He was raised by servants and educated at home by his elder brother. Tagore detested formal education, and later mentioned in *My Reminiscences* (1912)—

"The main object of teaching is not to explain meanings, but to knock at the door of the mind. If any boy is asked to give an account of what is awakened in him at such knocking, he will probably say something very silly. For what happens within is much bigger than what he can express in words. Those who pin their faith on University examinations as a test of all educational results take no account of this fact."

He began writing at an early age. The eleven-year-old Tagore, after his *upanayan* (coming-of-age) rite, set out with his father on an India tour. They spent several weeks at Debendranath's family estate in Shantiniketan, stayed in Amritsar for a month, and then travelled to Dalhousie. During this period, Tagore read English- and Sanskrit-language books, biographies, astronomy, history, modern science, and classical poetry of Kalidasa. While in Amritsar, he accompanied his father regularly to the Golden Temple and was influenced by the Gurbani and Nanak Bani.

After returning to Calcutta, he wrote a couple of poems and articles about Sikhism. The sixteen-year-old wrote his first short story, *Bhikharini (The Beggar Woman)*, in 1877. Published the same year in *Bharati*, it was the first short story written in Bengali language.

As per his father's wish, who wanted him to become a barrister, Tagore travelled to England in 1878 and entered a public school in Brighton, East Sussex. He studied law at the University College London for a brief period, and then returned to Calcutta without a degree.

He continued writing regularly and published stories, novels, and poems. The exposure to English culture influenced his works as he created new styles of drama, music, and poetry. Some of his works published during this period include the musical dramas *Valmiki Pratibha* (1881; *The Genius of Valmiki*) and *Kal Mrigaya* (1882; *The Fateful Hunt*), the poetry collections *Sandhya Sangeet* (1881; *Evening Songs*) and *Bhagna Hriday* (1881; *The Broken Heart*), *Alochana* (1885; *Discussions*), a collection of essays, and the short story *Ghater Katha* (1886; *The River Stairs*). At twenty-two, Tagore married the ten-year-old Mrinalini Devi. They had five children, only three of whom survived.

He moved to Shelaidaha (now a part of Bangladesh) in 1890 to manage his ancestral estates. In the same year, he also published a collection of poems called *Manasi* (*The Heart's Desire*). With youthful romanticism and profound love forming the subject matter of many poems in this collection, it is among his best-known works and marks the maturity of his poetic genius.

The years 1891 to 1895, known as his 'Sadhana' period (named after one of his magazines), was Tagore's most productive period. He produced a number of works during these years. A major part of the eighty-four stories included in his well-known three-volume collection of short stories titled *Golpoguchchho* (*Bunch of Stories*) were written during this period.

Khokababur Pratyabartan (1891; *My Lord, The Baby*), *Postmaster* (1891; *The Postmaster*), *Khata* (1891; *The Exercise Book*), *Sampatti Samarpan* (1891-92; *The Trust Property*), *Kabuliwallah* (1892; *The Cabuliwallah*), *Jibita o Mrita* (1892; *Living or Dead?*), *Chhuti* (1892-93; *The Home-Coming*), *Samasya Paran* (1893; *The Riddle Solved*), *Didi* (1895; *The Elder Sister*), *Kshudhita Pashaan* (1895; *The Hungry Stones*), *Atithi* (1895; *The Guest*) are some of the short stories written during these years. Inspired from his life in the countryside, these stories examine the lives of the poor and common people. Other notable works from this period include *Sonar Tari* (1895; *The Golden Boat*), a poetry collection, and *Chitrangada* (1892; *Chitra*), a play.

Tagore shifted to Shantiniketan in 1901 and established an ashram. The same year, he completed the first draft of his novel *Chokher Bali (Eye Sore)*. Serialized from 1902 to 1903 in *Bangadarshan*, a Bengali literary magazine, it was published in book form in 1903. One of his best-known works, the novel narrates the life of a young widow named Binodini and her relationships with the other three main characters. Tagore emphasised the social issues of child marriage and women literacy in the novel.

In 1909, he published one of his longest novels titled *Gora (Fair-faced)*. Caste, class, nationalism, universalism, feminism, tradition vs modernity, liberation, love and union, were some of the themes meticulously woven in his plots. Tagore started translating his poems into free verse. In August 1910, he published a collection of one hundred and fifty-six poems called *Gitanjali (Song Offerings)*. It was first published in English in 1912 by the Indian Society of London. The English edition, a translation by Tagore himself, contained a total of one hundred and three poems, fifty-three of which were from the Bengali *Gitanjali* and the rest were taken from his drama *Achalayatan* and other poetry collections.

In 1912 and 1913, Tagore travelled abroad with his translated works. A masterpiece, *Gitanjali* took the English world by storm. It was extremely well received, and Tagore was awarded the Nobel Prize in Literature in 1913. It was a major achievement in the history of Indian English literature. Tagore became the first non-European to receive the Nobel Prize in Literature. King George V granted him a knighthood in 1915, which he renounced in 1919 as a protest against the Jallianwala Bagh massacre in Amritsar.

Tagore travelled across the world to give lectures and raised the stature of India abroad. He denounced European imperialism and supported Indian nationalists. He also opposed nationalism, and delivered a series of lectures abroad on the same. His essay 'Nationlism in India' was regarded with contempt. Tagore wrote songs hailing the Indian independence movement. His poem 'Chitto Jetha Bhayshunyo' (Where the Mind is Without Fear), published in 1910, represents the poet's vision of an awakened India. Among his other protest songs were 'Ekla Chalo Re' and 'Amar Sonar Bangla' ('My Golden Bengal'), written during the Swadeshi movement and partition of Bengal in 1905. 'Amar Sonar Bangla' was chosen as the national anthem of Bangladesh.

Tagore composed 'Bharoto Bhagyo Bidhata' ('Dispenser of the destiny of India), a Brahmo hymn dedicated to the Supreme divine who is the dispenser of India's destiny, in 1911. First sung at the annual session of the Indian National Congress in Calcutta on December 27, 1911, it was published the following year in *Tatwabodhini Patrika*, a Brahmo Samaj journal edited by Tagore, under the title 'Bharat Bhagya Bidhata'. The song was translated into English by the poet himself in 1919 and titled 'The Morning Song of India'. On August 14, 1947, the day India attained freedom, the session of the Indian Constituent Assembly, which had assembled as a sovereign body for the first time, closed with a performance of 'Jana Gana Mana'. The first stanza of the five-stanza song was officially announced as the National Anthem of India on January 24, 1950.

Ghôre Baire (*The Home and the World*) was published in 1916. The novel depicts a traditional Indian household and narrates the story of the three main characters, their personal struggles, and the conflict between the ideas of Western culture and the revolt against them. While comparing differing views of truth, the novel also explores the themes of nationalism, religion vs nationalism, illusions, and tradition vs modernism.

Tagore established the college Visva-Bharati in Shantiniketan in December 1921. It was given the status of a university after Indian independence and renamed Visva-Bharati University. Tagore's literary pursuits continued and he kept experimenting with the styles and subjects in his poems, dramas, and stories. Though the last few years of his life were marked by illness, he continued writing and produced some of the finest poems during this period. He breathed his last on August 7, 1941, in his Jorasanko mansion where he was born and raised.

One of the leading figures of Bengali literature, Rabindranath Tagore remains one of the greatest poets the world has ever seen. Versatile, innovative, and experimental, the bibliography of his writing contains more than two hundred works and around two thousand two hundred songs. From poetic dramas, social plays, short stories, philosophical and critical essays, and travelogues to letters, memoirs, lyrics, drawings, and paintings, Tagore's life was marked by uninterrupted literary and artistic creations.

Inspired by the lives of common people and children, his character portrayals were vivid and colourful. Tagore skilfully explored the limitations, faults, imperfections, and peculiarities of the sensitive human relationships. His stories and novels were progressive and way ahead of his time with confident and strong-headed women protagonists who rebelled fearlessly. The charm of the old-world Bengal and the contemporary struggles of the times in which they were written are masterfully woven in his plots.

Many of Tagore's stories and novels have been adapted for film and television. His works continue to be translated into many languages worldwide.

About this Edition

A compilation of the Nobel laureate's literary masterpieces, this edition contains the English translations of his twenty-five classic short stories namely *The River Stairs, The Postmaster, The Cabuliwallah, Living or Dead?, The Supreme Night, The Home-Coming, The Hungry Stones, The Auspicious Vision, Master Mashai,* and *Mashi* among others. Also included is *Gitanjali,* his most celebrated collection of poetry; *My Reminiscences,* his memoir; and the well-known novel, *The Home and The World.*

A small editorial note precedes each work.

Contents

POETRY

MEMOIR

NOVEL

SHORT STORIES

ঘাটের কথা

The River Stairs

[*Ghater Katha* was written in 1886. This translation is taken from *Mashi and Other Stories* (1918), a collection translated by various writers. It has also been translated as *The Ghat's Story* and *The Bathing Ghat's Tale*.]

If you wish to hear of days gone by, sit on this step of mine, and lend your ears to the murmur of the rippling water.

The month of *Ashwin* (September) was about to begin. The river was in full flood. Only four of my steps peeped above the surface. The water had crept up to the low-lying parts of the bank, where the *kachu* plant grew dense beneath the branches of the mango grove. At that bend of the river, three old brick-heaps towered above the water around them. The fishing boats, moored to the trunks of the *bābla* trees on the bank, rocked on the heaving flow-tide at dawn. The path of tall grasses on the sandbank had caught the newly risen sun; they had just begun to flower, and were not yet in full bloom.

The little boats puffed out their tiny sails on the sunlit river. The Brahmin priest had come to bathe with his ritual vessels. The women arrived in twos and threes to draw water. I knew this was the time of Kusum's coming to the bathing stairs.

But that morning I missed her. Bhuban and Swarno mourned at the *ghat*.* They said that their friend had been led away to her

---

* Bathing place

husband's house, which was a place far away from the river, with strange people, strange houses, and strange roads.

In time she almost faded out of my mind. A year passed. The women at the ghat now rarely talked of Kusum. But one evening I was startled by the touch of the long familiar feet. Ah, yes, but those feet were now without anklets, they had lost their old music.

Kusum had become a widow. They said that her husband had worked in some far-off place, and that she had met him only once or twice. A letter brought her the news of his death. A widow at eight years old, she had rubbed out the wife's red mark from her forehead, stripped off her bangles, and come back to her old home by the Ganges. But she found few of her old playmates there. Of them, Bhuban, Swarno, and Amala were married, and gone away; only Sarat remained, and she too, they said, would be wed in December next.

As the Ganges rapidly grows to fullness with the coming of the rains, even so did Kusum day by day grow to the fullness of beauty and youth. But her dull-coloured robe, her pensive face, and quiet manners drew a veil over her youth, and hid it from men's eyes as in a mist. Ten years slipped away, and none seemed to have noticed that Kusum had grown up.

One morning such as this, at the end of a far-off September, a tall, young, fair-skinned Sanyasi, coming I know not whence, took shelter in the Shiva temple in front of me. His arrival was noised abroad in the village. The women left their pitchers behind, and crowded into the temple to bow to the holy man.

The crowd increased day by day. The Sanyasi's fame rapidly spread among the womankind. One day he would recite the Bhagbat, another day he would expound the Gita, or hold forth upon a holy book in the temple. Some sought him for counsel, some for spells, some for medicines.

So months passed away. In April, at the time of the solar eclipse, vast crowds came here to bathe in the Ganges. A fair was held under the bābla tree. Many of the pilgrims went to visit the Sanyasi, and among them were a party of women from the village where Kusum had been married.

It was morning. The Sanyasi was counting his beads on my steps, when all of a sudden one of the women pilgrims nudged another, and said: "Why! He is our Kusum's husband!" Another parted her veil a little in the middle with two fingers and cried out: "Oh dear me! So it is! He is the younger son of the Chattergi family of our village!" Said a third, who made little parade of her veil: "Ah! he has got exactly the same brow, nose, and eyes!" Yet another woman, without turning to the Sanyasi, stirred the water with her pitcher, and sighed: "Alas! That young man is no more; he will not come back. Bad luck to Kusum!"

But, objected one, "He had not such a big beard"; and another, "He was not so thin"; or "He was most probably not so tall." That settled the question for the time, and the matter spread no further.

One evening, as the full moon arose, Kusum came and sat upon my last step above the water, and cast her shadow upon me.

There was no other at the ghat just then. The crickets were chirping about me. The din of brass gongs and bells had ceased in the temple—the last wave of sound grew fainter and fainter, until it merged like the shade of a sound in the dim groves of the farther bank. On the dark water of the Ganges lay a line of glistening moonlight. On the bank above, in bush and hedge, under the porch of the temple, in the base of ruined houses, by the side of the tank, in the palm grove, gathered shadows of fantastic shape. The bats swung from the *chhatim* boughs. Near the houses the loud clamour of the jackals rose and sank into silence.

Slowly the Sanyasi came out of the temple. Descending a few steps of the ghat he saw a woman sitting alone, and was about to go back, when suddenly Kusum raised her head, and looked behind her. The veil slipped away from her. The moonlight fell upon her face, as she looked up.

The owl flew away hooting over their heads. Starting at the sound, Kusum came to herself and put the veil back on her head. Then she bowed low at the Sanyasi's feet.

He gave her blessing and asked: "Who are you?"

She replied: "I am called Kusum."

No other word was spoken that night. Kusum went slowly back to her house which was hard by. But the Sanyasi remained sitting on my steps for long hours that night. At last when the moon passed from the east to the west, and the Sanyasi's shadow, shifting from behind, fell in front of him, he rose up and entered the temple.

Henceforth I saw Kusum come daily to bow at his feet. When he expounded the holy books, she stood in a corner listening to him. After finishing his morning service, he used to call her to himself and speak on religion. She could not have understood it all; but, listening attentively in silence, she tried to understand it. As he directed her, so she acted implicitly. She daily served at the temple— ever alert in the god's worship—gathering flowers for the puja, and drawing water from the Ganges to wash the temple floor.

The winter was drawing to its close. We had cold winds. But now and then in the evening the warm spring breeze would blow unexpectedly from the south; the sky would lose its chilly aspect; pipes would sound, and music be heard in the village after a long silence. The boatmen would set their boats drifting down the current, stop rowing, and begin to sing the songs of Krishna. This was the season.

Just then I began to miss Kusum. For some time she had given up visiting the temple, the ghat, or the Sanyasi.

What happened next I do not know, but after a while the two met together on my steps one evening.

With downcast looks, Kusum asked: "Master, did you send for me?"

"Yes, why do I not see you? Why have you grown neglectful of late in serving the gods?"

She kept silent.

"Tell me your thoughts without reserve."

Half averting her face, she replied: "I am a sinner, Master, and hence I have failed in the worship."

The Sanyasi said: "Kusum, I know there is unrest in your heart."

She gave a slight start, and, drawing the end of her sari* over her face, she sat down on the step at the Sanyasi's feet, and wept.

He moved a little away, and said: "Tell me what you have in your heart, and I shall show you the way to peace."

---

* The sari is the dress of the Hindu woman.

She replied in a tone of unshaken faith, stopping now and then for words: "If you bid me, I must speak out. But, then, I cannot explain it clearly. You, Master, must have guessed it all. I adored one as a god, I worshipped him, and the bliss of that devotion filled my heart to fullness. But one night I dreamt that the lord of my heart was sitting in a garden somewhere, clasping my right hand in his left, and whispering to me of love. The whole scene did not appear to me at all strange. The dream vanished, but its hold on me remained. Next day when I beheld him he appeared in another light than before. That dream-picture continued to haunt my mind. I fled far from him in fear, and the picture clung to me. Thenceforth my heart has known no peace—all has grown dark within me!"

While she was wiping her tears and telling this tale, I felt that the Sanyasi was firmly pressing my stone surface with his right foot.

Her speech done, the Sanyasi said:

"You must tell me whom you saw in your dream."

With folded hands, she entreated: "I cannot."

He insisted: "You must tell me who he was."

Wringing her hands she asked: "Must I tell it?"

He replied: "Yes, you must."

Then crying, "You are he, Master!" she fell on her face on my stony bosom, and sobbed.

When she came to herself, and sat up, the Sanyasi said slowly: "I am leaving this place tonight that you may not see me again. Know that I am a Sanyasi, not belonging to this world. *You* must forget me."

Kusum replied in a low voice: "It will be so, Master."

The Sanyasi said: "I take my leave."

Without a word more Kusum bowed to him, and placed the dust of his feet on her head. He left the place.

The moon set; the night grew dark. I heard a splash in the water. The wind raved in the darkness, as if it wanted to blow out all the stars of the sky.

পোস্টমাস্টার

The Postmaster

[*Postmaster* was written in 1891. The first English edition appeared
in the collection *Mashi and Other Stories* (1918). This version is taken
from *Stories from Tagore* (1918).]

The postmaster first took up his duties in the village of
Ulapur. Though the village was a small one, there was an
indigo factory nearby, and the proprietor, an Englishman,
had managed to get a post office established.

Our postmaster belonged to Calcutta. He felt like a fish out of
water in this remote village. His office and living room were in a
dark thatched shed, not far from a green, slimy pond, surrounded on
all sides by a dense growth.

The men employed in the indigo factory had no leisure;
moreover, they were hardly desirable companions for decent folk.
Nor is a Calcutta boy an adept in the art of associating with others.
Among strangers he appears either proud or ill at ease. At any rate,
the postmaster had but little company; nor had he much to do.

At times he tried his hand at writing a verse or two. That the
movement of the leaves and the clouds of the sky were enough to fill
life with joy—such were the sentiments to which he sought to give
expression. But God knows that the poor fellow would have felt it
as the gift of a new life, if some genie of the *Arabian Nights* had in
one night swept away the trees, leaves and all, and replaced them

with a macadamised road, hiding the clouds from view with rows of tall houses.

The postmaster's salary was small. He had to cook his own meals, which he used to share with Ratan, an orphan girl of the village, who did odd jobs for him.

When in the evening the smoke began to curl up from the village cowsheds*, and the cicadas chirped in every bush; when the mendicants of the Baül sect sang their shrill songs in their daily meeting-place, when any poet, who had attempted to watch the movement of the leaves in the dense bamboo thickets, would have felt a ghostly shiver run down his back, the postmaster would light his little lamp, and call out "Ratan."

Ratan would sit outside waiting for this call, and, instead of coming in at once, would reply, "Did you call me, sir?"

"What are you doing?" the postmaster would ask.

"I must be going to light the kitchen fire," would be the answer.

And the postmaster would say: "Oh, let the kitchen fire be for awhile; light me my pipe first."

At last Ratan would enter, with puffed-out cheeks, vigorously blowing into a flame a live coal to light the tobacco. This would give the postmaster an opportunity of conversing. "Well, Ratan," perhaps he would begin, "do you remember anything of your mother?" That was a fertile subject. Ratan partly remembered, and partly didn't. Her father had been fonder of her than her mother; him she recollected more vividly. He used to come home in the evening after his work, and one or two evenings stood out more clearly than others, like pictures in her memory. Ratan would sit on the floor near the postmaster's feet, as memories crowded in upon her. She called to mind a little brother that she had—and how on some bygone cloudy day she had played at fishing with him on the edge of the pond, with a twig for a make-believe fishing-rod. Such little incidents would drive out greater events from her mind. Thus, as they talked, it would often get very late, and the postmaster would feel too lazy to do any cooking at all. Ratan would then hastily light

---

* Smoky fires are lit in the cowsheds to drive off mosquitoes.

the fire, and toast some unleavened bread, which, with the cold remnants of the morning meal, was enough for their supper.

On some evenings, seated at his desk in the corner of the big empty shed, the postmaster too would call up memories of his own home, of his mother and his sister, of those for whom in his exile his heart was sad—memories which were always haunting him, but which he could not talk about with the men of the factory, though he found himself naturally recalling them aloud in the presence of the simple little girl. And so it came about that the girl would allude to his people as mother, brother, and sister*, as if she had known them all her life. In fact, she had a complete picture of each one of them painted in her little heart.

One noon, during a break in the rains, there was a cool soft breeze blowing; the smell of the damp grass and leaves in the hot sun felt like the warm breathing of the tired earth on one's body. A persistent bird went on all the afternoon repeating the burden of its one complaint in Nature's audience chamber.

The postmaster had nothing to do. The shimmer of the freshly washed leaves, and the banked-up remnants of the retreating rain-clouds were sights to see; and the postmaster was watching them and thinking to himself: "Oh, if only some kindred soul were near—just one loving human being whom I could hold near my heart!" This was exactly, he went on to think, what that bird was trying to say, and it was the same feeling which the murmuring leaves were striving to express. But no one knows, or would believe, that such an idea might also take possession of an ill-paid village postmaster in the deep, silent midday interval of his work.

The postmaster sighed, and called out "Ratan." Ratan was then sprawling beneath the guava tree, busily engaged in eating unripe guavas. At the voice of her master, she ran up breathlessly, saying: "Were you calling me, Dada†?" "I was thinking," said the postmaster, "of teaching you to read." And then for the rest of the afternoon he taught her the alphabet.

---

* Family servants call the master and mistress father and mother and the children elder brothers and sisters.
† Dada = elder brother

Thus, in a very short time, Ratan had got as far as the double consonants.

It seemed as though the showers of the season would never end. Canals, ditches, and hollows were all overflowing with water. Day and night the patter of rain was heard, and the croaking of frogs. The village roads became impassable, and marketing had to be done in punts.

One heavily clouded morning, the postmaster's little pupil had been long waiting outside the door for her call, but, not hearing it as usual, she took up her dog-eared book, and slowly entered the room. She found her master stretched out on his bed, and, thinking that he was resting, she was about to retire on tip-toe, when she suddenly heard her name—"Ratan!" She turned at once and asked: "Were you sleeping, Dada?" The postmaster in a plaintive voice said: "I am not well. Feel my head; is it very hot?"

In the loneliness of his exile, and in the gloom of the rains, his ailing body needed a little tender nursing. He longed to remember the touch on the forehead of soft hands with tinkling bracelets, to imagine the presence of loving womanhood, the nearness of mother and sister. And the exile was not disappointed. Ratan ceased to be a little girl. She at once stepped into the post of mother, called in the village doctor, gave the patient his pills at the proper intervals, sat up all night by his pillow, cooked his gruel for him, and every now and then asked: "Are you feeling a little better, Dada?"

It was some time before the postmaster, with weakened body, was able to leave his sick-bed. "No more of this," said he with decision. "I must get a transfer." He at once wrote off to Calcutta an application for a transfer, on the ground of the unhealthiness of the place.

Relieved from her duties as nurse, Ratan again took up her old place outside the door. But she no longer heard the same old call. She would sometimes peep inside furtively to find the postmaster sitting on his chair, or stretched on his bed, and staring absent-mindedly into the air. While Ratan was awaiting her call, the postmaster was awaiting a reply to his application. The girl read her old lessons over and over again—her great fear was lest, when the call came, she might be found wanting in the double consonants. At last, after a week, the

25

call did come one evening. With an overflowing heart Ratan rushed into the room with her—"Were you calling me, Dada?"

The postmaster said: "I am going away tomorrow, Ratan."

"Where are you going, Dada?"

"I am going home."

"When will you come back?"

"I am not coming back."

Ratan asked no other question. The postmaster, of his own accord, went on to tell her that his application for a transfer had been rejected, so he had resigned his post and was going home.

For a long time neither of them spoke another word. The lamp went on dimly burning, and from a leak in one corner of the thatch water dripped steadily into an earthen vessel on the floor beneath it.

After a while Ratan rose, and went off to the kitchen to prepare the meal; but she was not so quick about it as on other days. Many new things to think of had entered her little brain. When the postmaster had finished his supper, the girl suddenly asked him: "Dada, will you take me to your home?"

The postmaster laughed. "What an idea!" said he; but he did not think it necessary to explain to the girl wherein lay the absurdity.

That whole night, in her waking and in her dreams, the postmaster's laughing reply haunted her—"What an idea!"

On getting up in the morning, the postmaster found his bath ready. He had stuck to his Calcutta habit of bathing in water drawn and kept in pitchers, instead of taking a plunge in the river as was the custom of the village. For some reason or other, the girl could not ask him about the time of his departure, so she had fetched the water from the river long before sunrise, that it should be ready as early as he might want it. After the bath came a call for Ratan. She entered noiselessly, and looked silently into her master's face for orders. The master said: "You need not be anxious about my going away, Ratan; I shall tell my successor to look after you." These words were kindly meant, no doubt: but inscrutable are the ways of a woman's heart!

Ratan had borne many a scolding from her master without complaint, but these kind words she could not bear. She burst out weeping, and said: "No, no, you need not tell anybody anything at all about me; I don't want to stay on here."

The postmaster was dumbfounded. He had never seen Ratan like this before.

The new incumbent duly arrived, and the postmaster, having given over charge, prepared to depart. Just before starting he called Ratan and said: "Here is something for you; I hope it will keep you for some little time." He brought out from his pocket the whole of his month's salary, retaining only a trifle for his travelling expenses. Then Ratan fell at his feet and cried: "Oh, Dada, I pray you, don't give me anything, don't in any way trouble about me," and then she ran away out of sight.

The postmaster heaved a sigh, took up his carpet bag, put his umbrella over his shoulder, and, accompanied by a man carrying his many-coloured tin trunk, he slowly made for the boat.

When he got in and the boat was under way, and the rain-swollen river, like a stream of tears welling up from the earth, swirled and sobbed at her bows, then he felt a pain at heart; the grief-stricken face of a village girl seemed to represent for him the great unspoken pervading grief of Mother Earth herself. At one time he had an impulse to go back, and bring away along with him that lonesome waif, forsaken of the world. But the wind had just filled the sails, the boat had got well into the middle of the turbulent current, and already the village was left behind, and its outlying burning-ground came in sight.

So the traveller, borne on the breast of the swift-flowing river, consoled himself with philosophical reflections on the numberless meetings and partings going on in the world—on death, the great parting, from which none returns.

But Ratan had no philosophy. She was wandering about the post office in a flood of tears. It may be that she had still a lurking hope in some corner of her heart that her Dada would return, and that is why she could not tear herself away. Alas for our foolish human nature! Its fond mistakes are persistent. The dictates of reason take a long time to assert their own sway. The surest proofs meanwhile are disbelieved. False hope is clung to with all one's might and main, till a day comes when it has sucked the heart dry and it forcibly breaks through its bonds and departs. After that comes the misery of awakening, and then once again the longing to get back into the maze of the same mistakes.

খোকাবাবুর প্রত্যাবর্তন

My Lord, The Baby

[*Khokababur Pratyabartan* was written in 1891. This English edition was published in 1916 in *The Hungry Stones and other stories*, a collection translated by Mr. C. F. Andrews and Tagore himself. It is also translated as *The Child's Return* and published in *Stories from Tagore* (1918).]

I

Raicharan was twelve years old when he came as a servant to his master's house. He belonged to the same caste as his master, and was given his master's little son to nurse. As time went on the boy left Raicharan's arms to go to school. From school he went on to college, and after college he entered the judicial service. Always, until he married, Raicharan was his sole attendant.

But, when a mistress came into the house, Raicharan found two masters instead of one. All his former influence passed to the new mistress. This was compensated for by a fresh arrival. Anukul had a son born to him, and Raicharan by his unsparing attentions soon got a complete hold over the child. He used to toss him up in his arms, call to him in absurd baby language, put his face close to the baby's and draw it away again with a grin.

Presently the child was able to crawl and cross the doorway. When Raicharan went to catch him, he would scream with mischievous laughter and make for safety. Raicharan was amazed at the profound skill and exact judgment the baby showed when pursued. He would say to his mistress with a look of awe and mystery: "Your son will be a judge someday."

New wonders came in their turn. When the baby began to toddle, that was to Raicharan an epoch in human history. When he called his father Ba-ba and his mother Ma-ma and Raicharan Chan-na, then Raicharan's ecstasy knew no bounds. He went out to tell the news to all the world.

After a while Raicharan was asked to show his ingenuity in other ways. He had, for instance, to play the part of a horse, holding the reins between his teeth and prancing with his feet. He had also to wrestle with his little charge, and if he could not, by a wrestler's trick, fall on his back defeated at the end, a great outcry was certain.

About this time Anukul was transferred to a district on the banks of the Padma. On his way through Calcutta he bought his son a little go-cart. He bought him also a yellow satin waistcoat, a gold-laced cap, and some gold bracelets and anklets. Raicharan was wont to take these out, and put them on his little charge with ceremonial pride, whenever they went for a walk.

Then came the rainy season, and day after day the rain poured down in torrents. The hungry river, like an enormous serpent, swallowed down terraces, villages, cornfields, and covered with its flood the tall grasses and wild casuarinas on the sand-banks. From time to time there was a deep thud, as the riverbanks crumbled. The unceasing roar of the rain current could be beard from far away. Masses of foam, carried swiftly past, proved to the eye the swiftness of the stream.

One afternoon the rain cleared. It was cloudy, but cool and bright. Raicharan's little despot did not want to stay in on such a fine afternoon. His lordship climbed into the go-cart. Raicharan, between the shafts, dragged him slowly along till he reached the rice-fields on the banks of the river. There was no one in the fields, and no boat on the stream. Across the water, on the farther side, the clouds were rifted in the west. The silent ceremonial of the setting sun was revealed in all its glowing splendour. In the midst of that stillness the child, all of a sudden, pointed with his finger in front of him and cried: "Chan-nal Pitty fow."

Close by on a mud-flat stood a large Kadamba tree in full flower. My lord, the baby, looked at it with greedy eyes, and Raicharan knew his meaning. Only a short time before he had made, out of these very flower balls, a small go-cart; and the child had been so entirely happy dragging it about with a string, that for the whole day Raicharan was not made to put on the reins at all. He was promoted from a horse into a groom.

But Raicharan had no wish that evening to go splashing knee-deep through the mud to reach the flowers. So he quickly pointed his finger in the opposite direction, calling out: "Oh, look, baby, look! Look at the bird." And with all sorts of curious noises he pushed the go-cart rapidly away from the tree.

But a child, destined to be a judge, cannot be put off so easily. And besides, there was at the time nothing to attract his eyes. And you cannot keep up for ever the pretence of an imaginary bird.

The little Master's mind was made up, and Raicharan was at his wits' end. "Very well, baby," he said at last, "you sit still in the cart, and I'll go and get you the pretty flower. Only mind you don't go near the water."

As he said this, he made his legs bare to the knee, and waded through the oozing mud towards the tree.

The moment Raicharan had gone, his little Master went off at racing speed to the forbidden water. The baby saw the river rushing by, splashing and gurgling as it went. It seemed as though the disobedient wavelets themselves were running away from some greater Raicharan with the laughter of a thousand children. At the sight of their mischief, the heart of the human child grew excited and restless. He got down stealthily from the go-cart and toddled off towards the river. On his way he picked up a small stick, and leant over the bank of the stream pretending to fish. The mischievous fairies of the river with their mysterious voices seemed inviting him into their play-house.

Raicharan had plucked a handful of flowers from the tree, and was carrying them back in the end of his cloth, with his face wreathed in smiles. But when he reached the go-cart, there was no one there. He looked on all sides and there was no one there. He looked back at the cart and there was no one there.

In that first terrible moment his blood froze within him. Before his eyes the whole universe swam round like a dark mist. From the depth of his broken heart he gave one piercing cry; "Master, Master, little Master."

But no voice answered "Chan-na." No child laughed mischievously back; no scream of baby delight welcomed his return. Only the river ran on, with its splashing, gurgling noise as before— as though it knew nothing at all, and had no time to attend to such a tiny human event as the death of a child.

As the evening passed by Raicharan's mistress became very anxious. She sent men out on all sides to search. They went with lanterns in their hands, and reached at last the banks of the Padma. There they found Raicharan rushing up and down the fields, like a stormy wind, shouting the cry of despair: "Master, Master, little Master!"

When they got Raicharan home at last, he fell prostrate at his mistress's feet. They shook him, and questioned him, and asked him repeatedly where he had left the child; but all he could say was, that he knew nothing.

Though everyone held the opinion that the Padma had swallowed the child, there was a lurking doubt left in the mind. For a band of gipsies had been noticed outside the village that afternoon, and some suspicion rested on them. The mother went so far in her wild grief as to think it possible that Raicharan himself had stolen the child. She called him aside with piteous entreaty and said: "Raicharan, give me back my baby. Oh! give me back my child. Take from me any money you ask, but give me back my child!"

Raicharan only beat his forehead in reply. His mistress ordered him out of the house.

Anukul tried to reason his wife out of this wholly unjust suspicion: "Why on earth," he said, "should he commit such a crime as that?"

The mother only replied: "The baby had gold ornaments on his body. Who knows?"

It was impossible to reason with her after that.

II

Raicharan went back to his own village. Up to this time he had had no son, and there was no hope that any child would now be born to him. But it came about before the end of a year that his wife gave birth to a son and died.

All overwhelming resentment at first grew up in Raicharan's heart at the sight of this new baby. At the back of his mind was resentful suspicion that it had come as a usurper in place of the little Master. He also thought it would be a grave offence to be happy with a son of his own after what had happened to his master's little child. Indeed, if it had not been for a widowed sister, who mothered the new baby, it would not have lived long.

But a change gradually came over Raicharan's mind. A wonderful thing happened. This new baby in turn began to crawl about, and cross the doorway with mischief in its face. It also showed an amusing cleverness in making its escape to safety. Its voice, its sounds of laughter and tears, its gestures, were those of the little Master. On some days, when Raicharan listened to its crying, his heart suddenly began thumping wildly against his ribs, and it seemed to him that his former little Master was crying somewhere in the unknown land of death because he had lost his Chan-na.

Phailna (for that was the name Raicharan's sister gave to the new baby) soon began to talk. It learnt to say Ba-ba and Ma-ma with a baby accent. When Raicharan heard those familiar sounds the mystery suddenly became clear. The little Master could not cast off the spell of his Chan-na, and therefore he had been reborn in his own house.

The arguments in favour of this were, to Raicharan, altogether beyond dispute:

(i) The new baby was born soon after his little master's death.
(ii) His wife could never have accumulated such merit as to give birth to a son in middle age.
(iii) The new baby walked with a toddle and called out Ba-ba and Ma-ma. There was no sign lacking which marked out the future judge.

Then suddenly Raicharan remembered that terrible accusation of the mother. "Ah," he said to himself with amazement, "the mother's heart was right. She knew I had stolen her child." When once he had come to this conclusion, he was filled with remorse for his past neglect. He now gave himself over, body and soul, to the new baby, and became its devoted attendant. He began to bring it up, as if it were the son of a rich man. He bought a go-cart, a yellow satin waistcoat, and a gold-embroidered cap. He melted down the ornaments of his dead wife, and made gold bangles and anklets. He refused to let the little child play with any one of the neighbourhood, and became himself its sole companion day and night. As the baby grew up to boyhood, he was so petted and spoilt and clad in such finery that the village children would call him "Your Lordship," and jeer at him; and older people regarded Raicharan as unaccountably crazy about the child.

At last the time came for the boy to go to school. Raicharan sold his small piece of land, and went to Calcutta. There he got employment with great difficulty as a servant, and sent Phailna to school. He spared no pains to give him the best education, the best clothes, the best food. Meanwhile he lived himself on a mere handful of rice, and would say in secret: "Ah! my little Master, my dear little Master, you loved me so much that you came back to my house. You shall never suffer from any neglect of mine."

Twelve years passed away in this manner. The boy was able to read and write well. He was bright and healthy and good-looking. He paid a great deal of attention to his personal appearance, and was specially careful in parting his hair. He was inclined to extravagance and finery, and spent money freely. He could never quite look on Raicharan as a father, because, though fatherly in affection, he had the manner of a servant. A further fault was this, that Raicharan kept secret from everyone that himself was the father of the child.

The students of the hostel, where Phailna was a boarder, were greatly amused by Raicharan's country manners, and I have to confess that behind his father's back Phailna joined in their fun. But, in the bottom of their hearts, all the students loved the innocent and tender-hearted old man, and Phailna was very fond of him also. But, as I have said before, he loved him with a kind of condescension.

Raicharan grew older and older, and his employer was continually finding fault with him for his incompetent work. He had been starving himself for the boy's sake. So he had grown physically weak, and no longer up to his work. He would forget things, and his mind became dull and stupid. But his employer expected a full servant's work out of him, and would not brook excuses. The money that Raicharan had brought with him from the sale of his land was exhausted. The boy was continually grumbling about his clothes, and asking for more money.

Raicharan made up his mind. He gave up the situation where he was working as a servant, and left some money with Phailna and said: "I have some business to do at home in my village, and shall be back soon."

He went off at once to Baraset where Anukul was magistrate. Anukul's wife was still broken down with grief. She had had no other child.

One day Anukul was resting after a long and weary day in court. His wife was buying, at an exorbitant price, a herb from a mendicant quack, which was said to ensure the birth of a child. A voice of greeting was heard in the courtyard. Anukul went out to see who was there. It was Raicharan. Anukul's heart was softened when he saw his old servant. He asked him many questions, and offered to take him back into service.

Raicharan smiled faintly, and said in reply; "I want to make obeisance to my mistress."

Anukul went with Raicharan into the house, where the mistress did not receive him as warmly as his old master. Raicharan took no notice of this, but folded his hands, and said: "It was not the Padma that stole your baby. It was I."

Anukul exclaimed: "Great God! Eh! What! Where is he?" Raicharan replied: "He is with me, I will bring him the day after tomorrow."

It was Sunday. There was no magistrate's court sitting. Both husband and wife were looking expectantly along the road, waiting from early morning for Raicharan's appearance. At ten o'clock he came, leading Phailna by the hand.

Anukul's wife, without a question, took the boy into her lap, and was wild with excitement, sometimes laughing, sometimes weeping, touching him, kissing his hair and his forehead, and gazing into his face with hungry, eager eyes. The boy was very good-looking and dressed like a gentleman's son. The heart of Anukul brimmed over with a sudden rush of affection.

Nevertheless the magistrate in him asked: "Have you any proofs?" Raicharan said: "How could there be any proof of such a deed? God alone knows that I stole your boy, and no one else in the world."

When Anukul saw how eagerly his wife was clinging to the boy, he realised the futility of asking for proofs. It would be wiser to believe. And then—where could an old man like Raicharan get such a boy from? And why should his faithful servant deceive him for nothing?

"But," he added severely, "Raicharan, you must not stay here."

"Where shall I go, Master?" said Raicharan, in a choking voice, folding his hands; "I am old. Who will take in an old man as a servant?"

The mistress said: "Let him stay. My child will be pleased. I forgive him."

But Anukul's magisterial conscience would not allow him. "No," he said, "he cannot be forgiven for what he has done."

Raicharan bowed to the ground, and clasped Anukul's feet. "Master," he cried, "let me stay. It was not I who did it. It was God."

Anukul's conscience was worse stricken than ever, when Raicharan tried to put the blame on God's shoulders.

"No," he said, "I could not allow it. I cannot trust you anymore. You have done an act of treachery."

Raicharan rose to his feet and said: "It was not I who did it."

"Who was it then?" asked Anukul.

Raicharan replied: "It was my fate."

But no educated man could take this for an excuse. Anukul remained obdurate.

When Phailna saw that he was the wealthy magistrate's son, and not Raicharan's, he was angry at first, thinking that he had been cheated all this time of his birthright. But seeing Raicharan in distress, he generously said to his father: "Father, forgive him.

Even if you don't let him live with us, let him have a small monthly pension."

After hearing this, Raicharan did not utter another word. He looked for the last time on the face of his son; he made obeisance to his old master and mistress. Then he went out, and was mingled with the numberless people of the world.

At the end of the month Anukul sent him some money to his village. But the money came back. There was no one there of the name of Raicharan.

সম্পত্তি সমর্পন

The Trust Property

[*Sampatti Samarpan* was written between 1891 and 1892. *The Trust Property*, its English translation, was published in 1918 in the collection *Mashi and Other Stories*. It has also been translated as *A Bequest of Property* and *Wealth Surrendered*.]

I

Brindaban Kundu came to his father in a rage and said: "I am off this moment."

"Ungrateful wretch!" sneered the father, Jaganath Kundu. "When you have paid me back all that I have spent on your food and clothing, it will be time enough to give yourself these airs."

Such food and clothing as was customary in Jaganath's household could not have cost very much. Our *rishis* of old managed to feed and clothe themselves on an incredibly small outlay. Jaganath's behaviour showed that his ideal in these respects was equally high. That he could not fully live up to it was due partly to the bad influence of the degenerate society around him, and partly to certain unreasonable demands of Nature in her attempt to keep body and soul together.

So long as Brindaban was single, things went smoothly enough, but after his marriage he began to depart from the high and rarefied standard cherished by his sire. It was clear that the son's ideas of comfort were moving away from the spiritual to the material, and imitating the ways of the world. He was unwilling to put up with the discomforts of heat and cold, thirst and hunger. His minimum of food and clothing rose apace.

Frequent were the quarrels between the father and the son. At last Brindaban's wife became seriously ill and a *kabiraj** was called in. But when the doctor prescribed a costly medicine for his patient, Jaganath took it as a proof of sheer incompetence, and turned him out immediately. At first Brindaban besought his father to allow the treatment to continue; then he quarrelled with him about it, but to no purpose. When his wife died, he abused his father and called him a murderer.

"Nonsense!" said the father. "Don't people die even after swallowing all kinds of drugs? If costly medicines could save life, how is it that kings and emperors are not immortal? You don't expect your wife to die with more pomp and ceremony than did your mother and your grandmother before her, do you?"

Brindaban might really have derived a great consolation from these words, had he not been overwhelmed with grief and incapable of proper thinking. Neither his mother nor his grandmother had taken any medicine before making their exit from this world, and this was the time-honoured custom of the family. But, alas, the younger generation was unwilling to die according to ancient custom. The English had newly come to the country at the time we speak of. Even in those remote days, the good old folks were horrified at the unorthodox ways of the new generation, and sat speechless, trying to draw comfort from their hookahs.

Be that as it may, the modern Brindaban said to his old fogy of a father: "I am off."

The father instantly agreed, and wished publicly that, should he ever give his son one single pice in future, the gods might reckon his act as shedding the holy blood of cows. Brindaban in his turn similarly wished that, should he ever accept anything from his father, his act might be held as bad as matricide.

---

* Country doctor, unqualified by any medical training

The people of the village looked upon this small revolution as a great relief after a long period of monotony. And when Jaganath disinherited his only son, everyone did his best to console him. All were unanimous in the opinion that to quarrel with a father for the sake of a wife was possible only in these degenerate days. And the reason they gave was sound too. "When your wife dies," they said, "you can find a second one without delay. But when your father dies, you can't get another to replace him for love or money." Their logic no doubt was perfect, but we suspect that the utter hopelessness of getting another father did not trouble the misguided son very much. On the contrary, he looked upon it as a mercy.

Nor did separation from Brindaban weigh heavily on the mind of his father. In the first place, his absence from home reduced the household expenses. Then, again, the father was freed from a great anxiety. The fear of being poisoned by his son and heir had always haunted him. When he ate his scanty fare, he could never banish the thought of poison from his mind. This fear had abated somewhat after the death of his daughter-in-law, and, now that the son was gone, it disappeared altogether.

But there was one tender spot in the old man's heart. Brindaban had taken away with him his four-year-old son, Gokul Chandra. Now, the expense of keeping the child was comparatively small, and so Jaganath's affection for him was without a drawback. Still, when Brindaban took him away, his grief, sincere as it was, was mingled at first with calculation as to how much he would save a month by the absence of the two, how much the sum would come to in the year, and what would be the capital to bring it in as interest.

But the empty house, without Gokul Chandra in it to make mischief, became more and more difficult for the old man to live in. There was no one now to play tricks upon him when he was engaged in his puja,* no one to snatch away his food and eat it, no one to run away with his inkpot, when he was writing up his accounts. His daily routine of life, now uninterrupted, became an intolerable burden to him. He bethought him that this unworried

---

* A ceremonial worship

39

peace was endurable only in the world to come. When he caught sight of the holes made in his quilt by his grandchild, and the pen-and-ink sketches executed by the same artist on his rush-mat, his heart was heavy with grief. Once upon a time he had reproached the boy bitterly because he had torn his dhoti into pieces within the short space of two years; now tears stood in Jaganath's eyes as he gazed upon the dirty remnants lying in the bedroom. He carefully put them away in his safe, and registered a vow that, should Gokul ever come back again, he should not be reprimanded even if he destroyed one dhoti a year.

But Gokul did not return, and poor Jaganath aged rapidly. His empty home seemed emptier every day.

No longer could the old man stay peacefully at home. Even in the middle of the day, when all respectable folks in the village enjoyed their after-dinner siesta, Jaganath might be seen roaming over the village, hookah in hand. The boys, at sight of him, would give up their play, and, retiring in a body to a safe distance, chant verses composed by a local poet, praising the old gentleman's economical habits. No one ventured to say his real name, lest he should have to go without his meal that day*—and so people gave him names after their own fancy. Elderly people called him Jaganash,† but the reason why the younger generation preferred to call him a vampire was hard to guess. It may be that the bloodless, dried-up skin of the old man had some physical resemblance to the vampire's.

II

One afternoon, when Jaganath was rambling as usual through the village lanes shaded by mango topes, he saw a boy, apparently a stranger, assuming the captaincy of the village boys and explaining to them the scheme of some new prank. Won by the force of his

---

* It is a superstition current in Bengal that if a man pronounces the name of a very miserly individual, he has to go without his meal that day.

† Jaganath is the Lord of Festivity, and *Jaganash* would mean the despoiler of it.

character and the startling novelty of his ideas, the boys had all sworn allegiance to him. Unlike the others, he did not run away from the old man as he approached, but came quite close to him and began to shake his own *chadar*. The result was that a live lizard sprang out of it on to the old man's body, ran down his back and off towards the jungle. Sudden fright made the poor man shiver from head to foot, to the great amusement of the other boys, who shouted with glee. Before Jaganath had gone far, cursing and swearing, the *gamcha* on his shoulder suddenly disappeared, and the next moment it was seen on the head of the new boy, transformed into a turban.

The novel attentions of this manikin came as a great relief to Jaganath. It was long since any boy had taken such freedom with him. After a good deal of coaxing and many fair promises, he at last persuaded the boy to come to him, and this was the conversation which followed:

"What's your name, my boy?"

"Nitai Pal."

"Where's your home?"

"Won't tell."

"Who's your father?"

"Won't tell."

"Why won't you?"

"Because I have run away from home."

"What made you do it?"

"My father wanted to send me to school."

It occurred to Jaganath that it would be useless extravagance to send such a boy to school, and his father must have been an unpractical fool not to have thought so.

"Well, well," said Jaganath, "how would you like to come and stay with me?"

"Don't mind," said the boy, and forthwith he installed himself in Jaganath's house. He felt as little hesitation as though it were the shadow of a tree by the wayside. And not only that. He began to proclaim his wishes as regards his food and clothing with such coolness that you would have thought he had paid his reckoning in full beforehand; and, when anything went wrong, he did not scruple

41

to quarrel with the old man. It had been easy enough for Jaganath to get the better of his own child; but, now, where another man's child was concerned, he had to acknowledge defeat.

III

The people of the village marvelled when Nitai Pal was unexpectedly made so much of by Jaganath. They felt sure that the old man's end was near, and the prospect of his bequeathing all his property to this unknown brat made their hearts sore. Furious with envy, they determined to do the boy an injury, but the old man took care of him as though he was a rib in his breast.

At times, the boy threatened that he would go away, and the old man used to say to him temptingly: "I will leave you all the property I possess." Young as he was, the boy fully understood the grandeur of this promise.

The village people then began to make inquiries after the father of the boy. Their hearts melted with compassion for the agonised parents, and they declared that the son must be a rascal to cause them so much suffering. They heaped abuses on his head, but the heat with which they did it betrayed envy rather than a sense of justice.

One day the old man learned from a wayfarer that one Damodar Pal was seeking his lost son, and was even now coming towards the village. Nitai, when he heard this, became very restless and was ready to run away, leaving his future wealth to take care of itself. Jaganath reassured him, saying: "I mean to hide you where nobody can find you—not even the village people themselves."

This whetted the curiosity of the boy and he said: "Oh, where? Do show me."

"People will know, if I show you now. Wait till it is night," said Jaganath.

The hope of discovering the mysterious hiding-place delighted Nitai. He planned to himself how, as soon as his father had gone away without him, he would have a bet with his comrades, and play hide-and-seek. Nobody would be able to find him. Wouldn't it be fun? His father, too, would ransack the whole village, and not find him—that would be rare fun also.

At noon, Jaganath shut the boy up in his house, and disappeared for some time. When he came home again, Nitai worried him with questions.

No sooner was it dark than Nitai said: "Grandfather, shall we go now?"

"It isn't night yet," replied Jaganath.

A little while later the boy exclaimed: "It is night now, grandfather; come let's go."

"The village people haven't gone to bed yet," whispered Jaganath.

Nitai waited but a moment, and said: "They have gone to bed now, grandfather; I am sure they have. Let's start now."

The night advanced. Sleep began to weigh heavily on the eyelids of the poor boy, and it was a hard struggle for him to keep awake. At midnight, Jaganath caught hold of the boy's arm, and left the house, groping through the dark lanes of the sleeping village. Not a sound disturbed the stillness, except the occasional howl of a dog, when all the other dogs far and near would join in chorus, or perhaps the flapping of a night-bird, scared by the sound of human footsteps at that unusual hour. Nitai trembled with fear, and held Jaganath fast by the arm.

Across many a field they went, and at last came to a jungle, where stood a dilapidated temple without a god in it. "What, here!" exclaimed Nitai in a tone of disappointment. It was nothing like what he had imagined. There was not much mystery about it. Often, since running away from home, he had passed nights in deserted temples like this. It was not a bad place for playing hide-and-seek; still it was quite possible that his comrades might track him there.

From the middle of the floor inside, Jaganath removed a slab of stone, and an underground room with a lamp burning in it was revealed to the astonished eyes of the boy. Fear and curiosity assailed his little heart. Jaganath descended by a ladder and Nitai followed him.

Looking around, the boy saw that there were brass *ghurras** on

---

* A water-pot holding about three gallons of water

all sides of him. In the middle lay spread an *assan**, and in front of it were arranged vermilion, sandal paste, flowers, and other articles of puja. To satisfy his curiosity the boy dipped his hand into some of the ghurras, and drew out their contents. They were rupees and gold *mohurs*.

Jaganath, addressing the boy, said: "I told you, Nitai, that I would give you all my money. I have not got much—these ghurras are all that I possess. These I will make over to you today."

The boy jumped with delight. "All?" he exclaimed; "you won't take back a rupee, will you?"

"If I do," said the old man in solemn tones, "may my hand be attacked with leprosy. But there is one condition. If ever my grandson, Gokul Chandra, or his son, or his grandson, or his great-grandson, or any of his progeny should happen to pass this way, then you must make over to him, or to them, every rupee and every mohur here."

The boy thought that the old man was raving. "Very well," he replied.

"Then sit on this assan," said Jaganath.

"What for?"

"Because puja will be done to you."

"But why?" said the boy, taken aback.

"This is the rule."

The boy squatted on the assan as he was told. Jaganath smeared his forehead with sandal paste, put a mark of vermilion between his eyebrows, flung a garland of flowers round his neck, and began to recite *mantras*.†

To sit there like a god, and hear mantras recited made poor Nitai feel very uneasy. "Grandfather," he whispered.

But Jaganath did not reply, and went on muttering his incantations.

Finally, with great difficulty he dragged each ghurra before the boy and made him repeat the following vow after him:

"I do solemnly promise that I will make over all this treasure to Gokul Chandra Kundu, the son of Brindaban Kundu, the grandson

---

* A prayer carpet
† Incantations

of Jaganath Kundu, or to the son or to the grandson or to the great-grandson of the said Gokul Chandra Kundu, or to any other progeny of his who may be the rightful heir."

The boy repeated this over and over again, until he felt stupefied, and his tongue began to grow stiff in his mouth. When the ceremony was over, the air of the cave was laden with the smoke of the earthen lamp and the breath-poison of the two. The boy felt that the roof of his mouth had become dry as dust, and his hands and feet were burning. He was nearly suffocated.

The lamp became dimmer and dimmer, and then went out altogether. In the total darkness that followed, Nitai could hear the old man climbing up the ladder. "Grandfather, where are you going to?" said he, greatly distressed.

"I am going now," replied Jaganath; "you remain here. No one will be able to find you. Remember the name Gokul Chandra, the son of Brindaban, and the grandson of Jaganath."

He then withdrew the ladder. In a stifled, agonised voice the boy implored: "I want to go back to father."

Jaganath replaced the slab. He then knelt down and placed his ear on the stone. Nitai's voice was heard once more—"Father"—and then came a sound of some heavy object falling with a bump—and then—everything was still.

Having thus placed his wealth in the hands of a *yak*,‡ Jaganath began to cover up the stone with earth. Then he piled broken bricks and loose mortar over it. On the top of all he planted turfs of grass and jungle weeds. The night was almost spent, but he could not tear himself away from the spot. Now and again he placed his ear to the ground, and tried to listen. It seemed to him that from far, far below—from the abysmal depth of the earth's interior—came a wailing. It seemed to him that the night sky was flooded with that one sound, that the sleeping humanity of all the world was awake, and was sitting on its beds, trying to listen.

---

‡ *Yak* or *Yaksa* is a supernatural being described in Sanskrit mythology and poetry. In Bengal, *Yak* has come to mean a ghostly custodian of treasure, under such circumstances as in this story.

The old man in his frenzy kept on heaping earth higher and higher. He wanted somehow to stifle that sound, but still he fancied he could hear "Father."

He struck the spot with all his might and said: "Be quiet—people might hear you." But still he imagined he heard "Father."

The sun lighted up the eastern horizon. Jaganath then left the temple, and came into the open fields.

There, too, somebody called out "Father." Startled at the sound, he turned back and saw his son at his heels.

"Father," said Brindaban, "I hear my boy is hiding himself in your house. I must have him back."

With eyes dilated and distorted mouth, the old man leaned forward and exclaimed: "Your boy?"

"Yes, my boy Gokul. He is Nitai Pal now, and I myself go by the name of Damodar Pal. Your *fame* has spread so widely in the neighbourhood, that we were obliged to cover up our origin, lest people should have refused to pronounce our names."

Slowly the old man lifted both his arms above his head. His fingers began to twitch convulsively, as though he was trying to catch hold of some imaginary object in the air. He then fell on the ground.

When he came to his senses again, he dragged his son towards the ruined temple. When they were both inside it, he said: "Do you hear any wailing sound?"

"No, I don't," said Brindaban.

"Just listen very carefully. Do you hear anybody calling out 'Father'?"

"No."

This seemed to relieve him greatly.

From that day forward, he used to go about asking people: "Do you hear any wailing sound?" They laughed at the raving dotard.

About four years later, Jaganath lay on his deathbed. When the light of this world was gradually fading away from his eyes, and his breathing became more and more difficult, he suddenly sat up in a state of delirium. Throwing both his hands in the air he seemed to grope about for something, muttering: "Nitai, who has removed my ladder?"

Unable to find the ladder to climb out of his terrible dungeon, where there was no light to see and no air to breathe, he fell on his bed once more, and disappeared into that region where no one has ever been found out in the world's eternal game of hide-and-seek.*

---

* The incidents described in this story, now happily a thing of the past, were by no means rare in Bengal at one time. Our author, however, slightly departs from the current accounts. Such criminally superstitious practices were resorted to by miserly persons under the idea that they themselves would re-acquire the treasure in a future state of existence. 'When you see me in a future birth passing this way, you must make over all this treasure to me. Guard it till then and stir not,'—was the usual promise exacted from the victim before he became *yak*. Many were the 'true' stories we heard in childhood of people becoming suddenly rich by coming across ghostly custodians of wealth belonging to them in a past birth.

কাবুলিওয়ালা

The Cabuliwallah

(THE FRUITSELLER FROM CABUL)

[*Kabuliwallah* was written in 1892. This is taken from the collection *The Hungry Stones and Other Stories* (1916) translated by the author and Mr. C. F. Andrews.]

My five-year-old daughter Mini cannot live without chattering. I really believe that in all her life she has not wasted a minute in silence. Her mother is often vexed at this, and would stop her prattle, but I would not. To see Mini quiet is unnatural, and I cannot bear it long. And so my own talk with her is always lively.

One morning, for instance, when I was in the midst of the seventeenth chapter of my new novel, my little Mini stole into the room, and putting her hand into mine, said: "Father! Ramdayal, the door-keeper, calls a crow a *krow*! He doesn't know anything, does he?"

Before I could explain to her the differences of language in this world, she was embarked on the full tide of another subject. "What do you think, Father? Bhola says there is an elephant in the clouds, blowing water out of his trunk, and that is why it rains!"

And then, darting off anew, while I sat still making ready some reply to this last saying, "Father! what relation is Mother to you?"

"My dear little sister in the law!" I murmured involuntarily to myself, but with a grave face contrived to answer: "Go and play with Bhola, Mini! I am busy!"

The window of my room overlooks the road. The child had seated herself at my feet near my table, and was playing softly, drumming on her knees. I was hard at work on my seventeenth chapter, where Protap Singh, the hero, had just caught Kanchanlata, the heroine, in his arms, and was about to escape with her by the third-storey window of the castle, when all of a sudden Mini left her play, and ran to the window, crying, "A Cabuliwallah! A Cabuliwallah!" Sure enough in the street below was a Cabuliwallah, passing slowly along. He wore the loose soiled clothing of his people, with a tall turban; there was a bag on his back, and he carried boxes of grapes in his hand.

I cannot tell what were my daughter's feelings at the sight of this man, but she began to call him loudly. "Ah!" I thought, "he will come in, and my seventeenth chapter will never be finished!" At which exact moment the Cabuliwallah turned, and looked up at the child. When she saw this, overcome by terror, she fled to her mother's protection, and disappeared. She had a blind belief that inside the bag, which the big man carried, there were perhaps two or three other children like herself. The pedlar meanwhile entered my doorway, and greeted me with a smiling face.

So precarious was the position of my hero and my heroine, that my first impulse was to stop and buy something, since the man had been called. I made some small purchases, and a conversation began about Abdur Rahman, the Russians, the English, and the Frontier Policy.

As he was about to leave, he asked: "And where is the little girl, sir?"

And I, thinking that Mini must get rid of her false fear, had her brought out.

She stood by my chair, and looked at the Cabuliwallah and his bag. He offered her nuts and raisins, but she would not be tempted, and only clung closer to me, with all her doubts increased.

This was their first meeting.

One morning, however, not many days later, as I was leaving the house, I was startled to find Mini, seated on a bench near the door, laughing and talking, with the great Cabuliwallah at her feet. In all her life, it appeared; my small daughter had never found so patient a listener, save her father. And already the corner of her little sari was stuffed with almonds and raisins, the gift of her visitor, "Why did you give her those?" I said, and taking out an eight-*anna* bit, I handed it to him. The man accepted the money without demur, and slipped it into his pocket.

Alas, on my return an hour later, I found the unfortunate coin had made twice its own worth of trouble! For the Cabuliwallah had given it to Mini, and her mother catching sight of the bright round object, had pounced on the child with: "Where did you get that eight-anna bit?"

"The Cabuliwallah gave it to me," said Mini cheerfully.

"The Cabuliwallah gave it to you!" cried her mother much shocked. "Oh, Mini! how could you take it from him?"

I, entering at the moment, saved her from impending disaster, and proceeded to make my own inquiries.

It was not the first or second time, I found, that the two had met. The Cabuliwallah had overcome the child's first terror by a judicious bribery of nuts and almonds, and the two were now great friends.

They had many quaint jokes, which afforded them much amusement. Seated in front of him, looking down on his gigantic frame in all her tiny dignity, Mini would ripple her face with laughter, and begin: "O Cabuliwallah, Cabuliwallah, what have you got in your bag?"

And he would reply, in the nasal accents of the mountaineer: "An elephant!" Not much cause for merriment, perhaps; but how they both enjoyed the witticism! And for me, this child's talk with a grown-up man had always in it something strangely fascinating.

Then the Cabuliwallah, not to be behindhand, would take his turn: "Well, little one, and when are you going to the father-in-law's house?"

Now most small Bengali maidens have heard long ago about the father-in-law's house; but we, being a little new-fangled, had kept these things from our child, and Mini at this question must have been a trifle bewildered. But she would not show it, and with ready tact replied: "Are *you* going there?"

Amongst men of the Cabuliwallah's class, however, it is well known that the words 'father-in-law's house' have a double meaning.

It is a euphemism for *jail*, the place where we are well cared for, at no expense to ourselves. In this sense would the sturdy pedlar take my daughter's question. "Ah," he would say, shaking his fist at an invisible policeman, "I will thrash my father-in-law!" Hearing this, and picturing the poor discomfited relative, Mini would go off into peals of laughter, in which her formidable friend would join.

These were autumn mornings, the very time of year when kings of old went forth to conquest; and I, never stirring from my little corner in Calcutta, would let my mind wander over the whole world. At the very name of another country, my heart would go out to it, and at the sight of a foreigner in the streets, I would fall to weaving a network of dreams—the mountains, the glens, and the forests of his distant home, with his cottage in its setting, and the free and independent life of faraway wilds. Perhaps the scenes of travel conjure themselves up before me, and pass and repass in my imagination all the more vividly, because I lead such a vegetable existence, that a call to travel would fall upon me like a thunderbolt. In the presence of this Cabuliwallah, I was immediately transported to the foot of arid mountain peaks, with narrow little defiles twisting in and out amongst their towering heights. I could see the string of camels bearing the merchandise, and the company of turbaned merchants, carrying some of their queer old firearms, and some of their spears, journeying downward towards the plains. I could see— but at some such point Mini's mother would intervene, imploring me to "beware of that man."

Mini's mother is unfortunately a very timid lady. Whenever she hears a noise in the street, or sees people coming towards the house, she always jumps to the conclusion that they are either thieves, or drunkards, or snakes, or tigers, or malaria or cockroaches, or caterpillars, or an English sailor. Even after all these years of experience, she is not able to overcome her terror. So she was full of doubts about the Cabuliwallah, and used to beg me to keep a watchful eye on him.

I tried to laugh her fear gently away, but then she would turn round on me seriously, and ask me solemn questions.

Were children never kidnapped?

Was it, then, not true that there was slavery in Cabul?

Was it so very absurd that this big man should be able to carry off a tiny child?

I urged that, though not impossible, it was highly improbable. But this was not enough, and her dread persisted. As it was indefinite, however, it did not seem right to forbid the man the house, and the intimacy went on unchecked.

Once a year in the middle of January Rahmun, the Cabuliwallah, was in the habit of returning to his country, and as the time approached he would be very busy, going from house to house collecting his debts. This year, however, he could always find time to come and see Mini. It would have seemed to an outsider that there was some conspiracy between the two, for when he could not come in the morning, he would appear in the evening.

Even to me it was a little startling now and then, in the corner of a dark room, suddenly to surprise this tall, loose-garmented, much bebagged man; but when Mini would run in smiling, with her, "O! Cabuliwallah! Cabuliwallah!" and the two friends, so far apart in age, would subside into their old laughter and their old jokes, I felt reassured.

One morning, a few days before he had made up his mind to go, I was correcting my proof sheets in my study. It was chilly weather. Through the window the rays of the sun touched my feet, and the slight warmth was very welcome. It was almost eight o'clock, and the early pedestrians were returning home, with their heads covered. All at once, I heard an uproar in the street, and, looking out, saw Rahmun being led away bound between two policemen, and behind them a crowd of curious boys. There were blood-stains on the clothes of the Cabuliwallah, and one of the policemen carried a knife. Hurrying out, I stopped them, and enquired what it all meant. Partly from one, partly from another, I gathered that a certain neighbour had owed the pedlar something for a Rampuri shawl, but had falsely denied having bought it, and that in the course of the quarrel, Rahmun had struck him. Now in the heat of his excitement, the prisoner began calling his enemy all sorts of names, when suddenly in a verandah of my house appeared my little Mini, with her usual exclamation: "O Cabuliwallah! Cabuliwallah!" Rahmun's face lighted up as he turned to her. He had no bag under his arm today, so she could not discuss the elephant with him. She at once therefore proceeded to the next question: "Are you going to the father-in-law's house?" Rahmun laughed and said: "Just where I am going, little one!" Then seeing that the reply did not amuse the child, he held up his fettered hands. "Ai," he said, "I would have thrashed that old father-in-law, but my hands are bound!"

On a charge of murderous assault, Rahmun was sentenced to some years' imprisonment.

Time passed away, and he was not remembered. The accustomed work in the accustomed place was ours, and the thought of the once-free mountaineer spending his years in prison seldom or never occurred to us. Even my light-hearted Mini, I am ashamed to say, forgot her old friend. New companions filled her life. As she grew older, she spent more of her time with girls. So much time indeed did she spend with them that she came no more, as she used to do, to her father's room. I was scarcely on speaking terms with her.

Years had passed away. It was once more autumn and we had made arrangements for our Mini's marriage. It was to take place during the Puja Holidays. With Durga returning to Kailas, the light of our home also was to depart to her husband's house, and leave her father's in the shadow.

The morning was bright. After the rains, there was a sense of ablution in the air, and the sunrays looked like pure gold. So bright were they that they gave a beautiful radiance even to the sordid brick walls of our Calcutta lanes. Since early dawn today the wedding-pipes had been sounding, and at each beat my own heart throbbed. The wail of the tune, *Bhairavi*, seemed to intensify my pain at the approaching separation. My Mini was to be married tonight.

From early morning noise and bustle had pervaded the house. In the courtyard the canopy had to be slung on its bamboo poles; the chandeliers with their tinkling sound must be hung in each room and verandah. There was no end of hurry and excitement. I was sitting in my study, looking through the accounts, when someone entered, saluting respectfully, and stood before me. It was Rahmun, the Cabuliwallah. At first I did not recognise him. He had no bag, nor the long hair, nor the same vigour that he used to have. But he smiled, and I knew him again.

"When did you come, Rahmun?" I asked him.

"Last evening," he said, "I was released from jail."

The words struck harsh upon my ears. I had never before talked with one who had wounded his fellow, and my heart shrank within itself, when I realised this, for I felt that the day would have been better-omened had he not turned up.

"There are ceremonies going on," I said, "and I am busy. Could you perhaps come another day?"

At once he turned to go; but as he reached the door he hesitated, and said: "May I not see the little one, sir, for a moment?" It was his belief that Mini was still the same. He had pictured her running to him as she used to, calling "O Cabuliwallah! Cabuliwallah!" He had imagined too that they would laugh and talk together, just as of old. In fact, in memory of former days he had brought, carefully wrapped up in paper, a few almonds and raisins and grapes, obtained somehow from a countryman, for his own little fund was dispersed.

I said again: "There is a ceremony in the house, and you will not be able to see anyone today."

The man's face fell. He looked wistfully at me for a moment, said "Good morning," and went out. I felt a little sorry, and would have called him back, but I found he was returning of his own accord. He came close up to me holding out his offerings and said: "I brought these few things, sir, for the little one. Will you give them to her?"

I took them and was going to pay him, but he caught my hand and said: "You are very kind, sir! Keep me in your recollection. Do not offer me money!—You have a little girl, I too have one like her in my own home. I think of her, and bring fruits to your child, not to make a profit for myself."

Saying this, he put his hand inside his big loose robe, and brought out a small and dirty piece of paper. With great care he unfolded this, and smoothed it out with both hands on my table. It bore the impression of a little hand. Not a photograph. Not a drawing. The impression of an ink-smeared hand laid flat on the paper. This touch of his own little daughter had been always on his heart, as he had come year after year to Calcutta, to sell his wares in the streets.

Tears came to my eyes. I forgot that he was a poor Cabuli fruit-seller, while I was—but no, what was I more than he? He also was a father. That impression of the hand of his little Parbati in her distant mountain home reminded me of my own little Mini.

I sent for Mini immediately from the inner apartment. Many difficulties were raised, but I would not listen. Clad in the red silk of her wedding-day, with the sandal paste on her forehead, and adorned as a young bride, Mini came, and stood bashfully before me.

The Cabuliwallah looked a little staggered at the apparition. He could not revive their old friendship. At last he smiled and said: "Little one, are you going to your father-in-law's house?"

But Mini now understood the meaning of the word "father-in-law," and she could not reply to him as of old. She flushed up at the question, and stood before him with her bride-like face turned down.

I remembered the day when the Cabuliwallah and my Mini had first met, and I felt sad. When she had gone, Rahmun heaved a deep sigh, and sat down on the floor. The idea had suddenly come to him that his daughter too must have grown in this long time, and that he would have to make friends with her anew. Assuredly he would not find her, as he used to know her. And besides, what might not have happened to her in these eight years?

The marriage-pipes sounded, and the mild autumn sun streamed round us. But Rahmun sat in the little Calcutta lane, and saw before him the barren mountains of Afghanistan.

I took out a bank-note, and gave it to him, saying: "Go back to your own daughter, Rahmun, in your own country, and may the happiness of your meeting bring good fortune to my child!"

Having made this present, I had to curtail some of the festivities. I could not have the electric lights I had intended, nor the military band, and the ladies of the house were despondent at it. But to me the wedding feast was all the brighter for the thought that in a distant land a long-lost father met again with his only child.

জয় পরাজয়

The Victory

[*Joy Porajoy* was written in 1892. This is the author's translation taken from the collection *The Hungry Stones and Other Stories* (1916).]

She was the Princess Ajita. And the court poet of King Narayan had never seen her. On the day he recited a new poem to the king he would raise his voice just to that pitch which could be heard by unseen hearers in the screened balcony high above the hall. He sent up his song towards the star-land out of his reach, where, circled with light, the planet who ruled his destiny shone unknown and out of ken.

He would espy some shadow moving behind the veil. A tinkling sound would come to his ear from afar, and would set him dreaming of the ankles whose tiny golden bells sang at each step. Ah, the rosy red tender feet that walked the dust of the earth like God's mercy on the fallen! The poet had placed them on the altar of his heart, where he wove his songs to the tune of those golden bells. Doubt never arose in his mind as to whose shadow it was that moved behind the screen, and whose anklets they were that sang to the time of his beating heart.

Manjari, the maid of the princess, passed by the poet's house on her way to the river, and she never missed a day to have a few words with him on the sly. When she found the road deserted, and the shadow of dusk on the land, she would boldly enter his room, and sit at the corner of his carpet. There was a suspicion of an added care in the choice of the colour of her veil, in the setting of the flower in her hair.

People smiled and whispered at this, and they were not to blame. For Shekhar the poet never took the trouble to hide the fact that these meetings were a pure joy to him.

The meaning of her name was the 'spray of flowers.' One must confess that for an ordinary mortal it was sufficient in its sweetness. But Shekhar made his own addition to this name, and called her the Spray of Spring Flowers. And ordinary mortals shook their heads and said, Ah, me!

In the spring songs that the poet sang the praise of the spray of spring flowers was conspicuously reiterated; and the king winked and smiled at him when he heard it, and the poet smiled in answer.

The king would put him the question: "Is it the business of the bee merely to hum in the court of the spring?"

The poet would answer: "No, but also to sip the honey of the spray of spring flowers."

And they all laughed in the king's hall. And it was rumoured that the Princess Ajita also laughed at her maid's accepting the poet's name for her, and Manjari felt glad in her heart.

Thus truth and falsehood mingle in life—and to what God builds man adds his own decoration.

Only those were pure truths which were sung by the poet. The theme was Krishna, the lover god, and Radha, the beloved, the Eternal Man and the Eternal Woman, the sorrow that comes from the beginning of time, and the joy without end. The truth of these songs was tested in his inmost heart by everybody from the beggar to the king himself. The poet's songs were on the lips of all. At the merest glimmer of the moon and the faintest whisper of the summer breeze his songs would break forth in the land from windows and courtyards, from sailing-boats, from shadows of the wayside trees, in numberless voices.

Thus passed the days happily. The poet recited, the king listened, the hearers applauded, Manjari passed and repassed by the poet's room on her way to the river—the shadow flitted behind the screened balcony, and the tiny golden bells tinkled from afar.

Just then set forth from his home in the south a poet on his path of conquest. He came to King Narayan, in the kingdom of Amarapur. He stood before the throne, and uttered a verse in praise of the king. He had challenged all the court poets on his way, and his career of victory had been unbroken.

The king received him with honour, and said: "Poet, I offer you welcome."

Pundarik, the poet, proudly replied: "Sire, I ask for war."

Shekhar, the court poet of the king did not know how the battle of the muse was to be waged. He had no sleep at night. The mighty figure of the famous Pundarik, his sharp nose curved like a scimitar, and his proud head tilted on one side, haunted the poet's vision in the dark.

With a trembling heart Shekhar entered the arena in the morning. The theatre was filled with the crowd.

The poet greeted his rival with a smile and a bow. Pundarik returned it with a slight toss of his head, and turned his face towards his circle of adoring followers with a meaning smile. Shekhar cast his glance towards the screened balcony high above, and saluted his lady in his mind, saying: "If I am the winner at the combat today, my lady, thy victorious name shall be glorified."

The trumpet sounded. The great crowd stood up, shouting victory to the king. The king, dressed in an ample robe of white, slowly came into the hall like a floating cloud of autumn, and sat on his throne.

Pundarik stood up, and the vast hall became still. With his head raised high and chest expanded, he began in his thundering voice to recite the praise of King Narayan. His words burst upon the walls of the hall like breakers of the sea, and seemed to rattle against the ribs of the listening crowd. The skill with which he gave varied meanings to the name Narayan, and wove each letter of it through the web of his verses in all manner of combinations, took away the breath of his amazed hearers.

For some minutes after he took his seat his voice continued to vibrate among the numberless pillars of the king's court and in thousands of speechless hearts. The learned professors who had come from distant lands raised their right hands, and cried, Bravo!

The king threw a glance on Shekhar's face, and Shekhar in

answer raised for a moment his eyes full of pain towards his master, and then stood up like a stricken deer at bay. His face was pale, his bashfulness was almost that of a woman, his slight youthful figure, delicate in its outline, seemed like a tensely strung *vina* ready to break out in music at the least touch.

His head was bent, his voice was low, when he began. The first few verses were almost inaudible. Then he slowly raised his head, and his clear sweet voice rose into the sky like a quivering flame of fire. He began with the ancient legend of the kingly line lost in the haze of the past, and brought it down through its long course of heroism and matchless generosity to the present age. He fixed his gaze on the king's face, and all the vast and unexpressed love of the people for the royal house rose like incense in his song, and enwreathed the throne on all sides. These were his last words when, trembling, he took his seat: "My master, I may be beaten in play of words, but not in my love for thee."

Tears filled the eyes of the hearers, and the stone walls shook with cries of victory.

Mocking this popular outburst of feeling, with an august shake of his head and a contemptuous sneer, Pundarik stood up, and flung this question to the assembly; "What is there superior to words?" In a moment the hall lapsed into silence again.

Then with a marvellous display of learning, he proved that the Word was in the beginning, that the Word was God. He piled up quotations from scriptures, and built a high altar for the Word to be seated above all that there is in heaven and in earth. He repeated that question in his mighty voice: "What is there superior to words?"

Proudly he looked around him. None dared to accept his challenge, and he slowly took his seat like a lion who had just made a full meal of its victim. The pandits shouted, Bravo! The king remained silent with wonder, and the poet Shekhar felt himself of no account by the side of this stupendous learning. The assembly broke up for that day.

Next day Shekhar began his song. It was of that day when the pipings of love's flute startled for the first time the hushed air of the Vrinda forest. The shepherd women did not know who was the player or whence came the music. Sometimes it seemed to come from the heart of the south wind, and sometimes from the straying clouds of the hilltops. It came with a message of tryst from the land of the sunrise, and it floated from the verge of sunset with its sigh of sorrow. The stars seemed to be the stops of the instrument that flooded the dreams of the night with melody. The music seemed to burst all at once from all sides, from fields and groves, from the shady lanes and lonely roads, from the melting blue of the sky, from the shimmering green of the grass. They neither knew its meaning nor could they find words to give utterance to the desire of their hearts. Tears filled their eyes, and their life seemed to long for a death that would be its consummation.

Shekhar forgot his audience, forgot the trial of his strength with a rival. He stood alone amid his thoughts that rustled and quivered round him like leaves in a summer breeze, and sang the Song of the Flute. He had in his mind the vision of an image that had taken its shape from a shadow, and the echo of a faint tinkling sound of a distant footstep.

He took his seat. His hearers trembled with the sadness of an indefinable delight, immense and vague, and they forgot to applaud him. As this feeling died away Pundarik stood up before the throne and challenged his rival to define who was this Lover and who was the Beloved. He arrogantly looked around him, he smiled at his followers and then put the question again: "Who is Krishna, the lover, and who is Radha, the beloved?"

Then he began to analyse the roots of those names—and various interpretations of their meanings. He brought before the bewildered audience all the intricacies of the different schools of metaphysics with consummate skill. Each letter of those names he divided from its fellow, and then pursued them with a relentless logic till they fell to the dust in confusion, to be caught up again and restored to a meaning never before imagined by the subtlest of word-mongers.

The pandits were in ecstasy; they applauded vociferously; and the crowd followed them, deluded into the certainty that they had witnessed, that day, the last shred of the curtains of Truth torn to pieces before their eyes by a prodigy of intellect. The performance of his tremendous feat so delighted them that they forgot to ask themselves if there was any truth behind it after all.

The king's mind was overwhelmed with wonder. The atmosphere was completely cleared of all illusion of music, and the vision of the world around seemed to be changed from its freshness of tender green to the solidity of a high road levelled and made hard with crushed stones.

To the people assembled their own poet appeared a mere boy in comparison with this giant, who walked with such ease, knocking down difficulties at each step in the world of words and thoughts. It became evident to them for the first time that the poems Shekhar wrote were absurdly simple, and it must be a mere accident that they did not write them themselves. They were neither new, nor difficult, nor instructive, nor necessary.

The king tried to goad his poet with keen glances, silently inciting him to make a final effort. But Shekhar took no notice, and remained fixed to his seat.

The king in anger came down from his throne—took off his pearl chain and put it on Pundarik's head. Everybody in the hall cheered. From the upper balcony came a slight sound of the movements of rustling robes and waist-chains hung with golden bells. Shekhar rose from his seat and left the hall.

It was a dark night of waning moon. The poet Shekhar took down his MSS. from his shelves and heaped them on the floor. Some of them contained his earliest writings, which he had almost forgotten. He turned over the pages, reading passages here and there. They all seemed to him poor and trivial—mere words and childish rhymes!

One by one he tore his books to fragments, and threw them into a vessel containing fire, and said: "To thee, to thee, O my beauty, my fire! Thou hast been burning in my heart all these futile years. If my life were a piece of gold it would come out of its trial brighter, but it is a trodden turf of grass, and nothing remains of it but this handful of ashes."

The night wore on. Shekhar opened wide his windows. He spread upon his bed the white flowers that he loved, the jasmines, tuberoses and chrysanthemums, and brought into his bedroom all the lamps he had in his house and lighted them. Then mixing with honey the juice of some poisonous root he drank it and lay down on his bed.

Golden anklets tinkled in the passage outside the door, and a subtle perfume came into the room with the breeze.

The poet, with his eyes shut, said: "My lady, have you taken pity upon your servant at last and come to see him?"

The answer came in a sweet voice: "My poet, I have come."

Shekhar opened his eyes—and saw before his bed the figure of a woman.

His sight was dim and blurred. And it seemed to him that the image made of a shadow that he had ever kept throned in the secret shrine of his heart had come into the outer world in his last moment to gaze upon his face.

The woman said: "I am the Princess Ajita."

The poet with a great effort sat up on his bed.

The princess whispered into his ear: "The king has not done you justice. It was you who won at the combat, my poet, and I have come to crown you with the crown of victory."

She took the garland of flowers from her own neck, and put it on his hair, and the poet fell down upon his bed stricken by death.

একটি আষাঢ়ে গল্প

The Kingdom of Cards

[*Ekti Ashare Golpo* was written in 1892. Here is a translation by Mr. C. F. Andrews and the author taken from *The Hungry Stones and Other Stories* (1916). The story has also been translated as *A Tale of Fantasy*, *A Fanciful Story*, and *An Absurd Story*.]

I

Once upon a time there was a lonely island in a distant sea where lived the Kings and Queens, the Aces and the Knaves, in the Kingdom of Cards. The Tens and Nines, with the Twos and Threes, and all the other members, had long ago settled there also. But these were not twice-born people, like the famous Court Cards.

The Ace, the King, and the Knave were the three highest castes. The fourth Caste was made up of a mixture of the lower Cards. The Twos and Threes were lowest of all. These inferior Cards were never allowed to sit in the same row with the great Court Cards.

Wonderful indeed were the regulations and rules of that island kingdom. The particular rank of each individual had been settled from time immemorial. Everyone had his own appointed work, and never did anything else. An unseen hand appeared to be directing them wherever they went—according to the Rules.

No one in the Kingdom of Cards had any occasion to think: no one had any need to come to any decision: no one was ever required to debate any new subject. The citizens all moved along in a listless groove without speech. When they fell, they made no noise. They lay down on their backs, and gazed upward at the sky with each prim feature firmly fixed for ever.

There was a remarkable stillness in the Kingdom of Cards. Satisfaction and contentment were complete in all their rounded wholeness. There was never any uproar or violence. There was never any excitement or enthusiasm.

The great ocean, crooning its lullaby with one unceasing melody, lapped the island to sleep with a thousand soft touches of its wave's white hands. The vast sky, like the outspread azure wings of the brooding mother-bird, nestled the island round with its downy plume. For on the distant horizon a deep blue line betokened another shore. But no sound of quarrel or strife could reach the Island of Cards, to break its calm repose.

II

In that far-off foreign land across the sea, there lived a young Prince whose mother was a sorrowing queen. This queen had fallen from favour, and was living with her only son on the seashore. The Prince passed his childhood alone and forlorn, sitting by his forlorn mother, weaving the net of his big desires. He longed to go in search of the Flying Horse, the Jewel in the Cobra's hood, the Rose of Heaven, the Magic Roads, or to find where the Princess Beauty was sleeping in the Ogre's castle over the thirteen rivers and across the seven seas.

From the Son of the Merchant at school the young Prince learnt the stories of foreign kingdoms. From the Son of the Kotwal he learnt the adventures of the Two Genii of the Lamp. And when the rain came beating down, and the clouds covered the sky, he would sit on the threshold facing the sea, and say to his sorrowing mother: "Tell me, mother, a story of some very far-off land."

And his mother would tell him an endless tale she had heard in her childhood of a wonderful country beyond the sea where dwelt the Princess Beauty. And the heart of the young Prince would become sick with longing, as he sat on the threshold, looking out on the ocean, listening to his mother's wonderful story, while the rain outside came beating down and the grey clouds covered the sky.

One day the Son of the Merchant came to the Prince, and said boldly: "Comrade, my studies are over. I am now setting out on my travels to seek my fortunes on the sea. I have come to bid you goodbye."

The Prince said: "I will go with you."

And the Son of Kotwal said also: "Comrades, trusty and true, you will not leave me behind. I also will be your companion."

Then the young Prince said to his sorrowing mother; "Mother, I am now setting out on my travels to seek my fortune. When I come back once more, I shall surely have found some way to remove all your sorrow."

So the Three Companions set out on their travels together. In the harbour were anchored the twelve ships of the merchant, and the Three Companions got on board. The south wind was blowing, and the twelve ships sailed away, as fast as the desires which rose in the Prince's breast.

At the Conch Shell Island they filled one ship with conchs. At the Sandal Wood Island they filled a second ship with sandalwood, and at the Coral Island they filled a third ship with coral.

Four years passed away, and they filled four more ships, one with ivory, one with musk, one with cloves, and one with nutmegs.

But when these ships were all loaded a terrible tempest arose. The ships were all of them sunk, with their cloves and nutmeg, and musk and ivory, and coral and sandalwood and conchs. But the ship with the Three Companions struck on an island reef, buried them safe ashore, and itself broke in pieces.

This was the famous Island of Cards, where lived the Ace and King and Queen and Knave, with the Nines and Tens and all the other Members—according to the Rules.

III

Up till now there had been nothing to disturb that island stillness. No new thing had ever happened. No discussion had ever been held.

And then, all of a sudden, the Three Companions appeared,

thrown up by the sea—and the Great Debate began. There were three main points of dispute.

First, to what caste should these unclassed strangers belong? Should they rank with the Court Cards? Or were they merely lower-caste people, to be ranked with the Nines and Tens? No precedent could be quoted to decide this weighty question.

Secondly, what was their clan? Had they the fairer hue and bright complexion of the Hearts, or was theirs the darker complexion of the Clubs? Over this question there were interminable disputes. The whole marriage system of the island, with its intricate regulations, would depend on its nice adjustment.

Thirdly, what food should they take? With whom should they live and sleep? And should their heads be placed south-west, north-west, or only north-east? In all the Kingdom of Cards a series of problems so vital and critical had never been debated before.

But the Three Companions grew desperately hungry. They had to get food in some way or other. So while this debate went on, with its interminable silence and pauses, and while the Aces called their own meeting, and formed themselves into a Committee, to find some obsolete dealing with the question, the Three Companions themselves were eating all they could find, and drinking out of every vessel, and breaking all regulations.

Even the Twos and Threes were shocked at this outrageous behaviour. The Threes said: "Brother Twos, these people are openly shameless!" And the Twos said: "Brother Threes, they are evidently of lower caste than ourselves!" After their meal was over, the Three Companions went for a stroll in the city.

When they saw the ponderous people moving in their dismal processions with prim and solemn faces, then the Prince turned to the Son of the Merchant and the Son of the Kotwal, and threw back his head, and gave one stupendous laugh.

Down Royal Street and across Ace Square and along the Knave Embankment ran the quiver of this strange, unheard-of laughter, the laughter that, amazed at itself, expired in the vast vacuum of silence.

The Son of the Kotwal and the Son of the Merchant were chilled through to the bone by the ghost-like stillness around them. They turned to the Prince, and said: "Comrade, let us away. Let us not stop for a moment in this awful land of ghosts."

But the Prince said: "Comrades, these people resemble men, so I am going to find out, by shaking them upside down and outside in, whether they have a single drop of warm living blood left in their veins."

IV

The days passed one by one, and the placid existence of the Island went on almost without a ripple. The Three Companions obeyed no rules nor regulations. They never did anything correctly either in sitting or standing or turning themselves round or lying on their back. On the contrary, wherever they saw these things going on precisely and exactly according to the Rules, they gave way to inordinate laughter. They remained unimpressed altogether by the eternal gravity of those eternal regulations.

One day the great Court Cards came to the Son of the Kotwal and the Son of the Merchant and the Prince.

"Why," they asked slowly, "are you not moving according to the Rules?"

The Three Companions answered: "Because that is our *Ichcha**."

The great Court Cards with hollow, cavernous voices, as if slowly awakening from an age-long dream, said together: "Ich-cha! And pray who is Ich-cha?"

They could not understand who Ichcha was then, but the whole island was to understand it by and by. The first glimmer of light passed the threshold of their minds when they found out, through watching the actions of the Prince, that they might move in a straight line in an opposite direction from the one in which they had always gone before. Then they made another startling discovery, that there was another side to the Cards which they had never yet noticed with attention. This was the beginning of the change.

Now that the change had begun, the Three Companions were able to initiate them more and more deeply into the mysteries of

---

* Wish

Ichcha. The Cards gradually became aware that life was not bound by regulations. They began to feel a secret satisfaction in the kingly power of choosing for themselves.

But with this first impact of Ichcha the whole pack of cards began to totter slowly, and then tumble down to the ground. The scene was like that of some huge python awaking from a long sleep, as it slowly unfolds its numberless coils with a quiver that runs through its whole frame.

V

Hitherto the Queens of Spades and Clubs and Diamonds and Hearts had remained behind curtains with eyes that gazed vacantly into space, or else remained fixed upon the ground.

And now, all of a sudden, on an afternoon in spring the Queen of Hearts from the balcony raised her dark eyebrows for a moment, and cast a single glance upon the Prince from the corner of her eye.

"Great God," cried the Prince, "I thought they were all painted images. But I am wrong. They are women after all."

Then the young Prince called to his side his two Companions, and said in a meditative voice: "My comrades! There is a charm about these ladies that I never noticed before. When I saw that glance of the Queen's dark, luminous eyes, brightening with new emotion, it seemed to me like the first faint streak of dawn in a newly created world."

The two Companions smiled a knowing smile, and said: "Is that really so, Prince?"

And the poor Queen of Hearts from that day went from bad to worse. She began to forget all rules in a truly scandalous manner. If, for instance, her place in the row was beside the Knave, she suddenly found herself quite accidentally standing beside the Prince instead. At this, the Knave, with motionless face and solemn voice, would say: "Queen, you have made a mistake."

And the poor Queen of Hearts' red cheeks would get redder than ever. But the Prince would come gallantly to her rescue and say: "No! There is no mistake. From today I am going to be Knave!"

Now it came to pass that, while everyone was trying to correct the improprieties of the guilty Queen of Hearts, they began to make mistakes themselves. The Aces found themselves elbowed out by the Kings. The Kings got muddled up with the Knaves. The Nines and Tens assumed airs as though they belonged to the Great Court Cards. The Twos and Threes were found secretly taking the places specially resented for the Fours and Fives. Confusion had never been so confounded before.

Many spring seasons had come and gone in that Island of Cards. The Kokil, the bird of Spring, had sung its song year after year. But it had never stirred the blood as it stirred it now. In days gone by the sea had sung its tireless melody. But, then, it had proclaimed only the inflexible monotony of the Rule. And suddenly its waves were telling, through all their flashing light and luminous shade and myriad voices, the deepest yearnings of the heart of love!

VI

Where are vanished now their prim, round, regular, complacent features? Here is a face full of love-sick longing. Here is a heart heating wild with regrets. Here is a mind racked sore with doubts. Music and sighing, and smiles and tears, are filling the air. Life is throbbing; hearts are breaking; passions are kindling.

Everyone is now thinking of his own appearance, and comparing himself with others. The Ace of Clubs is musing to himself, that the King of Spades may be just passably good-looking. "But," says he, "when I walk down the street you have only to see how people's eyes turn towards me." The King of Spades is saying; "Why on earth is that Ace of Clubs always straining his neck and strutting about like a peacock? He imagines all the Queens are dying of love for him, while the real fact is—" Here he pauses, and examines his face in the glass.

But the Queens were the worst of all. They began to spend all their time in dressing themselves up to the Nines. And the Nines would become their hopeless and abject slaves. But their cutting remarks about one another were more shocking still.

So the young men would sit listless on the leaves under the trees, lolling with outstretched limbs in the forest shade. And the young maidens, dressed in pale-blue robes, would come walking accidentally to the same shade of the same forest by the same trees, and turn their eyes as though they saw no one there, and look as though they came out to see nothing at all. And then one young man more forward than the rest in a fit of madness would dare to go near to a maiden in blue. But, as he drew near, speech would forsake him. He would stand there tongue-tied and foolish, and the favourable moment would pass.

The Kokil birds were singing in the boughs overhead. The mischievous South wind was blowing; it disarrayed the hair, it whispered in the ear, and stirred the music in the blood. The leaves of the trees were murmuring with rustling delight. And the ceaseless sound of the ocean made all the mute longings of the heart of man and maid surge backwards and forwards on the full springtide of love.

The Three Companions had brought into the dried-up channels of the Kingdom of Cards the full flood-tide of a new life.

VII

And, though the tide was full, there was a pause as though the rising waters would not break into foam but remain suspended for ever. There were no outspoken words, only a cautious going forward one step and receding two. All seemed busy heaping up their unfulfilled desires like castles in the air, or fortresses of sand. They were pale and speechless, their eyes were burning, their lips trembling with unspoken secrets.

The Prince saw what was wrong. He summoned everyone on the Island and said: "Bring hither the flutes and the cymbals, the pipes and drums. Let all be played together, and raise loud shouts of rejoicing. For the Queen of Hearts this very night is going to choose her Mate!"

So the Tens and Nines began to blow on their flutes and pipes; the Eights and Sevens played on their sackbuts and viols; and even the Twos and Threes began to beat madly on their drums.

When this tumultuous gust of music came, it swept away at one blast all those sighings and mopings. And then what a torrent of laughter and words poured forth! There were daring proposals and locking refusals, and gossip and chatter, and jests and merriment. It was like the swaying and shaking, and rustling and soughing, in a summer gale, of a million leaves and branches in the depth of the primeval forest.

But the Queen of Hearts, in a rose-red robe, sat silent in the shadow of her secret bower, and listened to the great uproarious sound of music and mirth, that came floating towards her. She shut her eyes, and dreamt her dream of lore. And when she opened them she found the Prince seated on the ground before her gazing up at her face. And she covered her eyes with both hands, and shrank back quivering with an inward tumult of joy.

And the Prince passed the whole day alone, walking by the side of the surging sea. He carried in his mind that startled look, that shrinking gesture of the Queen, and his heart beat high with hope.

That night the serried, gaily-dressed ranks of young men and maidens waited with smiling faces at the Palace Gates. The Palace Hall was lighted with fairy lamps and festooned with the flowers of spring. Slowly the Queen of Hearts entered, and the whole assembly rose to greet her. With a jasmine garland in her hand, she stood before the Prince with downcast eyes. In her lowly bashfulness she could hardly raise the garland to the neck of the Mate she had chosen. But the Prince bowed his head, and the garland slipped to its place. The assembly of youths and maidens had waited her choice with eager, expectant hush. And when the choice was made, the whole vast concourse rocked and swayed with a tumult of wild delight. And the sound of their shouts was heard in every part of the island, and by ships far out at sea. Never had such a shout been raised in the Kingdom of Cards before.

And they carried the Prince and his Bride, and seated them on the throne, and crowned them then and there in the Ancient Island of Cards.

And the sorrowing Mother Queen, on the far-off island shore on the other side of the sea, came sailing to her son's new kingdom in a ship adorned with gold.

And the citizens are no longer regulated according to the Rules, but are good or bad, or both, according to their Ichcha.

জীবিত ও মৃত

Living or Dead?

[*Jibita o Mrita*, a ghost story, was written in 1892. This translation is taken from *The Hungry Stones and Other Stories* (1916). It has also been translated as *Alive and Dead* and *The Living and the Dead*.]

I

The widow in the house of Saradasankar, the Ranihat zamindar, had no kinsmen of her father's family. One after another all had died. Nor had she in her husband's family any one she could call her own, neither husband nor son. The child of her brother-in-law Saradasankar was her darling. For a long time after his birth, his mother had been very ill, and the widow, his aunt Kadambini, had fostered him. If a woman fosters another's child, her love for him is all the stronger because she has no claim upon him—no claim of kinship, that is, but simply the claim of love. Love cannot prove its claim by any document which society accepts, and does not wish to prove it; it merely worships with double passion its life's uncertain treasure. Thus all the widow's thwarted love went out towards this little child. One night in *Sraban* Kadambini died suddenly. For some reason her heart stopped beating. Everywhere else the world held on its course; only in this gentle little breast, suffering with love, the watch of time stood still for ever.

Lest they should be harassed by the police, four of the zamindar's Brahmin servants took away the body, without ceremony, to be burned. The burning-ground of Ranihat was very far from the village. There was a hut beside a tank, a huge banyan near it, and nothing more. Formerly a river, now completely dried up, ran through the ground, and part of the watercourse had been dug out to make a tank for the performance of funeral rites. The people considered the tank as part of the river and reverenced it as such.

Taking the body into the hut, the four men sat down to wait for the wood. The time seemed so long that two of the four grew restless, and went to see why it did not come. Nitai and Gurucharan being gone, Bidhu and Banamali remained to watch over the body.

It was a dark night of Sraban. Heavy clouds hung in a starless sky. The two men sat silent in the dark room. Their matches and lamp were useless. The matches were damp, and would not light, for all their efforts, and the lantern went out.

After a long silence, one said: "Brother, it would be good if we had a bowl of tobacco. In our hurry we brought none."

The other answered: "I can run and bring all we want."

Understanding why Banamali wanted to go (From fear of ghosts, the burning-ground being considered haunted), Bidhu said: "I daresay! Meanwhile, I suppose I am to sit here alone!"

Conversation ceased again. Five minutes seemed like an hour. In their minds they cursed the two, who had gone to fetch the wood, and they began to suspect that they sat gossiping in some pleasant nook. There was no sound anywhere, except the incessant noise of frogs and crickets from the tank. Then suddenly they fancied that the bed shook slightly, as if the dead body had turned on its side. Bidhu and Banamali trembled, and began muttering: "Ram, Ram." A deep sigh was heard in the room. In a moment the watchers leapt out of the hut, and raced for the village.

After running about three miles, they met their colleagues coming back with a lantern. As a matter of fact, they *had* gone to smoke, and knew nothing about the wood. But they declared that a tree had been cut down, and that, when it was split up, it would be brought along at once. Then Bidhu and Banamali told them what had happened in the hut. Nitai and Gurucharan scoffed at the story, and abused Bidhu and Banamali angrily for leaving their duty.

Without delay all four returned to the hut. As they entered, they saw at once that the body was gone; nothing but an empty bed remained. They stared at one another. Could a jackal have taken it? But there was no scrap of clothing anywhere. Going outside, they saw that on the mud that had collected at the door of the hut there were a woman's tiny footprints, newly made. Saradasankar was no fool, and they could hardly persuade him to believe in this ghost story. So after much discussion the four decided that it would be best to say that the body had been burnt.

Towards dawn, when the men with the wood arrived they were told that, owing to their delay, the work had been done without them; there had been some wood in the hut after all. No one was likely to question this, since a dead body is not such a valuable property that any one would steal it.

II

Everyone knows that, even when there is no sign, life is often secretly present, and may begin again in an apparently dead body. Kadambini was not dead; only the machine of her life had for some reason suddenly stopped.

When consciousness returned, she saw dense darkness on all sides. It occurred to her that she was not lying in her usual place. She called out "Sister," but no answer came from the darkness. As she sat up, terror-stricken, she remembered her deathbed, the sudden pain at her breast, the beginning of a choking sensation. Her elder sister-in-law was warming some milk for the child, when Kadambini became faint, and fell on the bed, saying with a choking voice: "Sister, bring the child here. I am worried." After that everything was black, as when an inkpot is upset over an exercise-book. Kadambini's memory and consciousness, all the letters of the world's book, in a moment became formless. The widow could not remember whether the child, in the sweet voice of love, called her "Auntie," as if for the last time, or not; she could not remember whether, as she left the world she knew for death's endless unknown journey, she had received a parting gift of affection, love's passage-money for the silent land. At first, I fancy, she thought the lonely dark place was the House of Yama, where there is nothing to see, nothing to hear, nothing to do, only an eternal watch. But when a cold damp wind drove through the open door, and she heard the croaking of frogs, she remembered vividly and in a moment all the rains of her short life, and could feel her kinship with the earth. Then came a flash of lightning, and she saw the tank, the banyan, the great plain, the far-off trees. She remembered how at full moon she had sometimes come to bathe in this tank, and how dreadful death had seemed when she saw a corpse on the burning-ground.

Her first thought was to return home. But then she reflected: "I am dead. How can I return home? That would bring disaster on them. I have left the kingdom of the living; I am my own ghost!" If this were not so, she reasoned, how could she have got out of Saradasankar's well-guarded zenana, and come to this distant burning-ground at midnight? Also, if her funeral rites had not been finished, where had the men gone who should burn her? Recalling her death-moment in Saradasankar's brightly-lit house, she now found herself alone in a distant, deserted, dark burning-ground. Surely she was no member of earthly society! Surely she was a creature of horror, of ill-omen, her own ghost!

At this thought, all the bonds were snapped which bound her to the world. She felt that she had marvellous strength, endless freedom. She could do what she liked, go where she pleased. Mad with the inspiration of this new idea, she rushed from the hut like a gust of wind, and stood upon the burning-ground. All trace of shame or fear had left her.

But as she walked on and on, her feet grew tired, her body weak. The plain stretched on endlessly; here and there were paddy-fields; sometimes she found herself standing knee-deep in water.

At the first glimmer of dawn she heard one or two birds cry from the bamboo-clumps by the distant houses. Then terror seized her. She could not tell in what new relation she stood to the earth and to living folk. So long as she had been on the plain, on the burning-ground, covered by the dark night of Sraban, so long she had been fearless, a denizen of her own kingdom. By daylight the homes of men filled her with fear. Men and ghosts dread each other, for their tribes inhabit different banks of the river of death.

III

Her clothes were clotted in the mud; strange thoughts and walking by night had given her the aspect of a madwoman; truly, her apparition was such that folk might have been afraid of her, and children might have stoned her or run away. Luckily, the first to catch sight of her was a traveller. He came up, and said: "Mother, you look a respectable woman. Wherever are you going, alone and in this guise?"

Kadambini, unable to collect her thoughts, stared at him in silence. She could not think that she was still in touch with the world, that she looked like a respectable woman, that a traveller was asking her questions.

Again the min said: "Come, mother, I will see you home. Tell me where you live."

Kadambini thought. To return to her father-in-law's house would be absurd, and she had no father's house. Then she remembered the friend of her childhood. She had not seen Jogmaya since the days of her youth, but from time to time they had exchanged letters. Occasionally there had been quarrels between them, as was only right, since Kadambini wished to make it clear that her love for Jogmaya was unbounded, while her friend complained that Kadambini did not return a love equal to her own. They were both sure that, if they once met, they would be inseparable.

Kadambini said to the traveller: "I will go to Sripati's house at Nisindapur."

As he was going to Calcutta, Nisindapur, though not near, was on his way. So he took Kadambini to Sripati's house, and the friends met again. At first they did not recognise one another, but gradually each recognised the features of the other's childhood.

"What luck!" said Jogmaya. "I never dreamt that I should see you again. But how have you come here, sister? Your father-in-law's folk surely didn't let you go!"

Kadambini remained silent, and at last said: "Sister, do not ask about my father-in-law. Give me a corner, and treat me as a servant: I will do your work."

"What?" cried Jogmaya. "Keep you like a servant! Why, you are my closest friend, you are my—" and so on and so on.

Just then Sripati came in. Kadambini stared at him for some time, and then went out very slowly. She kept her head uncovered, and showed not the slightest modesty or respect. Jogmaya, fearing that Sripati would be prejudiced against her friend, began an elaborate explanation. But Sripati, who readily agreed to anything Jogmaya said, cut short her story, and left his wife uneasy in her mind.

Kadambini had come, but she was not at one with her friend: death was between them. She could feel no intimacy for others so long as her existence perplexed her and consciousness remained. Kadambini would look at Jogmaya, and brood. She would think: "She has her husband and her work, she lives in a world far away from mine. She shares affection and duty with the people of the world; I am an empty shadow. She is among the living; I am in eternity."

Jogmaya also was uneasy, but could not explain why. Women do not love mystery, because, though uncertainty may be transmuted into poetry, into heroism, into scholarship, it cannot be turned to account in household work. So, when a woman cannot understand a thing, she either destroys and forgets it, or she shapes it anew for her own use; if she fails to deal with it in one of these ways, she loses her temper with it. The greater Kadambini's abstraction became, the more impatient was Jogmaya with her, wondering what trouble weighed upon her mind.

Then a new danger arose. Kadambini was afraid of herself; yet she could not flee from herself. Those who fear ghosts fear those who are behind them; wherever they cannot see there is fear. But Kadambini's chief terror lay in herself, for she dreaded nothing external. At the dead of night, when alone in her room, she screamed; in the evening, when she saw her shadow in the lamplight, her whole body shook. Watching her fearfulness, the rest of the house fell into a sort of terror. The servants and Jogmaya herself began to see ghosts.

One midnight, Kadambini came out from her bedroom weeping, and wailed at Jogmaya's door: "Sister, sister, let me lie at your feet! Do not put me by myself!"

Jogmaya's anger was no less than her fear. She would have liked to drive Kadambini from the house that very second. The good-natured Sripati, after much effort, succeeded in quieting their guest, and put her in the next room.

Next day, Sripati was unexpectedly summoned to his wife's apartments. She began to upbraid him: "You, do you call yourself a man? A woman runs away from her father-in-law, and enters your house; a month passes, and you haven't hinted that she should go away, nor have I heard the slightest protest from you. I should cake it as a favour if you would explain yourself. You men are all alike."

Men, as a race, have a natural partiality for womankind in general, foe which women themselves hold them accountable. Although Sripati was prepared to touch Jogmaya's body, and swear that his kind feeling towards the helpless but beautiful Kadambini was no whit greater than it should be, he could not prove it by his behaviour. He thought that her father-in-law's people must have treated this forlorn widow abominably, if she could bear it no longer, and was driven to take refuge with him. As she had neither father nor mother, how could he desert her? So saying, he let the matter drop, for he had no mind to distress Kadambini by asking her unpleasant questions.

His wife, then, tried other means of her sluggish lord, until at last he saw that for the sake of peace he must send word to Kadambini's father-in-law. The result of a letter, he thought, might not be satisfactory; so he resolved to go to Ranihat, and act on what he learnt.

So Sripati went, and Jogmaya on her part said to Kadambini: "Friend, it hardly seems proper for you to stop here any longer. What will people say?"

Kadambini stared solemnly at Jogmaya, and said: "What have I to do with people?"

Jogmaya was astounded. Then she said sharply: "If you have nothing to do with people, we have. How can we explain the detention of a woman belonging to another house?"

Kadambini said: "Where is my father-in-law's house?"

"Confound it!" thought Jogmaya. "What will the wretched woman say next?"

Very slowly Kadambini said: "What have I to do with you? Am I of the earth? You laugh, weep, love; each grips and holds his own; I merely look. You are human, I a shadow. I cannot understand why God has kept me in this world of yours."

So strange were her look and speech that Jogmaya understood something of her drift, though not all. Unable either to dismiss her, or to ask her any more questions, she went away, oppressed with thought.

IV

It was nearly ten o'clock at night when Sripati returned from Ranihat. The earth was drowned in torrents of rain. It seemed that the downpour would never stop, that the night would never end.

Jogmaya asked: "Well?"

"I've lots to say, presently."

So saying, Sripati changed his clothes, and sat down to supper; then he lay down for a smoke. His mind was perplexed.

His wife stifled her curiosity for a long time; then she came to his couch and demanded: "What did you hear?"

"That you have certainly made a mistake."

Jogmaya was nettled. Women never make mistakes, or, if they do, a sensible man never mentions them; it is better to take them on his own shoulders. Jogmaya snapped: "May I be permitted to hear how?"

Sripati replied: "The woman you have taken into your house is not your Kadambini."

Hearing this, she was greatly annoyed, especially since it was her husband who said it. "What! I don't know my own friend? I must come to you to recognise her! You are clever, indeed!"

Sripati explained that there was no need to quarrel about his cleverness. He could prove what he said. There was no doubt that Jogmaya's Kadambini was dead.

Jogmaya replied: "Listen! You've certainly made some huge mistake. You've been to the wrong house, or are confused as to what you have heard. Who told you to go yourself? Write a letter, and everything will be cleared up."

Sripati was hurt by his wife's lack of faith in his executive ability; he produced all sorts of proof, without result. Midnight found them still asserting and contradicting. Although they both agreed now that Kadambini should be got out of the house, although Sripati believed that their guest had deceived his wife all the time by a pretended acquaintance, and Jogmaya that she was a prostitute, yet in the present discussion neither would acknowledge defeat. By degrees their voices became so loud that they forgot that Kadambini was sleeping in the next room.

The one said: "We're in a nice fix! I tell you, I heard it with my own ears!" And the other answered angrily: "What do I care about that? I can see with my own eyes, surely."

At length Jogmaya said: "Very well. Tell me when Kadambini died." She thought that if she could find a discrepancy between the day of death and the date of some letter from Kadambini, she could prove that Sripati erred.

He told her the date of Kadambini's death, and they both saw that it fell on the very day before she came to their house. Jogmaya's heart trembled, even Sripati was not unmoved.

Just then the door flew open; a damp wind swept in and blew the lamp out. The darkness rushed after it, and filled the whole house. Kadambini stood in the room. It was nearly one o'clock, the rain was pelting outside.

Kadambini spoke: "Friend, I am your Kadambini, but I am no longer living. I am dead."

Jogmaya screamed with terror; Sripati could speak.

"But, save in being dead, I have done you no wrong. If I have no place among the living, I have none among the dead. Oh! whither shall I go?"

Crying as if to wake the sleeping Creator in the dense night of rain, she asked again: "Oh! whither shall I go?"

So saying Kadambini left her friend fainting in the dark house, and went out into the world, seeking her own place.

V

It is hard to say how Kadambini reached Ranihat. At first she showed herself to no one, but spent the whole day in a ruined temple, starving. When the untimely afternoon of the rains was pitch-black, and people huddled into their houses for fear of the impending storm, then Kadambini came forth. Her heart trembled as she reached her father-in-law's house; and when, drawing a thick veil over her face, she entered, none of the doorkeepers objected, since they took her for a servant. And the rain was pouring down, and the wind howled.

The mistress, Saradasankar's wife, was playing cards with her widowed sister. A servant was in the kitchen, the sick child was sleeping in the bedroom. Kadambini, escaping every one's notice, entered this room. I do not know why she had come to her father-in-law's house; she herself did not know; she felt only that she wanted to see her child again. She had no thought where to go next, or what to do.

In the lighted room she saw the child sleeping, his fists clenched, his body wasted with fever. At sight of him, her heart became parched and thirsty. If only she could press that tortured body to her breast! Immediately the thought followed: "I do not exist. Who would see it? His mother loves company, loves gossip and cards. All the time that she left me in charge, she was herself free from anxiety, nor was she troubled about him in the least. Who will look after him now as I did?"

The child turned on his side, and cried, half-asleep: "Auntie, give me water." Her darling had not yet forgotten his auntie! In a fever of excitement, she poured out some water, and, taking him to her breast, she gave it him.

As long as he was asleep, the child felt no strangeness in taking water from the accustomed hand. But when Kadambini satisfied her long-starved longing, and kissed him and began rocking him asleep again, he awoke and embraced her. "Did you die, Auntie?" he asked.

"Yes, darling."

"And you have come back? Do not die again."

Before she could answer disaster overtook her. One of the maidservants coming in with a cup of sago dropped it, and fell down. At the crash the mistress left her cards, and entered the room. She stood like a pillar of wood, unable to flee or speak. Seeing all this, the child, too, became terrified, and burst out weeping: "Go away, Auntie," he said, "go away!"

Now at last Kadambini understood that she had not died. The old room, the old things, the same child, the same love, all returned to their living state, without change or difference between her and them. In her friend's house she had felt that her childhood's companion was dead. In her child's room she knew that the boy's 'Auntie' was not dead at all. In anguished tones she said: "Sister, why do you dread me? See, I am as you knew me."

Her sister-in-law could endure no longer, and fainted. Saradasankar himself entered the zenana. With folded hands, he said piteously: "Is this right? Satis is my only son. Why do you show yourself to him? Are we not your own kin? Since you went, he has wasted away daily; his fever has been incessant; day and night he cries: 'Auntie, Auntie.' You have left the world; break these bonds of maya*. We will perform all funeral honours."

Kadambini could bear no more. She said: "Oh, I am not dead, I am not dead. Oh, how can I persuade you that I am not dead? I am living, living!" She lifted a brass pot from the ground and dashed it against her forehead. The blood ran from her brow. "Look!" she cried, "I am living!" Saradasankar stood like an image; the child screamed with fear, the two fainted women lay still.

Then Kadambini, shouting "I am not dead, I am not dead," went down the steps to the zenana well, and plunged in. From the upper storey Saradasankar heard the splash.

All night the rain poured; it poured next day at dawn, was pouring still at noon. By dying, Kadambini had given proof that she was not dead.

---

* Illusory affection binding a soul to the world

ঙ

ত্যাগ

The Renunciation

[*Tyaga* was written in 1892. This translation by Mr. C. F. Andrews and the author is taken from *The Hungry Stones and Other Stories* published in 1916. It has also been translated as *Outcast* and *Sacrifice*.]

I

It was a night of full moon early in the month of *Phalgun*. The youthful spring was everywhere sending forth its breeze laden with the fragrance of mango-blossoms. The melodious notes of an untiring papiya*, concealed within the thick foliage of an old lichee tree by the side of a tank, penetrated a sleepless bedroom of the Mukerji family. There Hemanta now restlessly twisted a lock of his wife's hair round his finger, now beat her *churi* against her wristlet until it tinkled, now pulled at the chaplet of flowers about her head, and left it hanging over her face. His mood was that of an evening breeze, which played about a favourite flowering shrub, gently shaking her now this side, now that, in the hope of rousing her to animation.

But Kusum sat motionless, looking out of the open window,

---

* One of the sweetest songsters in Bengal. Anglo-Indian writers have nicknamed it the 'brain-fever bird,' which is a sheer libel.

with eyes immersed in the moonlit depth of never-ending space beyond. Her husband's caresses were lost on her.

At last Hemanta clasped both the hands of his wife, and, shaking them gently, said: "Kusum, where are you? A patient search through a big telescope would reveal you only as a small speck—you seem to have receded so far away. O, do come closer to me, dear. See how beautiful the night is."

Kusum turned her eyes from the void of space towards her husband, and said slowly: "I know a mantra*, which could in one moment shatter this spring night and the moon into pieces."

"If you do," laughed Hemanta, "pray don't utter it. If any mantra of yours could bring three or four Saturdays during the week, and prolong the nights till 5 p.m. the next day, say it by all means."

Saying this, he tried to draw his wife a little closer to him. Kusum, freeing herself from the embrace, said: "Do you know, tonight I feel a longing to tell you what I promised to reveal only on my deathbed. Tonight I feel that I could endure whatever punishment you might inflict on me."

Hemanta was on the point of making a jest about punishments by reciting a verse from Jayadeva, when the sound of an angry pair of slippers was heard approaching rapidly. They were the familiar footsteps of his father, Harihar Mukerji, and Hemanta, not knowing what it meant, was in a flutter of excitement.

Standing outside the door Harihar roared out: "Hemanta, turn your wife out of the house immediately."

Hemanta looked at his wife, and detected no trace of surprise in her features. She merely buried her face within the palms of her hands, and, with all the strength and intensity of her soul, wished that she could then and there melt into nothingness. It was the same papiya whose song floated into the room with the south breeze, and no one heard it. Endless are the beauties of the earth—but alas, how easily everything is twisted out of shape.

---

* A set of magic words

II

Returning from without, Hemanta asked his wife: "Is it true?"

"It is," replied Kusum.

"Why didn't you tell me long ago?"

"I did try many a time, and I always failed. I am a wretched woman."

"Then tell me everything now."

Kusum gravely told her story in a firm unshaken voice. She waded barefooted through fire, as it were, with slow unflinching steps, and nobody knew how much she was scorched. Having heard her to the end, Hemanta rose and walked out.

Kusum thought that her husband had gone, never to return to her again. It did not strike her as strange. She took it as naturally as any other incident of everyday life—so dry and apathetic had her mind become during the last few moments. Only the world and love seemed to her as a void and make-believe from beginning to end. Even the memory of the protestations of love, which her husband had made to her in days past, brought to her lips a dry, hard, joyless smile, like a sharp cruel knife which had cut through her heart. She was thinking, perhaps, that the love which seemed to fill so much of one's life, which brought in its train such fondness and depth of feeling, which made even the briefest separation so exquisitely painful and a moment's union so intensely sweet, which seemed boundless in its extent and eternal in its duration, the cessation of which could not be imagined even in births to come—that this was that love! So feeble was its support! No sooner does the priesthood touch it than your 'eternal' love crumbles into a handful of dust! Only a short while ago Hemanta had whispered to her: "What a beautiful night!" The same night was not yet at an end, the same papiya was still warbling, the same south breeze still blew into the roam, making the bed-curtain shiver; the same moonlight lay on the bed next the open window, sleeping like a beautiful heroine exhausted with gaiety. All this was unreal! Love was more falsely dissembling than she herself!

III

The next morning Hemanta, fagged after a sleepless night, and looking like one distracted, called at the house of Peari Sankar Ghosal. "What news, my son?" Peari Sankar greeted him.

Hemanta, flaring up like a big fire, said in a trembling voice: "You have defiled our caste. You have brought destruction upon us. And you will have to pay for it." He could say no more; he felt choked.

"And *you* have preserved my caste, presented my ostracism from the community, and patted me on the back affectionately!" said Peari Sankar with a slight sarcastic smile.

Hemanta wished that his Brahmin-fury could reduce Peari Sankar to ashes in a moment, but his rage burnt only himself. Peari Sankar sat before him unscathed, and in the best of health.

"Did I ever do you any harm?" demanded Hemanta in a broken voice.

"Let me ask you one question," said Peari Sankar. "My daughter—my only child—what harm had she done your father? You were very young then, and probably never heard. Listen, then. Now, don't you excite yourself. There is much humour in what I am going to relate.

"You were quite small when my son-in-law Nabakanta ran away to England after stealing my daughter's jewels. You might truly remember the commotion in the village when he returned as a barrister five years later. Or, perhaps, you were unaware of it, as you were at school in Calcutta at the time. Your father, arrogating to himself the headship of the community, declared that if I sent my daughter to her husband's home, I must renounce her for good, and never again allow her to cross my threshold. I fell at your father's feet, and implored him, saying: 'Brother, save me this once. I will make the boy swallow cow-dung, and go through the *prayaschittam* ceremony. Do take him back into caste.' But your father remained obdurate. For my part, I could not disown my only child, and, bidding goodbye to my village and my kinsmen, I betook myself to Calcutta. There, too, my troubles followed me. When I had made every arrangement for my nephew's marriage, your father stirred up the girl's people, and they broke the match off. Then I took a solemn vow that, if there was a drop of Brahmin blood flowing in my veins, I would avenge myself. You understand the business to some extent now, don't you? But wait a little longer. You will enjoy it, when I tell you the whole story; it is interesting.

"When you were attending college, one Bipradas Chatterji used to live next door to your lodgings. The poor fellow is dead now. In his house lived a child-widow called Kusum, the destitute orphan of a Kayestha gentleman. The girl was very pretty, and the old Brahmin desired to shield her from the hungry gaze of college students. But for a young girl to throw dust in the eyes of her old guardian was not at all a difficult task. She often went to the top of the roof, to hang her washing out to dry, and, I believe, you found your own roof best suited for your studies. Whether you two spoke to each other, when on your respective roofs, I cannot tell, but the girl's behaviour excited suspicion in the old man's mind. She made frequent mistakes in her household duties, and, like Parbati*, engaged in her devotions, began gradually to renounce food and sleep. Some evenings she would burst into tears in the presence of the old gentleman, without any apparent reason.

"At last he discovered that you two saw each other from the roofs pretty frequently, and that you even went the length of absenting yourself from college to sit on the roof at midday with a book in your hand, so fond had you grown suddenly of solitary study. Bipradas came to me for advice, and told me everything. 'Uncle,' said I to him, 'for a long while you have cherished a desire to go on a pilgrimage to Benares. You had better do it now, and leave the girl in my charge. I will take care of her.'

"So he went. I lodged the girl in the house of Sripati Chatterji, passing him off as her father. What happened next is known to you. I feel a great relief today, having told you everything from the beginning. It sounds like a romance, doesn't it? I think of turning it into a book, and getting it printed. But I am not a writing-man myself. They say my nephew has some aptitude that way—I will get him to write it for me. But the best thing would be, if you would collaborate with him, because the conclusion of the story is not known to me so well."

---

* The wife of Shiva, the Destroyer.

Without paying much attention to the concluding remarks of Peari Sankar, Hemanta asked: "Did not Kusum object to this marriage?"

"Well," said Peari Sankar, "it is very difficult to guess. You know, my boy, how women's minds are constituted. When they say 'no,' they mean 'yes.' During the first few days after her removal to the new home, she went almost crazy at not seeing you. You, too, seemed to have discovered her new address somehow, as you used to lose your way after starting for college, and loiter about in front of Sripati's house. Your eyes did not appear to be exactly in search of the Presidency College, as they were directed towards the barred windows of a private house, through which nothing but insects and the hearts of moon-struck young men could obtain access. I felt very sorry for you both. I could see that your studies were being seriously interrupted, and that the plight of the girl was pitiable also.

"One day I called Kusum to me, and said: 'Listen to me, my daughter. I am an old man, and you need feel no delicacy in my presence. I know whom you desire at heart. The young man's condition is hopeless too. I wish I could bring about your union.' At this Kusum suddenly melted into tears, and ran away. On several evenings after that, I visited Sripati's house, and, calling Kusum to me, discussed with her matters relating to you, and so I succeeded in gradually overcoming her shyness. At last, when I said that I would try to bring about a marriage, she asked me: 'How can it be?' 'Never mind,' I said, 'I would pass you off as a Brahmin maiden.' After a good deal of argument, she begged me to find out whether you would approve of it. 'What nonsense,' replied I, 'the boy is well-nigh mad as it were, what's the use of disclosing all these complications to him? Let the ceremony be over smoothly and then—all's well that ends well. Especially, as there is not the slightest risk of its ever leaking out, why go out of the way to make a fellow miserable for life?'

"I do not know whether the plan had Kusum's assent or not. At times she wept, and at other times she remained silent. If I said, 'Let us drop it then,' she would become very restless. When things were in this state, I sent Sripati to you with the proposal of marriage; you consented without a moment's hesitation. Everything was settled.

"Shortly before the day fixed, Kusum became so obstinate that I had the greatest difficulty in bringing her round again. 'Do let it drop, uncle,' she said to me constantly. 'What do you mean, you silly child,' I rebuked her, 'how can we back out now, when everything has been settled?'

"'Spread a rumour that I am dead,' she implored. 'Send me away somewhere.'

"'What would happen to the young man then?' said I. 'He is now in the seventh heaven of delight, expecting that his long cherished desire would be fulfilled tomorrow; and today you want me to send him the news of your death. The result would be that tomorrow I should have to bear the news of his death to you, and the same evening your death would be reported to me. Do you imagine, child, that I am capable of committing a girl-murder and a Brahmin-murder at my age?'

"Eventually the happy marriage was celebrated at the auspicious moment, and I felt relieved of a burdensome duty which I owed to myself. What happened afterwards you know best."

"Couldn't you stop after having done us an irreparable injury?" burst out Hemanta after a short silence. "Why have you told the secret now?"

With the utmost composure, Peari Sankar replied: "When I saw that all arrangements had been made for the wedding of your sister, I said to myself: 'Well, I have fouled the caste of one Brahmin, but that was only from a sense of duty. Here, another Brahmin's caste is imperilled, and this time it is my plain duty to prevent it.' So I wrote to them saying that I was in a position to prove that you had taken the daughter of a sudra to wife."

Controlling himself with a gigantic effort, Hemanta said: "What will become of this girl whom I shall abandon now? Would you give her food and shelter?"

"I have done what was mine to do," replied Peari Sankar calmly. "It is no part of my duty to look after the discarded wives of other people. Anybody there? Get a glass of coconut milk for Hemanta Babu with ice in it. And some paan* too."

Hemanta rose, and took his departure without waiting for this luxurious hospitality.

* Spices wrapped in betel leaf

IV

It was the fifth night of the waning of the moon—and the night was dark. No birds were singing. The lichee tree by the tank looked like a smudge of ink on a background a shade less deep. The south wind was blindly roaming about in the darkness like a sleep-walker. The stars in the sky with vigilant unblinking eyes were trying to penetrate the darkness, in their effort to fathom some profound mystery.

No light shone in the bedroom. Hemanta was sitting on the side of the bed next to the open window, gazing at the darkness in front of him. Kusum lay on the floor, clasping her husband's feet with both her arms, and her face resting on them. Time stood like an ocean hushed into stillness. On the background of eternal night, Fate seemed to have painted this one single picture for all time—annihilation on every side, the judge in the centre of it, and the guilty one at his feet.

The sound of slippers was heard again. Approaching the door, Harihar Mukerji said: "You have had enough time—I can't allow you more. Turn the girl out of the house."

Kusum, as she heard this, embraced her husband's feet with all the ardour of a lifetime, covered them with kisses, and touching her forehead to them reverentially, withdrew herself.

Hemanta rose, and walking to the door, said: "Father, I won't forsake my wife."

"What!" roared out Harihar, "would you lose your caste, sir?"

"I don't care for caste," was Hemanta's calm reply.

"Then you too I renounce."

কঙ্কাল

The Skeleton

[*Kankal* was written in 1892. *The Skeleton* is a translation by various writers taken from the collection *Mashi and Other Stories* (1918). The ghost story has also been translated as *A Study in Anatomy*.]

In the room next to the one in which we boys used to sleep, there hung a human skeleton. In the night it would rattle in the breeze which played about its bones. In the day these bones were rattled by us. We were taking lessons in osteology from a student in the Campbell Medical School, for our guardians were determined to make us masters of all the sciences. How far they succeeded we need not tell those who know us; and it is better hidden from those who do not.

Many years have passed since then. In the meantime the skeleton has vanished from the room, and the science of osteology from our brains, leaving no trace behind.

The other day, our house was crowded with guests, and I had to pass the night in the same old room. In these now unfamiliar surroundings, sleep refused to come, and, as I tossed from side to side, I heard all the hours of the night chimed, one after another, by the church clock nearby. At length the lamp in the corner of the room, after some minutes of choking and spluttering, went out altogether. One or two bereavements had recently happened in the family, so the going out of the lamp naturally led me to thoughts of death. In the great arena of nature, I thought, the light of a lamp losing itself in eternal darkness, and the going out of the light of our little human lives, by day or by night, were much the same thing.

My train of thought recalled to my mind the skeleton. While I was trying to imagine what the body which had clothed it could have been like, it suddenly seemed to me that something was walking round and round my bed, groping along the walls of the room. I could hear its rapid breathing. It seemed as if it was searching for something which it could not find, and pacing round the room with ever-hastier steps. I felt quite sure that this was a mere fancy of my sleepless, excited brain; and that the throbbing of the veins in my temples was really the sound which seemed like running footsteps. Nevertheless, a cold shiver ran all over me. To help to get rid of this hallucination, I called out aloud: "Who is there?" The footsteps seemed to stop at my bedside, and the reply came: "It is I. I have come to look for that skeleton of mine."

It seemed absurd to show any fear before the creature of my own imagination; so, clutching my pillow a little more tightly, I said in a casual sort of way: "A nice business for this time of night! Of what use will that skeleton be to you now?"

The reply seemed to come almost from my mosquito-curtain itself. "What a question! In that skeleton were the bones that encircled my heart; the youthful charm of my six-and-twenty years bloomed about it. Should I not desire to see it once more?"

"Of course," said I, "a perfectly reasonable desire. Well, go on with your search, while I try to get a little sleep."

Said the voice: "But I fancy you are lonely. All right; I'll sit down a while, and we will have a little chat. Years ago I used to sit by men and talk to them. But during the last thirty-five years I have only moaned in the wind in the burning-places of the dead. I would talk once more with a man as in the old times."

I felt that someone sat down just near my curtain. Resigning myself to the situation, I replied with as much cordiality as I could summon: "That will be very nice indeed. Let us talk of something cheerful."

"The funniest thing I can think of is my own life-story. Let me tell you that."

The church clock chimed the hour of two.

"When I was in the land of the living, and young, I feared one thing like death itself, and that was my husband. My feelings can be likened only to those of a fish caught with a hook. For it was as if a stranger had snatched me away with the sharpest of hooks from the peaceful calm of my childhood's home—and from him I had no means of escape. My husband died two months after my marriage, and my friends and relations moaned pathetically on my behalf. My husband's father, after scrutinising my face with great care, said to my mother-in-law: "Do you not see, she has the evil eye?"—Well, are you listening? I hope you are enjoying the story?"

"Very much indeed!" said I. "The beginning is extremely humorous."

"Let me proceed then. I came back to my father's house in great glee. People tried to conceal it from me, but I knew well that I was endowed with a rare and radiant beauty. What is your opinion?"

"Very likely," I murmured. "But you must remember that I never saw you."

"What! Not seen me? What about that skeleton of mine? Ha! ha! ha! Never mind. I was only joking. How can I ever make you believe that those two cavernous hollows contained the brightest of dark, languishing eyes? And that the smile which was revealed by those ruby lips had no resemblance whatever to the grinning teeth which you used to see? The mere attempt to convey to you some idea of the grace, the charm, the soft, firm, dimpled curves, which in the fullness of youth were growing and blossoming over those dry old bones makes me smile; it also makes me angry. The most eminent doctors of my time could not have dreamed of the bones of that body of mine as materials for teaching osteology. Do you know, one young doctor that I knew of, actually compared me to a golden champak blossom. It meant that to him the rest of humankind was fit only to illustrate the science of physiology, that I was a flower of beauty. Does anyone think of the skeleton of a champak flower?

"When I walked, I felt that, like a diamond scattering splendour, my every movement set waves of beauty radiating on every side. I used to spend hours gazing on my hands—hands which could gracefully have reined the liveliest of male creatures.

"But that stark and staring old skeleton of mine has borne false-witness to you against me, while I was unable to refute the shameless libel. That is why of all men I hate you most! I feel I would like once for all to banish sleep from your eyes with a vision of that warm rosy loveliness of mine, to sweep out with it all the wretched osteological stuff of which your brain is full."

"I could have sworn by your body," cried I, "if you had it still, that no vestige of osteology has remained in my head, and that the only thing that it is now full of is a radiant vision of perfect loveliness, glowing against the black background of night. I cannot say more than that."

"I had no girl-companions," went on the voice. "My only brother had made up his mind not to marry. In the zenana I was alone. Alone I used to sit in the garden under the shade of the trees, and dream that the whole world was in love with me; that the stars with sleepless gaze were drinking in my beauty; that the wind was languishing in sighs as on some pretext or other it brushed past me; and that the lawn on which my feet rested, had it been conscious, would have lost consciousness again at their touch. It seemed to me that all the young men in the world were as blades of grass at my feet; and my heart, I know not why, used to grow sad.

"When my brother's friend, Shekhar, had passed out of the Medical College, he became our family doctor. I had already often seen him from behind a curtain. My brother was a strange man, and did not care to look on the world with open eyes. It was not empty enough for his taste; so he gradually moved away from it, until he was quite lost in an obscure corner. Shekhar was his one friend, so he was the only young man I could ever get to see. And when I held my evening court in my garden, then the host of imaginary young men whom I had at my feet were each one a Shekhar.—Are you listening? What are you thinking of?"

I sighed as I replied: "I was wishing I was Shekhar!"

"Wait a bit. Hear the whole story first. One day, in the rains, I was feverish. The doctor came to see me. That was our first meeting. I was reclining opposite the window, so that the blush of the evening sky might temper the pallor of my complexion. When the doctor, coming in, looked up into my face, I put myself into his place, and gazed at myself in imagination. I saw in the glorious evening light that delicate wan face laid like a drooping flower against the soft white pillow, with the unrestrained curls playing over the forehead, and the bashfully lowered eyelids casting a pathetic shade over the whole countenance.

"The doctor, in a tone bashfully low, asked my brother: "Might I feel her pulse?"

"I put out a tired, well-rounded wrist from beneath the coverlet. "Ah!" thought I, as I looked on it, "if only there had been a sapphire bracelet."* I have never before seen a doctor so awkward about feeling a patient's pulse. His fingers trembled as they felt my wrist. He measured the heat of my fever, I gauged the pulse of his heart.— Don't you believe me?"

"Very easily," said I; "the human heartbeat tells its tale."

"After I had been taken ill and restored to health several times, I found that the number of the courtiers who attended my imaginary evening reception began to dwindle till they were reduced to only one! And at last in my little world there remained only one doctor and one patient.

"In these evenings I used to dress myself† secretly in a canary-coloured sari; twine about the braided knot into which I did my hair a garland of white jasmine blossoms; and with a little mirror in my hand betake myself to my usual seat under the trees.

"Well! Are you perhaps thinking that the sight of one's own beauty would soon grow wearisome? Ah no! for I did not see myself with my own eyes. I was then one and also two. I used to see myself as though I were the doctor; I gazed, I was charmed, I fell madly in love. But, in spite of all the caresses I lavished on myself, a sigh would wander about my heart, moaning like the evening breeze.

"Anyhow, from that time I was never alone. When I walked I watched with downcast eyes the play of my dainty little toes on the earth, and wondered what the doctor would have felt had he been there to see. At midday the sky would be filled with the glare of the sun, without a sound, save now and then the distant cry of a

---

* Widows are supposed to dress in white only, without ornaments or jewellery.
† Refer to the previous note

passing kite. Outside our garden walls the hawker would pass with his musical cry of 'Bangles for sale, crystal bangles.' And I, spreading a snow-white sheet on the lawn, would lie on it with my head on my arm. With studied carelessness the other arm would rest lightly on the soft sheet, and I would imagine to myself that someone had caught sight of the wonderful pose of my hand, that someone had clasped it in both of his and imprinted a kiss on its rosy palm, and was slowly walking away.—What if I ended the story here? How would it do?"

"Not half a bad ending," I replied thoughtfully. "It would no doubt remain a little incomplete, but I could easily spend the rest of the night putting in the finishing touches."

"But that would make the story too serious. Where would the laugh come in? Where would be the skeleton with its grinning teeth?

"So let me go on. As soon as the doctor had got a little practice, he took a room on the ground floor of our house for a consulting-chamber. I used then sometimes to ask him jokingly about medicines and poisons, and how much of this drug or that would kill a man. The subject was congenial and he would wax eloquent. These talks familiarised me with the idea of death; and so love and death were the only two things that filled my little world. My story is now nearly ended—there is not much left."

"Not much of the night is left either," I muttered.

"After a time I noticed that the doctor had grown strangely absent-minded, and it seemed as if he were ashamed of something which he was trying to keep from me. One day he came in, somewhat smartly dressed, and borrowed my brother's carriage for the evening.

"My curiosity became too much for me, and I went up to my brother for information. After some talk beside the point, I at last asked him: 'By the way, Dada, where is the doctor going this evening in your carriage?'

"My brother briefly replied: 'To his death.'

"'Oh, do tell me,' I importuned. 'Where is he really going?'

"'To be married,' he said, a little more explicitly.

"'Oh, indeed!' said I, as I laughed long and loudly.

"I gradually learnt that the bride was an heiress, who would bring the doctor a large sum of money. But why did he insult me by hiding all this from me? Had I ever begged and prayed him not to marry, because it would break my heart? Men are not to be trusted. I have known only one man in all my life, and in a moment I made this discovery.

"When the doctor came in after his work and was ready to start, I said to him, rippling with laughter all the while: 'Well, doctor, so you are to be married tonight?'

"My gaiety not only made the doctor lose countenance; it thoroughly irritated him.

"'How is it,' I went on, "that there is no illumination, no band of music?'

"With a sigh he replied: 'Is marriage then such a joyful occasion?'

"I burst out into renewed laughter. 'No, no,' said I, 'this will never do. Who ever heard of a wedding without lights and music?'

"I bothered my brother about it so much that he at once ordered all the trappings of a gay wedding.

"All the time I kept on gaily talking of the bride, of what would happen, of what I would do when the bride came home. 'And, doctor,' I asked, 'will you still go on feeling pulses?' Ha! ha! ha! Though the inner workings of people's, especially men's, minds are not visible, still I can take my oath that these words were piercing the doctor's bosom like deadly darts.

"The marriage was to be celebrated late at night. Before starting, the doctor and my brother were having a glass of wine together on the terrace, as was their daily habit. The moon had just risen.

"I went up smiling, and said: 'Have you forgotten your wedding, doctor? It is time to start.'

"I must here tell you one little thing. I had meanwhile gone down to the dispensary and got a little powder, which at a convenient opportunity I had dropped unobserved into the doctor's glass.

"The doctor, draining his glass at a gulp, in a voice thick with emotion, and with a look that pierced me to the heart, said: 'Then I must go.'

"The music struck up. I went into my room and dressed myself in my bridal robes of silk and gold. I took out my jewellery and ornaments from the safe and put them all on; I put the red mark of wifehood on the parting in my hair. And then under the tree in the garden I prepared my bed.

"It was a beautiful night. The gentle south wind was kissing away the weariness of the world. The scent of jasmine and bela filled the garden with rejoicing.

"When the sound of the music began to grow fainter and fainter, the light of the moon got dimmer and dimmer, the world with its lifelong associations of home and kin faded away from my perceptions like some illusion, then I closed my eyes and smiled.

"I fancied that when people came and found me they would see that smile of mine lingering on my lips like a trace of rose-coloured wine, that when I thus slowly entered my eternal bridal-chamber I should carry with me this smile, illuminating my face. But alas for the bridal-chamber! Alas for the bridal robes of silk and gold! When I woke at the sound of a rattling within me, I found three urchins learning osteology from my skeleton. Where in my bosom my joys and griefs used to throb, and the petals of youth to open one by one, there the master with his pointer was busy naming my bones. And as to that last smile, which I had so carefully rehearsed, did you see any sign of that?

"Well, well, how did you like the story?"

"It has been delightful," said I.

At this point the first crow began to caw. "Are you there?" I asked. There was no reply.

The morning light entered the room.

এক রাত্রি

The Supreme Night

[*Ek Ratri* was written in 1892. The translation reproduced below is as published in *Mashi and Other Stories* (1918). The story has also been translated as *A Single Night* and *One Night*.]

I used to go to the same dame's school with Surabala and play at marriage with her. When I paid visits to her house, her mother would pet me, and setting us side by side would say to herself: "What a lovely pair!"

I was a child then, but I could understand her meaning well enough. The idea became rooted in my mind that I had a special right to Surabala above that of people in general. So it happened that, in the pride of ownership, at times I punished and tormented her; and she, too, fagged for me and bore all my punishments without complaint. The village was wont to praise her beauty; but in the eyes of a young barbarian like me that beauty had no glory;—I knew only that Surabala had been born in her father's house solely to bear my yoke, and that therefore she was the particular object of my neglect.

My father was the land-steward of the Chaudhuris, a family of zamindars. It was his plan, as soon as I had learnt to write a good hand, to train me in the work of estate management and secure a rent collectorship for me somewhere. But in my heart I disliked the proposal. Nilratan of our village had run away to Calcutta, had learnt English there, and finally became the *Nazir** of the District Magistrate; *that* was my life's ideal: I was secretly determined to be the Head Clerk of the Judge's Court, even if I could not become the Magistrate's Nazir.

I saw that my father always treated these court officers with the greatest respect. I knew from my childhood that they had to be propitiated with gifts of fish, vegetables, and even money. For this reason I had given a seat of high honour in my heart to the court underlings, even to the bailiffs. These are the gods worshipped in our Bengal—a modern miniature edition of the 330 millions of deities of the Hindu pantheon. For gaining material success, people have more genuine faith in *them* than in the good Ganesh, the giver of success; hence the people now offer to these officers everything that was formerly Ganesh's due.

Fired by the example of Nilratan, I too seized a suitable opportunity and ran away to Calcutta. There I first put up in the house of a village acquaintance, and afterwards got some funds from my father for my education. Thus I carried on my studies regularly.

In addition, I joined political and benevolent societies. I had no doubt whatever that it was urgently necessary for me to give my life suddenly for my country. But I knew not how such a hard task could be carried out. Also no one showed me the way.

But, nevertheless, my enthusiasm did not abate at all. We country lads had not learnt to sneer at everything like the precocious boys of Calcutta, and hence our faith was very strong. The 'leaders' of our associations delivered speeches, and we went begging for subscriptions from door to door in the hot blaze of noon without breaking our fast; or we stood by the roadside distributing hand-bills, or arranged the chairs and benches in the lecture-hall, and, if anybody whispered a word against our leader, we got ready to fight him. For these things the city boys used to laugh at us as provincials.

I had come to Calcutta to be a Nazir or a Head Clerk, but I was preparing to become a Mazzini or a Garibaldi.

At this time Surabala's father and my father laid their heads together to unite us in marriage. I had come to Calcutta at the age of

---

* Superintendent of bailiffs

fifteen; Surabala was eight years old then. I was now eighteen, and in my father's opinion I was almost past the age of marriage. But it was my secret vow to remain unmarried all my life and to die for my country; so I told my father that I would not marry before I had finished my education.

In two or three months I learnt that Surabala had been married to a pleader named Ram Lochan. I was then busy collecting subscriptions for raising fallen India, and this news did not seem worth my thought.

I had matriculated, and was about to appear at the Intermediate Examination, when my father died. I was not alone in the world, but had to maintain my mother and two sisters. I had therefore to leave college and look out for employment. After a good deal of exertion I secured the post of second master in the matriculation school of a small town in the Noakhali District.

I thought, here is just the work for me! By my advice and inspiration I shall train up every one of my pupils as a general for future India.

I began to work, and then found that the impending examination was a more pressing affair than the future of India. The headmaster got angry whenever I talked of anything outside grammar or algebra. And in a few months my enthusiasm, too, flagged.

I am no genius. In the quiet of the home I may form vast plans; but when I enter the field of work, I have to bear the yoke of the plough on my neck like the Indian bullock, get my tail twisted by my master, break clods all day, patiently and with bowed head, and then at sunset have to be satisfied if I can get any cud to chew. Such a creature has not the spirit to prance and caper.

One of the teachers lived in the school-house, to guard against fires. As I was a bachelor, this work was thrown on me. I lodged in a thatched shed close to the large cottage in which the school sat.

The school-house stood at some distance from the inhabited portion of the town, and beside a big tank. Around it were betel nut, coconut, and *madar* trees, and very near to the school building two large ancient neem trees grew close together, and cast a cool shade around.

One thing I have forgotten to mention, and indeed I had not

so long considered it worth mentioning. The local Government pleader, Ram Lochan Ray, lived near our school. I also knew that his wife—my early playmate, Surabala—lived with him.

I got acquainted with Ram Lochan Babu. I cannot say whether he knew that I had known Surabala in childhood. I did not think fit to mention the fact at my first introduction to him. Indeed, I did not clearly remember that Surabala had been ever linked with my life in any way.

One holiday I paid a visit to Ram Lochan Babu. The subject of our conversation has gone out of my mind; probably it was the unhappy condition of present-day India. Not that he was very much concerned or heartbroken over the matter; but the subject was such that one could freely pour forth one's sentimental sorrow over it for an hour or two while puffing at one's hookah.

While thus engaged, I heard in a side-room the softest possible jingle of bracelets, crackle of dress, and footfall; and I felt certain that two curious eyes were watching me through a small opening of the window.

All at once there flashed upon my memory a pair of eyes—a pair of large eyes, beaming with trust, simplicity, and girlhood's love—black pupils—thick dark eyelashes—a calm fixed gaze. Suddenly some unseen force squeezed my heart in an iron grip, and it throbbed with intense pain.

I returned to my house, but the pain clung to me. Whether I read, wrote, or did any other work, I could not shake that weight off my heart; a heavy load seemed to be always swinging from my heartstrings.

In the evening, calming myself a little, I began to reflect: 'What ails me?' From within came the question: 'Where is *your* Surabala now?' I replied: 'I gave her up of my free will. Surely I did not expect her to wait for me for ever.'

But something kept saying: '*Then* you could have got her merely for the asking. *Now* you have not the right to look at her even once, do what you will. That Surabala of your boyhood may come very close to you; you may hear the jingle of her bracelets; you may breathe the air embalmed by the essence of her hair—but there will always be a wall between you two.'

I answered: 'Be it so. What is Surabala to me?'

My heart rejoined: 'Today Surabala is nobody to you. But what might she not have been to you?'

Ah! that's true. *What* might she not have been to me? Dearest to me of all things, closer to me than the world besides, the sharer of all my life's joys and sorrows—she might have been. And now, she is so distant, so much of a stranger, that to look on her is forbidden, to talk with her is improper, and to think of her is a sin!—while this Ram Lochan, coming suddenly from nowhere, has muttered a few set religious texts, and in one swoop has carried off Surabala from the rest of mankind!

I have not come to preach a new ethical code, or to revolutionise society; I have no wish to tear asunder domestic ties. I am only expressing the exact working of my mind, though it may not be reasonable. I could not by any means banish from my mind the sense that Surabala, reigning there within shelter of Ram Lochan's home, was mine far more than his. The thought was, I admit, unreasonable and improper—but it was not unnatural.

Thereafter I could not set my mind to any kind of work. At noon when the boys in my class hummed, when Nature outside simmered in the sun, when the sweet scent of the neem blossoms entered the room on the tepid breeze, I then wished—I know not what I wished for; but this I can say, that I did not wish to pass all my life in correcting the grammar exercises of those future hopes of India.

When school was over, I could not bear to live in my large lonely house; and yet, if anyone paid me a visit, it bored me. In the gloaming as I sat by the tank and listened to the meaningless breeze sighing through the betel nut and coconut palms, I used to muse that human society is a web of mistakes; nobody has the sense to do the right thing at the right time, and when the chance is gone we break our hearts over vain longings.

I could have married Surabala and lived happily. But I must be a Garibaldi—and I ended by becoming the second master of a village school! And pleader Ram Lochan Ray, who had no special call to be Surabala's husband—to whom, before his marriage, Surabala was no wise different from a hundred other maidens—has very quietly married her, and is earning lots of money as Government pleader;

when his dinner is badly cooked he scolds Surabala, and when he is in good humour he gives her a bangle! He is sleek and fat, tidily dressed, free from every kind of worry; *he* never passes his evenings by the tank gazing at the stars and sighing.

Ram Lochan was called away from our town for a few days by a big case elsewhere. Surabala in her house was as lonely as I was in my school building.

I remember it was a Monday. The sky was overcast with clouds from the morning. It began to drizzle at ten o'clock. At the aspect of the heavens our headmaster closed the school early. All day the black detached clouds began to run about in the sky as if making ready for some grand display. Next day, towards afternoon, the rain descended in torrents, accompanied by storm. As the night advanced the fury of wind and water increased. At first the wind was easterly; gradually it veered, and blew towards the south and south-west.

It was idle to try to sleep on such a night. I remembered that in this terrible weather Surabala was alone in her house. Our school was much more strongly built than her bungalow. Often and often did I plan to invite her to the school-house, while I meant to pass the night alone by the tank. But I could not summon up courage for it.

When it was half-past one in the morning, the roar of the tidal wave was suddenly heard—the sea was rushing on us! I left my room and ran towards Surabala's house. In the way stood one embankment of our tank, and as I was wading to it the flood already reached my knees. When I mounted the bank, a second wave broke on it. The highest part of the bank was more than seventeen feet above the plain.

As I climbed up the bank, another person reached it from the opposite side. Who she was, every fibre of my body knew at once, and my whole soul was thrilled with the consciousness. I had no doubt that she, too, had recognised me.

On an island some three yards in area stood we two; all else was covered with water.

It was a time of cataclysm; the stars had been blotted out of the sky; all the lights of the earth had been darkened; there would have been no harm if we had held converse *then*. But we could not bring ourselves to utter a word; neither of us made even a formal inquiry after the other's health. Only we stood gazing at the darkness. At our feet swirled the dense, black, wild, roaring torrent of death.

Today Surabala has come to *my* side, leaving the whole world. Today she has none besides *me*. In our far-off childhood this Surabala had come from some dark primeval realm of mystery, from a life in another orb, and stood by my side on this luminous peopled earth; and today, after a wide span of time, she has left that earth, so full of light and human beings, to stand alone by *my* side amidst this terrible desolate gloom of Nature's death-convulsion. The stream of birth had flung that tender bud before me, and the flood of death had wafted the same flower, now in full bloom, to *me* and to none else. One more wave and we shall be swept away from this extreme point of the earth, torn from the stalks on which we now sit apart, and made one in death.

May that wave never come! May Surabala live long and happily, girt round by husband and children, household and kinsfolk! This one night, standing on the brink of Nature's destruction, I have tasted eternal bliss.

The night wore out, the tempest ceased, the flood abated; without a word spoken, Surabala went back to her house, and I, too, returned to my shed without having uttered a word.

I reflected: True, I have become no Nazir or Head Clerk, nor a Garibaldi; I am only the second master of a beggarly school. But one night had for its brief space beamed upon my whole life's course.

That one night, out of all the days and nights of my allotted span, has been the supreme glory of my humble existence.

Subha

[*Subha* was written in 1892. This translation was published in *Mashi and Other Stories* in 1918. It has also been translated as *The Silent Girl* and *The Dumb Girl*.]

When the girl was given the name of Subhashini*, who could have guessed that she would prove dumb? Her two elder sisters were Sukeshini† and Suhasini,‡ and for the sake of uniformity her father named his youngest girl Subhashini. She was called Subha for short.

Her two elder sisters had been married with the usual cost and difficulty, and now the youngest daughter lay like a silent weight upon the heart of her parents. All the world seemed to think that, because she did not speak, therefore she did not feel; it discussed her future and its own anxiety freely in her presence. She had understood from her earliest childhood that God had sent her like a curse to her father's house, so she withdrew herself from ordinary people, and tried to live apart. If only they would all forget her she felt she could endure it. But who can forget pain? Night and day her parents' minds were aching on her account. Especially her mother looked upon her as a deformity in herself. To a mother a daughter is a more

---

* Sweetly speaking
† Lovely-locked
‡ Sweetly smiling

closely intimate part of herself than a son can be; and a fault in her is a source of personal shame. Banikantha, Subha's father, loved her rather better than his other daughters; her mother regarded her with aversion as a stain upon her own body.

If Subha lacked speech, she did not lack a pair of large dark eyes, shaded with long lashes; and her lips trembled like a leaf in response to any thought that rose in her mind.

When we express our thought in words, the medium is not found easily. There must be a process of translation, which is often inexact, and then we fall into error. But black eyes need no translating; the mind itself throws a shadow upon them. In them thought opens or shuts, shines forth, or goes out in darkness, hangs steadfast like the setting moon, or, like the swift and restless lightning, illumines all quarters of the sky. They who from birth have had no other speech than the trembling of their lips learn a language of the eyes, endless in expression, deep as the sea, clear as the heavens, wherein play dawn and sunset, light and shadow. The dumb have a lonely grandeur like Nature's own. Wherefore the other children almost dreaded Subha, and never played with her. She was silent and companionless as noontide.

The hamlet where she lived was Chandipur. Its river, small for a river of Bengal, kept to its narrow bounds like a daughter of the middle class. This busy streak of water never overflowed its banks, but went about its duties as though it were a member of every family in the villages beside it. On either side were houses and banks shaded with trees. So stepping from her queenly throne, the river-goddess became a garden deity of each home; and forgetful of herself, performed her task of endless benediction with swift and cheerful foot.

Banikantha's house looked upon the stream. Every hut and stack in the place could be seen by the passing boatmen. I know not if amid these signs of worldly wealth anyone noticed the little girl who, when her work was done, stole away to the waterside, and sat there. But here Nature fulfilled her want of speech, and spoke for her. The murmur of the brook, the voice of the village folk, the songs of the boatmen, the crying of the birds and rustle of trees mingled, and were one with the trembling of her heart. They became one vast wave of sound, which beat upon her restless soul. This murmur and movement of Nature were the dumb girl's language; that speech of the dark eyes, which the long lashes shaded, was the language of the world about her. From the trees, where the cicadas chirped, to the quiet stars there was nothing but signs and gestures, weeping and sighing. And in the deep mid-noon, when the boatmen and fisherfolk had gone to their dinner, when the villagers slept, and birds were still, when the ferry-boats were idle, when the great busy world paused in its toil, and became suddenly a lonely, awful giant, then beneath the vast impressive heavens there were only dumb Nature and a dumb girl, sitting very silent—one under the spreading sunlight, the other where a small tree cast its shadow.

But Subha was not altogether without friends. In the stall were two cows, Sarbbashi and Panguli. They had never heard their names from her lips, but they knew her footfall. Though she had no words, she murmured lovingly and they understood her gentle murmuring better than all speech. When she fondled them or scolded or coaxed them, they understood her better than men could do. Subha would come to the shed, and throw her arms round Sarbbashi's neck; she would rub her cheek against her friend's, and Panguli would turn her great kind eyes and lick her face. The girl paid them three regular visits every day, and others that were irregular. Whenever she heard any words that hurt her, she would come to these dumb friends out of due time. It was as though they guessed her anguish of spirit from her quiet look of sadness. Coming close to her, they would rub their horns softly against her arms, and in dumb, puzzled fashion try to comfort her. Besides these two, there were goats and a kitten; but Subha had not the same equality of friendship with them, though they showed the same attachment. Every time it got a chance, night or day, the kitten would jump into her lap, and settle down to slumber, and show its appreciation of an aid to sleep as Subha drew her soft fingers over its neck and back.

Subha had a comrade also among the higher animals, and it is hard to say what were the girl's relations with him, for he could speak, and his gift of speech left them without any common language. He was the youngest boy of the Gosains, Pratap by name, an idle fellow. After long effort, his parents had abandoned the hope that he would ever make his living. Now losels have this advantage, that, though their own folk disapprove of them, they are generally popular with everyone else. Having no work to chain them, they become public property. Just as every town needs an open space where all may breathe, so a village needs two or three gentlemen of leisure, who can give time to all; so that, if we are lazy and want a companion, one is to hand.

Pratap's chief ambition was to catch fish. He managed to waste a lot of time this way, and might be seen almost any afternoon so employed. It was thus most often that he met Subha. Whatever he was about, he liked a companion; and, when one is catching fish, a silent companion is best of all. Pratap respected Subha for her taciturnity, and, as every one called her Subha, he showed his affection by calling her Su. Subha used to sit beneath a tamarind, and Pratap, a little distance off, would cast his line. Pratap took with him a small allowance of betel, and Subha prepared it for him. And I think that, sitting and gazing a long while, she desired ardently to bring some great help to Pratap, to be of real aid, to prove by any means that she was not a useless burden to the world. But there was nothing to do. Then she turned to the Creator in prayer for some rare power, that by an astonishing miracle she might startle Pratap into exclaiming: "My! I never dreamt our Su could have done this!"

Only think! If Subha had been a water nymph, she might have risen slowly from the river, bringing the gem of a snake's crown to the landing-place. Then Pratap, leaving his paltry fishing, might dive into the lower world, and see there, on a golden bed in a palace of silver, whom else but dumb little Su, Banikantha's child? Yes, our Su, the only daughter of the king of that shining city of jewels! But that might not be, it was impossible. Not that anything is really impossible, but Su had been born, not into the royal house of Patalpur,* but into Banikantha's family, and she knew no means of astonishing the Gosains' boy.

Gradually she grew up. Gradually she began to find herself. A new inexpressible consciousness like a tide from the central places of

* The Lower World

the sea, when the moon is full, swept through her. She saw herself, questioned herself, but no answer came that she could understand.

Once upon a time, late on a night of full moon, she slowly opened her door, and peeped out timidly. Nature, herself at full moon, like lonely Subha, was looking down on the sleeping earth. Her strong young life beat within her; joy and sadness filled her being to its brim; she reached the limits even of her own illimitable loneliness, nay, passed beyond them. Her heart was heavy, and she could not speak! At the skirts of this silent, troubled Mother there stood a silent troubled girl.

The thought of her marriage filled her parents with an anxious care. People blamed them, and even talked of making them outcasts. Banikantha was well off; they had fish-curry twice daily; and consequently he did not lack enemies. Then the women interfered, and Bani went away for a few days. Presently he returned, and said: "We must go to Calcutta."

They got ready to go to this strange country. Subha's heart was heavy with tears, like a mist-wrapt dawn. With a vague fear that had been gathering for days, she dogged her father and mother like a dumb animal. With her large eyes wide open, she scanned their faces as though she wished to learn something. But not a word did they vouchsafe. One afternoon in the midst of all this, as Pratap was fishing, he laughed: "So then, Su, they have caught your bridegroom, and you are going to be married! Mind you don't forget me altogether!" Then he turned his mind again to his fish. As a stricken doe looks in the hunter's face, asking in silent agony: "What have I done to you?" so Subha looked at Pratap. That day she sat no longer beneath her tree. Banikantha, having finished his nap, was smoking in his bedroom when Subha dropped down at his feet and burst out weeping as she gazed towards him. Banikantha tried to comfort her, and his cheek grew wet with tears.

It was settled that on the morrow they should go to Calcutta. Subha went to the cow-shed to bid farewell to her childhood's comrades. She fed them with her hand; she clasped their necks; she looked into their faces, and tears fell fast from the eyes which spoke for her. That night was the tenth of the moon. Subha left her room, and flung herself down on her grassy couch beside her dear river. It

Subha

was as if she threw her arms about Earth, her strong, silent mother, and tried to say: "Do not let me leave you, mother. Put your arms about me, as I have put mine about you, and hold me fast."

One day in a house in Calcutta, Subha's mother dressed her up with great care. She imprisoned her hair, knotting it up in laces, she hung her about with ornaments, and did her best to kill her natural beauty, Subha's eyes filled with tears. Her mother, fearing they would grow swollen with weeping, scolded her harshly, but the tears disregarded the scolding. The bridegroom came with a friend to inspect the bride. Her parents were dizzy with anxiety and fear when they saw the god arrive to select the beast for his sacrifice. Behind the stage, the mother called her instructions aloud, and increased her daughter's weeping twofold, before she sent her into the examiner's presence. The great man, after scanning her a long time, observed: "Not so bad."

He took special note of her tears, and thought she must have a tender heart. He put it to her credit in the account, arguing that the heart, which today was distressed at leaving her parents, would presently prove a useful possession. Like the oyster's pearls, the child's tears only increased her value, and he made no other comment.

The almanac was consulted, and the marriage took place on an auspicious day. Having delivered over their dumb girl into another's hands, Subha's parents returned home. Thank God! Their caste in this and their safety in the next world were assured! The bridegroom's work lay in the west, and shortly after the marriage he took his wife thither.

In less than ten days everyone knew that the bride was dumb! At least, if anyone did not, it was not her fault, for she deceived no one. Her eyes told them everything, though no one understood her. She looked on every hand; she found no speech; she missed the faces, familiar from birth, of those who had understood a dumb girl's language. In her silent heart there sounded an endless, voiceless weeping, which only the Searcher of Hearts could hear.

Using both eyes and ears *this* time, her lord made another careful examination, using his ears this time as well as his eyes, and married a second wife who could speak.

ॐ

ছুটি

The Home-Coming

[*Chhuti* was written between 1892 and 1893. This English
translation by Mr. C. F. Andrews and the author was published in
The Hungry Stones and Other Stories in 1916. The short story has also
been translated as *Holiday* and *The School Closes*.]

P hatik Chakravorti was ringleader among the boys of the
village. A new mischief got into his head. There was a heavy
log lying on the mud-flat of the river waiting to be shaped
into a mast for a boat. He decided that they should all work together
to shift the log by main force from its place and roll it away. The
owner of the log would be angry and surprised, and they would all
enjoy the fun. Everyone seconded the proposal, and it was carried
unanimously.

But just as the fun was about to begin, Makhan, Phatik's
younger brother, sauntered up, and sat down on the log in front
of them all without a word. The boys were puzzled for a moment.
He was pushed, rather timidly, by one of the boys and told to
get up but he remained quite unconcerned. He appeared like a
young philosopher meditating on the futility of games. Phatik was
furious. "Makhan," he cried, "if you don't get down this minute
I'll thrash you!"

Makhan only moved to a more comfortable position.

Now, if Phatik was to keep his regal dignity before the public,
it was clear he ought to carry out his threat. But his courage failed

him at the crisis. His fertile brain, however, rapidly seized upon a new manoeuvre which would discomfit his brother and afford his followers an added amusement. He gave the word of command to roll the log and Makhan over together. Makhan heard the order, and made it a point of honour to stick on. But he overlooked the fact, like those who attempt earthly fame in other matters, that there was peril in it.

The boys began to heave at the log with all their might, calling out, "One, two, three, go!" At the word 'go' the log went; and with it went Makhan's philosophy, glory and all.

All the other boys shouted themselves hoarse with delight. But Phatik was a little frightened. He knew what was coming. And, sure enough, Makhan rose from Mother Earth blind as Fate and screaming like the Furies. He rushed at Phatik and scratched his face and beat him and kicked him, and then went crying home. The first act of the drama was over.

Phatik wiped his face, and sat down on the edge of a sunken barge on the riverbank, and began to chew a piece of grass. A boat came up to the landing, and a middle-aged man, with grey hair and dark moustache, stepped on shore. He saw the boy sitting there doing nothing, and asked him where the Chakravortis lived. Phatik went on chewing the grass, and said: "Over there," but it was quite impossible to tell where he pointed. The stranger asked him again. He swung his legs to and fro on the side of the barge, and said; "Go and find out," and continued to chew the grass as before.

But now a servant came down from the house and told Phatik his mother wanted him. Phatik refused to move. But the servant was the master on this occasion. He took Phatik up roughly and carried him, kicking and struggling in impotent rage.

When Phatik came into the house, his mother saw him. She called out angrily: "So you have been hitting Makhan again?"

Phatik answered indignantly: "No, I haven't! Who told you that?"

His mother shouted: "Don't tell lies! You have."

Phatik said suddenly: "I tell you, I haven't. You ask Makhan!"

But Makhan thought it best to stick to his previous statement. He said: "Yes, mother. Phatik did hit me."

Phatik's patience was already exhausted. He could not hear this injustice. He rushed at Makhan, and hammered him with blows: "Take that," he cried, "and that, and that, for telling lies."

His mother took Makhan's side in a moment, and pulled Phatik away, beating him with her hands. When Phatik pushed her aside, she shouted out: "What! you little villain! Would you hit your own mother?"

It was just at this critical juncture that the grey-haired stranger arrived. He asked what was the matter. Phatik looked sheepish and ashamed.

But when his mother stepped back and looked at the stranger, her anger was changed to surprise. For she recognised her brother, and cried: "Why, Dada! Where have you come from?" As she said these words, she bowed to the ground and touched his feet. Her brother had gone away soon after she had married, and he had started business in Bombay. His sister had lost her husband while he was in Bombay. Bishamber had now come back to Calcutta, and had at once made enquiries about his sister. He had then hastened to see her as soon as he found out where she was.

The next few days were full of rejoicing. The brother asked after the education of the two boys. He was told by his sister that Phatik was a perpetual nuisance. He was lazy, disobedient, and wild. But Makhan was as good as gold, as quiet as a lamb, and very fond of reading. Bishamber kindly offered to take Phatik off his sister's hands and educate him with his own children in Calcutta. The widowed mother readily agreed. When his uncle asked Phatik if he would like to go to Calcutta with him, his joy knew no bounds, and he said: "Oh, yes, uncle!" In a way that made it quite clear that he meant it.

It was an immense relief to the mother to get rid of Phatik. She had a prejudice against the boy, and no love was lost between the two brothers. She was in daily fear that he would either drown Makhan someday in the river, or break his head in a fight, or run him into some danger or other. At the same time she was somewhat distressed to see Phatik's extreme eagerness to get away.

Phatik, as soon as all was settled, kept asking his uncle every minute when they were to start. He was on pins and needles all day long with excitement, and lay awake most of the night. He bequeathed to Makhan, in perpetuity, his fishing-rod, his big kite and his marbles. Indeed, at this time of departure his generosity towards Makhan was unbounded.

When they reached Calcutta, Phatik made the acquaintance of his aunt for the first time. She was by no means pleased with this unnecessary addition to her family. She found her own three boys quite enough to manage without taking anyone else. And to bring a village lad of fourteen into their midst was terribly upsetting. Bishamber should really have thought twice before committing such an indiscretion.

In this world of human affairs there is no worse nuisance than a boy at the age of fourteen. He is neither ornamental, nor useful. It is impossible to shower affection on him as on a little boy; and he is always getting in the way. If he talks with a childish lisp he is called a baby, and if he answers in a grown-up way he is called impertinent. In fact any talk at all from him is resented. Then he is at the unattractive, growing age. He grows out of his clothes with indecent haste; his voice grows hoarse and breaks and quavers; his face grows suddenly angular and unsightly. It is easy to excuse the shortcomings of early childhood, but it is hard to tolerate even unavoidable lapses in a boy of fourteen. The lad himself becomes painfully self-conscious. When he talks with elderly people he is either unduly forward, or else so unduly shy that he appears ashamed of his very existence.

Yet it is at this very age when in his heart of hearts a young lad most craves for recognition and love; and he becomes the devoted slave of anyone who shows him consideration. But none dare openly love him, for that would be regarded as undue indulgence, and therefore bad for the boy. So, what with scolding and chiding, he becomes very much like a stray dog that has lost his master.

For a boy of fourteen, his own home is the only paradise. To live in a strange house with strange people is little short of torture, while the height of bliss is to receive the kind looks of women, and never to be slighted by them.

It was anguish to Phatik to be the unwelcome guest in his aunt's house, despised by this elderly woman, and slighted, on every occasion. If she ever asked him to do anything for her, he would be so overjoyed that he would overdo it; and then she would tell him not to be so stupid, but to get on with his lessons.

The cramped atmosphere of neglect in his aunt's house oppressed Phatik so much that he felt that he could hardly breathe. He wanted to go out into the open country and fill his lungs and breathe freely. But there was no open country to go to. Surrounded on all sides by Calcutta houses and walls, he would dream night after night of his village home, and long to be back there. He remembered the glorious meadow where he used to fly his kite all day long; the broad riverbanks where he would wander about the livelong day singing and shouting for joy; the narrow brook where he could go and dive and swim at any time he liked. He thought of his band of boy companions over whom he was despot; and, above all, the memory of that tyrant mother of his, who had such a prejudice against him, occupied him day and night. A kind of physical love like that of animals; a longing to be in the presence of the one who is loved; an inexpressible wistfulness during absence; a silent cry of the inmost heart for the mother, like the lowing of a calf in the twilight—this love, which was almost an animal instinct, agitated the shy, nervous, lean, uncouth and ugly boy. No one could understand it, but it preyed upon his mind continually.

There was no more backward boy in the whole school than Phatik. He gaped and remained silent when the teacher asked him a question, and like an overladen ass patiently suffered all the blows that came down on his back. When other boys were out at play, he stood wistfully by the window and gazed at the roofs of the distant houses. And if by chance he espied children playing on the open terrace of any roof, his heart would ache with longing.

One day he summoned up all his courage, and asked his uncle: "Uncle, when can I go home?"

His uncle answered: "Wait till the holidays come." But the holidays would not come till November, and there was a long time still to wait.

One day Phatik lost his lesson book. Even with the help of books he had found it very difficult indeed to prepare his lesson. Now it was impossible. Day after day the teacher would cane him unmercifully. His condition became so abjectly miserable that even his cousins were ashamed to own him. They began to jeer and insult him more than the other boys. He went to his aunt at last, and told her that he had lost his book.

His aunt pursed her lips in contempt, and said: "You great clumsy, country lout. How can I afford, with all my family, to buy you new books five times a month?"

That night, on his way back from school, Phatik had a bad headache with a fit of shivering. He felt he was going to have an attack of malarial fever. His one great fear was that he would be a nuisance to his aunt.

The next morning Phatik was nowhere to be seen. All searches in the neighbourhood proved futile. The rain had been pouring in torrents all night, and those who went out in search of the boy got drenched through to the skin. At last Bisbamber asked help from the police.

At the end of the day a police van stopped at the door before the house. It was still raining and the streets were all flooded. Two constables brought out Phatik in their arms and placed him before Bishamber. He was wet through from head to foot, muddy all over, his face and eyes flushed red with fever, and his limbs all trembling. Bishamber carried him in his arms, and took him into the inner apartments. When his wife saw him, she exclaimed; "What a heap of trouble this boy has given us. Hadn't you better send him home?"

Phatik heard her words, and sobbed out loud: "Uncle, I was just going home; but they dragged me back again."

The fever rose very high, and all that night the boy was delirious. Bishamber brought in a doctor. Phatik opened his eyes flushed with fever, and looked up to the ceiling, and said vacantly: "Uncle, have the holidays come yet? May I go home?"

Bishamber wiped the tears from his own eyes, and took Phatik's lean and burning hands in his own, and sat by him through the night. The boy began again to mutter. At last his voice became excited: "Mother," he cried, "don't beat me like that! Mother! I am telling the truth!"

The next day Phatik became conscious for a short time. He turned his eyes about the room, as if expecting someone to come.

117

At last, with an air of disappointment, his head sank back on the pillow. He turned his face to the wall with a deep sigh.

Bishamber knew his thoughts, and, bending down his head, whispered: "Phatik, I have sent for your mother." The day went by. The doctor said in a troubled voice that the boy's condition was very critical.

Phatik began to cry out; "By the mark!—three fathoms. By the mark—four fathoms. By the mark—." He had heard the sailor on the river-steamer calling out the mark on the plumb-line. Now he was himself plumbing an unfathomable sea.

Later in the day Phatik's mother burst into the room like a whirlwind, and began to toss from side to side and moan and cry in a loud voice.

Bishamber tried to calm her agitation, but she flung herself on the bed, and cried: "Phatik, my darling, my darling."

Phatik stopped his restless movements for a moment. His hands ceased beating up and down. He said: "Eh?"

The mother cried again: "Phatik, my darling, my darling."

Phatik very slowly turned his head and, without seeing anybody, said: "Mother, the holidays have come."

সমস্যা পারান

The Riddle Solved

[*Samasya Paran* was written in 1893. This translation was published in *Mashi and Other Stories* (1918). The story has also been translated as *A Problem Solved* and *The Solution of the Problem*.]

I

Krishna Gopal Sircar, zamindar of Jhikrakota, made over his estates to his eldest son, and retired to Kasi, as befits a good Hindu, to spend the evening of his life in religious devotion. All the poor and the destitute of the neighbourhood were in tears at the parting. Every one declared that such piety and benevolence were rare in these degenerate days.

His son, Bipin Bihari, was a young man well educated after the modern fashion, and had taken the degree of Bachelor of Arts. He sported a pair of spectacles, wore a beard, and seldom mixed with others. His private life was unsullied. He did not smoke, and never touched cards. He was a man of stern disposition, though he looked soft and pliable. This trait of his character soon came home to his tenantry in diverse ways. Unlike his father, he would on no account allow the remission of one single pice out of the rents justly due to him. In no circumstances would he grant any tenant one single day's grace in paying up.

On taking over the management of the property, Bipin Bihari discovered that his father had allowed a large number of Brahmins to hold land entirely rent-free, and a larger number at rents much below the prevailing rates. His father was incapable of resisting the importunate solicitation of others—such was the weakness of his character.

Bipin Bihari said this could never be. He could not abandon the income of half his property—and he reasoned with himself thus: *Firstly*, the persons who were in actual enjoyment of the concessions and getting fat at his expense were a lot of worthless people, and wholly undeserving of charity. Charity bestowed on such objects only encouraged idleness. *Secondly*, living nowadays had become much costlier than in the days of his ancestors. Wants had increased apace. For a gentleman to keep up his position had become four times as expensive as in days past. So he could not afford to scatter gifts right and left as his father had done. On the contrary, it was his bounden duty to call back as many of them as he possibly could.

So Bipin Bihari lost no time in carrying into effect what he conceived to be his duty. He was a man of strict principles.

What had gone out of his grasp, returned to him little by little. Only a very small portion of his father's grants did he allow to remain undisturbed, and he took good care to arrange that even those should not be deemed permanent.

The wails of the tenants reached Krishna Gopal at Benares through the post. Some even made a journey to that place to represent their grievances to him in person. Krishna Gopal wrote to his son intimating his displeasure. Bipin Bihari replied, pointing out that the times had changed. In former days, he said, the zamindar was compensated for the gifts he made by the many customary presents he received from his tenantry. Recent statutes had made all such impositions illegal. The zamindar had now to rest content with just the stipulated rent, and nothing more. "Unless," he continued, "we keep a strict watch over the payment of our just dues, what will be left to us? Since the tenants won't give us anything extra now, how can we allow them concessions? Our relations must henceforth be strictly commercial. We shall be ruined if we go on making gifts and endowments, and the preservation of our property and the keeping up of our position will be rendered very difficult."

Krishna Gopal became uneasy at finding that times should

have changed so much. "Well, well," he murmured to himself, "the younger generation knows best, I suppose. Our old-fashioned methods won't do now. If I interfere, my son might refuse to manage the property, and insist on my going back. No, thank you—I would rather not. I prefer to devote the few days that are left me to the service of my God."

II

So things went on. Bipin Bihari put his affairs in order after much litigation in the Courts, and by less constitutional methods outside. Most of the tenants submitted to his will out of fear. Only a fellow called Asimuddin, son of Mirza Bibi, remained refractory.

Bipin's displeasure was keenest against this man. He could quite understand his father having granted rent-free lands to Brahmins, but why this Mohammedan should be holding so much land, some free and some at rents lower than the prevailing rates, was a riddle to him. And what was he? The son of a low Mohammedan widow, giving himself airs and defying the whole world, simply because he had learnt to read and write a little at the village school. To Bipin it was intolerable.

He made inquiries of his clerks about Asimuddin's holdings. All that they could tell him was that Babu Krishna Gopal himself had made these grants to the family many years back, but they had no idea as to what his motive might have been. They imagined, however, that perhaps the widow won the compassion of the kind-hearted zamindar, by representing to him her woe and misery.

To Bipin these favours seemed to be utterly undeserved. He had not seen the pitiable condition of these people in days gone by. Their comparative ease at the present day and their arrogance drove him to the conclusion that they had impudently swindled his tender-hearted father out of a part of his lawful income.

Asimuddin was a stiff-necked sort of a fellow, too. He vowed that he would lay down his life sooner than give up an inch of his land. Then came open hostilities.

The poor old widow tried her best to pacify her son. "It is no good fighting with the zamindar," she would often say to him. "His kindness has kept us alive so long; let us depend upon him still, though he may curtail his favours. Surrender to him part of the lands as he desires."

"Oh, mother!" protested Asimuddin. "What do you know of these matters, pray?"

One by one, Asimuddin lost the cases instituted against him. The more he lost, the more his obstinacy increased. For the sake of his all, he staked all that was his.

One afternoon, Mirza Bibi collected some fruits and vegetables from her little garden, and unknown to her son went and sought an interview with Bipin Babu. She looked at him with a tenderness maternal in its intensity, and spoke: "May Allah bless you, my son. Do not destroy Asim—it wouldn't be right of you. To your charge I commit him. Take him as though he were one whom it is your duty to support—as though he were a ne'er-do-well younger brother of yours. Vast is your wealth—don't grudge him a small particle of it, my son."

This assumption of familiarity on the part of the garrulous old woman annoyed Bipin not a little. "What do you know of these things, my good woman?" he condescended to say. "If you have any representations to make, send your son to me."

Being assured for the second time that she knew nothing about these affairs, Mirza Bibi returned home, wiping her eyes with her apron all the way, and offering her silent prayers to Allah.

III

The litigation dragged its weary length from the Criminal to the Civil Courts, and thence to the High Court, where at last Asimuddin met with a partial success. Eighteen months passed in this way. But he was a ruined man now—plunged in debts up to his very ears. His creditors took this opportunity to execute the decrees they had obtained against him. A date was fixed for putting up to auction every stick and stone that he had left.

It was Monday. The village market had assembled by the side of a tiny river, now swollen by the rains. Buying and selling were going on, partly on the bank and partly in the boats moored there. The hubbub was great. Among the commodities for sale jackfruits preponderated, it being the month of *Asadh*. Hilsa fish were seen in large quantities also. The sky was cloudy. Many of the stall-holders, apprehending a downpour, had stretched a piece of cloth overhead, across bamboo poles put up for the purpose.

Asimuddin had come too—but he had not a copper with him. No shopkeepers allowed him credit nowadays. He therefore had brought a brass *thali** and a *dao*† with him. These he would pawn, and then buy what he needed.

Towards evening, Bipin Babu was out for a walk, attended by two or three retainers armed with *lathis*.‡ Attracted by the noise, he directed his steps towards the market. On his arrival, he stopped awhile before the stall of Dwari, the oilman, and made kindly inquiries about his business. All of a sudden, Asimuddin raised his dao and ran towards Bipin Babu, roaring like a tiger. The market people caught hold of him half-way, and quickly disarmed him. He was forthwith given in custody to the police. Business in the market then went on as usual.

We cannot say that Bipin Babu was not inwardly pleased at this incident. It is intolerable that the creature we are hunting down should turn and show fight. "The *badmash*," Bipin chuckled; "I have got him at last."

The ladies of Bipin Babu's house, when they heard the news, exclaimed with horror: "Oh, the ruffian! What a mercy they seized him in time!" They found consolation in the prospect of the man being punished as he richly deserved.

In another part of the village the same evening, the widow's humble cottage, devoid of bread and bereft of her son, became darker than death. Others dismissed the incident of the afternoon from their minds, sat down to their meals, retired to bed and went to sleep, but to the widow the event loomed larger than anything else in this wide world. But, alas, who was there to combat it? Only a bundle of wearied bones and a helpless mother's heart trembling with fear.

---

* Plate
† Knife
‡ Stick

IV

Three days have passed in the meanwhile. Tomorrow the case would come up for trial before a Deputy Magistrate. Bipin Babu would have to be examined as a witness. Never before this did a zamindar of Jhikrakota appear in the witness-box, but Bipin did not mind.

The next day at the appointed hour, Bipin Babu arrived at the Court in a palanquin in great state. He wore a turban on his head, and a watch-chain dangled on his breast. The Deputy Magistrate invited him to a seat on the daïs, beside his own. The courtroom was crowded to suffocation. So great a sensation had not been witnessed in this Court for many years.

When the time for the case to be called drew near, a *chaprasi** came and whispered something in Bipin Babu's ear. He got up very agitated and walked out, begging the Deputy Magistrate to excuse him for a few minutes.

Outside he saw his old father a little way off, standing under a banyan tree, barefooted and wrapped in a piece of *namabali*.† A string of beads was in his hand. His slender form shone with a gentle lustre, and tranquil compassion seemed to radiate from his forehead.

Bipin, hampered by his close-fitting trousers and his flowing *chapkan*, touched his father's feet with his forehead. As he did this his turban came off and kissed his nose, and his watch, popping out of his pocket, swung to and fro in the air. Bipin hurriedly straightened his turban, and begged his father to come to his pleader's house close by.

"No, thank you," Krishna Gopal replied, "I will tell you here what I have got to say."

A curious crowd had gathered by this time. Bipin's attendants pushed them back.

Then Krishna Gopal said: "You must do what you can to get Asim acquitted, and restore him the lands that you have taken away from him."

---

* Servants
† A garment with the name of Krishna printed over it.

"Is it for this, father," said Bipin, very much surprised, "that you have come all the way from Benares? Would you tell me why you have made these people the objects of your special favour?"

"What would you gain by knowing it, my boy?"

But Bipin persisted. "It is only this, father," he went on; "I have revoked many a grant because I thought the tenants were not deserving. There were many Brahmins among them, but of them you never said a word. Why are you so keen about these Mohammedans now? After all that has happened, if I drop this case against Asim, and give him back his lands, what shall I say to people?"

Krishna Gopal kept silence for some moments. Then, passing the beads through his shaky fingers with rapidity, he spoke with a tremulous voice: "Should it be necessary to explain your conduct to people, you may tell them that Asimuddin is my son—and your brother."

"What?" exclaimed Bipin in painful surprise. "From a Musalman's womb?"

"Even so, my son," was the calm reply.

Bipin stood there for some time in mute astonishment. Then he found words to say: "Come home, father; we will talk about it afterwards."

"No, my son," replied the old man, "having once relinquished the world to serve my God, I cannot go home again. I return hence. Now I leave you to do what your sense of duty may suggest." He then blessed his son, and, checking his tears with difficulty, walked off with tottering steps.

Bipin was dumbfounded, not knowing what to say nor what to do. "So, such was the piety of the older generation," he said to himself. He reflected with pride how much better he was than his father in point of education and morality. This was the result, he concluded, of not having a principle to guide one's actions.

Returning to the Court, he saw Asimuddin outside between two constables, awaiting his trial. He looked emaciated and worn out. His lips were pale and dry, and his eyes unnaturally bright. A dirty piece of cloth worn to shreds covered him. "This my brother!" Bipin shuddered at the thought.

The Deputy Magistrate and Bipin were friends, and the case

ended in a fiasco. In a few days Asimuddin was restored to his former condition. Why all this happened, he could not understand. The village people were greatly surprised also.

However, the news of Krishna Gopal's arrival just before the trial soon got abroad. People began to exchange meaning glances. The pleaders in their shrewdness guessed the whole affair. One of them, Ram Taran Babu, was beholden to Krishna Gopal for his education and his start in life. Somehow or other he had always suspected that the virtue and piety of his benefactor were shams. Now he was fully convinced that, if a searching inquiry were made, all 'pious' men might be found out. "Let them tell their beads as much as they like," he thought with glee, "everybody in this world is just as bad as myself. The only difference between a good and a bad man is that the good practises dissimulation while the bad doesn't." The revelation that Krishna Gopal's far-famed piety, benevolence, and magnanimity were nothing but a cloak of hypocrisy, settled a difficulty that had oppressed Ram Taran Babu for many years. By what process of reasoning, we do not know, the burden of gratitude was greatly lifted off his mind. It was a vast relief to him!

অসম্ভব কথা

Once There was a King

[*Asambhava Katha* was written in 1893. Here is a translation taken from *The Hungry Stones and Other Stories* (1916) translated by the author and Mr. C. F. Andrews.]

"Once upon a time there was a king." When we were children there was no need to know who the king in the fairy story was. It didn't matter whether he was called Shiladitya or Shaliban, whether he lived at Kashi or Kanauj. The thing that made a seven-year-old boy's heart go thump, thump with delight was this one sovereign truth; this reality of all realities: "Once there was a king."

But the readers of this modern age are far more exact and exacting. When they hear such an opening to a story, they are at once critical and suspicious. They apply the searchlight of science to its legendary haze and ask: "Which king?"

The storytellers have become more precise in their turn. They are no longer content with the old indefinite, "There was a king," but assume instead a look of profound learning, and begin: "Once there was a king named Ajatasatru."

The modern reader's curiosity, however, is not so easily satisfied. He blinks at the author through his scientific spectacles, and asks again: "Which Ajatasatru?"

"Every schoolboy knows," the author proceeds, "that there were three Ajatasatrus. The first was born in the twentieth century B.C., and died at the tender age of two years and eight months, I deeply regret that it is impossible to find, from any trustworthy source, a detailed account of his reign. The second Ajatasatru is better known to historians. If you refer to the new Encyclopaedia of History . . ."

By this time the modern reader's suspicions are dissolved. He feels he may safely trust his author. He says to himself: "Now we shall have a story that is both improving and instructive."

Ah! how we all love to be deluded! We have a secret dread of being thought ignorant. And we end by being ignorant after all, only we have done it in a long and roundabout way.

There is an English proverb: "Ask me no questions, and I will tell you no lies." The boy of seven who is listening to a fairy story understands that perfectly well; he withholds his questions, while the story is being told. So the pure and beautiful falsehood of it all remains naked and innocent as a babe; transparent as truth itself; limpid as afresh bubbling spring. But the ponderous and learned lie of our moderns has to keep its true character draped and veiled. And if there is discovered anywhere the least little peep-hole of deception, the reader turns away with a prudish disgust, and the author is discredited.

When we were young, we understood all sweet things; and we could detect the sweets of a fairy story by an unerring science of our own. We never cared for such useless things as knowledge. We only cared for truth. And our unsophisticated little hearts knew well where the Crystal Palace of Truth lay and how to reach it. But today we are expected to write pages of facts, while the truth is simply this:

"There was a king."

I remember vividly that evening in Calcutta when the fairy story began. The rain and the storm had been incessant. The whole of the city was flooded. The water was knee-deep in our lane. I had a straining hope, which was almost a certainty, that my tutor would be prevented from coming that evening. I sat on the stool in the far corner of the veranda looking down the lane, with a heart beating faster and faster. Every minute I kept my eye on the rain, and when it began to grow less I prayed with all my might; "Please, God, send some more rain till half-past seven is over." For I was quite ready to believe that there was no other need for rain except to protect one helpless boy one evening in one corner of Calcutta from the deadly clutches of his tutor.

If not in answer to my prayer, at any rate according to some grosser law of physical nature, the rain did not give up.

But, alas! nor did my teacher.

Exactly to the minute, in the bend of the lane, I saw his approaching umbrella. The great bubble of hope burst in my breast, and my heart collapsed. Truly, if there is a punishment to fit the crime after death, then my tutor will be born again as me, and I shall be born as my tutor.

As soon as I saw his umbrella I ran as hard as I could to my mother's room. My mother and my grandmother were sitting opposite one another playing cards by the light of a lamp. I ran into the room, and flung myself on the bed beside my mother, and said:

"Mother dear, the tutor has come, and I have such a bad headache; couldn't I have no lessons today?"

I hope no child of immature age will be allowed to read this story, and I sincerely trust it will not be used in textbooks or primers for schools. For what I did was dreadfully bad, and I received no punishment whatever. On the contrary, my wickedness was crowned with success.

My mother said to me: "All right," and turning to the servant added: "Tell the tutor that he can go back home."

It was perfectly plain that she didn't think my illness very serious, as she went on with her game as before, and took no further notice. And I also, burying my head in the pillow, laughed to my heart's content. We perfectly understood one another, my mother and I.

But everyone must know how hard it is for a boy of seven years old to keep up the illusion of illness for a long time. After about a minute I got hold of Grandmother, and said: "Grannie, do tell me a story."

I had to ask this many times. Grannie and Mother went on playing cards, and took no notice. At last Mother said to me: "Child, don't bother. Wait till we've finished our game." But I persisted: "Grannie, do tell me a story." I told Mother she could finish her game tomorrow, but she must let Grannie tell me a story there and then.

At last, Mother threw down the cards and said: "You had better do what he wants. I can't manage him." Perhaps she had it in her mind that she would have no tiresome tutor on the morrow, while I should be obliged to be back to those stupid lessons.

As soon as ever Mother had given way, I rushed at Grannie. I got hold of her hand, and, dancing with delight, dragged her inside my mosquito curtain on to the bed. I clutched hold of the bolster with both hands in my excitement, and jumped up and down with joy, and when I had got a little quieter, said: "Now, Grannie, let's have the story!"

Grannie went on: "And the king had a queen." That was good to begin with. He had only one.

It is usual for kings in fairy stories to be extravagant in queens. And whenever we hear that there are two queens, our hearts begin to sink. One is sure to be unhappy. But in Grannie's story that danger was past. He had only one queen.

We next hear that the king had not got any son. At the age of seven I didn't think there was any need to bother if a man had had no son. He might only have been in the way. Nor are we greatly excited when we hear that the king has gone away into the forest to practise austerities in order to get a son. There was only one thing that would have made me go into the forest, and that was to get away from my tutor!

But the king left behind with his queen a small girl, who grew up into a beautiful princess.

Twelve years pass away, and the king goes on practising austerities, and never thinks all this while of his beautiful daughter. The princess has reached the full bloom of her youth. The age of marriage has passed, but the king does not return. And the queen pines away with grief and cries: "Is my golden daughter destined to die unmarried? Ah me! What a fate is mine!"

Then the queen sent men to the king to entreat him earnestly to come back for a single night and take one meal in the palace. And the king consented.

The queen cooked with her own hand, and with the greatest care, sixty-four dishes, and made a seat for him of sandalwood, and arranged the food in plates of gold and cups of silver. The princess stood behind with the peacock-tail fan in her hand. The king, after twelve years' absence, came into the house, and the princess waved the fan, lighting up all the room with her beauty. The king looked in his daughter's face, and forgot to take his food.

At last he asked his queen: "Pray, who is this girl whose beauty shines as the gold image of the goddess? Whose daughter is she?"

The queen beat her forehead, and cried: "Ah, how evil is my fate! Do you not know your own daughter?"

The king was struck with amazement. He said at last: "My tiny daughter has grown to be a woman."

"What else?" the queen said with a sigh. "Do you not know that twelve years have passed by?"

"But why did you not give her in marriage?" asked the king.

"You were away," the queen said. "And how could I find her a suitable husband?"

The king became vehement with excitement. "The first man I see tomorrow," he said, "when I come out of the palace shall marry her."

The princess went on waving her fan of peacock feathers, and the king finished his meal.

The next morning, as the king came out of his palace, he saw the son of a Brahman gathering sticks in the forest outside the palace gates. His age was about seven or eight.

The king said: "I will marry my daughter to him."

Who can interfere with a king's command? At once the boy was called, and the marriage garlands were exchanged between him and the princess.

At this point I came up close to my wise Grannie and asked her eagerly: "What then?"

In the bottom of my heart there was a devout wish to substitute myself for that fortunate wood-gatherer of seven years old. The night was resonant with the patter of rain. The earthen lamp by my bedside was burning low. My grandmother's voice droned on as she told the story. And all these things served to create in a corner of my credulous heart the belief that I had been gathering sticks in the dawn of some indefinite time in the kingdom of some unknown king, and in a moment garlands had been exchanged between me and the princess, beautiful as the Goddess of Grace. She had a gold band on her hair and gold earrings in her ears. She bad a necklace and bracelets of gold, and a golden waist-chain round her waist, and a pair of golden anklets tinkled above her feet.

If my grandmother were an author how many explanations she would have to offer for this little story! First of all, everyone would ask why the king remained twelve years in the forest? Secondly, why should the king's daughter remain unmarried all that while? This would be regarded as absurd.

Even if she could have got so far without a quarrel, still there would have been a great hue and cry about the marriage itself. First, it never happened. Secondly, how could there be a marriage between a princess of the Warrior Caste and a boy of the priestly Brahman Caste? Her readers would have imagined at once that the writer was preaching against our social customs in an underhand way. And they would write letters to the papers.

So I pray with all my heart that my grandmother may be born a grandmother again, and not through some cursed fate take birth as her luckless grandson.

So with a throb of joy and delight, I asked Grannie: "What then?"

Grannie went on: Then the princess took her little husband away in great distress, and built a large palace with seven wings, and began to cherish her husband with great care.

I jumped up and down in my bed and clutched at the bolster more tightly than ever and said: "What then?"

Grannie continued: The little boy went to school and learnt many lessons from his teachers, and as he grew up his class-fellows began to ask him: "Who is that beautiful lady who lives with you in the palace with the seven wings?" The Brahman's son was eager to know who she was. He could only remember how one day he had been gathering sticks, and a great disturbance arose. But all that was so long ago, that he had no clear recollection.

Four or five years passed in this way. His companions always asked him: "Who is that beautiful lady in the palace with the seven wings?" And the Brahman's son would come back from school and sadly tell the princess: "My school companions always ask me who is that beautiful lady in the palace with the seven wings, and I can give them no reply. Tell me, oh, tell me, who you are!"

The princess said: "Let it pass today. I will tell you some other day." And every day the Brahman's son would ask; "Who are you?" and the princess would reply: "Let it pass today. I will tell you some other day." In this manner four or five more years passed away.

At last the Brahman's son became very impatient, and said: "If you do not tell me today who you are, O beautiful lady, I will leave this palace with the seven wings." Then the princess said: "I will certainly tell you tomorrow."

Next day the Brahman's son, as soon as he came home from school, said: "Now, tell me who you are." The princess said: "Tonight I will tell you after supper, when you are in bed."

The Brahman's son said: "Very well," and he began to count the hours in expectation of the night. And the princess, on her side, spread white flowers over the golden bed, and lighted a gold lamp with fragrant oil, and adorned her hair, and dressed herself in a beautiful robe of blue, and began to count the hours in expectation of the night.

That evening when her husband, the Brahman's son, had finished his meal, too excited almost to eat, and had gone to the golden bed in the bed-chamber strewn with flowers, he said to himself: "Tonight I shall surely know who this beautiful lady is in the palace with the seven wings."

The princess took for her the food that was left over by her husband, and slowly entered the bed-chamber. She had to answer that night the question, who was the beautiful lady who lived in the palace with the seven wings. And as she went up to the bed to tell him she found a serpent had crept out of the flowers and had bitten the Brahman's son. Her boy-husband was lying on the bed of flowers, with face pale in death.

My heart suddenly ceased to throb, and I asked with choking voice: "What then?"

Grannie said: "Then . . ."

But what is the use of going on any further with the story? It would only lead on to what was more and more impossible. The boy of seven did not know that, if there were some 'What then?' after death, no grandmother of a grandmother could tell us all about it.

But the child's faith never admits defeat, and it would snatch at the mantle of death itself to turn him back. It would be outrageous for him to think that such a story of one teacherless evening could so suddenly come to a stop. Therefore the grandmother had to call back her story from the ever-shut chamber of the great End, but she does it so simply: it is merely by floating the dead body on a banana stem on the river, and having some incantations read by a magician. But in that rainy night and in the dim light of a lamp death loses all its horror in the mind of the boy, and seems nothing more than a deep slumber of a single night. When the story ends the tired eyelids are weighed down with sleep. Thus it is that we send the little body of the child floating on the back of sleep over the still water of time, and then in the morning read a few verses of incantation to restore him to the world of life and light.

ক্ষুধিত পাষাণ

The Hungry Stones

[*Kshudhita Pashaan* was written in 1895. *The Hungry Stones* is taken from *The Hungry Stones and Other Stories* (1916), a collection translated by the author and Mr. C. F. Andrews. This ghost story has also been translated as *The Hunger of Stones* and *The Spirit of the Marble Palace*.]

My kinsman and myself were returning to Calcutta from our Puja trip when we met the man in a train. From his dress and bearing we took him at first for an up-country Mahomedan, but we were puzzled as we heard him talk. He discoursed upon all subjects so confidently that you might think the Disposer of All Things consulted him at all times in all that He did. Hitherto we had been perfectly happy, as we did not know that secret and unheard-of forces were at work, that the Russians had advanced close to us, that the English had deep and secret policies, that confusion among the native chiefs had come to a head. But our newly-acquired friend said with a sly smile: "There happen more things in heaven and earth, Horatio, than are reported in your newspapers." As we had never stirred out of our homes before, the demeanour of the man struck us dumb with wonder. Be the topic ever so trivial, he would quote science, or comment on the Vedas, or repeat quatrains from some Persian poet; and as we had no pretence to a knowledge of science or the Vedas or Persian, our admiration for him went on increasing, and my kinsman, a theosophist, was firmly convinced that our fellow-passenger must have been supernaturally inspired by some strange 'magnetism' or 'occult power,' by an 'astral body' or something of that kind. He listened to the tritest saying that fell from the lips of our extraordinary companion with devotional rapture, and secretly took down notes of his conversation. I fancy that the extraordinary man saw this, and was a little pleased with it.

When the train reached the junction, we assembled in the waiting room for the connection. It was then 10 p.m., and as the train, we heard, was likely to be very late, owing to something wrong in the lines, I spread my bed on the table and was about to lie down for a comfortable doze, when the extraordinary person deliberately set about spinning the following yarn. Of course, I could get no sleep that night.

When, owing to a disagreement about some questions of administrative policy, I threw up my post at Junagarh, and entered the service of the Nizam of Hyderabad, they appointed me at once, as a strong young man, collector of cotton duties at Barich.

Barich is a lovely place. The *Susta* 'chatters over stony ways and babbles on the pebbles,' tripping, like a skilful dancing girl, in through the woods below the lonely hills. A flight of 150 steps rises from the river, and above that flight, on the river's brim and at the foot of the hills, there stands a solitary marble palace. Around it there is no habitation of man—the village and the cotton mart of Barich being far off.

About 250 years ago the Emperor Mahmud Shah II had built this lonely palace for his pleasure and luxury. In his days jets of rose water spurted from its fountains, and on the cold marble floors of its spray-cooled rooms young Persian damsels would sit, their hair dishevelled before bathing, and, splashing their soft naked feet in the clear water of the reservoirs, would sing, to the tune of the guitar, the ghazals of their vineyards.

The fountains play no longer; the songs have ceased; no longer do snow-white feet step gracefully on the snowy marble. It is but the vast and solitary quarters of cess-collectors like us, men oppressed with solitude and deprived of the society of women. Now, Karim Khan, the old clerk of my office, warned me repeatedly not to take up my abode there. "Pass the day there, if you like," said he, "but never stay the night." I passed it off with a light laugh. The servants said that they would work till dark and go away at night. I gave my ready assent. The house had such a bad name that even thieves would not venture near it after dark.

At first the solitude of the deserted palace weighed upon me like a nightmare. I would stay out, and work hard as long as possible, then return home at night jaded and tired, go to bed and fall asleep.

Before a week had passed, the place began to exert a weird fascination upon me. It is difficult to describe or to induce people to believe; but I felt as if the whole house was like a living organism slowly and imperceptibly digesting me by the action of some stupefying gastric juice.

Perhaps the process had begun as soon as I set my foot in the house, but I distinctly remember the day on which I first was conscious of it.

It was the beginning of summer, and the market being dull I had no work to do. A little before sunset I was sitting in an arm-chair near the water's edge below the steps. The Susta had shrunk and sunk low; a broad patch of sand on the other side glowed with the hues of evening; on this side the pebbles at the bottom of the clear shallow waters were glistening. There was not a breath of wind anywhere, and the still air was laden with an oppressive scent from the spicy shrubs growing on the hills close by.

As the sun sank behind the hilltops a long dark curtain fell upon the stage of day, and the intervening hills cut short the time in which light and shade mingle at sunset. I thought of going out for a ride, and was about to get up when I heard a footfall on the steps behind. I looked back, but there was no one.

As I sat down again, thinking it to be an illusion, I heard many footfalls, as if a large number of persons were rushing down the steps. A strange thrill of delight, slightly tinged with fear, passed through my frame, and though there was not a figure before my eyes, methought I saw a bevy of joyous maidens coming down the steps to bathe in the Susta in that summer evening. Not a sound was in the valley, in the river, or in the palace, to break the silence, but I distinctly heard the maidens' gay and mirthful laugh, like the gurgle of a spring gushing forth in a hundred cascades, as they ran past me, in quick playful pursuit of each other, towards the river, without noticing me at all. As they were invisible to me, so I was, as it were, invisible to them. The river was perfectly calm, but I felt that its still, shallow, and clear waters were stirred suddenly by the splash of many an arm jingling with bracelets, that the girls laughed and dashed and spattered water at one another, that the feet of the fair swimmers tossed the tiny waves up in showers of pearl.

I felt a thrill at my heart—I cannot say whether the excitement was due to fear or delight or curiosity. I had a strong desire to see them more clearly, but naught was visible before me; I thought I could catch all that they said if I only strained my ears; but however hard I strained them, I heard nothing but the chirping of the cicadas in the woods. It seemed as if a dark curtain of 250 years was hanging before me, and I would fain lift a corner of it tremblingly and peer through, though the assembly on the other side was completely enveloped in darkness.

The oppressive closeness of the evening was broken by a sudden gust of wind, and the still surface of the Susta rippled and curled like the hair of a nymph, and from the woods wrapt in the evening gloom there came forth a simultaneous murmur, as though they were awakening from a black dream. Call it reality or dream, the momentary glimpse of that invisible mirage reflected from a far-off world, 250 years old, vanished in a flash. The mystic forms that brushed past me with their quick unbodied steps, and loud, voiceless laughter, and threw themselves into the river, did not go back wringing their dripping robes as they went. Like fragrance wafted away by the wind they were dispersed by a single breath of the spring.

Then I was filled with a lively fear that it was the Muse that had taken advantage of my solitude and possessed me—the witch had evidently come to ruin a poor devil like myself making a living by collecting cotton duties. I decided to have a good dinner—it is the empty stomach that all sorts of incurable diseases find an easy prey. I sent for my cook and gave orders for a rich, sumptuous Mughlai dinner, redolent of spices and ghee.

Next morning the whole affair appeared a queer fantasy. With a light heart I put on a *sola* hat like the sahibs, and drove out to my work. I was to have written my quarterly report that day, and expected to return late; but before it was dark I was strangely drawn to my house—by what I could not say—I felt they were all waiting, and that I should delay no longer. Leaving my report unfinished I rose, put on my sola hat, and startling the dark, shady, desolate path with the rattle of my carriage, I reached the vast silent palace standing on the gloomy skirts of the hills.

On the first floor the stairs led to a very spacious hall, its roof stretching wide over ornamental arches resting on three rows of massive pillars, and groaning day and night under the weight of its own intense solitude. The day had just closed, and the lamps had not yet been lighted. As I pushed the door open a great bustle seemed to follow within, as if a throng of people had broken up in confusion, and rushed out through the doors and windows and corridors and verandas and rooms, to make its hurried escape.

As I saw no one I stood bewildered, my hair on end in a kind of ecstatic delight, and a faint scent of attar and unguents almost effected by age lingered in my nostrils. Standing in the darkness of that vast desolate hall between the rows of those ancient pillars, I could hear the gurgle of fountains plashing on the marble floor, a strange tune on the guitar, the jingle of ornaments and the tinkle of anklets, the clang of bells tolling the hours, the distant note of *nahabat*, the din of the crystal pendants of chandeliers shaken by the breeze, the song of bulbuls from the cages in the corridors, the cackle of storks in the gardens, all creating round me a strange unearthly music.

Then I came under such a spell that this intangible, inaccessible, unearthly vision appeared to be the only reality in the world—and all else a mere dream. That I, that is to say, Srijut So-and-so, the eldest son of So-and-so of blessed memory, should be drawing a monthly salary of Rs. 450 by the discharge of my duties as collector of cotton duties, and driving in my dog-cart to my office every day in a short coat and sola hat, appeared to me to be such an astonishingly ludicrous illusion that I burst into a horse-laugh, as I stood in the gloom of that vast silent hall.

At that moment my servant entered with a lighted kerosene lamp in his hand. I do not know whether he thought me mad, but it came back to me at once that I was in very deed Srijut So-and-so, son of So-and-so of blessed memory, and that, while our poets, great and small, alone could say whether inside of or outside the earth there was a region where unseen fountains perpetually played and fairy guitars, struck by invisible fingers, sent forth an eternal harmony, this at any rate was certain, that I collected duties at the cotton market at Banch, and earned thereby Rs. 450 per mensem as my salary. I laughed in great glee at my curious illusion, as I sat over the newspaper at my camp-table, lighted by the kerosene lamp.

After I had finished my paper and eaten my Mughlai dinner, I put out the lamp, and lay down on my bed in a small side-room. Through the open window a radiant star, high above the Avalli hills skirted by the darkness of their woods, was gazing intently from millions and millions of miles away in the sky at Mr. Collector lying on a humble camp-bedstead. I wondered and felt amused at the idea, and do not know when I fell asleep or how long I slept; but I suddenly awoke with a start, though I heard no sound and saw no intruder—only the steady bright star on the hilltop had set, and the dim light of the new moon was stealthily entering the room through the open window, as if ashamed of its intrusion.

I saw nobody, but felt as if someone was gently pushing me. As I awoke she said not a word, but beckoned me with her five fingers bedecked with rings to follow her cautiously. I got up noiselessly, and, though not a soul save myself was there in the countless apartments of that deserted palace with its slumbering sounds and waiting echoes, I feared at every step lest anyone should wake up. Most of the rooms of the palace were always kept closed, and I had never entered them.

I followed breathless and with silent steps my invisible guide—I cannot now say where. What endless dark and narrow passages, what long corridors, what silent and solemn audience-chambers and close secret cells I crossed!

Though I could not see my fair guide, her form was not invisible to my mind's eye—an Arab girl, her arms, hard and smooth as marble, visible through her loose sleeves, a thin veil falling on her face from the fringe of her cap, and a curved dagger at her waist! Methought that one of the thousand and one Arabian Nights had been wafted to me from the world of romance, and that at the dead of night I was wending my way through the dark narrow alleys of slumbering Bagdad to a trysting-place fraught with peril.

At last my fair guide stopped abruptly before a deep blue screen, and seemed to point to something below. There was nothing there, but a sudden dread froze the blood in my heart—methought I saw there on the floor at the foot of the screen a terrible Negro eunuch dressed in rich brocade, sitting and dozing with outstretched legs, with a naked sword on his lap. My fair guide lightly tripped over his legs and held up a fringe of the screen. I could catch a glimpse of a part of the room spread with a Persian carpet—someone was sitting inside on a bed—I could not see her, but only caught a glimpse of two exquisite feet in gold-embroidered slippers, hanging out from loose saffron-coloured pyjamas and placed idly on the orange-coloured velvet carpet. On one side there was a bluish crystal tray on which a few apples, pears, oranges, and bunches of grapes in plenty, two small cups and a gold-tinted decanter were evidently waiting the guest. A fragrant intoxicating vapour, issuing from a strange sort of incense that burned within, almost overpowered my senses.

As with trembling heart I made an attempt to step across the outstretched legs of the eunuch, he woke up suddenly with a start, and the sword fell from his lap with a sharp clang on the marble floor. A terrific scream made me jump, and I saw I was sitting on that camp-bedstead of mine sweating heavily; and the crescent moon looked pale in the morning light like a weary sleepless patient at dawn; and our crazy Meher Ali was crying out, as is his daily custom, "Stand back! Stand back!!" while he went along the lonely road.

Such was the abrupt close of one of my Arabian Nights; but there were yet a thousand nights left.

Then followed a great discord between my days and nights. During the day I would go to my work worn and tired, cursing the bewitching night and her empty dreams, but as night came my daily life with its bonds and shackles of work would appear a petty, false, ludicrous vanity.

After nightfall I was caught and overwhelmed in the snare of a strange intoxication, I would then be transformed into some unknown personage of a bygone age, playing my part in unwritten

141

history; and my short English coat and tight breeches did not suit me in the least. With a red velvet cap on my head, loose pyjamas, an embroidered vest, a long flowing silk gown, and coloured handkerchiefs scented with attar, I would complete my elaborate toilet, sit on a high-cushioned chair, and replace my cigarette with a many-coiled *narghileh* filled with rose water, as if in eager expectation of a strange meeting with the beloved one.

I have no power to describe the marvellous incidents that unfolded themselves, as the gloom of the night deepened. I felt as if in the curious apartments of that vast edifice the fragments of a beautiful story, which I could follow for some distance, but of which I could never see the end, flew about in a sudden gust of the vernal breeze. And all the same I would wander from room to room in pursuit of them the whole night long.

Amid the eddy of these dream-fragments, amid the smell of henna and the twanging of the guitar, amid the waves of air charged with fragrant spray, I would catch like a flash of lightning the momentary glimpse of a fair damsel. She it was who had saffron-coloured pyjamas, white ruddy soft feet in gold-embroidered slippers with curved toes, a close-fitting bodice wrought with gold, a red cap, from which a golden frill fell on her snowy brow and cheeks.

She had maddened me. In pursuit of her I wandered from room to room, from path to path among the bewildering maze of alleys in the enchanted dreamland of the nether world of sleep.

Sometimes in the evening, while arraying myself carefully as a prince of the blood-royal before a large mirror, with a candle burning on either side, I would see a sudden reflection of the Persian beauty by the side of my own. A swift turn of her neck, a quick eager glance of intense passion and pain glowing in her large dark eyes, just a suspicion of speech on her dainty red lips, her figure, fair and slim crowned with youth like a blossoming creeper, quickly uplifted in her graceful tilting gait, a dazzling flash of pain and craving and ecstasy, a smile and a glance and a blaze of jewels and silk, and she melted away. A wild gust of wind, laden with all the fragrance of hills and woods, would put out my light, and I would fling aside my dress and lie down on my bed, my eyes closed and my body thrilling with delight, and there around me in the breeze, amid all the perfume of the woods and hills, floated through the silent gloom many a caress and many a kiss and many a tender touch of hands, and gentle murmurs in my ears, and fragrant breaths on my brow; or a sweetly-perfumed kerchief was wafted again and again on my cheeks. Then slowly a mysterious serpent would twist her stupefying coils about me; and heaving a heavy sigh, I would lapse into insensibility, and then into a profound slumber.

One evening I decided to go out on my horse—I do not know who implored me to stay—but I would listen to no entreaties that day. My English hat and coat were resting on a rack, and I was about to take them down when a sudden whirlwind, crested with the sands of the Susta and the dead leaves of the Avalli hills, caught them up, and whirled them round and round, while a loud peal of merry laughter rose higher and higher, striking all the chords of mirth till it died away in the land of sunset.

I could not go out for my ride, and the next day I gave up my queer English coat and hat for good.

That day again at dead of night I heard the stifled heartbreaking sobs of someone—as if below the bed, below the floor, below the stony foundation of that gigantic palace, from the depths of a dark damp grave, a voice piteously cried and implored me: "Oh, rescue me! Break through these doors of hard illusion, deathlike slumber and fruitless dreams, place by your side on the saddle, press me to your heart, and, riding through hills and woods and across the river, take me to the warm radiance of your sunny rooms above!"

Who am I? Oh, how can I rescue thee? What drowning beauty, what incarnate passion shall I drag to the shore from this wild eddy of dreams? O lovely ethereal apparition! Where didst thou flourish and when? By what cool spring, under the shade of what date-groves, wast thou born—in the lap of what homeless wanderer in the desert? What Bedouin snatched thee from thy mother's arms, an opening bud plucked from a wild creeper, placed thee on a horse swift as lightning, crossed the burning sands, and took thee to the slave-market of what royal city? And there, what officer of the Badshah, seeing the glory of thy bashful blossoming youth, paid for thee in gold, placed thee in a golden palanquin, and offered thee as a present for the seraglio of his master? And O, the history of that place! The music of the *sareng*, the jingle of anklets, the occasional flash of daggers and the glowing wine of Shiraz poison, and the piercing flashing glance! What infinite grandeur, what endless servitude!

The slave-girls to thy right and left waved the *chamar* as diamonds flashed from their bracelets; the Badshah, the king of kings, fell on his knees at thy snowy feet in bejewelled shoes, and outside the terrible Abyssinian eunuch, looking like a messenger of death, but clothed like an angel, stood with a naked sword in his hand! Then, O, thou flower of the desert, swept away by the blood-stained dazzling ocean of grandeur, with its foam of jealousy, its rocks and shoals of intrigue, on what shore of cruel death wast thou cast, or in what other land more splendid and more cruel?

Suddenly at this moment that crazy Meher Ali screamed out: "Stand back! Stand back!! All is false! All is false!!" I opened my eyes and saw that it was already light. My chaprasi came and handed me my letters, and the cook waited with a *salaam* for my orders.

I said: "No, I can stay here no longer." That very day I packed up, and moved to my office. Old Karim Khan smiled a little as he saw me. I felt nettled, but said nothing, and fell to my work.

As evening approached I grew absent-minded; I felt as if I had an appointment to keep; and the work of examining the cotton accounts seemed wholly useless; even the Nizamat of the Nizam did not appear to be of much worth. Whatever belonged to the present, whatever was moving and acting and working for bread seemed trivial, meaningless, and contemptible.

I threw my pen down, closed my ledgers, got into my dog-cart, and drove away. I noticed that it stopped of itself at the gate of the marble palace just at the hour of twilight. With quick steps I climbed the stairs, and entered the room.

A heavy silence was reigning within. The dark rooms were looking sullen as if they had taken offence. My heart was full of contrition, but there was no one to whom I could lay it bare, or of whom I could ask forgiveness. I wandered about the dark rooms with a vacant mind. I wished I had a guitar to which I could sing to the unknown: "O fire, the poor moth that made a vain effort to fly away has come back to thee! Forgive it but this once, burn its wings and consume it in thy flame!"

Suddenly two tear-drops fell from overhead on my brow. Dark masses of clouds overcast the top of the Avalli hills that day. The gloomy woods and the sooty waters of the Susta were waiting in terrible suspense and in an ominous calm. Suddenly land, water, and sky shivered, and a wild tempest-blast rushed howling through the distant pathless woods, showing its lightning-teeth like a raving maniac who had broken his chains. The desolate halls of the palace banged their doors, and moaned in the bitterness of anguish.

The servants were all in the office, and there was no one to light the lamps. The night was cloudy and moonless. In the dense gloom within I could distinctly feel that a woman was lying on her face on the carpet below the bed—clasping and tearing her long dishevelled hair with desperate fingers. Blood was tricking down her fair brow, and she was now laughing a hard, harsh, mirthless laugh, now bursting into violent wringing sobs, now rending her bodice and striking at her bare bosom, as the wind roared in through the open window, and the rain poured in torrents and soaked her through and through.

All night there was no cessation of the storm or of the passionate cry. I wandered from room to room in the dark, with unavailing sorrow. Whom could I console when no one was by? Whose was this intense agony of sorrow? Whence arose this inconsolable grief?

And the mad man cried out: "Stand back! Stand back!! All is false! All is false!!"

I saw that the day had dawned, and Meher Ali was going round and round the palace with his usual cry in that dreadful weather. Suddenly it came to me that perhaps he also had once lived in that house, and that, though he had gone mad, he came there every day, and went round and round, fascinated by the weird spell cast by the marble demon.

Despite the storm and rain I ran to him and asked: "Ho, Meher Ali, what is false?"

The man answered nothing, but pushing me aside went round and round with his frantic cry, like a bird flying fascinated about the jaws of a snake, and made a desperate effort to warn himself by repeating: "Stand back! Stand back!! All is false! All is false!!"

I ran like a mad man through the pelting rain to my office, and asked Karim Khan: "Tell me the meaning of all this!"

What I gathered from that old man was this: That at one time countless unrequited passions and unsatisfied longings and lurid flames of wild blazing pleasure raged within that palace, and that the curse of all the heartaches and blasted hopes had made its every stone thirsty and hungry, eager to swallow up like a famished ogress any living man who might chance to approach. Not one of those who lived there for three consecutive nights could escape these cruel jaws, save Meher Ali, who had escaped at the cost of his reason.

I asked: "Is there no means whatever of my release?" The old man said: "There is only one means, and that is very difficult. I will tell you what it is, but first you must hear the history of a young Persian girl who once lived in that pleasure-dome. A stranger or a more bitterly heart-rending tragedy was never enacted on this earth."

Just at this moment the coolies announced that the train was coming. So soon? We hurriedly packed up our luggage, as the tram steamed in. An English gentleman, apparently just aroused from slumber, was looking out of a first-class carriage endeavouring to read the name of the station. As soon as he caught sight of our fellow-passenger, he cried, "Hallo," and took him into his own compartment. As we got into a second-class carriage, we had no chance of finding out who the man was nor what was the end of his story.

I said: "The man evidently took us for fools and imposed upon us out of fun. The story is pure fabrication from start to finish." The discussion that followed ended in a lifelong rupture between my theosophist kinsman and myself.

ঠাকুরদা

The Babus of Nayanjore

[*Thakurda* was written in 1895. This edition is taken from *The Hungry Stones and Other Stories* (1916). It has also been translated as *Grandfather* and *Thakurda*.]

I

O nce upon a time the Babus of Nayanjore were famous landholders. They were noted for their princely extravagance. They would tear off the rough border of their Dacca muslin, because it rubbed against their skin. They could spend many thousands of rupees over the wedding of a kitten. On a certain grand occasion it is alleged that in order to turn night into day they lighted numberless lamps and showered silver threads from the sky to imitate sunlight. Those were the days before the flood. The flood came. The line of succession among these old-world Babus, with their lordly habits, could not continue for long. Like a lamp with too many wicks burning, the oil flared away quickly, and the light went out.

Kailas Babu, our neighbour, is the last relic of this extinct magnificence. Before he grew up, his family had very nearly reached its lowest ebb. When his father died, there was one dazzling outburst of funeral extravagance, and then insolvency. The property was sold to liquidate the debt. What little ready money was left over was altogether insufficient to keep up the past ancestral splendours.

Kailas Babu left Nayanjore, and came to Calcutta. His son did not remain long in this world of faded glory. He died, leaving behind him an only daughter.

In Calcutta we are Kailas Babu's neighbours. Curiously enough our own family history is just the opposite of his. My father got his money by his own exertions, and prided himself on never spending a penny more than was needed. His clothes were those of a working man, and his hands also. He never had any inclination to earn the title of Babu by extravagant display, and I myself his only son, owe him gratitude for that. He gave me the very best education, and I was able to make my way in the world. I am not ashamed of the fact that I am a self-made man. Crisp banknotes in my safe are dearer to me than a long pedigree in an empty family chest.

I believe this was why I disliked seeing Kailas Babu drawing his heavy cheques on the public credit from the bankrupt bank of his ancient Babu reputation I used to fancy that he looked down on me, because my father had earned money with his own hands.

I ought to have noticed that no one showed any vexation towards Kailas Babu except myself. Indeed it would have been difficult to find an old man who did less harm than he. He was always ready with his kindly little acts of courtesy in times of sorrow and joy. He would join in all the ceremonies and religious observances of his neighbours. His familiar smile would greet young and old alike. His politeness in asking details about domestic affairs was untiring. The friends who met him in the street were perforce ready to be button-holed, while a long string of questions of this kind followed one another from his lips:

"My dear friend, I am delighted to see you. Are quite well? How is Shashi? And Dada—is he all right? Do you know, I've only just heard that Madhu's son has got fever. How is he? Have you heard? And Hari Charan Babu—I've not seen him for a long time—I hope he is not ill. What's the matter with Rakkhal? And, er—er, how are the ladies of your family?"

Kailas Babu was spotlessly neat in his dress on all occasions, though his supply of clothes was sorely limited. Every day he used to air his shirts and vests and coats and trousers carefully, and put them out in the sun, along with his bed-quilt, his pillowcase, and the small carpet on which he always sat. After airing them he would shake them, and brush them, and put them on the rock. His little bits of furniture made his small room decent, and hinted that there was more in reserve if needed. Very often, for want of a servant, he would shut up his house for a while. Then he would iron out his shirts and linen with his own hands, and do other little menial tasks. After this he would open his door and receive his friends again.

Though Kailas Babu, as I have said, had lost all his landed property, he had still same family heirlooms left. There was a silver cruet for sprinkling scented water, a filigree box for otto-of-roses, a small gold salver, a costly ancient shawl, and the old-fashioned ceremonial dress and ancestral turban. These he had rescued with the greatest difficulty from the money-lenders' clutches. On every suitable occasion he would bring them out in state, and thus try to save the world-famed dignity of the Babus of Nayanjore. At heart the most modest of men, in his daily speech he regarded it as a sacred duty, owed to his rank, to give free play to his family pride. His friends would encourage this trait in his character with kindly good-humour, and it gave them great amusement.

The neighbourhood soon learnt to call him their Thakur Dada (Grandfather). They would flock to his house, and sit with him for hours together. To prevent his incurring any expense, one or other of his friends would bring him tobacco, and say: "Thakur Dada, this morning some tobacco was sent to me from Gaya. Do take it, and see how you like it."

Thakur Dada would take it, and say it was excellent. He would then go on to tell of a certain exquisite tobacco which they once smoked in the old days at Nayanjore at the cost of a guinea an ounce.

"I wonder," he used to say, "I wonder if anyone would like to try it now. I have some left, and can get it at once."

Everyone knew that, if they asked for it, then somehow or other the key of the cupboard would be missing; or else Ganesh, his old family servant, had put it away somewhere.

"You never can be sure," he would add, "where things go to when servants are about. Now, this Ganesh of mine—I can't tell you what a fool he is, but I haven't the heart to dismiss him."

Ganesh, for the credit of the family, was quite ready to bear all the blame without a word.

One of the company usually said at this point: "Never mind, Thakur Dada. Please don't trouble to look for it. This tobacco we're smoking will do quite well. The other would be too strong."

Then Thakur Dada would be relieved, and settle down again, and the talk would go on.

When his guests got up to go away, Thakur Dada would accompany them to the door, and say to them on the doorstep: "Oh, by the way, when are you all coming to dine with me?"

One or other of us would answer: "Not just yet, Thakur Dada, not just yet. We'll fix a day later."

"Quite right," he would answer. "Quite right. We had much better wait till the rains come. It's too hot now. And a grand rich dinner, such as I should want to give you, would upset us in weather like this."

But when the rains did come, every one careful not to remind him of his promise. If the subject was brought up, some friend would suggest gently that it was very inconvenient to get about when the rains were so severe, that it would be much better to wait till they were over. And so the game went on.

His poor lodging was much too small for his position, and we used to condole with him about it. His friends would assure him they quite understood his difficulties: it was next to impossible to get a decent house in Calcutta. Indeed, they had all been looking out for years for a house to suit him. But, I need hardly add, no friend had been foolish enough to find one. Thakur Dada used to say, after a long sigh of resignation: "Well, well, I suppose I shall have to put up with this house after all." Then he would add with a genial smile: "But, you know, I could never bear to be away from my friends. I must be near you. That really compensates for everything."

Somehow I felt all this very deeply indeed. I suppose the real reason was that when a man is young stupidity appears to him the worst of crimes. Kailas Babu was not really stupid. In ordinary business matters everyone was ready to consult him.

But with regard to Nayanjore his utterances were certainly void of common sense. Because, out of amused affection for him, no one contradicted his impossible statements, he refused to keep them in bounds. When people recounted in his hearing the glorious history of Nayanjore with absurd exaggerations he would accept all they said with the utmost gravity, and never doubted, even in his dreams, that anyone could disbelieve it.

II

When I sit down and try to analyse the thoughts and feelings that I had towards Kailas Babu, I see that there was a still deeper reason for my dislike. I will now explain.

Though I am the son of a rich man, and might have wasted time at college, my industry was such that I took my M.A. degree in Calcutta University when quite young. My moral character was flawless. In addition, my outward appearance was so handsome, that if I were to call myself beautiful, it might be thought a mark of self-estimation, but could not be considered an untruth.

There could be no question that among the young men of Bengal I was regarded by parents generally as a very eligible match. I was myself quite clear on the point, and had determined to obtain my full value in the marriage market. When I pictured my choice, I had before my mind's eye a wealthy father's only daughter, extremely beautiful and highly educated. Proposals came pouring in to me from far and near; large sums in cash were offered. I weighed these offers with rigid impartiality, in the delicate scales of my own estimation. But there was no one fit to be my partner. I became convinced, with the poet Bhabavuti, that

In this world's endless time and boundless space
One may be born at last to match my sovereign grace.

But in this puny modern age, and this contracted space of modern Bengal, it was doubtful if the peerless creature existed as yet.

Meanwhile my praises were sung in many tunes, and in different metres, by designing parents.

Whether I was pleased with their daughters or not, this worship which they offered was never unpleasing. I used to regard it as my proper due, because I was so good. We are told that when the gods withhold their boons from mortals they still expect their worshippers to pay them fervent honour, and are angry if it is withheld. I had that divine expectance strongly developed in myself.

I have already mentioned that Thakur Dada had an only granddaughter. I had seen her many times, but had never mistaken her for beautiful. No thought had ever entered my mind that she would be a possible partner for myself. All the same, it seemed quite certain to me that someday or other Kailas Babu would offer her, with all due worship, as an oblation at my shrine. Indeed—this was the secret of my dislike—I was thoroughly annoyed that he had not done it already.

I heard he had told his friends that the Babus of Nayanjore never craved a boon. Even if the girl remained unmarried, he would not break the family tradition. It was this arrogance of his that made me angry. My indignation smouldered for some time. But I remained perfectly silent, and bore it with the utmost patience, because I was so good.

As lightning accompanies thunder, so in my character a flash of humour was mingled with the mutterings of my wrath. It was, of course, impossible for me to punish the old man merely to give vent to my rage; and for a long time I did nothing at all. But suddenly one day such an amusing plan came into my head, that I could not resist the temptation of carrying it into effect.

I have already said that many of Kailas Babu's friends used to flatter the old man's vanity to the full. One, who was a retired Government servant, had told him that whenever he saw the Chota Lat Sahib he always asked for the latest news about the Babus of Nayanjore, and the Chota Lat had been heard to say that in all Bengal the only really respectable families were those of the Maharaja of Burdwan and the Babus of Nayanjore. When this monstrous falsehood was told to Kailas Babu he was extremely gratified, and often repeated the story. And wherever after that he met this Government servant in company he would ask, along with other questions:

"Oh! er—by the way, how is the Chota Lat Sahib? Quite well, did you say? Ah, yes, I am so delighted to hear it! And the dear Mem

Sahib, is she quite well too? Ah, yes! and the little children—are they quite well also? Ah, yes I that's very good news! Be sure and give them my compliments when you see them."

Kailas Babu would constantly express his intention of going some day and paying a visit to the Sahib.

But it may be taken for granted that many Chota Lats and Burro Lats also would come and go, and much water would pass down the Hoogly, before the family coach of Nayanjore would be furnished up to pay a visit to Government House.

One day I took Kailas Babu aside, and told him in a whisper: "Thakur Dada, I was at the Levee yesterday, and the Chota Lat happened to mention the Babus of Nayanjore. I told him that Kailas Babu had come to town. Do you know, he was terribly hurt because you hadn't called? He told me he was going to put etiquette on one side, and pay you a private visit himself this very afternoon."

Anybody else could have seen through this plot of mine in a moment. And, if it had been directed against another person, Kailas Babu would have understood the joke. But after all he had heard from his friend, the Government servant, and after all his own exaggerations, a visit from the Lieutenant-Governor seemed the most natural thing in the world. He became highly nervous and excited at my news. Each detail of the coming visit exercised him greatly—most of all his own ignorance of English. How on earth was that difficulty to be met? I told him there was no difficulty at all: it was aristocratic not to know English: and, besides, the Lieutenant-Governor always brought an interpreter with him, and he had expressly mentioned that this visit was to be private.

About midday, when most of our neighbours were at work, and the rest were asleep, a carriage and pair stopped before the lodging of Kailas Babu. Two flunkeys in livery came up the stairs, and announced in a loud voice, "The Chota Lat Sahib has arrived." Kailas Babu was ready, waiting for him, in his old-fashioned ceremonial robes and ancestral turban, and Ganesh was by his side, dressed in his master's best suit of clothes for the occasion. When the Chota Lat Sahib was announced, Kailas Babu ran panting and puffing and trembling to the door, and led in a friend of mine, in disguise, with repeated salaams, bowing low at each step, and walking backward as best he could. He had his old family shawl spread over a hard wooden chair, and he asked the Lat Sahib to be seated. He then made a high-flown speech in Urdu, the ancient Court language of the Sahibs, and presented on the golden salver a string of gold *mohurs*, the last relics of his broken fortune. The old family servant Ganesh, with an expression of awe bordering on terror, stood behind with the scent-sprinkler, drenching the Lord Sahib, touching him gingerly from time to time with the otto-of-roses from the filigree box.

Kailas Babu repeatedly expressed his regret at not being able to receive His Honour Bahadur with all the ancestral magnificence of his own family estate at Nayanjore. There he could have welcomed him properly with due ceremonial. But in Calcutta he was a mere stranger and sojourner—in fact a fish out of water.

My friend, with his tall silk hat on, very gravely nodded. I need hardly say that according to English custom the hat ought to have been removed inside the room. But my friend did not dare to take it off for fear of detection; and Kailas Babu and his old servant Ganesh were sublimely unconscious of the breach of etiquette.

After a ten minutes' interview, which consisted chiefly of nodding the head, my friend rose to his feet to depart. The two flunkeys in livery, as had been planned beforehand, carried off in state the string of gold mohurs, the gold salver, the old ancestral shawl, the silver scent-sprinkler, and the otto-of-roses filigree box; they placed them ceremoniously in the carriage. Kailas Babu regarded this as the usual habit of Chota Lat Sahibs.

I was watching all the while from the next room. My sides were aching with suppressed laughter. When I could hold myself in no longer, I rushed into a further room, suddenly to discover, in a corner, a young girl sobbing as if her heart would break. When she saw my uproarious laughter she stood upright in passion, flashing the lightning of her big dark eyes in mine, and said with a tear-choked voice:

"Tell me! What harm has my grandfather done to you? Why have you come to deceive him? Why have you come here? Why—"

She could say no more. She covered her face with her hands, and broke into sobs.

My laughter vanished in a moment. It had never occurred to me that there was anything but a supremely funny joke in this act of mine, and here I discovered that I had given the cruellest pain to this tender little heart. All the ugliness of my cruelty rose up to condemn me. I slunk out of the room in silence, like a kicked dog.

Hitherto I had only looked upon Kusum, the granddaughter of Kailas Babu, as a somewhat worthless commodity in the marriage market, waiting in vain to attract a husband. But now I found, with a shock of surprise, that in the corner of that room a human heart was beating.

The whole night through I had very little sleep. My mind was in a tumult. On the next day, very early in the morning, I took all those stolen goods back to Kailas Babu's lodgings, wishing to hand them over in secret to the servant Ganesh. I waited outside the door, and, not finding anyone, went upstairs to Kailas Babu's room. I heard from the passage Kusum asking her grandfather in the most winning voice: "Dada, dearest, do tell me all that the Chota Lat Sahib said to you yesterday. Don't leave out a single word. I am dying to hear it all over again."

And Dada needed no encouragement. His face beamed over with pride as he related all manner of praises, which the Lat Sahib had been good enough to utter concerning the ancient families of Nayanjore. The girl was seated before him, looking up into his face, and listening with rapt attention. She was determined, out of love for the old man, to play her part to the full.

My heart was deeply touched, and tears came to my eyes. I stood there in silence in the passage, while Thakur Dada finished all his embellishments of the Chota Lat Sahib's wonderful visit. When he left the room at last, I took the stolen goods and laid them at the feet of the girl and came away without a word.

Later in the day I called again to see Kailas Babu himself. According to our ugly modern custom, I had been in the habit of making no greeting at all to this old man when I came into the room. But on this day I made a low bow, and touched his feet. I am convinced, the old man thought, that the coming of the Chota Lat Sahib to his house was the cause of my new politeness. He was highly gratified by it, and an air of benign severity shone from his eyes. His friends had flocked in, and he had already begun to tell again at full length the story of the Lieutenant-Governor's visit with still further adornments of a most fantastic kind. The interview was already becoming an epic, both in quality and in length.

When the other visitors had taken their leave, I made my proposal to the old man in a humble manner. I told him that, "though I could never for a moment hope to be worthy of marriage connection with such an illustrious family, yet . . . etc. etc."

When I made clear my proposal of marriage, the old man embraced me, and broke out in a tumult of joy: "I am a poor man, and could never have expected such great good fortune."

That was the first and last time in his life that Kailas Babu confessed to being poor. It was also the first and last time in his life that he forgot, if only for a single moment, the ancestral dignity that belongs to the Babus of Nayanjore.

আপদ

The Castaway

[*Apad* was written in 1895. It was published in English in *Mashi and Other Stories* (1918). It has also been translated as *The Nuisance, Unwanted*, and *The Troublemaker.*]

Towards evening the storm was at its height. From the terrific downpour of rain, the crash of thunder, and the repeated flashes of lightning, you might think that a battle of the gods and demons was raging in the skies. Black clouds waved like the Flags of Doom. The Ganges was lashed into a fury, and the trees of the gardens on either bank swayed from side to side with sighs and groans.

In a closed room of one of the riverside houses at Chandernagore, a husband and his wife were seated on a bed spread on the floor, intently discussing. An earthen lamp burned beside them.

The husband, Sharat, was saying: "I wish you would stay on a few days more; you would then be able to return home quite strong again."

The wife, Kiran, was saying: "I have quite recovered already. It will not, cannot possibly, do me any harm to go home now."

Every married person will at once understand that the conversation was not quite so brief as I have reported it. The matter was not difficult, but the arguments for and against did not advance it towards a solution. Like a rudderless boat, the discussion kept turning round and round the same point; and at last it threatened to be overwhelmed in a flood of tears.

Sharat said: "The doctor thinks you should stop here a few days longer."

Kiran replied: "Your doctor knows everything!"

"Well," said Sharat, "you know that just now all sorts of illness are abroad. You would do well to stop here a month or two more."

"And at this moment I suppose everyone in this place is perfectly well!"

What had happened was this: Kiran was a universal favourite with her family and neighbours, so that, when she fell seriously ill, they were all anxious. The village wiseacres thought it shameless for her husband to make so much fuss about a mere wife and even to suggest a change of air, and asked if Sharat supposed that no woman had ever been ill before, or whether he had found out that the folk of the place to which he meant to take her were immortal. Did he imagine that the writ of Fate did not run there? But Sharat and his mother turned a deaf ear to them, thinking that the little life of their darling was of greater importance than the united wisdom of a village. People are wont to reason thus when danger threatens their loved ones. So Sharat went to Chandernagore, and Kiran recovered, though she was still very weak. There was a pinched look on her face which filled the beholder with pity, and made his heart tremble, as he thought how narrowly she had escaped death.

Kiran was fond of society and amusement; the loneliness of her riverside villa did not suit her at all. There was nothing to do, there were no interesting neighbours, and she hated to be busy all day with medicine and dieting. There was no fun in measuring doses and making fomentations. Such was the subject discussed in their closed room on this stormy evening.

So long as Kiran deigned to argue, there was a chance of a fair fight. When she ceased to reply, and with a toss of her head disconsolately looked the other way, the poor man was disarmed. He was on the point of surrendering unconditionally when a servant shouted a message through the shut door.

Sharat got up, and, opening the door, learnt that a boat had been upset in the storm, and that one of the occupants, a young Brahmin boy, had succeeded in swimming ashore in their garden.

Kiran was at once her own sweet self, and set to work to get out some dry clothes for the boy. She then warmed a cup of milk, and invited him to her room.

The boy had long curly hair, big expressive eyes, and no sign yet of hair on the face. Kiran, after getting him to drink some milk, asked him all about himself.

He told her that his name was Nilkanta, and that he belonged to a theatrical troupe. They were coming to play in a neighbouring villa when the boat had suddenly foundered in the storm. He had no idea what had become of his companions. He was a good swimmer, and had just managed to reach the shore.

The boy stayed with them. His narrow escape from a terrible death made Kiran take a warm interest in him. Sharat thought the boy's appearance at this moment rather a good thing, as his wife would now have something to amuse her, and might be persuaded to stay on for some time longer. Her mother-in-law, too, was pleased at the prospect of profiting their Brahmin guest by her kindness. And Nilkanta himself was delighted at his double escape from his master and from the other world, as well as at finding a home in this wealthy family.

But in a short while Sharat and his mother changed their opinion, and longed for his departure. The boy found a secret pleasure in smoking Sharat's hookas; he would calmly go off in pouring rain with Sharat's best silk umbrella for a stroll through the village, and make friends with all whom he met. Moreover, he had got hold of a mongrel village dog which he petted so recklessly that it came indoors with muddy paws, and left tokens of its visit on Sharat's spotless bed. Then he gathered about him a devoted band of boys of all sorts and sizes, and the result was that not a solitary mango in the neighbourhood had a chance of ripening that season.

There is no doubt that Kiran had a hand in spoiling the boy. Sharat often warned her about it, but she would not listen to him. She made a dandy of him with Sharat's cast-off clothes, and gave him new ones too. And because she felt drawn towards him, and also had a curiosity to know more about him, she was constantly calling him to her own room. After her bath and midday meal Kiran would be seated on the bedstead with her betel-leaf box by her side; and while her maid combed and dried her hair, Nilkanta would stand in front and recite pieces out of his repertory with appropriate gesture and song, his elf-locks waving wildly. Thus the long afternoon hours passed merrily away. Kiran would often try to persuade Sharat to sit with her as one of the audience, but Sharat, who had taken a cordial dislike to the boy, refused, nor could Nilkanta do his part half so well when Sharat was there. His mother would sometimes be lured by the hope of hearing sacred names in the recitation; but love of her midday sleep speedily overcame devotion, and she lay lapped in dreams.

The boy often got his ears boxed and pulled by Sharat, but as this was nothing to what he had been used to as a member of the troupe, he did not mind it in the least. In his short experience of the world he had come to the conclusion that, as the earth consisted of land and water, so human life was made up of eatings and beatings, and that the beatings largely predominated.

It was hard to tell Nilkanta's age. If it was about fourteen or fifteen, then his face was too old for his years; if seventeen or eighteen, then it was too young. He was either a man too early or a boy too late. The fact was that, joining the theatrical band when very young, he had played the parts of Radhika, Damayanti, Sita, and Bidya's Companion. A thoughtful Providence so arranged things that he grew to the exact stature that his manager required, and then growth ceased. Since every one saw how small he was, and he himself felt small, he did not receive due respect for his years. These causes, natural and artificial, combined to make him sometimes seem immature for seventeen years, and at other times a lad of fourteen but far too knowing for seventeen. And as no sign of hair appeared on his face, the confusion became greater. Either because he smoked or because he used language beyond his years, his lips puckered into lines that showed him to be old and hard; but innocence and youth shone in his large eyes. I fancy that his heart remained young, but the hot glare of publicity had been a forcing-house that ripened untimely his outward aspect.

In the quiet shelter of Sharat's house and garden at Chandernagore, Nature had leisure to work her way unimpeded. He had lingered in a kind of unnatural youth, but now he silently and swiftly overpassed that stage. His seventeen or eighteen years came to adequate revelation. No one observed the change, and its first sign was this, that when Kiran treated him like a boy, he felt ashamed. When the gay Kiran one day proposed that he should play the part of lady's companion, the idea of woman's dress hurt him, though he could not say why. So now, when she called for him to act over again his old characters, he disappeared. It never occurred to him that he was even now not much more than a lad-of-all-work in a strolling company. He even made up his mind to pick up a little education from Sharat's factor. But, because Nilkanta was the pet of his master's wife, the factor could not endure the sight of him. Also, his restless training made it impossible for him to keep his mind long engaged; presently, the alphabet did a misty dance before his eyes. He would sit long enough with an open book on his lap, leaning against a champak bush beside the Ganges. The waves sighed below, boats floated past, birds flitted and twittered restlessly above. What thoughts passed through his mind as he looked down on that book he alone knew, if indeed he did know. He never advanced from one word to another, but the glorious thought that he was actually reading a book filled his soul with exultation. Whenever a boat went by, he lifted his book, and pretended to be reading hard, shouting at the top of his voice. But his energy dropped as soon as the audience was gone.

Formerly he sang his songs automatically, but now their tunes stirred in his mind. Their words were of little import, and full of trifling alliteration. Even the little meaning they had was beyond his comprehension; yet when he sang—

Twice-born* bird! ah! wherefore stirred
To wrong our royal lady?
Goose, ah! say why wilt thou slay
Her in forest shady?

then he felt as if transported to another world, and to far other folk. This familiar earth and his own poor life became music, and he was transformed. That tale of goose and king's daughter flung upon the mirror of his mind a picture of surpassing beauty. It is impossible to

---

* Once in the egg, and again once out of the egg.

say what he imagined he himself was, but the destitute little slave of the theatrical troupe faded from his memory.

When with evening the child of want lies down, dirty and hungry, in his squalid home, and hears of prince and princess and fabled gold, then in the dark hovel with its dim flickering candle, his mind springs free from her bonds of poverty and misery, and walks in fresh beauty and glowing raiment, strong beyond all fear of hindrance, through that fairy realm where all is possible.

Even so, this drudge of wandering players fashioned himself and his world anew, as he moved in spirit amid his songs. The lapping water, rustling leaves, and calling birds; the goddess who had given shelter to him, the helpless, the Godforsaken; her gracious, lovely face, her exquisite arms with their shining bangles, her rosy feet as soft as flower-petals; all these by some magic became one with the music of his song. When the singing ended, the mirage faded, and Nilkanta of the stage appeared again, with his wild elf-locks. Fresh from the complaints of his neighbour, the owner of the despoiled mango-orchard, Sharat would come and box his ears, and cuff him. The boy Nilkanta, the misleader of adoring youths, went forth once more, to make ever new mischief by land and water and in the branches that are above the earth.

Shortly after the advent of Nilkanta, Sharat's younger brother, Satish, came to spend his college vacation with them. Kiran was hugely pleased at finding a fresh occupation. She and Satish were of the same age, and the time passed pleasantly in games and quarrels and makings-up and laughter and even tears. Suddenly she would clasp him over the eyes, from behind, with vermilion-stained hands, she would write 'monkey' on his back, and sometimes bolt the door on him from outside amidst peals of laughter. Satish in his turn did not take things lying down; he would take her keys and rings, he would put pepper among her betel; he would tie her to the bed when she was not looking.

Meanwhile, heaven only knows what possessed poor Nilkanta. He was suddenly filled with a bitterness which he must avenge on somebody or something. He thrashed his devoted boy-followers for no fault, and sent them away crying. He would kick his pet mongrel till it made the skies resound with its whinings. When he went out for a walk, he would litter his path with twigs and leaves beaten from the roadside shrubs with his cane.

Kiran liked to see people enjoying good fare. Nilkanta had an immense capacity for eating, and never refused a good thing, however often it was offered. So Kiran liked to send for him to have his meals in her presence, and ply him with delicacies, happy in the bliss of seeing this Brahmin boy eat to satiety. After Satish's arrival she had much less spare time on her hands, and was seldom present when Nilkanta's meals were served. Before, her absence made no difference to the boy's appetite, and he would not rise till he had drained his cup of milk, and rinsed it thoroughly with water.*

But now, if Kiran was not present to ask him to try this and that, he was miserable, and nothing tasted right. He would get up without eating much, and say to the serving-maid in a choking voice: "I am not hungry." He thought in imagination that the news of his repeated refusal, "I am not hungry," would reach Kiran; he pictured her concern, and hoped that she would send for him, and press him to eat. But nothing of the sort happened. Kiran never knew, and never sent for him; and the maid finished whatever he left. He would then put out the lamp in his room, and throw himself on his bed in the darkness, burying his head in the pillow in a paroxysm of sobs. What was his grievance? Against whom? And from whom did he expect redress? At last, when none else came, Mother Sleep soothed with her soft caresses the wounded heart of the motherless lad.

Nilkanta came to the unshakable conviction that Satish was poisoning Kiran's mind against him. If Kiran was absent-minded, and had not her usual smile, he would jump to the conclusion that some trick of Satish had made her angry with him. He took to praying to the gods, with all the fervour of his hate, to make him at the next rebirth Satish, and Satish him. He had an idea that a Brahmin's wrath could never be in vain; and the more he tried to consume Satish with the fire of his curses, the more did his own heart burn within him. And upstairs he would hear Satish laughing and joking with his sister-in-law.

---

* A habit which was relic from his days of poverty, when milk was too rare a luxury to allow of even its stains in the cup being wasted.

Nilkanta never dared openly to show his enmity to Satish. But he would contrive a hundred petty ways of causing him annoyance. When Satish went for a swim in the river, and left his soap on the steps of the bathing-place, on coming back for it he would find that it had disappeared. Once he found his favourite striped tunic floating past him on the water, and thought it had been blown away by the wind.

One day Kiran, desiring to entertain Satish, sent for Nilkanta to recite as usual, but he stood there in gloomy silence. Quite surprised, Kiran asked him what was the matter. But he remained silent. And when again pressed by her to repeat some particular favourite piece of hers, he answered: "I don't remember," and walked away.

At last the time came for their return home. Everybody was busy packing up. Satish was going with them. But to Nilkanta nobody said a word. The question whether he was to go or not seemed not to have occurred to anybody.

The question, as a matter of fact, had been raised by Kiran, who had proposed to take him along with them. But her husband and his mother and brother had all objected so strenuously that she let the matter drop. A couple of days before they were to start, she sent for the boy, and with kind words advised him to go back to his own home.

So many days had he felt neglected that this touch of kindness was too much for him; he burst into tears. Kiran's eyes were also brimming over. She was filled with remorse at the thought that she had created a tie of affection, which could not be permanent.

But Satish was much annoyed at the blubbering of this overgrown boy. "Why does the fool stand there howling instead of speaking?" said he. When Kiran scolded him for an unfeeling creature, he replied: "Sister mine, you do not understand. You are too good and trustful. This fellow turns up from the Lord knows where, and is treated like a king. Naturally the tiger has no wish to become a mouse again.* And he has evidently discovered that there is nothing like a tear or two to soften your heart."

Nilkanta hurriedly left the spot. He felt he would like to be a

---

* A reference to a folk-story of a saint who turned a pet mouse into a tiger.

knife to cut Satish to pieces; a needle to pierce him through and through; a fire to burn him to ashes. But Satish was not even scarred. It was only his own heart that bled and bled.

Satish had brought with him from Calcutta a grand inkstand. The inkpot was set in a mother-of-pearl boat drawn by a German-silver goose supporting a penholder. It was a great favourite of his, and he cleaned it carefully every day with an old silk handkerchief. Kiran would laugh and, tapping the silver bird's beak, would say—

Twice-born bird, ah! wherefore stirred
To wrong our royal lady?

and the usual war of words would break out between her and her brother-in-law.

The day before they were to start, the inkstand was missing, and could nowhere be found. Kiran smiled, and said: "Brother-in-law, your goose has flown off to look for your Damaynti."*

But Satish was in a great rage. He was certain that Nilkanta had stolen it—for several people said they had seen him prowling about the room the night before. He had the accused brought before him. Kiran also was there. "You have stolen my inkstand, you thief!" he blurted out. "Bring it back at once." Nilkanta had always taken punishment from Sharat, deserved or undeserved, with perfect equanimity. But, when he was called a thief in Kiran's presence, his eyes blazed with a fierce anger, his breast swelled, and his throat choked. If Satish had said another word he would have flown at him like a wild cat, and used his nails like claws.

Kiran was greatly distressed at the scene, and taking the boy into another room said in her sweet, kind way: "Nilu, if you really have taken that inkstand give it to me quietly, and I shall see that no one says another word to you about it." Big tears coursed down the boy's cheeks, till at last he hid his face in his hands, and wept bitterly. Kiran came back from the room, and said: "I am sure Nilkanta has not taken the inkstand." Sharat and Satish were equally positive that no other than Nilkanta could have done it.

* To find Satish a wife.

But Kiran said determinedly: "Never."

Sharat wanted to cross-examine the boy, but his wife refused to allow it.

Then Satish suggested that his room and box should be searched. And Kiran said: "If you dare do such a thing I will never, never forgive you. You shall not spy on the poor innocent boy." And as she spoke, her wonderful eyes filled with tears. That settled the matter, and effectually prevented any further molestation of Nilkanta!

Kiran's heart overflowed with pity at this attempted outrage on a homeless lad. She got two new suits of clothes and a pair of shoes, and with these and a banknote in her hand she quietly went into Nilkanta's room in the evening. She intended to put these parting presents into his box as a surprise. The box itself had been her gift.

From her bunch of keys she selected one that fitted, and noiselessly opened the box. It was so jumbled up with odds and ends that the new clothes would not go in. So she thought she had better take everything out and pack the box for him. At first knives, tops, kite-flying reels, bamboo twigs, polished shells for peeling green mangoes, bottoms of broken tumblers and such like things dear to a boy's heart were discovered. Then there came a layer of linen, clean and otherwise. And from under the linen there emerged the missing inkstand, goose and all!

Kiran, with flushed face, sat down helplessly with the inkstand in her hand, puzzled and wondering.

In the meantime, Nilkanta had come into the room from behind without Kiran knowing it. He had seen the whole thing, and thought that Kiran had come like a thief to catch him in his thieving—and that his deed was out. How could he ever hope to convince her that he was not a thief, and that only revenge had prompted him to take the inkstand, which he meant to throw into the river at the first chance? In a weak moment he had put it in his box instead. "He was not a thief," his heart cried out, "not a thief!" Then what was he? What could he say? He had stolen, and yet he was not a thief! He could never explain to Kiran how grievously wrong she was in taking him for a thief; how could he bear the thought that she had tried to spy on him?

At last Kiran with a deep sigh replaced the inkstand in the box, and, as if she were the thief herself, covered it up with the linen and the trinkets as they were before; and at the top she placed the presents together with the banknote which she had brought for him.

The next day the boy was nowhere to be found. The villagers had not seen him; the police could discover no trace of him. Said Sharat: "Now, as a matter of curiosity, let us have a look at his box." But Kiran was obstinate in her refusal to allow that to be done.

She had the box brought up to her own room; and taking out the inkstand alone, threw it into the river.

The whole family went home. In a day the garden became desolate. And only that starving mongrel of Nilkanta's remained prowling along the riverbank, whining and whining as if its heart would break.

ৠৄ

দিদি

The Elder Sister

[*Didi* was written in 1895. It was published in English as *The Elder Sister* in *Mashi and Other Stories* (1918).]

I

Having described at length the misdeeds of an unfortunate woman's wicked, tyrannical husband, Tara, the woman's neighbour in the village, very shortly declared her verdict: "Fire be to such a husband's mouth."

At this Joygopal Babu's wife felt much hurt; it did not become womankind to wish, in any circumstances whatever, a worse species of fire than that of a cigar in a husband's mouth.

When, therefore, she mildly disapproved the verdict, hard-hearted Tara cried with redoubled vehemence: "'Twere better to be a widow seven births over than the wife of such a husband," and saying this she broke up the meeting and left.

Sasi said within herself: "I can't imagine any offence in a husband that could so harden the heart against him." Even as she turned the matter over in her mind, all the tenderness of her loving soul gushed forth towards her own husband now abroad. Throwing herself with outstretched arms on that part of the bed whereon her husband was wont to lie, she kissed the empty pillow, caught the smell of her husband's head, and, shutting the door, brought out from a wooden box an old and almost faded photograph with some letters in his handwriting, and sat gazing upon them. Thus she passed the hushed noontide alone in her room, musing of old memories and shedding tears of sadness.

It was no new yoke between Sasikala and Joygopal. They had been married at an early age and had children. Their long companionship had made the days go by in an easy, commonplace sort of way. On neither side had there been any symptoms of excessive passion. They had lived together nearly sixteen years without a break, when her husband was suddenly called away from home on business, and then a great impulse of love awoke in Sasi's soul. As separation strained the tie, love's knot grew tighter, and the passion, whose existence Sasi had not felt, now made her throb with pain.

So it happened that after so many long years, and at such an age, and being the mother of children, Sasi, on this spring noon, in her lonely chamber, lying on the bed of separation, began to dream the sweet dream of a bride in her budding youth. That love of which hitherto she had been unconscious suddenly aroused her with its murmuring music. She wandered a long way up the stream, and saw many a golden mansion and many a grove on either bank; but no foothold could she find now amid the vanished hopes of happiness. She began to say to herself that, when next she met her husband, life should not be insipid nor should the spring come in vain. How very often, in idle disputation or some petty quarrel, had she teased her husband! With all the singleness of a penitent heart she vowed that she would never show impatience again, never oppose her husband's wishes, bear all his commands, and with a tender heart submit to whatever he wished of good or ill; for the husband was all-in-all, the husband was the dearest object of love, the husband was divine.

Sasikala was the only and much-petted daughter of her parents. For this reason, though he had only a small property of his own, Joygopal had no anxieties about the future. His father-in-law had enough to support them in a village with royal state.

And then in his old age a son was born untimely to Sasikala's father. To tell the truth, Sasi was very sore in her mind at this unlooked-for, improper, and unjust action of her parents; nor was Joygopal particularly pleased.

The parents' love centred in this son of their advanced years, and when the newly arrived, diminutive, sleepy brother-in-law seized with his two weak tiny fists all the hopes and expectations of Joygopal, Joygopal found a place in a tea-garden in Assam.

His friends urged him to look for employment hard-by, but whether out of a general feeling of resentment, or knowing the chances of rapid rise in a tea-garden, Joygopal would not pay heed to anybody. He sent his wife and children to his father-in-law's, and left for Assam. It was the first separation between husband and wife in their married life.

This incident made Sasikala very angry with her baby brother. The soreness which may not pass the lips is felt the more keenly within. When the little fellow sucked and slept at his ease, his big sister found a hundred reasons, such as the rice is cold, the boys are too late for school, to worry herself and others, day and night, with her petulant humours.

But in a short time the child's mother died. Before her death, she committed her infant son to her daughter's care.

Then did the motherless child easily conquer his sister's heart. With loud whoops he would fling himself upon her, and with right goodwill try to get her mouth, nose, eyes within his own tiny mouth; he would seize her hair within his little fists and refuse to give it up; awaking before the dawn, he would roll over to her side and thrill her with his soft touch, and babble like a noisy brook; later on, he would call her *jiji* and *jijima*, and in hours of work and rest, by doing forbidden things, eating forbidden food, going to forbidden places, would set up a regular tyranny over her; then Sasi could resist no longer. She surrendered herself completely to this wayward little tyrant. Since the child had no mother, his influence over her became the greater.

II

The child was named Nilmani. When he was two years old his father fell seriously ill. A letter reached Joygopal asking him to come as quickly as possible. When after much trouble he got leave and arrived, Kaliprasanna's last hour had come.

Before he died Kaliprasanna entrusted Joygopal with the charge of his son, and left a quarter of his estate to his daughter.

So Joygopal gave up his appointment, and came home to look after his property.

After a long time, husband and wife met again. When a material body breaks, it may be put together again. But when two human beings are divided, after a long separation, they never re-unite at the same place, and to the same time; for the mind is a living thing, and moment by moment it grows and changes.

In Sasi reunion stirred a new emotion. The numbness of age-long habit in their old marriage was entirely removed by the longing born of separation, and she seemed to win her husband much more closely than before. Had she not vowed in her mind that whatever days might come, and how long so ever they might be, she would never let the brightness of this glowing love for her husband be dimmed.

Of this reunion, however, Joygopal felt differently. When they were constantly together before he had been bound to his wife by his interests and idiosyncrasies. His wife was then a living truth in his life, and there would have been a great rent in the web of his daily habit if she were left out. Consequently Joygopal found himself in deep waters at first when he went abroad. But in time this breach in habit was patched up by a new habit.

And this was not all. Formerly his days went by in the most indolent and careless fashion. For the last two years, the stimulus of bettering his condition had stirred so powerfully in his breast that he had nothing else in his thoughts. As compared with the intensity of this new passion, his old life seemed like an unsubstantial shadow. The greatest changes in a woman's nature are wrought by love; in a man's, by ambition.

Joygopal, when he returned after two years, found his wife not quite the same as of old. To her life his infant brother-in-law had added a new breadth. This part of her life was wholly unfamiliar to him—here he had no communion with his wife. His wife tried hard to share her love for the child with him, but it cannot be said that she succeeded. Sasi would come with the child in her arms, and hold him before her husband with a smiling face—Nilmani would clasp Sasi's neck, and hide his face on her shoulder, and admit no

171

obligation of kindred. Sasi wished that her little brother might show Joygopal all the arts he had learnt to capture a man's mind. But Joygopal was not very keen about it. How could the child show any enthusiasm? Joygopal could not at all understand what there was in the heavy-pated, grave-faced, dusky child that so much love should be wasted on him.

Women quickly understand the ways of love. Sasi at once understood that Joygopal did not care for Nilmani. Henceforth she used to screen her brother with the greatest care—to keep him away from the unloving, repelling look of her husband. Thus the child came to be the treasure of her secret care, the object of her isolated love.

Joygopal was greatly annoyed when Nilmani cried; so Sasi would quickly press the child to her breast, and with her whole heart and soul try to soothe him. And when Nilmani's cry happened to disturb Joygopal's sleep at night, and Joygopal with an expression of displeasure, and in a tortured spirit, growled at the child, Sasi felt humbled and fluttered like a guilty thing. Then she would take up the child in her lap, retire to a distance, and in a voice of pleading love, with such endearments as 'my gold, my treasure, my jewel,' lull him to sleep.

Children will fall out for a hundred things. Formerly in such cases, Sasi would punish her children, and side with her brother, for he was motherless. Now the law changed with the judge. Nilmani had often to bear heavy punishment without fault and without inquiry. This wrong went like a dagger to Sasi's heart; so she would take her punished brother into her room, and with sweets and toys, and by caressing and kissing him, solace as much as she could his stricken heart.

Thus the more Sasi loved Nilmani, the more Joygopal was annoyed with him. On the other hand, the more Joygopal showed his contempt for Nilmani, the more would Sasi bathe the child with the nectar of her love.

And when the fellow Joygopal behaved harshly to his wife, Sasi would minister to him silently, meekly, and with loving kindness. But inwardly they hurt each other, moment by moment, about Nilmani.

The hidden clash of a silent conflict like this is far harder to bear than an open quarrel.

III

Nilmani's head was the largest part of him. It seemed as if the Creator had blown through a slender stick a big bubble at its top. The doctors feared sometimes that the child might be as frail and as quickly evanescent as a bubble. For a long time he could neither speak nor walk. Looking at his sad grave face, you might think that his parents had unburdened all the sad weight of their advanced years upon the head of this little child.

With his sister's care and nursing, Nilmani passed the period of danger, and arrived at his sixth year.

In the month of *Kartik*, on the *bhaiphoto** day, Sasi had dressed Nilmani up as a little Babu, in coat and chadar and red-bordered *dhoti*, and was giving him the 'brother's mark,' when her outspoken neighbour Tara came in and, for one reason or another, began a quarrel.

"'Tis no use," cried she, "giving the 'brother's mark' with so much show and ruining the brother in secret."

At this Sasi was thunderstruck with astonishment, rage, and pain. Tara repeated the rumour that Sasi and her husband had conspired together to put the minor Nilmani's property up for sale for arrears of rent, and to purchase it in the name of her husband's cousin. When Sasi heard this, she uttered a curse that those who could spread such a foul lie might be stricken with leprosy in the mouth. And then she went weeping to her husband, and told him of the gossip. Joygopal said: "Nobody can be trusted in these days. Upen is my aunt's son, and I felt quite safe in leaving him in charge of the property. He could not have allowed the *taluk* Hasilpur to fall into arrears and purchase it himself in secret, if I had had the least inkling about it.'

'Won't you sue then?' asked Sasi in astonishment.

---

* Lit. the 'brother's mark.' A beautiful and touching ceremony in which a Hindu sister makes a mark of sandalwood paste on the forehead of her brother and utters a formula, 'putting the barrier in Yama's doorway' (figurative for wishing long life). On these occasions, the sisters entertain their brothers and make them presents of clothes, etc.

'Sue one's cousin!' said Joygopal. 'Besides, it would be useless, a simple waste of money.'

It was Sasi's supreme duty to trust her husband's word, but Sasi could not. At last her happy home, the domesticity of her love seemed hateful to her. That home life which had once seemed her supreme refuge was nothing more than a cruel snare of self-interest, which had surrounded them, brother and sister, on all sides. She was a woman, single-handed, and she knew not how she could save the helpless Nilmani. The more she thought, the more her heart filled with terror, loathing, and an infinite love for her imperilled little brother. She thought that, if she only knew how, she would appear before the *Lat Sahib*,* nay, write to the Maharani herself, to save her brother's property. The Maharani would surely not allow Nilmani's *taluk*† of Hasilpur, with an income of seven hundred and fifty-eight rupees a year, to be sold.

When Sasi was thus thinking of bringing her husband's cousin to book by appealing to the Maharani herself, Nilmani was suddenly seized with fever and convulsions.

Joygopal called in the village doctor. When Sasi asked for a better doctor, Joygopal said: "Why, Matilal isn't a bad sort."

Sasi fell at his feet, and charged him with an oath on her own head; whereupon Joygopal said: "Well, I shall send for the doctor from town."

Sasi lay with Nilmani in her lap, nor would Nilmani let her out of his sight for a minute; he clung to her lest by some pretence she should escape; even while he slept he would not loosen his hold of her dress.

Thus the whole day passed, and Joygopal came after nightfall to say that the doctor was not at home; he had gone to see a patient at a distance. He added that he himself had to leave that very day on account of a lawsuit, and that he had told Matilal, who would regularly call to see the patient.

At night Nilmani wandered in his sleep. As soon as the morning dawned, Sasi, without the least scruple, took a boat with her sick

---

* The Viceroy
† Land

brother, and went straight to the doctor's house. The doctor was at home—he had not left the town. He quickly found lodgings for her, and having installed her under the care of an elderly widow, undertook the treatment of the boy.

The next day Joygopal arrived. Blazing with fury, he ordered his wife to return home with him at once.

"Even if you cut me to pieces, I won't return," replied his wife. "You all want to kill my Nilmani, who has no father, no mother, none other than me, but I will save him."

"Then you remain here, and don't come back to my house," cried Joygopal indignantly.

Sasi at length fired up. "*Your* house! Why, 'tis my brother's!"

"All right, we'll see," said Joygopal. The neighbours made a great stir over this incident. "If you want to quarrel with your husband," said Tara, "do so at home. What is the good of leaving your house? After all, Joygopal is your husband."

By spending all the money she had with her, and selling her ornaments, Sasi saved her brother from the jaws of death. Then she heard that the big property which they had in Dwarigram, where their dwelling-house stood, the income of which was more than Rs. 1500 a year, had been transferred by Joygopal into his own name with the help of the zamindar. And now the whole property belonged to them, not to her brother.

When he had recovered from his illness, Nilmani would cry plaintively: "Let us go home, sister." His heart was pining for his nephews and nieces, his companions. So he repeatedly said: "Let us go home, sister, to that old house of ours." At this Sasi wept. Where was their home?

But it was no good crying. Her brother had no one else besides herself in the world. Sasi thought of this, wiped her tears, and, entering the zenana of the Deputy Magistrate, Tarini Babu, appealed to his wife. The Deputy Magistrate knew Joygopal. That a woman should forsake her home, and engage in a dispute with her husband regarding matters of property, greatly incensed him against Sasi. However, Tarini Babu kept Sasi diverted, and instantly wrote to Joygopal. Joygopal put his wife and brother-in-law into a boat by force, and brought them home.

Husband and wife, after a second separation, met again for the second time! The decree of Prajapati!*

Having got back his old companions after a long absence, Nilmani was perfectly happy. Seeing his unsuspecting joy, Sasi felt as if her heart would break.

IV

The Magistrate was touring in the Mofussil during the cold weather and pitched his tent within the village to shoot. The Sahib met Nilmani on the village *maidan*. The other boys gave him a wide berth, varying Chanakya's couplet a little, and adding the Sahib to the list of 'the clawed, the toothed, and the horned beasts.' But grave-natured Nilmani in imperturbable curiosity serenely gazed at the Sahib.

The Sahib was amused and came up and asked in Bengali: "You read at the *pathsala*?"

The boy silently nodded. "What *pustaks*† do you read?" asked the Sahib.

As Nilmani did not understand the word pustak, he silently fixed his gaze on the Magistrate's face. Nilmani told his sister the story of his meeting the Magistrate with great enthusiasm.

At noon, Joygopal, dressed in trousers, *chapkan*,‡ and *pagri*,§ went to pay his salaams to the Sahib. A crowd of suitors, chaprasies, and constables stood about him. Fearing the heat, the Sahib had seated himself at a court-table outside the tent, in the open shade, and placing Joygopal in a chair, questioned him about the state of the village. Having taken the seat of honour in open view of the community, Joygopal swelled inwardly, and thought it would be a good thing if any of the Chakrabartis or Nandis came and saw him there.

At this moment, a woman, closely veiled, and accompanied by Nilmani, came straight up to the Magistrate. She said: "Sahib,

---

* The Hindu god of marriage
† A literary word for books. The colloquial will be *boi*.
‡ A *chapkan* is a long coat.
§ Turban

into your hands I resign my helpless brother. Save him." The Sahib, seeing the large-headed, solemn boy, whose acquaintance he had already made, and thinking that the woman must be of a respectable family, at once stood up and said: "Please enter the tent."

The woman said: "What I have to say I will say here."

Joygopal writhed and turned pale. The curious villagers thought it capital fun, and pressed closer. But the moment the Sahib lifted his cane they scampered off.

Holding her brother by the hand, Sasi narrated the history of the orphan from the beginning. As Joygopal tried to interrupt now and then, the Magistrate thundered with a flushed face, "*Chup raho*," and with the tip of his cane motioned to Joygopal to leave the chair and stand up.

Joygopal, inwardly raging against Sasi, stood speechless. Nilmani nestled up close to his sister, and listened awe-struck.

When Sasi had finished her story, the Magistrate put a few questions to Joygopal, and on hearing his answers, kept silence for a long while, and then addressed Sasi thus: "My good woman, though this matter may not come up before me, still rest assured I will do all that is needful about it. You can return home with your brother without the least misgiving."

Sasi said: "Sahib, so long as he does not get back his own home, I dare not take him there. Unless you keep Nilmani with you, none else will be able to save him."

"And what would you do?" queried the Sahib.

"I will retire to my husband's house," said Sasi; "there is nothing to fear for me."

The Sahib smiled a little, and, as there was nothing else to do, agreed to take charge of this lean, dusty, grave, sedate, gentle Bengali boy whose neck was ringed with amulets.

When Sasi was about to take her leave, the boy clutched her dress. "Don't be frightened, baba—come," said the Sahib. With tears streaming behind her veil, Sasi said: "Do go, my brother, my darling brother—you will meet your sister again!"

Saying this she embraced him and stroked his head and back, and releasing her dress, hastily withdrew; and just then the Sahib put his left arm round him. The child wailed out: "Sister, oh, my sister!"

Sasi turned round at once, and with outstretched arm made a sign of speechless solace, and with a bursting heart withdrew.

Again in that old, ever-familiar house husband and wife met. The decree of Prajapati!

But this union did not last long. For soon after the villagers learnt one morning that Sasi had died of cholera in the night, and had been instantly cremated.

None uttered a word about it. Only neighbour Tara would sometimes be on the point of bursting out, but people would shut up her mouth, saying, "Hush!"

At parting, Sasi gave her word to her brother they would meet again. Where that word was kept none can tell.

রাজটিকা

"We Crown Thee King"

[*Rajtika* was written in 1898. This English translation was published in *The Hungry Stones and other Stories* in 1916. It has also been translated as *The Royal Mark* and *The Raj Seal*.]

When Nabendu Sekhar was wedded to Arunlekha, the God of marriage smiled from behind the sacrificial fire. Alas! what is sport for the gods is not always a joke to us poor mortals.

Purnendu Sekhar, the father of Nabendu, was a man well known amongst the English officials of the Government. In the voyage of life he had arrived at the desert shores of Rai Bahadurship by diligently plying his oars of *salaams*. He held in reserve enough for further advancement, but at the age of fifty-five, his tender gaze still fixed on the misty peals of Raja-hood, he suddenly found himself transported to a region where earthly honours and decorations are naught, and his salaam-wearied neck found everlasting repose on the funeral pyre.

According to modern science, force is not destroyed, but is merely converted to another form, and applied to another point. So Purnendu's salaam-force, constant handmaid of the fickle Goddess of Fortune, descended from the shoulder of the father to that of his worthy son; and the youthful head of Nabendu Sekhar began to move up and down, at the doors of high-placed Englishmen, like a pumpkin swayed by the wind.

The traditions of the family into which he had married were entirely different. Its eldest son, Pramathanath, had won for himself the love of his kinsfolk and the regard of all who knew him. His kinsmen and his neighbours looked up to him as their ideal in all things.

Pramathanath was a Bachelor of Arts, and in addition was gifted with common sense. But he held no high official position; he had no handsome salary; nor did he exert any influence with his pen. There was no one in power to lend him a helping hand, because he desired to keep away from Englishmen, as much as they desired to keep away from him. So it happened that he shone only within the sphere of his family and his friends, and excited no admiration beyond it.

Yet this Pramathanath had once sojourned in England for some three years. The kindly treatment he received during his stay there overpowered him so much that he forgot the sorrow and the humiliation of his own country, and came back dressed in European clothes. This rather grieved his brothers and his sisters at first, but after a few days they began to think that European clothes suited nobody better, and gradually they came to share his pride and dignity.

On his return from England, Pramathanath resolved that he would show the world how to associate with Anglo-Indians on terms of equality. Those of our countrymen who think that no such association is possible, unless we bend our knees to them, showed their utter lack of self-respect, and were also unjust to the English— so thought Pramathanath.

He brought with him letters of introduction from many distinguished Englishmen at home, and these gave him some recognition in Anglo-Indian society. He and his wife occasionally enjoyed English hospitality at tea, dinner, sports, and other entertainments. Such good luck intoxicated him, and began to produce a tingling sensation in every vein of his body.

About this time, at the opening of a new railway line, many of the town, proud recipients of official favour, were invited by the Lieutenant-Governor to take the first trip. Pramathanath was among them. On the return journey, a European Sergeant of the Police expelled some Indian gentlemen from a railway-carriage with great insolence. Pramathanath, dressed in his European clothes, was there. He, too, was getting out, when the Sergeant said: "You needn't move, sir. Keep your seat, please."

At first Pramathanath felt flattered at the special respect thus shown to him. When, however, the train went on, the dull rays of the setting sun, at the west of the fields, now ploughed up and stripped of green, seemed in his eyes to spread a glow of shame over the whole country. Sitting near the window of his lonely compartment, he seemed to catch a glimpse of the downcast eyes of his Motherland, hidden behind the trees. As Pramathanath sat there, lost in reverie, burning tears flowed down his cheeks, and his heart burst with indignation.

He now remembered the story of a donkey who was drawing the chariot of an idol along the street. The wayfarers bowed down to the idol, and touched the dusty ground with their foreheads. The foolish donkey imagined that all this reverence was being shown to him. "The only difference," said Pramathanath to himself, "between the donkey and myself is this: I understand today that the respect I receive is not given to me but to the burden on my back."

Arriving home, Pramathanath called together all the children of the household, and lighting a big bonfire, threw all his European clothes into it one by one. The children danced round and round it, and the higher the flames shot up, the greater was their merriment. After that, Pramathanath gave up his sip of tea and bits of toast in Anglo-Indian houses, and once again sat inaccessible within the castle of his house, while his insulted friends went about from the door of one Englishman to that of another, bending their turbaned heads as before.

By an irony of fate, poor Nabendu Sekhar married the second daughter of this house. His sisters-in-law were well educated and handsome. Nabendu considered he had made a lucky bargain. But he lost no time in trying to impress on the family that it was a rare bargain on their side also. As if by mistake, he would often hand to his sisters-in-law sundry letters that his late father had received from Europeans. And when the cherry lips of those young ladies smiled sarcastically, and the point of a shining dagger peeped out of its sheath of red velvet, the unfortunate man saw his folly, and regretted it.

Labanyalekha, the eldest sister, surpassed the rest in beauty and cleverness. Finding an auspicious day, she put on the mantel-shelf of Nabendu's bedroom two pairs of English boots, daubed with vermilion, and arranged flowers, sandal-paste, incense and a couple of burning candles before them in true ceremonial fashion. When Nabendu came in, the two sisters-in-law stood on either side of him, and said with mock solemnity: "Bow down to your gods, and may you prosper through their blessings."

The third sister Kiranlekha spent many days in embroidering with red silk one hundred common English names such as Jones, Smith, Brown, Thomson, etc., on a chadar. When it was ready, she presented this *namavoli** to Nabendu Sekhar with great ceremony.

The fourth, Sasankalekha, of tender age and therefore of no account, said: "I will make you a string of beads, brother, with which to tell the names of your gods—the sahibs." Her sisters reproved her, saying: "Run away, you saucy girl."

Feelings of shame and irritation assailed by turns the mind of Nabendu Sekhar. Still he could not forego the company of his sisters-in-law, especially as the eldest one was beautiful. Her honey was no less than her gall, and Nabendu's mind tasted at once the sweetness of the one and the bitterness of the other. The butterfly, with its bruised wings, buzzes round the flower in blind fury, unable to depart.

The society of his sisters-in-law so much infatuated him that at last Nabendu began to disavow his craving for European favours. When he went to salaam the Burra Sahib, he used to pretend that he was going to listen to a speech by Mr. Surendranath Banerjea. When he went to the railway station to pay respects to the Chota Sahib, returning from Darjeeling, he would tell his sisters-in-law that he expected his youngest uncle.

It was a sore trial to the unhappy man placed between the crossfires of his Sahibs and his sisters-in-law. The sisters-in-law, however, secretly vowed that they would not rest till the Sahibs had been put to rout.

About this time it was rumoured that Nabendu's name would be included in the forthcoming list of Birthday honours, and that

---

* A *namavoli* is a sheet of cloth printed all over with the names of Hindu gods and goddesses and worn by pious Hindus when engaged in devotional exercises.

he would mount the first step of the ladder to Paradise by becoming
a Rai Bahadur. The poor fellow had not the courage to break the
joyful news to his sisters-in-law. One evening, however, when the
autumn moon was flooding the earth with its mischievous beams,
Nabendu's heart was so full that he could not contain himself any
longer, and he told his wife. The next day, Mrs. Nabendu betook
herself to her eldest sister's house in a palanquin, and in a voice
choked with tears bewailed her lot.

"He isn't going to grow a tail," said Labanya, "by becoming a
Rai Bahadur, is he? Why should you feel so very humiliated?"

"Oh, no, sister dear," replied Arunlekha, "I am prepared to
be anything—but not a Rai-Baha-durni." The fact was that in her
circle of acquaintances there was one Bhutnath Babu, who was a Rai
Bahadur, and that explained her intense aversion to that title.

Labanya said to her sister in soothing tones: "Don't be upset
about it, dear; I will see what I can do to prevent it."

Babu Nilratan, the husband of Labanya, was a pleader at Buxar.
When the autumn was over, Nabendu received an invitation from
Labanya to pay them a visit, and he started for Buxar greatly pleased.

The early winter of the western province endowed Labanyalekha
with new health and beauty, and brought a glowing colour to her
pale cheeks. She looked like the flower-laden kasa reeds on a clear
autumn day, growing by the lonely bank of a rivulet. To Nabendu's
enchanted eyes she appeared like a *malati* plant in full blossom,
showering dew-drops brilliant with the morning light.

Nabendu had never felt better in his life. The exhilaration of his
own health and the genial company of his pretty sister-in-law made
him think himself light enough to tread on air. The Ganges in front
of the garden seemed to him to be flowing ceaselessly to regions
unknown, as though it gave shape to his own wild fantasies.

As he returned in the early morning from his walk on the bank
of the river, the mellow rays of the winter sun gave his whole frame
that pleasing sensation of warmth which lovers feel in each other's
arms. Coming home, he would now and then find his sister-in-law
amusing herself by cooking some dishes. He would offer his help,
and display his want of skill and ignorance at every step. But Nabendu
did not appear to be at all anxious to improve himself by practice

183

and attention. On the contrary he thoroughly enjoyed the rebukes he received from his sister-in-law. He was at great pains to prove every day that he was inefficient and helpless as a newborn babe in mixing spices, handling the saucepan, and regulating the heat so as to prevent things getting burnt—and he was duly rewarded with pitiful smiles and scoldings.

In the middle of the day he ate a great deal of the good food set before him, incited by his keen appetite and the coaxing of his sister-in-law. Later on, he would sit down to a game of cards—at which he betrayed the same lack of ability. He would cheat, pry into his adversary's hand, quarrel—but never did he win a single rubber, and worse still, he would not acknowledge defeat. This brought him abuse every day, and still he remained incorrigible.

There was, however, one matter in which his reform was complete. For the time at least, he had forgotten that to win the smiles of Sahibs was the final goal of life. He was beginning to understand how happy and worthy we might feel by winning the affection and esteem of those near and dear to us.

Besides, Nabendu was now moving in a new atmosphere. Labanya's husband, Babu Nilratan, a leader of the bar, was reproached by many because he refused to pay his respects to European officials. To all such reproaches Nilratan would reply: "No, thank you—if they are not polite enough to return my call, then the politeness I offer them is a loss that can never be made up for. The sands of the desert may be very white and shiny, but I would much rather sow my seeds in black soil, where I can expect a return."

And Nabendu began to adopt similar ideas, all regardless of the future. His chance of Rai Bahadurship throve on the soil carefully prepared by his late father and also by himself in days gone by, nor was any fresh watering required. Had he not at great expense laid out a splendid race-course in a town, which was a fashionable resort of Europeans?

When the time of Congress drew near, Nilratan received a request from headquarters to collect subscriptions. Nabendu, free from anxiety, was merrily engaged in a game of cards with his sister-in-law, when Nilratan Babu came upon him with a subscription-book in his hand, and said: "Your signature, please."

From old habit Nabendu looked horrified. Labanya, assuming an air of great concern and anxiety, said: "Never do that. It would ruin your racecourse beyond repair."

Nabendu blurted out: "Do you suppose I pass sleepless nights through fear of that?"

"We won't publish your name in the papers," said Nilratan reassuringly.

Labanya, looking grave and anxious, said: "Still, it wouldn't be safe. Things spread so, from mouth to mouth—"

Nabendu replied with vehemence: "My name wouldn't suffer by appearing in the newspapers." So saying, he snatched the subscription list from Nilratan's hand, and signed away a thousand rupees. Secretly he hoped that the papers would not publish the news.

Labanya struck her forehead with her palm and gasped out: "What—have you—done?"

"Nothing wrong," said Nabendu boastfully.

"But—but—" drawled Labanya, "the Guard sahib of Sealdah Station, the shop-assistant at Whiteaway's, the syce-sahib of Hart Bros.—these gentlemen might be angry with you, and decline to come to your Poojah dinner to drink your champagne, you know. Just think, they mightn't pat you on the back, when you meet them again!"

"It wouldn't break my heart," Nabendu snapped out.

A few days passed. One morning Nabendu was sipping his tea, and glancing at a newspaper. Suddenly a letter signed 'X' caught his eye. The writer thanked him profusely for his donation, and declared that the increase of strength the Congress had acquired by having such a man within its fold, was inestimable.

Alas, father Purnendu Sekhar! Was it to increase the strength of the Congress, that you brought this wretch into the world?

Put the cloud of misfortune had its silver lining. That he was not a mere cypher was clear from the fact that the Anglo-Indian community on the one side and the Congress on the other were each waiting patiently, eager to hook him, and land him on their own side. So Nabendu, beaming with pleasure took the paper to his sister-in-law, and showed her the letter. Looking as though she knew nothing about it, Labanya exclaimed in surprise: "Oh, what a pity! Everything has come out! Who bore you such ill-will? Oh, how cruel of him, how wicked of him!"

Nabendu laughed out, saying: "Now—now—don't call him names, Labanya. I forgive him with all my heart, and bless him too."

A couple of days after this, an anti-Congress Anglo-Indian paper reached Nabendu through the post. There was a letter in it, signed "One who knows," and contradicting the above report. "Those who have the pleasure of Babu Nabendu Sekhar's personal acquaintance," the writer went on, "cannot for a moment believe this absurd libel to be true. For him to turn a Congresswallah is as impossible as it is for the leopard to change his spots. He is a man of genuine worth, and neither a disappointed candidate for Government employ nor a briefless barrister. He is not one of those who, after a brief sojourn in England, return aping our dress and manners, audaciously try to thrust themselves on Anglo-Indian society, and finally go back in dejection. So there is absolutely no reason why Babu Nabendu Sekhar," etc., etc.

Ah, father Purnendu Sekhar! What a reputation you had made with the Europeans before you died!

This letter also was paraded before his sister-in-law, for did it not assert that he was no mean, contemptible scallywag, but a man of real worth?

Labanya exclaimed again in feigned surprise: "Which of your friends wrote it now? Oh, come—is it the Ticket Collector, or the hide merchant, or is it the drum-major of the Fort?"

"You ought to send in a contradiction, I think," said Nilratan.

"Is it necessary?" said Nabendu loftily. "Must I contradict every little thing they choose to say against me?"

Labanya filled the room with a deluge of laughter. Nabendu felt a little disconcerted at this, and said: "Why? What's the matter?" She went on laughing, unable to check herself, and her youthful slender form waved to and fro. This torrent of merriment had the effect of overthrowing Nabendu completely, and he said in pitiable accents: "Do you imagine that I am afraid to contradict it?"

"Oh, dear, no," said Labanya; "I was thinking that you haven't yet ceased trying to save that racecourse of yours, so full of promise. While there is life, there is hope, you know."

"That's what I am afraid of, you think, do you? Very well, you shall see," said Nabendu desperately, and forthwith sat down to write his contradiction. When he had finished, Labanya and Nilratan read it through, and said: "It isn't strong enough. We must give them pretty hot, mustn't we?" And they kindly undertook to revise the composition. Thus it ran: "When one connected to us by ties of blood turns our enemy he becomes far more dangerous than any outsider. To the Government of India, the haughty Anglo-Indians are worse enemies than the Russians or the frontier Pathans themselves—they are the impenetrable barrier, forever hindering the growth of any bond of friendship between the Government and people of the country. It is the Congress which has opened up the royal road to a better understanding between the rulers and the ruled, and the Anglo-Indian papers have planted themselves like thorns across the whole breadth of that road," etc., etc.

Nabendu had an inward fear as to the mischief this letter might do, but at the same time he felt elated at the excellence of its composition, which he fondly imagined to be his own. It was duly published, and for some days comments, replies, and rejoinders went on in various newspapers, and the air was full of trumpet-notes, proclaiming the fact that Nabendu had joined the Congress, and the amount of his subscription.

Nabendu, now grown desperate, talked as though he was a patriot of the fiercest type. Labanya laughed inwardly, and said to herself: "Well—well—you have to pass through the ordeal of fire yet."

One morning when Nabendu, before his bath, had finished rubbing oil over his chest, and was trying various devices to reach the inaccessible portions of his back, the bearer brought in a card inscribed with the name of the District Magistrate himself! Good heavens!—What would he do? He could not possibly go, and receive the Magistrate Sahib, thus oil-besmeared. He shook and twitched like a koi-fish, ready dressed for the frying pan. He finished his bath in a great hurry, tugged on his clothes somehow, and ran breathlessly to the outer apartments. The bearer said that the Sahib had just left after waiting for a long time. How much of the blame for concocting this drama of invented incidents may be set down to Labanya, and how much to the bearer is a nice problem for ethical mathematics to solve.

Nabendu's heart was convulsed with pain within his breast, like the tail of a lizard just cut off. He moped like an owl all day long.

Labanya banished all traces of inward merriment from her face, and kept on enquiring in anxious tones: "What has happened to you? You are not ill, I hope?"

Nabendu made great efforts to smile, and find a humorous reply. "How can there be," he managed to say, "any illness within your jurisdiction, since you yourself are the Goddess of Health?"

But the smile soon flickered out. His thoughts were: "I subscribed to the Congress fund to begin with, published a nasty letter in a newspaper, and on the top of that, when the Magistrate Sahib himself did me the honour to call on me, I kept him waiting. I wonder what he is thinking of me."

Alas, father Purnendu Sekhar, by an irony of Fate I am made to appear what I am not.

The next morning, Nabendu decked himself in his best clothes, wore his watch and chain, and put a big turban on his head.

"Where are you off to?" enquired his sister-in-law.

"Urgent business," Nabendu replied. Labanya kept quiet.

Arriving at the Magistrate's gate, he took out his card-case.

"You cannot see him now," said the orderly peon icily.

Nabendu took out a couple of rupees from his pocket. The peon at once salaamed him and said: "There are five of us, sir." Immediately Nabendu pulled out a ten-rupee note, and handed it to him.

He was sent for by the Magistrate, who was writing in his dressing-gown and bedroom slippers. Nabendu salaamed him. The Magistrate pointed to a chair with his finger, and without raising his eyes from the paper before him said: "What can I do for you, Babu?"

Fingering his watch-chain nervously, Nabendu said is shaky tones: "Yesterday you were good enough to call at my place, sir—"

The Sahib knitted his brows, and, lifting just one eye from his paper, said: "I called at your place! Babu, what nonsense are you talking?"

"Beg your pardon, sir," faltered out Nabendu. "There has been a mistake—some confusion," and wet with perspiration, he tumbled out of the room somehow. And that night, as he lay tossing on his bed, a distant dream-like voice came into his ear with a recurring persistency: "Babu, you are a howling idiot."

On his way home, Nabendu came to the conclusion that the Magistrate denied having called, simply because he was highly offended.

So he explained to Labanya that he had been out purchasing rose-water. No sooner had he uttered the words than half-a-dozen chaprasis wearing the Collectorate badge made their appearance, and after salaaming Nabendu, stood there grinning.

"Have they come to arrest you because you subscribed to the Congress fund?" whispered Labanya with a smile.

The six peons displayed a dozen rows of teeth and said: "*Bakshish*—Babu-Sahib."

From a side room Nilratan came out, and said in an irritated manner: "Bakshish? What for?"

The peons, grinning as before, answered: "The Babu-Sahib went to see the Magistrate—so we have come for bakshish."

"I didn't know," laughed out Labanya, "that the Magistrate was selling rose-water nowadays. Coolness wasn't the special feature of his trade before."

Nabendu in trying to reconcile the story of his purchase with his visit to the Magistrate, uttered some incoherent words, which nobody could make sense of.

Nilratan spoke to the peons: "There has been no occasion for bakshish; you shan't have it."

Nabendu said, feeling very small: "Oh, they are poor men—what's the harm of giving them something?" And he took out a currency note. Nilratan snatched it way from Nabendu's hand, remarking: "There are poorer men in the world—I will give it to them for you."

Nabendu felt greatly distressed that he was not able to appease these ghostly retainers of the angry Siva. When the peons were leaving, with thunder in their eyes, he looked at them languishingly, as much as to say: "You know everything, gentlemen, it is not my fault."

189

The Congress was to be held at Calcutta this year. Nilratan went down thither with his wife to attend the sittings. Nabendu accompanied them.

As soon as they arrived at Calcutta, the Congress party surrounded Nabendu, and their delight and enthusiasm knew no bounds. They cheered him, honoured him, and extolled him up to the skies. Everybody said that, unless leading men like Nabendu devoted themselves to the Cause, there was no hope for the country. Nabendu was disposed to agree with them, and emerged out of the chaos of mistake and confusion as a leader of the country. When he entered the Congress Pavilion on the first day, everybody stood up, and shouted "Hip, hip, hurrah," in a loud outlandish voice, hearing which our Motherland reddened with shame to the root of her ears.

In due time the Queen's birthday came, and Nabendu's name was not found in the list of Rai Bahadurs.

He received an invitation from Labanya for that evening. When he arrived there, Labanya with great pomp and ceremony presented him with a robe of honour, and with her own hand put a mark of red sandal paste on the middle of his forehead. Each of the other sisters threw round his neck a garland of flowers woven by herself. Decked in a pink Sari and dazzling jewels, his wife Arunlekha was waiting in a side room, her face lit up with smiles and blushes. Her sisters rushed to her, and, placing another garland in her hand, insisted that she also should come, and do her part in the ceremony, but she would not listen to it; and that principal garland, cherishing a desire for Nabendu's neck, waited patiently for the still secrecy of midnight.

The sisters said to Nabendu: "Today we crown thee King. Such honour will not be done to anybody else in Hindoostan."

Whether Nabendu derived any consolation from this, he alone can tell; but we greatly doubt it. We believe, in fact, that he will become a Rai Bahadur before he has done, and the Englishman and the Pioneer will write heart-rending articles lamenting his demise at the proper time. So, in the meanwhile, Three Cheers for Babu Purnendu Sekhar! Hip, hip, hurrah—Hip, hip, hurrah—Hip, hip, hurrah.

শুভদৃষ্টি

The Auspicious Vision

[*Subhadristi* was written in 1900. Its English translation was collected in *Mashi and Other Stories* (1918).]

Kantichandra was young; yet after his wife's death he sought no second partner, and gave his mind to the hunting of beasts and birds. His body was long and slender, hard and agile; his sight keen; his aim unerring. He dressed like a countryman, and took with him Hira Singh the wrestler, Chakkanlal, Khan Sahib the musician, Mian Sahib, and many others. He had no lack of idle followers.

In the month of *Agrahayan*, Kanti had gone out shooting near the swamp of Nydighi with a few sporting companions. They were in boats, and an army of servants, in boats also, filled the bathing ghats. The village women found it well-nigh impossible to bathe or to draw water. All day long, land and water trembled to the firing of the guns; and every evening musicians killed the chance of sleep.

One morning as Kanti was seated in his boat cleaning a favourite gun, he suddenly started at what he thought was the cry of wild duck. Looking up, he saw a village maiden, coming to the water's edge, with two white ducklings clasped to her breast. The little stream was almost stagnant. Many weeds choked the current. The girl put the birds into the water, and watched them anxiously. Evidently the presence of the sportsmen was the cause of her care and not the wildness of the ducks.

The girl's beauty had a rare freshness—as if she had just come from Vishwakarma's* workshop. It was difficult to guess her age. Her figure was almost a woman's, but her face was so childish that clearly the world had left no impression there. She seemed not to know herself that she had reached the threshold of youth.

Kanti's gun-cleaning stopped for a while. He was fascinated. He had not expected to see such a face in such a spot. And yet its beauty suited its surroundings better than it would have suited a palace. A bud is lovelier on the bough than in a golden vase. That day the blossoming reeds glittered in the autumn dew and morning sun, and the fresh, simple face set in the midst was like a picture of festival to Kanti's enchanted mind. Kalidas has forgotten to sing how Siva's Mountain Queen herself sometimes has come to the young Ganges, with just such ducklings in her breast. As he gazed, the maiden started in terror, and hurriedly took back the ducks into her bosom with a half-articulate cry of pain. In another moment, she had left the riverbank and disappeared into the bamboo thicket hard by. Looking round, Kanti saw one of his men pointing an unloaded gun at the ducks. He at once went up to him, wrenched away his gun, and bestowed on his cheek a prodigious slap. The astonished humourist finished his joke on the floor. Kanti went on cleaning his gun.

But curiosity drove Kanti to the thicket wherein he had seen the girl disappear. Pushing his way through, he found himself in the yard of a well-to-do householder. On one side was a row of conical thatched barns, on the other a clean cow-shed, at the end of which grew a *zizyph* bush. Under the bush was seated the girl he had seen that morning, sobbing over a wounded dove, into whose yellow beak she was trying to wring a little water from the moist corner of her garment. A grey cat, its fore-paws on her knee, was looking eagerly at the bird, and every now and then, when it got too forward, she kept it in its place by a warning tap on the nose.

This little picture, set in the peaceful midday surroundings of the householder's yard, instantly impressed itself on Kanti's sensitive heart. The checkered light and shade, flickering beneath the delicate foliage of the zizyph, played on the girl's lap. Not far off a cow was

---

* The divine craftsman in Hindu mythology

chewing the cud, and lazily keeping off the flies with slow movements of its head and tail. The north wind whispered softly in the rustling bamboo thickets. And she who at dawn on the riverbank had looked like the Forest Queen, now in the silence of noon showed the eager pity of the Divine Housewife. Kanti, coming in upon her with his gun, had a sense of intrusion. He felt like a thief caught red-handed. He longed to explain that it was not he who had hurt the dove. As he wondered how he should begin, there came a call of "Sudha!" from the house. The girl jumped up. "Sudha!" came the voice again. She took up her dove, and ran within. "Sudha,"* thought Kanti, "what an appropriate name!"

Kanti returned to the boat, handed his gun to his men, and went over to the front door of the house. He found a middle-aged Brahmin, with a peaceful, clean-shaven face, seated on a bench outside, and reading a devotional book. Kanti saw in his kindly, thoughtful face something of the tenderness which shone in the face of the maiden.

Kanti saluted him, and said: "May I ask for some water, sir? I am very thirsty." The elder man welcomed him with eager hospitality, and, offering him a seat on the bench, went inside and fetched with his own hands a little brass plate of sugar wafers and a bell-metal vessel full of water.

After Kanti had eaten and drunk, the Brahmin begged him to introduce himself. Kanti gave his own name, his father's name, and the address of his home, and then said in the usual way: "If I can be of any service, sir, I shall deem myself fortunate."

"I require no service, my son," said Nabin Banerji; "I have only one care at present."

"What is that, sir?" said Kanti.

"It is my daughter, Sudha, who is growing up" (Kanti smiled as he thought of her babyish face), "and for whom I have not yet been able to find a worthy bridegroom. If I could only see her well married, all my debt to this world would be paid. But there is no suitable bridegroom here, and I cannot leave my charge of Gopinath here, to search for a husband elsewhere."

---

* *Sudha* means nectar, ambrosia.

"If you would see me in my boat, sir, we would have a talk about the marriage of your daughter." So saying, Kanti repeated his salute and went back. He then sent some of his men into the village to inquire, and in answer heard nothing but praise of the beauty and virtues of the Brahmin's daughter.

When next day the old man came to the boat on his promised visit, Kanti bent low in salutation, and begged the hand of his daughter for himself. The Brahmin was so much overcome by this undreamed-of piece of good fortune—for Kanti not only belonged to a well-known Brahmin family, but was also a landed proprietor of wealth and position—that at first he could hardly utter a word in reply. He thought there must have been some mistake, and at length mechanically repeated: "You desire to marry my daughter?"

"If you will deign to give her to me," said Kanti.

"You mean Sudha?" he asked again.

"Yes," was the reply.

"But will you not first see and speak to her——?"

Kanti, pretending he had not seen her already, said: "Oh, that we shall do at the moment of the Auspicious Vision."*

In a voice husky with emotion the old man said: "My Sudha is indeed a good girl, well skilled in all the household arts. As you are so generously taking her on trust, may she never cause you a moment's regret. This is my blessing!"

The brick-built mansion of the Mazumdars had been borrowed for the wedding ceremony, which was fixed for next *Magh*, as Kanti did not wish to delay. In due time the bridegroom arrived on his elephant, with drums and music and with a torchlight procession, and the ceremony began.

When the bridal couple were covered with the scarlet screen for the rite of the Auspicious Vision, Kanti looked up at his bride. In that bashful, downcast face, crowned with the wedding coronet and bedecked with sandal paste, he could scarcely recognise the village

---

* After betrothal the prospective bride and bridegroom are not supposed to see each other again till that part of the wedding ceremony which is called *the Auspicious Vision*.

maiden of his fancy, and in the fullness of his emotion a mist seemed to becloud his eyes.

At the gathering of women in the bridal chamber, after the wedding ceremony was over, an old village dame insisted that Kanti himself should take off his wife's bridal veil. As he did so he started back. It was not the same girl.

Something rose from within his breast and pierced into his brain. The light of the lamps seemed to grow dim, and darkness to tarnish the face of the bride herself.

At first he felt angry with his father-in-law. The old scoundrel had shown him one girl, and married him to another. But on calmer reflection he remembered that the old man had not shown him any daughter at all—that it was all his own fault. He thought it best not to show his arrant folly to the world, and took his place again with apparent calmness.

He could swallow the powder; he could not get rid of its taste. He could not bear the merry-makings of the festive throng. He was in a blaze of anger with himself as well as with everybody else.

Suddenly he felt the bride, seated by his side, give a little start and a suppressed scream; a leveret, scampering into the room, had brushed across her feet. Close upon it followed the girl he had seen before. She caught up the leveret into her arms, and began to caress it with an affectionate murmuring. "Oh, the mad girl!" cried the women as they made signs to her to leave the room. She heeded them not, however, but came and unconcernedly sat in front of the wedded pair, looking into their faces with a childish curiosity. When a maidservant came and took her by the arm to lead her away, Kanti hurriedly interposed, saying, "Let her be."

"What is your name?" he then went on to ask her.

The girl swayed backwards and forwards but gave no reply. All the women in the room began to titter.

Kanti put another question: "Have those ducklings of yours grown up?"

The girl stared at him as unconcernedly as before.

The bewildered Kanti screwed up courage for another effort, and asked tenderly after the wounded dove, but with no avail. The increasing laughter in the room betokened an amusing joke.

At last Kanti learned that the girl was deaf and dumb, the companion of all the animals and birds of the locality. It was but by chance that she rose the other day when the name of Sudha was called.

Kanti now received a second shock. A black screen lifted from before his eyes. With a sigh of intense relief, as of escape from calamity, he looked once more into the face of his bride. Then came the true Auspicious Vision. The light from his heart and from the smokeless lamps fell on her gracious face; and he saw it in its true radiance, knowing that Nabin's blessing would find fulfilment.

প্রতিবেশিনী

My Fair Neighbour

[*Pratibesini* was written in 1900. *My Fair Neighbour* was published in *Mashi and Other Stories* in 1918.]

My feelings towards the young widow who lived in the next house to mine were feelings of worship; at least, that is what I told to my friends and myself. Even my nearest intimate, Nabin, knew nothing of the real state of my mind. And I had a sort of pride that I could keep my passion pure by thus concealing it in the inmost recesses of my heart. She was like a dew-drenched *sephali*-blossom, untimely fallen to earth. Too radiant and holy for the flower-decked marriage-bed, she had been dedicated to Heaven.

But passion is like the mountain stream, and refuses to be enclosed in the place of its birth; it must seek an outlet. That is why I tried to give expression to my emotions in poems; but my unwilling pen refused to desecrate the object of my worship.

It happened curiously that just at this time my friend Nabin was afflicted with a madness of verse. It came upon him like an earthquake. It was the poor fellow's first attack, and he was equally unprepared for rhyme and rhythm. Nevertheless he could not refrain, for he succumbed to the fascination, as a widower to his second wife.

So Nabin sought help from me. The subject of his poems was the old, old one, which is ever new: his poems were all addressed to the beloved one. I slapped his back in jest, and asked him: "Well, old chap, who is she?"

Nabin laughed, as he replied: "That I have not yet discovered!"

I confess that I found considerable comfort in bringing help to my friend. Like a hen brooding on a duck's egg, I lavished all the warmth of my pent-up passion on Nabin's effusions. So vigorously did I revise and improve his crude productions, that the larger part of each poem became my own.

Then Nabin would say in surprise: "That is just what I wanted to say, but could not. How on earth do you manage to get hold of all these fine sentiments?"

Poet-like, I would reply: "They come from my imagination; for, as you know, truth is silent, and it is imagination only which waxes eloquent. Reality represses the flow of feeling like a rock; imagination cuts out a path for itself."

And the poor puzzled Nabin would say: "Y-e-s, I see, yes, of course"; and then after some thought would murmur again: "Yes, yes, you are right!"

As I have already said, in my own love there was a feeling of reverential delicacy which prevented me from putting it into words. But with Nabin as a screen, there was nothing to hinder the flow of my pen; and a true warmth of feeling gushed out into these vicarious poems.

Nabin in his lucid moments would say: "But these are yours! Let me publish them over your name."

"Nonsense!" I would reply. "They are yours, my dear fellow; I have only added a touch or two here and there."

And Nabin gradually came to believe it.

I will not deny that, with a feeling akin to that of the astronomer gazing into the starry heavens, I did sometimes turn my eyes towards the window of the house next door. It is also true that now and again my furtive glances would be rewarded with a vision. And the least glimpse of the pure light of that countenance would at once still and clarify all that was turbulent and unworthy in my emotions.

But one day I was startled. Could I believe my eyes? It was a hot summer afternoon. One of the fierce and fitful nor'-westers was threatening. Black clouds were massed in the north-west corner of the sky; and against the strange and fearful light of that background my fair neighbour stood, gazing out into empty space. And what a world of forlorn longing did I discover in the faraway look of those lustrous black eyes! Was there then, perchance, still some living volcano within the serene radiance of that moon of mine? Alas! that look of limitless yearning, which was winging its way through the clouds like an eager bird, surely sought—not heaven—but the nest of some human heart!

At the sight of the unutterable passion of that look I could hardly contain myself. I was no longer satisfied with correcting crude poems. My whole being longed to express itself in some worthy action. At last I thought I would devote myself to making widow-remarriage popular in my country. I was prepared not only to speak and write on the subject, but also to spend money on its cause.

Nabin began to argue with me. "Permanent widowhood," said he, "has in it a sense of immense purity and peace; a calm beauty like that of the silent places of the dead shimmering in the wan light of the eleventh moon.* Would not the mere possibility of remarriage destroy its divine beauty?"

Now this sort of sentimentality always makes me furious. In time of famine, if a well-fed man speaks scornfully of food, and advises a starving man at point of death to glut his hunger on the fragrance of flowers and the song of birds, what are we to think of him? I said with some heat: "Look here, Nabin, to the artist a ruin may be a beautiful object; but houses are built not only for the contemplation of artists, but that people may live therein; so they have to be kept in repair in spite of artistic susceptibilities. It is all very well for you to idealise widowhood from your safe distance, but you should remember that within widowhood there is a sensitive human heart, throbbing with pain and desire."

I had an impression that the conversion of Nabin would be a difficult matter, so perhaps I was more impassioned than I need have been. I was somewhat surprised to find at the conclusion of my little speech that Nabin after a single thoughtful sigh completely

---

* The eleventh day of the moon is a day of fasting and penance.

agreed with me. The even more convincing peroration which I felt I might have delivered was not needed!

After about a week Nabin came to me, and said that if I would help him he was prepared to lead the way by marrying a widow himself.

I was overjoyed. I embraced him effusively, and promised him any money that might be required for the purpose. Then Nabin told me his story.

I learned that Nabin's loved one was not an imaginary being. It appeared that Nabin, too, had for some time adored a widow from a distance, but had not spoken of his feelings to any living soul. Then the magazines in which Nabin's poems, or rather *my* poems, used to appear had reached the fair one's hands; and the poems had not been ineffective.

Not that Nabin had deliberately intended, as he was careful to explain, to conduct love-making in that way. In fact, said he, he had no idea that the widow knew how to read. He used to post the magazine, without disclosing the sender's name, addressed to the widow's brother. It was only a sort of fancy of his, a concession to his hopeless passion. It was flinging garlands before a deity; it is not the worshipper's affair whether the god knows or not, whether he accepts or ignores the offering.

And Nabin particularly wanted me to understand that he had no definite end in view when on diverse pretexts he sought and made the acquaintance of the widow's brother. Any near relation of the loved one needs must have a special interest for the lover.

Then followed a long story about how an illness of the brother at last brought them together. The presence of the poet himself naturally led to much discussion of the poems; nor was the discussion necessarily restricted to the subject out of which it arose.

After his recent defeat in argument at my hands, Nabin had mustered up courage to propose marriage to the widow. At first he could not gain her consent. But when he had made full use of my eloquent words, supplemented by a tear or two of his own, the fair one capitulated unconditionally. Some money was now wanted by her guardian to make arrangements.

"Take it at once," said I.

"But," Nabin went on, "you know it will be some months before I can appease my father sufficiently for him to continue my allowance. How are we to live in the meantime?" I wrote out the necessary cheque without a word, and then I said: "Now tell me who she is. You need not look on me as a possible rival, for I swear I will not write poems to her; and even if I do I will not send them to her brother, but to you!"

"Don't be absurd," said Nabin; "I have not kept back her name because I feared your rivalry! The fact is, she was very much perturbed at taking this unusual step, and had asked me not to talk about the matter to my friends. But it no longer matters, now that everything has been satisfactorily settled. She lives at No. 19, the house next to yours."

If my heart had been an iron boiler it would have burst. "So she has no objection to remarriage?" I simply asked.

"Not at the present moment," replied Nabin with a smile.

"And was it the poems alone which wrought the magic change?"

"Well, my poems were not so bad, you know," said Nabin, "were they?"

I swore mentally.

But at whom was I to swear? At him? At myself? At Providence? All the same, I swore.

মাস্টার মশাই

Master Mashai

[*Master Moshayi* was written in 1907. It was first published in English in *Stories from Tagore* in 1918.]

I

Adhar Babu lived upon the interest of the capital left him by his father. Only the brokers, negotiating loans, came to his drawing room and smoked the silver-chased hookah, and the clerks from the attorney's office discussed the terms of some mortgage or the amount of the stamp fees. He was so careful with his money that even the most dogged efforts of the boys from the local football club failed to make any impression on his pocket.

At the time this story opens, a new guest came into his household. After a long period of despair, his wife, Nanibala, bore him a son.

The child resembled his mother—large eyes, well-formed nose, and fair complexion. Ratikanta, Adharlal's protégé, gave verdict— "He is worthy of this noble house." They named him Venugopal.

Never before had Adharlal's wife expressed any opinion differing from her husband's on household expenses. There had been a hot discussion now and then about the propriety of some necessary item and up to this time she had merely acknowledged defeat with silent contempt. But now Adharlal could no longer maintain his supremacy. He had to give way little by little when things for his son were in question.

II

As Venugopal grew up, his father gradually became accustomed to spending money on him. He obtained an old teacher, who had a considerable repute for his learning and also for his success in dragging impassable boys through their examinations. But such a training does not lead to the cultivation of amiability. This man tried his best to win the boy's heart, but the little that was left in him of the natural milk of human kindness had turned sour, and the child repulsed his advances from the very beginning. The mother, in consequence, objected to him strongly, and complained that the very sight of him made her boy ill. So the teacher left.

Just then, Haralal made his appearance in a dirty dress and a torn pair of old canvas shoes. Haralal's mother, who was a widow, had kept him with great difficulty at a District school out of the scanty earnings which she made by cooking in strange houses and husking rice. He managed to pass the Matriculation and determined to go to college. As a result of his half-starved condition, his pinched face tapered to a point in an unnatural manner—like Cape Comorin in the map of India; and the only broad portion of it was his forehead, which resembled the ranges of the Himalayas.

The servant asked Haralal what he wanted, and he answered timidly that he wished to see the master.

The servant answered sharply: "You can't see him." Haralal was hesitating, at a loss what to do next, when Venugopal, who had finished his game in the garden, suddenly came to the door. The servant shouted at Haralal: "Get away." Quite unaccountably Venugopal grew excited and cried: "No, he shan't get away." And he dragged the stranger to his father.

Adharlal had just risen from his midday sleep and was sitting quietly on the upper verandah in his cane chair, rocking his legs. Ratikanta was enjoying his hookah, seated in a chair next to him. He asked Haralal how far he had got in his reading. The young man bent his head and answered that he had passed the Matriculation. Ratikanta looked stern and expressed surprise that he should be so backward for his age. Haralal kept silence. It was Ratikanta's special pleasure to torture his patron's dependants, whether actual or potential.

Suddenly it struck Adharlal that he would be able to employ this youth as a tutor for his son on next to nothing. He agreed, there and then, to take him at a salary of five rupees a month with board and lodging free.

III

This time the post of tutor remained occupied longer than before. From the very beginning of their acquaintance Haralal and his pupil became great friends. Never before did Haralal have such an opportunity of loving any young human creature. His mother had been so poor and dependent, that he had never had the privilege of playing with the children where she was employed at work. He had not hitherto suspected the hidden stores of love which lay all the while accumulating in his own heart.

Venu, also, was glad to find a companion in Haralal. He was the only boy in the house. His two younger sisters were looked down upon, as unworthy of being his playmates. So his new tutor became his only companion, patiently bearing the undivided weight of the tyranny of his child friend.

IV

Venu was now eleven. Haralal had passed his Intermediate, winning a scholarship. He was working hard for his B.A. degree. After college lectures were over, he would take Venu out into the public park and tell him stories about the heroes from Greek History and Victor Hugo's romances. The child used to get quite impatient to run to Haralal, after school hours, in spite of his mother's attempts to keep him by her side.

This displeased Nanibala. She thought that it was a deep-laid plot of Haralal's to captivate her boy, in order to prolong his own appointment. One day she talked to him from behind the purdah: "It is your duty to teach my son only for an hour or two in the morning and evening. But why are you always with him? The child has nearly forgotten his own parents. You must understand that a man of your position is no fit companion for a boy belonging to this house."

Haralal's voice choked a little as he answered that for the future he would merely be Venu's teacher and would keep away from him at other times.

It was Haralal's usual practice to begin his college study early before dawn. The child would come to him directly after he had washed himself. There was a small pool in the garden and they used to feed the fish in it with puffed rice. Venu was also engaged in building a miniature garden-house, at the corner of the garden, with its Lilliputian gates and hedges and gravel paths. When the sun became too hot they would go back into the house, and Venu would have his morning lesson from Haralal.

On the day in question, Venu had risen earlier than usual, because he wished to hear the end of the story which Haralal had begun the evening before. But he found his teacher absent. When asked about him, the door-servant said that he had gone out. At lesson time Venu remained unnaturally quiet. He never even asked Haralal why he had gone out, but went on mechanically with his lessons. When the child was with his mother taking his breakfast, she asked him what had happened to make him so gloomy, and why he was not eating his food. Venu gave no answer. After his meal his mother caressed him and questioned him repeatedly. Venu burst out crying and said, "Master Mashai." His mother asked Venu, "What about Master Mashai?" But Venu found it difficult to name the offence which his teacher had committed.

His mother said to Venu: "Has your Master Mashai been saying anything to you against *me*?"

Venu could not understand the question and went away.

V

There was a theft in Adhar Babu's house. The police were called in to investigate. Even Haralal's trunks were searched. Ratikanta said with meaning: "The man who steals anything, does not keep his thefts in his own box."

Adharlal called his son's tutor and said to him: "It will not be convenient for me to keep any of you in my own house. From today you will have to take up your quarters outside, only coming in to teach my son at the proper time."

Ratikanta said sagely, drawing at his hookah: "That is a good proposal—good for both parties."

Haralal did not utter a word, but he sent a letter saying that it would be no longer possible for him to remain as tutor to Venu.

When Venu came back from school, he found his tutor's room empty. Even that broken steel trunk of his was absent. The rope was stretched across the corner, but there were no clothes or towel hanging on it. Only on the table, which formerly was strewn with books and papers, stood a bowl containing some goldfish with a label on which was written the word 'Venu' in Haralal's handwriting. The boy ran up at once to his father and asked him what had happened. His father told him that Haralal had resigned his post. Venu went to his room and flung himself down and began to cry. Adharlal did not know what to do with him.

The next day, when Haralal was sitting on his wooden bedstead in the Hostel, debating with himself whether he should attend his college lectures, suddenly he saw Adhar Babu's servant coming into his room followed by Venu. Venu at once ran up to him and threw his arms round his neck asking him to come back to the house.

Haralal could not explain why it was absolutely impossible for him to go back, but the memory of those clinging arms and that pathetic request used to choke his breath with emotion long after.

VI

Haralal found out, after this, that his mind was in an unsettled state, and that he had but a small chance of winning the scholarship, even if he could pass the examination. At the same time, he knew that, without the scholarship, he could not continue his studies. So he tried to get employment in some office.

Fortunately for him, an English Manager of a big merchant firm took a fancy to him at first sight. After only a brief exchange of words the Manager asked him if he had any experience, and could he bring any testimonial. Haralal could only answer "No"; nevertheless a post was offered him of twenty rupees a month and fifteen rupees were allowed him in advance to help him to come properly dressed to the office.

The Manager made Haralal work extremely hard. He had to stay on after office hours and sometimes go to his master's house late in the evening. But, in this way, he learnt his work quicker than others, and his fellow clerks became jealous of him and tried to injure him, but without effect. He rented a small house in a narrow lane and brought his mother to live with him as soon as his salary was raised to forty rupees a month. Thus happiness came back to his mother after weary years of waiting.

Haralal's mother used to express a desire to see Venugopal, of whom she had heard so much. She wished to prepare some dishes with her own hand and to ask him to come just once to dine with her son. Haralal avoided the subject by saying that his house was not big enough to invite him for that purpose.

VII

The news reached Haralal that Venu's mother had died. He could not wait a moment, but went at once to Adharlal's house to see Venu. After that they began to see each other frequently.

But times had changed. Venu, stroking his budding moustache, had grown quite a young man of fashion. Friends, befitting his present condition, were numerous. That old dilapidated study chair and ink-stained desk had vanished, and the room now seemed to be bursting with pride at its new acquisitions—its looking-glasses, oleographs, and other furniture. Venu had entered college, but showed no haste in crossing the boundary of the Intermediate examination.

Haralal remembered his mother's request to invite Venu to dinner. After great hesitation, he did so. Venugopal, with his handsome face, at once won the mother's heart. But as soon as the meal was over he became impatient to go, and looking at his gold watch he explained that he had pressing engagements elsewhere.

Then he jumped into his carriage, which was waiting at the door, and drove away. Haralal with a sigh said to himself that he would never invite him again.

VIII

One day, on returning from office, Haralal noticed the presence of a man in the dark room on the ground floor of his house. Possibly he would have passed him by, had not the heavy scent of some foreign perfume attracted his attention. Haralal asked who was there, and the answer came:

"It is I, Master Mashai."

"What is the matter, Venu?" said Haralal. "When did you arrive?"

"I came hours ago," said Venu. "I did not know that you returned so late."

They went upstairs together and Haralal lighted the lamp and asked Venu whether all was well. Venu replied that his college classes were becoming a fearful bore, and his father did not realise how dreadfully hard it was for him to go on in the same class, year after year, with students much younger than himself. Haralal asked him what he wished to do. Venu then told him that he wanted to go to England and become a barrister. He gave an instance of a student, much less advanced than himself, who was getting ready to go. Haralal asked him if he had received his father's permission. Venu replied that his father would not hear a word of it until he had passed the Intermediate, and that was an impossibility in his present frame of mind. Haralal suggested that he himself should go and try to talk over his father.

"No," said Venu, "I can never allow that!"

Haralal asked Venu to stay for dinner and while they were waiting he gently placed his hand on Venu's shoulder and said:

"Venu, you should not quarrel with your father, or leave home."

Venu jumped up angrily and said that if he was not welcome, he could go elsewhere. Haralal caught him by the hand and implored him not to go away without taking his food. But Venu snatched away his hand and was just leaving the room when Haralal's mother brought the food in on a tray. On seeing Venu about to leave she pressed him to remain and he did so with bad grace.

While he was eating the sound of a carriage stopping at the door was heard. First a servant entered the room with creaking shoes and then Adhar Babu himself. Venu's face became pale. The mother left the room as soon as she saw strangers enter. Adhar Babu called out to Haralal in a voice thick with anger:

"Ratikanta gave me full warning, but I could not believe that you had such devilish cunning hidden in you. So, you think you're going to live upon Venu? This is sheer kidnapping, and I shall prosecute you in the Police Court."

Venu silently followed his father and went out of the house.

IX

The firm to which Haralal belonged began to buy up large quantities of rice and dhal from the country districts. To pay for this, Haralal had to take the cash every Saturday morning by the early train and disburse it. There were special centres where the brokers and middlemen would come with their receipts and accounts for settlement. Some discussion had taken place in the office about Haralal being entrusted with this work, without any security, but the Manager undertook all the responsibility and said that a security was not needed. This special work used to go on from the middle of December to the middle of April. Haralal would get back from it very late at night.

One day, after his return, he was told by his mother that Venu had called and that she had persuaded him to take his dinner at their house. This happened more than once. The mother said that it was because Venu missed his own mother, and the tears came into her eyes as she spoke about it.

One day Venu waited for Haralal to return and had a long talk with him.

"Master Mashai!" he said. "Father has become so cantankerous of late that I cannot live with him any longer. And, besides, I know that he is getting ready to marry again. Ratikanta is seeking a suitable match, and they are always conspiring about it. There used to be a time when my father would get anxious, if I were absent from home even for a few hours. Now, if I am away for more than a week, he takes no notice—indeed he is greatly relieved. If this marriage takes place, I feel that I cannot live in the house any longer. You must show me a way out of this. I want to become independent."

Haralal felt deeply pained, but he did not know how to help his former pupil. Venu said that he was determined to go to England and become a barrister. Somehow or other he must get the passage money out of his father: he could borrow it on a note of hand and his father would have to pay when the creditors filed a suit. With this borrowed money he would get away, and when he was in England his father was certain to remit his expenses.

"But who is there," Haralal asked, "who would advance you the money?"

"You!" said Venu.

"I!" exclaimed Haralal in amazement.

"Yes," said Venu, "I've seen the servant bringing heaps of money here in bags."

"The servant and the money belong to someone else."

Haralal explained why the money came to his house at night, like birds to their nest, to be scattered next morning.

"But can't the Manager advance the sum?" Venu asked.

"He may do so," said Haralal, "if your father stands security."

The discussion ended at this point.

X

One Friday night a carriage and pair stopped before Haralal's lodging house. When Venu was announced Haralal was counting money in his bedroom, seated on the floor. Venu entered the room dressed in a strange manner. He had discarded his Bengali dress and was wearing a Parsee coat and trousers and had a cap on his head. Rings were prominent on almost all the fingers of both hands, and a thick gold chain was hanging round his neck: there was a gold-watch in his pocket, and diamond studs could be seen peeping from his shirt sleeves. Haralal at once asked him what was the matter and why he was wearing that dress.

"My father's marriage," said Venu, "comes off tomorrow. He tried hard to keep it from me, but I found it out. I asked him to allow me to go to our garden-house at Barrackpur for a few days, and he was only too glad to get rid of me so easily. I am going there, and I wish to God I had never to come back."

Haralal looked pointedly at the rings on his fingers. Venu explained that they had belonged to his mother. Haralal then asked him if he had already had his dinner. He answered, "Yes, haven't you had yours?"

"No," said Haralal, "I cannot leave this room until I have all the money safely locked up in this iron chest."

"Go and take your dinner," said Venu, "while I keep guard here: your mother will be waiting for you."

For a moment Haralal hesitated, and then he went out and had his dinner. In a short time he came back with his mother and the three of them sat among the bags of money talking together. When it was about midnight, Venu took out his watch and looked at it and jumped up saying that he would miss his train. Then he asked Haralal to keep all his rings and his watch and chain until he asked for them again. Haralal put them all together in a leather bag and laid it in the iron safe. Venu went out.

The canvas bags containing the currency notes had already been placed in the safe: only the loose coins remained to be counted over and put away with the rest.

XI

Haralal lay down on the floor of the same room, with the key under his pillow, and went to sleep. He dreamt that Venu's mother was loudly reproaching him from behind the curtain. Her words were indistinct, but rays of different colours from the jewels on her body kept piercing the curtain like needles and violently vibrating. Haralal struggled to call Venu, but his voice seemed to forsake him. At last, with a noise, the curtain fell down. Haralal started up from his sleep and found darkness piled up round about him. A sudden gust of wind had flung open the window and put out the light. Haralal's whole body was wet with perspiration. He relighted the lamp and saw, by the clock, that it was four in the morning. There was no time to sleep again; for he had to get ready to start.

After Haralal had washed his face and hands his mother called from her own room—"Baba, why are you up so soon?"

It was the habit of Haralal to see his mother's face the first thing in the morning in order to bring a blessing upon the day. His mother said to him: "I was dreaming that you were going out to bring back a bride for yourself." Haralal went to his own bedroom and began to take out the bags containing the silver and the currency notes.

Suddenly his heart stopped beating. Three of the bags appeared to be empty. He knocked them against the iron safe, but this only proved his fear to be true. He opened them and shook them with all his might. Two letters from Venu dropped out from one of the bags. One was addressed to his father and one to Haralal.

Haralal tore open his own letter and began reading. The words seemed to run into one another. He trimmed the lamp, but felt as if he could not understand what he read. Yet the purport of the letter was clear. Venu had taken three thousand rupees, in currency notes, and had started for England. The steamer was to sail before daybreak that very morning. The letter ended with the words: "I am explaining everything in a letter to my father. He will pay off the debt; and then, again, my mother's ornaments, which I have left in your care, will more than cover the amount I have taken."

Haralal locked up his room and hired a carriage and went with all haste to the jetty. But he did not know even the name of the steamer which Venu had taken. He ran the whole length of the wharves from Prinsep's Ghat to Metiaburuj. He found that two steamers had started on their voyage to England early that morning. It was impossible for him to know which of them carried Venu, or how to reach him.

When Haralal got home, the sun was strong and the whole of Calcutta was awake. Everything before his eyes seemed blurred. He felt as if he were pushing against a fearful obstacle which was bodiless and without pity. His mother came on the verandah to ask him anxiously where he had gone. With a dry laugh he said to her—"To bring home a bride for myself," and then he fainted away.

On opening his eyes after a while, Haralal asked his mother

to leave him. Entering his room he shut the door from the inside while his mother remained seated on the floor of the verandah in the fierce glare of the sun. She kept calling to him fitfully, almost mechanically—"Baba, Baba!"

The servant came from the Manager's office and knocked at the door, saying that they would miss the train if they did not start out at once. Haralal called from inside, "It will not be possible for me to start this morning."

"Then where are we to go, Sir?"

"I will tell you later on."

The servant went downstairs with a gesture of impatience.

Suddenly Haralal thought of the ornaments which Venu had left behind. Up till now he had completely forgotten about them, but with the thought came instant relief. He took the leather bag containing them, and also Venu's letter to his father, and left the house.

Before he reached Adharlal's house he could hear the bands playing for the wedding, yet on entering he could feel that there had been some disturbance. Haralal was told that there had been a theft the night before and one or two servants were suspected. Adhar Babu was sitting in the upper verandah flushed with anger and Ratikanta was smoking his hookah. Haralal said to Adhar Babu, "I have something private to tell you." Adharlal flared up, "I have no time now!" He was afraid that Haralal had come to borrow money or to ask his help. Ratikanta suggested that if there was any delicacy in making the request in his presence he would leave the place. Adharlal told him angrily to sit where he was. Then Haralal handed over the bag which Venu had left behind. Adharlal asked what was inside it and Haralal opened it and gave the contents into his hands.

Then Adhar Babu said with a sneer: "It's a paying business that you two have started—you and your former pupil! You were certain that the stolen property would be traced, and so you come along with it to me to claim a reward!"

Haralal presented the letter which Venu had written to his father. This only made Adharlal all the more furious.

"What's all this?" he shouted, "I'll call for the police! My son has not yet come of age—and *you* have smuggled him out of the country! I'll bet my soul you've lent him a few hundred rupees, and then taken a note of hand for three thousand! But I am not going to be bound by *this*!"

"I never advanced him any money at all," said Haralal.

"Then how did he find it?" said Adharlal, "Do you mean to tell me he broke open your safe and stole it?"

Haralal stood silent.

Ratikanta sarcastically remarked: "I don't believe this fellow ever set hands on as much as three thousand rupees in his life."

When Haralal left the house he seemed to have lost the power of dreading anything, or even of being anxious. His mind seemed to refuse to work. Directly he entered the lane he saw a carriage waiting before his own lodging. For a moment he felt certain that it was Venu's. It was impossible to believe that his calamity could be so hopelessly final.

Haralal went up quickly, but found an English assistant from the firm sitting inside the carriage. The man came out when he saw Haralal and took him by the hand and asked him: "Why didn't you go out by train this morning?" The servant had told the Manager his suspicions and he had sent this man to find out.

Haralal answered: "Notes to the amount of three thousand rupees are missing."

The man asked how that could have happened.

Haralal remained silent.

The man said to Haralal: "Let us go upstairs together and see where you keep your money." They went up to the room and counted the money and made a thorough search of the house.

When the mother saw this she could not contain herself any longer. She came out before the stranger and said: "Baba, what has happened?" He answered in broken Hindustani that some money had been stolen.

"Stolen!" the mother cried, "Why! How could it be stolen? Who could do such a dastardly thing?" Haralal said to her: "Mother, don't say a word."

The man collected the remainder of the money and told Haralal to come with him to the Manager. The mother barred the way and said:

"Sir, where are you taking my son? I have brought him up, starving and straining to do honest work. My son would never touch money belonging to others."

The Englishman, not knowing Bengali, said, "Achcha! Achcha!" Haralal told his mother not to be anxious; he would explain it all to the Manager and soon be back again. The mother entreated him, with a distressed voice,

"Baba, you haven't taken a morsel of food all morning." Haralal stepped into the carriage and drove away, and the mother sank to the ground in the anguish of her heart.

The Manager said to Haralal: "Tell me the truth. What did happen?"

Haralal said to him, "I haven't taken any money."

"I fully believe it," said the Manager, "but surely you know who has taken it."

Haralal looked on the ground and remained silent.

"Somebody," said the Manager, "must have taken it away with your connivance."

"Nobody," replied Haralal, "could take it away with my knowledge without taking first my life."

"Look here, Haralal," said the Manager, "I trusted you completely. I took no security. I employed you in a post of great responsibility. Everyone in the office was against me for doing so. The three thousand rupees is a small matter, but the shame of all this to me is a great matter. I will do one thing. I will give you the whole day to bring back this money. If you do so, I shall say nothing about it and I will keep you on in your post."

It was now eleven o'clock. Haralal with bent head went out of the office. The clerks began to discuss the affair with exultation.

"What can I do? What can I do?" Haralal repeated to himself, as he walked along like one dazed, the sun's heat pouring down upon him. At last his mind ceased to think at all about what could be done, but the mechanical walk went on without ceasing.

This city of Calcutta, which offered its shelter to thousands and thousands of men had become like a steel trap. He could see no way out. The whole body of people were conspiring to surround and hold him captive—this most insignificant of men, whom no one knew.

Nobody had any special grudge against him, yet everybody was his enemy. The crowd passed by, brushing against him: the clerks of the offices were eating their lunch on the roadside from their plates made of leaves; a tired wayfarer on the Maidan, under the shade of a tree, was lying with one hand beneath his head and one leg upraised over the other: The up-country women, crowded into hackney carriages, were wending their way to the temple; a chaprasi came up with a letter and asked him the address on the envelope—so the afternoon went by.

Then came the time when the offices were all about to close. Carriages started off in all directions, carrying people back to their homes. The clerks, packed tightly on the seats of the trams, looked at the theatre advertisements as they returned to their lodgings. From today, Haralal had neither his work in the office, nor release from work in the evening. He had no need to hurry to catch the tram to take him to his home. All the busy occupations of the city— the buildings—the horses and carriages—the incessant traffic— seemed, now at one time, to swell into dreadful reality, and at another time, to subside into the shadowy unreal.

Haralal had taken neither food, nor rest, nor shelter all that day.

The street lamps were lighted from one road to another and it seemed to him that a watchful darkness, like some demon, was keeping its eyes wide open to guard every movement of its victim. Haralal did not even have the energy to enquire how late it was. The veins on his forehead throbbed, and he felt as if his head would burst. Through the paroxysms of pain, which alternated with the apathy of dejection, only one thought came again and again to his mind; among the innumerable multitudes in that vast city, only one name found its way through his dry throat—"Mother!"

He said to himself, "At the deep of night, when no one is awake to capture me—me, who am the least of all men—I will silently creep to my mother's arms and fall asleep, and may I never wake again!"

Haralal's one trouble was lest some police officer should molest him in the presence of his mother, and this kept him back from going home. When it became impossible for him at last to bear the weight of his own body, he hailed a carriage. The driver asked him where he wanted to go. He said: "Nowhere, I want to drive across the Maidan to get the fresh air." The man at first did not believe him and was about to drive on, when Haralal put a rupee into his hand as an advance payment. Thereupon the driver crossed, and then re-crossed, the Maidan from one side to the other, traversing the different roads.

Haralal laid his throbbing head on the side of the open window of the carriage and closed his eyes. Slowly all the pain abated. His body became cool. A deep and intense peace filled his heart and a supreme deliverance seemed to embrace him on every side. It was *not* true—the day's despair which threatened him with its grip of utter helplessness. It was *not* true, it was false. He knew now that it was only an empty fear of the mind. Deliverance was in the infinite sky and there was no end to peace. No king or emperor in the world had the power to keep captive this nonentity, this Haralal. In the sky, surrounding his emancipated heart on every side, he felt the presence of his mother, that one poor woman. She seemed to grow and grow till she filled the infinity of darkness. All the roads and buildings and shops of Calcutta gradually became enveloped by her. In her presence vanished all the aching pains and thoughts and consciousness of Haralal. It burst—that bubble filled with the hot vapour of pain. And now there was neither darkness nor light, but only one tensefulness.

The Cathedral clock struck one. The driver called out impatiently: "Babu, my horse can't go on any longer. Where do you want to go?"

There came no answer.

The driver came down and shook Haralal and asked him again where he wanted to go.

There came no answer.

And the answer was never received from Haralal, where he wanted to go.

বোষ্টমী

The Devotee

[*Boshtomi* was written in 1914. Its English translation was published in *The Hungry Stones and Other Stories* in 1916. It has also been translated as *The Baishnav Woman*.]

At a time, when my unpopularity with a part of my readers had reached the nadir of its glory, and my name had become the central orb of the journals, to be attended through space with a perpetual rotation of revilement, I felt the necessity to retire to some quiet place and endeavour to forget my own existence.

I have a house in the country some miles away from Calcutta, where I can remain unknown and unmolested. The villagers there have not, as yet, come to any conclusion about me. They know I am no mere holiday-maker or pleasure-seeker; for I never outrage the silence of the village nights with the riotous noises of the city. Nor do they regard me as ascetic, because the little acquaintance they have of me carries the savour of comfort about it. I am not, to them, a traveller; for, though I am a vagabond by nature, my wandering through the village fields is aimless. They are hardly even quite certain whether I am married or single; for they have never seen me with my children. So, not being able to classify me in any animal or vegetable kingdom that they know, they have long since given me up and left me stolidly alone.

But quite lately I have come to know that there is one person in the village who is deeply interested in me. Our acquaintance began on a sultry afternoon in July. There had been rain all the morning, and the air was still wet and heavy with mist, like eyelids when weeping is over.

I sat lazily watching a dappled cow grazing on the high bank of the river. The afternoon sun was playing on her glossy hide. The simple beauty of this dress of light made me wonder idly at man's deliberate waste of money in setting up tailors' shops to deprive his own skin of its natural clothing.

While I was thus watching and lazily musing, a woman of middle age came and prostrated herself before me, touching the ground with her forehead. She carried in her robe some bunches of flowers, one of which she offered to me with folded hands. She said to me, as she offered it: "This is an offering to my God."

She went away. I was so taken aback as she uttered these words, that I could hardly catch a glimpse of her before she was gone. The whole incident was entirely simple, but it left a deep impression on my mind; and as I turned back once more to look at the cattle in the field, the zest of life in the cow, who was munching the lush grass with deep breaths, while she whisked off the flies, appeared to me fraught with mystery. My readers may laugh at my foolishness, but my heart was full of adoration. I offered my worship to the pure joy of living, which is God's own life. Then, plucking a tender shoot from the mango tree, I fed the cow with it from my own hand, and as I did this I had the satisfaction of having pleased my God.

The next year when I returned to the village it was February. The cold season still lingered on. The morning sun came into my room, and I was grateful for its warmth. I was writing, when the servant came to tell me that a devotee, of the Vishnu cult, wanted to see me. I told him, in an absent way, to bring her upstairs, and went on with my writing. The Devotee came in, and bowed to me, touching my feet. I found that she was the same woman whom I had met, for a brief moment, a year ago.

I was able now to examine her more closely. She was past that age when one asks the question whether a woman is beautiful or not. Her stature was above the ordinary height, and she was strongly built; but her body was slightly bent owing to her constant attitude of veneration. Her manner had nothing shrinking about it. The most remarkable of her features were her two eyes. They seemed to have a penetrating power which could make distance near.

With those two large eyes of hers, she seemed to push me as she entered.

"What is this?" she asked. "Why have you brought me here before your throne, my God? I used to see you among the trees; and that was much better. That was the true place to meet you."

She must have seen me walking in the garden without my seeing her. For the last few days, however, I had suffered from a cold, and had been prevented from going out. I had, perforce, to stay indoors and pay my homage to the evening sky from my terrace. After a silent pause the Devotee said to me: "O my God, give me some words of good."

I was quite unprepared for this abrupt request, and answered her on the spur of the moment: "Good words I neither give nor receive. I simply open my eyes and keep silence, and then I can at once both hear and see, even when no sound is uttered. Now, while I am looking at you, it is as good as listening to your voice."

The Devotee became quite excited as I spoke, and exclaimed: "God speaks to me, not only with His mouth, but with His whole body."

I said to her: "When I am silent I can listen with my whole body. I have come away from Calcutta here to listen to that sound."

The Devotee said: "Yes, I know that, and therefore I have come here to sit by you."

Before taking her leave, she again bowed to me, and touched my feet. I could see that she was distressed, because my feet were covered. She wished them to be bare.

Early next morning I came out, and sat on my terrace on the roof. Beyond the line of trees southward I could see the open country chill and desolate. I could watch the sun rising over the sugarcane in the East, beyond the clump of trees at the side of the village. Out of the deep shadow of those dark trees the village road suddenly appeared. It stretched forward, winding its way to some distant villages on the horizon, till it was lost in the grey of the mist.

That morning it was difficult to say whether the sun had risen or not. A white fog was still clinging to the tops of the trees. I saw the Devotee walking through the blurred dawn, like a mist-wraith of the morning twilight. She was singing her chant to God, and sounding her cymbals.

The thick haze lifted at last; and the sun, like the kindly grandsire of the village, took his seat amid all the work that was going on in home and field.

When I had just settled down at my writing-table, to appease the hungry appetite of my editor in Calcutta, there came a sound of footsteps on the stair, and the Devotee, humming a tune to herself, entered, and bowed before me. I lifted my head from my papers.

She said to me: "My God, yesterday I took as sacred food what was left over from your meal."

I was startled, and asked her how she could do that.

"Oh," she said, "I waited at your door in the evening, while you were at dinner, and took some food from your plate when it was carried out."

This was a surprise to me, for everyone in the village knew that I had been to Europe, and had eaten with Europeans. I was a vegetarian, no doubt, but the sanctity of my cook would not bear investigation, and the orthodox regarded my food as polluted.

The Devotee, noticing my sign of surprise, said: "My God, why should I come to you at all, if I could not take your food?"

I asked her what her own caste people would say. She told me she had already spread the news far and wide all over the village. The caste people had shaken their heads, but agreed that she must go her own way.

I found out that the Devotee came from a good family in the country, and that her mother was well-to-do, and desired to keep her daughter. But she preferred to be a mendicant. I asked her how she made her living. She told me that her followers had given her a piece of land, and that she begged her food from door to door. She said to me: "The food which I get by begging is divine."

After I had thought over what she said, I understood her meaning. When we get our food precariously as alms, we remember God the giver. But when we receive our food regularly at home, as a matter of course, we are apt to regard it as ours by right.

I had a great desire to ask her about her husband. But as she never mentioned him even indirectly, I did not question her.

I found out very soon that the Devotee had no respect at all for that part of the village where the people of the higher castes lived.

"They never give," she said, "a single farthing to God's service; and yet they have the largest share of God's glebe. But the poor worship and starve."

I asked her why she did not go and live among these godless people, and help them towards a better life. "That," I said with some unction, "would be the highest form of divine worship."

I had heard sermons of this kind from time to time, and I am rather fond of copying them myself for the public benefit, when the chance comes.

But the Devotee was not at all impressed. She raised her big round eyes, and looked straight into mine, and said:

"You mean to say that because God is with the sinners, therefore when you do them any service you do it to God? Is that so?"

"Yes," I replied, "that is my meaning."

"Of course," she answered almost impatiently, "of course, God is with them: otherwise, how could they go on living at all? But what is that to me? My God is not there. My God cannot be worshipped among them; because I do not find Him there. I seek Him where I can find Him."

As she spoke, she made obeisance to me. What she meant to say was really this. A mere doctrine of God's omnipresence does not help us. That God is all-pervading—this truth may be a mere intangible abstraction, and therefore unreal to ourselves. Where I can see Him, there is His reality in my soul.

I need not explain that all the while she showered her devotion on me she did it to me not as an individual. I was simply a vehicle of her divine worship. It was not for me either to receive it or to refuse it: for it was not mine, but God's.

When the Devotee came again, she found me once more engaged with my books and papers.

"What have you been doing," she said, with evident vexation, "that my God should make you undertake such drudgery? Whenever I come, I find you reading and writing."

"God keeps his useless people busy," I answered; "otherwise they would be bound to get into mischief. They have to do all the least necessary things in life. It keeps them out of trouble."

The Devotee told me that she could not bear the encumbrances, with which, day by day, I was surrounded. If she wanted to see me, she was not allowed by the servants to come straight upstairs. If she wanted to touch my feet in worship, there were my socks always in the way. And when she wanted to have a simple talk with me, she found my mind lost in a wilderness of letters.

This time, before she left me, she folded her hands, and said: "My God! I felt your feet in my breast this morning. Oh, how cool! And they were bare, not covered. I held them upon my head for a long time in worship. That filled my very being. Then, after that, pray what was the use of my coming to you yourself? Why did I come? My Lord, tell me truly—wasn't it a mere infatuation?"

There were some flowers in my vase on the table. While she was there, the gardener brought some new flowers to put in their place. The Devotee saw him changing them.

"Is that all?" she exclaimed. "Have you done with the flowers? Then give them to me."

She held the flowers tenderly in the cup of her hands, and began to gaze at them with bent head. After a few moments' silence she raised her head again, and said to me: "You never look at these flowers; therefore they become stale to you. If you would only look into them, then your reading and writing would go to the winds."

She tied the flowers together in the end of her robe, and placed them, in an attitude of worship, on the top of her head, saying reverently: "Let me carry my God with me."

While she did this, I felt that flowers in our rooms do not receive their due meed of loving care at our hands. When we stick them in vases, they are more like a row of naughty schoolboys standing on a form to be punished.

The Devotee came again the same evening, and sat by my feet on the terrace of the roof.

"I gave away those flowers," she said, "as I went from house to house this morning, singing God's name. Beni, the head man of our village, laughed at me for my devotion, and said: 'Why do you waste all this devotion on Him? Don't you know He is reviled up and down the countryside?' Is that true, my God? Is it true that they are hard upon you?"

For a moment I shrank into myself. It was a shock to find that the stains of printers' ink could reach so far.

The Devotee went on: "Beni imagined that he could blow out the flame of my devotion at one breath! But this is no mere tiny flame: it is a burning fire. Why do they abuse you, my God?"

I said: "Because I deserved it. I suppose in my greed I was loitering about to steal people's hearts in secret."

The Devotee said: "Now you see for yourself how little their hearts are worth. They are full of poison, and this will cure you of your greed."

"When a man," I answered, "has greed in his heart, he is always on the verge of being beaten. The greed itself supplies his enemies with poison."

"Our merciful God," she replied, "beats us with His own hand, and drives away all the poison. He who endures God's beating to the end is saved."

II

That evening the Devotee told me the story of her life. The stars of evening rose and set behind the trees, as she went on to the end of her tale.

"My husband is very simple. Some people think that he is a simpleton; but I know that those who understand simply, understand truly. In business and household management he was able to hold his own. Because his needs were small, and his wants few, he could manage carefully on what we had. He would never meddle in other matters, nor try to understand them.

"Both my husband's parents died before we had been married long, and we were left alone. But my husband always needed someone to be over him. I am ashamed to confess that he had a sort of reverence for me, and looked upon me as his superior. But I am sure that he could understand things better than I, though I had greater powers of talking.

"Of all the people in the world he held his Guru Thakur (spiritual master) in the highest veneration. Indeed it was not veneration merely but love; and such love as his is rare.

"Guru Thakur was younger than my husband. Oh! how beautiful he was!

"My husband had played games with him when he was a boy; and from that time forward he had dedicated his heart and soul to this friend of his early days. Thakur knew how simple my husband was, and used to tease him mercilessly.

"He and his comrades would play jokes upon him for their own amusement; but he would bear them all with long suffering.

"When I married into this family, Guru Thakur was studying at Benares. My husband used to pay all his expenses. I was eighteen years old when he returned home to our village.

"At the age of fifteen I had my child. I was so young I did not know how to take care of him. I was fond of gossip, and liked to be with my village friends for hours together. I used to get quite cross with my boy when I was compelled to stay at home and nurse him. Alas! my child-God came into my life, but His playthings were not ready for Him. He came to the mother's heart, but the mother's heart lagged behind. He left me in anger; and ever since I have been searching for Him up and down the world.

"The boy was the joy of his father's life. My careless neglect used to pain my husband. But his was a mute soul. He has never been able to give expression to his pain.

"The wonderful thing was this, that in spite of my neglect the child used to love me more than anyone else. He seemed to have the dread that I would one day go away and leave him. So even when I was with him, he would watch me with a restless look in his eyes. He had me very little to himself, and therefore his desire to be with me was always painfully eager. When I went each day to the river, he used to fret and stretch out his little arms to be taken with me. But the bathing ghat was my place for meeting my friends, and I did not care to burden myself with the child.

"It was an early morning in August. Fold after fold of grey clouds had wrapped the midday round with a wet clinging robe. I asked the maid to take care of the boy, while I went down to the river. The child cried after me as I went away.

"There was no one there at the bathing ghat when I arrived. As a swimmer, I was the best among all the village women. The river was quite full with the rains. I swam out into the middle of the stream some distance from the shore.

"Then I heard a cry from the bank, 'Mother!' I turned my head and saw my boy coming down the steps, calling me as he came. I shouted to him to stop, but he went on, laughing and calling. My feet and hands became cramped with fear. I shut my eyes, afraid to see. When I opened them, there, at the slippery stairs, my boy's ripple of laughter had disappeared for ever.

"I got back to the shore. I raised him from the water. I took him in my arms, my boy, my darling, who had begged so often in vain for me to take him. I took him now, but he no more looked in my eyes and called 'Mother.'

"My child-God had come. I had ever neglected Him. I had ever made Him cry. And now all that neglect began to beat against my own heart, blow upon blow, blow upon blow. When my boy was with me, I had left him alone. I had refused to take him with me. And now, when he is dead, his memory clings to me and never leaves me.

"God alone knows all that my husband suffered. If he had only punished me for my sin, it would have been better for us both. But he knew only how to endure in silence, not how to speak.

"When I was almost mad with grief, Guru Thakur came back. In earlier days, the relation between him and my husband had been that of boyish friendship. Now, my husband's reverence for his sanctity and learning was unbounded. He could hardly speak in his presence, his awe of him was so great.

"My husband asked his Guru to try to give me some consolation. Guru Thakur began to read and explain to me the scriptures. But I do not think they had much effect on my mind. All their value for me lay in the voice that uttered them. God makes the draught of divine life deepest in the heart for man to drink, through the human voice. He has no better vessel in His hand than that; and He Himself drinks His divine draught out of the same vessel.

"My husband's love and veneration for his Guru filled our house, as incense fills a temple shrine. I showed that veneration, and had peace. I saw my God in the form of that Guru. He used to come to take his meal at our house every morning. The first thought that would come to my mind on waking from sleep was that of his food as a sacred gift from God. When I prepared the things for his meal, my fingers would sing for joy.

"When my husband saw my devotion to his Guru, his respect for me greatly increased. He noticed his Guru's eager desire to explain the scriptures to me. He used to think that he could never expect to earn any regard from his Guru himself, on account of his stupidity; but his wife had made up for it.

"Thus another five years went by happily, and my whole life would have passed like that; but beneath the surface some stealing was going on somewhere in secret. I could not detect it; but it was detected by the God of my heart. Then came a day when, in a moment our whole life was turned upside down.

"It was a morning in midsummer. I was returning home from bathing, my clothes all wet, down a shady lane. At the bend of the road, under the mango tree, I met my Guru Thakur. He had his towel on his shoulder and was repeating some Sanskrit verses as he was going to take his bath. With my wet clothes clinging all about me I was ashamed to meet him. I tried to pass by quickly, and avoid being seen. He called me by my name.

"I stopped, lowering my eyes, shrinking into myself. He fixed his gaze upon me, and said: 'How beautiful is your body!'

"All the universe of birds seemed to break into song in the branches overhead. All the bushes in the lane seemed ablaze with flowers. It was as though the earth and sky and everything had become a riot of intoxicating joy.

"I cannot tell how I got home. I only remember that I rushed into the room where we worship God. But the room seemed empty. Only before my eyes those same gold spangles of light were dancing which had quivered in front of me in that shady lane on my way back from the river.

"Guru Thakur came to take his food that day, and asked my husband where I had gone. He searched for me, but could not find me anywhere.

"Ah! I have not the same earth now any longer. The same

sunlight is not mine. I called on my God in my dismay, and He kept His face turned away from me.

"The day passed, I know not how. That night I had to meet my husband. But the night is dark and silent. It is the time when my husband's mind comes out shining, like stars at twilight. I had heard him speak things in the dark, and I had been surprised to find how deeply he understood.

"Sometimes I am late in the evening in going to rest on account of household work. My husband waits for me, seated on the floor, without going to bed. Our talk at such times had often begun with something about our Guru.

"That night, when it was past midnight, I came to my room, and found my husband sleeping on the floor. Without disturbing him I lay down on the ground at his feet, my head towards him. Once he stretched his feet, while sleeping, and struck me on the breast. That was his last bequest.

"Next morning, when my husband woke up from his sleep, I was already sitting by him. Outside the window, over the thick foliage of the jackfruit tree, appeared the first pale red of the dawn at the fringe of the night. It was so early that the crows had not yet begun to call.

"I bowed, and touched my husband's feet with my forehead. He sat up, starting as if waking from a dream, and looked at my face in amazement. I said:

"'I have made up my mind. I must leave the world. I cannot belong to you any longer. I must leave your home.'

"Perhaps my husband thought that he was still dreaming. He said not a word.

"'Ah! do hear me!' I pleaded with infinite pain. 'Do hear me and understand! You must marry another wife. I must take my leave.'

"My husband said: 'What is all this wild, mad talk? Who advises you to leave the world?'

"I said: 'My Guru Thakur.'

"My husband looked bewildered. 'Guru Thakur!' he cried. 'When did he give you this advice?'

"'In the morning,' I answered, 'yesterday, when I met him on my way back from the river.'

228

"His voice trembled a little. He turned, and looked in my face, and asked me: 'Why did he give you such a behest?'

"'I do not know,' I answered. 'Ask him! He will tell you himself, if he can.'

"My husband said: 'It is possible to leave the world, even when continuing to live in it. You need not leave my home. I will speak to my Guru about it.'

"'Your Guru,' I said, 'may accept your petition; but my heart will never give its consent. I must leave your home. From henceforth, the world is no more to me.'

"My husband remained silent, and we sat there on the floor in the dark. When it was light, he said to me: 'Let us both come to him.'

"I folded my hands and said: 'I shall never meet him again.'

"He looked into my face. I lowered my eyes. He said no more. I knew that, somehow, he had seen into my mind, and understood what was there. In this world of mine, there were only two who loved me best—my boy and my husband. That love was my God, and therefore it could brook no falsehood. One of these two left me, and I left the other. Now I must have truth, and truth alone."

She touched the ground at my feet, rose and bowed to me, and departed.

শেষের রাত্রি

Mashi

[*Shesher Ratri* was written in 1914. It was translated by various writers and published in 1918 in *Mashi and Other Stories*. It has also been translated as *Last Night*.]

I

"**M**ashi!"*
"Try to sleep, Jotin, it is getting late."
"Never mind if it is. I have not many days left. I was thinking that Mani should go to her father's house.—I forget where he is now."

"Sitarampur."

"Oh yes! Sitarampur. Send her there. She should not remain any longer near a sick man. She herself is not strong."

"Just listen to him! How can she bear to leave you in this state?"

"Does she know what the doctors——?"

"But she can see for herself! The other day she cried her eyes out at the merest hint of having to go to her father's house."

We must explain that in this statement there was a slight distortion of truth, to say the least of it. The actual talk with Mani was as follows:—

---

* The maternal aunt is addressed as Mashi.

"I suppose, my child, you have got some news from your father? I thought I saw your cousin Anath here."

"Yes! Next Friday will be my little sister's *annaprashan** ceremony. So I'm thinking——"

"All right, my dear. Send her a gold necklace. It will please your mother."

"I'm thinking of going myself. I've never seen my little sister, and I want to ever so much."

"Whatever do you mean? You surely don't think of leaving Jotin alone? Haven't you heard what the doctor says about him?"

"But he said that just now there's no special cause for——"

"Even if he did, you can see his state."

"This is the first girl after three brothers, and she's a great favourite.—I have heard that it's going to be a grand affair. If I don't go, mother will be very——"

"Yes, yes! I don't understand your mother. But I know very well that your father will be angry enough if you leave Jotin just now."

"You'll have to write a line to him saying that there is no special cause for anxiety, and that even if I go, there will be no——"

"You're right there; it will certainly be no great loss if you do go. But remember, if I write to your father, I'll tell him plainly what is in my mind."

"Then you needn't write. I shall ask my husband, and he will surely——"

"Look here, child, I've borne a good deal from you, but if you do that, I won't stand it for a moment. Your father knows you too well for you to deceive him."

When Mashi had left her, Mani lay down on her bed in a bad temper.

Her neighbour and friend came and asked what was the matter.

"Look here! What a shame it is! Here's my only sister's annaprashan coming, and they don't want to let me go to it!"

"Why! Surely you're never thinking of going, are you, with your husband so ill?"

---

* The *annaprashan* ceremony takes place when a child is first given rice. Usually it receives its name on that day.

231

"I don't do anything for him, and I couldn't if I tried. It's so deadly dull in this house, that I tell you frankly I can't bear it."

"You are a strange woman!"

"But I can't pretend, as you people do, and look glum lest anyone should think ill of me."

"Well, tell me your plan."

"I must go. Nobody can prevent me."

"Isss! What an imperious young woman you are!"

II

Hearing that Mani had wept at the mere thought of going to her father's house, Jotin was so excited that he sat up in bed. Pulling his pillow towards him, he leaned back, and said: "Mashi, open this window a little, and take that lamp away."

The still night stood silently at the window like a pilgrim of eternity; and the stars gazed in, witnesses through untold ages of countless death-scenes.

Jotin saw his Mani's face traced on the background of the dark night, and saw those two big dark eyes brimming over with tears, as it were for all eternity.

Mashi felt relieved when she saw him so quiet, thinking he was asleep.

Suddenly he started up, and said: "Mashi, you all thought that Mani was too frivolous ever to be happy in our house. But you see now——"

"Yes, I see now, my Baba,* I was mistaken—but trial tests a person."

"Mashi!"

"Do try to sleep, dear!"

"Let me think a little, let me talk. Don't be vexed, Mashi!"

"Very well."

"Once, when I used to think I could not win Mani's heart, I bore it silently. But you——"

---

* Baba literally means Father, but is often used by elders as a term of endearment. In the same way 'Ma' is used.

"No, dear, I won't allow you to say that; I also bore it."

"Our minds, you know, are not clods of earth which you can possess by merely picking up. I felt that Mani did not know her own mind, and that one day at some great shock——"

"Yes, Jotin, you are right."

"Therefore I never took much notice of her waywardness."

Mashi remained silent, suppressing a sigh. Not once, but often she had seen Jotin spending the night on the verandah wet with the splashing rain, yet not caring to go into his bedroom. Many a day he lay with a throbbing head, longing, she knew, that Mani would come and soothe his brow, while Mani was getting ready to go to the theatre. Yet when Mashi went to fan him, he sent her away petulantly. She alone knew what pain lay hidden in that distress. Again and again she had wanted to say to Jotin: "Don't pay so much attention to that silly child, my dear; let her learn to want—to cry for things." But these things cannot be said, and are apt to be misunderstood. Jotin had in his heart a shrine set up to the goddess Woman, and there Mani had her throne. It was hard for him to imagine that his own fate was to be denied his share of the wine of love poured out by that divinity. Therefore the worship went on, the sacrifice was offered, and the hope of a boon never ceased.

Mashi imagined once more that Jotin was sleeping, when he cried out suddenly:

"I know you thought that I was not happy with Mani, and therefore you were angry with her. But, Mashi, happiness is like those stars. They don't cover all the darkness; there are gaps between. We make mistakes in life and we misunderstand, and yet there remain gaps through which truth shines. I do not know whence comes this gladness that fills my heart tonight."

Mashi began gently to soothe Jotin's brow, her tears unseen in the dark.

"I was thinking, Mashi, she's so young! What will she do when I am——?"

"Young, Jotin? She's old enough. I too was young when I lost the idol of my life, only to find him in my heart for ever. Was that any loss, do you think? Besides, is happiness absolutely necessary?"

"Mashi, it seems as if just when Mani's heart shows signs of awakening I have to——"

"Don't you worry about that, Jotin. Isn't it enough if her heart awakes?"

Suddenly Jotin recollected the words of a village minstrel's song which he had heard long before:

O my heart! you woke not when the man of my heart came to my door.
At the sound of his departing steps you woke up.
Oh, you woke up in the dark!

"Mashi, what is the time now?"

"About nine."

"So early as that! Why, I thought it must be at least two or three o'clock. My midnight, you know, begins at sundown. But why did you want me to sleep, then?"

"Why, you know how late last night you kept awake talking; so today you must get to sleep early."

"Is Mani asleep?"

"Oh no, she's busy making some soup for you."

"You don't mean to say so, Mashi? Does she——?"

"Certainly! Why, she prepares all your food, the busy little woman."

"I thought perhaps Mani could not——"

"It doesn't take long for a woman to learn such things. With the need it comes of itself."

"The fish soup, that I had in the morning, had such a delicate flavour, I thought you had made it."

"Dear me, no! Surely you don't think Mani would let me do anything for you? Why, she does all your washing herself. She knows you can't bear anything dirty about you. If only you could see your sitting room, how spick and span she keeps it! If I were to let her haunt your sickroom, she would wear herself out. But that's what she really wants to do."

"Is Mani's health, then——?"

"The doctors think she should not be allowed to visit the sickroom too often. She's too tender-hearted."

"But, Mashi, how do you prevent her from coming?"
"Because she obeys me implicitly. But still I have constantly to
be giving her news of you."

The stars glistened in the sky like tear-drops. Jotin bowed his
head in gratitude to his life that was about to depart, and when Death
stretched out his right hand towards him through the darkness, he
took it in perfect trust.

Jotin sighed, and, with a slight gesture of impatience, said:
"Mashi, if Mani is still awake, then, could I—if only for a——?"
"Very well! I'll go and call her."
"I won't keep her long, only for five minutes. I have something
particular to tell her."
Mashi, sighing, went out to call Mani. Meanwhile Jotin's pulse
began to beat fast. He knew too well that he had never been able to
have an intimate talk with Mani. The two instruments were tuned
differently and it was not easy to play them in unison. Again and
again, Jotin had felt pangs of jealousy on hearing Mani chattering
and laughing merrily with her girl companions. Jotin blamed only
himself—why couldn't he talk irrelevant trifles as they did? Not
that he could not, for with his men friends he often chatted on all
sorts of trivialities. But the small talk that suits men is not suitable
for women. You can hold a philosophical discourse in monologue,
ignoring your inattentive audience altogether, but small talk requires
the cooperation of at least two. The bagpipes can be played singly, but
there must be a pair of cymbals. How often in the evenings had Jotin,
when sitting on the open verandah with Mani, made some strained
attempts at conversation, only to feel the thread snap. And the very
silence of the evening felt ashamed. Jotin was certain that Mani
longed to get away. He had even wished earnestly that a third person
would come. For talking is easy with three, when it is hard for two.
He began to think what he should say when Mani came. But
such manufactured talk would not satisfy him. Jotin felt afraid that
this five minutes of tonight would be wasted. Yet, for him, there
were but few moments left for intimate talk.

III

"What's this, child, you're not going anywhere, are you?"

"Of course, I'm going to Sitarampur."

"What do you mean? Who is going to take you?"

"Anath."

"Not today, my child, some other day."

"But the compartment has already been reserved."

"What does that matter? That loss can easily be borne. Go tomorrow, early in the morning."

"Mashi, I don't hold by your inauspicious days. What harm if I do go today?"

"Jotin wants to have a talk with you."

"All right! there's still some time. I'll just go and see him."

"But you mustn't say that you are going."

"Very well, I won't tell him, but I shan't be able to stay long. Tomorrow is my sister's annaprashan, and I must go today."

"Oh, my child! I beg you to listen to me this once. Quiet your mind for a while and sit by him. Don't let him see your hurry."

"What can I do? The train won't wait for me. Anath will be back in ten minutes. I can sit by him till then."

"No, that won't do. I shall never let you go to him in that frame of mind . . . Oh, you wretch! the man you are torturing is soon to leave this world; but I warn you, you will remember this day till the end of your days! That there is a God! that there is a God! you will someday understand!"

"Mashi, you mustn't curse me like that."

"Oh, my darling boy! my darling! why do you go on living longer? There is no end to this sin, yet I cannot check it!"

Mashi after delaying a little returned to the sickroom, hoping by that time Jotin would be asleep. But Jotin moved in his bed when she entered. Mashi exclaimed:

"Just look what she has done!"

"What's happened? Hasn't Mani come? Why have you been so long, Mashi?"

"I found her weeping bitterly because she had allowed the milk for your soup to get burnt! I tried to console her, saying, 'Why, there's more milk to be had!' But that she could be so careless about the preparation of *your* soup made her wild. With great trouble I managed to pacify her and put her to bed. So I haven't brought her today. Let her sleep it off."

Though Jotin was pained when Mani didn't come, yet he felt a certain amount of relief. He had half feared that Mani's bodily presence would do violence to his heart's image of her. Such things had happened before in his life. And the gladness of the idea that Mani was miserable at burning *his* milk filled his heart to overflowing.

"Mashi!"

"What is it, Baba?"

"I feel quite certain that my days are drawing to a close. But I have no regrets. Don't grieve for me."

"No, dear, I won't grieve. I don't believe that only life is good and not death."

"Mashi, I tell you truly that death seems sweet."

Jotin, gazing at the dark sky, felt that it was Mani herself who was coming to him in Death's guise. She had immortal youth and the stars were flowers of blessing, showered upon her dark tresses by the hand of the World-Mother. It seemed as if once more he had his first sight of his bride under the veil of darkness.* The immense night became filled with the loving gaze of Mani's dark eyes. Mani, the bride of this house, the little girl, became transformed into a world-image—her throne on the altar of the stars at the confluence of life and death. Jotin said to himself with clasped hands: "At last the veil is raised, the covering is rent in this deep darkness. Ah, beautiful one! How often have you wrung my heart, but no longer shall you forsake me!"

---

* The bride and the bridegroom see each other's face for the first time at the marriage ceremony under a veil thrown over their heads.

IV

"I'm suffering, Mashi, but nothing like you imagine. It seems to me as if my pain were gradually separating itself from my life. Like a laden boat, it was so long being towed behind, but the rope has snapped, and now it floats away with all my burdens. Still I can see it, but it is no longer mine . . . But, Mashi, I've not seen Mani even once for the last two days!"

"Jotin, let me give you another pillow."

"It almost seems to me, Mashi, that Mani also has left me like that laden boat of sorrow which drifts away."

"Just sip some pomegranate juice, dear! Your throat must be getting dry."

"I wrote my will yesterday; did I show it to you? I can't recollect."

"There's no need to show it to me, Jotin."

"When mother died, I had nothing of my own. You fed me and brought me up. Therefore I was saying——"

"Nonsense, child! I had only this house and a little property. You earned the rest."

"But this house——?"

"That's nothing. Why, you've added to it so much that it's difficult to find out where my house was!"

"I'm sure Mani's love for you is really——"

"Yes, yes! I know that, Jotin. Now you try to sleep."

"Though I have bequeathed all my property to Mani, it is practically yours, Mashi. She will never disobey you."

"Why are you worrying so much about that, dear?"

"All I have I owe to you. When you see my will don't think for a moment that——"

"What do you mean, Jotin? Do you think I shall mind for a moment because you give to Mani what belongs to you? Surely I'm not so mean as that?"

"But you also will have——"

"Look here, Jotin, I shall get angry with you. You want to console me with money!"

"Oh, Mashi, how I wish I could give you something better than money!"

"That you have done, Jotin!—more than enough. Haven't I had you to fill my lonely house? I must have won that great good-fortune in many previous births! You have given me so much that now, if my destiny's due is exhausted, I shall not complain. Yes, yes! Give away everything in Mani's name—your house, your money, your carriage, and your land—such burdens are too heavy for me!"

"Of course I know you have lost your taste for the enjoyments of life, but Mani is so young that——"

"No! you mustn't say that. If you want to leave her your property, it is all right, but as for enjoyment——"

"What harm if she does enjoy herself, Mashi?"

"No, no, it will be impossible. Her throat will become parched, and it will be dust and ashes to her."

Jotin remained silent. He could not decide whether it was true or not, and whether it was a matter of regret or otherwise, that the world would become distasteful to Mani for want of him. The stars seemed to whisper in his heart:

"Indeed it is true. We have been watching for thousands of years, and know that all these great preparations for enjoyment are but vanity."

Jotin sighed and said: "We cannot leave behind us what is really worth giving."

"It's no trifle you are giving, dearest. I only pray she may have the power to know the value of what is given her."

"Give me a little more of that pomegranate juice, Mashi, I'm thirsty. Did Mani come to me yesterday, I wonder?"

"Yes, she came, but you were asleep. She sat by your head, fanning you for a long time, and then went away to get your clothes washed."

"How wonderful! I believe I was dreaming that very moment that Mani was trying to enter my room. The door was slightly open, and she was pushing against it, but it wouldn't open. But, Mashi, you're going too far—you ought to let her see that I am dying; otherwise my death will be a terrible shock to her."

"Baba, let me put this shawl over your feet; they are getting cold."

"No, Mashi, I can't bear anything over me like that."

"Do you know, Jotin, Mani made this shawl for you? When she ought to have been asleep, she was busy at it. It was finished only yesterday."

Jotin took the shawl, and touched it tenderly with his hands. It seemed to him that the softness of the wool was Mani's own. Her loving thoughts had been woven night after night with its threads. It was not made merely of wool, but also of her touch. Therefore, when Mashi drew that shawl over his feet, it seemed as if, night after night, Mani had been caressing his tired limbs.

"But, Mashi, I thought Mani didn't know how to knit—at any rate she never liked it."

"It doesn't take long to learn a thing. Of course I had to teach her. Then there are a good many mistakes in it."

"Let there be mistakes; we're not going to send it to the Paris Exhibition. It will keep my feet warm in spite of its mistakes."

Jotin's mind began to picture Mani at her task, blundering and struggling, and yet patiently going on night after night. How sweetly pathetic it was! And again he went over the shawl with his caressing fingers.

"Mashi, is the doctor downstairs?"

"Yes, he will stay here tonight."

"But tell him it is useless for him to give me a sleeping draught. It doesn't bring me real rest and only adds to my pain. Let me remain properly awake. Do you know, Mashi, that my wedding took place on the night of the full moon in the month of *Baisakh*? Tomorrow will be that day, and the stars of that very night will be shining in the sky. Mani perhaps has forgotten. I want to remind her of it today; just call her to me for a minute or two . . . Why do you keep silent? I suppose the doctor has told you I am so weak that any excitement will——but I tell you truly, Mashi, tonight, if I can have only a few minutes' talk with her, there will be no need for any sleeping draughts. Mashi, don't cry like that! I am quite well. Today my heart is full as it has never been in my life before. That's why I want to see Mani. No, no, Mashi, I can't bear to see you crying! You have been so quiet all these last days. Why are you so troubled tonight?"

"Oh, Jotin, I thought that I had exhausted all my tears, but I find there are plenty left. I can't bear it any longer."

"Call Mani. I'll remind her of our wedding night, so that tomorrow she may——"

"I'm going, dear. Shombhu will wait at the door. If you want anything, call him."

Mashi went to Mani's bedroom and sat down on the floor crying—"Oh come, come once, you heartless wretch! Keep his last request who has given you his all! Don't kill him who is already dying!"

Jotin hearing the sound of footsteps started up, saying, "Mani!"

"I am Shombhu. Did you call me?"

"Ask your mistress to come?"

"Ask whom?"

"Your mistress."

"She has not yet returned."

"Returned? From where?"

"From Sitarampur."

"When did she go?"

"Three days ago."

For a moment Jotin felt numb all over, and his head began to swim. He slipped down from the pillows, on which he was reclining, and kicked off the woollen shawl that was over his feet.

When Mashi came back after a long time, Jotin did not mention Mani's name, and Mashi thought he had forgotten all about her.

Suddenly Jotin cried out: "Mashi, did I tell you about the dream I had the other night?"

"Which dream?"

"That in which Mani was pushing the door, and the door wouldn't open more than an inch. She stood outside unable to enter. Now I know that Mani has to stand outside my door till the last."

Mashi kept silent. She realised that the heaven she had been building for Jotin out of falsehood had toppled down at last. If sorrow comes, it is best to acknowledge it.—When God strikes, we cannot avoid the blow.

"Mashi, the love I have got from you will last through all my births. I have filled this life with it to carry it with me. In the next birth, I am sure you will be born as my daughter, and I shall tend you with all my love."

"What are you saying, Jotin? Do you mean to say I shall be born again as a woman? Why can't you pray that I should come to your arms as a son?"

"No, no, not a son! You will come to my house in that wonderful beauty which you had when you were young. I can even imagine how I shall dress you."

"Don't talk so much, Jotin, but try to sleep."

"I shall name you 'Lakshmi.'"

"But that is an old-fashioned name, Jotin!"

"Yes, but you are my old-fashioned Mashi. Come to my house again with those beautiful old-fashioned manners."

"I can't wish that I should come and burden your home with the misfortune of a girl-child!"

"Mashi, you think me weak, and are wanting to save me all trouble."

"My child, I am a woman, so I have my weakness. Therefore I have tried all my life to save you from all sorts of trouble—only to fail."

"Mashi, I have not had time in this life to apply the lessons I have learnt. But they will keep for my next birth. I shall show then what a man is able to do. I have learnt how false it is always to be looking after oneself."

"Whatever you may say, darling, you have never grasped anything for yourself, but given everything to others."

"Mashi, I can boast of one thing at any rate. I have never been a tyrant in my happiness, or tried to enforce my claims by violence. Because lies could not content me, I have had to wait long. Perhaps truth will be kind to me at last.—Who is that, Mashi, who is that?"

"Where? There's no one there, Jotin!"

"Mashi, just go and see in the other room. I thought I——"

"No, dear! I don't see anybody."

"But it seemed quite clear to me that——"

"No, Jotin, it's nothing. So keep quiet! The doctor is coming now."

When the doctor entered, he said:

"Look here, you mustn't stay near the patient so much, you excite him. You go to bed, and my assistant will remain with him."

"No, Mashi, I can't let you go."

"All right, Baba! I will sit quietly in that corner."

"No, no! you must sit by my side. I can't let go your hand, not till the very end. I have been made by your hand, and only from your hand shall God take me."

"All right," said the doctor, "you can remain there. But, Jotin Babu, you must not talk to her. It's time for you to take your medicine."

"Time for my medicine? Nonsense! The time for that is over. To give medicine now is merely to deceive; besides I am not afraid to die. Mashi, Death is busy with his physic; why do you add another nuisance in the shape of a doctor? Send him away, send him away! It is you alone I need now! No one else, none whatever! No more falsehood!"

"I protest, as a doctor, this excitement is doing you harm."

"Then go, doctor, don't excite me anymore!—Mashi, has he gone? . . . That's good! Now come and take my head in your lap."

"All right, dear! Now, Baba, try to sleep!"

"No, Mashi, don't ask me to sleep. If I sleep, I shall never wake. I still need to keep awake a little longer. Don't you hear a sound? Somebody is coming."

V

"Jotin dear, just open your eyes a little. She has come. Look once and see!"

"Who has come? A dream?"

"Not a dream, darling! Mani has come with her father."

"Who are you?"

"Can't you see? This is your Mani!"

"Mani? Has that door opened?"

"Yes, Baba, it is wide open."

"No, Mashi, not that shawl! not *that* shawl! That shawl is a fraud!"

"It is not a shawl, Jotin! It is our Mani, who has flung herself on your feet. Put your hand on her head and bless her. Don't cry like that, Mani! There will be time enough for that. Keep quiet now for a little."

POETRY

গীতাঞ্জলি
GITANJALI

A Collection of Prose Translations
made by the Author from
the Original Bengali

With an introduction by
W. B. YEATS

To
William Rothenstein

Introduction

A few days ago I said to a distinguished Bengali doctor of medicine, 'I know no German, yet if a translation of a German poet had moved me, I would go to the British Museum and find books in English that would tell me something of his life, and of the history of his thought. But though these prose translations from Rabindranath Tagore have stirred my blood as nothing has for years, I shall not know anything of his life, and of the movements of thoughts that have made them possible, if some Indian traveller will not tell me.' It seemed to him natural that I should be moved, for he said, 'I read Rabindranath every day, to read one line of his is to forget all the troubles of the world.' I said, 'An Englishman living in London in the reign of Richard the Second had he been shown translations from Petrarch or from Dante, would have found no books to answer his questions, but would have questioned some Florentine banker or Lambard merchant as I question you. For all I know, so abundant and simple is this poetry, the new Renaissance has been born in your country and I shall never know of it except by hearsay.' He answered, 'We have other poets, but none that are his equal; we call this the epoch of Rabindranath. No poet seems to me as famous in Europe as he is among us. He is as great in music as in poetry, and his songs are sung from the west of India into Burma wherever Bengali is spoken. He was already famous at nineteen when he wrote his first novel; and plays, written when he was but little older, are still played in Calcutta. I so much admire the completeness of his life; when he was very young he wrote much of natural objects, he would sit all day in his garden; from his twenty-fifth year or so to his thirty-fifth perhaps, when he had a great sorrow, he wrote the most beautiful love poetry in our language'; and then he said with deep emotion, 'words can never express what I owed at seventeen to his love poetry. After that his art grew deeper, it became religious and philosophical; all the aspirations of mankind are in his hymns. He is the first among our saints who has not refused to live, but has spoken out of Life itself, and that is why we give him our love.' I may have changed his well-chosen words in my memory but not his thought. 'A little while ago he was to read divine service in one of our churches—we of the Brahma Samaj use your word "church" in English—it was the largest in Calcutta and not only was it crowded, people even standing in the windows, but the streets were all but impassable because of the people.'

Other Indians came to see me and their reverence for this man sounded strange in our world, where we hide great and little things under the same veil of obvious comedy and half-serious depreciation. When we were making the cathedrals had we a like reverence for our great men? 'Every morning at three—I know, for I have seen it'—one said to me, 'he sits immovable in contemplation, and for two hours does not awake from his reverie upon the nature of God. His father, the Maha Rishi, would sometimes sit there all through the next day; once, upon a river, he fell into contemplation because of the beauty of the landscape, and the rowers waited for eight hours before they could continue their journey.' He then told me of Mr. Tagore's family and how for generations great men have come out of its cradles. 'Today,' he said, 'there are Gogonendranath and Abanindranath Tagore, who are artists; and Dwijendranath, Rabindranath's brother, who is a great philosopher. The squirrels come from the boughs and climb on to his knees and the birds alight upon his hands.' I notice in these men's thought a sense of visible beauty and meaning as though they held that doctrine of Nietzsche that we must not believe in the moral or intellectual beauty which does not sooner or later impress itself upon physical things. I said, 'In the East you know how to keep a family illustrious. The other day the curator of a museum pointed out to me a little dark-skinned man who was arranging their Chinese prints and said, "That is the hereditary connoisseur of the Mikado, he is the fourteenth of his family to hold the post." He answered, 'When Rabindranath was a boy he had all round him in his home literature and music.' I thought of the abundance, of the simplicity of the poems, and said, 'In your country is there much propagandist writing, much criticism? We have to do so much, especially in my own country, that our minds gradually cease to be creative, and yet we cannot help it. If our life was not a continual warfare, we would not have taste, we would not know what is good, we would not find hearers and readers. Four-fifths of our energy is spent in the quarrel with bad taste, whether in our own minds or in the minds of others.' 'I understand,' he replied, 'we too have our propagandist writing. In the villages they recite long mythological poems adapted from the Sanskrit in the Middle Ages, and they often insert passages telling the people that they must do their duties.'

II

I have carried the manuscript of these translations about with me for days, reading it in railway trains, or on the top of omnibuses and in restaurants, and I have often had to close it lest some stranger would see how much it moved me. These lyrics—which are in the original, my Indians tell me, full of subtlety of rhythm, of untrans-latable delicacies of colour, of metrical invention—display in their thought a world I have dreamed of all my life long. The work of a supreme culture, they yet appear as much the growth of the common soil as the grass and the rushes. A tradition, where poetry and religion are the same thing, has passed through the centuries, gathering from learned and unlearned metaphor and emotion, and carried back again to the multitude the thought of the scholar and of the noble. If the civilization of Bengal remains unbroken, if that common mind which—as one divines—runs through all, is not, as with us, broken into a dozen minds that know nothing of each other, something even of what is most subtle in these verses will have come, in a few generations, to the beggar on the roads. When there was but one mind in England, Chaucer wrote his *Troilus and Cressida,* and though he had written to be read, or to be read out—for our time was coming on apace—he was sung by minstrels for a while. Rabindranath Tagore, like Chaucer's forerunners, writes music for his words, and one understands at every moment that he is so abun-dant, so spontaneous, so daring in his passion, so full of surprise, because he is doing something which is never strange, unnatural,

251

or in need of defence. These verses will not lie in little well-printed books upon ladies' tables, who turn the pages with indolent hands that they may sigh over a life without meaning, which is yet all they can know of life, or be carried about by students at the university to be laid aside when the work of life begins, but, as the generations pass, travellers will hum them on the highway and men rowing upon rivers. Lovers, while they await one another, shall find, in murmuring them, this love of God a magic gulf wherein their own more bitter passion may bathe and renew its youth. At every moment the heart of this poet flows outward to these without derogation or condescension, for it has known that they will understand; and it has filled itself with the circumstance of their lives. The traveller in the red-brown clothes that he wears that dust may not show upon him, the girl searching in her bed for the petals fallen from the wreath of her royal lover, the servant or the bride awaiting the master's home-coming in the empty house, are images of the heart turning to God. Flowers and rivers, the blowing of conch shells, the heavy rain of the Indian July, or the parching heat, are images of the moods of that heart in union or in separation; and a man sitting in a boat upon a river playing upon a lute, like one of those figures full of mysterious meaning in a Chinese picture, is God Himself. A whole people, a whole civilization, immeasurably strange to us, seems to have been taken up into this imagination; and yet we are not moved because of its strangeness, but because we have met our own image, as though we had walked in Rossetti's willow wood, or heard, perhaps for the first time in literature, our voice as in a dream.

Since the Renaissance the writing of European saints—however familiar their metaphor and the general structure of their thought—has ceased to hold our attention. We know that we must at last forsake the world, and we are accustomed in moments of weariness or exaltation to consider a voluntary forsaking; but how can we, who have read so much poetry, seen so many paintings, listened to so much music, where the cry of the flesh and the cry of the soul seem one, forsake it harshly and rudely? What have we in common with St. Bernard covering his eyes that they may not dwell upon the beauty of the lakes of Switzerland, or with the violent rhetoric of the Book of Revelation? We would, if we might, find, as in this book, words full of courtesy. 'I have got my leave. Bid me farewell, my brothers! I bow to you all and take my departure. Here I give back the keys of my door—and I give up all claims to my house. I only ask for last kind words from you. We were neighbours for long, but I received more than I could give. Now the day has dawned and the lamp that lit my dark corner is out. A summons has come and I am ready for my journey.' And it is our own mood, when it is furthest from a Kempis or John of the Cross, that cries, 'And because I love this life, I know I shall love death as well.' Yet it is not only in our thoughts of the parting that this book fathoms all. We had not known that we loved God, hardly it may be that we believed in Him; yet looking backward upon our life we discover, in our exploration of the pathways of woods, in our delight in the lonely places of hills, in that mysterious claim that we have made, unavailingly, on the women that we have loved, the emotion that created this insidious sweetness. 'Entering my heart unbidden even as one of the common crowd, unknown to me, my king, thou didst press the signet of eternity upon many a fleeting moment.' This is no longer the sanctity of the cell and of the scourage; being but a lifting up, as it were, into a greater intensity of the mood of the painter, painting the dust and the sunlight, and we go for a like voice to St. Francis and to William Blake who have seemed so alien in our violent history.

III

We write long books where no page perhaps has any quality to make writing a pleasure, being confident in some general design, just as we fight and make money and fill our heads with politics—all dull things in the doing—while Mr. Tagore, like the Indian civilization itself, has been content to discover the soul and surrender himself to its spontaneity. He often seems to contrast his life with that of those who have lived more after our fashion, and have more seeming weight in the world, and always humbly as though he were only sure his way is best for him: 'Men going home glance at me and smile and fill me with shame. I sit like a beggar maid, drawing my skirt over my face, and when they ask me, what it is I want, I drop my eyes and answer them not.' At another time, remembering how his life had once a different shape, he will say, 'Many an hour have I spent in the strife of the good and the evil, but now it is the pleasure of my playmate of the empty days to draw my heart on to him; and I know not why is this sudden call to what useless inconsequence.' An innocence, a simplicity that one does not find elsewhere in literature makes the birds and the leaves seems as near to him as they are near to children, and the changes of the seasons great events as before our thoughts had arisen between them and us. At times I wonder if he has it from the literature of Bengal or from religion, and at other times, remembering the birds alighting on his brother's hands, I find pleasure in thinking it hereditary, a mystery that was growing through the centuries like the courtesy of a Tristan or a Pelanore. Indeed, when he is speaking of children, so much a part of himself this quality seems, one is not certain that he is not also speaking of the saints, 'they build their houses with sand and they play with empty shells. With withered leaves they weave their boats and smilingly float them on the vast deep. Children have their play on the seashore of worlds. They know not how to swim, they know not how to cast nets. Pearl fishers dive for pearls, merchants sail in their ships, while children gather pebbles and scatter them again. They seek not for hidden treasures, they know not how to cast nets.'

W. B. YEATS
September 1912

1

Thou hast made me endless, such is thy pleasure. This frail vessel thou emptiest again and again, and fillest it ever with fresh life.

This little flute of a reed thou hast carried over hills and dales, and hast breathed through it melodies eternally new.

At the immortal touch of thy hands my little heart loses its limits in joy and gives birth to utterance ineffable.

Thy infinite gifts come to me only on these very small hands of mine. Ages pass, and still thou pourest, and still there is room to fill.

2

When thou commandest me to sing it seems that my heart would break with pride; and I look to thy face, and tears come to my eyes.

All that is harsh and dissonant in my life melts into one sweet harmony—and my adoration spreads wings like a glad bird on its flight across the sea.

I know thou takes pleasure in my singing. I know that only as a singer I come before thy presence.

I touch by the edge of the far-spreading wing of my song thy feet which I could never aspire to reach.

Drunk with the joy of singing I forget myself and call thee friend who art my lord.

3

I know not how thou singest, my master! I ever listen in silent amazement.

The light of thy music illumines the world. The life breath of thy music runs from sky to sky. The holy stream of thy music breaks through all stony obstacles and rushes on.

My heart longs to join in thy song, but vainly struggles for a voice. I would speak, but speech breaks not into song, and I cry out baffled. Ah, thou hast made my heart captive in the endless meshes of thy music, my master!

4

Life of my life, I shall ever try to keep my body pure, knowing that thy living touch is upon all my limbs.

I shall ever try to keep all untruths out from my thoughts, knowing that thou art that truth which has kindled the light of reason in my mind.

I shall ever try to drive all evils away from my heart and keep my love in flower, knowing that thou hast thy seat in the inmost shrine of my heart.

And it shall be my endeavour to reveal thee in my actions, knowing it is thy power gives me strength to act.

5

I ask for a moment's indulgence to sit by thy side. The works that I have in hand I will finish afterwards.

Away from the sight of thy face my heart knows no rest nor respite, and my work becomes an endless toil in a shoreless sea of toil.

Today the summer has come at my window with its sighs and murmurs; and the bees are plying their minstrelsy at the court of the flowering grove.

Now it is time to sit quiet, face to face with thee, and to sing dedication of life in this silent and overflowing leisure.

6

Pluck this little flower and take it, delay not! I fear lest it droop and drop into the dust.

It may not find a place in thy garland, but honour it with a touch of pain from thy hand and pluck it. I fear lest the day end before I am aware, and the time of offering go by.

Though its colour be not deep and its smell be faint, use this flower in thy service and pluck it while there is time.

7

My song has put off her adornments. She has no pride of dress and decoration. Ornaments would mar our union; they would come between thee and me; their jingling would drown thy whispers.

My poet's vanity dies in shame before thy sight. O master poet, I have sat down at thy feet. Only let me make my life simple and straight, like a flute of reed for thee to fill with music.

8

The child who is decked with prince's robes and who has jewelled chains round his neck loses all pleasure in his play; his dress hampers him at every step.

In fear that it may be frayed, or stained with dust he keeps himself from the world, and is afraid even to move.

Mother, it is no gain, thy bondage of finery, if it keep one shut off from the healthful dust of the earth, if it rob one of the right of entrance to the great fair of common human life.

9

O fool, to try to carry thyself upon thy own shoulders!
O beggar, to come to beg at thy own door!

Leave all thy burdens on his hands who can bear all, and never look behind in regret.

Thy desire at once puts out the light from the lamp it touches with its breath. It is unholy—take not thy gifts through its unclean hands. Accept only what is offered by sacred love.

10

Here is thy footstool and there rest thy feet where live the poorest, and lowliest, and lost.

When I try to bow to thee, my obeisance cannot reach down to the depth where thy feet rest among the poorest, and lowliest, and lost.

Pride can never approach to where thou walkest in the clothes of the humble among the poorest, and lowliest, and lost.

My heart can never find its way to where thou keepest company with the companionless among the poorest, the lowliest, and the lost.

11

Leave this chanting and singing and telling of beads! Whom dost thou worship in this lonely dark corner of a temple with doors all shut? Open thine eyes and see thy God is not before thee!

He is there where the tiller is tilling the hard ground and where the pathmaker is breaking stones. He is with them in sun and in shower, and his garment is covered with dust. Put off thy holy mantle and even like him come down on the dusty soil!

Deliverance? Where is this deliverance to be found?

Our master himself has joyfully taken upon him the bonds of creation; he is bound with us all for ever.

Come out of thy meditations and leave aside thy flowers and incense! What harm is there if thy clothes become tattered and stained? Meet him and stand by him in toil and in sweat of thy brow.

12

The time that my journey takes is long and the way of it long.

I came out on the chariot of the first gleam of light, and pursued my voyage through the wildernesses of worlds leaving my track on many a star and planet.

It is the most distant course that comes nearest to thyself, and that training is the most intricate which leads to the utter simplicity of a tune.

The traveller has to knock at every alien door to come to his own, and one has to wander through all the outer worlds to reach the innermost shrine at the end.

My eyes strayed far and wide before I shut them and said, 'Here are thou!'

The question and the cry, 'Oh, where?' melt into tears of a thousand streams and deluge the world with the flood of the assurance, 'I am!'

13

The song that I came to sing remains unsung to this day.

I have spent my days in stringing and in unstringing my instrument.

The time has not come true, the words have not been rightly set; only there is the agony of wishing in my heart.

The blossom has not opened; only the wind is sighing by.

I have not seen his face, nor have I listened to his voice; only I have heard his gentle footsteps from the road before my house.

The livelong day has passed in spreading his seat on the floor; but the lamp has not been lit and I cannot ask him into my house.

I live in the hope of meeting with him; but this meeting is not yet.

14

My desires are many and my cry is pitiful, but ever didst thou save me by hard refusals; and this strong mercy has been wrought into my life through and through.

Day by day thou art making me worthy of the simple, great gifts that thou gavest to me unasked—this sky and the light, this body and the life and the mind—saving me from perils of overmuch desire.

There are times when I languidly linger and times when I awaken and hurry in search of my goal; but cruelly thou hidest thyself from before me.

Day by day thou art making me worthy of thy full acceptance by refusing me ever and anon, saving me from perils of weak, uncertain desire.

15

I am here to sing thee songs. In this hall of thine I have a corner seat.

In thy world I have no work to do; my useless life can only break out in tunes without a purpose.

When the hour strikes for thy silent worship at the dark temple of midnight, command me, my master, to stand before thee to sing.

When in the morning air the golden harp is tuned, honour me, commanding my presence.

16

I have had my invitation to this world's festival, and thus my life has been blessed. My eyes have seen and my ears have heard.

It was my part at this feast to play upon my instrument, and I have done all I could.

Now, I ask, has the time come at last when I may go in and see thy face and offer thee my silent salutation?

17

I am only waiting for love to give myself up at last into his hands. That is why it is so late and why I have been guilty of such omissions.

They come with their laws and their codes to bind me fast; but I evade them ever, for I am only waiting for love to give myself up at last into his hands.

People blame me and call me heedless; I doubt not they are right in their blame.

The market day is over and work is all done for the busy. Those who came to call me in vain have gone back in anger. I am only waiting for love to give myself up at last into his hands.

18

Clouds heap upon clouds and it darkens. Ah, love, why dost thou let me wait outside at the door all alone?

In the busy moments of the noontide work I am with the crowd, but on this dark lonely day it is only for thee that I hope.

If thou showest me not thy face, if thou leavest me wholly aside, I know not how I am to pass these long, rainy hours.

I keep gazing on the faraway gloom of the sky, and my heart wanders wailing with the restless wind.

19

If thou speakest not I will fill my heart with thy silence and endure it. I will keep still and wait like the night with starry vigil and its head bent low with patience.

The morning will surely come, the darkness will vanish, and thy voice pour down in golden streams breaking through the sky.

Then thy words will take wing in songs from every one of my birds' nests, and thy melodies will break forth in flowers in all my forest groves.

20

On the day when the lotus bloomed, alas, my mind was straying, and I knew it not. My basket was empty and the flower remained unheeded.

Only now and again a sadness fell upon me, and I started up from my dream and felt a sweet trace of a strange fragrance in the south wind.

That vague sweetness made my heart ache with longing and it seemed to me that it was the eager breath of the summer seeking for its completion.

I knew not then that it was no near, that it was mine, and that this perfect sweetness had blossomed in the depth of my own heart.

21

I must launch out my boat. The languid hours pass by on the shore—
Alas for me!

The spring has done its flowering and taken leave.

And now with the burden of faded futile flowers I wait and linger.

The waves have become clamorous, and upon the bank in the shady lane the yellow leaves flutter and fall.

What emptiness do you gaze upon! Do you not feel a thrill passing through the air with the notes of the faraway song floating from the other shore?

22

In the deep shadows of the rainy July, with secret steps, thou walkest, silent as night, eluding all watchers.

Today the morning has closed its eyes, heedless of the insistent calls of the loud east wind, and a thick veil has been drawn over the ever-wakeful blue sky.

The woodlands have hushed their songs, and doors are all shut at every house. Thou art the solitary wayfarer in this deserted street. Oh my only friend, my best beloved, the gates are open in my house—do not pass by like a dream.

23

Art thou abroad on this stormy night on thy journey of love, my friend? The sky groans like one in despair.

I have no sleep tonight. Ever and again I open my door and look out on the darkness, my friend!

I can see nothing before me. I wonder where lies thy path!

By what dim shore of the ink-black river, by what far edge of the frowning forest, through what mazy depth of gloom art thou threading thy course to come to me, my friend?

24

If the day is done, if birds sing no more, if the wind has flagged tired, then draw the veil of darkness thick upon me, even as thou hast wrapt the earth with the coverlet of sleep and tenderly closed the petals of the drooping lotus at dusk.

From the traveller, whose sack of provisions is empty before the voyage is ended, whose garment is torn and dust laden, whose strength is exhausted, remove shame and poverty, and renew his life like a flower under the cover of thy kindly night.

25

In the night of weariness let me give myself up to sleep without struggle, resting my trust upon thee.

Let me not force my flagging spirit into a poor preparation for thy worship.

It is thou who drawest the veil of night upon the tired eyes of the day to renew its sight in a fresher gladness of awakening.

26

He came and sat by my side but I woke not. What a cursed sleep it was, O miserable me!

He came when the night was still; he had his harp in his hands, and my dreams became resonant with its melodies.

Alas, why are my nights all thus lost? Ah, why do I ever miss his sight whose breath touches my sleep?

27

Light, oh where is the light? Kindle it with the burning fire of desire!

There is the lamp but never a flicker of a flame—is such thy fate, my heart? Ah, death were better by far for thee!

Misery knocks at thy door, and her message is that thy lord is wakeful, and he calls thee to the love-tryst through the darkness of night.

The sky is overcast with clouds and the rain is ceaseless. I know not what this is that stirs in me—I know not its meaning.

A moment's flash of lightning drags down a deeper gloom on my sight, and my heart gropes for the path to where the music of the night calls me.

Light, oh where is the light! Kindle it with the burning fire of desire! It thunders and the wind rushes screaming through the void. The night is black as a black stone. Let not the hours pass by in the dark. Kindle the lamp of love with thy life.

28

Obstinate are the trammels, but my heart aches when I try to break them.

Freedom is all I want, but to hope for it I feel ashamed.

I am certain that priceless wealth is in thee, and that thou art my best friend, but I have not the heart to sweep away the tinsel that fills my room.

The shroud that covers me is a shroud of dust and death; I hate it, yet hug it in love.

My debts are large, my failures great, my shame secret and heavy; yet when I come to ask for my good, I quake in fear lest my prayer be granted.

29

He whom I enclose with my name is weeping in this dungeon. I am ever busy building this wall all around; and as this wall goes up into the sky day by day I lose sight of my true being in its dark shadow.

I take pride in this great wall, am I plaster it with dust and sand lest a least hole should be left in this name; and for all the care I take I lose sight of my true being.

30

I came out alone on my way to my tryst. But who is this that follows me in the silent dark?

I move aside to avoid his presence but I escape him not.

He makes the dust rise from the earth with his swagger; he adds his loud voice to every word that I utter.

He is my own little self, my lord, he knows no shame; but I am ashamed to come to thy door in his company.

31

'Prisoner, tell me, who was it that bound you?'

'It was my master,' said the prisoner.

'I thought I could outdo everybody in the world in wealth and power, and I amassed in my own treasurehouse the money due to my king. When sleep overcame me I lay upon the bed that was for my lord, and on waking up I found I was a prisoner in my own treasurehouse.'

'Prisoner, tell me, who was it that wrought this unbreakable chain?'

'It was I,' said the prisoner, 'who forged this chain very carefully. I thought my invincible power would hold the world captive leaving me in a freedom undisturbed. Thus night and day I worked at the chain with huge fires and cruel hard strokes. When at last the work was done and the links were complete and unbreakable, I found that it held me in its grip.'

 272

32

By all means they try to hold me secure who love me in this world. But it is otherwise with thy love which is greater than theirs, and thou keepest me free.

Lest I forget them they never venture to leave me alone. But day passes by after day and thou art not seen.

If I call not thee in my prayers, if I keep not thee in my heart, thy love for me still waits for my love.

33

When it was day they came into my house and said, 'We shall only take the smallest room here.'

They said, 'We shall help you in the worship of your God and humbly accept only our own share of his grace'; and then they took their seat in a corner and they sat quiet and meek.

But in the darkness of night I find they break into my sacred shrine, strong and turbulent, and snatch with unholy greed the offerings from God's altar.

34

Let only that little be left of me whereby I may name thee my all.

Let only that little be left of my will whereby I may feel thee on every side, and come to thee in everything, and offer to thee my love every moment. Let only that little be left of me whereby I may never hide thee.

Let only that little of my fetters be left whereby I am bound with thy will, and thy purpose is carried out in my life—and that is the fetter of thy love.

35

Where the mind is without fear and the head is held high;

Where knowledge is free;

Where the world has not been broken up into fragments by narrow domestic walls;

Where words come out from the depth of truth;

Where tireless striving stretches its arms towards perfection;

Where the clear stream of reason has not lost its way into the dreary desert sand of dead habit;

Where the mind is led forward by thee into ever-widening thought and action—

Into that heaven of freedom, my Father, let my country awake.

36

This is my prayer to thee, my lord—strike, strike at the root of penury in my heart.

Give me the strength lightly to bear my joys and sorrows.

Give me the strength to make my love fruitful in service.

Give me the strength never to disown the poor or bend my knees before insolent might.

Give me the strength to raise my mind high above daily trifles.

And give me the strength to surrender my strength to thy will with love.

37

I thought that my voyage had come to its end at the last limit of my power—that the path before me was closed, that provisions were exhausted and the time come to take shelter in a silent obscurity.

But I find that thy will knows no end in me. And when old words die out on the tongue, new melodies break forth from the heart; and where the old tracks are lost, new country is revealed with its wonders.

38

That I want thee, only thee—let my heart repeat without end. All desires that distract me, day and night, are false and empty to the core.

As the night keeps hidden in its gloom the petition for light, even thus in the depth of my unconsciousness rings the cry—'I want thee, only thee.'

As the storm still seeks its end in peace when it strikes against peace with all its might, even thus my rebellion strikes against thy love and still its cry is—'I want thee, only thee.'

39

When the heart is hard and parched up, come upon me with a shower of mercy.

When grace is lost from life, come with a burst of song.

When tumultuous work raises its din on all sides shutting me out from beyond, come to me, my lord of silence, with thy peace and rest.

When my beggarly heart sits crouched, shut up in a corner, break open the door, my king, and come with the ceremony of a king.

When desire blinds the mind with delusion and dust, O thou holy one, thou wakeful, come with thy light and thy thunder.

40

The rain has held back for days and days, my God, in my arid heart. The horizon is fiercely naked—not the thinnest cover of a soft cloud, not the vaguest hint of a distant cool shower.

Send thy angry storm, dark with death, if it is thy wish, and with lashes of lightning startle the sky from end to end.

But call back, my lord, call back this pervading silent heat, still and keen and cruel, burning the heart with dire despair.

Let the cloud of grace bend low from above like the tearful look of the mother on the day of the father's wrath.

41

Where dost thou stand behind them all, my lover, hiding thyself in the shadows? They push thee and pass thee by on the dusty road, taking thee for naught. I wait here weary hours spreading my offerings for thee, while passers-by come and take my flowers, one by one, and my basket is nearly empty.

The morning time is past, and the noon. In the shade of evening my eyes are drowsy with sleep. Men going home glance at me and smile and fill me with shame. I sit like a beggar maid, drawing my skirt over my face, and when they ask me, what it is I want, I drop my eyes and answer them not.

Oh, how, indeed, could I tell them that for thee I wait, and that thou hast promised to come. How could I utter for shame that I keep for my dowry this poverty. Ah, I hug this pride in the secret of my heart.

I sit on the grass and gaze upon the sky and dream of the sudden splendour of thy coming—all the lights ablaze, golden pennons flying over thy car, and they at the roadside standing agape, when they see thee come down from thy seat to raise me from the dust, and set at thy side this ragged beggar girl a tremble with shame and pride, like a creeper in a summer breeze.

But time glides on and still no sound of the wheels of thy chariot. Many a procession passes by with noise and shouts and glamour of glory. Is it only thou who wouldst stand in the shadow silent and behind them all? And only I who would wait and weep and wear out my heart in vain longing?

42

Early in the day it was whispered that we should sail in a boat, only thou and I, and never a soul in the world would know of this, our pilgrimage to no country and to no end.

In that shoreless ocean, at thy silently listening smile my songs would swell in melodies, free as waves, free from all bondage of words.

Is the time not come yet? Are there works still to do? Lo, the evening has come down upon the shore and in the fading light the seabirds come flying to their nests.

Who knows when the chains will be off, and the boat, like the last glimmer of sunset, vanish into the night?

43

The day was when I did not keep myself in readiness for thee; and entering my heart unbidden even as one of the common crowd, unknown to me, my king, thou didst press the signet of eternity upon many a fleeting moment of my life.

And today when by chance I light upon them and see thy signature, I find they have lain scattered in the dust mixed with the memory of joys and sorrows of my trivial days forgotten.

Thou didst not turn in contempt from my childish play among dust, and the steps that I heard in my playroom are the same that are echoing from star to star.

44

This is my delight, thus to wait and watch at the wayside where shadow chases light and the rain comes in the wake of the summer.

Messengers, with tidings from unknown skies, greet me and speed along the road. My heart is glad within, and the breath of the passing breeze is sweet.

From dawn till dusk I sit here before my door, and I know that of a sudden the happy moment will arrive when I shall see.

In the meanwhile I smile and I sing all alone. In the meanwhile the air is filling with the perfume of promise.

45

Have you not heard his silent steps? He comes, comes, ever comes.

Every moment and every age, every day and every night he comes, comes, ever comes.

Many a song have I sung in many a mood of mind, but all their notes have always proclaimed, 'He comes, comes, ever comes.'

In the fragrant days of sunny April through the forest path he comes, comes, ever comes.

In the rainy gloom of July nights on the thundering chariot of clouds he comes, comes, ever comes.

In sorrow after sorrow it is his steps that press upon my heart, and it is the golden touch of his feet that makes my joy to shine.

46

I know not from what distant time thou art ever coming nearer to meet me. Thy sun and stars can never keep thee hidden from me for aye.

In many a morning and eve thy footsteps have been heard and thy messenger has come within my heart and called me in secret.

I know not why today my life is all astir, and a feeling of tremulous joy is passing through my heart.

It is as if the time were come to wind up my work, and I feel in the air a faint smell of thy sweet presence.

47

The night is nearly spent waiting for him in vain. I fear lest in the morning he suddenly come to my door when I have fallen asleep wearied out. Oh friends, leave the way open to him—forbid him not.

If the sound of his steps does not wake me, do not try to rouse me, I pray. I wish not to be called from my sleep by the clamorous choir of birds, by the riot of wind at the festival of morning light. Let me sleep undisturbed even if my lord comes of a sudden to my door.

Ah, my sleep, precious sleep, which only waits for his touch to vanish. Ah, my closed eyes that would open their lids only to the light of his smile when he stands before me like a dream emerging from darkness of sleep.

Let him appear before my sight as the first of all lights and all forms. The first thrill of joy to my awakened soul let it come from his glance. And let my return to myself be immediate return to him.

48

The morning sea of silence broke into ripples of bird songs; and the flowers were all merry by the roadside; and the wealth of gold was scattered through the rift of the clouds while we busily went on our way and paid no heed.

We sang no glad songs nor played; we went not to the village for barter; we spoke not a word nor smiled; we lingered not on the way. We quickened our pace more and more as the time sped by.

The sun rose to the mid sky and doves cooed in the shade. Withered leaves danced and whirled in the hot air of noon. The shepherd boy drowsed and dreamed in the shadow of the banyan tree, and I laid myself down by the water and stretched my tired limbs on the grass.

My companions laughed at me in scorn; they held their heads high and hurried on; they never looked back nor rested; they vanished in the distant blue haze. They crossed many meadows and hills, and passed through strange, faraway countries. All honour to you, heroic host of the interminable path! Mockery and reproach pricked me to rise, but found no response in me. I gave myself up for lost in the depth of a glad humiliation—in the shadow of a dim delight.

The repose of the sun-embroidered green gloom slowly spread over my heart. I forgot for what I had travelled, and I surrendered my mind without struggle to the maze of shadows and songs.

At last, when I woke from my slumber and opened my eyes, I saw thee standing by me, flooding my sleep with thy smile. How I had feared that the path was long and wearisome, and the struggle to reach thee was hard!

49

You came down from your throne and stood at my cottage door.

I was singing all alone in a corner, and the melody caught your ear. You came down and stood at my cottage door.

Masters are many in your hall, and songs are sung there at all hours. But the simple carol of this novice struck at your love. One plaintive little strain mingled with the great music of the world, and with a flower for a prize you came down and stopped at my cottage door.

50

I had gone a-begging from door to door in the village path, when thy golden chariot appeared in the distance like a gorgeous dream and I wondered who was this King of all kings!

My hopes rose high and methought my evil days were at an end, and I stood waiting for alms to be given unasked and for wealth scattered on all sides in the dust.

The chariot stopped where I stood. Thy glance fell on me and thou camest down with a smile. I felt that the luck of my life had come at last. Then of a sudden thou didst hold out thy right hand and say, 'What hast thou to give to me?'

Ah, what a kingly jest was it to open thy palm to a beggar to beg! I was confused and stood undecided, and then from my wallet I slowly took out the least little grain of corn and gave it to thee.

But how great my surprise when at the day's end I emptied my bag on the floor to find a least little gram of gold among the poor heap. I bitterly wept and wished that I had the heart to give thee my all.

51

The night darkened. Our day's works had been done. We thought that the last guest had arrived for the night and the doors in the village were all shut. Only some said the king was to come. We laughed and said, 'No, it cannot be!'

It seemed there were knocks at the door and we said it was nothing but the wind. We put out the lamps and lay down to sleep. Only some said, 'It is the messenger!' We laughed and said, 'No, it must be the wind!'

There came a sound in the dead of the night. We sleepily thought it was the distant thunder. The earth shook, the walls rocked, and it troubled us in our sleep. Only some said it was the sound of wheels. We said in a drowsy murmur, 'No, it must be the rumbling of clouds!'

The night was still dark when the drum sounded.

The voice came, 'Wake up! Delay not!' We pressed our hands on our hearts and shuddered with fear. Some said, 'Lo, there is the king's flag!' We stood up on our feet and cried, 'There is no time for delay!'

The king has come—but where are lights, where are wreaths? Where is the throne to seat him? Oh, shame! Oh utter shame! Where is the hall, the decorations? Someone has said, 'Vain is this cry! Greet him with empty hands, lead him into thy rooms all bare!'

Open the doors, let the conch-shells be sounded! In the depth of the night has come the king of our dark, dreary house. The thunder roars in the sky. The darkness shudders with lightning. Bring out thy tattered piece of mat and spread it in the courtyard. With the storm has come of a sudden our king of the fearful night.

52

I thought I should ask of thee—but I dared not—the rose wreath thou hadst on thy neck. Thus I waited for the morning, when thou didst depart, to find a few fragments on the bed. And like a beggar I searched in the dawn only for a stray petal or two.

Ah me, what is it I find? What token left of thy love?

It is no flower, no spices, no vase of perfumed water. It is thy mighty sword, flashing as a flame, heavy as a bolt of thunder. The young light of morning comes through the window and spread itself upon thy bed. The morning bird twitters and asks, 'Woman, what hast thou got?' No, it is no flower, nor spices, nor vase of perfumed water—it is thy dreadful sword.

I sit and muse in wonder, what gift is this of thine.

I can find no place where to hide it. I am ashamed to wear it, frail as I am, and it hurts me when I press it to my bosom. Yet shall I bear in my heart this honour of the burden of pain, this gift of thine.

From now there shall be no fear left for me in this world, and thou shalt be victorious in all my strife. Thou hast left death for my companion and I shall crown him with my life. Thy sword is with me to cut asunder my bonds, and there shall be no fear left for me in the world.

From now I leave off all petty decorations. Lord of my heart, no more shall there be for me waiting and weeping in corners, no more coyness and sweetness of demeanour. Thou hast given me thy sword for adornment. No more doll's decorations for me!

53

Beautiful is thy wristlet, decked with stars and cunningly wrought in myriad-coloured jewels. But more beautiful to me thy sword with its curve of lightning like the outspread wings of the divine bird of Vishnu, perfectly poised in the angry red light of the sunset.

It quivers like the one last response of life in ecstasy of pain at the final stroke of death; it shines like the pure flame of being burning up earthly sense with one fierce flash.

Beautiful is thy wristlet, decked with starry gems; but thy sword, O lord of thunder, is wrought with uttermost beauty, terrible to behold or to think of.

54

I asked nothing from thee; I uttered not my name to thine ear. When thou took'st thy leave I stood silent. I was alone by the well where the shadow of the tree fell aslant, and the women had gone home with their brown earthen pitchers full to the brim. They called me and shouted, 'Come with us, the morning is wearing on to noon.' But I languidly lingered awhile lost in the midst of vague musings.

I heard not thy steps as thou camest. Thine eyes were sad when they fell on me; thy voice was tired as thou spokest low—'Ah, I am a thirsty traveller.' I started up from my day-dreams and poured water from my jar on thy joined palms. The leaves rustled overhead; the cuckoo sang from the unseen dark, and perfume of *babla* flowers came from the bend of the road.

I stood speechless with shame when my name thou didst ask. Indeed, what had I done for thee to keep me in remembrance? But the memory that I could give water to thee to allay thy thirst will cling to my heart and enfold it in sweetness. The morning hour is late, the bird sings in weary notes, *neem* leaves rustle overhead and I sit and think and think.

55

Languor is upon your heart and the slumber is still on your eyes.

Has not the word come to you that the flower is reigning in splendour among thorns? Wake, oh awaken! Let not the time pass in vain!

At the end of the stony path, in the country of virgin solitude, my friend is sitting all alone. Deceive him not. Wake, oh awaken!

What if the sky pants and trembles with the heat of the midday sun—what if the burning sand spreads its mantle of thirst—

Is there no joy in the deep of your heart? At every footfall of yours, will not the harp of the road break out in sweet music of pain?

56

Thus it is that thy joy in me is so full. Thus it is that thou hast come down to me. O thou lord of all heavens, where would be thy love if I were not?

Thou hast taken me as thy partner of all this wealth.

In my heart is the endless play of thy delight. In my life thy will is ever taking shape.

And for this, thou who art the King of kings hast decked thyself in beauty to captivate my heart. And for this thy love loses itself in the love of thy lover, and there art thou seen in the perfect union of two.

57

Light, my light, the world-filling light, the eye-kissing light, heart-sweetening light!

Ah, the light dances, my darling, at the centre of my life; the light strikes, my darling, the chords of my love; the sky opens, the wind runs wild, laughter passes over the earth.

The butterflies spread their sails on the sea of light.

Lilies and jasmines surge up on the crest of the waves of light.

The light is shattered into gold on every cloud, my darling, and it scatters gems in profusion.

Mirth spreads from leaf to leaf, my darling, and gladness without measure. The heaven's river has drowned its banks and the flood of joy is abroad.

58

Let all the strains of joy mingle in my last song—the joy that makes the earth flow over in the riotous excess of the grass, the joy that sets the twin brothers, life and death, dancing over the wide world, the joy that sweeps in with the tempest, shaking and waking all life with laughter, the joy that sits still with its tears on the open red lotus of pain, and the joy that throws everything it has upon the dust, and knows not a word.

59

Yes, I know, this is nothing but thy love, O beloved of my heart—this golden light that dances upon the leaves, these idle clouds sailing across the sky, this passing breeze leaving its coolness upon my forehead.

The morning light has flooded my eyes—this is thy message to my heart. Thy face is bent from above, thy eyes look down on my eyes, and my heart has touched thy feet.

60

On the seashore of endless worlds children meet. The infinite sky is motionless overhead and the restless water is boisterous. On the seashore of endless worlds the children meet with shouts and dances.

They build their houses with sand and they play with empty shells. With withered leaves they weave their boats and smilingly float them on the vast deep. Children have their play on the seashore of worlds.

They know not how to swim, they know not how to cast nets. Pearl fishers dive for pearls, merchants sail in their ships, while children gather pebbles and scatter them again. They seek not for hidden treasures, they know not how to cast nets.

The sea surges up with laughter and pale gleams the smile of the sea beach. Death-dealing waves sing meaningless ballads to the children, even like a mother while rocking her baby's cradle. The sea plays with children, and pale gleams the smile of the sea beach.

On the seashore of endless worlds children meet.

Tempest roams in the pathless sky, ships get wrecked in the trackless water, death is abroad and children play. On the seashore of endless worlds is the great meeting of children.

61

The sleep that flits on baby's eyes—does anybody know from where it comes? Yes, there is a rumour that it has its dwelling where, in the fairy village among shadows of the forest dimly lit with glow-worms, there hang two timid buds of enchantment. From there it comes to kiss baby's eyes.

The smile that flickers on baby's lips when he sleeps—does anybody know where it was born? Yes, there is a rumour that a young pale beam of a crescent moon touched the edge of a vanishing autumn cloud, and there the smile was first born in the dream of a dew-washed morning—the smile that flickers on baby's lips when he sleeps.

The sweet, soft freshness that blooms on baby's limbs—does anybody know where it was hidden so long? Yes, when the mother was a young girl it lay pervading her heart in tender and silent mystery of love—the sweet, soft freshness that has bloomed on baby's limbs.

62

When I bring to you coloured toys, my child, I understand why there is such a play of colours on clouds, on water, and why flowers are painted in tints—when I give coloured toys to you, my child.

When I sing to make you dance I truly know why there is music in leaves, and why waves send their chorus of voices to the heart of the listening earth—when I sing to make you dance.

When I bring sweet things to your greedy hands I know why there is honey in the cup of the flower and why fruits are secretly filled with sweet juice—when I bring sweet things to your greedy hands.

When I kiss your face to make you smile, my darling, I surely understand what pleasure streams from the sky in morning light, and what delight that is which the summer breeze brings to my body—when I kiss you to make you smile.

63

Thou hast made me known to friend whom I knew not. Thou hast given me seats in homes not my own. Thou hast brought the distant near and made a brother of the stranger.

I am uneasy at heart when I have to leave my accustomed shelter; I forget that there abides the old in the new, and that there also thou abidest.

Through birth and death, in this world or in others, wherever thou leadest me it is thou, the same, the one companion of my endless life who ever linkest my heart with bonds of joy to the unfamiliar.

When one knows thee, then alien there is none, then no door is shut. Oh, grant me my prayer that I may never lose the bliss of the touch of the one in the play of the many.

64

On the slope of the desolate river among tall grasses I asked her, 'Maiden, where do you go shading your lamp with your mantle? My house is all dark and lonesome—lend me your light!' She raised her dark eyes for a moment and looked at my face through the dusk. 'I have come to the river,' she said, 'to float my lamp on the stream when the daylight wanes in the west.' I stood alone among tall grasses and watched the timid flame of her lamp uselessly drifting in the tide.

In the silence of gathering night I asked her, 'Maiden, your lights are all lit—then where do you go with your lamp? My house is all dark and lonesome—lend me light.' She raised her dark eyes on my face and stood for a moment doubtful. 'I have come,' she said at last, 'to dedicate my lamp to the sky.' I stood and watched her light uselessly burning in the void.

In the moonless gloom of midnight I asked her, 'Maiden, what is your quest, holding the lamp near your heart? My house is all dark and lonesome—lend me your light.' She stopped for a minute and thought and gazed at my face in the dark. 'I have brought my light,' she said, 'to join the carnival of lamps.' I stood and watched her little lamp uselessly lost among lights.

65

What divine drink wouldst thou have, my God, from this overflowing cup of life?

My poet, is it thy delight to see thy creation through my eyes and to stand at the portals of my ears silently to listen to thine own eternal harmony?

Thy world is weaving words in my mind and thy joy is adding music to them. Thou givest thyself to me in love and then feelest thine own entire sweetness in me.

66

She who ever had remained in the depth of my being, in the twilight of gleams and of glimpses; she who never opened her veils in the morning light, will be my last gift to thee, my God, folded in my final song.

Words have wooed yet failed to win her; persuasion has stretched to her its eager arms in vain.

I have roamed from country to country keeping her in the core of my heart, and around her have risen and fallen the growth and decay of my life.

Over my thoughts and actions, my slumbers and dreams, she reigned yet dwelled alone and apart.

Many a man knocked at my door and asked for her and turned away in despair.

There was none in the world who ever saw her face to face, and she remained in her loneliness waiting for thy recognition.

67

Thou art the sky and thou art the nest as well.

O thou beautiful, there in the nest it is thy love that encloses the soul with colours and sounds and odours.

There comes the morning with the golden basket in her right hand bearing the wreath of beauty, silently to crown the earth.

And there comes the evening over the lonely meadows deserted by herds, through trackless paths, carrying cool draughts of peace in her golden pitcher from the western ocean of rest.

But there, where spreads the infinite sky for the soul to take her flight in, reigns the stainless white radiance. There is no day nor night, nor form nor colour, and never, never a word.

68

Thy sunbeam comes upon this earth of mine with arms outstretched and stands at my door the livelong day to carry back to thy feet clouds made of my tears and sighs and songs.

With fond delight thou wrappest about thy starry breast that mantle of misty cloud, turning it into numberless shapes and folds and colouring it with hues everchanging.

It is so light and so fleeting, tender and tearful and dark, that is why thou lovest it, O thou spotless and serene. And that is why it may cover thy awful white light with its pathetic shadows.

69

The same stream of life that runs through my veins night and day runs through the world and dances in rhythmic measures.

It is the same life that shoots in joy through the dust of the earth in numberless blades of grass and breaks into tumultuous waves of leaves and flowers.

It is the same life that is rocked in the ocean-cradle of birth and of death, in ebb and in flow.

I feel my limbs are made glorious by the touch of this world of life. And my pride is from the life-throb of ages dancing in my blood this moment.

70

Is it beyond thee to be glad with the gladness of this rhythm? To be tossed and lost and broken in the whirl of this fearful joy?

All things rush on, they stop not, they look not behind, no power can hold them back, they rush on.

Keeping steps with that restless, rapid music, seasons come dancing and pass away—colours, tunes, and perfumes pour in endless cascades in the abounding joy that scatters and gives up and dies every moment.

71

That I should make much of myself and turn it on all sides, thus casting coloured shadows on thy radiance—such is thy *maya*.

Thou settest a barrier in thine own being and then callest thy severed self in myriad notes. This thy self-separation has taken body in me.

The poignant song is echoed through all the sky in many-coloured tears and smiles, alarms and hopes; waves rise up and sink again, dreams break and form. In me is thy own defeat of self.

This screen that thou hast raised is painted with innumerable figures with the brush of the night and the day. Behind it thy seat is woven in wondrous mysteries of curves, casting away all barren lines of straightness.

The great pageant of thee and me has overspread the sky. With the tune of thee and me all the air is vibrant, and all ages pass with the hiding and seeking of thee and me.

72

He it is, the innermost one, who awakens my being with his deep hidden touches.

He it is who puts his enchantment upon these eyes and joyfully plays on the chords of my heart in varied cadence of pleasure and pain.

He it is who weaves the web of this *maya* in evanescent hues of gold and silver, blue and green, and lets peep out through the folds his feet, at whose touch I forget myself.

Days come and ages pass, and it is ever he who moves my heart in many a name, in many a guise, in many a rapture of joy and of sorrow.

73

Deliverance is not for me in renunciation. I feel the embrace of freedom in a thousand bonds of delight.

Thou ever pourest for me the fresh draught of thy wine of various colours and fragrance, filling this earthen vessel to the brim.

My world will light its hundred different lamps with thy flame and place them before the altar of thy temple.

No, I will never shut the doors of my senses. The delights of sight and hearing and touch will bear thy delight.

Yes, all my illusions will burn into illumination of joy, and all my desires ripen into fruits of love.

74

The day is no more, the shadow is upon the earth. It is time that I go to the stream to fill my pitcher.

The evening air is eager with the sad music of the water. Ah, it calls me out into the dusk. In the lonely lane there is no passer-by, the wind is up, the ripples are rampant in the river.

I know not if I shall come back home. I know not whom I shall chance to meet. There at the fording in the little boat the unknown man plays upon his lute.

75

Thy gifts to us mortals fulfil all our needs and yet run back to thee undiminished.

The river has its everyday work to do and hastens through fields and hamlets; yet its incessant stream winds towards the washing of thy feet.

The flower sweetens the air with its perfume; yet its last service is to offer itself to thee.

Thy worship does not impoverish the world. From the words of the poet men take what meanings please them; yet their last meaning points to thee.

76

Day after day, O lord of my life, shall I stand before thee face to face. With folded hands, O lord of all worlds, shall I stand before thee face to face.

Under the great sky in solitude and silence, with humble heart shall I stand before thee face to face.

In this laborious world of thine, tumultuous with toil and with struggle, among hurrying crowds shall I stand before thee face to face.

And when my work shall be done in this world, O King of kings, alone and speechless shall I stand before thee face to face.

77

I know thee as my God and stand apart—I do not know thee as my own and come closer. I know thee as my father and bow before they feet—I do not grasp thy hand as my friend's.

I stand not where thou comest down and ownest thyself as mine, there to clasp thee to my heart and take thee as my comrade.

Thou art the Brother amongst my brothers, but I heed them not, I divide not my earnings with them, thus sharing my all with thee.

In pleasure and in pain I stand not by the side of men, and thus stand by thee. I shrink to give up my life, and thus do not plunge into the great waters of life.

78

When the creation was new and all the stars shone in their first splendour, the gods held their assembly in the sky and sang, 'Oh, the picture of perfection! the joy unalloyed!'

But one cried of a sudden—'It seems that somewhere there is a break in the chain of light and one of the stars has been lost.'

The golden string of their harp snapped, their song stopped, and they cried in dismay—'Yes, that lost star was the best, she was the glory of all heavens!'

From that day the search is unceasing for her, and the cry goes on from one to the other that in her the world has lost its one joy!

Only in the deepest silence of night the stars smile and whisper among themselves—'Vain is this seeking! Unbroken perfection is over all!'

79

If it is not my portion to meet thee in this my life then let me ever feel that I have missed thy sight—let me not forget for a moment, let me carry the pangs of this sorrow in my dreams and in my wakeful hours.

As my days pass in the crowded market of this world and my hands grow full with the daily profits, let me ever feel that I have gained nothing—let me not forget for a moment, let me carry the pangs of this sorrow in my dreams and in my wakeful hours.

When I sit by the roadside, tired and painting, when I spread my bed low in the dust, let me ever feel that the long journey is still before me—let me not forget for a moment, let me carry the pangs of this sorrow in my dreams and in my wakeful hours.

When my rooms have been decked out and the flutes sound and the laughter there is loud, let me ever feel that I have not invited thee to my house—let me not forget for a moment, let me carry the pangs of this sorrow in my dreams and in my wakeful hours.

80

I am like a remnant of a cloud of autumn uselessly roaming in the sky, O my sun ever-glorious! Thy touch has not yet melted my vapour, making me one with thy light, and thus I count months and years separated from thee.

If this be thy wish and if this be thy play, then take this fleeting emptiness of mine, paint it with colours, gild it with gold, float it on the wanton wind and spread it in varied wonders.

And again when it shall be thy wish to end this play at night, I shall melt and vanish away in the dark, or it may be in a smile of the white morning, in a coolness of purity transparent.

81

On many an idle day have I grieved over lost time. But it is never lost, my lord. Thou hast taken every moment of my life in thine own hands.

Hidden in the heart of things thou art nourishing seeds into sprouts, buds into blossoms, and ripening flowers into fruitfulness.

I was tired and sleeping on my idle bed and imagined all work had ceased. In the morning I woke up and found my garden full with wonders of flowers.

82

Time is endless in thy hands, my lord. There is none to count thy minutes.

Days and nights pass and ages bloom and fade like flowers. Thou knowest how to wait.

Thy centuries follow each other perfecting a small wild flower.

We have no time to lose, and having no time we must scramble for our chances.

We are too poor to be late.

And thus it is that time goes by while I give it to every querulous man who claims it, and thine altar is empty of all offerings to the last.

At the end of the day I hasten in fear lest thy gate be shut; but I find that yet there is time.

83

Mother, I shall weave a chain of pearls for thy neck with my tears of sorrow.

The stars have wrought their anklets of light to deck thy feet, but mine will hang upon thy breast.

Wealth and fame come from thee and it is for thee to give or to withhold them. But this my sorrow is absolutely mine own, and when I bring it to thee as my offering thou rewardest me with the grace.

84

It is the pang of separation that spreads throughout the world and gives birth to shapes innumerable in the infinite sky.

It is this sorrow of separation that gazes in silence all night from star to star and becomes lyric among rustling leaves in rainy darkness of July.

It is this overspreading pain that deepens into loves and desires, into sufferings and joys in human homes; and this it is that ever melts and flows in songs through my poet's heart.

85

When the warriors came out first from their master's hall, where had they hid their power? Where were their armour and their arms?

They looked poor and helpless, and the arrows were showered upon them on the day they came out from their master's hall.

When the warriors marched back again to their master's hall where did they hide their power?

They had dropped the sword and dropped the bow and the arrow; peace was on their foreheads, and they had left the fruits of their life behind them on the day they marched back again to their master's hall.

86

Death, thy servant, is at my door. He has crossed the unknown sea and brought thy call to my home.

The night is dark and my heart is fearful—yet I will take up the lamp, open my gates and bow to him my welcome. It is thy messenger who stands at my door.

I will worship him with folded hands, and with tears. I will worship him placing at his feet the treasure of my heart.

He will go back with his errand done, leaving a dark shadow on my morning; and in my desolate home only my forlorn self will remain as my last offering to thee.

87

In desperate hope I go and search for her in all the corners of my room; I find her not.

My house is small and what once has gone from it can never be regained.

But infinite is thy mansion, my lord, and seeking her I have come to thy door.

I stand under the golden canopy of thine evening sky and I lift my eager eyes to thy face.

I have come to the brink of eternity from which nothing can vanish—no hope, no happiness, no vision of a face seen through tears.

Oh, dip my emptied life into that ocean, plunge it into the deepest fullness. Let me for once feel that lost sweet touch in the allness of the universe.

88

Deity of the ruined temple! The broken strings of *Vina* sing no more your praise. The bells in the evening proclaim not your time of worship. The air is still and silent about you.

In your desolate dwelling comes the vagrant spring breeze. It brings the tidings of flowers—the flowers that for your worship are offered no more.

Your worshipper of old wanders ever longing for favour still refused. In the eventide, when fires and shadows mingle with the gloom of dust, he wearily comes back to the ruined temple with hunger in his heart.

Many a festival day comes to you in silence, deity of the ruined temple. Many a night of worship goes away with lamp unlit.

Many new images are built by masters of cunning art and carried to the holy stream of oblivion when their time is come.

Only the deity of the ruined temple remains unworshipped in deathless neglect.

89

No more noisy, loud words from me—such is my master's will. Henceforth I deal in whispers. The speech of my heart will be carried on in murmurings of a song.

Men hasten to the King's market. All the buyers and sellers are there. But I have my untimely leave in the middle of the day, in the thick of work.

Let then the flowers come out in my garden, though it is not their time; and let the midday bees strike up their lazy hum.

Full many an hour have I spent in the strife of the good and the evil, but now it is the pleasure of my playmate of the empty days to draw my heart on to him; and I know not why is this sudden call to what useless inconsequence!

90

On the day when death will knock at thy door what wilt thou offer to him?

Oh, I will set before my guest the full vessel of my life—I will never let him go with empty hands.

All the sweet vintage of all my autumn days and summer nights, all the earnings and gleanings of my busy life will I place before him at the close of my days when death will knock at my door.

91

O thou the last fulfilment of life, Death, my death, come and whisper to me!

Day after day have I kept watch for thee; for thee have I borne the joys and pangs of life.

All that I am, that I have, that I hope and all my love have ever flowed towards thee in depth of secrecy. One final glance from thine eyes and my life will be ever thine own.

The flowers have been woven and the garland is ready for the bridegroom. After the wedding the bride shall leave her home and meet her lord alone in the solitude of night.

92

I know that the day will come when my sight of this earth shall be lost, and life will take its leave in silence, drawing the last curtain over my eyes.

Yet stars will watch at night, and morning rise as before, and hours heave like sea waves casting up pleasures and pains.

When I think of this end of my moments, the barrier of the moments breaks and I see by the light of death thy world with its careless treasures. Rare is its lowliest seat, rare is its meanest of lives.

Things that I longed for in vain and things that I got—let them pass. Let me but truly possess the things that I ever spurned and overlooked.

93

I have got my leave. Bid me farewell, my brothers! I bow to you all and take my departure.

Here I give back the keys of my door—and I give up all claims to my house. I only ask for last kind words from you.

We were neighbours for long, but I received more than I could give. Now the day has dawned and the lamp that lit my dark corner is out. A summons has come and I am ready for my journey.

94

At this time of my parting, wish me good luck, my friends! The sky is flushed with the dawn and my path lies beautiful.

Ask not what I have with me to take there. I start on my journey with empty hands and expectant heart.

I shall put on my wedding garland. Mine is not the red-brown dress of the traveller, and though there are dangers on the way I have no fear in my mind.

The evening star will come out when my voyage is done and the plaintive notes of the twilight melodies be struck up from the King's gateway.

95

I was not aware of the moment when I first crossed the threshold of this life.

What was the power that made me open out into this vast mystery like a bud in the forest at midnight!

When in the morning I looked upon the light I felt in a moment that I was no stranger in this world, that the inscrutable without name and form had taken me in its arms in the form of my own mother.

Even so, in death the same unknown will appear as ever known to me. And because I love this life, I know I shall love death as well.

The child cries out when from the right breast the mother takes it away, in the very next moment to find in the left one its consolation.

96

When I go from hence let this be my parting word, that what I have seen is unsurpassable.

I have tasted of the hidden honey of this lotus that expands on the ocean of light, and thus am I blessed—let this be my parting word.

In this playhouse of infinite forms I have had my play and here have I caught sight of him that is formless.

My whole body and my limbs have thrilled with his touch who is beyond touch; and if the end comes here, let it come—let this be my parting word.

97

When my play was with thee I never questioned who thou wert. I knew nor shyness nor fear, my life was boisterous.

In the early morning thou wouldst call me from my sleep like my own comrade and lead me running from glade to glade.

On those days I never cared to know the meaning of songs thou sangest to me. Only my voice took up the tunes, and my heart danced in their cadence.

Now, when the playtime is over, what is this sudden sight that is come upon me? The world with eyes bent upon thy feet stands in awe with all its silent stars.

98

I will deck thee with trophies, garlands of my defeat. It is never in my power to escape unconquered.

I surely know my pride will go to the wall, my life will burst its bonds in exceeding pain, and my empty heart will sob out in music like a hollow reed, and the stone will melt in tears.

I surely know the hundred petals of a lotus will not remain closed for ever and the secret recess of its honey will be bared.

From the blue sky an eye shall gaze upon me and summon me in silence. Nothing will be left for me, nothing whatever, and utter death shall I receive at thy feet.

99

When I give up the helm I know that the time has come for thee to take it. What there is to do will be instantly done. Vain is this struggle.

Then take away your hands and silently put up with your defeat, my heart, and think it your good fortune to sit perfectly still where you are placed.

These my lamps are blown out at every little puff of wind, and trying to light them I forget all else again and again.

But I shall be wise this time and wait in the dark, spreading my mat on the floor; and whenever it is thy pleasure, my lord, come silently and take thy seat here.

100

I dive down into the depth of the ocean of forms, hoping to gain the perfect pearl of the formless.

No more sailing from harbour to harbour with this my weather-beaten boat. The days are long passed when my sport was to be tossed on waves.

And now I am eager to die into the deathless. Into the audience hall by the fathomless abyss where swells up the music of toneless strings I shall take this harp of my life.

I shall tune it to the notes of forever, and when it has sobbed out its last utterance, lay down my silent harp at the feet of the silent.

101

Ever in my life have I sought thee with my songs. It was they who led me from door to door, and with them have I felt about me, searching and touching my world.

It was my songs that taught me all the lessons I ever learnt; they showed me secret paths, they brought before my sight many a star on the horizon of my heart.

They guided me all the day long to the mysteries of the country of pleasure and pain, and, at last, to what palace gate have they brought me in the evening at the end of my journey?

102

I boasted among men that I had known you. They see your pictures in all works of mine. They come and ask me, 'Who is he?' I know not how to answer them. I say, 'Indeed, I cannot tell.' They blame me and they go away in scorn. And you sit there smiling.

I put my tales of you into lasting songs. The secret gushes out from my heart. They come and ask me, 'Tell me all your meanings.' I know not how to answer them. I say, 'Ah, who knows what they mean!' They smile and go away in utter scorn. And you sit there smiling.

103

In one salutation to thee, my God, let all my senses spread out and touch this world at thy feet.

Like a rain-cloud of July hung low with its burden of unshed showers let all my mind bend down at thy door in one salutation to thee.

Let all my songs gather together their diverse strains into a single current and flow to a sea of silence in one salutation to thee.

Like a flock of homesick cranes flying night and day back to their mountain nests let all my life take its voyage to its eternal home in one salutation to thee.

MEMOIR

জীবন স্মৃতি

MY REMINISCENCES

[*Jivan Smriti* was published in 1911. The English translation
reproduced here was first published in 1917.]

Translator's Preface

These Reminiscences were written and published by the Author in his fiftieth year, shortly before he started on a trip to Europe and America for his failing health in 1912. It was in the course of this trip that he wrote for the first time in the English language for publication.

In these memory pictures, so lightly, even casually presented by the author there is, nevertheless, revealed a connected history of his inner life together with that of the varying literary forms in which his growing self-found successive expression, up to the point at which both his soul and poetry attained maturity.

This lightness of manner and importance of matter form a combination the translation of which into a different language is naturally a matter of considerable difficulty. It was, in any case, a task which the present Translator, not being an original writer in the English language, would hardly have ventured to undertake, had there not been other considerations. The translator's familiarity, however, with the persons, scenes, and events herein depicted made it a temptation difficult for him to resist, as well as a responsibility which he did not care to leave to others not possessing these advantages, and therefore more liable to miss a point, or give a wrong impression.

The Translator, moreover, had the author's permission and advice to make a free translation, a portion of which was completed and approved by the latter before he left India on his recent tour to Japan and America.

In regard to the nature of the freedom taken for the purposes of the translation, it may be mentioned that those suggestions which might not have been as clear to the foreign as to the Bengali reader have been brought out in a slightly more elaborate manner than in the original text; while again, in rare cases, others which depend on allusions entirely unfamiliar to the non-Indian reader, have been omitted rather than spoil by an over-elaboration the simplicity and naturalness which is the great feature of the original.

There are no footnotes in the original. All the footnotes here given have been added by the Translator in the hope that they may be of further assistance to the foreign reader.

PART I

❧

1

My Reminiscences

I know not who paints the pictures on memory's canvas; but whoever he may be, what he is painting are pictures; by which I mean that he is not there with his brush simply to make a faithful copy of all that is happening. He takes in and leaves out according to his taste. He makes many a big thing small and small thing big. He has no compunction in putting into the background that which was to the fore, or bringing to the front that which was behind. In short he is painting pictures, and not writing history.

Thus, over Life's outward aspect passes the series of events, and within is being painted a set of pictures. The two correspond but are not one.

We do not get the leisure to view thoroughly this studio within us. Portions of it now and then catch our eye, but the greater part remains out of sight in the darkness. Why the ever-busy painter is painting; when he will have done; for what gallery his pictures are destined—who can tell?

Some years ago, on being questioned as to the events of my past life, I had occasion to pry into this picture-chamber. I had thought to be content with selecting some few materials for my Life's story. I then discovered, as I opened the door, that Life's memories are not Life's history, but the original work of an unseen Artist. The variegated colours scattered about are not reflections of outside lights, but belong to the painter himself, and come passion-tinged from his heart; thereby unfitting the record on the canvas for use as evidence in a court of law.

But though the attempt to gather precise history from memory's storehouse may be fruitless, there is a fascination in looking over the pictures, a fascination which cast its spell on me.

The road over which we journey, the wayside shelter in which we pause, are not pictures while yet we travel—they are too necessary, too obvious. When, however, before turning into the evening rest house, we look back upon the cities, fields, rivers and hills which we have been through in Life's morning, then, in the light of the passing day, are they pictures indeed. Thus, when my opportunity came, did I look back, and was engrossed.

Was this interest aroused within me solely by a natural affection for my own past? Some personal feeling, of course, there must have been, but the pictures had also an independent artistic value of their own. There is no event in my reminiscences worthy of being preserved for all time. But the quality of the subject is not the only justification for a record. What one has truly felt, if only it can be made sensible to others, is always of importance to one's fellow men. If pictures which have taken shape in memory can be brought out in words, they are worth a place in literature.

It is as literary material that I offer my memory pictures. To take them as an attempt at autobiography would be a mistake. In such a view these reminiscences would appear useless as well as incomplete.

2
Teaching Begins

We three boys were being brought up together. Both my companions were two years older than I. When they were placed under their tutor, my teaching also began, but of what I learnt nothing remains in my memory.

What constantly recurs to me is 'The rain patters, the leaf quivers.'* I am just come to anchor after crossing the stormy region of the *kara, khala*† series; and I am reading 'The rain patters, the leaf quivers,' for me the first poem of the Arch Poet. Whenever the joy of that day comes back to me, even now, I realise why rhyme is so needful in poetry. Because of it the words come to an end, and yet end not; the utterance is over, but not its ring; and the ear and the mind can go on and on with their game of tossing the rhyme to each other. Thus did the rain patter and the leaves quiver again and again, the live-long day in my consciousness.

Another episode of this period of my early boyhood is held fast in my mind.

We had an old cashier, Kailash by name, who was like one of the family. He was a great wit, and would be constantly cracking jokes with everybody, old and young; recently married sons-in-law, new comers into the family circle, being his special butts. There was room for the suspicion that his humour had not deserted him even after death. Once my elders were engaged in an attempt to start a postal service with the other world by means of a planchette. At one of the sittings the pencil scrawled out the name of Kailash. He was asked as to the sort of life one led where he was. Not a bit of it, was the reply. "Why should you get so cheap what I had to die to learn?"

This Kailash used to rattle off for my special delectation a doggerel ballad of his own composition. The hero was myself and there was a glowing anticipation of the arrival of a heroine. And as I

---

* A jingling sentence in the Bengali Child's Primer.

† Exercises in two-syllables

listened my interest would wax intense at the picture of this world-charming bride illuminating the lap of the future in which she sat enthroned. The list of the jewellery with which she was bedecked from head to foot, and the unheard of splendour of the preparations for the bridal, might have turned older and wiser heads; but what moved the boy, and set wonderful joy pictures flitting before his vision, was the rapid jingle of the frequent rhymes and the swing of the rhythm.

These two literary delights still linger in my memory—and there is the other, the infants' classic: 'The rain falls pit-a-pat, the tide comes up the river.'

The next thing I remember is the beginning of my school-life. One day I saw my elder brother, and my sister's son Satya, also a little older than myself, starting off to school, leaving me behind, accounted unfit. I had never before ridden in a carriage nor even been out of the house. So when Satya came back, full of unduly glowing accounts of his adventures on the way, I felt I simply could not stay at home. Our tutor tried to dispel my illusion with sound advice and a resounding slap: "You're crying to go to school now, you'll have to cry a lot more to be let off later on." I have no recollection of the name, features or disposition of this tutor of ours, but the impression of his weighty advice and weightier hand has not yet faded. Never in my life have I heard a truer prophecy.

My crying drove me prematurely into the Oriental Seminary. What I learnt there I have no idea, but one of its methods of punishment I still bear in mind. The boy who was unable to repeat his lessons was made to stand on a bench with arms extended, and on his upturned palms were piled a number of slates. It is for psychologists to debate how far this method is likely to conduce to a better grasp of things. I thus began my schooling at an extremely tender age.

My initiation into literature had its origin, at the same time, in the books which were in vogue in the servants' quarters. Chief among these were a Bengali translation of Chanakya's aphorisms, and the Ramayana of Krittivasa.

A picture of one day's reading of the Ramayana comes clearly back to me.

Rabindranath Tagore in 1877

The day was a cloudy one. I was playing about in the long verandah* overlooking the road. All of a sudden Satya, for some reason I do not remember, wanted to frighten me by shouting, "Policeman! Policeman!" My ideas of the duties of policemen were of an extremely vague description. One thing I was certain about, that a person charged with crime once placed in a policeman's hands would, as sure as the wretch caught in a crocodile's serrated grip, go under and be seen no more. Not knowing how an innocent boy could escape this relentless penal code, I bolted towards the inner apartments, with shudders running down my back for blind

---

* Roofed colonnade or balcony. The writer's family house is an irregular three-storied mass of buildings, which had grown with the joint family it sheltered, built round several courtyards or quadrangles, with long colonnades along the outer faces, and narrower galleries running round each quadrangle, giving access to the single rows of rooms.

fear of pursuing policemen. I broke to my mother the news of my impending doom, but it did not seem to disturb her much. However, not deeming it safe to venture out again, I sat down on the sill of my mother's door to read the dog-eared Ramayana, with a marbled paper cover, which belonged to her old aunt. Alongside stretched the verandah running round the four sides of the open inner quadrangle, on which had fallen the faint afternoon glow of the clouded sky, and finding me weeping over one of its sorrowful situations my great-aunt came and took away the book from me.

3

Within and Without

Luxury was a thing almost unknown in the days of my infancy. The standard of living was then, as a whole, much more simple than it is now. Apart from that, the children of our household were entirely free from the fuss of being too much looked after. The fact is that, while the process of looking after may be an occasional treat for the guardians, to the children it is always an unmitigated nuisance.

We used to be under the rule of the servants. To save themselves trouble they had almost suppressed our right of free movement. But the freedom of not being petted made up even for the harshness of this bondage, for our minds were left clear of the toils of constant coddling, pampering and dressing up.

Our food had nothing to do with delicacies. A list of our articles of clothing would only invite the modern boy's scorn. On no pretext did we wear socks or shoes till we had passed our tenth year. In the cold weather a second cotton tunic over the first one sufficed. It never entered our heads to consider ourselves ill-off for that reason. It was only when old Niyamat, the tailor, would forget to put a pocket into one of our tunics that we complained, for no boy has yet been born so poor as not to have the wherewithal to stuff his pockets; nor, by a merciful dispensation of providence, is there much difference between the wealth of boys of rich and of poor parentage. We used to have a pair of slippers each, but not always where we had our feet. Our habit of kicking the slippers on ahead, and catching them up again, made them work none the less hard, through effectually defeating at every step the reason of their being.

Our elders were in every way at a great distance from us, in their dress and food, living and doing, conversation and amusement. We caught glimpses of these, but they were beyond our reach. Elders have become cheap to modern children; they are too readily accessible, and so are all objects of desire. Nothing ever came so easily to us. Many a trivial thing was for us a rarity, and we lived mostly in the hope of attaining, when we were old enough, the things which the distant future held in trust for us. The result was that what little we did get we enjoyed to the utmost; from skin to core nothing was thrown away. The modern child of a well-to-do family nibbles at only half the things he gets; the greater part of his world is wasted on him.

Our days were spent in the servants' quarters in the south-east corner of the outer apartments. One of our servants was Shyam, a dark chubby boy with curly locks, hailing from the District of Khulna. He would put me into a selected spot and, tracing a chalk line all round, warn me with solemn face and uplifted finger of the perils of transgressing this ring. Whether the threatened danger was material or spiritual I never fully understood, but a great fear used to possess me. I had read in the Ramayana of the tribulations of Sita for having left the ring drawn by Lakshman, so it was not possible for me to be sceptical of its potency.

Just below the window of this room was a tank with a flight of masonry steps leading down into the water; on its west bank, along the garden wall, an immense banyan tree; to the south a fringe of coconut palms. Ringed round as I was near this window I would spend the whole day peering through the drawn Venetian shutters, gazing and gazing on this scene as on a picture book. From early morning our neighbours would drop in one by one to have their bath. I knew the time for each one to arrive. I was familiar with the peculiarities of each one's toilet. One would stop up his ears with his fingers as he took his regulation number of dips, after which he would depart. Another would not venture on a complete immersion but be content with only squeezing his wet towel repeatedly over his head. A third would carefully drive the surface impurities away from him with a rapid play of his arms, and then on a sudden impulse take his plunge. There was one who jumped in from the top steps without any preliminaries at all. Another would walk slowly in, step by step, muttering his morning prayers the while. One was always in a hurry, hastening home as soon as he was through with his dip. Another was in no sort of hurry at all, taking his bath leisurely, followed with a good rub-down, and a change from wet bathing clothes into clean ones, including a careful adjustment of the folds of his waist cloth, ending with a turn or two in the outer* garden, and the gathering of flowers, with which he would finally saunter slowly homewards, radiating the cool comfort of his refreshed body, as he went. This would go on till it was past noon. Then the bathing places would be deserted and become silent. Only the ducks remained, paddling about after water snails, or busy preening their feathers, the live-long day.

When solitude thus reigned over the water, my whole attention would be drawn to the shadows under the banyan tree. Some of its aerial roots, creeping down along its trunk, had formed a dark complication of coils at its base. It seemed as if into this mysterious region the laws of the universe had not found entrance; as if some old-world dreamland had escaped the divine vigilance and lingered on into the light of modern day. Whom I used to see there, and what those beings did, it is not possible to express in intelligible language. It was about this banyan tree that I wrote later:

> With tangled roots hanging down from your branches, O ancient banyan tree,
> You stand still day and night, like an ascetic at his penances,
> Do you ever remember the child whose fancy played with your shadows?

Alas! that banyan tree is no more, nor the piece of water which served to mirror the majestic forest-lord! Many of those who used to bathe there have also followed into oblivion the shade of the banyan

---

* The men's portion of the house is the outer; and the women's the inner.

332

tree. And that boy, grown older, is counting the alternations of light and darkness which penetrate the complexities with which the roots he has thrown off on all sides have encircled him.

Going out of the house was forbidden to us, in fact we had not even the freedom of all its parts. We perforce took our peeps at nature from behind the barriers. Beyond my reach there was this limitless thing called the Outside, of which flashes and sounds and scents used momentarily to come and touch me through its interstices. It seemed to want to play with me through the bars with so many gestures. But it was free and I was bound—there was no way of meeting. So the attraction was all the stronger. The chalk line has been wiped away today, but the confining ring is still there. The distant is just as distant, the outside is still beyond me; and I am reminded of the poem I wrote when I was older:

The tame bird was in a cage, the free bird was in the forest,
They met when the time came, it was a decree of fate.
The free bird cries, "O my love, let us fly to wood."
The cage bird whispers, "Come hither, let us both live in the cage."
Says the free bird, "Among bars, where is there room to spread one's
wings?"
"Alas," cries the cage bird, "I should not know where to sit perched in
the sky."

The parapets of our terraced roofs were higher than my head. When I had grown taller; when the tyranny of the servants had relaxed; when, with the coming of a newly married bride into the house, I had achieved some recognition as a companion of her leisure, then did I sometimes come up to the terrace in the middle of the day. By that time everybody in the house would have finished their meal; there would be an interval in the business of the household; over the inner apartments would rest the quiet of the midday siesta; the wet bathing clothes would be hanging over the parapets to dry; the crows would be picking at the leavings thrown on the refuse heap at the corner of the yard; in the solitude of that interval the caged bird would, through the gaps in the parapet, commune bill to bill with the free bird!

The Inner Garden was My Paradise

I would stand and gaze . . . My glance first falls on the row of coconut trees on the further edge of our inner garden. Through these are seen the 'Singhi's Garden' with its cluster of huts* and tank, and on the edge of the tank the dairy of our milkwoman, Tara; still further on, mixed up with the tree-tops, the various shapes and different heights of the terraced roofs of Calcutta, flashing back the blazing whiteness of the midday sun, stretch right away into the greyish blue of the eastern horizon. And some of these far distant dwellings from which stand forth their roofed stairways leading up to the terrace, look as if with uplifted finger and a wink they are hinting to me of the mysteries of their interiors. Like the beggar at the palace door who imagines impossible treasures to be held in the strong rooms closed to him, I can hardly tell of the wealth of play

---

* These Bustis or settlements consisting of tumbledown hovels, existing side by side with palatial buildings, are still one of the anomalies of Calcutta.

and freedom which these unknown dwellings seem to me crowded with. From the furthest depth of the sky full of burning sunshine overhead the thin shrill cry of a kite reaches my ear; and from the lane adjoining Singhi's Garden comes up, past the houses silent in their noonday slumber, the sing-song of the bangle-seller—*chai choori chai* . . . and my whole being would fly away from the work-a-day world.

My father hardly ever stayed at home, he was constantly roaming about. His rooms on the third storey used to remain shut up. I would pass my hands through the venetian shutters, and thus opening the latch get the door open, and spend the afternoon lying motionless on his sofa at the south end. First of all it was a room always closed, and then there was the stolen entry, this gave it a deep flavour of mystery; further the broad empty expanse of terrace to the south, glowing in the rays of the sun would set me day-dreaming.

There was yet another attraction. The water-works had just been started in Calcutta, and in the first exuberance of its triumphant entry it did not stint even the Indian quarters of their supply. In that golden age of pipe water, it used to flow even up to my father's third storey rooms. And turning on the shower tap I would indulge to my heart's content in an untimely bath. Not so much for the comfort of it, as to give rein to my desire to do just as I fancied. The alternation of the joy of liberty, and the fear of being caught, made that shower of municipal water send arrows of delight thrilling into me.

It was perhaps because the possibility of contact with the outside was so remote that the joy of it came to me so much more readily. When material is in profusion, the mind gets lazy and leaves everything to it, forgetting that for a successful feast of joy its internal equipment counts for more than the external. This is the chief lesson which his infant state has to teach to man. There his possessions are few and trivial, yet he needs no more for his happiness. The world of play is spoilt for the unfortunate youngster who is burdened with an unlimited quantity of playthings.

To call our inner garden a garden is to say a deal too much. Its properties consisted of a citron tree, a couple of plum trees of different varieties, and a row of coconut trees. In the centre was a paved circle the cracks of which various grasses and weeds had invaded and planted in them their victorious standards. Only those flowering plants which refused to die of neglect continued uncomplainingly to perform their respective duties without casting any aspersions on the gardener. In the northern corner was a rice-husking shed, where the inmates of the inner apartments would occasionally foregather when household necessity demanded. This last vestige of rural life has since owned defeat and slunk away ashamed and unnoticed.

None the less I suspect that Adam's garden of Eden could hardly have been better adorned than this one of ours; for he and his paradise were alike naked; they needed not to be furnished with material things. It is only since his tasting of the fruit of the tree of knowledge, and till he can fully digest it, that man's need for external furniture and embellishment persistently grows. Our inner garden was my paradise; it was enough for me. I well remember how in the early autumn dawn I would run there as soon as I was awake. A scent of dewy grass and foliage would rush to meet me, and the morning with its cool fresh sunlight would peep out at me over the top of the Eastern garden wall from below the trembling tassels of the coconut palms.

There is another piece of vacant land to the north of the house which to this day we call the *golabari* (barn house). The name shows that in some remote past this must have been the place where the year's store of grain used to be kept in a barn. Then, as with brother and sister in infancy, the likeness between town and country was visible all over. Now the family resemblance can hardly be traced. This golabari would be my holiday haunt if I got the chance. It would hardly be correct to say that I went there to play—it was the place not play, which drew me. Why this was so, is difficult to tell. Perhaps its being a deserted bit of waste land lying in an out-of-the-way corner gave it its charm for me. It was entirely outside the living quarters and bore no stamp of usefulness; moreover it was as unadorned as it was useless, for no one had ever planted anything there; it was doubtless for these reasons that this desert spot offered no resistance to the free play of the boy's imagination. Whenever I got any loop-hole to evade the vigilance of my warders and could contrive to reach the golabari I felt I had a holiday indeed.

There was yet another place in our house which I have even yet not succeeded in finding out. A little girl playmate of my own age called this the "King's palace."* "I have just been there," she would sometimes tell me. But somehow the propitious moment never turned up when she could take me along with her. That was a wonderful place, and its playthings were as wonderful as the games that were played there. It seemed to me it must be somewhere very near—perhaps in the first or second storey; the only thing was one never seemed to be able to get there. How often have I asked my companion, "Only tell me, is it really inside the house or outside?" And she would always reply, "No, no, it's in this very house." I would sit and wonder: "Where then can it be? Don't I know all the rooms of the house?" Who the king might be I never cared to inquire; where his palace is still remains undiscovered; this much was clear—the king's palace was within our house.

Looking back on childhood's days the thing that recurs most often is the mystery which used to fill both life and world. Something undreamt of was lurking everywhere and the uppermost question every day was: when, Oh! when would we come across it? It was as if nature held something in her closed hands and was smilingly asking us: "What d'you think I have?" What was impossible for her to have was the thing we had no idea of.

Well do I remember the custard apple seed which I had planted and kept in a corner of the south verandah, and used to water every day. The thought that the seed might possibly grow into a tree kept me in a great state of fluttering wonder. Custard apple seeds still have the habit of sprouting, but no longer to the accompaniment of that feeling of wonder. The fault is not in the custard apple but in the mind. We had once stolen some rocks from an elder cousin's rockery and started a little rockery of our own. The plants which we sowed in its interstices were cared for so excessively that it was only because of their vegetable nature that they managed to put up with it till their untimely death. Words cannot recount the endless joy and wonder which this miniature mountain-top held for us. We had no doubt that this creation of ours would be a wonderful thing to our

---

* Corresponding to 'Wonderland'

elders also. The day that we sought to put this to the proof, however, the hillock in the corner of our room, with all its rocks, and all its vegetation, vanished. The knowledge that the schoolroom floor was not a proper foundation for the erection of a mountain was imparted so rudely, and with such suddenness, that it gave us a considerable shock. The weight of stone of which the floor was relieved settled on our minds when we realised the gulf between our fancies and the will of our elders.

How intimately did the life of the world throb for us in those days! Earth, water, foliage and sky, they all spoke to us and would not be disregarded. How often were we struck by the poignant regret that we could only see the upper storey of the earth and knew nothing of its inner storey. All our planning was as to how we could pry beneath its dust-coloured cover. If, thought we, we could drive in bamboo after bamboo, one over the other, we might perhaps get into some sort of touch with its inmost depths.

During the *Magh* festival a series of wooden pillars used to be planted round the outer courtyard for supporting the chandeliers. Digging holes for these would begin on the first of Magh. The preparations for festivity are ever interesting to young folk. But this digging had a special attraction for me. Though I had watched it done year after year—and seen the hole grow bigger and bigger till the digger had completely disappeared inside, and yet nothing extraordinary, nothing worthy of the quest of prince or knight, had ever appeared—yet every time I had the feeling that the lid being lifted off a chest of mystery. I felt that a little bit more digging would do it. Year after year passed, but that bit never got done. There was a pull at the curtain but it was not drawn. The elders, thought I, can do whatever they please, why do they rest content with such shallow delving? If we young folk had the ordering of it, the inmost mystery of the earth would no longer be allowed to remain smothered in its dust covering.

And the thought that behind every part of the vault of blue reposed the mysteries of the sky would also spur our imaginings. When our Pundit, in illustration of some lesson in our Bengali science primer, told us that the blue sphere was not an enclosure, how thunderstruck we were! "Put ladder upon ladder," said he, "and go on mounting away, but you will never bump your head." He must be sparing of his ladders, I opined, and questioned with a rising inflection, "And what if we put more ladders, and more, and more?" When I realised that it was fruitless multiplying ladders I remained dumbfounded pondering over the matter. Surely, I concluded, such an astounding piece of news must be known only to those who are the world's schoolmasters!

PART II

4

Servocracy

In the history of India the regime of the Slave Dynasty was not a happy one. In going back to the reign of the servants in my own life's history I can find nothing glorious or cheerful touching the period. There were frequent changes of king, but never a variation in the code of restraints and punishments with which we were afflicted. We, however, had no opportunity at the time for philosophising on the subject; our backs bore as best they could the blows which befell them: and we accepted as one of the laws of the universe that it is for the Big to hurt and for the Small to be hurt. It has taken me a long time to learn the opposite truth that it is the Big who suffer and the Small who cause suffering.

The quarry does not view virtue and vice from the standpoint of the hunter. That is why the alert bird, whose cry warns its fellows before the shot has sped, gets abused as vicious. We howled when we were beaten, which our chastisers did not consider good manners; it was in fact counted sedition against the servocracy. I cannot forget how, in order effectively to suppress such sedition, our heads used to be crammed into the huge water jars then in use; distasteful, doubtless, was this outcry to those who caused it; moreover, it was likely to have unpleasant consequences.

I now sometimes wonder why such cruel treatment was meted out to us by the servants. I cannot admit that there was on the whole anything in our behaviour or demeanour to have put us beyond the pale of human kindness. The real reason must have been that the whole of our burden was thrown on the servants, and the whole burden is a thing difficult to bear even for those who are nearest and dearest. If children are only allowed to be children, to run and play about and satisfy their curiosity, it becomes quite simple. Insoluble problems are only created if you try to confine them inside, keep them still or hamper their play. Then does the burden of the child, so lightly borne by its own childishness, fall heavily on the guardian— like that of the horse in the fable which was carried instead of being allowed to trot on its own legs: and though money procured bearers even for such a burden it could not prevent them taking it out of the unlucky beast at every step.

Of most of these tyrants of our childhood I remember only their cuffings and boxings, and nothing more. Only one personality stands out in my memory.

His name was Iswar. He had been a village schoolmaster before. He was a prim, proper and sedately dignified personage. The Earth seemed too earthy for him, with too little water to keep it sufficiently clean; so that he had to be in a constant state of warfare with its chronic soiled state. He would shoot his water-pot into the tank with a lightning movement so as to get his supply from an uncontaminated depth. It was he who, when bathing in the tank, would be continually thrusting away the surface impurities till he took a sudden plunge expecting, as it were, to catch the water unawares. When walking his right arm stood out at an angle from his body, as if, so it seemed to us, he could not trust the cleanliness even of his own garments. His whole bearing had the appearance of an effort to keep clear of the imperfections which, through unguarded avenues, find entrance into earth, water and air, and into the ways of men. Unfathomable was the depth of his gravity. With head slightly tilted he would mince his carefully selected words in a deep voice. His literary diction would give food for merriment to our elders behind his back, some of his high-flown phrases finding a permanent place in our family repertoire of witticisms. But I doubt whether the expressions he used would sound as remarkable today; showing how the literary and spoken languages, which used to be as sky from earth asunder, are now coming nearer each other.

This erstwhile schoolmaster had discovered a way of keeping us quiet in the evenings. Every evening he would gather us round the cracked castor-oil lamp and read out to us stories from the Ramayana and Mahabharata. Some of the other servants would also come and join the audience. The lamp would be throwing huge shadows right up to the beams of the roof, the little house lizards catching insects on the walls, the bats doing a mad dervish dance round and round the verandahs outside, and we listening in silent open-mouthed wonder.

I still remember, on the evening we came to the story of Kusha and Lava, and those two valiant lads were threatening to humble to the dust the renown of their father and uncles, how the tense silence of that dimly lighted room was bursting with eager anticipation. It was getting late, our prescribed period of wakefulness was drawing to a close, and yet the denouement was far off.

At this critical juncture my father's old follower Kishori came to the rescue, and finished the episode for us, at express speed, to the quickstep of Dasuraya's jingling verses. The impression of the soft slow chant of Krittivasa's* fourteen-syllabled measure was swept clean away and we were left overwhelmed by a flood of rhymes and alliterations.

On some occasions these readings would give rise to shastric discussions, which would at length be settled by the depth of Iswar's wise pronouncements. Though, as one of the children's servants, his rank in our domestic society was below that of many, yet, as with old Grandfather Bhisma in the Mahabharata, his supremacy would assert itself from his seat, below his juniors.

Our grave and reverend servitor had one weakness to which, for the sake of historical accuracy, I feel bound to allude. He used to take opium. This created a craving for rich food. So that when he brought us our morning goblets of milk the forces of attraction in his mind would be greater than those of repulsion. If we gave the least expression to our natural repugnance for this meal, no sense

---

* There are innumerable renderings of the Ramayana in the Indian languages.

of responsibility for our health could prompt him to press it on us a second time.

Iswar also held somewhat narrow views as to our capacity for solid nourishment. We would sit down to our evening repast and a quantity of *luchis** heaped on a thick round wooden tray would be placed before us. He would begin by gingerly dropping a few on each platter, from a sufficient height to safeguard himself from contamination†—like unwilling favours, wrested from the gods by dint of importunity, did they descend, so dexterously inhospitable was he. Next would come the inquiry whether he should give us any more. I knew the reply which would be most gratifying, and could not bring myself to deprive him by asking for another help.

Then again Iswar was entrusted with a daily allowance of money for procuring our afternoon light refreshment. He would ask us every morning what we should like to have. We knew that to mention the cheapest would be accounted best, so sometimes we ordered a light refection of puffed rice, and at others an indigestible one of boiled gram or roasted groundnuts. It was evident that Iswar was not as painstakingly punctilious in regard to our diet as with the shastric proprieties.

5

The Normal School

While at the Oriental Seminary I had discovered a way out of the degradation of being a mere pupil. I had started a class of my own in a corner of our verandah. The wooden bars of the railing were my pupils, and I would act the schoolmaster, cane in hand, seated on a chair in front of them. I had decided which were the good boys and which the bad—nay, further, I could distinguish clearly the quiet from the naughty, the clever from the stupid. The bad

---

* A kind of crisp unsweetened pancake taken like bread along with the other courses.
† Food while being eaten, and utensils or anything else touched by the hand engaged in conveying food to the mouth, are considered ceremonially unclean.

rails had suffered so much from my constant caning that they must have longed to give up the ghost had they been alive. And the more scarred they got with my strokes the worse they angered me, till I knew not how to punish them enough. None remain to bear witness today how tremendously I tyrannised over that poor dumb class of mine. My wooden pupils have since been replaced by cast-iron railings, nor have any of the new generation taken up their education in the same way—they could never have made the same impression.

I have since realised how much easier it is to acquire the manner than the matter. Without an effort had I assimilated all the impatience, the short temper, the partiality and the injustice displayed by my teachers to the exclusion of the rest of their teaching. My only consolation is that I had not the power of venting these barbarities on any sentient creature. Nevertheless the difference between my wooden pupils and those of the Seminary did not prevent my psychology from being identical with that of its schoolmasters.

I could not have been long at the Oriental Seminary, for I was still of tender age when I joined the Normal School. The only one of its features which I remember is that before the classes began all the boys had to sit in a row in the gallery and go through some kind of singing or chanting of verses—evidently an attempt at introducing an element of cheerfulness into the daily routine.

Unfortunately the words were English and the tune quite as foreign, so that we had not the faintest notion what sort of incantation we were practising; neither did the meaningless monotony of the performance tend to make us cheerful. This failed to disturb the serene self-satisfaction of the school authorities at having provided such a treat; they deemed it superfluous to inquire into the practical effect of their bounty; they would probably have counted it a crime for the boys not to be dutifully happy. Anyhow they rested content with taking the song as they found it, words and all, from the self-same English book which had furnished the theory.

The language into which this English resolved itself in our mouths cannot but be edifying to philologists. I can recall only one line:

Kallokee pullokee singill mellaling mellaling mellaling.

After much thought I have been able to guess at the original of a part of it. Of what words *kallokee* is the transformation still baffles me. The rest I think was:

. . . full of glee, singing merrily, merrily, merrily!

As my memories of the Normal School emerge from haziness and become clearer they are not the least sweet in any particular. Had I been able to associate with the other boys, the woes of learning might not have seemed so intolerable. But that turned out to be impossible—so nasty were most of the boys in their manners and habits. So, in the intervals of the classes, I would go up to the second storey and while away the time sitting near a window overlooking the street. I would count: one year—two years—three years—; wondering how many such would have to be got through like this.

Of the teachers I remember only one, whose language was so foul that, out of sheer contempt for him, I steadily refused to answer any one of his questions. Thus I sat silent throughout the year at the bottom of his class, and while the rest of the class was busy I would be left alone to attempt the solution of many an intricate problem.

One of these, I remember, on which I used to cogitate profoundly, was how to defeat an enemy without having arms. My preoccupation with this question, amidst the hum of the boys reciting their lessons, comes back to me even now. If I could properly train up a number of dogs, tigers and other ferocious beasts, and put a few lines of these on the field of battle, that, I thought, would serve very well as an inspiriting prelude. With our personal prowess let loose thereafter, victory should by no means be out of reach. And, as the picture of this wonderfully simple strategy waxed vivid in my imagination, the victory of my side became assured beyond doubt.

While work had not yet come into my life I always found it easy to devise short cuts to achievement; since I have been working I find that what is hard is hard indeed, and what is difficult remains difficult. This, of course, is less comforting; but nowhere near so bad as the discomfort of trying to take shortcuts.

When at length a year of that class had passed, we were examined in Bengali by Pandit Madhusudan Vachaspati. I got the largest number of marks of all the boys. The teacher complained to the school authorities that there had been favouritism in my case. So I was examined a second time, with the superintendent of the school seated beside the examiner. This time, also, I got a top place.

6

Versification

I could not have been more than eight years old at the time. Jyoti, a son of a niece of my father's, was considerably older than I. He had just gained an entrance into English literature, and would recite Hamlet's soliloquy with great gusto. Why he should have taken it into his head to get a child, as I was, to write poetry I cannot tell. One afternoon he sent for me to his room, and asked me to try and make up a verse; after which he explained to me the construction of the *payar* metre of fourteen syllables.

I had up to then only seen poems in printed books—no mistakes penned through, no sign to the eye of doubt or trouble or any human weakness. I could not have dared even to imagine that any effort of mine could produce such poetry.

One day a thief had been caught in our house. Overpowered by curiosity, yet in fear and trembling, I ventured to the spot to take a peep at him. I found he was just an ordinary man! And when he was somewhat roughly handled by our door-keeper I felt a great pity. I had a similar experience with poetry.

When, after stringing together a few words at my own sweet will, I found them turned into a payar verse I felt I had no illusions left about the glories of poetising. So when poor Poetry is mishandled, even now I feel as unhappy as I did about the thief. Many a time have I been moved to pity and yet been unable to restrain impatient hands itching for the assault. Thieves have scarcely suffered so much, and from so many.

The first feeling of awe once overcome there was no holding me back. I managed to get hold of a blue-paper manuscript book by the favour of one of the officers of our estate. With my own hands I ruled it with pencil lines, at not very regular intervals, and thereon I began to write verses in a large childish scrawl.

Like a young deer which butts here, there and everywhere with its newly sprouting horns, I made myself a nuisance with my budding poetry. More so my elder* brother, whose pride in my performance impelled him to hunt about the house for an audience.

I recollect how, as the pair of us, one day, were coming out of the estate offices on the ground floor, after a conquering expedition against the officers, we came across the editor of *The National Paper*, Nabagopal Mitter, who had just stepped into the house. My brother tackled him without further ado: "Look here, Nabagopal Babu! Won't you listen to a poem which Rabi has written?" The reading forthwith followed.

My works had not as yet become voluminous. The poet could carry all his effusions about in his pockets. I was writer, printer and publisher, all in one; my brother, as advertiser, being my only colleague. I had composed some verses on The Lotus which I recited to Nabagopal Babu then and there, at the foot of the stairs, in a voice pitched as high as my enthusiasm. "Well done!" said he with a smile. "But what is a *dwirepha*?"†

How I had got hold of this word I do not remember. The ordinary name would have fitted the metre quite as well. But this was the one word in the whole poem on which I had pinned my hopes. It had doubtless duly impressed our officers. But curiously enough Nabagopal Babu did not succumb to it—on the contrary he smiled! He could not be an understanding man, I felt sure. I never read poetry to him again. I have since added many years to my age but have not been able to improve upon my test of what does or does not constitute understanding in my hearer. However Nabagopal Babu might smile, the word *dwirepha*, like a bee drunk with honey, stuck to its place, unmoved.

---

* The writer is the youngest of seven brothers. The sixth brother is here meant.
† Obsolete word meaning bee

7

Various Learning

One of the teachers of the Normal School also gave us private lessons at home. His body was lean, his features dry, his voice sharp. He looked like a cane incarnate. His hours were from six to half-past-nine in the morning. With him our reading ranged from popular literary and science readers in Bengali to the epic of Meghnadvadha.

My third brother was very keen on imparting to us a variety of knowledge. So at home we had to go through much more than what was required by the school course. We had to get up before dawn and, clad in loin-cloths, begin with a bout or two with a blind wrestler. Without a pause we donned our tunics on our dusty bodies, and started on our courses of literature, mathematics, geography and history. On our return from school our drawing and gymnastic masters would be ready for us. In the evening Aghore Babu came for our English lessons. It was only after nine that we were free.

On Sunday morning we had singing lessons with Vishnu. Then, almost every Sunday, came Sitanath Dutta to give us demonstrations in physical science. The last were of great interest to me. I remember distinctly the feeling of wonder which filled me when he put some water, with sawdust in it, on the fire in a glass vessel, and showed us how the lightened hot water came up, and the cold water went down and how finally the water began to boil. I also felt a great elation the day I learnt that water is a separable part of milk, and that milk thickens when boiled because the water frees itself as vapour from the connexion. Sunday did not feel Sunday-like unless Sitanath Babu turned up.

There was also an hour when we would be told all about human bones by a pupil of the Campbell Medical School, for which purpose a skeleton, with the bones fastened together by wires was hung up in our schoolroom. And finally, time was also found for Pandit Heramba Tatwaratna to come and get us to learn by rote rules of Sanskrit grammar. I am not sure which of them, the names of the bones or the *sutras* of the grammarian, were the more jaw-breaking. I think the latter took the palm.

We began to learn English after we had made considerable progress in learning through the medium of Bengali. Aghore Babu, our English tutor, was attending the Medical College, so he came to teach us in the evening.

Books tell us that the discovery of fire was one of the biggest discoveries of man. I do not wish to dispute this. But I cannot help feeling how fortunate the little birds are that their parents cannot light lamps of an evening. They have their language lessons early in the morning and you must have noticed how gleefully they learn them. Of course we must not forget that they do not have to learn the English language!

The health of this medical-student tutor of ours was so good that even the fervent and united wishes of his three pupils were not enough to cause his absence even for a day. Only once was he laid up with a broken head when, on the occasion of a fight between the Indian and Eurasian students of the Medical College, a chair was thrown at him. It was a regrettable occurrence; nevertheless we were not able to take it as a personal sorrow, and his recovery somehow seemed to us needlessly swift.

It is evening. The rain is pouring in lance-like showers. Our lane is under knee-deep water. The tank has overflown into the garden, and the bushy tops of the Bael trees are seen standing out over the waters. Our whole being, on this delightful rainy evening, is radiating rapture like the *Kadamba* flower its fragrant spikes. The time for the arrival of our tutor is over by just a few minutes. Yet there is no certainty . . .! We are sitting on the verandah overlooking the lane* watching and watching with a piteous gaze. All of a sudden, with a great big thump, our hearts seem to fall in a swoon. The familiar black umbrella has turned the corner undefeated even by such weather! Could it not be somebody else? It certainly could not! In the wide wide world there might be found another, his equal in pertinacity, but never in this little lane of ours.

Looking back on his period as a whole, I cannot say that Aghore Babu was a hard man. He did not rule us with a rod. Even his

---

* The lane, a blind one, leads, at right angles to the front verandah, from the public main road to the grounds round the house.

rebukes did not amount to scoldings. But whatever may have been his personal merits, his time was *evening*, and his subject *English*! I am certain that even an angel would have seemed a veritable messenger of Yama* to any Bengali boy if he came to him at the end of his miserable day at school, and lighted a dismally dim lamp to teach him English.

How well do I remember the day our tutor tried to impress on us the attractiveness of the English language. With this object he recited to us with great unction some lines—prose or poetry we could not tell—out of an English book. It had a most unlooked for effect on us. We laughed so immoderately that he had to dismiss us for that evening. He must have realised that he held no easy brief—that to get us to pronounce in his favour would entail a contest ranging over years.

Aghore Babu would sometimes try to bring the zephyr of outside knowledge to play on the arid routine of our schoolroom. One day he brought a paper parcel out of his pocket and said: "I'll show you today a wonderful piece of work of the Creator." With this he untied the paper wrapping and, producing a portion of the vocal organs of a human being, proceeded to expound the marvels of its mechanism.

I can still call to mind the shock this gave me at the time. I had always thought the whole man spoke—had never even imagined that the act of speech could be viewed in this detached way. However wonderful the mechanism of a part may be, it is certainly less so than the whole man. Not that I put it to myself in so many words, but that was the cause of my dismay. It was perhaps because the tutor had lost sight of this truth that the pupil could not respond to the enthusiasm with which he was discoursing on the subject.

Another day he took us to the dissecting room of the Medical College. The body of an old woman was stretched on the table. This did not disturb me so much. But an amputated leg which was lying on the floor upset me altogether. To view man in this fragmentary way seemed to me so horrid, so absurd that I could not get rid of the impression of that dark, unmeaning leg for many a day.

---

* God of Death

350

After getting through Peary Sarkar's first and second English readers we entered upon McCulloch's Course of Reading. Our bodies were weary at the end of the day, our minds yearning for the inner apartments, the book was black and thick with difficult words, and the subject-matter could hardly have been more inviting, for in those days, Mother Saraswati's* maternal tenderness was not in evidence. Children's books were not full of pictures then as they are now. Moreover, at the gateway of every reading lesson stood sentinel an array of words, with separated syllables, and forbidding accent marks like fixed bayonets, barring the way to the infant mind. I had repeatedly attacked their serried ranks in vain.

Our tutor would try to shame us by recounting the exploits of some other brilliant pupil of his. We felt duly ashamed, and also not well-disposed towards that other pupil, but this did not help to dispel the darkness which clung to that black volume.

Providence, out of pity for mankind, has instilled a soporific charm into all tedious things. No sooner did our English lessons begin than our heads began to nod. Sprinkling water into our eyes, or taking a run round the verandahs, were palliatives which had no lasting effect. If by any chance my eldest brother happened to be passing that way, and caught a glimpse of our sleep-tormented condition, we would get let off for the rest of the evening. It did not take our drowsiness another moment to get completely cured.

8

My First Outing

Once, when the dengue fever was raging in Calcutta, some portion of our extensive family had to take shelter in Chhatu Babu's riverside villa. We were among them.

This was my first outing. The bank of the Ganges welcomed me into its lap like a friend of a former birth. There, in front of the servants' quarters, was a grove of guava trees; and, sitting in the

---

* Goddess of Learning

verandah under the shade of these, gazing at the flowing current through the gaps between their trunks, my days would pass. Every morning, as I awoke, I somehow felt the day coming to me like a new gilt-edged letter, with some unheard-of news awaiting me on the opening of the envelope. And, lest I should lose any fragment of it, I would hurry through my toilet to my chair outside. Every day there was the ebb and flow of the tide on the Ganges; the various gait of so many different boats; the shifting of the shadows of the trees from west to east; and, over the fringe of shade-patches of the woods on the opposite bank, the gush of golden life-blood through the pierced breast of the evening sky. Some days would be cloudy from early morning; the opposite woods black; black shadows moving over the river. Then with a rush would come the vociferous rain, blotting out the horizon; the dim line of the other bank taking its leave in tears: the river swelling with suppressed heavings; and the moist wind making free with the foliage of the trees overhead.

I felt that out of the bowels of wall, beam and rafter, I had a new birth into the outside. In making fresh acquaintance with things, the dingy covering of petty habits seemed to drop off the world. I am sure that the sugar-cane molasses, which I had with cold luchis for my breakfast, could not have tasted different from the ambrosia which *Indra** quaffs in his heaven; for, the immortality is not in the nectar but in the taster, and thus is missed by those who seek it.

Behind the house was a walled-in enclosure with a tank and a flight of steps leading into the water from a bathing platform. On one side of the platform was an immense Jambolan tree, and all round were various fruit trees, growing in thick clusters, in the shade of which the tank nestled in its privacy. The veiled beauty of this retired little inner garden had a wonderful charm for me, so different from the broad expanse of the riverbank in front. It was like the bride of the house, in the seclusion of her midday siesta, resting on a many-coloured quilt of her own embroidering, murmuring low the secrets of her heart. Many a midday hour did

---

* The Jupiter Pluvius of Hindu Mythology

I spend alone under that Jambolan tree dreaming of the fearsome kingdom of the Yakshas* within the depths of the tank.

I had a great curiosity to see a Bengal village. Its clusters of cottages, its thatched pavilions, its lanes and bathing places, its games and gatherings, its fields and markets, its life as a whole as I saw it in imagination, greatly attracted me. Just such a village was right on the other side of our garden wall, but it was forbidden to us. We had come out, but not into freedom. We had been in a cage, and were now on a perch, but the chain was still there.

One morning two of our elders went out for a stroll into the village. I could not restrain my eagerness any longer, and, slipping out unperceived, followed them for some distance. As I went along the deeply shaded lane, with its close thorny *seora* hedges, by the side of the tank covered with green water weeds, I rapturously took in picture after picture. I still remember the man with bare body, engaged in a belated toilet on the edge of the tank, cleaning his teeth with the chewed end of a twig. Suddenly my elders became aware of my presence behind them. "Get away, get away, go back at once!" they scolded. They were scandalised. My feet were bare, I had no scarf or upper-robe over my tunic, I was not dressed fit to come out; as if it was my fault! I never owned any socks or superfluous apparel, so not only went back disappointed for that morning, but had no chance of repairing my shortcomings and being allowed to come out any other day. However though the Beyond was thus shut out from behind, in front the Ganges freed me from all bondage, and my mind, whenever it listed, could embark on the boats gaily sailing along, and hie away to lands not named in any geography.

This was forty years ago. Since then I have never set foot again in that champak-shaded villa garden. The same old house and the same old trees must still be there, but I know it cannot any longer be the same—for where am I now to get that fresh feeling of wonder which made it what it was?

We returned to our Jorasanko house in town. And my days were as so many mouthfuls offered up to be gulped down into the yawning interior of the Normal School.

---

* The King of the Yakshas is the Pluto of Hindu Mythology.

9
Practising Poetry

That blue manuscript book was soon filled, like the hive of some insect, with a network of variously slanting lines and the thick and thin strokes of letters. The eager pressure of the boy writer soon crumpled its leaves; and then the edges got frayed, and twisted up claw-like as if to hold fast the writing within, till at last, down what river *Baitarani** I know not, its pages were swept away by merciful oblivion. Anyhow they escaped the pangs of a passage through the printing press and need fear no birth into this vale of woe.

I cannot claim to have been a passive witness of the spread of my reputation as a poet. Though Satkari Babu was not a teacher of our class he was very fond of me. He had written a book on Natural History—wherein I hope no unkind humorist will try to find a reason for such fondness. He sent for me one day and asked: "So you write poetry, do you?" I did not conceal the fact. From that time on, he would now and then ask me to complete a quatrain by adding a couplet of my own to one given by him.

Gobinda Babu of our school was very dark, and short and fat. He was the Superintendent. He sat, in his black suit, with his account books, in an office room on the second storey. We were all afraid of him, for he was the rod-bearing judge. On one occasion I had escaped from the attentions of some bullies into his room. The persecutors were five or six older boys. I had no one to bear witness on my side—except my tears. I won my case and since then Govinda Babu had a soft corner in his heart for me.

One day he called me into his room during the recess. I went in fear and trembling but had no sooner stepped before him than he also accosted me with the question: "So you write poetry?" I did not hesitate to make the admission. He commissioned me to write a poem on some high moral precept which I do not remember. The amount of condescension and affability which such a request

---

* Corresponding to Lethe

coming from him implied can only be appreciated by those who were his pupils. When I finished and handed him the verses next day, he took me to the highest class and made me stand before the boys. "Recite," he commanded. And I recited loudly.

The only praiseworthy thing about this moral poem was that it soon got lost. Its moral effect on that class was far from encouraging—the sentiment it aroused being not one of regard for its author. Most of them were certain that it was not my own composition. One said he could produce the book from which it was copied, but was not pressed to do so; the process of proving is such a nuisance to those who want to believe. Finally the number of seekers after poetic fame began to increase alarmingly; moreover their methods were not those which are recognised as roads to moral improvement.

Nowadays there is nothing strange in a youngster writing verses. The glamour of poesy is gone. I remember how the few women who wrote poetry in those days were looked upon as miraculous creations of the Deity. If one hears today that some young lady does not write poems one feels sceptical. Poetry now sprouts long before the highest Bengali class is reached; so that no modern Gobinda Babu would have taken any notice of the poetic exploit I have recounted.

PART III

❧

10
Srikantha Babu

At this time I was blessed with a hearer the like of whom I shall never get again. He had so inordinate a capacity for being pleased as to have utterly disqualified him for the post of critic in any of our monthly Reviews. The old man was like a perfectly ripe Alfonso mango—not a trace of acid or coarse fibre in his composition. His tender clean-shaven face was rounded off by an all-pervading baldness; there was not the vestige of a tooth to worry the inside of his mouth; and his big smiling eyes gleamed with a constant delight. When he spoke in his soft deep voice, his mouth and eyes and hands all spoke likewise. He was of the old school of Persian culture and knew not a word of English. His inseparable companions were a hubble-bubble at his left, and a sitar on his lap; and from his throat flowed song unceasing.

Srikantha Babu had no need to wait for a formal introduction, for none could resist the natural claims of his genial heart. Once he took us to be photographed with him in some big English photographic studio. There he so captivated the proprietor with his artless story, in a jumble of Hindusthani and Bengali, of how he was a poor man, but badly wanted this particular photograph taken, that the man smilingly allowed him a reduced rate. Nor did such bargaining sound at all incongruous in that unbending English establishment, so naïve was Srikantha Babu, so unconscious of any possibility of giving offence. He would sometimes take me along to a European missionary's house. There, also, with his playing and singing, his caresses of the missionary's little girl and his unstinted admiration of the little booted feet of the missionary's lady, he would enliven the gathering as no one else could have done. Another behaving so absurdly would have been deemed a bore, but his transparent simplicity pleased all and drew them to join in his gaiety.

Srikantha Babu was impervious to rudeness or insolence. There was at the time a singer of some repute retained in our establishment. When the latter was the worse for liquor he would rail at poor Srikantha Babu's singing in no very choice terms. This he would bear unflinchingly, with no attempt at retort. When at last the man's incorrigible rudeness brought about his dismissal Srikantha Babu anxiously interceded for him. "It was not he, it was the liquor," he insisted.

The Ganges

He could not bear to see anyone sorrowing or even to hear of it. So when any one of the boys wanted to torment him they had only to read out passages from Vidyasagar's *Banishment of Sita*; whereat he would be greatly exercised, thrusting out his hands in protest and begging and praying of them to stop.

This old man was the friend alike of my father, my elder brothers and ourselves. He was of an age with each and every one of us. As any piece of stone is good enough for the freshet to dance round and gambol with, so the least provocation would suffice to make him beside himself with joy. Once I had composed a hymn, and had not failed to make due allusion to the trials and tribulations of this world. Srikantha Babu was convinced that my father would be overjoyed at such a perfect gem of a devotional poem. With unbounded enthusiasm he volunteered personally to acquaint him with it. By a piece of good fortune I was not there at the time but heard afterwards that my father was hugely amused that the sorrows of the world should have so early moved his youngest son to the point of versification. I am sure Gobinda Babu, the superintendent, would have shown more respect for my effort on so serious a subject.

In singing I was Srikantha Babu's favourite pupil. He had taught me a song: "No more of Vraja* for me," and would drag me about to everyone's rooms and get me to sing it to them. I would sing and he would thrum an accompaniment on his sitar and when we came to the chorus he would join in, and repeat it over and over again, smiling and nodding his head at each one in turn, as if nudging them on to a more enthusiastic appreciation.

He was a devoted admirer of my father. A hymn had been set to one of his tunes, "For He is the heart of our hearts." When he sang this to my father Srikantha Babu got so excited that he jumped up from his seat and in alternation violently twanged his sitar as he sang: "For He is the heart of our hearts" and then waved his hand about my father's face as he changed the words to "For *you* are the heart of our hearts."

When the old man paid his last visit to my father, the latter, himself bed-ridden, was at a riverside villa in Chinsurah. Srikantha

---

* Krishna's playground

Babu, stricken with his last illness, could not rise unaided and had to push open his eyelids to see. In this state, tended by his daughter, he journeyed to Chinsurah from his place in Birbhoom. With a great effort he managed to take the dust of my father's feet and then return to his lodgings in Chinsurah where he breathed his last a few days later. I heard afterwards from his daughter that he went to his eternal youth with the song "How sweet is thy mercy, Lord!" on his lips.

11

Our Bengali Course Ends

At School we were then in the class below the highest one. At home we had advanced in Bengali much further than the subjects taught in the class. We had been through Akshay Datta's book on Popular Physics, and had also finished the epic of Meghnadvadha. We read our physics without any reference to physical objects and so our knowledge of the subject was correspondingly bookish. In fact the time spent on it had been thoroughly wasted; much more so to my mind than if it had been wasted in doing nothing. The Meghnadvadha, also, was not a thing of joy to us. The tastiest tit-bit may not be relished when thrown at one's head. To employ an epic to teach language is like using a sword to shave with—sad for the sword, bad for the chin. A poem should be taught from the emotional standpoint; inveigling it into service as grammar-cum-dictionary is not calculated to propitiate the divine Saraswati.

All of a sudden our Normal School career came to an end; and thereby hangs a tale. One of our school teachers wanted to borrow a copy of my grandfather's life by Mitra from our library. My nephew and classmate Satya managed to screw up courage enough to volunteer to mention this to my father. He came to the conclusion that everyday Bengali would hardly do to approach him with. So he concocted and delivered himself of an archaic phrase with such meticulous precision that my father must have felt our study of the Bengali language had gone a bit too far and was in danger of over-reaching itself. So the next morning, when according to our wont our table had been placed in the south verandah, the blackboard hung up on a nail in the wall, and everything was in readiness for our lessons with Nilkamal Babu, we three were sent for by my father to his room upstairs. "You need not do any more Bengali lessons," he said. Our minds danced for very joy.

Nilkamal Babu was waiting downstairs, our books were lying open on the table, and the idea of getting us once more to go through the Meghnadvadha doubtless still occupied his mind. But as on one's deathbed the various routine of daily life seems unreal, so, in a moment, did everything, from the Pandit down to the nail on which the blackboard was hung, become for us as empty as a mirage. Our sole trouble was how to give this news to Nilkamal Babu with due decorum. We did it at last with considerable restraint, while the geometrical figures on the blackboard stared at us in wonder and the blank verse of the Meghnadvadha looked blankly on.

Our Pandit's parting words were: "At the call of duty I may have been sometimes harsh with you—do not keep that in remembrance. You will learn the value of what I have taught you later on."

Indeed I have learnt that value. It was because we were taught in our own language that our minds quickened. Learning should as far as possible follow the process of eating. When the taste begins from the first bite, the stomach is awakened to its function before it is loaded, so that its digestive juices get full play. Nothing like this happens, however, when the Bengali boy is taught in English. The first bite bids fair to wrench loose both rows of teeth—like a veritable earthquake in the mouth! And by the time he discovers that the morsel is not of the genus stone, but a digestible bonbon, half his allotted span of life is over. While one is choking and spluttering over the spelling and grammar, the inside remains starved, and when at length the taste is felt, the appetite has vanished. If the whole mind does not work from the beginning its full powers remain undeveloped to the end. While all around was the cry for English teaching, my third brother was brave enough to keep us to our Bengali course. To him in heaven my grateful reverence.

12

The Professor

On leaving the Normal School we were sent to the Bengal Academy, a Eurasian institution. We felt we had gained an access of dignity, that we had grown up—at least into the first storey of freedom. In point of fact the only progress we made in that academy was towards freedom. What we were taught there we never understood, nor did we make any attempt to learn, nor did it seem to make any difference to anybody that we did not. The boys here were annoying but not disgusting—which was a great comfort. They wrote ASS on their palms and slapped it on to our backs with a cordial "hello!" They gave us a dig in the ribs from behind and looked innocently another way. They dabbed banana pulp on our heads and made away unperceived. Nevertheless it was like coming out of slime on to rock—we were worried but not soiled.

This school had one great advantage for me. No one there cherished the forlorn hope that boys of our sort could make any advance in learning. It was a petty institution with an insufficient income, so that we had one supreme merit in the eyes of its authorities—we paid our fees regularly. This prevented even the Latin Grammar from proving a stumbling block, and the most egregious of blunders left our backs unscathed. Pity for us had nothing to do with it—the school authorities had spoken to the teachers!

Still, harmless though it was, after all it was a school. The rooms were cruelly dismal with their walls on guard like policemen. The house was more like a pigeon-holed box than a human habitation. No decoration, no pictures, not a touch of colour, not an attempt to attract the boyish heart. The fact that likes and dislikes form a large part of the child mind was completely ignored. Naturally our whole being was depressed as we stepped through its doorway into the narrow quadrangle—and playing truant became chronic with us.

In this we found an accomplice. My elder brothers had a Persian tutor. We used to call him Munshi. He was of middle age and all skin and bone, as though dark parchment had been stretched over his skeleton without any filling of flesh and blood. He probably knew Persian well, his knowledge of English was quite fair, but in neither of these directions lay his ambition. His belief was that his proficiency in singlestick was matched only by his skill in song. He would stand in the sun in the middle of our courtyard and go through a wonderful series of antics with a staff—his own shadow being his antagonist. I need hardly add that his shadow never got the better of him and when at the end he gave a great big shout and whacked it on the head with a victorious smile, it lay submissively prone at his feet. His singing, nasal and out of tune, sounded like a gruesome mixture of groaning and moaning coming from some ghost-world. Our singing master Vishnu would sometimes chaff him: "Look here, Munshi, you'll be taking the bread out of our mouths at this rate!" To which his only reply would be a disdainful smile.

This shows that the Munshi was amenable to soft words; and in fact, whenever we wanted we could persuade him to write to the school authorities to excuse us from attendance. The school authorities took no pains to scrutinise these letters, they knew it would be all the same whether we attended or not, so far as educational results were concerned.

I have now a school of my own in which the boys are up to all kinds of mischief, for boys will be mischievous—and schoolmasters unforgiving. When any of us are beset with undue uneasiness at their conduct and are stirred into a resolution to deal out condign punishment, the misdeeds of my own schooldays confront me in a row and smile at me.

I now clearly see that the mistake is to judge boys by the standard of grown-ups, to forget that a child is quick and mobile like a running stream; and that, in the case of such, any touch of imperfection need cause no great alarm, for the speed of the flow is itself the best corrective. When stagnation sets in then comes the danger. So it is for the teacher, more than the pupil, to beware of wrongdoing.

There was a separate refreshment room for Bengali boys for meeting their caste requirements. This was where we struck up a friendship with some of the others. They were all older than we. One of these will bear to be dilated upon.

His specialty was the art of Magic, so much so that he had

actually written and published a little booklet on it, the front page of which bore his name with the title of Professor. I had never before come across a schoolboy whose name had appeared in print, so that my reverence for him—as a professor of magic I mean—was profound. How could I have brought myself to believe that anything questionable could possibly find place in the straight and upright ranks of printed letters? To be able to record one's own words in indelible ink—was that a slight thing? To stand unscreened yet unabashed, self-confessed before the world—how could one withhold belief in the face of such supreme self-confidence? I remember how once I got the types for the letters of my name from some printing press, and what a memorable thing it seemed when I inked and pressed them on paper and found my name imprinted.

We used to give a lift in our carriage to this schoolfellow and author-friend of ours. This led to visiting terms. He was also great at theatricals. With his help we erected a stage on our wrestling ground with painted paper stretched over a split bamboo framework. But a peremptory negative from upstairs prevented any play from being acted thereon.

A comedy of errors was however played later on without any stage at all. The author of this has already been introduced to the reader in these pages. He was none other than my nephew Satya. Those who behold his present calm and sedate demeanour would be shocked to learn of the tricks of which he was the originator.

Satya

The event of which I am writing happened sometime afterwards when I was twelve or thirteen. Our magician friend had told of so many strange properties of things that I was consumed with curiosity to see them for myself. But the materials of which he spoke were invariably so rare or distant that one could hardly hope to get hold of them without the help of Sindbad the sailor. Once, as it happened, the Professor forgot himself so far as to mention accessible things. Who could ever believe that a seed dipped and dried twenty-one times in the juice of a species of cactus would sprout and flower and fruit all in the space of an hour? I was determined to test this, not daring withal to doubt the assurance of a Professor whose name appeared in a printed book.

I got our gardener to furnish me with a plentiful supply of the milky juice, and betook myself, on a Sunday afternoon, to our mystic nook in a corner of the roof terrace, to experiment with the stone of a mango. I was wrapt in my task of dipping and drying—but the grown-up reader will probably not wait to ask me the result. In the meantime, I little knew that Satya, in another corner, had, in the space of an hour, caused to root and sprout a mystical plant of his own creation. This was to bear curious fruit later on.

After the day of this experiment the Professor rather avoided me, as I gradually came to perceive. He would not sit on the same side in the carriage, and altogether seemed to fight shy of me.

One day, all of a sudden, he proposed that each one in turn should jump off the bench in our schoolroom. He wanted to observe the differences in style, he said. Such scientific curiosity did not appear queer in a professor of magic. Everyone jumped, so did I. He shook his head with a subdued "h'm." No amount of persuasion could draw anything further out of him.

Another day he informed us that some good friends of his wanted to make our acquaintance and asked us to accompany him to their house. Our guardians had no objection, so off we went. The crowd in the room seemed full of curiosity. They expressed their eagerness to hear me sing. I sang a song or two. Mere child as I was I could hardly have bellowed like a bull. "Quite a sweet voice," they all agreed.

When refreshments were put before us they sat round and watched us eat. I was bashful by nature and not used to strange company; moreover the habit I acquired during the attendance of our servant Iswar left me a poor eater for good. They all seemed impressed with the delicacy of my appetite.

In the fifth act I got some curiously warm letters from our Professor which revealed the whole situation. And here let the curtain fall.

I subsequently learnt from Satya that while I had been practising magic on the mango seed, he had successfully convinced the Professor that I was dressed as a boy by our guardians merely for getting me a better schooling, but that really this was only a disguise. To those who are curious in regard to imaginary science I should explain that a girl is supposed to jump with her left foot forward, and this is what I had done on the occasion of the Professor's trial. I little realised at the time what a tremendously false step mine had been!

13

My Father

Shortly after my birth my father took to constantly travelling about. So it is no exaggeration to say that in my early childhood I hardly knew him. He would now and then come back home all of a sudden, and with him came foreign servants with whom I felt extremely eager to make friends. Once there came in this way a young Panjabi servant named Lenu. The cordiality of the reception he got from us would have been worthy of Ranjit Singh himself. Not only was he a foreigner, but a Panjabi to boot—what wonder he stole our hearts away?

We had the same reverence for the whole Panjabi nation as for Bhima and Arjuna of the Mahabharata. They were warriors; and if they had sometimes fought and lost, that was clearly the enemy's fault. It was glorious to have Lenu, of the Panjab, in our very home.

My sister-in-law had a model warship under a glass case, which, when wound up, rocked on blue-painted silken waves to the tinkling of a musical box. I would beg hard for the loan of this to display its marvels to the admiring Lenu.

Caged in the house as we were, anything savouring of foreign parts had a peculiar charm for me. This was one of the reasons why I made so much of Lenu. This was also the reason why Gabriel, the Jew, with his embroidered gaberdine, who came to sell *attars* and scented oils, stirred me so; and the huge Kabulis, with their dusty, baggy trousers and knapsacks and bundles, wrought on my young mind a fearful fascination.

Anyhow, when my father came, we would be content with wandering round about his entourage and in the company of his servants. We did not reach his immediate presence.

Once while my father was away in the Himalayas, that old bogey of the British Government, the Russian invasion, came to be a subject of agitated conversation among the people. Some well-meaning lady friend had enlarged on the impending danger to my mother with all the circumstance of a prolific imagination. How could a body tell from which of the Tibetan passes the Russian host might suddenly flash forth like a baleful comet?

My mother was seriously alarmed. Possibly the other members of the family did not share her misgivings; so, despairing of grown-up sympathy, she sought my boyish support. "Won't you write to your father about the Russians?" she asked.

That letter, carrying the tidings of my mother's anxieties, was my first one to my father. I did not know how to begin or end a letter, or anything at all about it. I went to Mahananda, the estate munshi.* The resulting style of address was doubtless correct enough, but the sentiments could not have escaped the musty flavour inseparable from literature emanating from an estate office.

I got a reply to my letter. My father asked me not to be afraid; if the Russians came he would drive them away himself. This confident assurance did not seem to have the effect of relieving my mother's fears, but it served to free me from all timidity as regards my father. After that I wanted to write to him every day and pestered Mahananda accordingly. Unable to withstand my importunity he would make out drafts for me to copy. But I did not know that there was the postage to be paid for. I had an idea that letters placed in

---

* Correspondence clerk

Mahananda's hands got to their destination without any need for further worry. It is hardly necessary to mention that, Mahananda being considerably older than myself, these letters never reached the Himalayan hill-tops.

When, after his long absences, my father came home even for a few days, the whole house seemed filled with the weight of his presence. We would see our elders at certain hours, formally robed in their *chogas*, passing to his rooms with restrained gait and sobered mien, casting away any paan they might have been chewing. Everyone seemed on the alert. To make sure of nothing going wrong, my mother would superintend the cooking herself. The old mace-bearer, Kinu, with his white livery and crested turban, on guard at my father's door, would warn us not to be boisterous in the verandah in front of his rooms during his midday siesta. We had to walk past quietly, talking in whispers, and dared not even take a peep inside.

On one occasion my father came home to invest the three of us with the sacred thread. With the help of Pandit Vedantavagish he had collected the old Vedic rites for the purpose. For days together we were taught to chant in correct accents the selections from the Upanishads, arranged by my father under the name of 'Brahma Dharma,' seated in the prayer hall with Becharam Babu. Finally, with shaven heads and gold rings in our ears, we three budding Brahmins went into a three-days' retreat in a portion of the third storey.

It was great fun. The earrings gave us a good handle to pull each other's ears with. We found a little drum lying in one of the rooms; taking this we would stand out in the verandah, and, when we caught sight of any servant passing alone in the storey below, we would rap a tattoo on it. This would make the man look up, only to beat a hasty retreat the next moment with averted eyes.* In short we cannot claim that these days of our retirement were passed in ascetic meditation.

I am however persuaded that boys like ourselves could not have been rare in the hermitages of old. And if some ancient document

---

* It is considered sinful for non-brahmins to cast glances on neophytes during the process of their sacred-thread investiture, before the ceremony is complete.

has it that the ten or twelve-year old Saradwata or Sarngarava* is spending the whole of the days of his boyhood offering oblations and chanting mantras, we are not compelled to put unquestioning faith in the statement; because the book of Boy Nature is even older and also more authentic.

After we had attained full brahminhood I became very keen on repeating the *gayatri.*† I would meditate on it with great concentration. It is hardly a text the full meaning of which I could have grasped at that age. I well remember what efforts I made to extend the range of my consciousness with the help of the initial invocation of "Earth, firmament and heaven." How I felt or thought it is difficult to express clearly, but this much is certain that to be clear about the meaning of words is not the most important function of the human understanding.

The main object of teaching is not to explain meanings, but to knock at the door of the mind. If any boy is asked to give an account of what is awakened in him at such knocking, he will probably say something very silly. For what happens within is much bigger than what he can express in words. Those who pin their faith on University examinations as a test of all educational results take no account of this fact.

I can recollect many things which I did not understand, but which stirred me deeply. Once, on the roof terrace of our riverside villa, my eldest brother, at the sudden gathering of clouds, repeated aloud some stanzas from Kalidas's 'Cloud Messenger.' I could not, nor had I the need to, understand a word of the Sanskrit. His ecstatic declamation of the sonorous rhythm was enough for me.

Then, again, before I could properly understand English, a profusely illustrated edition of *The Old Curiosity Shop* fell into my hands. I went through the whole of it, though at least nine-tenths of the words were unknown to me. Yet, with the vague ideas I conjured up from the rest, I spun out a variously coloured thread on which to string the illustrations. Any university examiner would have given

---

* Two novices in the hermitage of the sage Kanva, mentioned in the Sanskrit drama, Sakuntala.
† The text for self-realisation.

me a great big zero, but the reading of the book had not proved for me quite so empty as all that.

Another time I had accompanied my father on a trip on the Ganges in his houseboat. Among the books he had with him was an old Fort William edition of Jayadeva's *Gita Govinda*. It was in the Bengali character. The verses were not printed in separate lines, but ran on like prose. I did not then know anything of Sanskrit, yet because of my knowledge of Bengali many of the words were familiar. I cannot tell how often I read that *Gita Govinda*. I can well remember this line:

The night that was passed in the lonely forest cottage.

It spread an atmosphere of vague beauty over my mind. That one Sanskrit word, Nibhrita-nikunja-griham, meaning 'the lonely forest cottage' was quite enough for me.

I had to discover for myself the intricate metre of Jayadeva, because its divisions were lost in the clumsy prose form of the book. And this discovery gave me very great delight. Of course I did not fully comprehend Jayadeva's meaning. It would hardly be correct to aver that I had got it even partly. But the sound of the words and the lilt of the metre filled my mind with pictures of wonderful beauty, which impelled me to copy out the whole of the book for my own use.

The same thing happened, when I was a little older, with a verse from Kalidas's *Birth of the War-God*. The verse moved me greatly, though the only words of which I gathered the sense, were 'the breeze carrying the spray-mist of the falling waters of the sacred Mandakini and shaking the deodar leaves.' These left me pining to taste the beauties of the whole. When, later, a Pandit explained to me that in the next two lines the breeze went on 'splitting the feathers of the peacock plume on the head of the eager deer-hunter,' the thinness of this last conceit disappointed me. I was much better off when I had relied only upon my imagination to complete the verse.

Whoever goes back to his early childhood will agree that his greatest gains were not in proportion to the completeness of his understanding. Our *Kathakas** I know this truth well. So their

* Bards or reciters

narratives always have a good proportion of ear-filling Sanskrit words and abstruse remarks not calculated to be fully understood by their simple hearers, but only to be suggestive.

The value of such suggestion is by no means to be despised by those who measure education in terms of material gains and losses. These insist on trying to sum up the account and find out exactly how much of the lesson imparted can be rendered up. But children, and those who are not over-educated, dwell in that primal paradise where men can come to know without fully comprehending each step. And only when that paradise is lost comes the evil day when everything needs must be understood. The road which leads to knowledge, without going through the dreary process of understanding, that is the royal road. If that be barred, though the world's marketing may yet go on as usual, the open sea and the mountain top cease to be possible of access.

So, as I was saying, though at that age I could not realise the full meaning of the *Gayatri*, there was something in me which could do without a complete understanding. I am reminded of a day when, as I was seated on the cement floor in a corner of our schoolroom meditating on the text, my eyes overflowed with tears. Why those tears came I knew not; and to a strict cross-questioner I would probably have given some explanation having nothing to do with the *Gayatri*. The fact of the matter is that what is going on in the inner recesses of consciousness is not always known to the dweller on the surface.

14

A Journey with my Father

My shaven head after the sacred thread ceremony caused me one great anxiety. However partial Eurasian lads may be to things appertaining to the Cow, their reverence for the Brahmin* is notoriously lacking. So that, apart from other missiles, our shaven

---

* The Cow and the Brahmin are watchwords of modern Hindu Orthodoxy.

heads were sure to be pelted with jeers. While I was worrying over this possibility I was one day summoned upstairs to my father. How would I like to go with him to the Himalayas, I was asked. Away from the Bengal Academy and off to the Himalayas! Would I like it? O that I could have rent the skies with a shout, that might have given some idea of the How!

On the day of our leaving home my father, as was his habit, assembled the whole family in the prayer hall for divine service. After I had taken the dust of the feet of my elders I got into the carriage with my father. This was the first time in my life that I had a full suit of clothes made for me. My father himself had selected the pattern and colour. A gold embroidered velvet cap completed my costume. This I carried in my hand, being assailed with misgivings as to its effect in juxtaposition to my hairless head. As I got into the carriage my father insisted on my wearing it, so I had to put it on. Every time he looked another way I took it off. Every time I caught his eye it had to resume its proper place.

My father was very particular in all his arrangements and orderings. He disliked leaving things vague or undetermined and never allowed slovenliness or makeshifts. He had a well-defined code to regulate his relations with others and theirs with him. In this he was different from the generality of his countrymen. With the rest of us a little carelessness this way or that did not signify; so in our dealings with him we had to be anxiously careful. It was not so much the little less or more that he objected to as the failure to be up to the standard.

My father had also a way of picturing to himself every detail of what he wanted done. On the occasion of any ceremonial gathering, at which he could not be present, he would think out and assign the place for each thing, the duty for each member of the family, the seat for each guest; nothing would escape him. After it was all over he would ask each one for a separate account and thus gain a complete impression of the whole for himself. So, while I was with him on his travels, though nothing would induce him to put obstacles in the way of my amusing myself as I pleased, he left no loophole in the strict rules of conduct which he prescribed for me in other respects.

Our first halt was to be for a few days at Bolpur. Satya had been there a short time before with his parents. No self-respecting nineteenth century infant would have credited the account of his travels which he gave us on his return. But we were different, and had had no opportunity of learning to determine the line between the possible and the impossible. Our Mahabharata and Ramayana gave us no clue to it. Nor had we then any children's illustrated books to guide us in the way a child should go. All the hard and fast laws which govern the world we learnt by knocking up against them.

Satya had told us that, unless one was very very expert, getting into a railway carriage was a terribly dangerous affair—the least slip, and it was all up. Then, again, a fellow had to hold on to his seat with all his might, otherwise the jolt at starting was so tremendous there was no telling where one would get thrown off to. So when we got to the railway station I was all a-quiver. So easily did we get into our compartment, however, that I felt sure the worst was yet to come. And when, at length, we made an absurdly smooth start, without any semblance of adventure, I felt woefully disappointed.

The train sped on; the broad fields with their blue-green border trees, and the villages nestling in their shade flew past in a stream of pictures which melted away like a flood of mirages. It was evening when we reached Bolpur. As I got into the palanquin I closed my eyes. I wanted to preserve the whole of the wonderful vision to be unfolded before my waking eyes in the morning light. The freshness of the experience would be spoilt, I feared, by incomplete glimpses caught in the vagueness of the dusk.

When I woke at dawn my heart was thrilling tremulously as I stepped outside. My predecessor had told me that Bolpur had one feature which was to be found nowhere else in the world. This was the path leading from the main buildings to the servants' quarters which, though not covered over in any way, did not allow a ray of the sun or a drop of rain to touch anybody passing along it. I started to hunt for this wonderful path, but the reader will perhaps not wonder at my failure to find it to this day.

Town bred as I was, I had never seen a rice-field, and I had a charming portrait of the cowherd boy, of whom we had read, pictured on the canvas of my imagination. I had heard from Satya that the Bolpur house was surrounded by fields of ripening rice, and that playing in these with cowherd boys was an everyday affair, of which the plucking, cooking and eating of the rice was the crowning feature. I eagerly looked about me. But where, oh, where was the rice-field on all that barren heath? Cowherd boys there might have been somewhere about, yet how to distinguish them from any other boys, that was the question!

However it did not take me long to get over what I could not see—what I did see was quite enough. There was no servant rule here, and the only ring which encircled me was the blue of the horizon which the presiding goddess of these solitudes had drawn round them. Within this I was free to move about as I chose.

Though I was yet a mere child my father did not place any restriction on my wanderings. In the hollows of the sandy soil the rainwater had ploughed deep furrows, carving out miniature mountain ranges full of red gravel and pebbles of various shapes through which ran tiny streams, revealing the geography of Lilliput. From this region I would gather in the lap of my tunic many curious pieces of stone and take the collection to my father. He never made light of my labours. On the contrary he waxed enthusiastic.

"How wonderful!" he exclaimed. "Wherever did you get all these?"

"There are many many more, thousands and thousands!" I burst out. "I could bring as many every day."

"That *would* be nice!" he replied. "Why not decorate my little hill with them?"

An attempt had been made to dig a tank in the garden, but the subsoil water proving too low, it had been abandoned, unfinished, with the excavated earth left piled up into a hillock. On the top of this height my father used to sit for his morning prayer, and as he sat the sun would rise at the edge of the undulating expanse which stretched away to the eastern horizon in front of him. This was the hill he asked me to decorate.

I was very troubled, on leaving Bolpur, that I could not carry away with me my store of stones. It is still difficult for me to realise that I have no absolute claim to keep up a close relationship with things, merely because I have gathered them together. If my fate had granted me the prayer, which I had pressed with such insistence, and undertaken that I should carry this load of stones about with me for ever, then I should scarcely have had the hardihood to laugh at it today.

In one of the ravines I came upon a hollow full of spring water which overflowed as a little rivulet, where sported tiny fish battling their way up the current.

"I've found such a lovely spring," I told my father. "Couldn't we get our bathing and drinking water from there?"

"The very thing," he agreed, sharing my rapture, and gave orders for our water supply to be drawn from that spring.

I was never tired of roaming about among those miniature hills and dales in hopes of lighting on something never known before. I was the Livingstone of this undiscovered land which looked as if seen through the wrong end of a telescope. Everything there, the dwarf date palms, the scrubby wild plums and the stunted jambolans, was in keeping with the miniature mountain ranges, the little rivulet and the tiny fish I had discovered.

Singing to My Father

Probably in order to teach me to be careful my father placed a little small change in my charge and required me to keep an account of it. He also entrusted me with the duty of winding his valuable gold watch for him. He overlooked the risk of damage in his desire to train me to a sense of responsibility. When we went out together for our morning walk he would ask me to give alms to any beggars we came across. But I never could render him a proper account at the end of it. One day my balance was larger than the account warranted.

"I really must make you my cashier," observed my father. "Money seems to have a way of growing in your hands!"

That watch of his I wound up with such indefatigable zeal that it had very soon to be sent to the watchmaker's in Calcutta.

I am reminded of the time when, later in life, I was appointed to manage the estate and had to lay before my father, owing to his failing eyesight, a statement of accounts on the second or third of every month. I had first to read out the totals under each head, and if he had any doubts on any point he would ask for the details. If I made any attempt to slur over or keep out of sight any item which I feared he would not like, it was sure to come out. So these first few days of the month were very anxious ones for me.

As I have said, my father had the habit of keeping everything clearly before his mind—whether figures of accounts, or ceremonial arrangements, or additions or alterations to property. He had never seen the new prayer hall built at Bolpur, and yet he was familiar with every detail of it from questioning those who came to see him after a visit to Bolpur. He had an extraordinary memory, and when once he got hold of a fact it never escaped him.

My father had marked his favourite verses in his copy of the Bhagavad Gita. He asked me to copy these out, with their translation, for him. At home, I had been a boy of no account, but here, when these important functions were entrusted to me, I felt the glory of the situation.

By this time I was rid of my blue manuscript book and had got hold of a bound volume of one of Lett's diaries. I now saw to it that my poetising should not lack any of the dignity of outward circumstance. It was not only a case of writing poems, but of holding myself forth as a poet before my own imagination. So when I wrote poetry at

Bolpur I loved to do it sprawling under a young coconut palm. This seemed to me the true poetic way. Resting thus on the hard unturfed gravel in the burning heat of the day I composed a martial ballad on the 'Defeat of King Prithwi.' In spite of the superabundance of its martial spirit, it could not escape an early death. That bound volume of Lett's diary has now followed the way of its elder sister, the blue manuscript book, leaving no address behind.

We left Bolpur and making short halts on the way at Sahebganj, Dinapore, Allahabad and Cawnpore we stopped at last at Amritsar.

An incident on the way remains engraved on my memory. The train had stopped at some big station. The ticket examiner came and punched our tickets. He looked at me curiously as if he had some doubt which he did not care to express. He went off and came back with a companion. Both of them fidgetted about for a time near the door of our compartment and then again retired. At last came the station master himself. He looked at my half-ticket and then asked:

"Is not the boy over twelve?"

"No," said my father.

I was then only eleven, but looked older than my age.

"You must pay the full fare for him," said the station master.

My father's eyes flashed as, without a word, he took out a currency note from his box and handed it to the station master. When they brought my father his change he flung it disdainfully back at them, while the station master stood abashed at this exposure of the meanness of his implied doubt.

The golden temple of Amritsar comes back to me like a dream. Many a morning have I accompanied my father to this *Gurudarbar* of the Sikhs in the middle of the lake. There the sacred chanting resounds continually. My father, seated amidst the throng of worshippers, would sometimes add his voice to the hymn of praise, and finding a stranger joining in their devotions they would wax enthusiastically cordial, and we would return loaded with the sanctified offerings of sugar crystals and other sweets.

One day my father invited one of the chanting choir to our place and got him to sing us some of their sacred songs. The man went away probably more than satisfied with the reward he received. The result was that we had to take stern measures of self-defence—such an insistent army of singers invaded us. When they found our house impregnable, the musicians began to waylay us in the streets. And as we went out for our walk in the morning, every now and then would appear a *Tambura,** slung over a shoulder, at which we felt like game birds at the sight of the muzzle of the hunter's gun. Indeed, so wary did we become that the twang of the Tambura, from a distance, scared us away and utterly failed to bag us.

When evening fell, my father would sit out in the verandah facing the garden. I would then be summoned to sing to him. The moon has risen; its beams, passing though the trees, have fallen on the verandah floor; I am singing in the *Behaga* mode:

O Companion in the darkest passage of life . . .

My father with bowed head and clasped hands is intently listening. I can recall this evening scene even now.

I have told of my father's amusement on hearing from Srikantha Babu of my maiden attempt at a devotional poem. I am reminded how, later, I had my recompense. On the occasion of one of our Magh festivals several of the hymns were of my composition. One of them was

'The eye sees thee not, who art the pupil of every eye . . .'

My father was then bed-ridden at Chinsurah. He sent for me and my brother Jyoti. He asked my brother to accompany me on the harmonium and got me to sing all my hymns one after the other— some of them I had to sing twice over. When I had finished he said: "If the king of the country had known the language and could appreciate its literature, he would doubtless have rewarded the poet. Since that is not so, I suppose I must do it." With which he handed me a cheque.

My father had brought with him some volumes of the Peter Parley series from which to teach me. He selected the life of Benjamin Franklin to begin with. He thought it would read like a story book and be both entertaining and instructive. But he found out his mistake soon after we began it. Benjamin Franklin was much too business-like a person. The narrowness of his calculated morality disgusted my father. In some cases he would get so impatient at

---

*   An instrument on which the keynote is strummed to accompany singing.

the worldly prudence of Franklin that he could not help using strong words of denunciation. Before this I had nothing to do with Sanskrit beyond getting some rules of grammar by rote. My father started me on the second Sanskrit reader at one bound, leaving me to learn the declensions as we went on. The advance I had made in Bengali* stood me in good stead. My father also encouraged me to try Sanskrit composition from the very outset. With the vocabulary acquired from my Sanskrit reader I built up grandiose compound words with a profuse sprinkling of sonorous 'm's and 'n's making altogether a most diabolical medley of the language of the gods. But my father never scoffed at my temerity.

Then there were the readings from Proctor's Popular Astronomy which my father explained to me in easy language and which I then rendered into Bengali.

Among the books which my father had brought for his own use, my attention would be mostly attracted by a ten or twelve volume edition of Gibbon's Rome. They looked remarkably dry. "Being a boy," I thought, "I am helpless and read many books because I have to. But why should a grown up person, who need not read unless he pleases, bother himself so?"

15

At the Himalayas

We stayed about a month in Amritsar, and, towards the middle of April, started for the Dalhousie Hills. The last few days at Amritsar seemed as if they would never pass, the call of the Himalayas was so strong upon me.

The terraced hill sides, as we went up in a *jhampan*, were all aflame with the beauty of the flowering spring crops. Every morning we would make a start after our bread and milk, and before sunset take shelter for the night in the next staging bungalow. My eyes had no

---

* A large proportion of words in the literary Bengali are derived unchanged from the Sanskrit.

rest the livelong day, so great was my fear lest anything should escape them. Wherever, at a turn of the road into a gorge, the great forest trees were found clustering closer, and from underneath their shade a little waterfall trickling out, like a little daughter of the hermitage playing at the feet of hoary sages wrapt in meditation, babbling its way over the black moss-covered rocks, there the jhampan bearers would put down their burden, and take a rest. Why, oh why, had we to leave such spots behind, cried my thirsting heart, why could we not stay on there for ever?

This is the great advantage of the first vision: the mind is not then aware that there are many more such to come. When this comes to be known to that calculating organ it promptly tries to make a saving in its expenditure of attention. It is only when it believes something to be rare that the mind ceases to be miserly in assigning values. So in the streets of Calcutta I sometimes imagine myself a foreigner, and only then do I discover how much is to be seen, which is lost so long as its full value in attention is not paid. It is the hunger to really see which drives people to travel to strange places.

My father left his little cash-box in my charge. He had no reason to imagine that I was the fittest custodian of the considerable sums he kept in it for use on the way. He would certainly have felt safer with it in the hands of Kishori, his attendant. So I can only suppose he wanted to train me to the responsibility. One day as we reached the staging bungalow, I forgot to make it over to him and left it lying on a table. This earned me a reprimand.

Every time we got down at the end of a stage, my father had chairs placed for us outside the bungalow and there we sat. As dusk came on the stars blazed out wonderfully through the clear mountain atmosphere, and my father showed me the constellations or treated me to an astronomical discourse.

The house we had taken at Bakrota was on the highest hill-top. Though it was nearing May it was still bitterly cold there, so much so that on the shady side of the hill the winter frosts had not yet melted.

My father was not at all nervous about allowing me to wander about freely even here. Some way below our house there stretched a spur thickly wooded with Deodars. Into this wilderness I would venture alone with my iron-spiked staff. These lordly forest trees, with their huge shadows, towering there like so many giants—what immense lives had they lived through the centuries! And yet this boy of only the other day was crawling round about their trunks unchallenged. I seemed to feel a presence, the moment I stepped into their shade, as of the solid coolness of some old-world saurian, and the checkered light and shade on the leafy mould seemed like its scales.

My room was at one end of the house. Lying on my bed I could see, through the uncurtained windows, the distant snowy peaks shimmering dimly in the starlight. Sometimes, at what hour I could not make out, I, half awakened, would see my father, wrapped in a red shawl, with a lighted lamp in his hand, softly passing by to the glazed verandah where he sat at his devotions. After one more sleep I would find him at my bedside, rousing me with a push, before yet the darkness of night had passed. This was my appointed hour for memorising Sanskrit declensions. What an excruciatingly wintry awakening from the caressing warmth of my blankets!

By the time the sun rose, my father, after his prayers, finished with me our morning milk, and then, I standing at his side, he would once more hold communion with God, chanting the Upanishads.

Then we would go out for a walk. But how should I keep pace with him? Many an older person could not! So, after a while, I would give it up and scramble back home through some short cut up the mountain side.

After my father's return I had an hour of English lessons. After ten o'clock came the bath in icy-cold water; it was no use asking the servants to temper it with even a jug full of hot water without my father's permission. To give me courage my father would tell of the unbearably freezing baths he had himself been through in his younger days.

Another penance was the drinking of milk. My father was very fond of milk and could take quantities of it. But whether it was a failure to inherit this capacity, or that the unfavourable environment of which I have told proved the stronger, my appetite for milk was grievously wanting. Unfortunately we used to have our milk together. So I had to throw myself on the mercy of the servants; and to their human kindness (or frailty) I was indebted for my goblet being thenceforth more than half full of foam.

After our midday meal lessons began again. But this was more than flesh and blood could stand. My outraged morning sleep *would* have its revenge and I would be toppling over with uncontrollable drowsiness. Nevertheless, no sooner did my father take pity on my plight and let me off, than my sleepiness was off likewise. Then ho! for the mountains.

Staff in hand I would often wander away from one peak to another, but my father did not object. To the end of his life, I have observed, he never stood in the way of our independence. Many a time have I said or done things repugnant alike to his taste and his judgment; with a word he could have stopped me; but he preferred to wait till the prompting to refrain came from within. A passive acceptance by us of the correct and the proper did not satisfy him; he wanted us to love truth with our whole hearts; he knew that mere acquiescence without love is empty. He also knew that truth, if strayed from, can be found again, but a forced or blind acceptance of it from the outside effectually bars the way in.

The Himalayas

In my early youth I had conceived a fancy to journey along the Grand Trunk Road, right up to Peshawar, in a bullock cart. No one else supported the scheme, and doubtless there was much to be urged against it as a practical proposition. But when I discoursed on it to my father he was sure it was a splendid idea—travelling by railroad was not worth the name! With which observation he proceeded to recount to me his own adventurous wanderings on foot and horseback. Of any chance of discomfort or peril he had not a word to say.

Another time, when I had just been appointed Secretary of the Adi Brahma Samaj, I went over to my father, at his Park Street residence, and informed him that I did not approve of the practice of only Brahmins conducting divine service to the exclusion of other castes. He unhesitatingly gave me permission to correct this if I could. When I got the authority I found I lacked the power. I was able to discover imperfections but could not create perfection! Where were the men? Where was the strength in me to attract the right man? Had I the means to build in the place of what I might break? Till the right man comes any form is better than none—this, I felt, must have been my father's view of the existing order. But he did not for a moment try to discourage me by pointing out the difficulties.

As he allowed me to wander about the mountains at my will, so in the quest for truth he left me free to select my path. He was not deterred by the danger of my making mistakes, he was not alarmed at the prospect of my encountering sorrow. He held up a standard, not a disciplinary rod.

I would often talk to my father of home. Whenever I got a letter from anyone at home I hastened to show it to him. I verily believe I was thus the means of giving him many a picture he could have got from none else. My father also let me read letters to him from my elder brothers. This was his way of teaching me how I ought to write to him; for he by no means underrated the importance of outward forms and ceremonial.

I am reminded of how in one of my second brother's letters he was complaining in somewhat sanskritised phraseology of being worked to death tied by the neck to his post of duty. My father asked me to explain the sentiment. I did it in my way, but he thought a different explanation would fit better. My overweening conceit made me stick to my guns and argue the point with him at length. Another would have shut me up with a snub, but my father patiently heard me out and took pains to justify his view to me.

My father would sometimes tell me funny stories. He had many an anecdote of the gilded youth of his time. There were some exquisites for whose delicate skins the embroidered borders of even Dacca muslins were too coarse, so that to wear muslins with the border torn off became, for a time, the tip-top thing to do.

I was also highly amused to hear from my father for the first time the story of the milkman who was suspected of watering his milk, and the more men one of his customers detailed to look after his milking the bluer the fluid became, till, at last, when the customer himself interviewed him and asked for an explanation, the milkman avowed that if more superintendents had to be satisfied it would only make the milk fit to breed fish!

After I had thus spent a few months with him my father sent me back home with his attendant Kishori.

PART IV

16

My Return

The chains of the rigorous regime which had bound me snapped for good when I set out from home. On my return I gained an accession of rights. In my case my very nearness had so long kept me out of mind; now that I had been out of sight I came back into view.

I got a foretaste of appreciation while still on the return journey. Travelling alone as I was, with an attendant, brimming with health and spirits, and conspicuous with my gold-worked cap, all the English people I came across in the train made much of me.

When I arrived it was not merely a home-coming from travel, it was also a return from my exile in the servants' quarters to my proper place in the inner apartments. Whenever the inner household assembled in my mother's room I now occupied a seat of honour. And she who was then the youngest bride of our house lavished on me a wealth of affection and regard.

In infancy the loving care of woman is to be had without the asking, and, being as much a necessity as light and air, is as simply accepted without any conscious response; rather does the growing child often display an eagerness to free itself from the encircling web of woman's solicitude. But the unfortunate creature who is deprived of this in its proper season is beggared indeed. This had been my plight. So after being brought up in the servants' quarters when

I suddenly came in for a profusion of womanly affection, I could hardly remain unconscious of it.

In the days when the inner apartments were as yet far away from me, they were the elysium of my imagination. The zenana, which from an outside view is a place of confinement, for me was the abode of all freedom. Neither school nor Pandit were there; nor, it seemed to me, did anybody have to do what they did not want to. Its secluded leisure had something mysterious about it; one played about, or did as one liked and had not to render an account of one's doings. Specially so with my youngest sister, to whom, though she attended Nilkamal Pandit's class with us, it seemed to make no difference in his behaviour whether she did her lessons well or ill. Then again, while, by ten o'clock, we had to hurry through our breakfast and be ready for school, she, with her queue dangling behind, walked unconcernedly away, withinwards, tantalising us to distraction.

And when the new bride, adorned with her necklace of gold, came into our house, the mystery of the inner apartments deepened. She, who came from outside and yet became one of us, who was unknown and yet our own, attracted me strangely—with her I burned to make friends. But if by much contriving I managed to draw near, my youngest sister would hustle me off with: "What d'you boys want here—get away outside." The insult added to the disappointment cut me to the quick. Through the glass doors of their cabinets one could catch glimpses of all manner of curious playthings—creations of porcelain and glass—gorgeous in colouring and ornamentation. We were not deemed worthy even to touch them, much less could we muster up courage to ask for any to play with. Nevertheless these rare and wonderful objects, as they were to us boys, served to tinge with an additional attraction the lure of the inner apartments.

Thus had I been kept at arm's length with repeated rebuffs. As the outer world, so, for me, the interior, was unattainable. Wherefore the impressions of it that I did get appeared to me like pictures.

After nine in the evening, my lessons with Aghore Babu over, I am retiring within for the night. A murky flickering lantern is hanging in the long venetian-screened corridor leading from the outer to the inner apartments. At its end this passage turns into a flight of four or five steps, to which the light does not reach, and down which I pass into the galleries running round the first inner quadrangle. A shaft of moonlight slants from the eastern sky into the western angle of these verandahs, leaving the rest in darkness. In this patch of light the maids have gathered and are squatting close together, with legs outstretched, rolling cotton waste into lamp-wicks, and chatting in undertones of their village homes. Many such pictures are indelibly printed on my memory.

Then after our supper, the washing of our hands and feet on the verandah before stretching ourselves on the ample expanse of our bed; whereupon one of the nurses Tinkari or Sankari comes and sits by our heads and softly croons to us the story of the prince travelling on and on over the lonely moor, and, as it comes to an end, silence falls on the room. With my face to the wall I gaze at the black and white patches, made by the plaster of the walls fallen off here and there, showing faintly in the dim light; and out of these I conjure up many a fantastic image as I drop off to sleep. And sometimes, in the middle of the night, I hear through my half-broken sleep the shouts of old Swarup, the watchman, going his rounds from verandah to verandah.

Then came the new order, when I got in profusion from this inner unknown dreamland of my fancies the recognition for which I had all along been pining; when that which naturally should have come day by day was suddenly made good to me with accumulated arrears. I cannot say that my head was not turned.

The little traveller was full of the story of his travels, and, with the strain of each repetition, the narrative got looser and looser till it utterly refused to fit into the facts. Like everything else, alas, a story also gets stale and the glory of the teller suffers likewise; that is why he has to add fresh colouring every time to keep up its freshness.

After my return from the hills I was the principal speaker at my mother's open air gatherings on the roof terrace in the evenings. The temptation to become famous in the eyes of one's mother is as difficult to resist as such fame is easy to earn. While I was at the Normal School, when I first came across the information in some reader that the Sun was hundreds and thousands of times as big as the Earth, I at once disclosed it to my mother. It served to prove that he who was small to look at might yet have a considerable amount of bigness about him. I used also to recite to her the scraps of poetry used as illustrations in the chapter on prosody or rhetoric of our Bengali grammar. Now I retailed at her evening gatherings the astronomical tit-bits I had gleaned from Proctor.

My father's follower Kishori belonged at one time to a band of reciters of Dasarathi's jingling versions of the Epics. While we were together in the hills he often said to me: "Oh, my little brother," if I only had had you in our troupe we could have got up a splendid performance." This would open up to me a tempting picture of wandering as a minstrel boy from place to place, reciting and singing. I learnt from him many of the songs in his repertoire and these were in even greater request than my talks about the photosphere of the Sun or the many moons of Saturn.

But the achievement of mine which appealed most to my mother was that while the rest of the inmates of the inner apartments had to be content with Krittivasa's Bengali rendering of the Ramayana, I had been reading with my father the original of Maharshi Valmiki himself, Sanskrit metre and all. "Read me some of that Ramayana, *do*!" she said, overjoyed at this news which I had given her.

The Servant-maids in the Verandah

---

* Servants call the master and mistress father, and mother, and the children brothers and sisters.

Alas, my reading of Valmiki had been limited to the short extract from his Ramayana given in my Sanskrit reader, and even that I had not fully mastered. Moreover, on looking over it now, I found that my memory had played me false and much of what I thought I knew had become hazy. But I lacked the courage to plead "I have forgotten" to the eager mother awaiting the display of her son's marvellous talents; so that, in the reading I gave, a large divergence occurred between Valmiki's intention and my explanation. That tender-hearted sage, from his seat in heaven, must have forgiven the temerity of the boy seeking the glory of his mother's approbation, but not so Madhusudan,* the taker down of Pride.

My mother, unable to contain her feelings at my extraordinary exploit, wanted all to share her admiration. "You must read this to Dwijendra," (my eldest brother), she said.

"In for it!" thought I, as I put forth all the excuses I could think of, but my mother would have none of them. She sent for my brother Dwijendra, and, as soon as he arrived, greeted him, with: "Just hear Rabi read Valmiki's Ramayan, how splendidly he does it."

It had to be done! But Madhusudan relented and let me off with just a taste of his pride-reducing power. My brother must have been called away while busy with some literary work of his own. He showed no anxiety to hear me render the Sanskrit into Bengali, and as soon as I had read out a few verses he simply remarked "Very good" and walked away.

After my promotion to the inner apartments I felt it all the more difficult to resume my school life. I resorted to all manner of subterfuges to escape the Bengal Academy. Then they tried putting me at St. Xavier's. But the result was no better.

My elder brothers, after a few spasmodic efforts, gave up all hopes of me—they even ceased to scold me. One day my eldest sister said: "We had all hoped Rabi would grow up to be a man, but he has disappointed us the worst." I felt that my value in the social world was distinctly depreciating; nevertheless I could not make up my mind to be tied to the eternal grind of the school mill which,

* Name of Vishnu in his aspect of slayer of the proud demon, Madhu.

divorced as it was from all life and beauty, seemed such a hideously cruel combination of hospital and gaol.

One precious memory of St. Xavier's I still hold fresh and pure—the memory of its teachers. Not that they were all of the same excellence. In particular, in those who taught in our class I could discern no reverential resignation of spirit. They were in nowise above the teaching-machine variety of school masters. As it is, the educational engine is remorselessly powerful; when to it is coupled the stone mill of the outward forms of religion the heart of youth is crushed dry indeed. This power-propelled grindstone type we had at St. Xavier's. Yet, as I say, I possess a memory which elevates my impression of the teachers there to an ideal plane.

This is the memory of Father DePeneranda. He had very little to do with us—if I remember right he had only for a while taken the place of one of the masters of our class. He was a Spaniard and seemed to have an impediment in speaking English. It was perhaps for this reason that the boys paid but little heed to what he was saying. It seemed to me that this inattentiveness of his pupils hurt him, but he bore it meekly day after day. I know not why, but my heart went out to him in sympathy. His features were not handsome, but his countenance had for me a strange attraction. Whenever I looked on him his spirit seemed to be in prayer, a deep peace to pervade him within and without.

We had half-an-hour for writing our copybooks; that was a time when, pen in hand, I used to become absent-minded and my thoughts wandered hither and thither. One day Father DePeneranda was in charge of this class. He was pacing up and down behind our benches. He must have noticed more than once that my pen was not moving. All of a sudden he stopped behind my seat. Bending over me he gently laid his hand on my shoulder and tenderly inquired: "Are you not well, Tagore?" It was only a simple question, but one I have never been able to forget.

I cannot speak for the other boys but I felt in him the presence of a great soul, and even today the recollection of it seems to give me a passport into the silent seclusion of the temple of God.

There was another old Father whom all the boys loved. This

was Father Henry. He taught in the higher classes; so I did not know him well. But one thing about him I remember. He knew Bengali. He once asked Nirada, a boy in his class, the derivation of his name. Poor Nirada* had so long been supremely easy in mind about himself—the derivation of his name, in particular, had never troubled him in the least; so that he was utterly unprepared to answer this question. And yet, with so many abstruse and unknown words in the dictionary, to be worsted by one's own name would have been as ridiculous a mishap as getting run over by one's own carriage, so Nirada unblushingly replied: "*Ni*—privative, *rode*—sun-rays; thence Nirode—that which causes an absence of the sun's rays!"

17

Home Studies

Gyan Babu, son of Pandit Vedantavagish, was now our tutor at home. When he found he could not secure my attention for the school course, he gave up the attempt as hopeless and went on a different tack. He took me through Kalidas's *Birth of the War-God*, translating it to me as we went on. He also read *Macbeth* to me, first explaining the text in Bengali, and then confining me to the school room till I had rendered the day's reading into Bengali verse. In this way he got me to translate the whole play. I was fortunate enough to lose this translation and so am relieved to that extent of the burden of my *karma*.

It was Pandit Ramsarvaswa's duty to see to the progress of our Sanskrit. He likewise gave up the fruitless task of teaching grammar to his unwilling pupil, and read Sakuntala with me instead. One day he took it into his head to show my translation of *Macbeth* to Pandit Vidyasagar and took me over to his house.

Rajkrishna Mukherji had called at the time and was seated with

---

* Nirada is a Sanskrit word meaning *cloud*, being a compound of *nira* = water and *da* = giver. In Bengali it is pronounced *nirode*.

him. My heart went pit-a-pat as I entered the great Pandit's study, packed full of books; nor did his austere visage assist in reviving my courage. Nevertheless, as this was the first time I had had such a distinguished audience, my desire to win renown was strong within me. I returned home, I believe, with some reason for an access of enthusiasm. As for Rajkrishna Babu, he contented himself with admonishing me to be careful to keep the language and metre of the Witches' parts different from that of the human characters.

During my boyhood Bengali literature was meagre in body, and I think I must have finished all the readable and unreadable books that there were at the time. Juvenile literature in those days had not evolved a distinct type of its own—but that I am sure did me no harm. The watery stuff into which literary nectar is now diluted for being served up to the young takes full account of their childishness, but none of them as growing human beings. Children's books should be such as can partly be understood by them and partly not. In our childhood we read every available book from one end to the other; and both what we understood, and what we did not, went on working within us. That is how the world itself reacts on the child consciousness. The child makes its own what it understands, while that which is beyond leads it on a step forward.

When Dinabandhu Mitra's satires came out I was not of an age for which they were suitable. A kinswoman of ours was reading a copy, but no entreaties of mine could induce her to lend it to me. She used to keep it under lock and key. Its inaccessibility made me want it all the more and I threw out the challenge that read the book I must and would.

One afternoon she was playing cards, and her keys, tied to a corner of her sari, hung over her shoulder. I had never paid any attention to cards, in fact I could not stand card games. But my behaviour that day would hardly have borne this out, so engrossed was I in their playing. At last, in the excitement of one side being about to make a score, I seized my opportunity and set about untying the knot which held the keys. I was not skilful, and moreover excited and hasty and so got caught. The owner of the sari and of the keys took the fold off her shoulder with a smile, and laid the keys on her lap as she went on with the game.

Then I hit on a stratagem. My kinswoman was fond of paan, and I hastened to place some before her. This entailed her rising later on to get rid of the chewed paan, and, as she did so, her keys fell off her lap and were replaced over her shoulder. This time they got stolen, the culprit got off, and the book got read! Its owner tried to scold me, but the attempt was not a success, we both laughed so.

Dr. Rajendralal Mitra used to edit an illustrated monthly miscellany. My third brother had a bound annual volume of it in his bookcase. This I managed to secure and the delight of reading it through, over and over again, still comes back to me. Many a holiday noontide has passed with me stretched on my back on my bed, that square volume on my breast, reading about the Narwhal whale, or the curiosities of justice as administered by the Kazis of old, or the romantic story of Krishna-kumari.

Why do we not have such magazines now-a-days? We have philosophical and scientific articles on the one hand, and insipid stories and travels on the other, but no such unpretentious miscellanies which the ordinary person can read in comfort—such as Chambers's or Cassell's or the Strand in England—which supply the general reader with a simple, but satisfying fare and are of the greatest use to the greatest number.

I came across another little periodical in my young days called the *Abodhabandhu* (ignorant man's friend). I found a collection of its monthly numbers in my eldest brother's library and devoured them day after day, seated on the doorsill of his study, facing a bit of terrace to the South. It was in the pages of this magazine that I made my first acquaintance with the poetry of Viharilal Chakravarti. His poems appealed to me the most of all that I read at the time. The artless flute-strains of his lyrics awoke within me the music of fields and forest-glades.

Into these same pages I have wept many a tear over a pathetic translation of Paul and Virginie. That wonderful sea, the breeze-stirred coconut forests on its shore, and the slopes beyond lively with the gambols of mountain goats—a delightfully refreshing mirage they conjured up on that terraced roof in Calcutta. And oh! the romantic courting that went on in the forest paths of that secluded island, between the Bengali boy reader and little Virginie with the many-coloured kerchief round her head!

Then came Bankim's *Bangadarsan*, taking the Bengali heart by storm. It was bad enough to have to wait till the next monthly number was out, but to be kept waiting further till my elders had done with it was simply intolerable! Now he who will may swallow at a mouthful the whole of *Chandrashekhar* or *Bishabriksha* but the process of longing and anticipating, month after month; of spreading over the long intervals the concentrated joy of each short reading, revolving every instalment over and over in the mind while watching and waiting for the next; the combination of satisfaction with unsatisfied craving, of burning curiosity with its appeasement; these long drawn out delights of going through the original serial none will ever taste again.

The compilations from the old poets by Sarada Mitter and Akshay Sarkar were also of great interest to me. Our elders were subscribers, but not very regular readers, of these series, so that it was not difficult for me to get at them. Vidyapati's quaint and corrupt Maithili language attracted me all the more because of its unintelligibility. I tried to make out his sense without the help of the compiler's notes, jotting down in my own note book all the more obscure words with their context as many times as they occurred. I also noted grammatical peculiarities according to my lights.

18
My Home Environment

One great advantage which I enjoyed in my younger days was the literary and artistic atmosphere which pervaded our house. I remember how, when I was quite a child, I would be leaning against the verandah railings which overlooked the detached building comprising the reception rooms. These rooms would be lighted up every evening. Splendid carriages would draw up under the portico, and visitors would be constantly coming and going. What was happening I could not very well make out, but would keep staring at the rows of lighted casements from my place in the darkness. The intervening space was not great but the gulf between my infant world and these lights was immense.

My elder cousin Ganendra had just got a drama written by Pandit Tarkaratna and was having it staged in the house. His enthusiasm for literature and the fine arts knew no bounds. He was the centre of the group who seem to have been almost consciously striving to bring about from every side the renascence which we see today. A pronounced nationalism in dress, literature, music, art and the drama had awakened in and around him. He was a keen student of the history of different countries and had begun but could not complete a historical work in Bengali. He had translated and published the Sanskrit drama, Vikramorvasi, and many a well-known hymn is his composition. He may be said to have given us the lead in writing patriotic poems and songs. This was in the days when the Hindu Mela was an annual institution and there his song 'Ashamed am I to sing of India's glories' used to be sung.

I was still a child when my cousin Ganendra died in the prime of his youth, but for those who have once beheld him it is impossible to forget his handsome, tall and stately figure. He had an irresistible social influence. He could draw men round him and keep them bound to him; while his powerful attraction was there, disruption was out of the question. He was one of those—a type peculiar to our country—who, by their personal magnetism, easily establish themselves in the centre of their family or village. In any other country, where large political, social or commercial groups are being formed, such would as naturally become national leaders. The power of organising a large number of men into a corporate group depends on a special kind of genius. Such genius in our country runs to waste, a waste, as pitiful, it seems to me, as that of pulling down a star from the firmament for use as a lucifer match.

I remember still better his younger brother, my cousin Gunendra.* He likewise kept the house filled with his personality. His large, gracious heart embraced alike relatives, friends, guests

---

* Father of the well-known artists Gaganendra and Abanindra.

and dependants. Whether in his broad south verandah, or on the lawn by the fountain, or at the tank-edge on the fishing platform, he presided over self-invited gatherings, like hospitality incarnate. His wide appreciation of art and talent kept him constantly radiant with enthusiasm. New ideas of festivity or frolic, theatricals or other entertainments, found in him a ready patron, and with his help would flourish and find fruition.

We were too young then to take any part in these doings, but the waves of merriment and life to which they gave rise came and beat at the doors of our curiosity. I remember how a burlesque composed by my eldest brother was once being rehearsed in my cousin's big drawing room. From our place against the verandah railings of our house we could hear, through the open windows opposite, roars of laughter mixed with the strains of a comic song, and would also occasionally catch glimpses of Akshay Mazumdar's extraordinary antics. We could not gather exactly what the song was about, but lived in hopes of being able to find that out sometime.

I recall how a trifling circumstance earned for me the special regard of cousin Gunendra. Never had I got a prize at school except once for good conduct. Of the three of us my nephew Satya was the best at his lessons. He once did well at some examination and was awarded a prize. As we came home I jumped off the carriage to give the great news to my cousin who was in the garden. "Satya has got a prize," I shouted as I ran to him. He drew me to his knees with a smile. "And have *you* not got a prize?" he asked. "No," said I, "not I, it's Satya." My genuine pleasure at Satya's success seemed to touch my cousin particularly. He turned to his friends and remarked on it as a very creditable trait. I well remember how mystified I felt at this, for I had not thought of my feeling in that light. This prize that I got for not getting a prize did not do me good. There is no harm in making gifts to children, but they should not be rewards. It is not healthy for youngsters to be made self-conscious.

After the mid-day meal cousin Gunendra would attend the estate offices in our part of the house. The office room of our elders was a sort of club where laughter and conversation were freely mixed with matters of business. My cousin would recline on a couch, and I would seize some opportunity of edging up to him.

My Eldest Brother

He usually told me stories from Indian History. I still remember the surprise with which I heard how Clive, after establishing British rule in India, went back home and cut his own throat. On the one hand new history being made, on the other a tragic chapter hidden away in the mysterious darkness of a human heart. How could there be such dismal failure within and such brilliant success outside? This weighed heavily on my mind the whole day.

Some days cousin Gunendra would not be allowed to remain in any doubt as to the contents of my pocket. At the least encouragement out would come my manuscript book, unabashed. I need hardly state that my cousin was not a severe critic; in point of fact the opinions he expressed would have done splendidly as advertisements. None the less, when in any of my poetry my childishness became too obtrusive, he could not restrain his hearty "Ha! Ha!"

One day it was a poem on 'Mother India' and as at the end of one line the only rhyme I could think of meant a cart, I had to drag in that cart in spite of there not being the vestige of a road by which it could reasonably arrive—the insistent claims of rhyme would not hear of any excuses mere reason had to offer. The storm of laughter with which cousin Gunendra greeted it blew away the cart back over the same impossible path it had come by, and it has not been heard of since.

My eldest brother was then busy with his masterpiece 'The Dream Journey,' his cushion seat placed in the south verandah, a low desk before him. Cousin Gunendra would come and sit there for a time every morning. His immense capacity for enjoyment, like the breezes of spring, helped poetry to sprout. My eldest brother would go on alternately writing and reading out what he had written, his boisterous mirth at his own conceits making the verandah tremble. My brother wrote a great deal more than he finally used in his finished work, so fertile was his poetic inspiration. Like the superabounding mango flowerets which carpet the shade of the mango topes in spring time, the rejected pages of his 'Dream Journey' were to be found scattered all over the house. Had anyone preserved them they would have been today a basketful of flowers adorning our Bengali literature.

Eavesdropping at doors and peeping round corners, we used to get our full share of this feast of poetry, so plentiful was it, with so much to spare. My eldest brother was then at the height of his wonderful powers; and from his pen surged, in untiring wave after wave, a tidal flood of poetic fancy, rhyme and expression, filling and overflowing its banks with an exuberantly joyful pæan of triumph. Did we quite understand 'The Dream Journey'? But then did we need absolutely to understand in order to enjoy it? We might not have got at the wealth in the ocean depths—what could we have done with it if we had?—but we revelled in the delights of the waves on the shore; and how gaily, at their buffettings, did our life-blood course through every vein and artery!

The more I think of that period the more I realise that we have no longer the thing called a *mujlis.** In our boyhood we beheld the dying rays of that intimate sociability which was characteristic of

---

* In Bengali this word has come to mean an informal uninvited gathering.

the last generation. Neighbourly feelings were then so strong that the mujlis was a necessity, and those who could contribute to its amenities were in great request. People now-a-days call on each other on business, or as a matter of social duty, but not to foregather by way of mujlis. They have not the time, nor are there the same intimate relations! What goings and comings we used to see, how merry were the rooms and verandahs with the hum of conversation and the snatches of laughter! The faculty our predecessors had of becoming the centre of groups and gatherings, of starting and keeping up animated and amusing gossip, has vanished. Men still come and go, but those same verandahs and rooms seem empty and deserted.

In those days everything from furniture to festivity was designed to be enjoyed by the many, so that whatever of pomp or magnificence there might have been did not savour of hauteur. These appendages have since increased in quantity, but they have become unfeeling, and know not the art of making high and low alike feel at home. The bare-bodied, the indigently clad, no longer have the right to use and occupy them, without a permit, on the strength of their smiling faces alone. Those whom we now-a-days seek to imitate in our house-building and furnishing, they have their own society, with its wide hospitality. The mischief with us is that we have lost what we had, but have not the means of building up afresh on the European standard, with the result that our home-life has become joyless. We still meet for business or political purposes, but never for the pleasure of simply meeting one another. We have ceased to contrive opportunities to bring men together simply because we love our fellow-men. I can imagine nothing more ugly than this social miserliness; and, when I look back on those whose ringing laughter, coming straight from their hearts, used to lighten for us the burden of household cares, they seem to have been visitors from some other world.

19

Literary Companions

There came to me in my boyhood a friend whose help in my literary progress was invaluable. Akshay Chowdhury was a school-fellow of my fourth brother. He was an M.A. in English Literature for which his love was as great as his proficiency therein. On the other hand he had an equal fondness for our older Bengali authors and Vaishnava Poets. He knew hundreds of Bengali songs of unknown authorship, and on these he would launch, with voice uplifted, regardless of tune, or consequence, or of the express disapproval of his hearers. Nor could anything, within him or without, prevent his loudly beating time to his own music, for which the nearest table or book served his nimble fingers to rap a vigorous tattoo on, to help to enliven the audience.

He was also one of those with an inordinate capacity for extracting enjoyment from all and sundry. He was as ready to absorb every bit of goodness in a thing as he was lavish in singing its praises. He had an extraordinary gift as a lightning composer of lyrics and songs of no mean merit, but in which he himself had no pride of authorship. He took no further notice of the heaps of scattered scraps of paper on which his pencil writings had been indited. He was as indifferent to his powers as they were prolific.

One of his longer poetic pieces was much appreciated when it appeared in the *Bangadarsan*, and I have heard his songs sung by many who knew nothing at all about their composer.

A genuine delight in literature is much rarer than erudition, and it was this enthusiastic enjoyment in Akshay Babu which used to awaken my own literary appreciation. He was as liberal in his friendships as in his literary criticisms. Among strangers he was as a fish out of water, but among friends discrepancies in wisdom or age made no difference to him. With us boys he was a boy. When he took his leave, late in the evening, from the mujlis of our elders, I would buttonhole and drag him to our school room. There, with undiminished geniality he would make himself the life and soul of our little gathering, seated on the top of our study table. On many such occasions I have listened to him going into a rapturous dissertation on some English poem; engaged him in some appreciative discussion, critical inquiry, or hot dispute; or read to him some of my own writings and been rewarded in return with praise unsparing.

My fourth brother Jyotirindra was one of the chief helpers in my literary and emotional training. He was an enthusiast himself and loved to evoke enthusiasm in others. He did not allow the difference between our ages to be any bar to my free intellectual and sentimental intercourse with him. This great boon of freedom which he allowed me, none else would have dared to do; many even blamed him for it. His companionship made it possible for me to shake off my shrinking sensitiveness. It was as necessary for my soul after its rigorous repression during my infancy as are the monsoon clouds after a fiery summer.

But for such snapping of my shackles I might have become crippled for life. Those in authority are never tired of holding forth the possibility of the abuse of freedom as a reason for withholding it, but without that possibility freedom would not be really free. And the only way of learning how to use properly a thing is through its misuse. For myself, at least, I can truly say that what little mischief resulted from my freedom always led the way to the means of curing mischief. I have never been able to make my own anything which they tried to compel me to swallow by getting hold of me, physically or mentally, by the ears. Nothing but sorrow have I ever gained except when left freely to myself.

My brother Jyotirindra unreservedly let me go my own way to self-knowledge, and only since then could my nature prepare to put forth its thorns, it may be, but likewise its flowers. This experience of mine has led me to dread, not so much evil itself, as tyrannical attempts to create goodness. Of punitive police, political or moral, I have a wholesome horror. The state of slavery which is thus brought on is the worst form of cancer to which humanity is subject.

My brother at one time would spend days at his piano engrossed in the creation of new tunes. Showers of melody would stream from under his dancing fingers, while Akshay Babu and I, seated on either side, would be busy fitting words to the tunes as they grew into shape to help to hold them in our memories.* This is how I served my apprenticeship in the composition of songs.

While we were growing to boyhood music was largely cultivated in our family. This had the advantage of making it possible for me to imbibe it, without an effort, into my whole being. It had also the disadvantage of not giving me that technical mastery which the effort of learning step by step alone can give. Of what may be called proficiency in music, therefore, I acquired none.

Ever since my return from the Himalayas it was a case of my getting more freedom, more and more. The rule of the servants came to an end; I saw to it with many a device that the bonds of my school life were also loosened; nor to my home tutors did I give much scope. Gyan Babu, after taking me through *The Birth of the War-God* and one or two other books in a desultory fashion, went off to take up a legal career. Then came Braja Babu. The first day he put me on to translate *The Vicar of Wakefield*. I found that I did not dislike the book; but when this encouraged him to make more elaborate arrangements for the advancement of my learning I made myself altogether scarce.

As I have said, my elders gave me up. Neither I nor they were troubled with any more hopes of my future. So I felt free to devote myself to filling up my manuscript book. And the writings which thus filled it were no better than could have been expected. My mind had nothing in it but hot vapour, and vapour-filled bubbles frothed and eddied round a vortex of lazy fancy, aimless and unmeaning. No forms were evolved, there was only the distraction of movement, a bubbling up, a bursting back into froth. What little of matter there was in it was not mine, but borrowed from other poets. What was my own was the restlessness, the seething tension within me. When motion has been born, while yet the balance of forces has not matured, then is there blind chaos indeed.

---

* Systems of notation were not then in use. One of the most popular of the present-day systems was subsequently devised by the writer's brother here mentioned.

My sister-in-law* was a great lover of literature. She did not read simply to kill time, but the Bengali books which she read filled her whole mind. I was a partner in her literary enterprises. She was a devoted admirer of 'The Dream Journey.' So was I; the more particularly as, having been brought up in the atmosphere of its creation, its beauties had become intertwined with every fibre of my heart. Fortunately it was entirely beyond my power of imitation, so it never occurred to me to attempt anything like it.

'The Dream Journey' may be likened to a superb palace of Allegory, with innumerable halls, chambers, passages, corners and niches full of statuary and pictures, of wonderful design and workmanship; and in the grounds around gardens, bowers, fountains and shady nooks in profusion. Not only do poetic thought and fancy abound, but the richness and variety of language and expression is also marvellous. It is not a small thing, this creative power which can bring into being so magnificent a structure complete in all its artistic detail, and that is perhaps why the idea of attempting an imitation never occurred to me.

At this time Viharilal Chakravarti's series of songs called *Sarada Mangal* were coming out in the *Arya Darsan*. My sister-in-law was greatly taken with the sweetness of these lyrics. Most of them she knew by heart. She used often to invite the poet to our house and had embroidered for him a cushion-seat with her own hands. This gave me the opportunity of making friends with him. He came to have a great affection for me, and I took to dropping in at his house at all times of the day, morning, noon or evening. His heart was as large as his body, and a halo of fancy used to surround him like a poetic astral body which seemed to be his truer image. He was always full of true artistic joy, and whenever I have been to him I have breathed in my share of it. Often have I come upon him in his little room on the third storey, in the heat of noonday, sprawling on the cool polished cement floor, writing his poems. Mere boy though I was, his welcome was always so genuine and hearty that I never felt the least awkwardness in approaching him. Then, wrapt in his inspiration and forgetful of all surroundings, he would read out his

---

* The new bride of the house, wife of the writer's fourth brother, above-mentioned.

poems or sing his songs to me. Not that he had much of the gift of song in his voice; but then he was not altogether tuneless, and one could get a fair idea of the intended melody.* When with eyes closed he raised his rich deep voice, its expressiveness made up for what it lacked in execution. I still seem to hear some of his songs as he sang them. I would also sometimes set his words to music and sing them to him.

He was a great admirer of Valmiki and Kalidas. I remember how once after reciting a description of the Himalayas from Kalidas with the full strength of his voice, he said: "The succession of long ā sounds here is not an accident. The poet has deliberately repeated this sound all the way from *Devatatma* down to *Nagadhiraja* as an assistance in realising the glorious expanse of the Himalayas."

At the time the height of my ambition was to become a poet like Vihari Babu. I might have even succeeded in working myself up to the belief that I was actually writing like him, but for my sister-in-law, his zealous devotee, who stood in the way. She would keep reminding me of a Sanskrit saying that the unworthy aspirant after poetic fame departs in jeers! Very possibly she knew that if my vanity was once allowed to get the upper hand it would be difficult afterwards to bring it under control. So neither my poetic abilities nor my powers of song readily received any praise from her; rather would she never let slip an opportunity of praising somebody else's singing at my expense; with the result that I gradually became quite convinced of the defects of my voice. Misgivings about my poetic powers also assailed me; but, as this was the only field of activity left in which I had any chance of retaining my self-respect, I could not allow the judgment of another to deprive me of all hope; moreover, so insistent was the spur within me that to stop my poetic adventure was a matter of sheer impossibility.

---

* It may be helpful to the foreign reader to explain that the expert singer of Indian music improvises more or less on the tune outline made over to him by the original composer, so that the latter need not necessarily do more than give a correct idea of such outline.

20

Publishing

My writings so far had been confined to the family circle. Then was started the monthly called the *Gyanankur*, Sprouting Knowledge, and, as befitted its name it secured an embryo poet as one of its contributors. It began to publish all my poetic ravings indiscriminately, and to this day I have, in a corner of my mind, the fear that, when the day of judgment comes for me, some enthusiastic literary police-agent will institute a search in the inmost zenana of forgotten literature, regardless of the claims of privacy, and bring these out before the pitiless public gaze.

My first prose writing also saw the light in the pages of the *Gyanankur*. It was a critical essay and had a bit of a history.

A book of poems had been published entitled *Bhubanmohini Pratibha*.* Akshay Babu in the *Sadharani* and Bhudeb Babu in the *Education Gazette* hailed this new poet with effusive acclamation. A friend of mine, older than myself, whose friendship dates from then, would come and show me letters he had received signed *Bhubanmohini*. He was one of those whom the book had captivated and used frequently to send reverential offerings of books or cloth† to the address of the reputed authoress.

Some of these poems were so wanting in restraint both of thought and language that I could not bear the idea of their being written by a woman. The letters that were shown to me made it still less possible for me to believe in the womanliness of the writer. But my doubts did not shake my friend's devotion and he went on with the worship of his idol.

Then I launched into a criticism of the work of this writer. I let myself go, and eruditely held forth on the distinctive features of

---

* This would mean 'the genius of Bhubanmohini' if that be taken as the author's name.

† Gifts of cloth for use as wearing apparel are customary by way of ceremonial offerings of affection, respect or seasonable greeting.

lyrics and other short poems, my great advantage being that printed matter is so unblushing, so impassively unbetraying of the writer's real attainments. My friend turned up in a great passion and hurled at me the threat that a B.A. was writing a reply. A B.A.! I was struck speechless. I felt the same as in my younger days when my nephew Satya had shouted for a policeman. I could see the triumphal pillar of argument, erected upon my nice distinctions, crumbling before my eyes at the merciless assaults of authoritative quotations; and the door effectually barred against my ever showing my face to the reading public again. Alas, my critique, under what evil star wert thou born! I spent day after day in the direst suspense. But, like Satya's policeman, the B.A. failed to appear.

21

Bhanu Singha

As I have said I was a keen student of the series of old Vaishnava poems which were being collected and published by Babus Akshay Sarkar and Saroda Mitter. Their language, largely mixed with Maithili, I found difficult to understand; but for that very reason I took all the more pains to get at their meaning. My feeling towards them was that same eager curiosity with which I regarded the ungerminated sprout within the seed, or the undiscovered mystery under the dust covering of the earth. My enthusiasm was kept up with the hope of bringing to light some unknown poetical gems as I went deeper and deeper into the unexplored darkness of this treasure-house.

While I was so engaged, the idea got hold of me of enfolding my own writings in just such a wrapping of mystery. I had heard from Akshay Chowdhury the story of the English boy-poet Chatterton. What his poetry was like I had no idea, nor perhaps had Akshay Babu himself. Had we known, the story might have lost its charm. As it happened the melodramatic element in it fired my imagination; for had not so many been deceived by his successful imitation of the classics? And at last the unfortunate youth had died by his own hand. Leaving aside the suicide part I girded up my loins to emulate young Chatterton's exploits.

One noon the clouds had gathered thickly. Rejoicing in the grateful shade of the cloudy midday rest-hour, I lay prone on the bed in my inner room and wrote on a slate the imitation *Maithili* poem *Gahana kusuma kunja majhe*. I was greatly pleased with it and lost no time in reading it out to the first one I came across; of whose understanding a word of it there happened to be not the slightest danger, and who consequently could not but gravely nod and say, "Good, very good indeed!"

To my friend mentioned a while ago I said one day: "A tattered old manuscript has been discovered while rummaging in the *Adi Brahma Samaj* library and from this I have copied some poems by an old Vaishnava Poet named Bhanu Singha;"[*] with which I read some of my imitation poems to him. He was profoundly stirred. "These could not have been written even by *Vidyapati* or *Chandidas*!" he rapturously exclaimed. "I really must have that MS. to make over to Akshay Babu for publication."

Then I showed him my manuscript book and conclusively proved that the poems could not have been written by either *Vidyapati* or *Chandidas* because the author happened to be myself. My friend's face fell as he muttered, "Yes, yes, they're not half bad."

When these Bhanu Singha poems were coming out in the *Bharati*, Dr. Nishikanta Chatterjee was in Germany. He wrote a thesis on the lyric poetry of our country comparing it with that of Europe. Bhanu Singha was given a place of honour as one of the old poets such as no modern writer could have aspired to. This was the thesis on which Nishikanta Chatterjee got his Ph.D.!

Whoever Bhanu Singha might have been, had his writings fallen into the hands of latter-day me, I swear I would not have been deceived. The language might have passed muster; for that which the old poets wrote in was not their mother tongue, but an artificial language varying in the hands of different poets. But there was nothing artificial about their sentiments. Any attempt to test Bhanu

---

* The old Vaishnava poets used to bring their name into the last stanza of the poem, this serving as their signature. Bhanu and Rabi both mean the Sun.

Singha's poetry by its ring would have shown up the base metal. It had none of the ravishing melody of our ancient pipes, but only the tinkle of a modern, foreign barrel organ.

22

Patriotism

From an outside point of view many a foreign custom would appear to have gained entry into our family, but at its heart flames a national pride which has never flickered. The genuine regard which my father had for his country never forsook him through all the revolutionary vicissitudes of his life, and this in his descendants has taken shape as a strong patriotic feeling. Love of country was, however, by no means a characteristic of the times of which I am writing. Our educated men then kept at arms' length both the language and thought of their native land. Nevertheless my elder brothers had always cultivated Bengali literature. When on one occasion some new connection by marriage wrote my father an English letter it was promptly returned to the writer.

The *Hindu Mela* was an annual fair which had been instituted with the assistance of our house. Babu Nabagopal Mitter was appointed its manager. This was perhaps the first attempt at a reverential realisation of India as our motherland. My second brother's popular national anthem *Bharater Jaya*, was composed, then. The singing of songs glorifying the motherland, the recitation of poems of the love of country, the exhibition of indigenous arts and crafts and the encouragement of national talent and skill were the features of this *Mela*.

On the occasion of Lord Curzon's Delhi durbar I wrote a prose-paper—at the time of Lord Lytton's it was a poem. The British Government of those days feared the Russians it is true, but not the pen of a fourteen-year-old poet. So, though my poem lacked none of the fiery sentiments appropriate to my age, there were no signs of any consternation in the ranks of the authorities from Commander-in-chief down to Commissioner of Police. Nor did any lachrymose letter in the *Times* predict a speedy downfall of the Empire for this apathy of its local guardians. I recited my poem under a tree at the Hindu Mela and one of my hearers was Nabin Sen, the poet. He reminded me of this after I had grown up.

My fourth brother, Jyotirindra, was responsible for a political association of which old Rajnarain Bose was the president. It held its sittings in a tumbledown building in an obscure Calcutta lane. Its proceedings were enshrouded in mystery. This mystery was its only claim to be awe-inspiring, for as a matter of fact there was nothing in our deliberations or doings of which government or people need have been afraid. The rest of our family had no idea where we were spending our afternoons. Our front door would be locked, the meeting room in darkness, the watchword a Vedic mantra, our talk in whispers. These alone provided us with enough of a thrill, and we wanted nothing more. Mere child as I was, I also was a member. We surrounded ourselves with such an atmosphere of pure frenzy that we always seemed to be soaring aloft on the wings of our enthusiasm. Of bashfulness, diffidence or fear we had none, our main object being to bask in the heat of our own fervour.

Bravery may sometimes have its drawbacks; but it has always maintained a deep hold on the reverence of mankind. In the literature of all countries we find an unflagging endeavour to keep alive this reverence. So in whatever state a particular set of men in a particular locality may be, they cannot escape the constant impact of these stimulating shocks. We had to be content with responding to such shocks, as best we could, by letting loose our imagination, coming together, talking tall and singing fervently.

There can be no doubt that closing up all outlets and barring all openings to a faculty so deep-seated in the nature of man, and moreover so prized by him, creates an unnatural condition favourable to degenerate activity. It is not enough to keep open only the avenues to clerical employment in any comprehensive scheme of Imperial Government—if no road be left for adventurous daring the soul of man will pine for deliverance, and secret passages still be sought, of which the pathways are tortuous and the end unthinkable. I firmly believe that if in those days Government had paraded a frightfulness born of suspicion, then the comedy which the youthful members of this association had been at might have turned into grim tragedy. The play, however, is over, not a brick of Fort-William is any the worse, and we are now smiling at its memory.

My brother Jyotirindra began to busy himself with a national costume for all India, and submitted various designs to the association. The *Dhoti* was not deemed business-like; trousers were too foreign; so he hit upon a compromise which considerably detracted from the dhoti while failing to improve the trousers. That is to say, the trousers were decorated with the addition of a false dhoti-fold in front and behind. The fearsome thing that resulted from combining a turban with a *Sola-topee* our most enthusiastic member would not have had the temerity to call ornamental. No person of ordinary courage could have dared it, but my brother unflinchingly wore the complete suit in broad daylight, passing through the house of an afternoon to the carriage waiting outside, indifferent alike to the stare of relation or friend, door-keeper or coachman. There may be many a brave Indian ready to die for his country, but there are but few, I am sure, who even for the good of the nation would face the public streets in such pan-Indian garb.

Every Sunday my brother would get up a *Shikar* party. Many of those who joined in it, uninvited, we did not even know. There was a carpenter, a smith and others from all ranks of society. Bloodshed was the only thing lacking in this *shikar*, at least I cannot recall any. Its other appendages were so abundant and satisfying that we felt the absence of dead or wounded game to be a trifling circumstance of no account. As we were out from early morning, my sister-in-law furnished us with a plentiful supply of luchis with appropriate accompaniments; and as these did not depend upon the fortunes of our chase we never had to return empty.

The neighbourhood of Maniktola is not wanting in Villa-gardens. We would turn into any one of these at the end, and high- and low-born alike, seated on the bathing platform of a tank, would fling ourselves on the luchis in right good earnest, all that was left of them being the vessels they were brought in.

Braja Babu was one of the most enthusiastic of these blood-thirstless *shikaris*. He was the Superintendent of the Metropolitan Institution and had also been our private tutor for a time. One day he had the happy idea of accosting the *mali* (gardener) of a villa-garden into which we had thus trespassed with: "Hallo, has uncle been here lately!" The mali lost no time in saluting him respectfully before he replied: "No, Sir, the master hasn't been lately." "All right, get us some green coconuts off the trees." We had a fine drink after our luchis that day.

A Zamindar in a small way was among our party. He owned a villa on the river side. One day we had a picnic there together, in defiance of caste rules. In the afternoon there was a tremendous storm. We stood on the riverside stairs leading into the water and shouted out songs to its accompaniment. I cannot truthfully assert that all the seven notes of the scale could properly be distinguished in Rajnarain Babu's singing, nevertheless he sent forth his voice and, as in the old Sanskrit works the text is drowned by the notes, so in Rajnarain Babu's musical efforts the vigorous play of his limbs and features overwhelmed his feebler vocal performance; his head swung from side to side marking time, while the storm played havoc with his flowing beard. It was late in the night when we turned homewards in a hackney carriage. By that time the storm clouds had dispersed and the stars twinkled forth. The darkness had become intense, the atmosphere silent, the village roads deserted, and the thickets on either side filled with fireflies like a carnival of sparks scattered in some noiseless revelry.

One of the objects of our association was to encourage the manufacture of lucifer matches, and similar small industries. For this purpose each member had to contribute a tenth of his income. Matches had to be made, but matchwood was difficult to get; for though we all know with what fiery energy a bundle of *khangras** can be wielded in capable hands, the thing that burns at its touch is not a lamp wick. After many experiments we succeeded in making a boxful of matches. The patriotic enthusiasm which was thus evidenced did

---

* The dried and stripped centre-vein of a coconut leaf gives a long tapering stick of the average thickness of a match stick, and a bundle of these goes to make the common Bengal household broom which in the hands of the housewife is popularly supposed to be useful in keeping the whole household in order from husband downwards. Its effect on a bare back is here alluded to.

not constitute their only value, for the money that was spent in their making might have served to light the family hearth for the space of a year. Another little defect was that these matches could not be got to burn unless there was a light handy to touch them up with. If they could only have inherited some of the patriotic flame of which they were born they might have been marketable even today.

News came to us that some young student was trying to make a power loom. Off we went to see it. None of us had the knowledge with which to test its practical usefulness, but in our capacity for believing and hoping we were inferior to none. The poor fellow had got into a bit of debt over the cost of his machine which we repaid for him. Then one day we found Braja Babu coming over to our house with a flimsy country towel tied round his head. "Made in our loom!" he shouted as with hands uplifted he executed a war-dance. The outside of Braja Babu's head had then already begun to ripen into grey!

At last some worldly-wise people came and joined our society, made us taste of the fruit of knowledge, and broke up our little paradise.

When I first knew Rajnarain Babu, I was not old enough to appreciate his many-sidedness. In him were combined many opposites. In spite of his hoary hair and beard he was as young as the youngest of us, his venerable exterior serving only as a white mantle for keeping his youth perpetually fresh. Even his extensive learning had not been able to do him any damage, for it left him absolutely simple. To the end of his life the incessant flow of his hearty laughter suffered no check, neither from the gravity of age, nor ill-health, nor domestic affliction, nor profundity of thought, nor variety of knowledge, all of which had been his in ample measure. He had been a favourite pupil of Richardson and brought up in an atmosphere of English learning, nevertheless he flung aside all obstacles due to his early habit and gave himself up lovingly and devotedly to Bengali literature. Though the meekest of men, he was full of fire which flamed its fiercest in his patriotism, as though to burn to ashes the shortcomings and destitution of his country. The memory of this smile-sweetened fervour-illumined lifelong-youthful saint is one that is worth cherishing by our countrymen.

23

The Bharati

On the whole the period of which I am writing was for me one of ecstatic excitement. Many a night have I spent without sleep, not for any particular reason but from a mere desire to do the reverse of the obvious. I would keep up reading in the dim light of our school room all alone; the distant church clock would chime every quarter as if each passing hour was being put up to auction; and the loud *Haribols* of the bearers of the dead, passing along Chitpore Road on their way to the Nimtollah cremation ground, would now and then resound. Through some summer moonlight nights I would be wandering about like an unquiet spirit among the lights and shadows of the tubs and pots on the garden of the roof-terrace.

Those who would dismiss this as sheer poetising would be wrong. The very earth in spite of its having aged considerably surprises us occasionally by its departure from sober stability; in the days of its youth, when it had not become hardened and crusty, it was effusively volcanic and indulged in many a wild escapade. In the days of man's first youth the same sort of thing happens. So long as the materials which go to form his life have not taken on their final shape they are apt to be turbulent in the process of their formation.

This was the time when my brother Jyotirindra decided to start the *Bharati* with our eldest brother as editor, giving us fresh food for enthusiasm. I was then just sixteen, but I was not left out of the editorial staff. A short time before, in all the insolence of my youthful vanity, I had written a criticism of the *Meghanadabadha*. As acidity is characteristic of the unripe mango so is abuse of the immature critic. When other powers are lacking, the power of pricking seems to be at its sharpest. I had thus sought immortality by leaving my scratches on that immortal epic. This impudent criticism was my first contribution to the Bharati.

In the first volume I also published a long poem called *Kavikahini*, The Poet's Story. It was the product of an age when the writer had seen practically nothing of the world except an exaggerated image of his own nebulous self. So the hero of the story was naturally a poet, not the writer as he was, but as he imagined or desired himself to seem. It would hardly be correct to say that he desired to *be* what he portrayed; that represented more what he thought was expected of him, what would make the world admiringly nod and say: "Yes, a poet indeed, quite the correct thing." In it was a great parade of universal love, that pet subject of the budding poet, which sounds as big as it is easy to talk about. While yet any truth has not dawned upon one's own mind, and others' words are one's only stock-in-trade, simplicity and restraint in expression are not possible. Then, in the endeavour to display magnified that which is really big in itself, it becomes impossible to avoid a grotesque and ridiculous exhibition.

When I blush to read these effusions of my boyhood I am also struck with the fear that very possibly in my later writings the same distortion, wrought by straining after effect, lurks in a less obvious form. The loudness of my voice, I doubt not, often drowns the thing I would say; and some day or other Time will find me out.

The *Kavikahini* was the first work of mine to appear in book form. When I went with my second brother to Ahmedabad, some enthusiastic friend of mine took me by surprise by printing and publishing it and sending me a copy. I cannot say that he did well, but the feeling that was roused in me at the time did not resemble that of an indignant judge. He got his punishment, however, not from the author, but from the public who hold the purse strings. I have heard that the dead load of the books lay, for many a long day, heavy on the shelves of the booksellers and the mind of the luckless publisher.

Writings of the age at which I began to contribute to the *Bharati* cannot possibly be fit for publication. There is no better way of ensuring repentance at maturity than to rush into print too early. But it has one redeeming feature: the irresistible impulse to see one's writings in print exhausts itself during early life. Who are the readers, what do they say, what printers' errors have remained uncorrected, these and the like worries run their course as infantile maladies and leave one leisure in later life to attend to one's literary work in a healthier frame of mind.

413

Bengali literature is not old enough to have elaborated those internal checks which can serve to control its votaries. As experience in writing is gained the Bengali writer has to evolve the restraining force from within himself. This makes it impossible for him to avoid the creation of a great deal of rubbish during a considerable length of time. The ambition to work wonders with the modest gifts at one's disposal is bound to be an obsession in the beginning, so that the effort to transcend at every step one's natural powers, and therewith the bounds of truth and beauty, is always visible in early writings. To recover one's normal self, to learn to respect one's powers as they are, is a matter of time.

However that may be, I have left much of youthful folly to be ashamed of, besmirching the pages of the *Bharati*; and this shames me not for its literary defects alone but for its atrocious impudence, its extravagant excesses and its high-sounding artificiality. At the same time I am free to recognise that the writings of that period were pervaded with an enthusiasm the value of which cannot be small. It was a period to which, if error was natural, so was the boyish faculty of hoping, believing and rejoicing. And if the fuel of error was necessary for feeding the flame of enthusiasm then while that which was fit to be reduced to ashes will have become ash, the good work done by the flame will not have been in vain in my life.

PART V

24

Ahmedabad

When the *Bharati* entered upon its second year, my second brother proposed to take me to England; and when my father gave his consent, this further unasked favour of providence came on me as a surprise.

As a first step I accompanied my brother to Ahmedabad where he was posted as judge. My sister-in-law with her children was then in England, so the house was practically empty.

The Judge's house is known as *Shahibagh* and was a palace of the Badshahs of old. At the foot of the wall supporting a broad terrace flowed the thin summer stream of the Savarmati river along one edge of its ample bed of sand. My brother used to go off to his court, and I would be left all alone in the vast expanse of the palace, with only the cooing of the pigeons to break the midday stillness; and an unaccountable curiosity kept me wandering about the empty rooms.

Into the niches in the wall of a large chamber my brother had put his books. One of these was a gorgeous edition of Tennyson's works, with big print and numerous pictures. The book, for me, was as silent as the palace, and, much in the same way I wandered among its picture plates. Not that I could not make anything of the text, but it spoke to me more like inarticulate cooings than words. In my brother's library I also found a book of collected Sanskrit poems edited by Dr. Haberlin and printed at the old Serampore press. This was also beyond my understanding but the sonorous Sanskrit words, and the march of the metre, kept me tramping among the *Amaru Shataka* poems to the mellow roll of their drum call.

In the upper room of the palace tower was my lonely hermit cell, my only companions being a nest of wasps. In the unrelieved darkness of the night I slept there alone. Sometimes a wasp or two would drop off the nest on to my bed, and if perchance I happened to roll on one, the meeting was unpleasing to the wasp and keenly discomforting to me.

On moonlight nights pacing round and round the extensive terrace overlooking the river was one of my caprices. It was while so doing that I first composed my own tunes for my songs. The song addressed to the Rose-maiden was one of these, and it still finds a place in my published works.

Finding how imperfect was my knowledge of English I set to work reading through some English books with the help of a dictionary. From my earliest years it was my habit not to let any want of complete comprehension interfere with my reading on, quite satisfied with the structure which my imagination reared on the bits which I understood here and there. I am reaping even today both the good and bad effects of this habit.

25

England

After six months thus spent in Ahmedabad we started for England. In an unlucky moment I began to write letters about my journey to my relatives and to the *Bharati*. Now it is beyond my power to call them back. These were nothing but the outcome of youthful bravado. At that age the mind refuses to admit that its greatest pride is in its power to understand, to accept, to respect; and that modesty is the best means of enlarging its domain. Admiration and praise are looked upon as a sign of weakness or surrender, and the desire to cry down and hurt and demolish with argument gives rise to this kind of intellectual fireworks. These attempts of mine to establish my superiority by revilement might have occasioned me amusement today, had not their want of straightness and common courtesy been too painful.

From my earliest years I had had practically no commerce with the outside world. To be plunged in this state, at the age of seventeen, into the midst of the social sea of England would have justified considerable misgiving as to my being able to keep afloat. But as my sister-in-law happened to be in Brighton with her children I weathered the first shock of it under her shelter.

Winter was then approaching. One evening as we were chatting round the fireside, the children came running to us with the exciting news that it had been snowing. We at once went out. It was bitingly cold, the sky filled with white moonlight, the earth covered with white snow. It was not the face of Nature familiar to me, but something quite different—like a dream. Everything near seemed to have receded far away, leaving the still white figure of an ascetic steeped in deep meditation. The sudden revelation, on the mere stepping outside a door, of such wonderful, such immense beauty had never before come upon me.

My days passed merrily under the affectionate care of my sister-in-law and in boisterous rompings with the children. They were greatly tickled at my curious English pronunciation, and though in the rest of their games I could whole-heartedly join, this I failed to see the fun of. How could I explain to them that there was no logical means of distinguishing between the sound of *a* in warm and *o* in worm. Unlucky that I was, I had to bear the brunt of the ridicule which was more properly the due of the vagaries of English spelling.

I became quite an adept in inventing new ways of keeping the children occupied and amused. This art has stood me in good stead many a time thereafter, and its usefulness for me is not yet over. But I no longer feel in myself the same unbounded profusion of ready contrivance. That was the first opportunity I had for giving my heart to children, and it had all the freshness and overflowing exuberance of such a first gift.

But I had not set out on this journey to exchange a home beyond the seas for the one on this side. The idea was that I should study Law and come back a barrister. So one day I was put into a public school in Brighton. The first thing the Headmaster said after scanning my features was: "What a splendid head you have!" This detail lingers in my memory because she, who at home was an enthusiast in her self-imposed duty of keeping my vanity in check, had impressed on me that my cranium* and features generally, compared with that of many another were barely of a medium order. I hope the reader will not fail to count it to my credit that I implicitly believed her, and inwardly deplored the parsimony of the Creator in the matter of my making. On many another occasion, finding myself estimated by my English acquaintances differently from what I had been accustomed to be by her, I was led to seriously worry my mind over the divergence in the standard of taste between the two countries!

One thing in the Brighton school seemed very wonderful: the other boys were not at all rude to me. On the contrary they would often thrust oranges and apples into my pockets and run away. I can only ascribe this uncommon behaviour of theirs to my being a foreigner.

I was not long in this school either—but that was no fault of the school. Mr. Tarak Palit† was then in England. He could see that this was not the way for me to get on, and prevailed upon my brother to allow him to take me to London, and leave me there to myself in a lodging house. The lodgings selected faced the Regent Gardens. It was then the depth of winter. There was not a leaf on the row of trees in front which stood staring at the sky with their scraggy snow-covered branches—a sight which chilled my very bones.

For the newly arrived stranger there can hardly be a more cruel place than London in winter. I knew no one near by, nor could I find my way about. The days of sitting alone at a window, gazing at the outside world, came back into my life. But the scene in this case was not attractive. There was a frown on its countenance; the sky turbid; the light lacking lustre like a dead man's eye; the horizon shrunk upon itself; with never an inviting smile from a broad hospitable world. The room was but scantily furnished, but there happened to be a harmonium which, after the daylight came to its untimely end, I

---

* There was a craze for phrenology at the time.
† Latterly Sir Tarak Palit, a life-long friend of the writer's second brother.

used to play upon according to my fancy. Sometimes Indians would come to see me; and, though my acquaintance with them was but slight, when they rose to leave I felt inclined to hold them back by their coat-tails.

While living in these rooms there was one who came to teach me Latin. His gaunt figure with its worn-out clothing seemed no more able than the naked trees to withstand the winter's grip. I do not know what his age was but he clearly looked older than his years. Some days in the course of our lessons he would suddenly be at a loss for some word and look vacant and ashamed. His people at home counted him a crank. He had become possessed of a theory. He believed that in each age some one dominant idea is manifested in every human society in all parts of the world; and though it may take different shapes under different degrees of civilisation, it is at bottom one and the same; nor is such idea taken from one by another by any process of adoption, for this truth holds good even where there is no intercourse. His great preoccupation was the gathering and recording of facts to prove this theory. And while so engaged his home lacked food, his body clothes. His daughters had but scant respect for his theory and were perhaps constantly upbraiding him for his infatuation. Some days one could see from his face that he had lighted upon some new proof, and that his thesis had correspondingly advanced. On these occasions I would broach the subject, and wax enthusiastic at his enthusiasm. On other days he would be steeped in gloom, as if his burden was too heavy to bear. Then would our lessons halt at every step; his eyes wander away into empty space; and his mind refuse to be dragged into the pages of the first Latin Grammar. I felt keenly for the poor body-starved theory-burdened soul, and though I was under no delusion as to the assistance I got in my Latin, I could not make up my mind to get rid of him. This pretence of learning Latin lasted as long as I was at these lodgings. When on the eve of leaving them I offered to settle his dues he said piteously: "I have done nothing, and only wasted your time, I cannot accept any payment from you." It was with great difficulty that I got him at last to take his fees.

Though my Latin tutor had never ventured to trouble me with the proofs of his theory, yet up to this day I do not disbelieve it. I am convinced that the minds of men are connected through some deep-lying continuous medium, and that a disturbance in one part is by it secretly communicated to others.

Mr. Palit next placed me in the house of a coach named Barker. He used to lodge and prepare students for their examinations. Except his mild little wife there was not a thing with any pretensions to attractiveness about this household. One can understand how such a tutor can get pupils, for these poor creatures do not often get the chance of making a choice. But it is painful to think of the conditions under which such men get wives. Mrs. Barker had attempted to console herself with a pet dog, but when Barker wanted to punish his wife he tortured the dog. So that her affection for the unfortunate animal only made for an enlargement of her field of sensibility.

From these surroundings, when my sister-in-law sent for me to Torquay in Devonshire, I was only too glad to run off to her. I cannot tell how happy I was with the hills there, the sea, the flower-covered meadows, the shade of the pine woods, and my two little restlessly playful companions. I was nevertheless sometimes tormented with questionings as to why, when my eyes were so surfeited with beauty, my mind saturated with joy, and my leisure-filled days crossing over the limitless blue of space freighted with unalloyed happiness, there should be no call of poetry to me. So one day off I went along the rocky shore, armed with MS. book and umbrella, to fulfil my poet's destiny. The spot I selected was of undoubted beauty, for that did not depend on my rhyme or fancy. There was a flat bit of overhanging rock reaching out as with a perpetual eagerness over the waters; rocked on the foam-flecked waves of the liquid blue in front, the sunny sky slept smilingly to its lullaby; behind, the shade of the fringe of pines lay spread like the slipped off garment of some languorous wood nymph. Enthroned on that seat of stone I wrote a poem *Magnatari* (the sunken boat). I might have believed today that it was good, had I taken the precaution of sinking it then in the sea. But such consolation is not open to me, for it happens to be existing in the body; and though banished from my published works, a writ might yet cause it to be produced.

The messenger of duty however was not idle. Again came its

call and I returned to London. This time I found a refuge in the household of Dr. Scott. One fine evening with bag and baggage I invaded his home. Only the white haired Doctor, his wife and their eldest daughter were there. The two younger girls, alarmed at this incursion of an Indian stranger had gone off to stay with a relative. I think they came back home only after they got the news of my not being dangerous.

In a very short time I became like one of the family. Mrs. Scott treated me as a son, and the heartfelt kindness I got from her daughters is rare even from one's own relations.

One thing struck me when living in this family—that human nature is everywhere the same. We are fond of saying, and I also believed, that the devotion of an Indian wife to her husband is something unique, and not to be found in Europe. But I at least was unable to discern any difference between Mrs. Scott and an ideal Indian wife. She was entirely wrapped up in her husband. With their modest means there was no fussing about of too many servants, and Mrs. Scott attended to every detail of her husband's wants herself. Before he came back home from his work of an evening, she would arrange his arm-chair and woollen slippers before the fire with her own hands. She would never allow herself to forget for a moment the things he liked, or the behaviour which pleased him. She would go over the house every morning, with their only maid, from attic to kitchen, and the brass rods on the stairs and the door knobs and fittings would be scrubbed and polished till they shone again. Over and above this domestic routine there were the many calls of social duty. After getting through all her daily duties she would join with zest in our evening readings and music, for it is not the least of the duties of a good housewife to make real the gaiety of the leisure hour.

Some evenings I would join the girls in a table-turning seance. We would place our fingers on a small tea table and it would go capering about the room. It got to be so that whatever we touched began to quake and quiver. Mrs. Scott did not quite like all this. She would sometimes gravely shake her head and say she had her doubts about its being right. She bore it bravely, however, not liking to put a damper on our youthful spirits. But one day when we put our hands on Dr. Scott's chimneypot to make it turn, that was too much for her. She rushed up in a great state of mind and forbade us to touch it. She could not bear the idea of Satan having anything to do, even for a moment, with her husband's head-gear.

In all her actions her reverence for her husband was the one thing that stood out. The memory of her sweet self-abnegation makes it clear to me that the ultimate perfection of all womanly love is to be found in reverence; that where no extraneous cause has hampered its true development woman's love naturally grows into worship. Where the appointments of luxury are in profusion, and frivolity tarnishes both day and night, this love is degraded, and woman's nature finds not the joy of its perfection.

I spent some months here. Then it was time for my brother to return home, and my father wrote to me to accompany him. I was delighted at the prospect. The light of my country, the sky of my country, had been silently calling me. When I said good bye Mrs. Scott took me by the hand and wept. "Why did you come to us," she said, "if you must go so soon?" That household no longer exists in London. Some of the members of the Doctor's family have departed to the other world, others are scattered in places unknown to me. But it will always live in my memory.

One winter's day, as I was passing through a street in Tunbridge Wells, I saw a man standing on the road side. His bare toes were showing through his gaping boots, his breast was partly uncovered. He said nothing to me, perhaps because begging was forbidden, but he looked up at my face just for a moment. The coin I gave him was perhaps more valuable than he expected, for, after I had gone on a bit, he came after me and said: "Sir, you have given me a gold piece by mistake," with which he offered to return it to me. I might not have particularly remembered this, but for a similar thing which happened on another occasion. When I first reached the Torquay railway station a porter took my luggage to the cab outside. After searching my purse for small change in vain, I gave him half-a-crown as the cab started. After a while he came running after us, shouting to the cabman to stop. I thought to myself that finding me to be such an innocent he had hit upon some excuse for demanding more. As the cab stopped he said: "You must have mistaken a half-crown piece for a penny, Sir!"

I cannot say that I have never been cheated while in England, but not in any way which it would be fair to hold in remembrance. What grew chiefly upon me, rather, was the conviction that only those who are trustworthy know how to trust. I was an unknown foreigner, and could have easily evaded payment with impunity, yet no London shopkeeper ever mistrusted me.

During the whole period of my stay in England I was mixed up in a farcical comedy which I had to play out from start to finish. I happened to get acquainted with the widow of some departed high Anglo-Indian official. She was good enough to call me by the pet-name Ruby. Some Indian friend of hers had composed a doleful poem in English in memory of her husband. It is needless to expatiate on its poetic merit or felicity of diction. As my ill-luck would have it, the composer had indicated that the dirge was to be chanted to the mode *Behaga*. So the widow one day entreated me to sing it to her thus. Like the silly innocent that I was, I weakly acceded. There was unfortunately no one there but I who could realise the atrociously ludicrous way in which the *Behaga* mode combined with those absurd verses. The widow seemed intensely touched to hear the Indian's lament for her husband sung to its native melody. I thought that there the matter ended, but that was not to be.

I frequently met the widowed lady at different social gatherings, and when after dinner we joined the ladies in the drawing room, she would ask me to sing that *Behaga*. Everyone else would anticipate some extraordinary specimen of Indian music and would add their entreaties to hers. Then from her pocket would come forth printed copies of that fateful composition, and my ears begin to redden and tingle. And at last, with bowed head and quavering voice I would have to make a beginning—but too keenly conscious that to none else in the room but me was this performance sufficiently heartrending. At the end, amidst much suppressed tittering, there would come a chorus of "Thank you very much!" "How interesting!" And in spite of its being winter I would perspire all over. Who would have predicted at my birth or at his death what a severe blow to me would be the demise of this estimable Anglo-Indian!

Then, for a time, while I was living with Dr. Scott and attending lectures at the University College, I lost touch with the widow. She was in a suburban locality some distance away from London, and I frequently got letters from her inviting me there. But my dread of that dirge kept me from accepting these invitations. At length I got a pressing telegram from her. I was on my way to college when this telegram reached me and my stay in England was then about to come to its close. I thought to myself I ought to see the widow once more before my departure, and so yielded to her importunity.

Instead of coming home from college I went straight to the railway station. It was a horrible day, bitterly cold, snowing and foggy. The station I was bound for was the terminus of the line. So I felt quite easy in mind and did not think it worthwhile to inquire about the time of arrival.

All the station platforms were coming on the right hand side, and in the right hand corner seat I had ensconced myself reading a book. It had already become so dark that nothing was visible outside. One by one the other passengers got down at their destinations. We reached and left the station just before the last one. Then the train stopped again, but there was nobody to be seen, nor any lights or platform. The mere passenger has no means of divining why trains should sometimes stop at the wrong times and places, so, giving up the attempt, I went on with my reading. Then the train began to move backwards. There seems to be no accounting for railway eccentricity, thought I as I once more returned to my book. But when we came right back to the previous station, I could remain indifferent no longer. "When are we getting to ——" I inquired at the station. "You are just coming from there," was the reply. "Where are we going now, then?" I asked, thoroughly flurried. "To London." I thereupon understood that this was a shuttle train. On inquiring about the next train to —— I was informed that there were no more trains that night. And in reply to my next question I gathered that there was no inn within five miles.

I had left home after breakfast at ten in the morning, and had had nothing since. When abstinence is the only choice, an ascetic frame of mind comes easy. I buttoned up my thick overcoat to the neck and seating myself under a platform lamp went on with my reading. The book I had with me was Spencer's *Data of Ethics*, then recently published. I consoled myself with the thought that I might never get another such opportunity of concentrating my whole attention on such a subject.

After a short time a porter came and informed me that a special was running and would be in in half an hour. I felt so cheered up by the news that I could not go on any longer with the *Data of Ethics*. Where I was due at seven I arrived at length at nine. "What is this, Ruby?" asked my hostess. "Whatever have you been doing with yourself?" I was unable to take much pride in the account of my wonderful adventures which I gave her. Dinner was over; nevertheless, as my misfortune was hardly my fault, I did not expect condign punishment, especially as the dispenser was a woman. But all that the widow of the high Anglo-Indian official said to me was: "Come along, Ruby, have a cup of tea."

I never was a tea-drinker, but in the hope that it might be of some assistance in allaying my consuming hunger I managed to swallow a cup of strong decoction with a couple of dry biscuits. When I at length reached the drawing room I found a gathering of elderly ladies and among them one pretty young American who was engaged to a nephew of my hostess and seemed busy going through the usual premarital love passages.

"Let's have some dancing," said my hostess. I was neither in the mood nor bodily condition for that exercise. But it is the docile who achieve the most impossible things in this world; so, though the dance was primarily got up for the benefit of the engaged couple, I had to dance with the ladies of considerably advanced age, with only the tea and biscuits between myself and starvation.

But my sorrows did not end here. "Where are you putting up for the night?" asked my hostess. This was a question for which I was not prepared. While I stared at her, speechless, she explained that as the local inn would close at midnight I had better betake myself thither without further delay. Hospitality, however, was not entirely wanting for I had not to find the inn unaided, a servant showing me the way there with a lantern. At first I thought this might prove a blessing in disguise, and at once proceeded to make inquiries for food: flesh, fish or vegetable, hot or cold, anything! I was told that drinks I could have in any variety but nothing to eat. Then I looked to slumber for forgetfulness, but there seemed to be no room even in her world-embracing lap. The sand-stone floor of the bedroom was icy cold, an old bedstead and worn-out wash-stand being its only furniture.

In the morning the Anglo-Indian widow sent for me to breakfast. I found a cold repast spread out, evidently the remnants of last night's dinner. A small portion of this, lukewarm or cold, offered to me last night could not have hurt anyone, while my dancing might then have been less like the agonised wrigglings of a landed carp.

After breakfast my hostess informed me that the lady for whose delectation I had been invited to sing was ill in bed, and that I would have to serenade her from her bedroom door. I was made to stand up on the staircase landing. Pointing to a closed door the widow said: "That's where she is." And I gave voice to that *Behaga* dirge facing the mysterious unknown on the other side. Of what happened to the invalid as the result I have yet received no news.

After my return to London I had to expiate in bed the consequences of my fatuous complaisance. Dr. Scott's girls implored me, on my conscience, not to take this as a sample of English hospitality. It was the effect of India's salt, they protested.

26

Loken Palit

While I was attending lectures on English literature at the University College, Loken Palit was my class fellow. He was about four years younger than I. At the age I am writing these reminiscences a difference of four years is not perceptible. But it is difficult for friendship to bridge the gulf between seventeen and thirteen. Lacking the weight of years the boy is always anxious to keep up the dignity of seniority. But this did not raise any barrier in my mind in the case of the boy Loken, for I could not feel that he was in any way my junior.

Boy and girl students sat together in the College library for study. This was the place for our tete-a-tete. Had we been fairly quiet about it none need have complained, but my young friend was so surcharged with high spirits that at the least provocation they would burst forth as laughter. In all countries girls have a perverse degree of application to their studies, and I feel repentant as I recall the multitude of reproachful blue eyes which vainly showered disapprobation on our unrestrained merriment. But in those days I felt not the slightest sympathy with the distress of disturbed studiousness. By the grace of Providence I have never had a headache in my life, nor a moment of compunction for interrupted school studies.

With our laughter as an almost unbroken accompaniment we managed also to do a bit of literary discussion, and, though Loken's reading of Bengali literature was less extensive than mine, he made up for that by the keenness of his intellect. Among the subjects we discussed was Bengali orthography.

The way it arose was this. One of the Scott girls wanted me to teach her Bengali. When taking her through the alphabet I expressed my pride that Bengali spelling has a conscience, and does not delight in overstepping rules at every step. I made clear to her how laughable would have been the waywardness of English spelling but for the tragic compulsion we were under to cram it for our examinations. But my pride had a fall. It transpired that Bengali spelling was quite as impatient of bondage, but that habit had blinded me to its transgressions.

Then I began to search for the laws regulating its lawlessness. I was quite surprised at the wonderful assistance which Loken proved to be in this matter.

After Loken had got into the Indian Civil Service, and returned home, the work, which had in the University College library had its source in rippling merriment, flowed on in a widening stream. Loken's boisterous delight in literature was as the wind in the sails of my literary adventure. And when at the height of my youth I was driving the tandem of prose and poetry at a furious rate, Loken's unstinted appreciation kept my energies from flagging for a moment. Many an extraordinary prose or poetical flight have I taken in his bungalow in the moffussil. On many an occasion did our literary and musical gatherings assemble under the auspices of the evening star to disperse, as did the lamplights at the breezes of dawn, under the morning star.

Of the many lotus flowers at *Saraswati's** feet the blossom of friendship must be her favourite. I have not come across much of golden pollen in her lotus bank, but have nothing to complain of as regards the profusion of the sweet savour of good-fellowship.

27

The Broken Heart

While in England I began another poem, which I went on with during my journey home, and finished after my return. This was published under the name of *Bhagna Hriday*, The Broken Heart. At the time I thought it very good. There was nothing strange in the writer's thinking so; but it did not fail to gain the appreciation of the readers of the time as well. I remember how, after it came out, the chief minister of the late Raja of Tipperah called on me solely to deliver the message that the Raja admired the poem and entertained high hopes of the writer's future literary career.

About this poem of my eighteenth year let me set down here what I wrote in a letter when I was thirty:

> When I began to write the *Bhagna Hriday* I was eighteen—neither in my childhood nor my youth. This borderland age is not illumined with the direct rays of Truth;—its reflection is seen here and there, and the rest is shadow. And like twilight shades its imaginings are long-drawn and vague, making the real world seem like a world of phantasy. The curious part of it is that not only was I eighteen, but everyone around me seemed to be eighteen likewise; and we all flitted about in the same baseless, substanceless world of imagination, where even the most intense joys and sorrows seemed like the joys and sorrows of dreamland. There being

---

* Saraswati, the goddess of learning, is depicted in Bengal as clad in white and seated among a mass of lotus flowers.

nothing real to weigh them against, the trivial did duty for the great.

This period of my life, from the age of fifteen or sixteen to twenty-two or twenty-three, was one of utter disorderliness.

When, in the early ages of the Earth, land and water had not yet distinctly separated, huge misshapen amphibious creatures walked the trunk-less forests growing on the oozing silt. Thus do the passions of the dim ages of the immature mind, as disproportionate and curiously shaped, haunt the unending shades of its trackless, nameless wildernesses. They know not themselves, nor the aim of their wanderings; and, because they do not, they are ever apt to imitate something else. So, at this age of unmeaning activity, when my undeveloped powers, unaware of and unequal to their object, were jostling each other for an outlet, each sought to assert superiority through exaggeration.

When milk-teeth are trying to push their way through, they work the infant into a fever. All this agitation finds no justification till the teeth are out and have begun assisting in the absorption of food. In the same way do our early passions torment the mind, like a malady, till they realise their true relationship with the outer world.

The lessons I learnt from my experiences at that stage are to be found in every moral text-book, but are not therefore to be despised. That which keeps our appetites confined within us, and checks their free access to the outside, poisons our life. Such is selfishness which refuses to give free play to our desires, and prevents them from reaching their real goal, and that is why it is always accompanied by festering untruths and extravagances. When our desires find unlimited freedom in good work they shake off their diseased condition and come back to their own nature;—that is their true end, there also is the joy of their being.

The condition of my immature mind which I have described was fostered both by the example and precept of the time, and I am not sure that the effects of these are not lingering on to the present day. Glancing back at the period of which I tell, it strikes me that we had gained more of stimulation than of nourishment out of English Literature. Our literary gods then were Shakespeare, Milton and Byron; and the quality in their work which stirred us most was strength of passion. In the social life of Englishmen passionate outbursts are kept severely in check, for which very reason, perhaps, they so dominate their literature, making its characteristic to be the working out of extravagantly vehement feelings to an inevitable conflagration. At least this uncontrolled excitement was what we learnt to look on as the quintessence of English literature.

Moonlight

In the impetuous declamation of English poetry by Akshay Chowdhury, our initiator into English literature, there was the wildness of intoxication. The frenzy of Romeo's and Juliet's love, the fury of King Lear's impotent lamentation, the all-consuming fire of Othello's jealousy, these were the things that roused us to enthusiastic admiration. Our restricted social life, our narrower field of activity, was hedged in with such monotonous uniformity that tempestuous feelings found no entrance;—all was as calm and quiet as could be. So our hearts naturally craved the life-bringing shock of the passionate emotion in English literature. Ours was not the æsthetic enjoyment of literary art, but the jubilant welcome by stagnation of a turbulent wave, even though it should stir up to the surface the slime of the bottom.

Shakespeare's contemporary literature represents the war-dance of the day when the Renascence came to Europe in all the violence of its reaction against the severe curbing and cramping of the hearts of men. The examination of good and evil, beauty and ugliness, was not the main object—man then seemed consumed with the anxiety to break through all barriers to the inmost sanctuary of his being, there to discover the ultimate image of his own violent desire. That is why in this literature we find such poignant, such exuberant, such unbridled expression.

The spirit of this bacchanalian revelry of Europe found entrance into our demurely well-behaved social world, woke us up, and made us lively. We were dazzled by the glow of unfettered life which fell upon our custom-smothered heart, pining for an opportunity to disclose itself.

There was another such day in English literature when the slow-measure of Pope's common time gave place to the dance-rhythm of the French revolution. This had Byron for its poet. And the impetuosity of his passion also moved our veiled heart-bride in the seclusion of her corner.

In this wise did the excitement of the pursuit of English literature come to sway the heart of the youth of our time, and at mine the waves of this excitement kept beating from every side. The first awakening is the time for the play of energy, not its repression.

And yet our case was so different from that of Europe. There the excitability and impatience of bondage was a reflection from its history into its literature. Its expression was consistent with its feeling. The roaring of the storm was heard because a storm was really raging. The breeze therefrom that ruffled our little world sounded in reality but little above a murmur. Therein it failed to satisfy our minds, so that our attempts to imitate the blast of a hurricane led us easily into exaggeration—a tendency which still persists and may not prove easy of cure.

And for this, the fact that in English literature the reticence of true art has not yet appeared, is responsible. Human emotion is only one of the ingredients of literature and not its end—which is the beauty of perfect fullness consisting in simplicity and restraint. This is a proposition which English literature does not yet fully admit.

Our minds from infancy to old age are being moulded by this English literature alone. But other literatures of Europe, both classical and modern, of which the art-form shows the well-nourished development due to a systematic cultivation of self-control, are not subjects of our study; and so, as it seems to me, we are yet unable to arrive at a correct perception of the true aim and method of literary work.

Akshay Babu, who had made the passion in English literature living to us, was himself a votary of the emotional life. The importance of realising truth in the fullness of its perfection seemed less apparent to him than that of feeling it in the heart. He had no intellectual respect for religion, but songs of *Shyāmā*, the dark Mother, would bring tears to his eyes. He felt no call to search for ultimate reality; whatever moved his heart served him for the time as the truth, even obvious coarseness not proving a deterrent.

Atheism was the dominant note of the English prose writings then in vogue—Bentham, Mill and Comte being favourite authors. Theirs was the reasoning in terms of which our youths argued. The age of Mill constitutes a natural epoch in English History. It represents a healthy reaction of the body politic; these destructive forces having been brought in, temporarily, to rid it of accumulated thought-rubbish. In our country we received these in the letter, but never sought to make practical use of them, employing them only as a stimulant to incite ourselves to moral revolt. Atheism was thus for us a mere intoxication.

For these reasons educated men then fell mainly into two classes. One class would be always thrusting themselves forward with unprovoked argumentation to cut to pieces all belief in God. Like the hunter whose hands itch, no sooner he spies a living creature on the top or at the foot of a tree, to kill it, whenever these came to learn of a harmless belief lurking anywhere in fancied security, they felt stirred up to sally forth and demolish it. We had for a short time a tutor of whom this was a pet diversion. Though I was a mere boy, even I could not escape his onslaughts. Not that his attainments were of any account, or that his opinions were the result of any enthusiastic search for the truth, being mostly gathered from others' lips. But though I fought him with all my strength, unequally matched in age as we were, I suffered many a bitter defeat. Sometimes I felt so mortified I almost wanted to cry.

The other class consisted not of believers, but religious epicureans, who found comfort and solace in gathering together, and steeping themselves in pleasing sights, sounds and scents galore, under the garb of religious ceremonial; they luxuriated in the paraphernalia of worship. In neither of these classes was doubt or denial the outcome of the travail of their quest.

Though these religious aberrations pained me, I cannot say I was not at all influenced by them. With the intellectual impudence of budding youth this revolt also found a place. The religious services which were held in our family I would have nothing to do with, I had not accepted them for my own. I was busy blowing up a raging flame with the bellows of my emotions. It was only the worship of fire, the giving of oblations to increase its flame—with no other aim. And because my endeavour had no end in view it was measureless, always reaching beyond any assigned limit.

As with religion, so with my emotions, I felt no need for any underlying truth, my excitement being an end in itself. I call to mind some lines of a poet of that time:

My heart is mine
I have sold it to none,
Be it tattered and torn and worn away,
My heart is mine!

From the standpoint of truth the heart need not worry itself so; for nothing compels it to wear itself to tatters. In truth sorrow is not desirable, but taken apart its pungency may appear savoury. This savour our poets often made much of; leaving out the god in whose worship they were indulging. This childishness our country has not yet succeeded in getting rid of. So even today, when we fail to see the truth of religion, we seek in its observance an artistic gratification. So, also, much of our patriotism is not service of the motherland, but the luxury of bringing ourselves into a desirable attitude of mind toward the country.

PART VI

28

European Music

W hen I was in Brighton I once went to hear some Prima
Donna. I forget her name. It may have been Madame
Neilson or Madame Albani. Never before had I come
across such an extraordinary command over the voice. Even our
best singers cannot hide their sense of effort; nor are they ashamed
to bring out, as best they can, top notes or bass notes beyond their
proper register. In our country the understanding portion of the
audience think no harm in keeping the performance up to standard
by dint of their own imagination. For the same reason they do
not mind any harshness of voice or uncouthness of gesture in the
exponent of a perfectly formed melody; on the contrary, they seem
sometimes to be of opinion that such minor external defects serve
better to set off the internal perfection of the composition—as with
the outward poverty of the Great Ascetic, Mahadeva, whose divinity
shines forth naked.

This feeling seems entirely wanting in Europe. There, outward
embellishment must be perfect in every detail, and the least defect
stands shamed and unable to face the public gaze. In our musical
gatherings nothing is thought of spending half-an-hour in tuning
up the *Tanpuras*, or hammering into tone the drums, little and big. In
Europe such duties are performed beforehand, behind the scenes,
for all that comes in front must be faultless. There is thus no room

for any weak spot in the singer's voice. In our country a correct and artistic exposition* of the melody is the main object, thereon is concentrated all the effort. In Europe the voice is the object of culture, and with it they perform impossibilities. In our country the virtuoso is satisfied if he has heard the song; in Europe, they go to hear the singer.

That is what I saw that day in Brighton. To me it was as good as a circus. But, admire the performance as I did, I could not appreciate the song. I could hardly keep from laughing when some of the *cadenzas* imitated the warbling of birds. I felt all the time that it was a misapplication of the human voice. When it came to the turn of a male singer I was considerably relieved. I specially liked the tenor voices which had more of human flesh and blood in them, and seemed less like the disembodied lament of a forlorn spirit.

After this, as I went on hearing and learning more and more of European music, I began to get into the spirit of it; but up to now I am convinced that our music and theirs abide in altogether different apartments, and do not gain entry to the heart by the self-same door.

European music seems to be intertwined with its material life, so that the text of its songs may be as various as that life itself. If we attempt to put our tunes to the same variety of use they tend to lose their significance, and become ludicrous; for our melodies transcend the barriers of everyday life, and only thus can they carry us so deep into Pity, so high into Aloofness; their function being to reveal a picture of the inmost inexpressible depths of our being, mysterious and impenetrable, where the devotee may find his hermitage ready, or even the epicurean his bower, but where there is no room for the busy man of the world.

I cannot claim that I gained admittance to the soul of European music. But what little of it I came to understand from the outside attracted me greatly in one way. It seemed to me so romantic. It is somewhat difficult to analyse what I mean by that word. What I would refer to is the aspect of variety, of abundance, of the waves on

---

* With Indian music it is not a mere question of correctly rendering a melody exactly as composed, but the theme of the original composition is the subject of an improvised interpretative elaboration by the expounding Artist.

the sea of life, of the ever-changing light and shade on their ceaseless undulations. There is the opposite aspect—of pure extension, of the unwinking blue of the sky, of the silent hint of immeasureability in the distant circle of the horizon. However that may be, let me repeat, at the risk of not being perfectly clear, that whenever I have been moved by European music I have said to myself: it is romantic, it is translating into melody the evanescence of life.

Not that we wholly lack the same attempt in some forms of our music; but it is less pronounced, less successful. Our melodies give voice to the star-spangled night, to the first reddening of dawn. They speak of the sky-pervading sorrow which lowers in the darkness of clouds; the speechless deep intoxication of the forest-roaming spring.

29

Valmiki Pratibha

We had a profusely decorated volume of Moore's Irish Melodies: and often have I listened to the enraptured recitation of these by Akshay Babu. The poems combined with the pictorial designs to conjure up for me a dream picture of the Ireland of old. I had not then actually heard the original tunes, but had sung these Irish Melodies to myself to the accompaniment of the harps in the pictures. I longed to hear the real tunes, to learn them, and sing them to Akshay Babu. Some longings unfortunately do get fulfilled in this life, and die in the process. When I went to England I did hear some of the Irish Melodies sung, and learnt them too, but that put an end to my keenness to learn more. They were simple, mournful and sweet, but they somehow did not fit in with the silent melody of the harp which filled the halls of the Old Ireland of my dreams.

When I came back home I sung the Irish melodies I had learnt to my people. "What is the matter with Rabi's voice?" they exclaimed. "How funny and foreign it sounds!" They even felt my speaking voice had changed its tone.

From this mixed cultivation of foreign and native melody was born the *Valmiki Pratibha.** The tunes in this musical drama are mostly Indian, but they have been dragged out of their classic dignity; that which soared in the sky was taught to run on the earth. Those who have seen and heard it performed will, I trust, bear witness that the harnessing of Indian melodic modes to the service of the drama has proved neither derogatory nor futile. This conjunction is the only special feature of *Valmiki Pratibha*. The pleasing task of loosening the chains of melodic forms and making them adaptable to a variety of treatment completely engrossed me.

Several of the songs of *Valmiki Pratibha* were set to tunes originally severely classic in mode; some of the tunes were composed by my brother Jyotirindra; a few were adapted from European sources. The *Telena*[†] style of Indian modes specially lends itself to dramatic purposes and has been frequently utilized in this work. Two English tunes served for the drinking songs of the robber band, and an Irish melody for the lament of the wood nymphs.

Valmiki Pratibha is not a composition which will bear being read. Its significance is lost if it is not heard sung and seen acted. It is not what Europeans call an Opera, but a little drama set to music. That is to say, it is not primarily a musical composition. Very few of the songs are important or attractive by themselves; they all serve merely as the musical text of the play.

Before I went to England we occasionally used to have gatherings of literary men in our house, at which music, recitations and light refreshments were served up. After my return one more such gathering was held, which happened to be the last. It was for an entertainment in this connection that the *Valmiki Pratibha* was

---

* *Valmiki Pratibha* means the genius of Valmiki. The plot is based on the story of Valmiki, the robber chief, being moved to pity and breaking out into a metrical lament on witnessing the grief of one of a pair of cranes whose mate was killed by a hunter. In the metre which so came to him he afterwards composed his Ramayana.

† Some Indian classic melodic compositions are designed on a scheme of accentuation, for which purpose the music is set, not to words, but to unmeaning notation-sounds representing drum-beats or plectrum-impacts which in Indian music are of a considerable variety of tone, each having its own sound-symbol. The *Telena* is one such style of composition.

composed. I played Valmiki and my niece, Pratibha, took the part of Saraswati—which bit of history remains recorded in the name.

I had read in some work of Herbert Spencer's that speech takes on tuneful inflexions whenever emotion comes into play. It is a fact that the tone or tune is as important to us as the spoken word for the expression of anger, sorrow, joy and wonder. Spencer's idea that, through a development of these emotional modulations of voice, man found music, appealed to me. Why should it not do, I thought to myself, to act a drama in a kind of recitative based on this idea. The Kathakas of our country attempt this to some extent, for they frequently break into a chant which, however, stops short of full melodic form. As blank verse is more elastic than rhymed, so such chanting, though not devoid of rhythm, can more freely adapt itself to the emotional interpretation of the text, because it does not attempt to conform to the more rigorous canons of tune and time required by a regular melodic composition. The expression of feeling being the object, these deficiencies in regard to form do not jar on the hearer.

Encouraged by the success of this new line taken in the *Valmiki Pratibha*, I composed another musical play of the same class. It was called the *Kal Mrigaya*, The Fateful Hunt. The plot was based on the story of the accidental killing of the blind hermit's only son by King Dasaratha. It was played on a stage erected on our roof-terrace, and the audience seemed profoundly moved by its pathos. Afterwards, much of it was, with slight changes, incorporated in the *Valmiki Pratibha*, and this play ceased to be separately published in my works.

Long afterwards, I composed a third musical play, *Mayar Khela*, the Play of *Maya*, an operetta of a different type. In this the songs were important, not the drama. In the others a series of dramatic situations were strung on a thread of melody; this was a garland of songs with just a thread of dramatic plot running through. The play of feeling, and not action, was its special feature. In point of fact I was, while composing it, saturated with the mood of song.

The enthusiasm which went to the making of *Valmiki Pratibha* and *Kal Mrigaya* I have never felt for any other work of mine. In these two the creative musical impulse of the time found expression.

My brother, Jyotirindra, was engaged the live-long day at his piano, refashioning the classic melodic forms at his pleasure. And, at every turn of his instrument, the old modes took on unthought-of shapes and expressed new shades of feeling. The melodic forms which had become habituated to their pristine stately gait, when thus compelled to march to more lively unconventional measures, displayed an unexpected agility and power; and moved us correspondingly. We could plainly hear the tunes speak to us while Akshay Babu and I sat on either side fitting words to them as they grew out of my brother's nimble fingers. I do not claim that our *libretto* was good poetry but it served as a vehicle for the tunes.

In the riotous joy of this revolutionary activity were these two musical plays composed, and so they danced merrily to every measure, whether or not technically correct, indifferent as to the tunes being homelike or foreign.

On many an occasion has the Bengali reading public been grievously exercised over some opinion or literary form of mine, but it is curious to find that the daring with which I had played havoc with accepted musical notions did not rouse any resentment; on the contrary those who came to hear departed pleased. A few of Akshay Babu's compositions find place in the *Valmiki Pratibha* and also adaptations from Vihari Chakravarti's *Sarada Mangal* series of songs.

I used to take the leading part in the performance of these musical dramas. From my early years I had a taste for acting, and firmly believed that I had a special aptitude for it. I think I proved that my belief was not ill-founded. I had only once before done the part of Aleek Babu in a farce written by my brother Jyotirindra. So these were really my first attempts at acting. I was then very young and nothing seemed to fatigue or trouble my voice.

In our house, at the time, a cascade of musical emotion was gushing forth day after day, hour after hour, its scattered spray reflecting into our being a whole gamut of rainbow colours. Then, with the freshness of youth, our new-born energy, impelled by its virgin curiosity, struck out new paths in every direction. We felt we would try and test everything, and no achievement seemed impossible. We wrote, we sang, we acted, we poured ourselves out on every side. This was how I stepped into my twentieth year.

Of these forces which so triumphantly raced our lives along, my brother Jyotirindra was the charioteer. He was absolutely fearless. Once, when I was a mere lad, and had never ridden a horse before, he made me mount one and gallop by his side, with no qualms about his unskilled companion. When at the same age, while we were at Shelidah, (the head-quarters of our estate,) news was brought of a tiger, he took me with him on a hunting expedition. I had no gun—it would have been more dangerous to me than to the tiger if I had. We left our shoes at the outskirts of the jungle and crept in with bare feet. At last we scrambled up into a bamboo thicket, partly stripped of its thorn-like twigs, where I somehow managed to crouch behind my brother till the deed was done; with no means of even administering a shoe-beating to the unmannerly brute had he dared lay his offensive paws on me!

Thus did my brother give me full freedom both internal and external in the face of all dangers. No usage or custom was a bondage for him, and so was he able to rid me of my shrinking diffidence.

30

Evening Songs

In the state of being confined within myself, of which I have been telling, I wrote a number of poems which have been grouped together, under the title of the *Heart-Wilderness*, in Mohita Babu's edition of my works. In one of the poems subsequently published in a volume called *Morning Songs*, the following lines occur:

There is a vast wilderness whose name is *Heart*;
Whose interlacing forest branches dandle and rock
    darkness like an infant.
I lost my way in its depths.

from which came the idea of the name for this group of poems.

Much of what I wrote, when thus my life had no commerce with the outside, when I was engrossed in the contemplation of my own heart, when my imaginings wandered in many a disguise amidst causeless emotions and aimless longings, has been left out of that edition; only a few of the poems originally published in the volume entitled *Evening Songs* finding a place there, in the *Heart-Wilderness* group.

My brother Jyotirindra and his wife had left home travelling on a long journey, and their rooms on the third storey, facing the terraced-roof, were empty. I took possession of these and the terrace, and spent my days in solitude. While thus left in communion with my self alone, I know not how I slipped out of the poetical groove into which I had fallen. Perhaps being cut off from those whom I sought to please, and whose taste in poetry moulded the form I tried to put my thoughts into, I naturally gained freedom from the style they had imposed on me.

I began to use a slate for my writing. That also helped in my emancipation. The manuscript books in which I had indulged before seemed to demand a certain height of poetic flight, to work up to which I had to find my way by a comparison with others. But the slate was clearly fitted for my mood of the moment. "Fear not," it seemed to say. "Write just what you please, one rub will wipe all away!"

As I wrote a poem or two, thus unfettered, I felt a great joy well up within me. "At last," said my heart, "what I write is my own!" Let no one mistake this for an accession of pride. Rather did I feel a pride in my former productions, as being all the tribute I had to pay them. But I refuse to call the realisation of self, self-sufficiency. The joy of parents in their first-born is not due to any pride in its appearance, but because it is their very own. If it happens to be an extraordinary child they may also glory in that—but that is different.

In the first flood-tide of that joy I paid no heed to the bounds of metrical form, and as the stream does not flow straight on but winds about as it lists, so did my verse. Before, I would have held this to be a crime, but now I felt no compunction. Freedom first breaks the law and then makes laws which brings it under true Self-rule.

The only listener I had for these erratic poems of mine was Akshay Babu. When he heard them for the first time he was as surprised as he was pleased, and with his approbation my road to freedom was widened.

The poems of Vihari Chakravarti were in a three-beat metre. This triple time produces a rounded-off globular effect, unlike the square-cut multiple of two. It rolls on with ease, it glides as it dances to the tinkling of its anklets. I was once very fond of this metre. It felt more like riding a bicycle than walking. And to this stride I had got accustomed. In the *Evening Songs*, without thinking of it, I somehow broke off this habit. Nor did I come under any other particular bondage. I felt entirely free and unconcerned. I had no thought or fear of being taken to task.

The strength I gained by working, freed from the trammels of tradition, led me to discover that I had been searching in impossible places for that which I had within myself. Nothing but want of self-confidence had stood in the way of my coming into my own. I felt like rising from a dream of bondage to find myself unshackled. I cut extraordinary capers just to make sure I was free to move.

To me this is the most memorable period of my poetic career. As poems my *Evening Songs* may not have been worth much, in fact as such they are crude enough. Neither their metre, nor language, nor thought had taken definite shape. Their only merit is that for the first time I had come to write what I really meant, just according to my pleasure. What if those compositions have no value, that pleasure certainly had.

31

An Essay on Music

I had been proposing to study for the bar when my father had recalled me home from England. Some friends concerned at this cutting short of my career pressed him to send me off once again. This led to my starting on a second voyage towards England, this time with a relative as my companion. My fate, however, had so strongly vetoed my being called to the bar that I was not even to reach England this time. For a certain reason we had to disembark at Madras and return home to Calcutta. The reason was by no means as grave as its outcome, but as the laugh was not against *me*, I refrain from setting it down here. From both my attempted pilgrimages to *Lakshmi's** shrine I had thus to come back repulsed. I hope, however, that the Law-god, at least, will look on me with a favourable eye for that I have not added to the encumbrances on the Bar-library premises.

My father was then in the Mussoorie hills. I went to him in fear and trembling. But he showed no sign of irritation, he rather seemed pleased. He must have seen in this return of mine the blessing of Divine Providence.

The evening before I started on this voyage I read a paper at the Medical College Hall on the invitation of the Bethune Society. This was my first public reading. The Reverend K. M. Banerji was the president. The subject was Music. Leaving aside instrumental music, I tried to make out that to bring out better what the words sought to express was the chief end and aim of vocal music. The text of my paper was but meagre. I sang and acted songs throughout illustrating my theme. The only reason for the flattering eulogy which the President bestowed on me at the end must have been the moving effect of my young voice together with the earnestness and variety of its efforts. But I must make the confession today that the opinion I voiced with such enthusiasm that evening was wrong.

The art of vocal music has its own special functions and features. And when it happens to be set to words the latter must not presume too much on their opportunity and seek to supersede the melody of which they are but the vehicle. The song being great in its own wealth, why should it wait upon the words? Rather does it begin where mere words fail. Its power lies in the region of the inexpressible; it tells us what the words cannot.

So the less a song is burdened with words the better. In the classic style of Hindustan† the words are of no account and leave the melody to make its appeal in its own way. Vocal music reaches

---

* The Goddess of Wealth

† As distinguished generally from different provincial styles, but chiefly from the Dravidian style prevalent in the South.

its perfection when the melodic form is allowed to develop freely, and carry our consciousness with it to its own wonderful plane. In Bengal, however, the words have always asserted themselves so, that our provincial song has failed to develop her full musical capabilities, and has remained content as the handmaiden of her sister art of poetry. From the old Vaishnava songs down to those of Nidhu Babu she has displayed her charms from the background. But as in our country the wife rules her husband through acknowledging her dependence, so our music, though professedly in attendance only, ends by dominating the song.

I have often felt this while composing my songs. As I hummed to myself and wrote the lines:

Do not keep your secret to yourself, my love,
But whisper it gently to me, only to me.

I found that the words had no means of reaching by themselves the region into which they were borne away by the tune. The melody told me that the secret, which I was so importunate to hear, had mingled with the green mystery of the forest glades, was steeped in the silent whiteness of moonlight nights, peeped out of the veil of the illimitable blue behind the horizon—and is the one intimate secret of Earth, Sky and Waters.

In my early boyhood I heard a snatch of a song:

Who dressed you, love, as a foreigner?

This one line painted such wonderful pictures in my mind that it haunts me still. One day I sat down to set to words a composition of my own while full of this bit of song. Humming my tune I wrote to its accompaniment:

I know you, O Woman from the strange land!
Your dwelling is across the Sea.

Had the tune not been there I know not what shape the rest of the poem might have taken; but the magic of the melody revealed to me the stranger in all her loveliness. It is she, said my soul, who comes and goes, a messenger to this world from the other shore of the ocean of mystery. It is she, of whom we now and again catch glimpses in the dewy Autumn mornings, in the scented nights of Spring, in the inmost recesses of our hearts—and sometimes we strain skywards to hear her song. To the door of this world-charming stranger the melody, as I say, wafted me, and so to her were the rest of the words addressed.

Long after this, in a street in Bolpur, a mendicant *Baul* was singing as he walked along:

How does the unknown bird flit in and out of the cage!
Ah, could I but catch it, I'd ring its feet with my love!

I found this *Baul* to be saying the very same thing. The unknown bird sometimes surrenders itself within the bars of the cage to whisper tidings of the bondless unknown beyond. The heart would fain hold it near to itself for ever, but cannot. What but the melody of song can tell us of the goings and comings of the unknown bird?

That is why I am always reluctant to publish books of the words of songs, for therein the soul must needs be lacking.

32

The Riverside

When I returned home from the outset of my second voyage to England, my brother Jyotirindra and sister-in-law were living in a riverside villa at Chandernagore, and there I went to stay with them.

The Ganges again! Again those ineffable days and nights, languid with joy, sad with longing, attuned to the plaintive babbling of the river along the cool shade of its wooded banks. This Bengal sky-full of light, this south breeze, this flow of the river, this right royal laziness, this broad leisure stretching from horizon to horizon and from green earth to blue sky, all these were to me as food and drink to the hungry and thirsty. Here it felt indeed like home, and in these I recognised the ministrations of a Mother.

That was not so very long ago, and yet time has wrought many changes. Our little riverside nests, clustering under their surrounding greenery, have been replaced by mills which now, dragon-like, everywhere rear their hissing heads, belching forth black smoke. In the midday glare of modern life even our hours of mental siesta have been narrowed down to the lowest limit, and hydra-headed unrest has invaded every department of life. Maybe, this is for the better, but I, for one, cannot account it wholly to the good.

The Ganges Again

These lovely days of mine at the riverside passed by like so many dedicated lotus blossoms floating down the sacred stream. Some rainy afternoons I spent in a veritable frenzy, singing away old Vaishnava songs to my own tunes, accompanying myself on a harmonium. On other afternoons, we would drift along in a boat, my brother Jyotirindra accompanying my singing with his violin.

And as, beginning with the *Puravi*,* we went on varying the mode of our music with the declining day, we saw, on reaching the *Behaga*,* the western sky close the doors of its factory of golden toys, and the moon on the east rise over the fringe of trees.

Then we would row back to the landing steps of the villa and seat ourselves on a quilt spread on the terrace facing the river. By then a silvery peace rested on both land and water, hardly any boats were about, the fringe of trees on the bank was reduced to a deep shadow, and the moonlight glimmered over the smooth flowing stream.

The villa we were living in was known as 'Moran's Garden'. A flight of stone-flagged steps led up from the water to a long, broad verandah which formed part of the house. The rooms were not regularly arranged, nor all on the same level, and some had to be reached by short flights of stairs. The big sitting room overlooking the landing steps had stained glass windows with coloured pictures.

One of the pictures was of a swing hanging from a branch half-hidden in dense foliage, and in the checkered light and shade of this bower, two persons were swinging; and there was another of a broad flight of steps leading into some castle-like palace, up and down which men and women in festive garb were going and coming. When the light fell on the windows, these pictures shone wonderfully, seeming to fill the riverside atmosphere with holiday music. Some faraway long-forgotten revelry seemed to be expressing itself in silent words of light; the love thrills of the swinging couple making alive with their eternal story the woodlands of the riverbank.

The topmost room of the house was in a round tower with windows opening to every side. This I used as my room for writing poetry. Nothing could be seen from thence save the tops of the surrounding trees, and the open sky. I was then busy with the *Evening Songs* and of this room I wrote:

There, where in the breast of limitless space clouds are laid to sleep,
I have built my house for thee, O Poesy!

---

* Many of the Hindustani classic modes are supposed to be best in keeping with particular seasons of the year, or times of the day.

33

More About the Evening Songs

At this time my reputation amongst literary critics was that of being a poet of broken cadence and lisping utterance. Everything about my work was dubbed misty, shadowy. However little I might have relished this at the time, the charge was not wholly baseless. My poetry did in fact lack the backbone of worldly reality. How, amidst the ringed-in seclusion of my early years, was I to get the necessary material?

But one thing I refuse to admit. Behind this charge of vagueness was the sting of the insinuation of its being a deliberate affectation—for the sake of effect. The fortunate possessor of good eyesight is apt to sneer at the youth with glasses, as if he wears them for ornament. While a reflection on the poor fellow's infirmity may be permissible, it is too bad to charge him with pretending not to see.

The nebula is not an outside creation—it merely represents a phase; and to leave out all poetry which has not attained definiteness would not bring us to the truth of literature. If any phase of man's nature has found true expression, it is worth preserving—it may be cast aside only if not expressed truly. There is a period in man's life when his feelings are the pathos of the inexpressible, the anguish of vagueness. The poetry which attempts its expression cannot be called baseless—at worst it may be worthless; but it is not necessarily even that. The sin is not in the thing expressed, but in the failure to express it.

There is a duality in man. Of the inner person, behind the outward current of thoughts, feelings and events, but little is known or recked; but for all that, he cannot be got rid of as a factor in life's progress. When the outward life fails to harmonise with the inner, the dweller within is hurt, and his pain manifests itself in the outer consciousness in a manner to which it is difficult to give a name, or even to describe, and of which the cry is more akin to an inarticulate wail than words with more precise meaning.

The sadness and pain which sought expression in the *Evening Songs* had their roots in the depths of my being. As one's sleep-smothered consciousness wrestles with a nightmare in its efforts to awake, so the submerged inner self struggles to free itself from its complexities and come out into the open. These *Songs* are the history of that struggle. As in all creation, so in poetry, there is the opposition of forces. If the divergence is too wide, or the unison too close, there is, it seems to me, no room for poetry. Where the pain of discord strives to attain and express its resolution into harmony, there does poetry break forth into music, as breath through a flute.

When the *Evening Songs* first saw the light they were not hailed with any flourish of trumpets, but none the less they did not lack admirers. I have elsewhere told the story of how at the wedding of Mr. Ramesh Chandra Dutt's eldest daughter, Bankim Babu was at the door, and the host was welcoming him with the customary garland of flowers. As I came up Bankim Babu eagerly took the garland and placing it round my neck said: "The wreath to him, Ramesh, have you not read his *Evening Songs*?" And when Mr. Dutt avowed he had not yet done so, the manner in which Bankim Babu expressed his opinion of some of them amply rewarded me.

The *Evening Songs* gained for me a friend whose approval, like the rays of the sun, stimulated and guided the shoots of my newly sprung efforts. This was Babu Priyanath Sen. Just before this the *Broken Heart* had led him to give up all hopes of me. I won him back with these *Evening Songs*. Those who are acquainted with him know him as an expert navigator of all the seven seas* of literature, whose highways and byways, in almost all languages, Indian and foreign, he is constantly traversing. To converse with him is to gain glimpses of even the most out of the way scenery in the world of ideas. This proved of the greatest value to me.

He was able to give his literary opinions with the fullest confidence, for he had not to rely on his unaided taste to guide his likes and dislikes. This authoritative criticism of his also assisted me more than I can tell. I used to read to him everything I wrote, and but for the timely showers of his discriminate appreciation it is hard to say whether these early ploughings of mine would have yielded as they have done.

---

* The world, as the Indian boy knows it from fairy tale and folklore, has seven seas and thirteen rivers.

34

Morning Songs

At the riverside I also did a bit of prose writing, not on any definite subject or plan, but in the spirit that boys catch butterflies. When spring comes within, many-coloured short-lived fancies are born and flit about in the mind, ordinarily unnoticed. In these days of my leisure, it was perhaps the mere whim to collect them which had come upon me. Or it may have been only another phase of my emancipated self which had thrown out its chest and decided to write just as it pleased; what I wrote not being the object, it being sufficient unto itself that it was I who wrote. These prose pieces were published later under the name of *Vividha Prabandha*, Various Topics, but they expired with the first edition and did not get a fresh lease of life in a second.

At this time, I think, I also began my first novel, *Bauthakuranir Hat*.

After we had stayed for a time by the river, my brother Jyotirindra took a house in Calcutta, on Sudder Street near the Museum. I remained with him. While I went on here with the novel and the *Evening Songs*, a momentous revolution of some kind came about within me.

One day, late in the afternoon, I was pacing the terrace of our Jorasanko house. The glow of the sunset combined with the wan twilight in a way which seemed to give the approaching evening a specially wonderful attractiveness for me. Even the walls of the adjoining house seemed to grow beautiful. Is this uplifting of the cover of triviality from the everyday world, I wondered, due to some magic in the evening light? Never!

I could see at once that it was the effect of the evening which had come within me; its shades had obliterated my *self*. While the self was rampant during the glare of day, everything I perceived was mingled with and hidden by it. Now, that the self was put into the background, I could see the world in its own true aspect. And that aspect has nothing of triviality in it, it is full of beauty and joy.

Since this experience I tried the effect of deliberately suppressing my *self* and viewing the world as a mere spectator, and was invariably rewarded with a sense of special pleasure. I remember I tried also to explain to a relative how to see the world in its true light, and the incidental lightening of one's own sense of burden which follows such vision; but, as I believe, with no success.

Then I gained a further insight which has lasted all my life.

The end of Sudder Street, and the trees on the Free School grounds opposite, were visible from our Sudder Street house. One morning I happened to be standing on the verandah looking that way. The sun was just rising through the leafy tops of those trees. As I continued to gaze, all of a sudden a covering seemed to fall away from my eyes, and I found the world bathed in a wonderful radiance, with waves of beauty and joy swelling on every side. This radiance pierced in a moment through the folds of sadness and despondency which had accumulated over my heart, and flooded it with this universal light.

That very day the poem, *The Awakening of the Waterfall*, gushed forth and coursed on like a veritable cascade. The poem came to an end, but the curtain did not fall upon the joy aspect of the Universe. And it came to be so that no person or thing in the world seemed to me trivial or unpleasing. A thing that happened the next day or the day following seemed specially astonishing.

There was a curious sort of person who came to me now and then, with a habit of asking all manner of silly questions. One day he had asked: "Have you, sir, seen God with your own eyes?" And on my having to admit that I had not, he averred that he had. "What was it you saw?" I asked. "He seethed and throbbed before my eyes!" was the reply.

It can well be imagined that one would not ordinarily relish being drawn into abstruse discussions with such a person. Moreover, I was at the time entirely absorbed in my own writing. Nevertheless as he was a harmless sort of fellow I did not like the idea of hurting his susceptibilities and so tolerated him as best I could.

This time, when he came one afternoon, I actually felt glad to see him, and welcomed him cordially. The mantle of his oddity and foolishness seemed to have slipped off, and the person I so joyfully hailed was the real man whom I felt to be in nowise inferior to myself, and moreover closely related. Finding no trace of annoyance within me at sight of him, nor any sense of my time being wasted with him, I was filled with an immense gladness, and felt rid of some enveloping tissue of untruth which had been causing me so much needless and uncalled for discomfort and pain.

As I would stand on the balcony, the gait, the figure, the features of each one of the passers-by, whoever they might be, seemed to me all so extraordinarily wonderful, as they flowed past—waves on the sea of the universe. From infancy I had seen only with my eyes, I now began to see with the whole of my consciousness. I could not look upon the sight of two smiling youths, nonchalantly going their way, the arm of one on the other's shoulder, as a matter of small moment; for, through it I could see the fathomless depths of the eternal spring of Joy from which numberless sprays of laughter leap up throughout the world.

I had never before marked the play of limbs and lineaments which always accompanies even the least of man's actions; now I was spellbound by their variety, which I came across on all sides, at every moment. Yet I saw them not as being apart by themselves, but as parts of that amazingly beautiful greater dance which goes on at this very moment throughout the world of men, in each of their homes, in their multifarious wants and activities.

Friend laughs with friend, the mother fondles her child, one cow sidles up to another and licks its body, and the immeasurability behind these comes direct to my mind with a shock which almost savours of pain.

When of this period I wrote:

I know not how of a sudden my heart flung open its doors,
And let the crowd of worlds rush in, greeting each other—

it was no poetic exaggeration. Rather I had not the power to express all I felt.

For some time together I remained in this self-forgetful state of bliss. Then my brother thought of going to the Darjeeling hills. So much the better, thought I. On the vast Himalayan tops I shall be able to see more deeply into what has been revealed to me in Sudder Street; at any rate I shall see how the Himalayas display themselves to my new gift of vision.

But the victory was with that little house in Sudder Street. When, after ascending the mountains, I looked around, I was at once aware I had lost my new vision. My sin must have been in imagining that I could get still more of truth from the outside. However sky-piercing the king of mountains may be, he can have nothing in his gift for me; while He who is the Giver can vouchsafe a vision of the eternal universe in the dingiest of lanes, and in a moment of time.

I wandered about amongst the firs, I sat near the falls and bathed in their waters, I gazed at the grandeur of Kinchinjunga through a cloudless sky, but in what had seemed to me these likeliest of places, I found *it* not. I had come to know it, but could see it no longer. While I was admiring the gem the lid had suddenly closed, leaving me staring at the enclosing casket. But, for all the attractiveness of its workmanship, there was no longer any danger of my mistaking it for merely an empty box.

My *Morning Songs* came to an end, their last echo dying out with *The Echo* which I wrote at Darjeeling. This apparently proved such an abstruse affair that two friends laid a wager as to its real meaning. My only consolation was that, as I was equally unable to explain the enigma to them when they came to me for a solution, neither of them had to lose any money over it. Alas! The days when I wrote excessively plain poems about *The Lotus* and *A Lake* had gone forever.

But does one write poetry to explain any matter? What is felt within the heart tries to find outside shape as a poem. So when after listening to a poem anyone says he has not understood, I feel nonplussed. If someone smells a flower and says he does not understand, the reply to him is: there is nothing to understand, it is only a scent. If he persists, saying: *that* I know, but what does it all *mean?* Then one has either to change the subject, or make it more abstruse by saying that the scent is the shape which the universal joy takes in the flower.

That words have meanings is just the difficulty. That is why the poet has to turn and twist them in metre and verse, so that the meaning may be held somewhat in check, and the feeling allowed a chance to express itself.

This utterance of feeling is not the statement of a fundamental truth, or a scientific fact, or a useful moral precept. Like a tear or a smile it is but a picture of what is taking place within. If Science or Philosophy may gain anything from it they are welcome, but that is not the reason of its being. If while crossing a ferry you can catch a fish you are a lucky man, but that does not make the ferry boat a fishing boat, nor should you abuse the ferryman if he does not make fishing his business.

The Echo was written so long ago that it has escaped attention and I am now no longer called upon to render an account of its meaning. Nevertheless, whatever its other merits or defects may be, I can assure my readers that it was not my intention to propound a riddle, or insidiously convey any erudite teaching. The fact of the matter was that a longing had been born within my heart, and, unable to find any other name, I had called the thing I desired an Echo.

When from the original fount in the depths of the Universe streams of melody are sent forth abroad, their echo is reflected into our heart from the faces of our beloved and the other beauteous things around us. It must be, as I suggested, this Echo which we love, and not the things themselves from which it happens to be reflected; for that which one day we scarce deign to glance at, may be, on another, the very thing which claims our whole devotion.

I had so long viewed the world with external vision only, and so had been unable to see its universal aspect of joy. When of a sudden, from some innermost depth of my being, a ray of light found its way out, it spread over and illuminated for me the whole universe, which then no longer appeared like heaps of things and happenings, but was disclosed to my sight as one whole. This experience seemed to tell me of the stream of melody issuing from the very heart of the universe and spreading over space and time, re-echoing thence as waves of joy which flow right back to the source.

When the artist sends his song forth from the depths of a full heart that is joy indeed. And the joy is redoubled when this same song is wafted back to him as hearer. If, when the creation of the Arch-Poet is thus returning back to him in a flood of joy, we allow it to flow over our consciousness, we at once, immediately, become aware, in an inexpressible manner, of the end to which this flood is streaming. And as we become aware our love goes forth; and our *selves* are moved from their moorings and would fain float down the stream of joy to its infinite goal. This is the meaning of the longing which stirs within us at the sight of Beauty.

The stream which comes from the Infinite and flows toward the finite—that is the True, the Good; it is subject to laws, definite in form. Its echo which returns towards the Infinite is Beauty and Joy; which are difficult to touch or grasp, and so make us beside ourselves. This is what I tried to say by way of a parable or a song in *The Echo*. That the result was not clear is not to be wondered at, for neither was the attempt then clear unto itself.

Let me set down here part of what I wrote in a letter, at a more advanced age, about the *Morning Songs*.

> "There is none in the World, all are in my heart"—is a state of mind belonging to a particular age. When the heart is first awakened it puts forth its arms and would grasp the whole world, like the teething infant which thinks everything meant for its mouth. Gradually it comes to understand what it really wants and what it does not. Then do its nebulous emanations shrink upon themselves, get heated, and heat in their turn.
>
> To begin by wanting the whole world is to get nothing. When desire is concentrated, with the whole strength of one's being upon any one object whatsoever it might be, then does the gateway to the Infinite become visible. The morning songs were the first throwing forth of my inner self outwards, and consequently they lack any signs of such concentration.

This all-pervading joy of a first outflow, however, has the effect of leading us to an acquaintance with the particular. The lake in its fullness seeks an outlet as a river. In this sense the permanent later love is narrower than first love. It is more definite in the direction of its activities, desires to realise the whole in each of its parts, and is thus impelled on towards the infinite. What it finally reaches is no longer the former indefinite extension of the heart's own inner joy, but a merging in the infinite reality which was outside itself, and thereby the attainment of the complete truth of its own longings.

In Mohita Babu's edition these *Morning Songs* have been placed in the group of poems entitled *Nishkraman*, The Emergence. For in these was to be found the first news of my coming out of the *Heart Wilderness* into the open world. Thereafter did this pilgrim heart make its acquaintance with that world, bit by bit, part by part, in many a mood and manner. And at the end, after gliding past all the numerous landing steps of ever-changing impermanence, it will reach the infinite—not the vagueness of indeterminate possibility, but the consummation of perfect fullness of Truth.

From my earliest years I enjoyed a simple and intimate communion with Nature. Each one of the coconut trees in our garden had for me a distinct personality. When, on coming home from the Normal School, I saw behind the skyline of our roof-terrace blue-grey water-laden clouds thickly banked up, the immense depth of gladness which filled me, all in a moment, I can recall clearly even now. On opening my eyes every morning, the blithely awakening world used to call me to join it like a playmate; the perfervid noonday sky, during the long silent watches of the siesta hours, would spirit me away from the work-a-day world into the recesses of its hermit cell; and the darkness of night would open the door to its phantom paths, and take me over all the seven seas and thirteen rivers, past all possibilities and impossibilities, right into its wonderland.

Then one day, when, with the dawn of youth, my hungry heart began to cry out for its sustenance, a barrier was set up between this play of inside and outside. And my whole being eddied round and round my troubled heart, creating a vortex within itself, in the whirls of which its consciousness was confined.

This loss of the harmony between inside and outside, due to the over-riding claims of the heart in its hunger, and consequent restriction of the privilege of communion which had been mine, was mourned by me in the *Evening Songs*. In the *Morning Songs* I celebrated the sudden opening of a gate in the barrier, by what shock I know not, through which I regained the lost one, not only as I knew it before, but more deeply, more fully, by force of the intervening separation.

Thus did the First Book of my life come to an end with these chapters of union, separation and reunion. Or, rather, it is not true to say it has come to an end. The same subject has still to be continued through more elaborate solutions of worse complexities, to a greater conclusion. Each one comes here to finish but one book of life, which, during the progress of its various parts, grows spiral-wise on an ever-increasing radius. So, while each segment may appear different from the others at a cursory glance, they all really lead back to the self-same starting centre.

The prose writings of the *Evening Songs* period were published, as I have said, under the name of *Vividha Prabandha*. Those others which correspond to the time of my writing the *Morning Songs* came out under the title of *Alochana*, Discussions. The difference between the characteristics of these two would be a good index of the nature of the change that had in the meantime taken place within me.

PART VII

35

Rajendrahal Mitra

I t was about this time that my brother Jyotirindra had the idea of
founding a Literary Academy by bringing together all the men
of letters of repute. To compile authoritative technical terms for
the Bengali language and in other ways to assist in its growth was
to be its object—therein differing but little from the lines on which
the modern *Sahitya Parishat*, Academy of Literature, has taken shape.

Dr. Rajendrahal Mitra took up the idea of this Academy with
enthusiasm, and he was eventually its president for the short time it
lasted. When I went to invite Pandit Vidyasagar to join it, he gave
a hearing to my explanation of its objects and the names of the
proposed members, then said: "My advice to you is to leave us out—
you will never accomplish anything with big wigs; they can never be
got to agree with one another." With which he refused to come in.
Bankim Babu became a member, but I cannot say that he took much
interest in the work.

To be plain, so long as this academy lived Rajendrahal Mitra did
everything single-handed. He began with Geographical terms. The
draft list was made out by Dr. Rajendrahal himself and was printed
and circulated for the suggestions of the members. We had also an
idea of transliterating in Bengali the name of each foreign country
as pronounced by itself.

Pandit Vidyasagar's prophecy was fulfilled. It did not prove possible to get the big wigs to do anything. And the academy withered away shortly after sprouting. But Rajendrahal Mitra was an all-round expert and was an academy in himself. My labours in this cause were more than repaid by the privilege of his acquaintance. I have met many Bengali men of letters in my time but none who left the impression of such brilliance.

I used to go and see him in the office of the Court of Wards in Maniktala. I would go in the mornings and always find him busy with his studies, and with the inconsiderateness of youth, I felt no hesitation in disturbing him. But I have never seen him the least bit put out on that account. As soon as he saw me he would put aside his work and begin to talk to me. It is a matter of common knowledge that he was somewhat hard of hearing, so he hardly ever gave me occasion to put him any question. He would take up some broad subject and talk away upon it, and it was the attraction of these discourses which drew me there. Converse with no other person ever gave me such a wealth of suggestive ideas on so many different subjects. I would listen enraptured.

I think he was a member of the text-book committee and every book he received for approval, he read through and annotated in pencil. On some occasions he would select one of these books for the text of discourses on the construction of the Bengali language in particular or Philology in general, which were of the greatest benefit to me. There were few subjects which he had not studied and anything he had studied he could clearly expound.

If we had not relied on the other members of the Academy we had tried to found, but left everything to Dr. Rajendrahal, the present *Sahitya Parishat* would have doubtless found the matters it is now occupied with left in a much more advanced state by that one man alone.

Dr. Rajendrahal Mitra was not only a profound scholar, but he had likewise a striking personality which shone through his features. Full of fire as he was in his public life, he could also unbend graciously so as to talk on the most difficult subjects to a stripling like myself without any trace of a patronising tone. I even took advantage of his condescension to the extent of getting a contribution, *Yama's Dog*, from him for the Bharabi. There were other great contemporaries of his with whom I would not have ventured to take such liberties, nor would I have met with the like response if I had.

And yet when he was on the war path his opponents on the Municipal Corporation or the Senate of the University were mortally afraid of him. In those days Kristo Das Pal was the tactful politician, and Rajendrahal Mitra the valiant fighter.

For the purposes of the Asiatic Society's publications and researches, he had to employ a number of Sanskrit Pandits to do the mechanical work for him. I remember how this gave certain envious and mean-minded detractors the opportunity of saying that everything was really done by these Pandits while Rajendrahal fraudulently appropriated all the credit. Even today we very often find the tools arrogating to themselves the lion's share of the achievement, imagining the wielder to be a mere ornamental figurehead. If the poor pen had a mind it would as certainly have bemoaned the unfairness of its getting all the stain and the writer all the glory!

It is curious that this extraordinary man should have got no recognition from his countrymen even after his death. One of the reasons may be that the national mourning for Vidyasagar, whose death followed shortly after, left no room for a recognition of the other bereavement. Another reason may be that his main contributions being outside the pale of Bengali literature, he had been unable to reach the heart of the people.

36

Karwar

Our Sudder Street party next transferred itself to Karwar on the West Sea coast. Karwar is the headquarters of the Kanara district in the Southern portion of the Bombay Presidency. It is the tract of the Malaya Hills of Sanskrit literature where grow the cardamum creeper and the Sandal Tree. My second brother was then Judge there.

The little harbour, ringed round with hills, is so secluded that it has nothing of the aspect of a port about it. Its crescent shaped beach throws out its arms to the shoreless open sea like the very image of an eager striving to embrace the infinite. The edge of the broad sandy beach is fringed with a forest of casuarinas, broken at one end by the *Kalanadi* river which here flows into the sea after passing through a gorge flanked by rows of hills on either side.

I remember how one moonlit evening we went up this river in a little boat. We stopped at one of Shivaji's old hill forts, and stepping ashore found our way into the clean-swept little yard of a peasant's home. We sat on a spot where the moonbeams fell glancing off the top of the outer enclosure, and there dined off the eatables we had brought with us. On our way back we let the boat glide down the river. The night brooded over the motionless hills and forests, and on the silent flowing stream of this little *Kalanadi*, throwing over all its moonlight spell. It took us a good long time to reach the mouth of the river, so, instead of returning by sea, we got off the boat there and walked back home over the sands of the beach. It was then far into the night, the sea was without a ripple, even the ever-troubled murmur of the casuarinas was at rest. The shadow of the fringe of trees along the vast expanse of sand hung motionless along its border, and the ring of blue-grey hills around the horizon slept calmly beneath the sky.

Karwar Beach

Through the deep silence of this illimitable whiteness we few human creatures walked along with our shadows, without a word. When we reached home my sleep had lost itself in something still deeper. The poem which I then wrote is inextricably mingled with that night on the distant seashore. I do not know how it will appeal to the reader apart from the memories with which it is entwined. This doubt led to its being left out of Mohita Babu's edition of my works. I trust that a place given to it among my reminiscences may not be deemed unfitting.

> Let me sink down, losing myself in the depths of midnight.
> Let the Earth leave her hold of me, let her free me from
>   her obstacle of dust.
> Keep your watch from afar, O stars, drunk though you be
>   with moonlight,
> And let the horizon hold its wings still around me.
> Let there be no song, no word, no sound, no touch; nor
>   sleep, nor awakening—
> But only the moonlight like a swoon of ecstasy over the sky
>   and my being.
> The world seems to me like a ship with its countless
>   pilgrims,
> Vanishing in the faraway blue of the sky,
> Its sailors' song becoming fainter and fainter in the air,
> While I sink in the bosom of the endless night, fading
>   away from myself, dwindling into a point.

It is necessary to remark here that merely because something has been written when feelings are brimming over, it is not therefore necessarily good. Such is rather a time when the utterance is thick with emotion. Just as it does not do to have the writer entirely removed from the feeling to which he is giving expression, so also it does not conduce to the truest poetry to have him too close to it. Memory is the brush which can best lay on the true poetic colour. Nearness has too much of the compelling about it and the imagination is not sufficiently free unless it can get away from its influence. Not only in poetry, but in all art, the mind of the artist must attain a certain degree of aloofness—the *creator* within man must be allowed the sole control. If the subject matter gets the better of the creation, the result is a mere replica of the event, not a reflection of it through the Artist's mind.

37

Nature's Revenge

Here in Karwar I wrote the *Prakritir Pratishodha*, Nature's Revenge, a dramatic poem. The hero was a Sanyasi (hermit) who had been striving to gain a victory over Nature by cutting away the bonds of all desires and affections and thus to arrive at a true and profound knowledge of self. A little girl, however, brought him back from his communion with the infinite to the world and into the bondage of human affection. On so coming back the *Sanyasi* realised that the great is to be found in the small, the infinite within the bounds of form, and the eternal freedom of the soul in love. It is only in the light of love that all limits are merged in the limitless.

The sea beach of Karwar is certainly a fit place in which to realise that the beauty of Nature is not a mirage of the imagination, but reflects the joy of the Infinite and thus draws us to lose ourselves in it. Where the universe is expressing itself in the magic of its laws it may not be strange if we miss its infinitude; but where the heart gets into immediate touch with immensity in the beauty of the meanest of things, is any room left for argument?

Nature took the *Sanyasi* to the presence of the Infinite, enthroned on the finite, by the pathway of the heart. In the *Nature's Revenge* there were shown on the one side the wayfarers and the villagers, content with their home-made triviality and unconscious of anything beyond; and on the other the *Sanyasi* busy casting away his all, and himself, into the self-evolved infinite of his imagination. When love bridged the gulf between the two, and the hermit and the householder met, the seeming triviality of the finite and the seeming emptiness of the infinite alike disappeared.

This was to put in a slightly different form the story of my own experience, of the entrancing ray of light which found its way into the depths of the cave into which I had retired away from all touch with the outer world, and made me more fully one with Nature again. This *Nature's Revenge* may be looked upon as an introduction to the whole of my future literary work; or, rather this has been the subject on which all my writings have dwelt—the joy of attaining the Infinite within the finite.

On our way back from Karwar I wrote some songs for the *Nature's Revenge* on board ship. The first one filled me with a great gladness as I sang, and wrote it sitting on the deck:

> *Mother, leave your darling boy to us,*
> *And let us take him to the field where we graze our cattle.*[*]

The sun has risen, the buds have opened, the cowherd boys are going to the pasture; and they would not have the sunlight, the flowers, and their play in the grazing grounds empty. They want their *Shyam* (Krishna) to be with them there, in the midst of all these. They want to see the Infinite in all its carefully adorned loveliness; they have turned out so early because they want to join in its gladsome play, in the midst of these woods and fields and hills and dales—not to admire from a distance, nor in the majesty of power. Their equipment is of the slightest. A simple yellow garment and a garland of wild-flowers are all the ornaments they require. For where joy reigns on every side, to hunt for it arduously, or amidst pomp and circumstances, is to lose it.

Shortly after my return from Karwar, I was married. I was then twenty-two years of age.

---

[*] This is addressed to Yashoda, mother of Krishna, by his playmates. Yashoda would dress up her darling every morning in his yellow garment with a peacock plume in his hair. But when it came to the point, she was nervous about allowing him, young as he was, to join the other cowherd boys at the pasturage. So it often required a great deal of persuasion before they would be allowed to take charge of him. This is part of the Vaishnava parable of the child aspect of Krishna's play with the world.

38

Pictures and Songs

Chhabi o Gan, Picture and Songs, was the title of a book of poems most of which were written at this time.

We were then living in a house with a garden in Lower Circular Road. Adjoining it on the south was a large *Busti.** I would often sit near a window and watch the sights of this populous little settlement. I loved to see them at their work and play and rest, and in their multifarious goings and comings. To me it was all like a living story.

A faculty of many-sightedness possessed me at this time. Each little separate picture I ringed round with the light of my imagination and the joy of my heart; every one of them, moreover, being variously coloured by a pathos of its own. The pleasure of thus separately marking off each picture was much the same as that of painting it, both being the outcome of the desire to see with the mind what the eye sees, and with the eye what the mind imagines.

Had I been a painter with the brush I would doubtless have tried to keep a permanent record of the visions and creations of that period when my mind was so alertly responsive. But that instrument was not available to me. What I had was only words and rhythms, and even with these I had not yet learnt to draw firm strokes, and the colours went beyond their margins. Still, like young folk with their first paint box, I spent the livelong day painting away with the many coloured fancies of my new-born youth. If these pictures are now viewed in the light of that twenty-second year of my life, some features may be discerned even through their crude drawing and blurred colouring.

I have said that the first book of my literary life came to an

---

* A *Busti* is an area thickly packed with shabby tiled huts, with narrow pathways running through, and connecting it with the main street. These are inhabited by domestic servants, the poorer class of artisans and the like. Such settlements were formerly scattered throughout the town even in the best localities, but are now gradually disappearing from the latter.

end with the *Morning Songs*. The same subject was then continued under a different rendering. Many a page at the outset of this Book, I am sure, is of no value. In the process of making a new beginning much in the way of superfluous preliminary has to be gone through. Had these been leaves of trees they would have duly dropped off. Unfortunately, leaves of books continue to stick fast even when they are no longer wanted. The feature of these poems was the closeness of attention devoted even to trifling things. *Pictures and Songs* seized every opportunity of giving value to these by colouring them with feelings straight from the heart.

Or, rather, that was not it. When the string of the mind is properly attuned to the universe then at each point the universal song can awaken its sympathetic vibrations. It was because of this music roused within that nothing then felt trivial to the writer. Whatever my eyes fell upon found a response within me. Like children who can play with sand or stones or shells or whatever they can get (for the spirit of play is within them), so also we, when filled with the song of youth, become aware that the harp of the universe has its variously tuned strings everywhere stretched, and the nearest may serve as well as any other for our accompaniment, there is no need to seek afar.

39

An Intervening Period

Between the *Pictures and Songs* and the *Sharps and Flats*, a child's magazine called the *Balaka* sprang up and ended its brief days like an annual plant. My second sister-in-law felt the want of an illustrated magazine for children. Her idea was that the young people of the family would contribute to it, but as she felt that that alone would not be enough, she took up the editorship herself and asked me to help with contributions. After one or two numbers of the *Balaka* had come out I happened to go on a visit to Rajnarayan Babu at Deoghur. On the return journey the train was crowded and as there was an unshaded light just over the only berth I could get, I could

not sleep. I thought I might as well take this opportunity of thinking out a story for the *Balaka*. In spite of my efforts to get hold of the story it eluded me, but sleep came to the rescue instead. I saw in a dream the stone steps of a temple stained with the blood of victims of the sacrifice;—a little girl standing there with her father asking him in piteous accents: "Father, what is this, why all this blood?" and the father, inwardly moved, trying with a show of gruffness to quiet her questioning. As I awoke I felt I had got my story. I have many more such dream-given stories and other writings as well. This dream episode I worked into the annals of King Gobinda Manikya of Tipperah and made out of it a little serial story, *Rajarshi*, for the *Balaka*.

Those were days of utter freedom from care. Nothing in particular seemed to be anxious to express itself through my life or writings. I had not yet joined the throng of travellers on the path of Life, but was a mere spectator from my roadside window. Many a person hied by on many an errand as I gazed on, and every now and then Spring or Autumn, or the Rains would enter unasked and stay with me for a while.

But I had not only to do with the seasons. There were men of all kinds of curious types who, floating about like boats adrift from their anchorage, occasionally invaded my little room. Some of them sought to further their own ends, at the cost of my inexperience, with many an extraordinary device. But they need not have taken any extraordinary pains to get the better of me. I was then entirely unsophisticated, my own wants were few, and I was not at all clever in distinguishing between good and bad faith. I have often gone on imagining that I was assisting with their school fees students to whom fees were as superfluous as their unread books.

Once a long-haired youth brought me a letter from an imaginary sister in which she asked me to take under my protection this brother of hers who was suffering from the tyranny of a stepmother as imaginary as herself. The brother was not imaginary, that was evident enough. But his sister's letter was as unnecessary for me as expert marksmanship to bring down a bird which cannot fly.

Another young fellow came and informed me that he was studying for the B.A., but could not go up for his examination as he

was afflicted with some brain trouble. I felt concerned, but being far from proficient in medical science, or in any other science, I was at a loss what advice to give him. But he went on to explain that he had seen in a dream that my wife had been his mother in a former birth, and that if he could but drink some water which had touched her feet he would get cured. "Perhaps you don't believe in such things," he concluded with a smile. My belief, I said, did not matter, but if he thought he could get cured, he was welcome, with which I procured him a phial of water which was supposed to have touched my wife's feet. He felt immensely better, he said. In the natural course of evolution from water he came to solid food. Then he took up his quarters in a corner of my room and began to hold smoking parties with his friends, till I had to take refuge in flight from the smoke laden air. He gradually proved beyond doubt that his brain might have been diseased, but it certainly was not weak.

After this experience it took no end of proof before I could bring myself to put my trust in children of previous births. My reputation must have spread for I next received a letter from a daughter. Here, however, I gently but firmly drew the line.

All this time my friendship with Babu Srish Chandra Magundar ripened apace. Every evening he and Prija Babu would come to this little room of mine and we would discuss literature and music far into the night. Sometimes a whole day would be spent in the same way. The fact is my *self* had not yet been moulded and nourished into a strong and definite personality and so my life drifted along as light and easy as an autumn cloud.

40
Bankim Chandra

This was the time when my acquaintance with Bankim Babu began. My first sight of him was a matter of long before. The old students of Calcutta University had then started an annual reunion, of which Babu Chandranath Basu was the leading spirit. Perhaps he entertained a hope that at some future time I might acquire

the right to be one of them; anyhow I was asked to read a poem on the occasion. Chandranath Babu was then quite a young man. I remember he had translated some martial German poem into English which he proposed to recite himself on the day, and came to rehearse it to us full of enthusiasm. That a warrior poet's ode to his beloved sword should at one time have been his favourite poem will convince the reader that even Chandranath Babu was once young; and moreover that those times were indeed peculiar.

While wandering about in the crush at the Students' reunion, I suddenly came across a figure which at once struck me as distinguished beyond that of all the others and who could not have possibly been lost in any crowd. The features of that tall fair personage shone with such a striking radiance that I could not contain my curiosity about him—he was the only one there whose name I felt concerned to know that day. When I learnt he was Bankim Babu I marvelled all the more, it seemed to me such a wonderful coincidence that his appearance should be as distinguished as his writings. His sharp aquiline nose, his compressed lips, and his keen glance all betokened immense power. With his arms folded across his breast he seemed to walk as one apart, towering above the ordinary throng—this is what struck me most about him. Not only that he looked an intellectual giant, but he had on his forehead the mark of a true prince among men.

One little incident which occurred at this gathering remains indelibly impressed on my mind. In one of the rooms a Pandit was reciting some Sanskrit verses of his own composition and explaining them in Bengali to the audience. One of the allusions was not exactly coarse, but somewhat vulgar. As the Pandit was proceeding to expound this Bankim Babu, covering his face with his hands, hurried out of the room. I was near the door and can still see before me that shrinking, retreating figure.

After that I often longed to see him, but could not get an opportunity. At last one day, when he was Deputy Magistrate of Hawrah, I made bold to call on him. We met, and I tried my best to make conversation. But I somehow felt greatly abashed while returning home, as if I had acted like a raw and bumptious youth in thus thrusting myself upon him unasked and unintroduced.

Shortly after, as I added to my years, I attained a place as the youngest of the literary men of the time; but what was to be my position in order of merit was not even then settled. The little reputation I had acquired was mixed with plenty of doubt and not a little of condescension. It was then the fashion in Bengal to assign each man of letters a place in comparison with a supposed compeer in the West. Thus one was the Byron of Bengal, another the Emerson and so forth. I began to be styled by some the Bengal Shelley. This was insulting to Shelley and only likely to get me laughed at.

My recognised cognomen was the Lisping Poet. My attainments were few, my knowledge of life meagre, and both in my poetry and my prose the sentiment exceeded the substance. So that there was nothing there on which anyone could have based his praise with any degree of confidence. My dress and behaviour were of the same anomalous description. I wore my hair long and indulged probably in an ultra-poetical refinement of manner. In a word I was eccentric and could not fit myself into everyday life like the ordinary man.

At this time Babu Akshay Sarkar had started his monthly review, the *Nabajiban*, New Life, to which I used occasionally to contribute. Bankim Babu had just closed the chapter of his editorship of the *Banga Darsan*, the Mirror of Bengal, and was busy with religious discussions for which purpose he had started the monthly, *Prachar*, the Preacher. To this also I contributed a song or two and an effusive appreciation of Vaishnava lyrics.

From now I began constantly to meet Bankim Babu. He was then living in Bhabani Dutt's street. I used to visit him frequently, it is true, but there was not much of conversation. I was then of the age to listen, not to talk. I fervently wished we could warm up into some discussion, but my diffidence got the better of my conversational powers. Some days Sanjib Babu* would be there reclining on his bolster. The sight would gladden me, for he was a genial soul. He delighted in talking and it was a delight to listen to his talk. Those who have read his prose writing must have noticed how gaily and airily it flows on like the sprightliest of conversation. Very few have this gift of conversation, and fewer still the art of translating it into writing.

---

* One of Bankim Babu's brothers

This was the time when Pandit Sashadhar rose into prominence. Of him I first heard from Bankim Babu. If I remember right Bankim Babu was also responsible for introducing him to the public. The curious attempt made by Hindu orthodoxy to revive its prestige with the help of western science soon spread all over the country. Theosophy for some time previously had been preparing the ground for such a movement. Not that Bankim Babu even thoroughly identified himself with this cult. No shadow of Sashadhar was cast on his exposition of Hinduism as it found expression in the *Prachar*—that was impossible.

I was then coming out of the seclusion of my corner as my contributions to these controversies will show. Some of these were satirical verses, some farcical plays, others letters to newspapers. I thus came down into the arena from the regions of sentiment and began to spar in right earnest.

In the heat of the fight I happened to fall foul of Bankim Babu. The history of this remains recorded in the *Prachar* and *Bharati* of those days and need not be repeated here. At the close of this period of antagonism Bankim Babu wrote me a letter which I have unfortunately lost. Had it been here the reader could have seen with what consummate generosity Bankim Babu had taken the sting out of that unfortunate episode.

PART VIII

41

The Steamer Hulk

L ured by an advertisement in some paper my brother
Jyotirindra went off one afternoon to an auction sale, and
on his return informed us that he had bought a steel hulk
for seven thousand rupees; all that now remained being to put in an
engine and some cabins for it to become a full-fledged steamer.

My brother must have thought it a great shame that our
countrymen should have their tongues and pens going, but not a
single line of steamers. As I have narrated before, he had tried to light
matches for his country, but no amount of rubbing availed to make
them strike. He had also wanted power-looms to work, but after all
his travail only one little country towel was born, and then the loom
stopped. And now that he wanted Indian steamers to ply, he bought
an empty old hulk, which in due course, was filled, not only with
engines and cabins, but with loss and ruin as well. And yet we should
remember that all the loss and hardship due to his endeavours fell
on him alone, while the gain of experience remained in reserve for
the whole country. It is these uncalculating, unbusinesslike spirits
who keep the business-fields of the country flooded with their
activities. And, though the flood subsides as rapidly as it comes, it
leaves behind fertilising silt to enrich the soil. When the time for
reaping arrives no one thinks of these pioneers; but those who have

cheerfully staked and lost their all, during life, are not likely, after death, to mind this further loss of being forgotten.

On one side was the European Flotilla Company, on the other my brother Jyotirindra alone; and how tremendous waxed that battle of the mercantile fleets, the people of Khulna and Barisal may still remember. Under the stress of competition steamer was added to steamer, loss piled on loss, while the income dwindled till it ceased to be worthwhile to print tickets. The golden age dawned on the steamer service between Khulna and Barisal. Not only were the passengers carried free of charge, but they were offered light refreshments *gratis* as well! Then was formed a band of volunteers who, with flags and patriotic songs, marched the passengers in procession to the Indian line of steamers. So while there was no want of passengers to carry, every other kind of want began to multiply apace.

My Brother Jyotirindra

Arithmetic remained uninfluenced by patriotic fervour; and while enthusiasm flamed higher and higher to the tune of patriotic songs, three times three went on steadily making nine on the wrong side of the balance sheet.

One of the misfortunes which always pursues the unbusinesslike is that, while they are as easy to read as an open book, they never learn to read the character of others. And since it takes them the whole of their lifetime and all their resources to find out this weakness of theirs, they never get the chance of profiting by experience. While the passengers were having free refreshments, the staff showed no signs of being starved either, but nevertheless the greatest gain remained with my brother in the ruin he so valiantly faced.

The daily bulletins of victory or disaster which used to arrive from the theatre of action kept us in a fever of excitement. Then one day came the news that the steamer *Swadeshi* had fouled the Howrah bridge and sunk. With this last loss my brother completely overstepped the limits of his resources, and there was nothing for it but to wind up the business.

42

Bereavements

In the meantime death made its appearance in our family. Before this, I had never met Death face to face. When my mother died I was quite a child. She had been ailing for quite a long time, and we did not even know when her malady had taken a fatal turn. She used all along to sleep on a separate bed in the same room with us. Then in the course of her illness she was taken for a boat trip on the river, and on her return a room on the third storey of the inner apartments was set apart for her.

On the night she died we were fast asleep in our room downstairs. At what hour I cannot tell, our old nurse came running in weeping and crying: "O my little ones, you have lost your all!" My sister-in-law rebuked her and led her away, to save us the sudden shock at dead of night. Half awakened by her words, I felt my heart sink within me, but could not make out what had happened. When in the morning we were told of her death, I could not realise all that it meant for me.

As we came out into the verandah we saw my mother laid on

a bedstead in the courtyard. There was nothing in her appearance which showed death to be terrible. The aspect which death wore in that morning light was as lovely as a calm and peaceful sleep, and the gulf between life and its absence was not brought home to us.

Only when her body was taken out by the main gateway, and we followed the procession to the cremation ground, did a storm of grief pass through me at the thought that mother would never return by this door and take again her accustomed place in the affairs of her household. The day wore on, we returned from the cremation, and as we turned into our lane I looked up at the house towards my father's rooms on the third storey. He was still in the front verandah sitting motionless in prayer.

She who was the youngest daughter-in-law of the house took charge of the motherless little ones. She herself saw to our food and clothing and all other wants, and kept us constantly near, so that we might not feel our loss too keenly. One of the characteristics of the living is the power to heal the irreparable, to forget the irreplaceable. And in early life this power is strongest, so that no blow penetrates too deeply, no scar is left permanently. Thus the first shadow of death which fell on us left no darkness behind; it departed as softly as it came, only a shadow.

When, in later life, I wandered about like a madcap, at the first coming of spring, with a handful of half-blown jessamines tied in a corner of my muslin scarf, and as I stroked my forehead with the soft, rounded, tapering buds, the touch of my mother's fingers would come back to me; and I clearly realised that the tenderness which dwelt in the tips of those lovely fingers was the very same as that which blossoms every day in the purity of these jessamine buds; and that whether we know it or not, this tenderness is on the earth in boundless measure.

The acquaintance which I made with Death at the age of twenty-four was a permanent one, and its blow has continued to add itself to each succeeding bereavement in an ever lengthening chain of tears. The lightness of infant life can skip aside from the greatest of calamities, but with age evasion is not so easy, and the shock of that day I had to take full on my breast.

That there could be any gap in the unbroken procession of the joys and sorrows of life was a thing I had no idea of. I could therefore see nothing beyond, and this life I had accepted as all in all. When of a sudden death came and in a moment made a gaping rent in its smooth-seeming fabric, I was utterly bewildered. All around, the trees, the soil, the water, the sun, the moon, the stars, remained as immovably true as before; and yet the person who was as truly there, who, through a thousand points of contact with life, mind, and heart, was ever so much more true for me, had vanished in a moment like a dream. What perplexing self-contradiction it all seemed to me as I looked around! How was I ever to reconcile that which remained with that which had gone?

The terrible darkness which was disclosed to me through this rent, continued to attract me night and day as time went on. I would ever and anon return to take my stand there and gaze upon it, wondering what there was left in place of what had gone. Emptiness is a thing man cannot bring himself to believe in; that which is *not*, is untrue; that which is untrue, is not. So our efforts to find something, where we see nothing, are unceasing.

Just as a young plant, surrounded by darkness, stretches itself, as it were on tiptoe, to find its way out into the light, so when death suddenly throws the darkness of negation round the soul it tries and tries to rise into the light of affirmation. And what other sorrow is comparable to the state wherein darkness prevents the finding of a way out of the darkness?

And yet in the midst of this unbearable grief, flashes of joy seemed to sparkle in my mind, now and again, in a way which quite surprised me. That life was not a stable permanent fixture was itself the sorrowful tidings which helped to lighten my mind. That we were not prisoners for ever within a solid stone wall of life was the thought which unconsciously kept coming uppermost in rushes of gladness. That which I had held I was made to let go—this was the sense of loss which distressed me—but when at the same moment I viewed it from the standpoint of freedom gained, a great peace fell upon me.

The all-pervading pressure of worldly existence compensates itself by balancing life against death, and thus it does not crush us. The terrible weight of an unopposed life force has not to be endured by man—this truth came upon me that day as a sudden, wonderful revelation.

With the loosening of the attraction of the world, the beauty of nature took on for me a deeper meaning. Death had given me the correct perspective from which to perceive the world in the fullness of its beauty, and as I saw the picture of the Universe against the background of Death I found it entrancing.

At this time I was attacked with a recrudescence of eccentricity in thought and behaviour. To be called upon to submit to the customs and fashions of the day, as if they were something soberly and genuinely real, made me want to laugh. I *could* not take them seriously. The burden of stopping to consider what other people might think of me was completely lifted off my mind. I have been about in fashionable book shops with a coarse sheet draped round me as my only upper garment, and a pair of slippers on my bare feet. Through hot and cold and wet I used to sleep out on the verandah of the third storey. There the stars and I could gaze at each other, and no time was lost in greeting the dawn.

This phase had nothing to do with any ascetic feeling. It was more like a holiday spree as the result of discovering the schoolmaster Life with his cane to be a myth, and thereby being able to shake myself free from the petty rules of his school. If, on waking one fine morning we were to find gravitation reduced to only a fraction of itself, would we still demurely walk along the high road? Would we not rather skip over many-storied houses for a change, or on encountering the monument take a flying jump, rather than trouble to walk round it? That was why, with the weight of worldly life no longer clogging my feet, I could not stick to the usual course of convention.

Alone on the terrace in the darkness of night I groped all over like a blind man trying to find upon the black stone gate of death some device or sign. Then when I woke with the morning light falling on that unscreened bed of mine, I felt, as I opened my eyes, that my enveloping haze was becoming transparent; and, as on the clearing of the mist the hills and rivers and forests of the scene shine forth, so the dew-washed picture of the world-life, spread out before me, seemed to become renewed and ever so beautiful.

43

The Rains and Autumn

According to the Hindu calendar, each year is ruled by a particular planet. So have I found that in each period of life a particular season assumes a special importance. When I look back to my childhood I can best recall the rainy days. The wind-driven rain has flooded the verandah floor. The row of doors leading into the rooms are all closed. Peari, the old scullery maid, is coming from the market, her basket laden with vegetables, wading through the slush and drenched with the rain. And for no rhyme or reason I am careering about the verandah in an ecstasy of joy.

This also comes back to me:—I am at school, our class is held in a colonnade with mats as outer screens; cloud upon cloud has come up during the afternoon, and they are now heaped up, covering the sky; and as we look on, the rain comes down in close thick showers, the thunder at intervals rumbling long and loud; some mad woman with nails of lightning seems to be rending the sky from end to end; the mat walls tremble under the blasts of wind as if they would be blown in; we can hardly see to read, for the darkness. The Pandit gives us leave to close our books. Then leaving the storm to do the romping and roaring for us, we keep swinging our dangling legs; and my mind goes right away across the far-off unending moor through which the Prince of the fairy tale passes.

I remember, moreover, the depth of the *Sravan** nights. The pattering of the rain finding its way through the gaps of my slumber, creates within a gladsome restfulness deeper than the deepest sleep. And in the wakeful intervals I pray that the morning may see the rain continue, our lane under water, and the bathing platform of the tank submerged to the last step.

But at the age of which I have just been telling, Autumn is on the throne beyond all doubt. Its life is to be seen spread under the clear

---

* The month corresponding to July-August, the height of the rainy season.

transparent leisure of *Ashwin*.* And in the molten gold of this autumn sunshine, softly reflected from the fresh dewy green outside, I am pacing the verandah and composing, in the mode *Jogiya*, the song:

In this morning light I do not know what it is that my heart desires.

The autumn day wears on, the house gong sounds 12 noon, the mode changes; though my mind is still filled with music, leaving no room for call of work or duty; and I sing:

What idle play is this with yourself, my heart, through the listless hours?

Then in the afternoon I am lying on the white floorcloth of my little room, with a drawing book trying to draw pictures—by no means an arduous pursuit of the pictorial muse, but just a toying with the desire to make pictures. The most important part is that which remains in the mind, and of which not a line gets drawn on the paper. And in the meantime the serene autumn afternoon is filtering through the walls of this little Calcutta room filling it, as a cup, with golden intoxication.

I know not why, but all my days of that period I see as if through this autumn sky, this autumn light—the autumn which ripened for me my songs as it ripens the corn for the tillers; the autumn which filled my granary of leisure with radiance; the autumn which flooded my unburdened mind with an unreasoning joy in fashioning song and story.

The great difference which I see between the Rainy-season of my childhood and the Autumn of my youth is that in the former it is outer Nature which closely hemmed me in keeping me entertained with its numerous troupe, its variegated make-up, its medley of music; while the festivity which goes on in the shining light of autumn is in man himself. The play of cloud and sunshine is left in the background, while the murmurs of joy and sorrow occupy the mind. It is our gaze which gives to the blue of the autumn sky

---

* The month of Ashwin corresponds to September-October, the long vacation time for Bengal.

its wistful tinge and human yearning which gives poignancy to the breath of its breezes.

My poems have now come to the doors of men. Here informal goings and comings are not allowed. There is door after door, chamber within chamber. How many times have we to return with only a glimpse of the light in the window, only the sound of the pipes from within the palace gates lingering in our ears. Mind has to treat with mind, will to come to terms with will, through many tortuous obstructions, before giving and taking can come about. The foundation of life, as it dashes into these obstacles, splashes and foams over in laughter and tears, and dances and whirls through eddies from which one cannot get a definite idea of its course.

44

Sharps and Flats

Sharps and Flats is a serenade from the streets in front of the dwelling of man, a plea to be allowed an entry and a place within that house of mystery.

This world is sweet—I do not want to die.
I wish to dwell in the ever-living life of Man.

This is the prayer of the individual to the universal life.

When I started for my second voyage to England, I made the acquaintance on board ship of Asutosh Chaudhuri. He had just taken the M.A. degree of the Calcutta University and was on his way to England to join the Bar. We were together only during the few days the steamer took from Calcutta to Madras, but it became quite evident that depth of friendship does not depend upon length of acquaintance. Within this short time he so drew me to him by his simple natural qualities of heart, that the previous life-long gap in our acquaintance seemed always to have been filled with our friendship.

When Ashu came back from England he became one of us.* He had not as yet had time or opportunity to pierce through all the barriers with which his profession is hedged in, and so become completely immersed in it. The money-bags of his clients had not yet sufficiently loosened the strings which held their gold, and Ashu was still an enthusiast in gathering honey from various gardens of literature. The spirit of literature which then saturated his being had nothing of the mustiness of library morocco about it, but was fragrant with the scent of unknown exotics from over the seas. At his invitation I enjoyed many a picnic amidst the spring time of those distant woodlands.

He had a special taste for the flavour of French literature. I was then writing the poems which came to be published in the volume entitled *Kadi o Komal*, Sharps and Flats. Ashu could discern resemblances between many of my poems and old French poems he knew. According to him the common element in all these poems was the attraction which the play of world-life had for the poet, and this had found varied expression in each and every one of them. The unfulfilled desire to enter into this larger life was the fundamental motive throughout.

"I will arrange and publish these poems for you," said Ashu, and accordingly that task was entrusted to him. The poem beginning *This world is sweet* was the one he considered to be the keynote of the whole series and so he placed it at the beginning of the volume.

Ashu was very possibly right. When in childhood I was confined to the house, I offered my heart in my wistful gaze to outside nature in all its variety through the openings in the parapet of our inner roof-terrace. In my youth the world of men in the same way exerted a powerful attraction on me. To that also I was then an outsider and looked out upon it from the roadside. My mind standing on the brink called out, as it were, with an eager waving of hands to the ferryman sailing away across the waves to the other side. For Life longed to start on life's journey.

It is not true that my peculiarly isolated social condition was the bar to my plunging into the midst of the world-life. I see no sign that

---

* Referring to his marriage with the writer's niece, Pratibha.

those of my countrymen who have been all their lives in the thick of society feel, any more than I did, the touch of its living intimacy. The life of our country has its high banks, and its flight of steps, and, on its dark waters falls the cool shade of the ancient trees, while from within the leafy branches over-head the *koel* cooes forth its ravishing old-time song. But for all that it is stagnant water. Where is its current, where are the waves, when does the high tide rush in from the sea?

Did I then get from the neighbourhood on the other side of our lane an echo of the victorious pæan with which the river, falling and rising, wave after wave, cuts its way through walls of stone to the sea? No! My life in its solitude was simply fretting for want of an invitation to the place where the festival of world-life was being held.

Man is overcome by a profound depression while nodding through his voluptuously lazy hours of seclusion, because in this way he is deprived of full commerce with life. Such is the despondency from which I have always painfully struggled to get free. My mind refused to respond to the cheap intoxication of the political movements of those days, devoid, as they seemed, of all strength of national consciousness, with their complete ignorance of the country, their supreme indifference to real service of the motherland. I was tormented by a furious impatience, an intolerable dissatisfaction with myself and all around me. Much rather, I said to myself, would I be an Arab Bedouin!

While in other parts of the world there is no end to the movement and clamour of the revelry of free life, we, like the beggar maid, stand outside and longingly look on. When have we had the wherewithal to deck ourselves for the occasion and go and join in it? Only in a country where the spirit of separation reigns supreme, and innumerable petty barriers divide one from another, need this longing to realise the larger life of the world in one's own remain unsatisfied.

I strained with the same yearning towards the world of men in my youth, as I did in my childhood towards outside nature from within the chalk-ring drawn round me by the servants. How rare, how unattainable, how far away it seemed! And yet if we cannot get into touch with it, if from it no breeze can blow, no current come, if no road be there for the free goings and comings of travellers, then the dead things that accumulate around us never get removed, but continue to be heaped up till they smother all life.

During the Rains there are only dark clouds and showers. And in the Autumn there is the play of light and shade in the sky, but that is not all-absorbing; for there is also the promise of corn in the fields. So in my poetical career, when the rainy season was in the ascendant there were only my vaporous fancies which stormed and showered; my utterance was misty, my verses were wild. And with the *Sharps and Flats* of my Autumn, not only was there the play of cloud-effects in the sky, but out of the ground crops were to be seen rising. Then, in the commerce with the world of reality, both language and metre attempted definiteness and variety of form.

Thus ends another Book. The days of coming together of inside and outside, kin and stranger, are closing in upon my life. My life's journey has now to be completed through the dwelling places of men. And the good and evil, joy and sorrow, which it thus encountered, are not to be lightly viewed as pictures. What makings and breakings, victories and defeats, clashings and minglings, are here going on!

I have not the power to disclose and display the supreme art with which the Guide of my life is joyfully leading me through all its obstacles, antagonisms and crookednesses towards the fulfilment of its innermost meaning. And if I cannot make clear all the mystery of this design, whatever else I may try to show is sure to prove misleading at every step. To analyse the image is only to get at its dust, not at the joy of the artist.

So having escorted them to the door of the inner sanctuary I take leave of my readers.

NOVEL

ঘরে বাইরে
THE HOME AND
THE WORLD

[*Ghôre Baire* was first published in 1916. This is a translation by
Surendranath Tagore, published in 1919.]

CHAPTER ONE

Bimala's Story

I

Mother, today there comes back to mind the vermilion mark* at the parting of your hair, the sari which you used to wear, with its wide red border, and those wonderful eyes of yours, full of depth and peace. They came at the start of my life's journey, like the first streak of dawn, giving me golden provision to carry me on my way.

The sky which gives light is blue, and my mother's face was dark, but she had the radiance of holiness, and her beauty would put to shame all the vanity of the beautiful.

Everyone says that I resemble my mother. In my childhood I used to resent this. It made me angry with my mirror. I thought that it was God's unfairness which was wrapped round my limbs—that my dark features were not my due, but had come to me by some misunderstanding. All that remained for me to ask of my God in reparation was, that I might grow up to be a model of what woman should be, as one reads it in some epic poem.

When the proposal came for my marriage, an astrologer was sent, who consulted my palm and said, "This girl has good signs. She will become an ideal wife."

---

* The mark of Hindu wifehood and the symbol of all the devotion that it implies.

And all the women who heard it said: "No wonder, for she resembles her mother."

I was married into a Rajah's house. When I was a child, I was quite familiar with the description of the Prince of the fairy story. But my husband's face was not of a kind that one's imagination would place in fairyland. It was dark, even as mine was. The feeling of shrinking, which I had about my own lack of physical beauty, was lifted a little; at the same time a touch of regret was left lingering in my heart.

But when the physical appearance evades the scrutiny of our senses and enters the sanctuary of our hearts, then it can forget itself. I know, from my childhood's experience, how devotion is beauty itself, in its inner aspect. When my mother arranged the different fruits, carefully peeled by her own loving hands, on the white stone plate, and gently waved her fan to drive away the flies while my father sat down to his meals, her service would lose itself in a beauty which passed beyond outward forms. Even in my infancy I could feel its power. It transcended all debates, or doubts, or calculations: it was pure music.

I distinctly remember after my marriage, when, early in the morning, I would cautiously and silently get up and take the dust* of my husband's feet without waking him, how at such moments I could feel the vermilion mark upon my forehead shining out like the morning star.

One day, he happened to awake, and smiled as he asked me: "What is that, Bimala? What *are* you doing?"

I can never forget the shame of being detected by him. He might possibly have thought that I was trying to earn merit secretly. But no, no! That had nothing to do with merit. It was my woman's heart, which must worship in order to love.

My father-in-law's house was old in dignity from the days of the *Badshahs*. Some of its manners were of the Moguls and Pathans, some of its customs of Manu and Parashar. But my husband was absolutely modern. He was the first of the house to go through a college course and take his M.A. degree. His elder brother had

---

* Taking the dust of the feet is a formal offering of reverence and is done by lightly touching the feet of the revered one and then one's own head with the same hand. The wife does not ordinarily do this to the husband.

died young, of drink, and had left no children. My husband did not drink and was not given to dissipation. So foreign to the family was this abstinence, that to many it hardly seemed decent! Purity, they imagined, was only becoming in those on whom fortune had not smiled. It is the moon which has room for stains, not the stars.

My husband's parents had died long ago, and his old grandmother was mistress of the house. My husband was the apple of her eye, the jewel on her bosom. And so he never met with much difficulty in overstepping any of the ancient usages. When he brought in Miss Gilby, to teach me and be my companion, he stuck to his resolve in spite of the poison secreted by all the wagging tongues at home and outside.

My husband had then just got through his B.A. examination and was reading for his M.A. degree; so he had to stay in Calcutta to attend college. He used to write to me almost every day, a few lines only, and simple words, but his bold, round handwriting would look up into my face, oh, so tenderly! I kept his letters in a sandalwood box and covered them every day with the flowers I gathered in the garden.

At that time the Prince of the fairy tale had faded, like the moon in the morning light. I had the Prince of my real world enthroned in my heart. I was his queen. I had my seat by his side. But my real joy was, that my true place was at his feet.

Since then, I have been educated, and introduced to the modern age in its own language, and therefore these words that I write seem to blush with shame in their prose setting. Except for my acquaintance with this modern standard of life, I should know, quite naturally, that just as my being born a woman was not in my own hands, so the element of devotion in woman's love is not like a hackneyed passage quoted from a romantic poem to be piously written down in round hand in a schoolgirl's copy-book.

But my husband would not give me any opportunity for worship. That was his greatness. They are cowards who claim absolute devotion from their wives as their right; that is a humiliation for both.

His love for me seemed to overflow my limits by its flood of wealth and service. But my necessity was more for giving than for receiving; for love is a vagabond, who can make his flowers bloom in the wayside dust, better than in the crystal jars kept in the drawing room.

My husband could not break completely with the old-time traditions which prevailed in our family. It was difficult, therefore, for us to meet at any hour of the day we pleased.* I knew exactly the time that he could come to me, and therefore our meeting had all the care of loving preparation. It was like the rhyming of a poem; it had to come through the path of the metre.

After finishing the day's work and taking my afternoon bath, I would do up my hair and renew my vermilion mark and put on my sari, carefully crinkled; and then, bringing back my body and mind from all distractions of household duties, I would dedicate it at this special hour, with special ceremonies, to one individual. That time, each day, with him was short; but it was infinite.

My husband used to say, that man and wife are equal in love because of their equal claim on each other. I never argued the point with him, but my heart said that devotion never stands in the way of true equality; it only raises the level of the ground of meeting. Therefore the joy of the higher equality remains permanent; it never slides down to the vulgar level of triviality.

My beloved, it was worthy of you that you never expected worship from me. But if you had accepted it, you would have done me a real service. You showed your love by decorating me, by educating me, by giving me what I asked for, and what I did not. I have seen what depth of love there was in your eyes when you gazed at me. I have known the secret sigh of pain you suppressed in your love for me. You loved my body as if it were a flower of paradise. You loved my whole nature as if it had been given you by some rare providence.

Such lavish devotion made me proud to think that the wealth was all my own which drove you to my gate. But vanity such as this only checks the flow of free surrender in a woman's love. When I sit on the queen's throne and claim homage, then the claim only goes on magnifying itself; it is never satisfied. Can there be any real happiness for a woman in merely feeling that she has power over a man? To surrender one's pride in devotion is woman's only salvation.

---

* It would not be reckoned good form for the husband to be continually going into the zenana, except at particular hours for meals or rest.

It comes back to me today how, in the days of our happiness, the fires of envy sprung up all around us. That was only natural, for had I not stepped into my good fortune by a mere chance, and without deserving it? But providence does not allow a run of luck to last for ever, unless its debt of honour be fully paid, day by day, through many a long day, and thus made secure. God may grant us gifts, but the merit of being able to take and hold them must be our own. Alas for the boons that slip through unworthy hands!

My husband's grandmother and mother were both renowned for their beauty. And my widowed sister-in-law was also of a beauty rarely to be seen. When, in turn, fate left them desolate, the grandmother vowed she would not insist on having beauty for her remaining grandson when he married. Only the auspicious marks with which I was endowed gained me an entry into this family—otherwise, I had no claim to be here.

In this house of luxury, but few of its ladies had received their meed of respect. They had, however, got used to the ways of the family, and managed to keep their heads above water, buoyed up by their dignity as Ranis of an ancient house, in spite of their daily tears being drowned in the foam of wine, and by the tinkle of the dancing girls' anklets. Was the credit due to me that my husband did not touch liquor, nor squander his manhood in the markets of woman's flesh? What charm did I know to soothe the wild and wandering mind of men? It was my good luck, nothing else. For fate proved utterly callous to my sister-in-law. Her festivity died out, while yet the evening was early, leaving the light of her beauty shining in vain over empty halls—burning and burning, with no accompanying music!

His sister-in-law affected a contempt for my husband's modern notions. How absurd to keep the family ship, laden with all the weight of its time-honoured glory, sailing under the colours of his slip of a girl-wife alone! Often have I felt the lash of scorn. "A thief who had stolen a husband's love!" "A sham hidden in the shamelessness of her new-fangled finery!" The many-coloured garments of modern fashion with which my husband loved to adorn me roused jealous wrath. "Is not she ashamed to make a show-window of herself—and with her looks, too!"

My husband was aware of all this, but his gentleness knew no bounds. He used to implore me to forgive her.

I remember I once told him: "Women's minds are so petty, so crooked!" "Like the feet of Chinese women," he replied. "Has not the pressure of society cramped them into pettiness and crookedness? They are but pawns of the fate which gambles with them. What responsibility have they of their own?"

My sister-in-law never failed to get from my husband whatever she wanted. He did not stop to consider whether her requests were right or reasonable. But what exasperated me most was that she was not grateful for this. I had promised my husband that I would not talk back at her, but this set me raging all the more, inwardly. I used to feel that goodness has a limit, which, if passed, somehow seems to make men cowardly. Shall I tell the whole truth? I have often wished that my husband had the manliness to be a little less good.

My sister-in-law, the Bara Rani,* was still young and had no pretensions to saintliness. Rather, her talk and jest and laugh inclined to be forward. The young maids with whom she surrounded herself were also impudent to a degree. But there was none to gainsay her—for was not this the custom of the house? It seemed to me that my good fortune in having a stainless husband was a special eyesore to her. He, however, felt more the sorrow of her lot than the defects of her character.

II

My husband was very eager to take me out of *purdah*.†

One day I said to him: "What do I want with the outside world?"

"The outside world may want you," he replied.

"If the outside world has got on so long without me, it may go on for some time longer. It need not pine to death for want of me."

---

* *Bara* = Senior; *Chota* = Junior. In joint families of rank, though the widows remain entitled only to a life-interest in their husbands' share, their rank remains to them according to seniority, and the titles 'Senior' and 'Junior' continue to distinguish the elder and younger branches, even though the junior branch be the one in power.

† The seclusion of the zenana, and all the customs peculiar to it, are designated by the general term 'Purdah,' which means Screen.

"Let it perish, for all I care! That is not troubling me. I am thinking about myself."

"Oh, indeed. Tell me what about yourself?"

My husband was silent, with a smile.

I knew his way, and protested at once: "No, no, you are not going to run away from me like that! I want to have this out with you."

"Can one ever finish a subject with words?"

"Do stop speaking in riddles. Tell me . . ."

"What I want is, that I should have you, and you should have me, more fully in the outside world. That is where we are still in debt to each other."

"Is anything wanting, then, in the love we have here at home?"

"Here you are wrapped up in me. You know neither what you have, nor what you want."

"I cannot bear to hear you talk like this."

"I would have you come into the heart of the outer world and meet reality. Merely going on with your household duties, living all your life in the world of household conventions and the drudgery of household tasks—you were not made for that! If we meet, and recognise each other, in the real world, then only will our love be true."

"If there be any drawback here to our full recognition of each other, then I have nothing to say. But as for myself, I feel no want."

"Well, even if the drawback is only on my side, why shouldn't you help to remove it?"

Such discussions repeatedly occurred. One day he said: "The greedy man who is fond of his fish stew has no compunction in cutting up the fish according to his need. But the man who loves the fish wants to enjoy it in the water; and if that is impossible he waits on the bank; and even if he comes back home without a sight of it he has the consolation of knowing that the fish is all right. Perfect gain is the best of all; but if that is impossible, then the next best gain is perfect losing."

I never liked the way my husband had of talking on this subject, but that is not the reason why I refused to leave the zenana. His grandmother was still alive. My husband had filled more than a hundred and twenty per cent of the house with the twentieth century, against her taste; but she had borne it uncomplaining. She would have borne it, likewise, if the daughter-in-law* of the Rajah's house had left its seclusion. She was even prepared for this happening. But I did not consider it important enough to give her the pain of it. I have read in books that we are called 'caged birds.' I cannot speak for others, but I had so much in this cage of mine that there was not room for it in the universe—at least that is what I then felt.

The grandmother, in her old age, was very fond of me. At the bottom of her fondness was the thought that, with the conspiracy of favourable stars which attended me, I had been able to attract my husband's love. Were not men naturally inclined to plunge downwards? None of the others, for all their beauty, had been able to prevent their husbands going headlong into the burning depths which consumed and destroyed them. She believed that I had been the means of extinguishing this fire, so deadly to the men of the family. So she kept me in the shelter of her bosom, and trembled if I was in the least bit unwell.

His grandmother did not like the dresses and ornaments my husband brought from European shops to deck me with. But she reflected: "Men will have some absurd hobby or other, which is sure to be expensive. It is no use trying to check their extravagance; one is glad enough if they stop short of ruin. If my Nikhil had not been busy dressing up his wife there is no knowing whom else he might have spent his money on!" So whenever any new dress of mine arrived she used to send for my husband and make merry over it.

Thus it came about that it was her taste which changed. The influence of the modern age fell so strongly upon her, that her evenings refused to pass if I did not tell her stories out of English books.

After his grandmother's death, my husband wanted me to go and live with him in Calcutta. But I could not bring myself to do that. Was not this our House, which she had kept under her sheltering care through all her trials and troubles? Would not a curse come upon me if I deserted it and went off to town? This was the thought that kept me back, as her empty seat reproachfully looked up at

---

* The prestige of the daughter-in-law is of the first importance in a Hindu household of rank.—*Translator*

me. That noble lady had come into this house at the age of eight, and had died in her seventy-ninth year. She had not spent a happy life. Fate had hurled shaft after shaft at her breast, only to draw out more and more the imperishable spirit within. This great house was hallowed with her tears. What should I do in the dust of Calcutta, away from it?

My husband's idea was that this would be a good opportunity for leaving to my sister-in-law the consolation of ruling over the household, giving our life, at the same time, more room to branch out in Calcutta. That is just where my difficulty came in. She had worried my life out, she ill brooked my husband's happiness, and for this she was to be rewarded! And what of the day when we should have to come back here? Should I then get back my seat at the head?

"What do you want with that seat?" my husband would say. "Are there not more precious things in life?"

Men never understand these things. They have their nests in the outside world; they little know the whole of what the household stands for. In these matters they ought to follow womanly guidance. Such were my thoughts at that time.

I felt the real point was, that one ought to stand up for one's rights. To go away, and leave everything in the hands of the enemy, would be nothing short of owning defeat.

But why did not my husband compel me to go with him to Calcutta? I know the reason. He did not use his power, just because he had it.

III

If one had to fill in, little by little, the gap between day and night, it would take an eternity to do it. But the sun rises and the darkness is dispelled—a moment is sufficient to overcome an infinite distance.

One day there came the new era of Swadeshi* in Bengal; but as to how it happened, we had no distinct vision. There was no gradual slope connecting the past with the present. For that reason,

---

* The Nationalist movement, which began more as an economic than a political one, having as its main object the encouragement of indigenous industries.—*Translator*

I imagine, the new epoch came in like a flood, breaking down the dykes and sweeping all our prudence and fear before it. We had no time even to think about, or understand, what had happened, or what was about to happen.

My sight and my mind, my hopes and my desires, became red with the passion of this new age. Though, up to this time, the walls of the home—which was the ultimate world to my mind—remained unbroken, yet I stood looking over into the distance, and I heard a voice from the far horizon, whose meaning was not perfectly clear to me, but whose call went straight to my heart.

From the time my husband had been a college student he had been trying to get the things required by our people produced in our own country. There are plenty of date trees in our district. He tried to invent an apparatus for extracting the juice and boiling it into sugar and treacle. I heard that it was a great success, only it extracted more money than juice. After a while he came to the conclusion that our attempts at reviving our industries were not succeeding for want of a bank of our own. He was, at the time, trying to teach me political economy. This alone would not have done much harm, but he also took it into his head to teach his countrymen ideas of thrift, so as to pave the way for a bank; and then he actually started a small bank. Its high rate of interest, which made the villagers flock so enthusiastically to put in their money, ended by swamping the bank altogether.

The old officers of the estate felt troubled and frightened. There was jubilation in the enemy's camp. Of all the family, only my husband's grandmother remained unmoved. She would scold me, saying: "Why are you all plaguing him so? Is it the fate of the estate that is worrying you? How many times have I seen this estate in the hands of the court receiver! Are men like women? Men are born spendthrifts and only know how to waste. Look here, child, count yourself fortunate that your husband is not wasting himself as well!"

My husband's list of charities was a long one. He would assist to the bitter end of utter failure anyone who wanted to invent a new loom or rice-husking machine. But what annoyed me most was the way that Sandip Babu used to fleece him on the pretext of Swadeshi work. Whenever he wanted to start a newspaper, or travel about preaching the Cause, or take a change of air by the advice of his doctor, my husband would unquestioningly supply him with the money. This was over and above the regular living allowance which Sandip Babu also received from him. The strangest part of it was that my husband and Sandip Babu did not agree in their opinions.

As soon as the Swadeshi storm reached my blood, I said to my husband: "I must burn all my foreign clothes."

"Why burn them?" said he. "You need not wear them as long as you please."

"As long as I please! Not in this life . . ."

"Very well, do not wear them for the rest of your life, then. But why this bonfire business?"

"Would you thwart me in my resolve?"

"What I want to say is this: Why not try to build up something? You should not waste even a tenth part of your energies in this destructive excitement."

"Such excitement will give us the energy to build."

"That is as much as to say, that you cannot light the house unless you set fire to it."

Then there came another trouble. When Miss Gilby first came to our house there was a great flutter, which afterwards calmed down when they got used to her. Now the whole thing was stirred up afresh. I had never bothered myself before as to whether Miss Gilby was European or Indian, but I began to do so now. I said to my husband: "We must get rid of Miss Gilby."

He kept silent.

I talked to him wildly, and he went away sad at heart.

After a fit of weeping, I felt in a more reasonable mood when we met at night. "I cannot," my husband said, "look upon Miss Gilby through a mist of abstraction, just because she is English. Cannot you get over the barrier of her name after such a long acquaintance? Cannot you realise that she loves you?"

I felt a little ashamed and replied with some sharpness: "Let her remain. I am not over anxious to send her away." And Miss Gilby remained.

But one day I was told that she had been insulted by a young fellow on her way to church. This was a boy whom we were supporting. My husband turned him out of the house. There was not a single soul, that day, who could forgive my husband for that act—not even I. This time Miss Gilby left of her own accord. She shed tears when she came to say goodbye, but my mood would not melt. To slander the poor boy so—and such a fine boy, too, who would forget his daily bath and food in his enthusiasm for Swadeshi.

My husband escorted Miss Gilby to the railway station in his own carriage. I was sure he was going too far. When exaggerated accounts of the incident gave rise to a public scandal, which found its way to the newspapers, I felt he had been rightly served.

I had often become anxious at my husband's doings, but had never before been ashamed; yet now I had to blush for him! I did not know exactly, nor did I care, what wrong poor Noren might, or might not, have done to Miss Gilby, but the idea of sitting in judgement on such a matter at such a time! I should have refused to damp the spirit which prompted young Noren to defy the Englishwoman. I could not but look upon it as a sign of cowardice in my husband, that he should fail to understand this simple thing. And so I blushed for him.

And yet it was not that my husband refused to support Swadeshi, or was in any way against the Cause. Only he had not been able whole-heartedly to accept the spirit of *Bande Mataram*.*

"I am willing," he said, "to serve my country; but my worship I reserve for Right which is far greater than my country. To worship my country as a god is to bring a curse upon it."

---

* Lit.: 'Hail Mother'; the opening words of a song by Bankim Chatterjee, the famous Bengali novelist. The song has now become the national anthem, and Bande Mataram the national cry, since the days of the Swadeshi movement.—*Translator*

CHAPTER TWO

Bimala's Story

IV

This was the time when Sandip Babu with his followers came to our neighbourhood to preach Swadeshi.

There is to be a big meeting in our temple pavilion. We women are sitting there, on one side, behind a screen. Triumphant shouts of Bande Mataram come nearer: and to them I am thrilling through and through. Suddenly a stream of barefooted youths in turbans, clad in ascetic ochre, rushes into the quadrangle, like a silt-reddened freshet into a dry river bed at the first burst of the rains. The whole place is filled with an immense crowd, through which Sandip Babu is borne, seated in a big chair hoisted on the shoulders of ten or twelve of the youths.

Bande Mataram! Bande Mataram! Bande Mataram! It seems as though the skies would be rent and scattered into a thousand fragments.

I had seen Sandip Babu's photograph before. There was something in his features which I did not quite like. Not that he was bad-looking—far from it: he had a splendidly handsome face. Yet, I know not why, it seemed to me, in spite of all its brilliance, that too much of base alloy had gone into its making. The light in his eyes somehow did not shine true. That was why I did not like it when my husband unquestioningly gave in to all his demands. I could bear the waste of money; but it vexed me to think that he was imposing on my husband, taking advantage of friendship. His bearing was not that of an ascetic, nor even of a person of moderate means, but foppish all over. Love of comfort seemed to . . . any number of such reflections come back to me today, but let them be.

When, however, Sandip Babu began to speak that afternoon, and the hearts of the crowd swayed and surged to his words, as though they would break all bounds, I saw him wonderfully transformed. Especially when his features were suddenly lit up by a shaft of light from the slowly setting sun, as it sunk below the roof-line of the pavilion, he seemed to me to be marked out by the gods as their messenger to mortal men and women.

From beginning to end of his speech, each one of his utterances was a stormy outburst. There was no limit to the confidence of his assurance. I do not know how it happened, but I found I had impatiently pushed away the screen from before me and had fixed my gaze upon him. Yet there was none in that crowd who paid any heed to my doings. Only once, I noticed, his eyes, like stars in fateful Orion, flashed full on my face.

I was utterly unconscious of myself. I was no longer the lady of the Rajah's house, but the sole representative of Bengal's womanhood. And he was the champion of Bengal. As the sky had shed its light over him, so he must receive the consecration of a woman's benediction . . .

It seemed clear to me that, since he had caught sight of me, the fire in his words had flamed up more fiercely. Indra's* steed refused to be reined in, and there came the roar of thunder and the flash of lightning. I said within myself that his language had caught fire from my eyes; for we women are not only the deities of the household fire, but the flame of the soul itself.

I returned home that evening radiant with a new pride and joy. The storm within me had shifted my whole being from one centre to another. Like the Greek maidens of old, I fain would cut off my long, resplendent tresses to make a bowstring for my hero. Had my outward ornaments been connected with my inner feelings, then my

* The Jupiter Pluvius of Hindu mythology

necklet, my armlets, my bracelets, would all have burst their bonds and flung themselves over that assembly like a shower of meteors. Only some personal sacrifice, I felt, could help me to bear the tumult of my exaltation.

When my husband came home later, I was trembling lest he should utter a sound out of tune with the triumphant paean which was still ringing in my ears, lest his fanaticism for truth should lead him to express disapproval of anything that had been said that afternoon. For then I should have openly defied and humiliated him. But he did not say a word . . . which I did not like either.

He should have said: "Sandip has brought me to my senses. I now realise how mistaken I have been all this time."

I somehow felt that he was spitefully silent, that he obstinately refused to be enthusiastic. I asked how long Sandip Babu was going to be with us.

"He is off to Rangpur early tomorrow morning," said my husband.

"Must it be tomorrow?"

"Yes, he is already engaged to speak there."

I was silent for a while and then asked again: "Could he not possibly stay a day longer?"

"That may hardly be possible, but why?"

"I want to invite him to dinner and attend on him myself."

My husband was surprised. He had often entreated me to be present when he had particular friends to dinner, but I had never let myself be persuaded. He gazed at me curiously, in silence, with a look I did not quite understand.

I was suddenly overcome with a sense of shame. "No, no," I exclaimed, "that would never do!"

"Why not!" said he. "I will ask him myself, and if it is at all possible he will surely stay on for tomorrow."

It turned out to be quite possible.

I will tell the exact truth. That day I reproached my Creator because he had not made me surpassingly beautiful—not to steal any heart away, but because beauty is glory. In this great day the men of the country should realise its goddess in its womanhood. But, alas, the eyes of men fail to discern the goddess, if outward beauty be lacking. Would Sandip Babu find the *Shakti* of the Motherland manifest in me? Or would he simply take me to be an ordinary, domestic woman?

That morning I scented my flowing hair and tied it in a loose knot, bound by a cunningly intertwined red silk ribbon. Dinner, you see, was to be served at midday, and there was no time to dry my hair after my bath and do it up plaited in the ordinary way. I put on a gold-bordered white sari, and my short-sleeve muslin jacket was also gold-bordered.

I felt that there was a certain restraint about my costume and that nothing could well have been simpler. But my sister-in-law, who happened to be passing by, stopped dead before me, surveyed me from head to foot and with compressed lips smiled a meaning smile. When I asked her the reason, "I am admiring your get-up!" she said.

"What is there so entertaining about it?" I enquired, considerably annoyed.

"It's superb," she said. "I was only thinking that one of those low-necked English bodices would have made it perfect." Not only her mouth and eyes, but her whole body seemed to ripple with suppressed laughter as she left the room.

I was very, very angry, and wanted to change everything and put on my everyday clothes. But I cannot tell exactly why I could not carry out my impulse. Women are the ornaments of society—thus I reasoned with myself—and my husband would never like it, if I appeared before Sandip Babu unworthily clad.

My idea had been to make my appearance after they had sat down to dinner. In the bustle of looking after the serving the first awkwardness would have passed off. But dinner was not ready in time, and it was getting late. Meanwhile my husband had sent for me to introduce the guest.

I was feeling horribly shy about looking Sandip Babu in the face. However, I managed to recover myself enough to say: "I am so sorry dinner is getting late."

He boldly came and sat right beside me as he replied: "I get a dinner of some kind every day, but the Goddess of Plenty keeps behind the scenes. Now that the goddess herself has appeared, it matters little if the dinner lags behind."

He was just as emphatic in his manners as he was in his public speaking. He had no hesitation and seemed to be accustomed to occupy, unchallenged, his chosen seat. He claimed the right to intimacy so confidently, that the blame would seem to belong to those who should dispute it.

I was in terror lest Sandip Babu should take me for a shrinking, old-fashioned bundle of inanity. But, for the life of me, I could not sparkle in repartees such as might charm or dazzle him. What could have possessed me, I angrily wondered, to appear before him in such an absurd way?

I was about to retire when dinner was over, but Sandip Babu, as bold as ever, placed himself in my way.

"You must not," he said, "think me greedy. It was not the dinner that kept me staying on, it was your invitation. If you were to run away now, that would not be playing fair with your guest."

If he had not said these words with a careless ease, they would have been out of tune. But, after all, he was such a great friend of my husband that I was like his sister.

While I was struggling to climb up this high wave of intimacy, my husband came to the rescue, saying: "Why not come back to us after you have taken your dinner?"

"But you must give your word," said Sandip Babu, "before we let you off."

"I will come," said I, with a slight smile.

"Let me tell you," continued Sandip Babu, "why I cannot trust you. Nikhil has been married these nine years, and all this while you have eluded me. If you do this again for another nine years, we shall never meet again."

I took up the spirit of his remark as I dropped my voice to reply: "Why even then should we not meet?"

"My horoscope tells me I am to die early. None of my forefathers have survived their thirtieth year. I am now twenty-seven."

He knew this would go home. This time there must have been a shade of concern in my low voice as I said: "The blessings of the whole country are sure to avert the evil influence of the stars."

"Then the blessings of the country must be voiced by its goddess. This is the reason for my anxiety that you should return, so that my talisman may begin to work from today."

Sandip Babu had such a way of taking things by storm that I got no opportunity of resenting what I never should have permitted in another.

"So," he concluded with a laugh, "I am going to hold this husband of yours as a hostage till you come back."

As I was coming away, he exclaimed: "May I trouble you for a trifle?"

I started and turned round.

"Don't be alarmed," he said. "It's merely a glass of water. You might have noticed that I did not drink any water with my dinner. I take it a little later."

Upon this I had to make a show of interest and ask him the reason. He began to give the history of his dyspepsia. I was told how he had been a martyr to it for seven months, and how, after the usual course of nuisances, which included different allopathic and homoeopathic misadventures, he had obtained the most wonderful results by indigenous methods.

"Do you know," he added, with a smile, "God has built even my infirmities in such a manner that they yield only under the bombardment of Swadeshi pills."

My husband, at this, broke his silence. "You must confess," said he, "that you have as immense an attraction for foreign medicine as the earth has for meteors. You have three shelves in your sitting room full of . . ."

Sandip Babu broke in: "Do you know what they are? They are the punitive police. They come, not because they are wanted, but because they are imposed on us by the rule of this modern age, exacting fines and inflicting injuries."

My husband could not bear exaggerations, and I could see he disliked this. But all ornaments are exaggerations. They are not made by God, but by man. Once I remember in defence of some untruth of mine I said to my husband: "Only the trees and beasts and birds tell unmitigated truths, because these poor things have not the power to invent. In this men show their superiority to the lower creatures, and women beat even men. Neither is a profusion of ornament unbecoming for a woman, nor a profusion of untruth."

As I came out into the passage leading to the zenana I found my sister-in-law, standing near a window overlooking the reception rooms, peeping through the venetian shutter.

"You here?" I asked in surprise.

"Eavesdropping!" she replied.

V

When I returned, Sandip Babu was tenderly apologetic. "I am afraid we have spoilt your appetite," he said.

I felt greatly ashamed. Indeed, I had been too indecently quick over my dinner. With a little calculation, it would become quite evident that my non-eating had surpassed the eating. But I had no idea that anyone could have been deliberately calculating.

I suppose Sandip Babu detected my feeling of shame, which only augmented it. "I was sure," he said, "that you had the impulse of the wild deer to run away, but it is a great boon that you took the trouble to keep your promise with me."

I could not think of any suitable reply and so I sat down, blushing and uncomfortable, at one end of the sofa. The vision that I had of myself, as the Shakti of Womanhood, incarnate, crowning Sandip Babu simply with my presence, majestic and unashamed, failed me altogether.

Sandip Babu deliberately started a discussion with my husband. He knew that his keen wit flashed to the best effect in an argument. I have often since observed, that he never lost an opportunity for a passage at arms whenever I happened to be present.

He was familiar with my husband's views on the cult of Bande Mataram, and began in a provoking way: "So you do not allow that there is room for an appeal to the imagination in patriotic work?"

"It has its place, Sandip, I admit, but I do not believe in giving it the whole place. I would know my country in its frank reality, and for this I am both afraid and ashamed to make use of hypnotic texts of patriotism."

"What you call hypnotic texts I call truth. I truly believe my country to be my God. I worship Humanity. God manifests Himself both in man and in his country."

"If that is what you really believe, there should be no difference for you between man and man, and so between country and country."

"Quite true. But my powers are limited, so my worship of Humanity is continued in the worship of my country."

"I have nothing against your worship as such, but how is it you propose to conduct your worship of God by hating other countries in which He is equally manifest?"

"Hate is also an adjunct of worship. Arjuna won Mahadeva's favour by wrestling with him. God will be with us in the end, if we are prepared to give Him battle."

"If that be so, then those who are serving and those who are harming the country are both His devotees. Why, then, trouble to preach patriotism?"

"In the case of one's own country, it is different. There the heart clearly demands worship."

"If you push the same argument further you can say that since God is manifested in us, our *self* has to be worshipped before all else; because our natural instinct claims it."

"Look here, Nikhil, this is all merely dry logic. Can't you recognise that there is such a thing as feeling?"

"I tell you the truth, Sandip," my husband replied. "It is my feelings that are outraged, whenever you try to pass off injustice as a duty, and unrighteousness as a moral ideal. The fact, that I am incapable of stealing, is not due to my possessing logical faculties, but to my having some feeling of respect for myself and love for ideals."

I was raging inwardly. At last I could keep silent no longer. "Is not the history of every country," I cried, "whether England, France, Germany, or Russia, the history of stealing for the sake of one's own country?"

"They have to answer for these thefts; they are doing so even now; their history is not yet ended."

"At any rate," interposed Sandip Babu, "why should we not follow suit? Let us first fill our country's coffers with stolen goods and then take centuries, like these other countries, to answer for them, if we must. But, I ask you, where do you find this 'answering' in history?"

507

"When Rome was answering for her sin no one knew it. All that time, there was apparently no limit to her prosperity. But do you not see one thing: how these political bags of theirs are bursting with lies and treacheries, breaking their backs under their weight?"

Never before had I had any opportunity of being present at a discussion between my husband and his men friends. Whenever he argued with me I could feel his reluctance to push me into a corner. This arose out of the very love he bore me. Today for the first time I saw his fencer's skill in debate.

Nevertheless, my heart refused to accept my husband's position. I was struggling to find some answer, but it would not come. When the word 'righteousness' comes into an argument, it sounds ugly to say that a thing can be too good to be useful.

All of a sudden Sandip Babu turned to me with the question: "What do *you* say to this?"

"I do not care about fine distinctions," I broke out. "I will tell you broadly what I feel. I am only human. I am covetous. I would have good things for my country. If I am obliged, I would snatch them and filch them. I have anger. I would be angry for my country's sake. If necessary, I would smite and slay to avenge her insults. I have my desire to be fascinated, and fascination must be supplied to me in bodily shape by my country. She must have some visible symbol casting its spell upon my mind. I would make my country a Person, and call her Mother, Goddess, Durga—for whom I would redden the earth with sacrificial offerings. I am human, not divine."

Sandip Babu leapt to his feet with uplifted arms and shouted "Hurrah!"—The next moment he corrected himself and cried: "Bande Mataram."

A shadow of pain passed over the face of my husband. He said to me in a very gentle voice: "Neither am I divine: I am human. And therefore I dare not permit the evil which is in me to be exaggerated into an image of my country—never, never!"

Sandip Babu cried out: "See, Nikhil, how in the heart of a woman Truth takes flesh and blood. Woman knows how to be cruel: her virulence is like a blind storm. It is beautifully fearful. In man it is ugly, because it harbours in its centre the gnawing worms of reason and thought. I tell you, Nikhil, it is our women who will save the country. This is not the time for nice scruples. We must be unswervingly, unreasoningly brutal. We must sin. We must give our women red sandal paste with which to anoint and enthrone our sin. Don't you remember what the poet says:

Come, Sin, O beautiful Sin,
Let thy stinging red kisses pour down fiery red wine into
    our blood.
Sound the trumpet of imperious evil
And cross our forehead with the wreath of exulting
    lawlessness,
O Deity of Desecration,
Smear our breasts with the blackest mud of disrepute,
    unashamed.

Down with that righteousness, which cannot smilingly bring rack and ruin."

When Sandip Babu, standing with his head high, insulted at a moment's impulse all that men have cherished as their highest, in all countries and in all times, a shiver went right through my body.

But, with a stamp of his foot, he continued his declamation: "I can see that you are that beautiful spirit of fire, which burns the home to ashes and lights up the larger world with its flame. Give to us the indomitable courage to go to the bottom of Ruin itself. Impart grace to all that is baneful."

It was not clear to whom Sandip Babu addressed his last appeal. It might have been She whom he worshipped with his Bande Mataram. It might have been the Womanhood of his country. Or it might have been its representative, the woman before him. He would have gone further in the same strain, but my husband suddenly rose from his seat and touched him lightly on the shoulder saying: "Sandip, Chandranath Babu is here."

I started and turned round, to find an aged gentleman at the door, calm and dignified, in doubt as to whether he should come in or retire. His face was touched with a gentle light like that of the setting sun.

My husband came up to me and whispered: "This is my master, of whom I have so often told you. Make your obeisance to him."

I bent reverently and took the dust of his feet. He gave me his blessing saying: "May God protect you always, my little mother."

I was sorely in need of such a blessing at that moment.

Nikhil's Story

I

One day I had the faith to believe that I should be able to bear whatever came from my God. I never had the trial. Now I think it has come.

I used to test my strength of mind by imagining all kinds of evil which might happen to me—poverty, imprisonment, dishonour, death—even Bimala's. And when I said to myself that I should be able to receive these with firmness, I am sure I did not exaggerate. Only I could never even imagine one thing, and today it is that of which I am thinking, and wondering whether I can really bear it. There is a thorn somewhere pricking in my heart, constantly giving me pain while I am about my daily work. It seems to persist even when I am asleep. The very moment I wake up in the morning, I find that the bloom has gone from the face of the sky. What is it? What has happened?

My mind has become so sensitive, that even my past life, which came to me in the disguise of happiness, seems to wring my very heart with its falsehood; and the shame and sorrow which are coming close to me are losing their cover of privacy, all the more because they try to veil their faces. My heart has become all eyes. The things that should not be seen, the things I do not want to see—these I must see.

The day has come at last when my ill-starred life has to reveal its destitution in a long-drawn series of exposures. This penury, all unexpected, has taken its seat in the heart where plenitude seemed to reign. The fees which I paid to delusion for just nine years of my youth have now to be returned with interest to Truth till the end of my days.

What is the use of straining to keep up my pride? What harm if I confess that I have something lacking in me? Possibly it is that unreasoning forcefulness which women love to find in men. But is strength mere display of muscularity? Must strength have no scruples in treading the weak underfoot?

But why all these arguments? Worthiness cannot be earned merely by disputing about it. And I am unworthy, unworthy, unworthy.

What if I *am* unworthy? The true value of love is this, that it can ever bless the unworthy with its own prodigality. For the worthy there are many rewards on God's earth, but God has specially reserved love for the unworthy.

Up till now Bimala was my home-made Bimala, the product of the confined space and the daily routine of small duties. Did the love which I received from her, I asked myself, come from the deep spring of her heart, or was it merely like the daily provision of pipe water pumped up by the municipal steam-engine of society?

I longed to find Bimala blossoming fully in all her truth and power. But the thing I forgot to calculate was, that one must give up all claims based on conventional rights, if one would find a person freely revealed in truth.

Why did I fail to think of this? Was it because of the husband's pride of possession over his wife? No. It was because I placed the fullest trust upon love. I was vain enough to think that I had the power in me to bear the sight of truth in its awful nakedness. It was tempting Providence, but still I clung to my proud determination to come out victorious in the trial.

Bimala had failed to understand me in one thing. She could not fully realise that I held as weakness all imposition of force. Only the weak dare not be just. They shirk their responsibility of fairness and try quickly to get at results through the shortcuts of injustice. Bimala has no patience with patience. She loves to find in men the turbulent, the angry, the unjust. Her respect must have its element of fear.

I had hoped that when Bimala found herself free in the outer world she would be rescued from her infatuation for tyranny. But now I feel sure that this infatuation is deep down in her nature. Her love is for the boisterous. From the tip of her tongue to the pit of her stomach she must tingle with red pepper in order to enjoy the simple fare of life. But my determination was, never to do my duty with frantic impetuosity, helped on by the fiery liquor of excitement. I know Bimala finds it difficult to respect me for this, taking my scruples for feebleness—and she is quite angry with me because I am not running amuck crying Bande Mataram.

For the matter of that, I have become unpopular with all my countrymen because I have not joined them in their carousals. They are certain that either I have a longing for some title, or else that I am afraid of the police. The police on their side suspect me of harbouring some hidden design and protesting too much in my mildness.

What I really feel is this, that those who cannot find food for their enthusiasm in a knowledge of their country as it actually is, or those who cannot love men just because they are men—who needs must shout and deify their country in order to keep up their excitement—these love excitement more than their country.

To try to give our infatuation a higher place than Truth is a sign of inherent slavishness. Where our minds are free we find ourselves lost. Our moribund vitality must have for its rider either some fantasy, or someone in authority, or a sanction from the pundits, in order to make it move. So long as we are impervious to truth and have to be moved by some hypnotic stimulus, we must know that we lack the capacity for self-government. Whatever may be our condition, we shall either need some imaginary ghost or some actual medicine-man to terrorize over us.

The other day when Sandip accused me of lack of imagination, saying that this prevented me from realising my country in a visible image, Bimala agreed with him. I did not say anything in my defence, because to win in argument does not lead to happiness. Her difference of opinion is not due to any inequality of intelligence, but rather to dissimilarity of nature.

They accuse me of being unimaginative—that is, according to

them, I may have oil in my lamp, but no flame. Now this is exactly the accusation which I bring against them. I would say to them: "You are dark, even as the flints are. You must come to violent conflicts and make a noise in order to produce your sparks. But their disconnected flashes merely assist your pride, and not your clear vision."

I have been noticing for some time that there is a gross cupidity about Sandip. His fleshly feelings make him harbour delusions about his religion and impel him into a tyrannical attitude in his patriotism. His intellect is keen, but his nature is coarse, and so he glorifies his selfish lusts under high-sounding names. The cheap consolations of hatred are as urgently necessary for him as the satisfaction of his appetites. Bimala has often warned me, in the old days, of his hankering after money. I understood this, but I could not bring myself to haggle with Sandip. I felt ashamed even to own to myself that he was trying to take advantage of me.

It will, however, be difficult to explain to Bimala today that Sandip's love of country is but a different phase of his covetous self-love. Bimala's hero-worship of Sandip makes me hesitate all the more to talk to her about him, lest some touch of jealousy may lead me unwittingly into exaggeration. It may be that the pain at my heart is already making me see a distorted picture of Sandip. And yet it is better perhaps to speak out than to keep my feelings gnawing within me.

II

I have known my master these thirty years. Neither calumny, nor disaster, nor death itself has any terrors for him. Nothing could have saved me, born as I was into the traditions of this family of ours, but that he has established his own life in the centre of mine, with its peace and truth and spiritual vision, thus making it possible for me to realise goodness in its truth.

My master came to me that day and said: "Is it necessary to detain Sandip here any longer?"

His nature was so sensitive to all omens of evil that he had at once understood. He was not easily moved, but that day he felt the dark shadow of trouble ahead. Do I not know how well he loves me?

At teatime I said to Sandip: "I have just had a letter from Rangpur. They are complaining that I am selfishly detaining you. When will you be going there?"

Bimala was pouring out the tea. Her face fell at once. She threw just one enquiring glance at Sandip.

"I have been thinking," said Sandip, "that this wandering up and down means a tremendous waste of energy. I feel that if I could work from a centre I could achieve more permanent results."

With this he looked up at Bimala and asked: "Do you not think so too?"

Bimala hesitated for a reply and then said: "Both ways seem good—to do the work from a centre, as well as by travelling about. That in which you find greater satisfaction is the way for you."

"Then let me speak out my mind," said Sandip. "I have never yet found any one source of inspiration suffice me for good. That is why I have been constantly moving about, rousing enthusiasm in the people, from which in turn I draw my own store of energy. Today you have given me the message of my country. Such fire I have never beheld in any man. I shall be able to spread the fire of enthusiasm in my country by borrowing it from you. No, do not be ashamed. You are far above all modesty and diffidence. You are the Queen Bee of our hive, and we the workers shall rally around you. You shall be our centre, our inspiration."

Bimala flushed all over with bashful pride and her hand shook as she went on pouring out the tea.

Another day my master came to me and said: "Why don't you two go up to Darjeeling for a change? You are not looking well. Have you been getting enough sleep?"

I asked Bimala in the evening whether she would care to have a trip to the hills. I knew she had a great longing to see the Himalayas. But she refused . . . The country's Cause, I suppose!

I must not lose my faith: I shall wait. The passage from the narrow to the larger world is stormy. When she is familiar with this freedom, then I shall know where my place is. If I discover that I do not fit in with the arrangement of the outer world, then I shall not quarrel with my fate, but silently take my leave . . . Use force? But for what? Can force prevail against Truth?

Sandip's Story

I

The impotent man says: "That which has come to my share is mine." And the weak man assents. But the lesson of the whole world is: "That is really mine which I can snatch away." My country does not become mine simply because it is the country of my birth. It becomes mine on the day when I am able to win it by force.

Every man has a natural right to possess, and therefore greed is natural. It is not in the wisdom of nature that we should be content to be deprived. What my mind covets, my surroundings must supply. This is the only true understanding between our inner and outer nature in this world. Let moral ideals remain merely for those poor anaemic creatures of starved desire whose grasp is weak. Those who can desire with all their soul and enjoy with all their heart, those who have no hesitation or scruple, it is they who are the anointed of Providence. Nature spreads out her riches and loveliest treasures for their benefit. They swim across streams, leap over walls, kick open doors, to help themselves to whatever is worth taking. In such a getting one can rejoice; such wresting as this gives value to the thing taken.

Nature surrenders herself, but only to the robber. For she delights in this forceful desire, this forceful abduction. And so she does not put the garland of her acceptance round the lean, scraggy neck of the ascetic. The music of the wedding march is struck. The time of the wedding I must not let pass. My heart therefore is eager. For, who is the bridegroom? It is I. The bridegroom's place belongs to him who, torch in hand, can come in time. The bridegroom in Nature's wedding hall comes unexpected and uninvited.

Ashamed? No, I am never ashamed! I ask for whatever I want, and I do not always wait to ask before I take it. Those who are deprived by their own diffidence dignify their privation by the name of modesty. The world into which we are born is the world of reality. When a man goes away from the market of real things with empty hands and empty stomach, merely filling his bag with big sounding words, I wonder why he ever came into this hard world at all. Did these men get their appointment from the epicures of the religious world, to play set tunes on sweet, pious texts in that pleasure garden where blossom airy nothings? I neither affect those tunes nor do I find any sustenance in those blossoms.

What I desire, I desire positively, superlatively. I want to knead it with both my hands and both my feet; I want to smear it all over my body; I want to gorge myself with it to the full. The scrannel pipes of those who have worn themselves out by their moral fastings, till they have become flat and pale like starved vermin infesting a long-deserted bed, will never reach my ear.

I would conceal nothing, because that would be cowardly. But if I cannot bring myself to conceal when concealment is needful, that also is cowardly. Because you have your greed, you build your walls. Because I have my greed, I break through them. You use your power: I use my craft. These are the realities of life. On these depend kingdoms and empires and all the great enterprises of men.

As for those *avatars* who come down from their paradise to talk to us in some holy jargon—their words are not real. Therefore, in spite of all the applause they get, these sayings of theirs only find a place in the hiding corners of the weak.

They are despised by those who are strong, the rulers of the world. Those who have had the courage to see this have won success, while those poor wretches who are dragged one way by nature and the other way by these avatars, they set one foot in the boat of the real and the other in the boat of the unreal, and thus are in a pitiable plight, able neither to advance nor to keep their place.

There are many men who seem to have been born only with an obsession to die. Possibly there is a beauty, like that of a sunset, in this lingering death in life which seems to fascinate them. Nikhil lives this kind of life, if life it may be called. Years ago, I had a great argument with him on this point.

"It is true," he said, "that you cannot get anything except by force. But then what *is* this force? And then also, what *is* this getting? The strength I believe in is the strength of renouncing."

"So you," I exclaimed, "are infatuated with the glory of bankruptcy."

"Just as desperately as the chick is infatuated about the bankruptcy of its shell," he replied. "The shell is real enough, yet it is given up in exchange for intangible light and air. A sorry exchange, I suppose you would call it?"

When once Nikhil gets on to metaphor, there is no hope of making him see that he is merely dealing with words, not with realities. Well, well, let him be happy with his metaphors. We are the flesh-eaters of the world; we have teeth and nails; we pursue and grab and tear. We are not satisfied with chewing in the evening the cud of the grass we have eaten in the morning. Anyhow, we cannot allow your metaphor-mongers to bar the door to our sustenance. In that case we shall simply steal or rob, for we must live.

People will say that I am starting some novel theory just because those who are moving in this world are in the habit of talking differently though they are really acting up to it all the time. Therefore they fail to understand, as I do, that this is the only working moral principle. In point of fact, I know that my idea is not an empty theory at all, for it has been proved in practical life. I have found that my way always wins over the hearts of women, who are creatures of this world of reality and do not roam about in cloud-land, as men do, in idea-filled balloons.

Women find in my features, my manner, my gait, my speech, a masterful passion—not a passion dried thin with the heat of asceticism, not a passion with its face turned back at every step in doubt and debate, but a full-blooded passion. It roars and rolls on, like a flood, with the cry: "I want, I want, I want." Women feel, in their own heart of hearts, that this indomitable passion is the lifeblood of the world, acknowledging no law but itself, and therefore victorious. For this reason they have so often abandoned themselves to be swept away on the flood-tide of my passion, recking naught as to whether it takes them to life or to death. This power which wins these women is the power of mighty men, the power which wins the world of reality.

Those who imagine the greater desirability of another world

merely shift their desires from the earth to the skies. It remains to be seen how high their gushing fountain will play, and for how long. But this much is certain: women were not created for these pale creatures—these lotus-eaters of idealism.

"Affinity!" When it suited my need, I have often said that God has created special pairs of men and women, and that the union of such is the only legitimate union, higher than all unions made by law. The reason of it is, that though man wants to follow nature, he can find no pleasure in it unless he screens himself with some phrase—and that is why this world is so overflowing with lies.

"Affinity!" Why should there be only one? There may be affinity with thousands. It was never in my agreement with nature that I should overlook all my innumerable affinities for the sake of only one. I have discovered many in my own life up to now, yet that has not closed the door to one more—and that one is clearly visible to my eyes. She has also discovered her own affinity to me.

And then?

Then, if I do not win I am a coward.

CHAPTER THREE

Bimala's Story

VI

I wonder what could have happened to my feeling of shame. The fact is, I had no time to think about myself. My days and nights were passing in a whirl, like an eddy with myself in the centre. No gap was left for hesitation or delicacy to enter.

One day my sister-in-law remarked to my husband: "Up to now the women of this house have been kept weeping. Here comes the men's turn.

"We must see that they do not miss it," she continued, turning to me. "I see you are out for the fray, Chota* Rani! Hurl your shafts straight at their hearts."

Her keen eyes looked me up and down. Not one of the colours into which my toilet, my dress, my manners, my speech, had blossomed out had escaped her. I am ashamed to speak of it today, but I felt no shame then. Something within me was at work of which I was not even conscious. I used to overdress, it is true, but more like an automaton, with no particular design. No doubt I knew which effort of mine would prove especially pleasing to Sandip Babu, but that required no intuition, for he would discuss it openly before all of them.

One day he said to my husband: "Do you know, Nikhil, when

---

* Bimala, the younger brother's wife, was the Chota or Junior Rani.

I first saw our Queen Bee, she was sitting there so demurely in her gold-bordered sari. Her eyes were gazing inquiringly into space, like stars which had lost their way, just as if she had been for ages standing on the edge of some darkness, looking out for something unknown. But when I saw her, I felt a quiver run through me. It seemed to me that the gold border of her sari was her own inner fire flaming out and twining round her. That is the flame we want, visible fire! Look here, Queen Bee, you really must do us the favour of dressing once more as a living flame."

So long I had been like a small river at the border of a village. My rhythm and my language were different from what they are now. But the tide came up from the sea, and my breast heaved; my banks gave way and the great drumbeats of the sea waves echoed in my mad current. I could not understand the meaning of that sound in my blood. Where was that former self of mine? Whence came foaming into me this surging flood of glory? Sandip's hungry eyes burnt like the lamps of worship before my shrine. All his gaze proclaimed that I was a wonder in beauty and power; and the loudness of his praise, spoken and unspoken, drowned all other voices in my world. Had the Creator created me afresh, I wondered? Did he wish to make up now for neglecting me so long? I who before was plain had become suddenly beautiful. I who before had been of no account now felt in myself all the splendour of Bengal itself.

For Sandip Babu was not a mere individual. In him was the confluence of millions of minds of the country. When he called me the Queen Bee of the hive, I was acclaimed with a chorus of praise by all our patriot workers. After that, the loud jests of my sister-in-law could not touch me any longer. My relations with all the world underwent a change. Sandip Babu made it clear how all the country was in need of me. I had no difficulty in believing this at the time, for I felt that I had the power to do everything. Divine strength had come to me. It was something which I had never felt before, which was beyond myself. I had no time to question it to find out what was its nature. It seemed to belong to me, and yet to transcend me. It comprehended the whole of Bengal.

Sandip Babu would consult me about every little thing touching the Cause. At first I felt very awkward and would hang back, but that soon wore off. Whatever I suggested seemed to astonish him. He would go into raptures and say: "Men can only think. You women have a way of understanding without thinking. Woman was created out of God's own fancy. Man, He had to hammer into shape."

Letters used to come to Sandip Babu from all parts of the country which were submitted to me for my opinion. Occasionally he disagreed with me. But I would not argue with him. Then after a day or two—as if a new light had suddenly dawned upon him—he would send for me and say: "It was my mistake. Your suggestion was the correct one." He would often confess to me that wherever he had taken steps contrary to my advice he had gone wrong. Thus I gradually came to be convinced that behind whatever was taking place was Sandip Babu, and behind Sandip Babu was the plain common sense of a woman. The glory of a great responsibility filled my being.

My husband had no place in our counsels. Sandip Babu treated him as a younger brother, of whom personally one may be very fond and yet have no use for his business advice. He would tenderly and smilingly talk about my husband's childlike innocence, saying that his curious doctrine and perversities of mind had a flavour of humour which made them all the more lovable. It was seemingly this very affection for Nikhil which led Sandip Babu to forbear from troubling him with the burden of the country.

Nature has many anodynes in her pharmacy, which she secretly administers when vital relations are being insidiously severed, so that none may know of the operation, till at last one awakes to know what a great rent has been made. When the knife was busy with my life's most intimate tie, my mind was so clouded with fumes of intoxicating gas that I was not in the least aware of what a cruel thing was happening. Possibly this is woman's nature. When her passion is roused she loses her sensibility for all that is outside it. When, like the river, we women keep to our banks, we give nourishment with all that we have: when we overflow them we destroy with all that we are.

Sandip's Story

II

I can see that something has gone wrong. I got an inkling of it the other day.

Ever since my arrival, Nikhil's sitting room had become a thing amphibious—half women's apartment, half men's: Bimala had access to it from the zenana, it was not barred to me from the outer side. If we had only gone slow, and made use of our privileges with some restraint, we might not have fallen foul of other people. But we went ahead so vehemently that we could not think of the consequences.

Whenever Bee comes into Nikhil's room, I somehow get to know of it from mine. There are the tinkle of bangles and other little sounds; the door is perhaps shut with a shade of unnecessary vehemence; the bookcase is a trifle stiff and creaks if jerked open. When I enter I find Bee, with her back to the door, ever so busy selecting a book from the shelves. And as I offer to assist her in this difficult task she starts and protests; and then we naturally get on to other topics.

The other day, on an inauspicious* Thursday afternoon, I sallied forth from my room at the call of these same sounds. There was a man on guard in the passage. I walked on without so much as glancing at him, but as I approached the door he put himself in my way saying: "Not that way, sir."

"Not that way! Why?"

"The Rani Mother is there."

"Oh, very well. Tell your Rani Mother that Sandip Babu wants to see her."

"That cannot be, sir. It is against orders."

I felt highly indignant. "I order you!" I said in a raised voice. "Go and announce me."

The fellow was somewhat taken aback at my attitude. In the meantime I had neared the door. I was on the point of reaching it,

---

* According to the Hindu calendar.—*Translator*

when he followed after me and took me by the arm saying: "No, sir, you must not."

What! To be touched by a flunkey! I snatched away my arm and gave the man a sounding blow. At this moment Bee came out of the room to find the man about to insult me.

I shall never forget the picture of her wrath! That Bee is beautiful is a discovery of my own. Most of our people would see nothing in her. Her tall, slim figure these boors would call 'lanky.' But it is just this lithesomeness of hers that I admire—like an up-leaping fountain of life, coming direct out of the depths of the Creator's heart. Her complexion is dark, but it is the lustrous darkness of a sword-blade, keen and scintillating.

"Nanku!" she commanded, as she stood in the doorway, pointing with her finger, "Leave us."

"Do not be angry with him," said I. "If it is against orders, it is I who should retire."

Bee's voice was still trembling as she replied: "You must not go. Come in."

It was not a request, but again a command! I followed her in, and taking a chair fanned myself with a fan which was on the table. Bee scribbled something with a pencil on a sheet of paper and, summoning a servant, handed it to him saying: "Take this to the Maharaja."

"Forgive me," I resumed. "I was unable to control myself, and hit that man of yours."

"You served him right," said Bee.

"But it was not the poor fellow's fault, after all. He was only obeying his orders."

Here Nikhil came in, and as he did so I left my seat with a rapid movement and went and stood near the window with my back to the room.

"Nanku, the guard, has insulted Sandip Babu," said Bee to Nikhil.

Nikhil seemed to be so genuinely surprised that I had to turn round and stare at him. Even an outrageously good man fails in keeping up his pride of truthfulness before his wife—if she be the proper kind of woman.

523

"He insolently stood in the way when Sandip Babu was coming in here," continued Bee. "He said he had orders . . ."

"Whose orders?" asked Nikhil.

"How am I to know?" exclaimed Bee impatiently, her eyes brimming over with mortification.

Nikhil sent for the man and questioned him. "It was not my fault," Nanku repeated sullenly. "I had my orders."

"Who gave you the order?"

"The Bara Rani Mother."

We were all silent for a while. After the man had left, Bee said: "Nanku must go!"

Nikhil remained silent. I could see that his sense of justice would not allow this. There was no end to his qualms. But this time he was up against a tough problem. Bee was not the woman to take things lying down. She would have to get even with her sister-in-law by punishing this fellow. And as Nikhil remained silent, her eyes flashed fire. She knew not how to pour her scorn upon her husband's feebleness of spirit. Nikhil left the room after a while without another word.

The next day Nanku was not to be seen. On inquiry, I learnt that he had been sent off to some other part of the estates, and that his wages had not suffered by such transfer.

I could catch glimpses of the ravages of the storm raging over this, behind the scenes. All I can say is, that Nikhil is a curious creature, quite out of the common.

The upshot was, that after this Bee began to send for me to the sitting room, for a chat, without any contrivance, or pretence of its being an accident. Thus from bare suggestion we came to broad hint: the implied came to be expressed. The daughter-in-law of a princely house lives in a starry region so remote from the ordinary outsider that there is not even a regular road for his approach. What a triumphal progress of Truth was this which, gradually but persistently, thrust aside veil after veil of obscuring custom, till at length Nature herself was laid bare.

Truth? Of course it was the truth! The attraction of man and woman for each other is fundamental. The whole world of matter, from the speck of dust upwards, is ranged on its side. And yet men would keep it hidden away out of sight, behind a tissue of words; and with home-made sanctions and prohibitions make of it a domestic utensil. Why, it's as absurd as melting down the solar system to make a watch-chain for one's son-in-law!*

When, in spite of all, reality awakes at the call of what is but naked truth, what a gnashing of teeth and beating of breasts is there! But can one carry on a quarrel with a storm? It never takes the trouble to reply, it only gives a shaking.

I am enjoying the sight of this truth, as it gradually reveals itself. These tremblings of steps, these turnings of the face, are sweet to me: and sweet are the deceptions which deceive not only others, but also Bee herself. When Reality has to meet the unreal, deception is its principal weapon; for its enemies always try to shame Reality by calling it gross, and so it needs must hide itself, or else put on some disguise. The circumstances are such that it dare not frankly avow: "Yes, I am gross, because I am true. I am flesh. I am passion. I am hunger, unashamed and cruel."

All is now clear to me. The curtain flaps, and through it I can see the preparations for the catastrophe. The little red ribbon, which peeps through the luxuriant masses of her hair, with its flush of secret longing, it is the lolling tongue of the red storm cloud. I feel the warmth of each turn of her sari, each suggestion of her raiment, of which even the wearer may not be fully conscious.

Bee was not conscious, because she was ashamed of the reality; to which men have given a bad name, calling it Satan; and so it has to steal into the garden of paradise in the guise of a snake, and whisper secrets into the ears of man's chosen consort and make her rebellious; then farewell to all ease; and after that comes death!

My poor little Queen Bee is living in a dream. She knows not which way she is treading. It would not be safe to awaken her before the time. It is best for me to pretend to be equally unconscious.

The other day, at dinner, she was gazing at me in a curious sort of way, little realising what such glances mean! As my eyes met hers, she turned away with a flush. "You are surprised at my appetite," I remarked. "I can hide everything, except that I am greedy! Anyhow, why trouble to blush for me, since I am shameless?"

* The son-in-law is the pet of a Hindu household.

This only made her colour more furiously, as she stammered: "No, no, I was only . . ."

"I know," I interrupted. "Women have a weakness for greedy men; for it is this greed of ours which gives them the upper hand. The indulgence which I have always received at their hands has made me all the more shameless. I do not mind your watching the good things disappear, not one bit. I mean to enjoy every one of them."

The other day I was reading an English book in which sex-problems were treated in an audaciously realistic manner. I had left it lying in the sitting room. As I went there the next afternoon, for something or other, I found Bee seated with this book in her hand. When she heard my footsteps she hurriedly put it down and placed another book over it—a volume of Mrs. Hemans's poems.

"I have never been able to make out," I began, "why women are so shy about being caught reading poetry. We men—lawyers, mechanics, or what not—may well feel ashamed. If we must read poetry, it should be at dead of night, within closed doors. But you women are so akin to poesy. The Creator Himself is a lyric poet, and Jayadeva* must have practised the divine art seated at His feet."

Bee made no reply, but only blushed uncomfortably. She made as if she would leave the room. Whereupon I protested: "No, no, pray read on. I will just take a book I left here, and run away." With which I took up my book from the table. "Lucky you did not think of glancing over its pages," I continued, "or you would have wanted to chastise me."

"Indeed! Why?" asked Bee.

"Because it is not poetry," said I. "Only blunt things, bluntly put, without any finicking niceness. I wish Nikhil would read it."

Bee frowned a little as she murmured: "What makes you wish that?"

"He is a man, you see, one of us. My only quarrel with him is that he delights in a misty vision of this world. Have you not observed how this trait of his makes him look on Swadeshi as if it

---

* A Vaishnava poet (Sanskrit) whose lyrics of the adoration of the Divinity serve as well to express all shades of human passion.—*Translator*

was some poem of which the metre must be kept correct at every step? We, with the clubs of our prose, are the iconoclasts of metre."

"What has your book to do with Swadeshi?"

"You would know if you only read it. Nikhil wants to go by made-up maxims, in Swadeshi as in everything else; so he knocks up against human nature at every turn, and then falls to abusing it. He never will realise that human nature was created long before phrases were, and will survive them too."

Bee was silent for a while and then gravely said: "Is it not a part of human nature to try and rise superior to itself?"

I smiled inwardly. "These are not your words", I thought to myself. "You have learnt them from Nikhil. You are a healthy human being. Your flesh and blood have responded to the call of reality. You are burning in every vein with life-fire—do I not know it? How long should they keep you cool with the wet towel of moral precepts?"

"The weak are in the majority," I said aloud. "They are continually poisoning the ears of men by repeating these shibboleths. Nature has denied them strength—it is thus that they try to enfeeble others."

"We women are weak," replied Bimala. "So I suppose we must join in the conspiracy of the weak."

"Women weak!" I exclaimed with a laugh. "Men belaud you as delicate and fragile, so as to delude you into thinking yourselves weak. But it is you women who are strong. Men make a great outward show of their so-called freedom, but those who know their inner minds are aware of their bondage. They have manufactured scriptures with their own hands to bind themselves; with their very idealism they have made golden fetters of women to wind round their body and mind. If men had not that extraordinary faculty of entangling themselves in meshes of their own contriving, nothing could have kept them bound. But as for you women, you have desired to conceive reality with body and soul. You have given birth to reality. You have suckled reality at your breasts."

Bee was well read for a woman, and would not easily give in to my arguments. "If that were true," she objected, "men would not have found women attractive."

"Women realise the danger," I replied. "They know that

men love delusions, so they give them full measure by borrowing their own phrases. They know that man, the drunkard, values intoxication more than food, and so they try to pass themselves off as an intoxicant. As a matter of fact, but for the sake of man, woman has no need for any make-believe."

"Why, then, are you troubling to destroy the illusion?"

"For freedom. I want the country to be free. I want human relations to be free."

III

I was aware that it is unsafe suddenly to awake a sleep-walker. But I am so impetuous by nature, a halting gait does not suit me. I knew I was overbold that day. I knew that the first shock of such ideas is apt to be almost intolerable. But with women it is always audacity that wins.

Just as we were getting on nicely, who should walk in but Nikhil's old tutor Chandranath Babu. The world would have been not half a bad place to live in but for these schoolmasters, who make one want to quit in disgust. The Nikhil type wants to keep the world always a school. This incarnation of a school turned up that afternoon at the psychological moment.

We all remain schoolboys in some corner of our hearts, and I, even I, felt somewhat pulled up. As for poor Bee, she at once took her place solemnly, like the topmost girl of the class on the front bench. All of a sudden she seemed to remember that she had to face her examination.

Some people are so like eternal pointsmen lying in wait by the line, to shunt one's train of thought from one rail to another.

Chandranath Babu had no sooner come in than he cast about for some excuse to retire, mumbling: "I beg your pardon, I . . ."

Before he could finish, Bee went up to him and made a profound obeisance, saying: "Pray do not leave us, sir. Will you not take a seat?" She looked like a drowning person clutching at him for support— the little coward!

But possibly I was mistaken. It is quite likely that there was a touch of womanly wile in it. She wanted, perhaps, to raise her value in my eyes. She might have been pointedly saying to me: "Please don't imagine for a moment that I am entirely overcome by you. My respect for Chandranath Babu is even greater."

Well, indulge in your respect by all means! Schoolmasters thrive on it. But not being one of them, I have no use for that empty compliment.

Chandranath Babu began to talk about Swadeshi. I thought I would let him go on with his monologues. There is nothing like letting an old man talk himself out. It makes him feel that he is winding up the world, forgetting all the while how far away the real world is from his wagging tongue.

But even my worst enemy would not accuse me of patience. And when Chandranath Babu went on to say: "If we expect to gather fruit where we have sown no seed, then we . . ." I had to interrupt him.

"Who wants fruit?" I cried. "We go by the Author of the Gita who says that we are concerned only with the doing, not with the fruit of our deeds."

"What is it then that you *do* want?" asked Chandranath Babu.

"Thorns!" I exclaimed, "which cost nothing to plant."

"Thorns do not obstruct others only," he replied. "They have a way of hurting one's own feet."

"That is all right for a copy-book," I retorted. "But the real thing is that we have this burning at heart. Now we have only to cultivate thorns for other's soles; afterwards when they hurt us we shall find leisure to repent. But why be frightened even of that? When at last we have to die it will be time enough to get cold. While we are on fire let us seethe and boil."

Chandranath Babu smiled. "Seethe by all means," he said, "but do not mistake it for work, or heroism. Nations which have got on in the world have done so by action, not by ebullition. Those who have always lain in dread of work, when with a start they awake to their sorry plight, they look to shortcuts and scamping for their deliverance."

I was girding up my loins to deliver a crushing reply, when Nikhil came back. Chandranath Babu rose, and looking towards Bee, said: "Let me go now, my little mother, I have some work to attend to."

As he left, I showed Nikhil the book in my hand. "I was telling Queen Bee about this book," I said.

Ninety-nine per cent of people have to be deluded with lies, but it is easier to delude this perpetual pupil of the schoolmaster with the truth. He is best cheated openly. So, in playing with him, the simplest course was to lay my cards on the table.

Nikhil read the title on the cover, but said nothing. "These writers," I continued, "are busy with their brooms, sweeping away the dust of epithets with which men have covered up this world of ours. So, as I was saying, I wish you would read it."

"I have read it," said Nikhil.

"Well, what do you say?"

"It is all very well for those who really care to think, but poison for those who shirk thought."

"What do you mean?"

"Those who preach 'Equal Rights of Property' should not be thieves. For, if they are, they would be preaching lies. When passion is in the ascendant, this kind of book is not rightly understood."

"Passion," I replied, "is the street lamp which guides us. To call it untrue is as hopeless as to expect to see better by plucking out our natural eyes."

Nikhil was visibly growing excited. "I accept the truth of passion," he said, "only when I recognise the truth of restraint. By pressing what we want to see right into our eyes we only injure them: we do not see. So does the violence of passion, which would leave no space between the mind and its object, defeat its purpose."

"It is simply your intellectual foppery," I replied, "which makes you indulge in moral delicacy, ignoring the savage side of truth. This merely helps you to mystify things, and so you fail to do your work with any degree of strength."

"The intrusion of strength," said Nikhil impatiently, "where strength is out of place, does not help you in your work . . . But why are we arguing about these things? Vain arguments only brush off the fresh bloom of truth."

I wanted Bee to join in the discussion, but she had not said a word up to now. Could I have given her too rude a shock, leaving her assailed with doubts and wanting to learn her lesson afresh from the schoolmaster? Still, a thorough shaking up is essential. One must begin by realising that things supposed to be unshakeable can be shaken.

"I am glad I had this talk with you," I said to Nikhil, "for I was on the point of lending this book to Queen Bee to read."

"What harm?" said Nikhil. "If I could read the book, why not Bimala too? All I want to say is, that in Europe people look at everything from the viewpoint of science. But man is neither mere physiology, nor biology, nor psychology, nor even sociology. For God's sake don't forget that. Man is infinitely more than the natural science of himself. You laugh at me, calling me the schoolmaster's pupil, but that is what you are, not I. You want to find the truth of man from your science teachers, and not from your own inner being."

"But why all this excitement?" I mocked.

"Because I see you are bent on insulting man and making him petty."

"Where on earth do you see all that?"

"In the air, in my outraged feelings. You would go on wounding the great, the unselfish, the beautiful in man."

"What mad idea is this of yours?"

Nikhil suddenly stood up. "I tell you plainly, Sandip," he said, "man may be wounded unto death, but he will not die. This is the reason why I am ready to suffer all, knowing all, with eyes open."

With these words he hurriedly left the room.

I was staring blankly at his retreating figure, when the sound of a book, falling from the table, made me turn to find Bee following him with quick, nervous steps, making a detour to avoid passing too near me.

A curious creature, that Nikhil! He feels the danger threatening his home, and yet why does he not turn me out? I know, he is waiting for Bimal to give him the cue. If Bimal tells him that their mating has been a misfit, he will bow his head and admit that it may have been a blunder! He has not the strength of mind to understand that to acknowledge a mistake is the greatest of all mistakes. He is a typical example of how ideas make for weakness. I have not seen another like him—so whimsical a product of nature! He would hardly do as a character in a novel or drama, to say nothing of real life.

And Bee? I am afraid her dream-life is over from today. She

has at length understood the nature of the current which is bearing her along. Now she must either advance or retreat, open-eyed. The chances are she will now advance a step, and then retreat a step. But that does not disturb me. When one is on fire, this rushing to and fro makes the blaze all the fiercer. The fright she has got will only fan her passion.

Perhaps I had better not say much to her, but simply select some modern books for her to read. Let her gradually come to the conviction that to acknowledge and respect passion as the supreme reality, is to be modern—not to be ashamed of it, not to glorify restraint. If she finds shelter in some such word as 'modern,' she will find strength.

Be that as it may, I must see this out to the end of the Fifth Act. I cannot, unfortunately, boast of being merely a spectator, seated in the royal box, applauding now and again. There is a wrench at my heart, a pang in every nerve. When I have put out the light and am in my bed, little touches, little glances, little words flit about and fill the darkness. When I get up in the morning, I thrill with lively anticipations, my blood seems to course through me to the strains of music . . .

There was a double photo frame on the table with Bee's photograph by the side of Nikhil's. I had taken out hers. Yesterday I showed Bee the empty side and said: "Theft becomes necessary only because of miserliness, so its sin must be divided between the miser and the thief. Do you not think so?"

"It was not a good one," observed Bee simply, with a little smile.

"What is to be done?" said I. "A portrait cannot be better than a portrait. I must be content with it, such as it is."

Bee took up a book and began to turn over the pages. "If you are annoyed," I went on, "I must make a shift to fill up the vacancy."

Today I have filled it up. This photograph of mine was taken in my early youth. My face was then fresher, and so was my mind. Then I still cherished some illusions about this world and the next. Faith deceives men, but it has one great merit: it imparts a radiance to the features.

My portrait now reposes next to Nikhil's, for are not the two of us old friends?

CHAPTER FOUR

Nikhil's Story

III

I was never self-conscious. But nowadays I often try to take an outside view—to see myself as Bimal sees me. What a dismally solemn picture it makes, my habit of taking things too seriously!

Better, surely, to laugh away the world than flood it with tears. That is, in fact, how the world gets on. We relish our food and rest, only because we can dismiss, as so many empty shadows, the sorrows scattered everywhere, both in the home and in the outer world. If we took them as true, even for a moment, where would be our appetite, our sleep?

But I cannot dismiss myself as one of these shadows, and so the load of my sorrow lies eternally heavy on the heart of my world.

Why not stand out aloof in the highway of the universe, and feel yourself to be part of the all? In the midst of the immense, age-long concourse of humanity, what is Bimal to you? Your wife? What is a wife? A bubble of a name blown big with your own breath, so carefully guarded night and day, yet ready to burst at any pin-prick from outside.

My wife—and so, forsooth, my very own! If she says: "No, I am myself"—am I to reply: "How can that be? Are you not mine?"

"My wife"—Does that amount to an argument, much less the truth? Can one imprison a whole personality within that name?

533

My wife!—Have I not cherished in this little world all that is purest and sweetest in my life, never for a moment letting it down from my bosom to the dust? What incense of worship, what music of passion, what flowers of my spring and of my autumn, have I not offered up at its shrine? If, like a toy paper-boat, she be swept along into the muddy waters of the gutter—would I not also . . .?

There it is again, my incorrigible solemnity! Why 'muddy'? What 'gutter'? Names, called in a fit of jealousy, do not change the facts of the world. If Bimal is not mine, she is not; and no fuming, or fretting, or arguing will serve to prove that she is. If my heart is breaking—let it break! That will not make the world bankrupt—nor even me; for man is so much greater than the things he loses in this life. The very ocean of tears has its other shore, else none would have ever wept.

But then there is Society to be considered . . . which let Society consider! If I weep it is for myself, not for Society. If Bimal should say she is not mine, what care I where my Society wife may be?

Suffering there must be; but I must save myself, by any means in my power, from one form of self-torture: I must never think that my life loses its value because of any neglect it may suffer. The full value of my life does not all go to buy my narrow domestic world; its great commerce does not stand or fall with some petty success or failure in the bartering of my personal joys and sorrows.

The time has come when I must divest Bimala of all the ideal decorations with which I decked her. It was owing to my own weakness that I indulged in such idolatry. I was too greedy. I created an angel of Bimala, in order to exaggerate my own enjoyment. But Bimala is what she is. It is preposterous to expect that she should assume the role of an angel for my pleasure. The Creator is under no obligation to supply me with angels, just because I have an avidity for imaginary perfection.

I must acknowledge that I have merely been an accident in Bimala's life. Her nature, perhaps, can only find true union with one like Sandip. At the same time, I must not, in false modesty, accept my rejection as my desert. Sandip certainly has attractive qualities, which had their sway also upon myself; but yet, I feel sure, he is not a greater man than I. If the wreath of victory falls to his lot today, and I am overlooked, then the dispenser of the wreath will be called to judgement.

I say this in no spirit of boasting. Sheer necessity has driven me to the pass, that to secure myself from utter desolation I must recognise all the value that I truly possess. Therefore, through the, terrible experience of suffering let there come upon me the joy of deliverance—deliverance from self-distrust.

I have come to distinguish what is really in me from what I foolishly imagined to be there. The profit and loss account has been settled, and that which remains is myself—not a crippled self, dressed in rags and tatters, not a sick self to be nursed on invalid diet, but a spirit which has gone through the worst, and has survived.

My master passed through my room a moment ago and said with his hand on my shoulder. "Get away to bed, Nikhil, the night is far advanced."

The fact is, it has become so difficult for me to go to bed till late—till Bimal is fast asleep. In the daytime we meet, and even converse, but what am I to say when we are alone together, in the silence of the night?—so ashamed do I feel in mind and body.

"How is it, sir, you have not yet retired?" I asked in my turn. My master smiled a little, as he left me, saying: "My sleeping days are over. I have now attained the waking age."

I had written thus far, and was about to rise to go off bedwards when, through the window before me, I saw the heavy pall of July cloud suddenly part a little, and a big star shine through. It seemed to say to me: "Dreamland ties are made, and dreamland ties are broken, but I am here for ever—the everlasting lamp of the bridal night."

All at once my heart was full with the thought that my Eternal Love was steadfastly waiting for me through the ages, behind the veil of material things. Through many a life, in many a mirror, have I seen her image—broken mirrors, crooked mirrors, dusty mirrors. Whenever I have sought to make the mirror my very own, and shut it up within my box, I have lost sight of the image. But what of that. What have I to do with the mirror, or even the image?

My beloved, your smile shall never fade, and every dawn there shall appear fresh for me the vermilion mark on your forehead!

"What childish cajolery of self-deception," mocks some devil from his dark corner—"silly prattle to make children quiet!"

That may be. But millions and millions of children, with their million cries, have to be kept quiet. Can it be that all this multitude is quieted with only a lie? No, my Eternal Love cannot deceive me, for she is true!

She is true; that is why I have seen her and shall see her so often, even in my mistakes, even through the thickest mist of tears. I have seen her and lost her in the crowd of life's marketplace, and found her again; and I shall find her once more when I have escaped through the loophole of death.

Ah, cruel one, play with me no longer! If I have failed to track you by the marks of your footsteps on the way, by the scent of your tresses lingering in the air, make me not weep for that forever. The unveiled star tells me not to fear. That which is eternal must always be there.

Now let me go and see my Bimala. She must have spread her tired limbs on the bed, limp after her struggles, and be asleep. I will leave a kiss on her forehead without waking her—that shall be the flower-offering of my worship. I believe I could forget everything after death—all my mistakes, all my sufferings—but some vibration of the memory of that kiss would remain; for the wreath which is being woven out of the kisses of many a successive birth is to crown the Eternal Beloved.

As the gong of the watch rang out, sounding the hour of two, my sister-in-law came into the room. "Whatever are you doing, brother dear?"* she cried. "For pity's sake go to bed and stop worrying so. I cannot bear to look on that awful shadow of pain on your face." Tears welled up in her eyes and overflowed as she entreated me thus.

I could not utter a word, but took the dust of her feet, as I went off to bed.

---

* When a relationship is established by marriage, or by mutual understanding arising out of special friendship or affection, the persons so related call each other in terms of such relationship, and not by name.—*Translator*

Bimala's Story

VII

At first I suspected nothing, feared nothing; I simply felt dedicated to my country. What a stupendous joy there was in this unquestioning surrender. Verily had I realised how, in thoroughness of self-destruction, man can find supreme bliss.

For aught I know, this frenzy of mine might have come to a gradual, natural end. But Sandip Babu would not have it so, he would insist on revealing himself. The tone of his voice became as intimate as a touch, every look flung itself on its knees in beggary. And, through it all, there burned a passion which in its violence made as though it would tear me up by the roots, and drag me along by the hair.

I will not shirk the truth. This cataclysmal desire drew me by day and by night. It seemed desperately alluring—this making havoc of myself. What a shame it seemed, how terrible, and yet how sweet! Then there was my overpowering curiosity, to which there seemed no limit. He of whom I knew but little, who never could assuredly be mine, whose youth flared so vigorously in a hundred points of flame—oh, the mystery of his seething passions, so immense, so tumultuous!

I began with a feeling of worship, but that soon passed away. I ceased even to respect Sandip; on the contrary, I began to look down upon him. Nevertheless this flesh-and-blood lute of mine, fashioned with my feeling and fancy, found in him a master-player. What though I shrank from his touch, and even came to loathe the lute itself; its music was conjured up all the same.

I must confess there was something in me which . . . what shall I say? . . . which makes me wish I could have died!

Chandranath Babu, when he finds leisure, comes to me. He has the power to lift my mind up to an eminence from where I can see in a moment the boundary of my life extended on all sides and so realise that the lines, which I took from my bounds, were merely imaginary.

But what is the use of it all? Do I really desire emancipation? Let suffering come to our house; let the best in me shrivel up and become black; but let this infatuation not leave me—such seems to be my prayer.

When, before my marriage, I used to see a brother-in-law of mine, now dead, mad with drink—beating his wife in his frenzy, and then sobbing and howling in maudlin repentance, vowing never to touch liquor again, and yet, the very same evening, sitting down to drink and drink—it would fill me with disgust. But my intoxication today is still more fearful. The stuff has not to be procured or poured out: it springs within my veins, and I know not how to resist it.

Must this continue to the end of my days? Now and again I start and look upon myself, and think my life to be a nightmare which will vanish all of a sudden with all its untruth. It has become so frightfully incongruous. It has no connection with its past. What it is, how it could have come to this pass, I cannot understand.

One day my sister-in-law remarked with a cutting laugh: "What a wonderfully hospitable Chota Rani we have! Her guest absolutely will not budge. In our time there used to be guests, too; but they had not such lavish looking after—we were so absurdly taken up with our husbands. Poor brother Nikhil is paying the penalty of being born too modern. He should have come as a guest if he wanted to stay on. Now it looks as if it were time for him to quit . . . O you little demon, do your glances never fall, by chance, on his agonized face?"

This sarcasm did not touch me; for I knew that these women had it not in them to understand the nature of the cause of my devotion. I was then wrapped in the protecting armour of the exaltation of sacrifice, through which such shafts were powerless to reach and shame me.

VIII

For some time all talk of the country's cause has been dropped. Our conversation nowadays has become full of modern sex-problems, and various other matters, with a sprinkling of poetry, both old Vaishnava and modern English, accompanied by a running undertone of melody, low down in the bass, such as I have never in my life heard before, which seems to me to sound the true manly note, the note of power.

The day had come when all cover was gone. There was no longer even the pretence of a reason why Sandip Babu should linger on, or why I should have confidential talks with him every now and then. I felt thoroughly vexed with myself, with my sister-in-law, with the ways of the world, and I vowed I would never again go to the outer apartments, not if I were to die for it.

For two whole days I did not stir out. Then, for the first time, I discovered how far I had travelled. My life felt utterly tasteless. Whatever I touched I wanted to thrust away. I felt myself waiting—from the crown of my head to the tips of my toes—waiting for something, somebody; my blood kept tingling with some expectation.

I tried busying myself with extra work. The bedroom floor was clean enough but I insisted on its being scrubbed over again under my eyes. Things were arranged in the cabinets in one kind of order; I pulled them all out and rearranged them in a different way. I found no time that afternoon even to do up my hair; I hurriedly tied it into a loose knot, and went and worried everybody, fussing about the storeroom. The stores seemed short, and pilfering must have been going on of late, but I could not muster up the courage to take any particular person to task—for might not the thought have crossed somebody's mind: "Where were your eyes all these days!"

In short, I behaved that day as one possessed. The next day I tried to do some reading. What I read I have no idea, but after a spell of absent-mindedness I found I had wandered away, book in hand, along the passage leading towards the outer apartments, and was standing by a window looking out upon the verandah running along the row of rooms on the opposite side of the quadrangle. One of these rooms, I felt, had crossed over to another shore, and the ferry had ceased to ply. I felt like the ghost of myself of two days ago, doomed to remain where I was, and yet not really there, blankly looking out for ever.

As I stood there, I saw Sandip come out of his room into the verandah, a newspaper in his hand. I could see that he looked extraordinarily disturbed. The courtyard, the railings, in front, seemed to rouse his wrath. He flung away his newspaper with a gesture which seemed to want to rend the space before him.

I felt I could no longer keep my vow. I was about to move on towards the sitting room, when I found my sister-in-law behind me. "O Lord, this beats everything!" she ejaculated, as she glided away. I could not proceed to the outer apartments.

The next morning when my maid came calling, "Rani Mother, it is getting late for giving out the stores," I flung the keys to her, saying, "Tell Harimati to see to it," and went on with some embroidery of English pattern on which I was engaged, seated near the window.

Then came a servant with a letter. "From Sandip Babu," said he. What unbounded boldness! What must the messenger have thought? There was a tremor within my breast as I opened the envelope. There was no address on the letter, only the words:

An urgent matter—touching the Cause. Sandip.

I flung aside the embroidery. I was up on my feet in a moment, giving a touch or two to my hair by the mirror. I kept the sari I had on, changing only my jacket—for one of my jackets had its associations.

I had to pass through one of the verandahs, where my sister-in-law used to sit in the morning slicing betel nut. I refused to feel awkward. "Whither away, Chota Rani?" she cried.

"To the sitting room outside."

"So early! A matinée, eh?"

And, as I passed on without further reply, she hummed after me a flippant song.

IX

When I was about to enter the sitting room, I saw Sandip immersed in an illustrated catalogue of British Academy pictures, with his back to the door. He has a great notion of himself as an expert in matters of Art.

One day my husband said to him: "If the artists ever want a teacher, they need never lack for one so long as you are there." It had not been my husband's habit to speak cuttingly, but latterly there has been a change and he never spares Sandip.

"What makes you suppose that artists need no teachers?" Sandip retorted.

"Art is a creation," my husband replied. "So we should humbly be content to receive our lessons about Art from the work of the artist."

Sandip laughed at this modesty, saying: "You think that meekness is a kind of capital which increases your wealth the more you use it. It is my conviction that those who lack pride only float about like water reeds which have no roots in the soil."

My mind used to be full of contradictions when they talked thus. On the one hand I was eager that my husband should win in argument and that Sandip's pride should be shamed. Yet, on the other, it was Sandip's unabashed pride which attracted me so. It shone like a precious diamond, which knows no diffidence, and sparkles in the face of the sun itself.

I entered the room. I knew Sandip could hear my footsteps as I went forward, but he pretended not to, and kept his eyes on the book.

I dreaded his Art talks, for I could not overcome my delicacy about the pictures he talked of, and the things he said, and had much ado in putting on an air of overdone insensibility to hide my qualms. So, I was almost on the point of retracing my steps, when, with a deep sigh, Sandip raised his eyes, and affected to be startled at the sight of me. "Ah, you have come!" he said.

In his words, in his tone, in his eyes, there was a world of suppressed reproach, as if the claims he had acquired over me made my absence, even for these two or three days, a grievous wrong. I knew this attitude was an insult to me, but, alas, I had not the power to resent it.

I made no reply, but though I was looking another way, I could not help feeling that Sandip's plaintive gaze had planted itself right on my face, and would take no denial. I did so wish he would say something, so that I could shelter myself behind his words. I cannot tell how long this went on, but at last I could stand it no longer. "What is this matter," I asked, "you are wanting to tell me about?"

Sandip again affected surprise as he said: "Must there always be some matter? Is friendship by itself a crime? Oh, Queen Bee, to think that you should make so light of the greatest thing on earth! Is the heart's worship to be shut out like a stray cur?"

There was again that tremor within me. I could feel the crisis coming, too importunate to be put off. Joy and fear struggled for the mastery. Would my shoulders, I wondered, be broad enough to stand its shock, or would it not leave me overthrown, with my face in the dust?

I was trembling all over. Steadying myself with an effort I repeated: "You summoned me for something touching the Cause, so I have left my household duties to attend to it."

"That is just what I was trying to explain," he said, with a dry laugh. "Do you not know that I come to worship? Have I not told you that, in you, I visualize the Shakti of our country? The Geography of a country is not the whole truth. No one can give up his life for a map! When I see you before me, then only do I realise how lovely my country is. When you have anointed me with your own hands, then shall I know I have the sanction of my country; and if, with that in my heart, I fall fighting, it shall not be on the dust of some map-made land, but on a lovingly spread skirt—do you know what kind of skirt?—like that of the earthen-red sari you wore the other day, with a broad blood-red border. Can I ever forget it? Such are the visions which give vigour to life, and joy to death!"

Sandip's eyes took fire as he went on, but whether it was the fire of worship, or of passion, I could not tell. I was reminded of the day on which I first heard him speak, when I could not be sure whether he was a person, or just a living flame.

I had not the power to utter a word. You cannot take shelter behind the walls of decorum when in a moment the fire leaps up and, with the flash of its sword and the roar of its laughter, destroys all the miser's stores. I was in terror lest he should forget himself and take me by the hand. For he shook like a quivering tongue of fire; his eyes showered scorching sparks on me.

"Are you for ever determined," he cried after a pause, "to make gods of your petty household duties—you who have it in you to send us to life or to death? Is this power of yours to be kept veiled in a zenana? Cast away all false shame, I pray you; snap your fingers at the whispering around. Take your plunge today into the freedom of the outer world."

When, in Sandip's appeals, his worship of the country gets to be subtly interwoven with his worship of me, then does my blood dance, indeed, and the barriers of my hesitation totter. His talks about Art and Sex, his distinctions between Real and Unreal, had but clogged my attempts at response with some revolting nastiness. This, however, now burst again into a glow before which my repugnance faded away. I felt that my resplendent womanhood made me indeed a goddess. Why should not its glory flash from my forehead with visible brilliance? Why does not my voice find a word, some audible cry, which would be like a sacred spell to my country for its fire initiation?

All of a sudden my maid Khema rushed into the room, dishevelled. "Give me my wages and let me go," she screamed. "Never in all my life have I been so . . ." The rest of her speech was drowned in sobs.

"What is the matter?"

Thako, the Bara Rani's maid, it appeared, had for no rhyme or reason reviled her in unmeasured terms. She was in such a state, it was no manner of use trying to pacify her by saying I would look into the matter afterwards.

The slime of domestic life that lay beneath the lotus bank of womanhood came to the surface. Rather than allow Sandip a prolonged vision of it, I had to hurry back within.

X

My sister-in-law was absorbed in her betel nuts, the suspicion of a smile playing about her lips, as if nothing untoward had happened. She was still humming the same song.

"Why has your Thako been calling poor Khema names?" I burst out.

"Indeed? The wretch! I will have her broomed out of the house. What a shame to spoil your morning out like this! As for Khema, where are the hussy's manners to go and disturb you when you are engaged? Anyhow, Chota Rani, don't you worry yourself with these domestic squabbles. Leave them to me, and return to your friend."

How suddenly the wind in the sails of our mind veers round! This going to meet Sandip outside seemed, in the light of the zenana code, such an extraordinarily out-of-the-way thing to do that I went off to my own room, at a loss for a reply. I knew this was my sister-in-law's doing and that she had egged her maid on to contrive this scene. But I had brought myself to such an unstable poise that I dared not have my fling.

Why, it was only the other day that I found I could not keep up to the last the unbending hauteur with which I had demanded from my husband the dismissal of the man Nanku. I felt suddenly abashed when the Bara Rani came up and said: "It is really all my fault, brother dear. We are old-fashioned folk, and I did not quite like the ways of your Sandip Babu, so I only told the guard . . . but how was I to know that our Chota Rani would take this as an insult?—I thought it would be the other way about! Just my incorrigible silliness!"

The thing which seems so glorious when viewed from the heights of the country's cause, looks so muddy when seen from the bottom. One begins by getting angry, and then feels disgusted.

I shut myself into my room, sitting by the window, thinking how easy life would be if only one could keep in harmony with one's surroundings. How simply the senior Rani sits in her verandah with her betel nuts and how inaccessible to me has become my natural seat beside my daily duties! Where will it all end, I asked myself? Shall I ever recover, as from a delirium, and forget it all; or am I to be dragged to depths from which there can be no escape in this life? How on earth did I manage to let my good fortune escape me, and spoil my life so? Every wall of this bedroom of mine, which I first entered nine years ago as a bride, stares at me in dismay.

When my husband came home, after his M.A. examination, he brought for me this orchid belonging to some faraway land beyond the seas. From beneath these few little leaves sprang such a cascade of blossoms, it looked as if they were pouring forth from some overturned urn of Beauty. We decided, together, to hang it here, over this window. It flowered only that once, but we have always been in hope of its doing so once more. Curiously enough I have kept on watering it these days, from force of habit, and it is still green.

It is now four years since I framed a photograph of my husband in ivory and put it in the niche over there. If I happen to look that way I have to lower my eyes. Up to last week I used regularly to put there the flowers of my worship, every morning after my bath. My husband has often chided me over this.

"It shames me to see you place me on a height to which I do not belong," he said one day.

"What nonsense!"

"I am not only ashamed, but also jealous!"

"Just hear him! Jealous of whom, pray?"

"Of that false me. It only shows that I am too petty for you, that you want some extraordinary man who can overpower you with his superiority, and so your needs must take refuge in making for yourself another 'me.'"

"This kind of talk only makes me angry," said I.

"What is the use of being angry with me?" he replied. "Blame your fate which allowed you no choice, but made you take me blindfold. This keeps you trying to retrieve its blunder by making me out a paragon."

I felt so hurt at the bare idea that tears started to my eyes that day. And whenever I think of that now, I cannot raise my eyes to the niche.

For now there is another photograph in my jewel case. The other day, when arranging the sitting room, I brought away that double photo frame, the one in which Sandip's portrait was next to my husband's. To this portrait I have no flowers of worship to offer, but it remains hidden away under my gems. It has all the greater fascination because kept secret. I look at it now and then with doors closed. At night I turn up the lamp, and sit with it in my hand, gazing and gazing. And every night I think of burning it in the flame of the lamp, to be done with it forever; but every night I heave a sigh and smother it again in my pearls and diamonds.

Ah, wretched woman! What a wealth of love was twined round each one of those jewels! Oh, why am I not dead?

Sandip had impressed it on me that hesitation is not in the nature of woman. For her, neither right nor left has any existence—she only moves forward. When the women of our country wake up, he repeatedly insisted, their voice will be unmistakably confident in its utterance of the cry: "I want."

"I want!" Sandip went on one day—this was the primal word at the root of all creation. It had no maxim to guide it, but it became fire and wrought itself into suns and stars. Its partiality is terrible. Because it had a desire for man, it ruthlessly sacrificed millions of beasts for millions of years to achieve that desire. That terrible word 'I want' has taken flesh in woman, and therefore men, who are cowards, try with all their might to keep back this primeval flood with their earthen dykes. They are afraid lest, laughing and dancing as it goes, it should wash away all the hedges and props of their pumpkin field. Men, in every age, flatter themselves that they have secured this force within the bounds of their convenience, but it gathers and grows. Now it is calm and deep like a lake, but gradually its pressure will increase, the dykes will give way, and the force which has so long been dumb will rush forward with the roar: "I want!"

These words of Sandip echo in my heartbeats like a war-drum. They shame into silence all my conflicts with myself. What do I care what people may think of me? Of what value are that orchid and that niche in my bedroom? What power have they to belittle me, to put me to shame? The primal fire of creation burns in me.

I felt a strong desire to snatch down the orchid and fling it out of the window, to denude the niche of its picture, to lay bare and naked the unashamed spirit of destruction that raged within me. My arm was raised to do it, but a sudden pang passed through my breast, tears started to my eyes. I threw myself down and sobbed: "What is the end of all this, what is the end?"

Sandip's Story

IV

When I read these pages of the story of my life I seriously question myself: Is this Sandip? Am I made of words? Am I merely a book with a covering of flesh and blood?

The earth is not a dead thing like the moon. She breathes. Her rivers and oceans send up vapours in which she is clothed. She is covered with a mantle of her own dust which flies about the air. The onlooker, gazing upon the earth from the outside, can see only the light reflected from this vapour and this dust. The tracks of the mighty continents are not distinctly visible.

The man, who is alive as this earth is, is likewise always enveloped in the mist of the ideas which he is breathing out. His real land and water remain hidden, and he appears to be made of only lights and shadows.

It seems to me, in this story of my life, that, like a living plant, I am displaying the picture of an ideal world. But I am not merely what I want, what I think—I am also what I do not love, what I do not wish to be. My creation had begun before I was born. I had no choice in regard to my surroundings and so must make the best of such material as comes to my hand.

My theory of life makes me certain that the Great is cruel. To be just is for ordinary men—it is reserved for the great to be unjust. The surface of the earth was even. The volcano butted it with its fiery horn and found its own eminence—its justice was not towards its obstacle, but towards itself. Successful injustice and genuine cruelty have been the only forces by which individual or nation has become millionaire or monarch.

That is why I preach the great discipline of Injustice. I say to everyone: Deliverance is based upon injustice. Injustice is the fire which must keep on burning something in order to save itself from becoming ashes. Whenever an individual or nation becomes incapable of perpetrating injustice it is swept into the dustbin of the world.

As yet this is only my idea—it is not completely myself. There are rifts in the armour through which something peeps out which is extremely soft and sensitive. Because, as I say, the best part of myself was created before I came to this stage of existence.

From time to time I try my followers in their lesson of cruelty. One day we went on a picnic. A goat was grazing by. I asked them: "Who is there among you that can cut off a leg of that goat, alive, with this knife, and bring it to me?" While they all hesitated, I went myself and did it. One of them fainted at the sight. But when they saw me unmoved they took the dust of my feet, saying that I was above all human weaknesses. That is to say, they saw that day the vaporous envelope which was my idea, but failed to perceive the inner me, which by a curious freak of fate has been created tender and merciful.

In the present chapter of my life, which is growing in interest every day round Bimala and Nikhil, there is also much that remains hidden underneath. This malady of ideas which afflicts me is shaping my life within: nevertheless a great part of my life remains outside its influence; and so there is set up a discrepancy between my outward life and its inner design which I try my best to keep concealed even from myself; otherwise it may wreck not only my plans, but my very life.

Life is indefinite—a bundle of contradictions. We men, with our ideas, strive to give it a particular shape by melting it into a particular mould—into the definiteness of success. All the world-conquerors, from Alexander down to the American millionaires, mould themselves into a sword or a mint, and thus find that distinct image of themselves which is the source of their success.

The chief controversy between Nikhil and myself arises from this: that though I say "know thyself", and Nikhil also says "know thyself", his interpretation makes this "knowing" tantamount to "not knowing".

"Winning your kind of success," Nikhil once objected, "is success gained at the cost of the soul: but the soul is greater than success."

I simply said in answer: "Your words are too vague."

"That I cannot help," Nikhil replied. "A machine is distinct enough, but not so life. If to gain distinctness you try to know life as a machine, then such mere distinctness cannot stand for truth. The soul is not as distinct as success, and so you only lose your soul if you seek it in your success."

"Where, then, is this wonderful soul?"

"Where it knows itself in the infinite and transcends its success."

"But how does all this apply to our work for the country?"

"It is the same thing. Where our country makes itself the final object, it gains success at the cost of the soul. Where it recognises the Greatest as greater than all, there it may miss success, but gains its soul."

"Is there any example of this in history?"

"Man is so great that he can despise not only the success, but also the example. Possibly example is lacking, just as there is no example of the flower in the seed. But there is the urgence of the flower in the seed all the same."

It is not that I do not at all understand Nikhil's point of view; that is rather where my danger lies. I was born in India and the poison of its spirituality runs in my blood. However loudly I may proclaim the madness of walking in the path of self-abnegation, I cannot avoid it altogether.

This is exactly how such curious anomalies happen nowadays in our country. We must have our religion and also our nationalism; our Bhagavad Gita and also our 'Bande Mataram.' The result is that both of them suffer. It is like performing with an English military band, side by side with our Indian festive pipes. I must make it the purpose of my life to put an end to this hideous confusion.

I want the western military style to prevail, not the Indian. We shall then not be ashamed of the flag of our passion, which mother Nature has sent with us as our standard into the battlefield of life. Passion is beautiful and pure—pure as the lily that comes out of the slimy soil. It rises superior to its defilement and needs no Pears' soap to wash it clean.

V

A question has been worrying me the last few days. Why am I allowing my life to become entangled with Bimala's? Am I a drifting log to be caught up at any and every obstacle?

Not that I have any false shame at Bimala becoming an object of my desire. It is only too clear how she wants me, and so I look on her as quite legitimately mine. The fruit hangs on the branch by the stem, but that is no reason why the claim of the stem should be eternal. Ripe fruit cannot for ever swear by its slackening stem-hold. All its sweetness has been accumulated for me; to surrender itself to my hand is the reason of its existence, its very nature, its true morality. So I must pluck it, for it becomes me not to make it futile.

But what is teasing me is that I am getting entangled. Am I not born to rule?—to bestride my proper steed, the crowd, and drive it as I will; the reins in my hand, the destination known only to me, and for it the thorns, the mire, on the road? This steed now awaits me at the door, pawing and champing its bit, its neighing filling the skies. But where am I, and what am I about, letting day after day of golden opportunity slip by?

I used to think I was like a storm—that the torn flowers with which I strewed my path would not impede my progress. But I am only wandering round and round a flower like a bee—not a storm. So, as I was saying, the colouring of ideas which man gives himself is only superficial. The inner man remains as ordinary as ever. If someone, who could see right into me, were to write my biography, he would make me out to be no different from that lout of a Panchu, or even from Nikhil!

Last night I was turning over the pages of my old diary . . . I had just graduated, and my brain was bursting with philosophy. Even so early I had vowed not to harbour any illusions, whether of my own or other's imagining, but to build my life on a solid basis of reality. But what has since been its actual story? Where is its solidity? It has rather been a network, where, though the thread be continuous, more space is taken up by the holes. Fight as I may, these will not own defeat. Just as I was congratulating myself on steadily following the thread, here I am badly caught in a hole! For I have become susceptible to compunctions.

"I want it; it is here; let me take it."—This is a clear-cut, straightforward policy. Those who can pursue its course with vigour needs must win through in the end. But the gods would not have it that such journey should be easy, so they have deputed the siren Sympathy to distract the wayfarer, to dim his vision with her tearful mist.

I can see that poor Bimala is struggling like a snared deer. What a piteous alarm there is in her eyes! How she is torn with straining at her bonds! This sight, of course, should gladden the heart of a true hunter. And so do I rejoice; but, then, I am also touched; and therefore I dally, and standing on the brink I am hesitating to pull the noose fast.

There have been moments, I know, when I could have bounded up to her, clasped her hands and folded her to my breast, unresisting. Had I done so, she would not have said one word. She was aware that some crisis was impending, which in a moment would change the meaning of the whole world. Standing before that cavern of the incalculable but yet expected, her face went pale and her eyes glowed with a fearful ecstasy. Within that moment, when it arrives, an eternity will take shape, which our destiny awaits, holding its breath.

But I have let this moment slip by. I did not, with uncompromising strength, press the almost certain into the absolutely assured. I now see clearly that some hidden elements in my nature have openly ranged themselves as obstacles in my path.

That is exactly how Ravana, whom I look upon as the real hero of the Ramayana, met with his doom. He kept Sita in his Asoka garden, awaiting her pleasure, instead of taking her straight into his harem. This weak spot in his otherwise grand character made the whole of the abduction episode futile. Another such touch of compunction made him disregard, and be lenient to, his traitorous brother Bibhisan, only to get himself killed for his pains.

Thus does the tragic in life come by its own. In the beginning it lies, a little thing, in some dark under-vault, and ends by overthrowing the whole superstructure. The real tragedy is, that man does not know himself for what he really is.

551

VI

Then again there is Nikhil. Crank though he be, laugh at him as I may, I cannot get rid of the idea that he is my friend. At first I gave no thought to his point of view, but of late it has begun to shame and hurt me. Therefore I have been trying to talk and argue with him in the same enthusiastic way as of old, but it does not ring true. It is even leading me at times into such a length of unnaturalness as to pretend to agree with him. But such hypocrisy is not in my nature, nor in that of Nikhil either. This, at least, is something we have in common. That is why, nowadays, I would rather not come across him, and have taken to fighting shy of his presence.

All these are signs of weakness. No sooner is the possibility of a wrong admitted than it becomes actual, and clutches you by the throat, however you may then try to shake off all belief in it. What I should like to be able to tell Nikhil frankly is, that happenings such as these must be looked in the face—as great Realities—and that which is the Truth should not be allowed to stand between true friends.

There is no denying that I have really weakened. It was not this weakness which won over Bimala; she burnt her wings in the blaze of the full strength of my unhesitating manliness. Whenever smoke obscures its lustre she also becomes confused, and draws back. Then comes a thorough revulsion of feeling, and she fain would take back the garland she has put round my neck, but cannot; and so she only closes her eyes, to shut it out of sight.

But all the same I must not swerve from the path I have chalked out. It would never do to abandon the cause of the country, especially at the present time. I shall simply make Bimala one with my country. The turbulent west wind which has swept away the country's veil of conscience, will sweep away the veil of the wife from Bimala's face, and in that uncovering there will be no shame. The ship will rock as it bears the crowd across the ocean, flying the pennant of Bande Mataram, and it will serve as the cradle to my power, as well as to my love.

Bimala will see such a majestic vision of deliverance, that her bonds will slip from about her, without shame, without her even being aware of it. Fascinated by the beauty of this terrible wrecking power, she will not hesitate a moment to be cruel. I have seen in Bimala's nature the cruelty which is the inherent force of existence—the cruelty which with its unrelenting might keeps the world beautiful.

If only women could be set free from the artificial fetters put round them by men, we could see on earth the living image of Kali, the shameless, pitiless goddess. I am a worshipper of Kali, and one day I shall truly worship her, setting Bimala on her altar of Destruction. For this let me get ready.

The way of retreat is absolutely closed for both of us. We shall despoil each other: get to hate each other: but never more be free.

CHAPTER FIVE

Nikhil's Story

IV

Everything is rippling and waving with the flood of August. The young shoots of rice have the sheen of an infant's limbs. The water has invaded the garden next to our house. The morning light, like the love of the blue sky, is lavished upon the earth . . . Why cannot I sing? The water of the distant river is shimmering with light; the leaves are glistening; the rice-fields, with their fitful shivers, break into gleams of gold; and in this symphony of Autumn, only I remain voiceless. The sunshine of the world strikes my heart, but is not reflected back.

When I realise the lack of expressiveness in myself, I know why I am deprived. Who could bear my company day and night without a break? Bimala is full of the energy of life, and so she has never become stale to me for a moment, in all these nine years of our wedded life.

My life has only its dumb depths; but no murmuring rush. I can only receive: not impart movement. And therefore my company is like fasting. I recognise clearly today that Bimala has been languishing because of a famine of companionship.

Then whom shall I blame? Like Vidyapati I can only lament:

It is August, the sky breaks into a passionate rain;
Alas, empty is my house.

My house, I now see, was built to remain empty, because its doors cannot open. But I never knew till now that its divinity had been sitting outside. I had fondly believed that she had accepted my sacrifice, and granted in return her boon. But, alas, my house has all along been empty.

Every year, about this time, it was our practice to go in a houseboat over the broads of Samalda. I used to tell Bimala that a song must come back to its refrain over and over again. The original refrain of every song is in Nature, where the rain-laden wind passes over the rippling stream, where the green earth, drawing its shadow-veil over its face, keeps its ear close to the speaking water. There, at the beginning of time, a man and a woman first met—not within walls. And therefore we two must come back to Nature, at least once a year, to tune our love anew to the first pure note of the meeting of hearts.

The first two anniversaries of our married life I spent in Calcutta, where I went through my examinations. But from the next year onwards, for seven years without a break, we have celebrated our union among the blossoming water-lilies. Now begins the next octave of my life.

It was difficult for me to ignore the fact that the same month of August had come round again this year. Does Bimala remember it, I wonder?—she has given me no reminder. Everything is mute about me.

It is August, the sky breaks into a passionate rain;
Alas, empty is my house.

The house which becomes empty through the parting of lovers, still has music left in the heart of its emptiness. But the house that is empty because hearts are asunder, is awful in its silence. Even the cry of pain is out of place there.

This cry of pain must be silenced in me. So long as I continue to suffer, Bimala will never have true freedom. I *must* free her completely, otherwise I shall never gain my freedom from untruth . . .

I think I have come to the verge of understanding one thing. Man has so fanned the flame of the loves of men and women, as to make it overpass its rightful domain, and now, even in the name of humanity itself, he cannot bring it back under control. Man's worship has idolized his passion. But there must be no more human sacrifices at its shrine . . .

I went into my bedroom this morning, to fetch a book. It is long since I have been there in the daytime. A pang passed through me as I looked round it today, in the morning light. On the clothes rack was hanging a sari of Bimala's, crinkled ready for wear. On the dressing-table were her perfumes, her comb, her hair-pins, and with them, still, her vermilion box! Underneath were her tiny gold-embroidered slippers.

Once, in the old days, when Bimala had not yet overcome her objections to shoes, I had got these out from Lucknow, to tempt her. The first time she was ready to drop for very shame, to go in them even from the room to the verandah. Since then she has worn out many shoes, but has treasured up this pair. When first showing her the slippers, I chaffed her over a curious practice of hers: "I have caught you taking the dust of my feet, thinking me asleep! These are the offerings of my worship to ward the dust off the feet of my wakeful divinity."

"You must not say such things," she protested, "or I will never wear your shoes!"

This bedroom of mine—it has a subtle atmosphere which goes straight to my heart. I was never aware, as I am today, how my thirsting heart has been sending out its roots to cling round each and every familiar object. The severing of the main root, I see, is not enough to set life free. Even these little slippers serve to hold one back.

My wandering eyes fall on the niche. My portrait there is looking the same as ever, in spite of the flowers scattered round it having been withered black! Of all the things in the room their greeting strikes me as sincere. They are still here simply because it was not felt worthwhile even to remove them. Never mind; let me welcome truth, albeit in such sere and sorry garb, and look forward to the time when I shall be able to do so unmoved, as does my photograph.

As I stood there, Bimal came in from behind. I hastily turned my eyes from the niche to the shelves as I muttered: "I came to get Amiel's Journal." What need had I to volunteer an explanation? I felt like a wrong-doer, a trespasser, prying into a secret not meant for me. I could not look Bimal in the face, but hurried away.

V

I had just made the discovery that it was useless to keep up a pretence of reading in my room outside, and also that it was equally beyond me to busy myself attending to anything at all—so that all the days of my future bid fair to congeal into one solid mass and settle heavily on my breast for good—when Panchu, the tenant of a neighbouring zamindar, came up to me with a basketful of coconuts and greeted me with a profound obeisance.

"Well, Panchu," said I. "What is all this for?"

I had got to know Panchu through my master. He was extremely poor, nor was I in a position to do anything for him; so I supposed this present was intended to procure a tip to help the poor fellow to make both ends meet. I took some money from my purse and held it out towards him, but with folded hands he protested: "I cannot take that, sir!"

"Why, what is the matter?"

"Let me make a clean breast of it, sir. Once, when I was hard pressed, I stole some coconuts from the garden here. I am getting old, and may die any day, so I have come to pay them back."

Amiel's Journal could not have done me any good that day. But these words of Panchu lightened my heart. There are more things in life than the union or separation of man and woman. The great world stretches far beyond, and one can truly measure one's joys and sorrows when standing in its midst.

Panchu was devoted to my master. I know well enough how he manages to eke out a livelihood. He is up before dawn every day, and with a basket of paan leaves, twists of tobacco, coloured cotton yarn, little combs, looking-glasses, and other trinkets beloved of the village women, he wades through the knee-deep water of the marsh and goes over to the *Namasudra* quarters. There he barters his goods for rice, which fetches him a little more than their price in money. If he can get back soon enough he goes out again, after a hurried meal, to the sweetmeat seller's, where he assists in beating sugar for wafers. As soon as he comes home he sits at his shell-bangle making, plodding on often till midnight. All this cruel toil does not earn, for himself and his family, a bare two meals a day during much more than half the year. His method of eating is to begin with a good filling draught of water, and his staple food is the cheapest kind of seedy banana. And yet the family has to go with only one meal a day for the rest of the year.

At one time I had an idea of making him a charity allowance, "But," said my master, "your gift may destroy the man, it cannot destroy the hardship of his lot. Mother Bengal has not only this one Panchu. If the milk in her breasts has run dry, that cannot be supplied from the outside."

These are thoughts which give one pause, and I decided to devote myself to working it out. That very day I said to Bimal: "Let us dedicate our lives to removing the root of this sorrow in our country."

"You are my Prince Siddhartha,* I see," she replied with a smile. "But do not let the torrent of your feelings end by sweeping me away also!"

"Siddhartha took his vows alone. I want ours to be a joint arrangement."

The idea passed away in talk. The fact is, Bimala is at heart what is called a 'lady.' Though her own people are not well off, she was born a Rani. She has no doubts in her mind that there is a lower unit of measure for the trials and troubles of the 'lower classes.' Want is, of course, a permanent feature of their lives, but does not necessarily mean 'want' to them. Their very smallness protects them, as the banks protect the pool; by widening bounds only the slime is exposed.

---

* The name by which Buddha was known when a Prince, before renouncing the world.

The real fact is that Bimala has only come into my home, not into my life. I had magnified her so, leaving her such a large place, that when I lost her, my whole way of life became narrow and confined. I had thrust aside all other objects into a corner to make room for Bimala—taken up as I was with decorating her and dressing her and educating her and moving round her day and night; forgetting how great is humanity and how nobly precious is man's life. When the actualities of everyday things get the better of the man, then is Truth lost sight of and freedom missed. So painfully important did Bimala make the mere actualities, that the truth remained concealed from me. That is why I find no gap in my misery, and spread this minute point of my emptiness over all the world. And so, for hours on this Autumn morning, the refrain has been humming in my ears:

> *It is the month of August, and the sky breaks into a passionate rain; Alas, my house is empty.*

Bimala's Story

XI

The change which had, in a moment, come over the mind of Bengal was tremendous. It was as if the Ganges had touched the ashes of the sixty thousand sons of Sagar* which no fire could enkindle, no other water knead again into living clay. The ashes of lifeless Bengal suddenly spoke up: "Here am I."

I have read somewhere that in ancient Greece a sculptor had the good fortune to impart life to the image made by his own

---

* The condition of the curse which had reduced them to ashes was such that they could only be restored to life if the stream of the Ganges was brought down to them.—*Translator*

hand. Even in that miracle, however, there was the process of form preceding life. But where was the unity in this heap of barren ashes? Had they been hard like stone, we might have had hopes of some form emerging, even as Ahalya, though turned to stone, at last won back her humanity. But these scattered ashes must have dropped to the dust through gaps in the Creator's fingers, to be blown hither and thither by the wind. They had become heaped up, but were never before united. Yet in this day which had come to Bengal, even this collection of looseness had taken shape, and proclaimed in a thundering voice, at our very door: "Here I am."

How could we help thinking that it was all supernatural? This moment of our history seemed to have dropped into our hand like a jewel from the crown of some drunken god. It had no resemblance to our past; and so we were led to hope that all our wants and miseries would disappear by the spell of some magic charm, that for us there was no longer any boundary line between the possible and the impossible. Everything seemed to be saying to us: "It is coming; it has come!"

Thus we came to cherish the belief that our history needed no steed, but that like heaven's chariot it would move with its own inherent power.—At least no wages would have to be paid to the charioteer; only his wine cup would have to be filled again and again. And then in some impossible paradise the goal of our hopes would be reached.

My husband was not altogether unmoved, but through all our excitement it was the strain of sadness in him which deepened and deepened. He seemed to have a vision of something beyond the surging present.

I remember one day, in the course of the arguments he continually had with Sandip, he said: "Good fortune comes to our gate and announces itself, only to prove that we have not the power to receive it—that we have not kept things ready to be able to invite it into our house."

"No," was Sandip's answer. "You talk like an atheist because you do not believe in our gods. To us it has been made quite visible that the Goddess has come with her boon, yet you distrust the obvious signs of her presence."

"It is because I strongly believe in my God," said my husband, "that I feel so certain that our preparations for his worship are lacking. God has power to give the boon, but we must have power to accept it."

This kind of talk from my husband would only annoy me. I could not keep from joining in: "You think this excitement is only a fire of drunkenness, but does not drunkenness, up to a point, give strength?"

"Yes," my husband replied. "It may give strength, but not weapons."

"But strength is the gift of God," I went on. "Weapons can be supplied by mere mechanics."

My husband smiled. "The mechanics will claim their wages before they deliver their supplies," he said.

Sandip swelled his chest as he retorted: "Don't you trouble about that. Their wages shall be paid."

"I shall bespeak the festive music when the payment has been made, not before," my husband answered.

"You needn't imagine that we are depending on your bounty for the music," said Sandip scornfully. "Our festival is above all money payments."

And in his thick voice he began to sing:

My lover of the unpriced love, spurning payments,
Plays upon the simple pipe, bought for nothing,
Drawing my heart away.

Then with a smile he turned to me and said: "If I sing, Queen Bee, it is only to prove that when music comes into one's life, the lack of a good voice is no matter. When we sing merely on the strength of our tunefulness, the song is belittled. Now that a full flood of music has swept over our country, let Nikhil practise his scales, while we rouse the land with our cracked voices:

My house cries to me: Why go out to lose your all?
My life says: All that you have, fling to the winds!
If we must lose our all, let us lose it: what is it worth after all?
If I must court ruin, let me do it smilingly;
For my quest is the death-draught of immortality.

"The truth is, Nikhil, that we have all lost our hearts. None can hold us any longer within the bounds of the easily possible, in our forward rush to the hopelessly impossible.

Those who would draw us back,
They know not the fearful joy of recklessness.
They know not that we have had our call
From the end of the crooked path.
All that is good and straight and trim—
Let it topple over in the dust."

I thought that my husband was going to continue the discussion, but he rose silently from his seat and left us.

The thing that was agitating me within was merely a variation of the stormy passion outside, which swept the country from one end to the other. The car of the wielder of my destiny was fast approaching, and the sound of its wheels reverberated in my being. I had a constant feeling that something extraordinary might happen any moment, for which, however, the responsibility would not be mine. Was I not removed from the plane in which right and wrong, and the feelings of others, have to be considered? Had I ever wanted this—had I ever been waiting or hoping for any such thing? Look at my whole life and tell me then, if I was in any way accountable.

Through all my past I had been consistent in my devotion— but when at length it came to receiving the boon, a different god appeared! And just as the awakened country, with its Bande Mataram, thrills in salutation to the unrealised future before it, so do all my veins and nerves send forth shocks of welcome to the unthought-of, the unknown, the importunate Stranger.

One night I left my bed and slipped out of my room on to the open terrace. Beyond our garden wall are fields of ripening rice. Through the gaps in the village groves to the North, glimpses of the river are seen. The whole scene slept in the darkness like the vague embryo of some future creation.

In that future I saw my country, a woman like myself, standing expectant. She has been drawn forth from her home corner by the sudden call of some Unknown. She has had no time to pause or ponder, or to light herself a torch, as she rushes forward into the darkness ahead. I know well how her very soul responds to the distant flute-strains which call her; how her breast rises and falls; how she feels she nears it, nay it is already hers, so that it matters not even if she runs blindfold. She is no mother. There is no call to her of children in their hunger, no home to be lighted of an evening, no household work to be done. So; she hies to her tryst, for this is the land of the Vaishnava Poets. She has left home, forgotten domestic duties; she has nothing but an unfathomable yearning which hurries her on—by what road, to what goal, she recks not.

I, also, am possessed of just such a yearning. I likewise have lost my home and also lost my way. Both the end and the means have become equally shadowy to me. There remain only the yearning and the hurrying on. Ah! wretched wanderer through the night, when the dawn reddens you will see no trace of a way to return. But why return? Death will serve as well. If the Dark which sounded the flute should lead to destruction, why trouble about the hereafter? When I am merged in its blackness, neither I, nor good and bad, nor laughter, nor tears, shall be any more!

XII

In Bengal the machinery of time being thus suddenly run at full pressure, things which were difficult became easy, one following soon after another. Nothing could be held back any more, even in our corner of the country. In the beginning our district was backward, for my husband was unwilling to put any compulsion on the villagers. "Those who make sacrifices for their country's sake are indeed her servants," he would say, "but those who compel others to make them in her name are her enemies. They would cut freedom at the root, to gain it at the top."

But when Sandip came and settled here, and his followers began to move about the country, speaking in towns and marketplaces, waves of excitement came rolling up to us as well. A band of young fellows of the locality attached themselves to him, some even who had been known as a disgrace to the village. But the glow of their genuine enthusiasm lighted them up, within as well as without. It became quite clear that when the pure breezes of a great joy and hope sweep through the land, all dirt and decay are cleansed away. It is hard, indeed, for men to be frank and straight and healthy, when their country is in the throes of dejection.

Then were all eyes turned on my husband, from whose estates alone foreign sugar and salt and cloths had not been banished. Even the estate officers began to feel awkward and ashamed over it. And yet, some time ago, when my husband began to import country-made articles into our village, he had been secretly and openly twitted for his folly, by old and young alike. When Swadeshi had not yet become a boast, we had despised it with all our hearts.

My husband still sharpens his Indian-made pencils with his Indian-made knife, does his writing with reed pens, drinks his water out of a bell-metal vessel, and works at night in the light of an old-fashioned castor-oil lamp. But this dull, milk-and-water Swadeshi of his never appealed to us. Rather, we had always felt ashamed of the inelegant, unfashionable furniture of his reception rooms, especially when he had the magistrate, or any other European, as his guest.

My husband used to make light of my protests. "Why allow such trifles to upset you?" he would say with a smile.

"They will think us barbarians, or at all events wanting in refinement."

"If they do, I will pay them back by thinking that their refinement does not go deeper than their white skins."

My husband had an ordinary brass pot on his writing-table which he used as a flower-vase. It has often happened that, when I had news of some European guest, I would steal into his room and put in its place a crystal vase of European make. "Look here, Bimala," he objected at length, "that brass pot is as unconscious of itself as those blossoms are; but this thing protests its purpose so loudly, it is only fit for artificial flowers."

The Bara Rani, alone, pandered to my husband's whims. Once she comes panting to say: "Oh, brother, have you heard? Such lovely Indian soaps have come out! My days of luxury are gone by; still, if they contain no animal fat, I should like to try some."

This sort of thing makes my husband beam all over, and the house is deluged with Indian scents and soaps. Soaps indeed! They are more like lumps of caustic soda. And do I not know that what my sister-in-law uses on herself are the European soaps of old, while these are made over to the maids for washing clothes?

Another time it is: "Oh, brother dear, do get me some of these new Indian pen-holders."

Her 'brother' bubbles up as usual, and the Bara Rani's room becomes littered with all kinds of awful sticks that go by the name of Swadeshi pen-holders. Not that it makes any difference to her, for reading and writing are out of her line. Still, in her writing-case, lies the selfsame ivory pen-holder, the only one ever handled.

The fact is, all this was intended as a hit at me, because I would not keep my husband company in his vagaries. It was no good trying to show up my sister-in-law's insincerity; my husband's face would set so hard, if I barely touched on it. One only gets into trouble, trying to save such people from being imposed upon!

The Bara Rani loves sewing. One day I could not help blurting out: "What a humbug you are, sister! When your 'brother' is present, your mouth waters at the very mention of Swadeshi scissors, but it is the English-made article every time when you work."

"What harm?" she replied. "Do you not see what pleasure it gives him? We have grown up together in this house, since he was a boy. I simply cannot bear, as you can, the sight of the smile leaving his face. Poor dear, he has no amusement except this playing at shop-keeping. You are his only dissipation, and you will yet be his ruin!"

"Whatever you may say, it is not right to be double-faced," I retorted.

My sister-in-law laughed out in my face. "Oh, our artless little Chota Rani!—straight as a schoolmaster's rod, eh? But a woman is not built that way. She is soft and supple, so that she may bend without being crooked."

I could not forget those words: "You are his dissipation, and will be his ruin!" Today I feel—if a man needs must have some intoxicant, let it not be a woman.

XIII

Suksar, within our estates, is one of the biggest trade centres in the district. On one side of a stretch of water there is held a daily bazar; on the other, a weekly market. During the rains when this piece of water gets connected with the river, and boats can come through, great quantities of cotton yarns, and woollen stuffs for the coming winter, are brought in for sale.

At the height of our enthusiasm, Sandip laid it down that all foreign articles, together with the demon of foreign influence, must be driven out of our territory.

"Of course!" said I, girding myself up for a fight.

"I have had words with Nikhil about it," said Sandip. "He tells me, he does not mind speechifying, but he will not have coercion."

"I will see to that," I said, with a proud sense of power. I knew how deep was my husband's love for me. Had I been in my senses I should have allowed myself to be torn to pieces rather than assert my claim to that, at such a time. But Sandip had to be impressed with the full strength of my Shakti.

Sandip had brought home to me, in his irresistible way, how the cosmic Energy was revealed for each individual in the shape of some special affinity. Vaishnava Philosophy, he said, speaks of the Shakti of Delight that dwells in the heart of creation, ever attracting the heart of her Eternal Lover. Men have a perpetual longing to bring out this Shakti from the hidden depths of their own nature, and those of us who succeed in doing so at once clearly understand the meaning of the music coming to us from the Dark. He broke out singing:

My flute, that was busy with its song,
Is silent now when we stand face to face.
My call went seeking you from sky to sky
When you lay hidden;
But now all my cry finds its smile
In the face of my beloved.

Listening to his allegories, I had forgotten that I was plain and simple Bimala. I was Shakti; also an embodiment of Universal joy.

The Home and The World

Nothing could fetter me, nothing was impossible for me; whatever I touched would gain new life. The world around me was a fresh creation of mine; for behold, before my heart's response had touched it, there had not been this wealth of gold in the Autumn sky! And this hero, this true servant of the country, this devotee of mine—this flaming intelligence, this burning energy, this shining genius—him also was I creating from moment to moment. Have I not seen how my presence pours fresh life into him time after time?

The other day Sandip begged me to receive a young lad, Amulya, an ardent disciple of his. In a moment I could see a new light flash out from the boy's eyes, and knew that he, too, had a vision of Shakti manifest, that my creative force had begun its work in his blood. "What sorcery is this of yours!" exclaimed Sandip next day. "Amulya is a boy no longer, the wick of his life is all ablaze. Who can hide your fire under your home-roof? Every one of them must be touched up by it, sooner or later, and when every lamp is alight what a grand carnival of a Diwali we shall have in the country!"

Blinded with the brilliance of my own glory I had decided to grant my devotee this boon. I was overweeningly confident that none could baulk me of what I really wanted. When I returned to my room after my talk with Sandip, I loosed my hair and tied it up over again. Miss Gilby had taught me a way of brushing it up from the neck and piling it in a knot over my head. This style was a favourite one with my husband. "It is a pity," he once said, "that Providence should have chosen poor me, instead of poet Kalidas, for revealing all the wonders of a woman's neck. The poet would probably have likened it to a flower-stem; but I feel it to be a torch, holding aloft the black flame of your hair." With which he . . . but why, oh why, do I go back to all that?

I sent for my husband. In the old days I could contrive a hundred and one excuses, good or bad, to get him to come to me. Now that all this had stopped for days I had lost the art of contriving.

Nikhil's Story

VI

Panchu's wife has just died of a lingering consumption. Panchu must undergo a purification ceremony to cleanse himself of sin and to propitiate his community. The community has calculated and informed him that it will cost one hundred and twenty-three rupees.

"How absurd!" I cried, highly indignant. "Don't submit to this, Panchu. What can they do to you?"

Raising to me his patient eyes like those of a tired-out beast of burden, he said: "There is my eldest girl, sir, she will have to be married. And my poor wife's last rites have to be put through."

"Even if the sin were yours, Panchu," I mused aloud, "you have surely suffered enough for it already."

"That is so, sir," he naïvely assented. "I had to sell part of my land and mortgage the rest to meet the doctor's bills. But there is no escape from the offerings I have to make the Brahmins."

What was the use of arguing? When will come the time, I wondered, for the purification of the Brahmins themselves who can accept such offerings?

After his wife's illness and funeral, Panchu, who had been tottering on the brink of starvation, went altogether beyond his depth. In a desperate attempt to gain consolation of some sort he took to sitting at the feet of a wandering ascetic, and succeeded in acquiring philosophy enough to forget that his children went hungry. He kept himself steeped for a time in the idea that the world is vanity, and if of pleasure it has none, pain also is a delusion. Then, at last, one night he left his little ones in their tumble-down hovel, and started off wandering on his own account.

I knew nothing of this at the time, for just then a veritable ocean-churning by gods and demons was going on in my mind. Nor did my master tell me that he had taken Panchu's deserted children under his own roof and was caring for them, though alone in the house, with his school to attend to the whole day.

After a month Panchu came back, his ascetic fervour considerably worn off. His eldest boy and girl nestled up to him, crying: "Where have you been all this time, father?" His youngest boy filled his lap; his second girl leant over his back with her arms around his neck; and they all wept together. "O sir!" sobbed Panchu, at length, to my master. "I have not the power to give these little ones enough to eat—I am not free to run away from them. What has been my sin that I should be scourged so, bound hand and foot?"

In the meantime the thread of Panchu's little trade connections had snapped and he found he could not resume them. He clung on to the shelter of my master's roof, which had first received him on his return, and said not a word of going back home. "Look here, Panchu," my master was at last driven to say. "If you don't take care of your cottage, it will tumble down altogether. I will lend you some money with which you can do a bit of peddling and return it me little by little."

Panchu was not excessively pleased—was there then no such thing as charity on earth? And when my master asked him to write out a receipt for the money, he felt that this favour, demanding a return, was hardly worth having. My master, however, did not care to make an outward gift which would leave an inward obligation. To destroy self-respect is to destroy caste, was his idea.

After signing the note, Panchu's obeisance to my master fell off considerably in its reverence—the dust-taking was left out. It made my master smile; he asked nothing better than that courtesy should stoop less low. "Respect given and taken truly balances the account between man and man," was the way he put it, "but veneration is overpayment."

Panchu began to buy cloth at the market and peddle it about the village. He did not get much of cash payment, it is true, but what he could realise in kind, in the way of rice, jute, and other field produce, went towards settlement of his account. In two month's time he was able to pay back an instalment of my master's debt, and with it there was a corresponding reduction in the depth of his bow. He must have begun to feel that he had been revering as a saint a mere man, who had not even risen superior to the lure of lucre.

While Panchu was thus engaged, the full shock of the Swadeshi flood fell on him.

VII

It was vacation time, and many youths of our village and its neighbourhood had come home from their schools and colleges. They attached themselves to Sandip's leadership with enthusiasm, and some, in their excess of zeal, gave up their studies altogether. Many of the boys had been free pupils of my school here, and some held college scholarships from me in Calcutta. They came up in a body, and demanded that I should banish foreign goods from my Suksar market.

I told them I could not do it.

They were sarcastic: "Why, Maharaja, will the loss be too much for you?"

I took no notice of the insult in their tone, and was about to reply that the loss would fall on the poor traders and their customers, not on me, when my master, who was present, interposed.

"Yes, the loss will be his—not yours, that is clear enough," he said.

"But for one's country . . ."

"The country does not mean the soil, but the men on it," interrupted my master again. "Have you yet wasted so much as a glance on what was happening to them? But now you would dictate what salt they shall eat, what clothes they shall wear. Why should they put up with such tyranny, and why should we let them?"

"But we have taken to Indian salt and sugar and cloth ourselves."

"You may do as you please to work off your irritation, to keep up your fanaticism. You are well off, you need not mind the cost. The poor do not want to stand in your way, but you insist on their submitting to your compulsion. As it is, every moment of theirs is a life-and-death struggle for a bare living; you cannot even imagine the difference a few pice means to them—so little have you in common. You have spent your whole past in a superior compartment, and now you come down to use them as tools for the wreaking of your wrath. I call it cowardly."

They were all old pupils of my master, so they did not venture to be disrespectful, though they were quivering with indignation.

They turned to me. "Will you then be the only one, Maharaja, to put obstacles in the way of what the country would achieve?"

"Who am I, that I should dare do such a thing? Would I not rather lay down my life to help it?"

The M.A. student smiled a crooked smile, as he asked: "May we enquire what you are actually doing to help?"

"I have imported Indian mill-made yarn and kept it for sale in my Suksar market, and also sent bales of it to markets belonging to neighbouring zamindars."

"But we have been to your market, Maharaja," the same student exclaimed, "and found nobody buying this yarn."

"That is neither my fault nor the fault of my market. It only shows the whole country has not taken your vow."

"That is not all," my master went on. "It shows that what you have pledged yourselves to do is only to pester others. You want dealers, who have not taken your vow, to buy that yarn; weavers, who have not taken your vow, to make it up; then their wares eventually to be foisted on to consumers who, also, have not taken your vow. The method? Your clamour, and the zamindars' oppression. The result: all righteousness yours, all privations theirs!"

"And may we venture to ask, further, what your share of the privation has been?" pursued a science student.

"You want to know, do you?" replied my master. "It is Nikhil himself who has to buy up that Indian mill yarn; he has had to start a weaving school to get it woven; and to judge by his past brilliant business exploits, by the time his cotton fabrics leave the loom their cost will be that of cloth-of-gold; so they will only find a use, perhaps, as curtains for his drawing room, even though their flimsiness may fail to screen him. When you get tired of your vow, you will laugh the loudest at their artistic effect. And if their workmanship is ever truly appreciated at all, it will be by foreigners."

I have known my master all my life, but have never seen him so agitated. I could see that the pain had been silently accumulating in his heart for some time, because of his surpassing love for me, and that his habitual self-possession had become secretly undermined to the breaking point.

"You are our elders," said the medical student. "It is unseemly that we should bandy words with you. But tell us, pray, finally, are you determined not to oust foreign articles from your market?"

"I will not," I said, "because they are not mine."

"Because that will cause you a loss!" smiled the M.A. student.

"Because he, whose is the loss, is the best judge," retorted my master.

With a shout of Bande Mataram they left us.

CHAPTER SIX

Nikhil's Story

VIII

A few days later, my master brought Panchu round to me. His zamindar, it appeared, had fined him a hundred rupees, and was threatening him with ejectment.

"For what fault?" I enquired.

"Because," I was told, "he has been found selling foreign cloths. He begged and prayed Harish Kundu, his zamindar, to let him sell off his stock, bought with borrowed money, promising faithfully never to do it again; but the zamindar would not hear of it, and insisted on his burning the foreign stuff there and then, if he wanted to be let off. Panchu in his desperation blurted out defiantly: "I can't afford it! You are rich; why not buy it up and burn it?" This only made Harish Kundu red in the face as he shouted: "The scoundrel must be taught manners, give him a shoe-beating!" So poor Panchu got insulted as well as fined.

"What happened to the cloth?"

"The whole bale was burnt."

"Who else was there?"

"Any number of people, who all kept shouting Bande Mataram. Sandip was also there. He took up some of the ashes, crying: 'Brothers! This is the first funeral pyre lighted by your village in celebration of the last rites of foreign commerce. These are sacred ashes. Smear yourselves with them in token of your Swadeshi vow."'

"Panchu," said I, turning to him, "you must lodge a complaint."

"No one will bear me witness," he replied.

"None bear witness?—Sandip! Sandip!"

Sandip came out of his room at my call. "What is the matter?" he asked.

"Won't you bear witness to the burning of this man's cloth?"

Sandip smiled. "Of course I shall be a witness in the case," he said. "But I shall be on the opposite side."

"What do you mean," I exclaimed, "by being a witness on this or that side? Will you not bear witness to the truth?"

"Is the thing which happens the only truth?"

"What other truths can there be?"

"The things that ought to happen! The truth we must build up will require a great deal of untruth in the process. Those who have made their way in the world have created truth, not blindly followed it."

"And so—"

"And so I will bear what you people are pleased to call false witness, as they have done who have created empires, built up social systems, founded religious organizations. Those who would rule do not dread untruths; the shackles of truth are reserved for those who will fall under their sway. Have you not read history? Do you not know that in the immense cauldrons, where vast political developments are simmering, untruths are the main ingredients?"

"Political cookery on a large scale is doubtless going on, but—"

"Oh, I know! You, of course, will never do any of the cooking. You prefer to be one of those down whose throats the hotchpotch which is being cooked will be crammed. They will partition Bengal and say it is for your benefit. They will seal the doors of education and call it raising the standard. But you will always remain good boys, snivelling in your corners. We bad men, however, must see whether we cannot erect a defensive fortification of untruth."

"It is no use arguing about these things, Nikhil," my master interposed. "How can they who do not feel the truth within them, realise that to bring it out from its obscurity into the light is man's highest aim—not to keep on heaping material outside?"

Sandip laughed. "Right, sir!" said he. "Quite a correct speech for a schoolmaster. That is the kind of stuff I have read in books; but in the real world I have seen that man's chief business is the accumulation of outside material. Those who are masters in the art, advertise the biggest lies in their business, enter false accounts in their political ledgers with their broadest-pointed pens, launch their newspapers daily laden with untruths, and send preachers abroad to disseminate falsehood like flies carrying pestilential germs. I am a humble follower of these great ones. When I was attached to the Congress party I never hesitated to dilute ten per cent of truth with ninety per cent of untruth. And now, merely because I have ceased to belong to that party, I have not forgotten the basic fact that man's goal is not truth but success."

"True success," corrected my master.

"Maybe," replied Sandip, "but the fruit of true success ripens only by cultivating the field of untruth, after tearing up the soil and pounding it into dust. Truth grows up by itself like weeds and thorns, and only worms can expect to get fruit from it!" With this he flung out of the room.

My master smiled as he looked towards me. "Do you know, Nikhil," he said, "I believe Sandip is not irreligious—his religion is of the obverse side of truth, like the dark moon, which is still a moon, for all that its light has gone over to the wrong side."

"That is why," I assented, "I have always had an affection for him, though we have never been able to agree. I cannot condemn him, even now; though he has hurt me sorely, and may yet hurt me more."

"I have begun to realise that," said my master. "I have long wondered how you could go on putting up with him. I have, at times, even suspected you of weakness. I now see that though you two do not rhyme, your rhythm is the same."

"Fate seems bent on writing *Paradise Lost* in blank verse, in my case, and so has no use for a rhyming friend!" I remarked, pursuing his conceit.

"But what of Panchu?" resumed my master.

"You say Harish Kundu wants to eject him from his ancestral holding. Supposing I buy it up and then keep him on as my tenant?"

"And his fine?"

"How can the zamindar realise that if he becomes my tenant?"

"His burnt bale of cloth?"

"I will procure him another. I should like to see anyone interfering with a tenant of mine, for trading as he pleases!"

"I am afraid, sir," interposed Panchu despondently, "while you big folk are doing the fighting, the police and the law vultures will merrily gather round, and the crowd will enjoy the fun, but when it comes to getting killed, it will be the turn of only poor me!"

"Why, what harm can come to you?"

"They will burn down my house, sir, children and all!"

"Very well, I will take charge of your children," said my master. "You may go on with any trade you like. They shan't touch you."

That very day I bought up Panchu's holding and entered into formal possession. Then the trouble began.

Panchu had inherited the holding of his grandfather as his sole surviving heir. Everybody knew this. But at this juncture an aunt turned up from somewhere, with her boxes and bundles, her rosary, and a widowed niece. She ensconced herself in Panchu's home and laid claim to a life interest in all he had.

Panchu was dumbfounded. "My aunt died long ago," he protested.

In reply he was told that he was thinking of his uncle's first wife, but that the former had lost no time in taking to himself a second.

"But my uncle died before my aunt," exclaimed Panchu, still more mystified. "Where was the time for him to marry again?"

This was not denied. But Panchu was reminded that it had never been asserted that the second wife had come after the death of the first, but the former had been married by his uncle during the latter's lifetime. Not relishing the idea of living with a co-wife she had remained in her father's house till her husband's death, after which she had got religion and retired to holy Brindaban, whence she was now coming. These facts were well known to the officers of Harish Kundu, as well as to some of his tenants. And if the zamindar's summons should be peremptory enough, even some of those who had partaken of the marriage feast would be forthcoming!

IX

One afternoon, when I happened to be specially busy, word came to my office room that Bimala had sent for me. I was startled.

"Who did you say had sent for me?" I asked the messenger.

"The Rani Mother."

"The Bara Rani?"

"No, sir, the Chota Rani Mother."

The Chota Rani! It seemed a century since I had been sent for by her. I kept them all waiting there, and went off into the inner apartments. When I stepped into our room I had another shock of surprise to find Bimala there with a distinct suggestion of being dressed up. The room, which from persistent neglect had latterly acquired an air of having grown absent-minded, had regained something of its old order this afternoon. I stood there silently, looking enquiringly at Bimala.

She flushed a little and the fingers of her right hand toyed for a time with the bangles on her left arm. Then she abruptly broke the silence. "Look here! Is it right that ours should be the only market in all Bengal which allows foreign goods?"

"What, then, would be the right thing to do?" I asked.

"Order them to be cleared out!"

"But the goods are not mine."

"Is not the market yours?"

"It is much more theirs who use it for trade."

"Let them trade in Indian goods, then."

"Nothing would please me better. But suppose they do not?"

"Nonsense! How dare they be so insolent? Are you not ..."

"I am very busy this afternoon and cannot stop to argue it out. But I must refuse to tyrannize."

"It would not be tyranny for selfish gain, but for the sake of the country."

"To tyrannize for the country is to tyrannize over the country. But that I am afraid you will never understand." With this I came away.

All of a sudden the world shone out for me with a fresh clearness. I seemed to feel it in my blood, that the Earth had lost the weight of its earthiness, and its daily task of sustaining life no longer appeared a burden, as with a wonderful access of power it whirled through space telling its beads of days and nights. What endless work, and withal what illimitable energy of freedom! None shall check it, oh, none can ever check it! From the depths of my being an uprush of joy, like a waterspout, sprang high to storm the skies.

I repeatedly asked myself the meaning of this outburst of feeling. At first there was no intelligible answer. Then it became clear that the bond against which I had been fretting inwardly, night and day, had broken. To my surprise I discovered that my mind was freed from all mistiness. I could see everything relating to Bimala as if vividly pictured on a camera screen. It was palpable that she had specially dressed herself up to coax that order out of me. Till that moment, I had never viewed Bimala's adornment as a thing apart from herself. But today the elaborate manner in which she had done up her hair, in the English fashion, made it appear a mere decoration. That which before had the mystery of her personality about it, and was priceless to me, was now out to sell itself cheap.

As I came away from that broken cage of a bedroom, out into the golden sunlight of the open, there was the avenue of bauhinias, along the gravelled path in front of my verandah, suffusing the sky with a rosy flush. A group of starlings beneath the trees were noisily chattering away. In the distance an empty bullock cart, with its nose on the ground, held up its tail aloft—one of its unharnessed bullocks grazing, the other resting on the grass, its eyes dropping for very comfort, while a crow on its back was pecking away at the insects on its body.

I seemed to have come closer to the heartbeats of the great earth in all the simplicity of its daily life; its warm breath fell on me with the perfume of the bauhinia blossoms; and an anthem, inexpressibly sweet, seemed to peal forth from this world, where I, in my freedom, live in the freedom of all else.

We, men, are knights whose quest is that freedom to which our ideals call us. She who makes for us the banner under which we fare forth is the true Woman for us. We must tear away the disguise of her who weaves our net of enchantment at home, and know her for what she is. We must beware of clothing her in the witchery of our own longings and imaginings, and thus allow her to distract us from our true quest.

Today I feel that I shall win through. I have come to the gateway of the simple; I am now content to see things as they are. I have gained freedom myself; I shall allow freedom to others. In my work will be my salvation.

I know that, time and again, my heart will ache, but now that I understand its pain in all its truth, I can disregard it. Now that I know it concerns only me, what after all can be its value? The suffering which belongs to all mankind shall be my crown.

Save me, Truth! Never again let me hanker after the false paradise of Illusion. If I must walk alone, let me at least tread your path. Let the drumbeats of Truth lead me to Victory.

Sandip's Story

VII

Bimala sent for me that day, but for a time she could not utter a word; her eyes kept brimming up to the verge of overflowing. I could see at once that she had been unsuccessful with Nikhil. She had been so proudly confident that she would have her own way—but I had never shared her confidence. Woman knows man well enough where he is weak, but she is quite unable to fathom him where he is strong. The fact is that man is as much a mystery to woman as woman is to man. If that were not so, the separation of the sexes would only have been a waste of Nature's energy.

Ah pride, pride! The trouble was, not that the necessary thing had failed of accomplishment, but that the entreaty, which had cost her such a struggle to make, should have been refused. What a wealth of colour and movement, suggestion and deception, group themselves round this 'me' and 'mine' in woman. That is just where her beauty lies—she is ever so much more personal than man. When man was being made, the Creator was a schoolmaster—His bag full of commandments and principles; but when He came to woman, He resigned His headmastership and turned artist, with only His brush and paint box.

When Bimala stood silently there, flushed and tearful in her broken pride, like a storm-cloud, laden with rain and charged with lightning, lowering over the horizon, she looked so absolutely sweet that I had to go right up to her and take her by the hand. It was trembling, but she did not snatch it away.

"Bee," said I, "we two are colleagues, for our aims are one. Let us sit down and talk it over."

I led her, unresisting, to a seat. But strange! at that very point the rush of my impetuosity suffered an unaccountable check—just as the current of the mighty Padma, roaring on in its irresistible course, all of a sudden gets turned away from the bank it is crumbling by some trifling obstacle beneath the surface. When I pressed Bimala's hand my nerves rang music, like tuned-up strings; but the symphony stopped short at the first movement.

What stood in the way? Nothing singly; it was a tangle of a multitude of things—nothing definitely palpable, but only that unaccountable sense of obstruction. Anyhow, this much has become plain to me, that I cannot swear to what I really am. It is because I am such a mystery to my own mind that my attraction for myself is so strong! If once the whole of myself should become known to me, I would then fling it all away—and reach beatitude!

As she sat down, Bimala went ashy pale. She, too, must have realised what a crisis had come and gone, leaving her unscathed. The comet had passed by, but the brush of its burning tail had overcome her. To help her to recover herself I said: "Obstacles there will be, but let us fight them through, and not be down-hearted. Is not that best, Queen?"

Bimala cleared her throat with a little cough, but simply to murmur: "Yes."

"Let us sketch out our plan of action," I continued, as I drew a piece of paper and a pencil from my pocket.

I began to make a list of the workers who had joined us from Calcutta and to assign their duties to each. Bimala interrupted me before I was through, saying wearily: "Leave it now; I will join you again this evening" and then she hurried out of the room. It was evident she was not in a state to attend to anything. She must be alone with herself for a while—perhaps lie down on her bed and have a good cry!

When she left me, my intoxication began to deepen, as the cloud colours grow richer after the sun is down. I felt I had let the moment of moments slip by. What an awful coward I had been! She must have left me in sheer disgust at my qualms—and she was right!

While I was tingling all over with these reflections, a servant came in and announced Amulya, one of our boys. I felt like sending him away for the time, but he stepped in before I could make up my mind. Then we fell to discussing the news of the fights which were raging in different quarters over cloth and sugar and salt; and the air was soon clear of all fumes of intoxication. I felt as if awakened from a dream. I leapt to my feet feeling quite ready for the fray—Bande Mataram!

The news was various. Most of the traders who were tenants of Harish Kundu had come over to us. Many of Nikhil's officials were also secretly on our side, pulling the wires in our interest. The Marwari shopkeepers were offering to pay a penalty, if only allowed to clear their present stocks. Only some Mahomedan traders were still obdurate.

One of them was taking home some German-made shawls for his family. These were confiscated and burnt by one of our village boys. This had given rise to trouble. We offered to buy him Indian woollen stuffs in their place. But where were cheap Indian woollens to be had? We could not very well indulge him in Cashmere shawls! He came and complained to Nikhil, who advised him to go to law. Of course Nikhil's men saw to it that the trial should come to nothing, even his law-agent being on our side!

The point is, if we have to replace burnt foreign clothes with Indian cloth every time, and on the top of that fight through a law-suit, where is the money to come from? And the beauty of it is that this destruction of foreign goods is increasing their demand and sending up the foreigner's profits—very like what happened to the fortunate shopkeeper whose chandeliers the nabob delighted in smashing, tickled by the tinkle of the breaking glass.

The next problem is—since there is no such thing as cheap and gaudy Indian woollen stuff, should we be rigorous in our boycott of foreign flannels and merinos, or make an exception in their favour?

"Look here!" said I at length on the first point, "we are not going to keep on making presents of Indian stuff to those who have got their foreign purchases confiscated. The penalty is intended to fall on them, not on us. If they go to law, we must retaliate by burning down their granaries!—What startles you, Amulya? It is not the prospect of a grand illumination that delights me! You must remember, this is War. If you are afraid of causing suffering, go in for love-making, you will never do for this work!"

The second problem I solved by deciding to allow no compromise with foreign articles, in any circumstance whatever. In the good old days, when these gaily coloured foreign shawls were unknown, our peasantry used to manage well enough with plain cotton quilts—they must learn to do so again. They may not look as gorgeous, but this is not the time to think of looks.

Most of the boatmen had been won over to refuse to carry foreign goods, but the chief of them, Mirjan, was still insubordinate.

"Could you not get his boat sunk?" I asked our manager here.

"Nothing easier, sir," he replied. "But what if afterwards I am held responsible?"

"Why be so clumsy as to leave any loophole for responsibility? However, if there must be any, my shoulders will be there to bear it."

Mirjan's boat was tied near the landing-place after its freight had been taken over to the marketplace. There was no one on it, for the manager had arranged for some entertainment to which all had been invited. After dusk the boat, loaded with rubbish, was holed and set adrift. It sank in mid-stream.

Mirjan understood the whole thing. He came to me in tears to beg for mercy. "I was wrong, sir—" he began.

"What makes you realise that all of a sudden?" I sneered.

He made no direct reply. "The boat was worth two thousand rupees," he said. "I now see my mistake, and if excused this time I will never . . ." with which he threw himself at my feet.

I asked him to come ten days later. If only we could pay him that two thousand rupees at once, we could buy him up body and soul.

This is just the sort of man who could render us immense service, if won over. We shall never be able to make any headway unless we can lay our hands on plenty of money.

As soon as Bimala came into the sitting room, in the evening, I said as I rose up to receive her: "Queen! Everything is ready, success is at hand, but we must have money."

"Money? How much money?"

"Not so very much, but by hook or by crook we must have it!"

"But how much?"

"A mere fifty thousand rupees will do for the present."

Bimala blenched inwardly at the figure, but tried not to show it. How could she again admit defeat?

"Queen!" said I, "you only can make the impossible possible. Indeed you have already done so. Oh, that I could show you the extent of your achievement—then you would know it. But the time for that is not now. Now we want money!"

"You shall have it," she said.

I could see that the thought of selling her jewels had occurred to her. So I said: "Your jewels must remain in reserve. One can never tell when they may be wanted." And then, as Bimala stared blankly at me in silence, I went on: "This money must come from your husband's treasury."

Bimala was still more taken aback. After a long pause she said: "But how am I to get his money?"

"Is not his money yours as well?"

"Ah, no!" she said, her wounded pride hurt afresh.

"If not," I cried, "neither is it his, but his country's, whom he has deprived of it, in her time of need!"

"But how am I to get it?" she repeated.

"Get it you shall and must. You know best how. You must get it for Her to whom it rightfully belongs. Bande Mataram! These are the magic words which will open the door of his iron safe, break through the walls of his strongroom, and confound the hearts of those who are disloyal to its call. Say Bande Mataram, Bee!"

"Bande Mataram!"

CHAPTER SEVEN

Sandip's Story

VIII

We are men, we are kings, we must have our tribute. Ever since we have come upon the Earth we have been plundering her; and the more we claimed, the more she submitted. From primeval days, we men have been plucking fruits, cutting down trees, digging up the soil, killing beast, bird and fish. From the bottom of the sea, from underneath the ground, from the very jaws of death, it has all been grabbing and grabbing and grabbing—no strong-box in Nature's storeroom has been respected or left unrifled. The one delight of this Earth is to fulfil the claims of those who are men. She has been made fertile and beautiful and complete through her endless sacrifices to them. But for this, she would be lost in the wilderness, not knowing herself, the doors of her heart shut, her diamonds and pearls never seeing the light.

Likewise, by sheer force of our claims, we men have opened up all the latent possibilities of women. In the process of surrendering themselves to us, they have ever gained their true greatness. Because they had to bring all the diamonds of their happiness and the pearls of their sorrow into our royal treasury, they have found their true wealth. So for men to accept is truly to give: for women to give is truly to gain.

The demand I have just made from Bimala, however, is indeed a large one! At first I felt scruples; for is it not the habit of man's mind to be in purposeless conflict with itself? I thought I had imposed too hard a task. My first impulse was to call her back, and tell her I would rather not make her life wretched by dragging her into all these troubles. I forgot, for the moment, that it was the mission of man to be aggressive, to make woman's existence fruitful by stirring up disquiet in the depth of her passivity, to make the whole world blessed by churning up the immeasurable abyss of suffering! This is why man's hands are so strong, his grip so firm.

Bimala had been longing with all her heart that I, Sandip, should demand of her some great sacrifice—should call her to her death. How else could she be happy? Had she not waited all these weary years only for an opportunity to weep out her heart—so satiated was she with the monotony of her placid happiness? And therefore, at the very sight of me, her heart's horizon darkened with the rain clouds of her impending days of anguish. If I pity her and save her from her sorrows, what then was the purpose of my being born a man?

The real reason of my qualms is that my demand happens to be for money. That savours of beggary, for money is man's, not woman's. That is why I had to make it a big figure. A thousand or two would have the air of petty theft. Fifty thousand has all the expanse of romantic brigandage. Ah, but riches should really have been mine! So many of my desires have had to halt, again and again, on the road to accomplishment simply for want of money. This does not become me! Had my fate been merely unjust, it could be forgiven—but its bad taste is unpardonable. It is not simply a hardship that a man like me should be at his wit's end to pay his house rent, or should have to carefully count out the coins for an Intermediate Class railway ticket—it is vulgar!

It is equally clear that Nikhil's paternal estates are a superfluity to him. For him it would not have been at all unbecoming to be poor. He would have cheerfully pulled in the double harness of indigent mediocrity with that precious master of his. I should love to have, just for once, the chance to fling about fifty thousand rupees in the service of my country and to the satisfaction of myself. I am a nabob born, and it is a great dream of mine to get rid of this disguise of poverty, though it be for a day only, and to see myself in my true character. I have grave misgivings, however, as to Bimala ever getting that fifty thousand rupees within her reach, and it will probably be only a thousand or two which will actually come to hand. Be it so. The wise man is content with half a loaf, or any fraction for that matter, rather than no bread. I must return to these personal reflections of mine later. News comes that I am wanted at once. Something has gone wrong . . .

It seems that the police have got a clue to the man who sank Mirjan's boat for us. He was an old offender. They are on his trail, but he should be too practised a hand to be caught blabbing. However, one never knows. Nikhil's back is up, and his manager may not be able to have things his own way.

"If I get into trouble, sir," said the manager when I saw him, "I shall have to drag you in!"

"Where is the noose with which you can catch me?" I asked.

"I have a letter of yours, and several of Amulya Babu's." I could not see that the letter marked 'urgent' to which I had been hurried into writing a reply was wanted urgently for this purpose only! I am getting to learn quite a number of things.

The point now is, that the police must be bribed and hush-money paid to Mirjan for his boat. It is also becoming evident that much of the cost of this patriotic venture of ours will find its way as profit into the pockets of Nikhil's manager. However, I must shut my eyes to that for the present, for is he not shouting Bande Mataram as lustily as I am?

This kind of work has always to be carried on with leaky vessels which let as much through as they fetch in. We all have a hidden fund of moral judgement stored away within us, and so I was about to wax indignant with the manager, and enter in my diary a tirade against the unreliability of our countrymen. But, if there be a god, I must acknowledge with gratitude to him that he has given me a clear-seeing mind, which allows nothing inside or outside it to remain vague. I may delude others, but never myself. So I was unable to continue angry.

Whatever is true is neither good nor bad, but simply true, and that is Science. A lake is only the remnant of water which has not been sucked into the ground. Underneath the cult of Bande Mataram, as indeed at the bottom of all mundane affairs, there is a region of slime, whose absorbing power must be reckoned with. The manager will take what he wants; I also have my own wants. These lesser wants form a part of the wants of the great Cause—the horse must be fed and the wheels must be oiled if the best progress is to be made.

The long and short of it is that money we must have, and that soon. We must take whatever comes the readiest, for we cannot afford to wait. I know that the immediate often swallows up the ultimate; that the five thousand rupees of today may nip in the bud the fifty thousand rupees of tomorrow. But I must accept the penalty. Have I not often twitted Nikhil that they who walk in the paths of restraint have never known what sacrifice is? It is we greedy folk who have to sacrifice our greed at every step!

Of the cardinal sins of man, Desire is for men who are men— but Delusion, which is only for cowards, hampers them. Because delusion keeps them wrapped up in past and future, but is the very deuce for confounding their footsteps in the present. Those who are always straining their ears for the call of the remote, to the neglect of the call of the imminent, are like Sakuntala* absorbed in the memories of her lover. The guest comes unheeded, and the curse descends, depriving them of the very object of their desire.

The other day I pressed Bimala's hand, and that touch still stirs her mind, as it vibrates in mine. Its thrill must not be deadened by repetition, for then what is now music will descend to mere argument. There is at present no room in her mind for the question 'why?' So I must not deprive Bimala, who is one of those creatures for whom illusion is necessary, of her full supply of it.

As for me, I have so much else to do that I shall have to be content for the present with the foam of the wine cup of passion. O man of desire! Curb your greed, and practise your hand on the harp of illusion till you can bring out all the delicate nuances of suggestion. This is not the time to drain the cup to the dregs.

---

* Sakuntala, after the king, her lover, went back to his kingdom, promising to send for her, was so lost in thoughts of him, that she failed to hear the call of her hermit guest who thereupon cursed her, saying that the object of her love would forget all about her.—*Translator*

IX

Our work proceeds apace. But though we have shouted ourselves hoarse, proclaiming the Mussulmans to be our brethren, we have come to realise that we shall never be able to bring them wholly round to our side. So they must be suppressed altogether and made to understand that we are the masters. They are now showing their teeth, but one day they shall dance like tame bears to the tune we play.

"If the idea of a United India is a true one," objects Nikhil, "Mussulmans are a necessary part of it."

"Quite so," said I, "but we must know their place and keep them there, otherwise they will constantly be giving trouble."

"So you want to make trouble to prevent trouble?"

"What, then, is your plan?"

"There is only one well-known way of avoiding quarrels," said Nikhil meaningly.

I know that, like tales written by good people, Nikhil's discourse always ends in a moral. The strange part of it is that with all his familiarity with moral precepts, he still believes in them! He is an incorrigible schoolboy. His only merit is his sincerity. The mischief with people like him is that they will not admit the finality even of death, but keep their eyes always fixed on a hereafter.

I have long been nursing a plan which, if only I could carry it out, would set fire to the whole country. True patriotism will never be roused in our countrymen unless they can visualize the motherland. We must make a goddess of her. My colleagues saw the point at once. "Let us devise an appropriate image!" they exclaimed. "It will not do if you devise it," I admonished them. "We must get one of the current images accepted as representing the country—the worship of the people must flow towards it along the deep-cut grooves of custom."

But Nikhil's needs must argue even about this. "We must not seek the help of illusions," he said to me some time ago, "for what we believe to be the true cause."

"Illusions are necessary for lesser minds," I said, "and to this class the greater portion of the world belongs. That is why divinities are set up in every country to keep up the illusions of the people, for men are only too well aware of their weakness."

"No," he replied. "God is necessary to clear away our illusions. The divinities which keep them alive are false gods."

"What of that? If need be, even false gods must be invoked, rather than let the work suffer. Unfortunately for us, our illusions are alive enough, but we do not know how to make them serve our purpose. Look at the Brahmins. In spite of our treating them as demi-gods, and untiringly taking the dust of their feet, they are a force going to waste.

"There will always be a large class of people, given to grovelling, who can never be made to do anything unless they are bespattered with the dust of somebody's feet, be it on their heads or on their backs! What a pity if after keeping Brahmins saved up in our armoury for all these ages—keen and serviceable—they cannot be utilized to urge on this rabble in the time of our need."

But it is impossible to drive all this into Nikhil's head. He has such a prejudice in favour of truth—as though there exists such an objective reality! How often have I tried to explain to him that where untruth truly exists, there it is indeed the truth. This was understood in our country in the old days, and so they had the courage to declare that for those of little understanding untruth is the truth. For them, who can truly believe their country to be a goddess, her image will do duty for the truth. With our nature and our traditions we are unable to realise our country as she is, but we can easily bring ourselves to believe in her image. Those who want to do real work must not ignore this fact.

Nikhil only got excited. "Because you have lost the power of walking in the path of truth's attainment," he cried, "you keep waiting for some miraculous boon to drop from the skies! That is why when your service to the country has fallen centuries into arrears all you can think of is, to make of it an image and stretch out your hands in expectation of gratuitous favours."

"We want to perform the impossible," I said. "So our country needs must be made into a god."

"You mean you have no heart for possible tasks," replied Nikhil. "Whatever is already there is to be left undisturbed; yet there must be a supernatural result:"

"Look here, Nikhil," I said at length, thoroughly exasperated.

"The things you have been saying are good enough as moral lessons. These ideas have served their purpose, as milk for babes, at one stage of man's evolution, but will no longer do, now that man has cut his teeth.

"Do we not see before our very eyes how things, of which we never even dreamt of sowing the seed, are sprouting up on every side? By what power? That of the deity in our country who is becoming manifest. It is for the genius of the age to give that deity its image. Genius does not argue, it creates. I only give form to what the country imagines.

"I will spread it abroad that the goddess has vouchsafed me a dream. I will tell the Brahmins that they have been appointed her priests, and that their downfall has been due to their dereliction of duty in not seeing to the proper performance of her worship. Do you say I shall be uttering lies? No, say I, it is the truth—nay more, the truth which the country has so long been waiting to learn from my lips. If only I could get the opportunity to deliver my message, you would see the stupendous result."

"What I am afraid of," said Nikhil, "is, that my lifetime is limited and the result you speak of is not the final result. It will have after-effects which may not be immediately apparent."

"I only seek the result," said I, "which belongs to today."

"The result I seek," answered Nikhil, "belongs to all time."

Nikhil may have had his share of Bengal's greatest gift—imagination, but he has allowed it to be overshadowed and nearly killed by an exotic conscientiousness. Just look at the worship of Durga which Bengal has carried to such heights. That is one of her greatest achievements. I can swear that Durga is a political goddess and was conceived as the image of the Shakti of patriotism in the days when Bengal was praying to be delivered from Mussulman domination. What other province of India has succeeded in giving such wonderful visual expression to the ideal of its quest?

Nothing betrayed Nikhil's loss of the divine gift of imagination more conclusively than his reply to me. "During the Mussulman domination," he said, "the Maratha and the Sikh asked for fruit from the arms which they themselves took up. The Bengali contented himself with placing weapons in the hands of his goddess and muttering incantations to her; and as his country did not really happen to be a goddess the only fruit he got was the lopped-off heads of the goats and buffaloes of the sacrifice. The day that we seek the good of the country along the path of righteousness, He who is greater than our country will grant us true fruition."

The unfortunate part of it is that Nikhil's words sound so fine when put down on paper. My words, however, are not meant to be scribbled on paper, but to be scored into the heart of the country. The Pandit records his Treatise on Agriculture in printer's ink; but the cultivator at the point of his plough impresses his endeavour deep in the soil.

X

When I next saw Bimala I pitched my key high without further ado. "Have we been able," I began, "to believe with all our heart in the god for whose worship we have been born all these millions of years, until he actually made himself visible to us?

"How often have I told you," I continued, "that had I not seen you I never would have known all my country as One. I know not yet whether you rightly understand me. The gods are invisible only in their heaven—on earth they show themselves to mortal men."

Bimala looked at me in a strange kind of way as she gravely replied: "Indeed I understand you, Sandip." This was the first time she called me plain Sandip.

"Krishna," I continued, "whom Arjuna ordinarily knew only as the driver of his chariot, had also His universal aspect, of which, too, Arjuna had a vision one day, and that day he saw the Truth. I have seen your Universal Aspect in my country. The Ganges and the Brahmaputra are the chains of gold that wind round and round your neck; in the woodland fringes on the distant banks of the dark waters of the river, I have seen your collyrium-darkened eyelashes; the changeful sheen of your sari moves for me in the play of light and shade amongst the swaying shoots of green corn; and the blazing summer heat, which makes the whole sky lie gasping like a red-tongued lion in the desert, is nothing but your cruel radiance.

"Since the goddess has vouchsafed her presence to her votary

591

in such wonderful guise, it is for me to proclaim her worship throughout our land, and then shall the country gain new life. 'Your image make we in temple after temple.'* But this our people have not yet fully realised. So I would call on them in your name and offer for their worship an image from which none shall be able to withhold belief. Oh give me this boon, this power."

Bimala's eyelids drooped and she became rigid in her seat like a figure of stone. Had I continued she would have gone off into a trance. When I ceased speaking she opened wide her eyes, and murmured with fixed gaze, as though still dazed: "O Traveller in the path of Destruction! Who is there that can stay your progress? Do I not see that none shall stand in the way of your desires? Kings shall lay their crowns at your feet; the wealthy shall hasten to throw open their treasure for your acceptance; those who have nothing else shall beg to be allowed to offer their lives. O my king, my god! What you have seen in me I know not, but I have seen the immensity of your grandeur in my heart. Who am I, what am I, in its presence? Ah, the awful power of Devastation! Never shall I truly live till it kills me utterly! I can bear it no longer, my heart is breaking!"

Bimala slid down from her seat and fell at my feet, which she clasped, and then she sobbed and sobbed and sobbed.

This is hypnotism indeed—the charm which can subdue the world! No materials, no weapons—but just the delusion of irresistible suggestion. Who says "Truth shall Triumph"?† Delusion shall win in the end. The Bengali understood this when he conceived the image of the ten-handed goddess astride her lion, and spread her worship in the land. Bengal must now create a new image to enchant and conquer the world. Bande Mataram!

I gently lifted Bimala back into her chair, and lest reaction should set in, I began again without losing time: "Queen! The Divine Mother has laid on me the duty of establishing her worship in the land. But, alas, I am poor!"

Bimala was still flushed, her eyes clouded, her accents thick, as she replied: "You poor? Is not all that each one has yours? What are

---

* A line from Bankim Chatterjee's national song 'Bande Mataram.'
† A quotation from the Upanishads

my caskets full of jewellery for? Drag away from me all my gold and gems for your worship. I have no use for them!"

Once before Bimala had offered up her ornaments. I am not usually in the habit of drawing lines, but I felt I had to draw the line there.* I know why I feel this hesitation. It is for man to give ornaments to woman; to take them from her wounds his manliness.

But I must forget myself. Am I taking them? They are for the Divine Mother, to be poured in worship at her feet. Oh, but it must be a grand ceremony of worship such as the country has never beheld before. It must be a landmark in our history. It shall be my supreme legacy to the Nation. Ignorant men worship gods. I, Sandip, shall create them.

But all this is a far cry. What about the urgent immediate? At least three thousand is indispensably necessary—five thousand would do roundly and nicely. But how on earth am I to mention money after the high flight we have just taken? And yet time is precious!

I crushed all hesitation under foot as I jumped up and made my plunge: "Queen! Our purse is empty, our work about to stop!"

Bimala winced. I could see she was thinking of that impossible fifty thousand rupees. What a load she must have been carrying within her bosom, struggling under it, perhaps, through sleepless nights! What else had she with which to express her loving worship? Debarred from offering her heart at my feet, she hankers to make this sum of money, so hopelessly large for her, the bearer of her imprisoned feelings. The thought of what she must have gone through gives me a twinge of pain; for she is now wholly mine. The

---

* There is a world of sentiment attached to the ornaments worn by women in Bengal. They are not merely indicative of the love and regard of the giver, but the wearing of them symbolizes all that is held best in wifehood—the constant solicitude for her husband's welfare, the successful performance of the material and spiritual duties of the household entrusted to her care. When the husband dies, and the responsibility for the household changes hands, then all ornaments are cast aside as a sign of the widow's renunciation of worldly concerns. At any other time the giving up of ornaments is always a sign of supreme distress and as such appeals acutely to the sense of chivalry of any Bengali who may happen to witness it. —*Translator*

wrench of plucking up the plant by the roots is over. It is now only careful tending and nurture that is needed.

"Queen!" said I, "that fifty thousand rupees is not particularly wanted just now. I calculate that, for the present, five thousand or even three will serve."

The relief made her heart rebound. "I shall fetch you five thousand," she said in tones which seemed like an outburst of song—the song which Radhika of the Vaishnava lyrics sang:

For my lover will I bind in my hair
The flower which has no equal in the three worlds!

—it is the same tune, the same song: five thousand will I bring! That flower will I bind in my hair!

The narrow restraint of the flute brings out this quality of song. I must not allow the pressure of too much greed to flatten out the reed, for then, as I fear, music will give place to the questions "Why?" "What is the use of so much?" "How am I to get it?"—not a word of which will rhyme with what Radhika sang! So, as I was saying, illusion alone is real—it is the flute itself; while truth is but its empty hollow. Nikhil has of late got a taste of that pure emptiness—one can see it in his face, which pains even me. But it was Nikhil's boast that he wanted the Truth, while mine was that I would never let go illusion from my grasp. Each has been suited to his taste, so why complain?

To keep Bimala's heart in the rarefied air of idealism, I cut short all further discussion over the five thousand rupees. I reverted to the demon-destroying goddess and her worship. When was the ceremony to be held and where? There is a great annual fair at Ruimari, within Nikhil's estates, where hundreds of thousands of pilgrims assemble. That would be a grand place to inaugurate the worship of our goddess!

Bimala waxed intensely enthusiastic. This was not the burning of foreign cloth or the people's granaries, so even Nikhil could have no objection—so thought she. But I smiled inwardly. How little these two persons, who have been together, day and night, for nine whole years, know of each other! They know something perhaps of their home life, but when it comes to outside concerns they are entirely at sea. They had cherished the belief that the harmony of the home with the outside was perfect. Today they realise to their cost that it is too late to repair their neglect of years, and seek to harmonize them now.

What does it matter? Let those who have made the mistake learn their error by knocking against the world. Why need I bother about their plight? For the present I find it wearisome to keep Bimala soaring much longer, like a captive balloon, in regions ethereal. I had better get quite through with the matter in hand.

When Bimala rose to depart and had neared the door I remarked in my most casual manner: "So, about the money . . ."

Bimala halted and faced back as she said: "On the expiry of the month, when our personal allowances become due . . ."

"That, I am afraid, would be much too late."

"When do you want it then?"

"Tomorrow.

"Tomorrow you shall have it."

CHAPTER EIGHT

Nikhil's Story

X

Paragraphs and letters against me have begun to come out in the local papers; cartoons and lampoons are to follow, I am told. Jets of wit and humour are being splashed about, and the lies thus scattered are convulsing the whole country. They know that the monopoly of mud-throwing is theirs, and the innocent passer-by cannot escape unsoiled.

They are saying that the residents in my estates, from the highest to the lowest, are in favour of Swadeshi, but they dare not declare themselves, for fear of me. The few who have been brave enough to defy me have felt the full rigour of my persecution. I am in secret league with the police, and in private communication with the magistrate, and these frantic efforts of mine to add a foreign title of my own earning to the one I have inherited, will not, it is opined, go in vain.

On the other hand, the papers are full of praise for those devoted sons of the motherland, the Kundu and the Chakravarti zamindars. If only, say they, the country had a few more of such staunch patriots, the mills of Manchester would have, had to sound their own dirge to the tune of 'Bande Mataram.'

Then comes a letter in blood-red ink, giving a list of the traitorous zamindars whose treasuries have been burnt down because of their failing to support the Cause. Holy Fire, it goes on to say, has been aroused to its sacred function of purifying the country; and other agencies are also at work to see that those who are not true sons of the motherland do cease to encumber her lap. The signature is an obvious *nom-de-plume*.

I could see that this was the doing of our local students. So I sent for some of them and showed them the letter.

The B.A. student gravely informed me that they also had heard that a band of desperate patriots had been formed who would stick at nothing in order to clear away all obstacles to the success of Swadeshi.

"If," said I, "even one of our countrymen succumbs to these overbearing desperadoes, that will indeed be a defeat for the country!"

"We fail to follow you, Maharaja," said the history student.

"Our country," I tried to explain, "has been brought to death's door through sheer fear—from fear of the gods down to fear of the police; and if you set up, in the name of freedom, the fear of some other bogey, whatever it may be called; if you would raise your victorious standard on the cowardice of the country by means of downright oppression, then no true lover of the country can bow to your decision."

"Is there any country, sir," pursued the history student, "where submission to Government is not due to fear?"

"The freedom that exists in any country," I replied, "may be measured by the extent of this reign of fear. Where its threat is confined to those who would hurt or plunder, there the Government may claim to have freed man from the violence of man. But if fear is to regulate how people are to dress, where they shall trade, or what they must eat, then is man's freedom of will utterly ignored, and manhood destroyed at the root."

"Is not such coercion of the individual will seen in other countries too?" continued the history student.

"Who denies it?" I exclaimed. "But in every country man has destroyed himself to the extent that he has permitted slavery to flourish."

"Does it not rather show," interposed a Master of Arts, "that trading in slavery is inherent in man—a fundamental fact of his nature?"

"Sandip Babu made the whole thing clear," said a graduate. "He gave us the example of Harish Kundu, your neighbouring zamindar. From his estates you cannot ferret out a single ounce of foreign salt. Why? Because he has always ruled with an iron hand. In the case of those who are slaves by nature, the lack of a strong master is the greatest of all calamities."

"Why, sir!" chimed in an undergraduate, "have you not heard of the obstreperous tenant of Chakravarti, the other zamindar close by—how the law was set on him till he was reduced to utter destitution? When at last he was left with nothing to eat, he started out to sell his wife's silver ornaments, but no one dared buy them. Then Chakravarti's manager offered him five rupees for the lot. They were worth over thirty, but he had to accept or starve. After taking over the bundle from him the manager coolly said that those five rupees would be credited towards his rent! We felt like having nothing more to do with Chakravarti or his manager after that, but Sandip Babu told us that if we threw over all the live people, we should have only dead bodies from the burning-grounds to carry on the work with! These live men, he pointed out, know what they want and how to get it—they are born rulers. Those who do not know how to desire for themselves, must live in accordance with, or die by virtue of, the desires of such as these. Sandip Babu contrasted them—Kundu and Chakravarti—with you, Maharaja. You, he said, for all your good intentions, will never succeed in planting Swadeshi within your territory."

"It is my desire," I said, "to plant something greater than Swadeshi. I am not after dead logs but living trees—and these will take time to grow."

"I am afraid, sir," sneered the history student, "that you will get neither log nor tree. Sandip Babu rightly teaches that in order to get, you must snatch. This is taking all of us some time to learn, because it runs counter to what we were taught at school. I have seen with my own eyes that when a rent-collector of Harish Kundu's found one of the tenants with nothing which could be sold up to pay his rent, he was made to sell his young wife! Buyers were not wanting, and the zamindar's demand was satisfied. I tell you, sir, the sight of that man's distress prevented my getting sleep for nights together! But, feel it as I did, this much I realised, that the man who knows how to get the money he is out for, even by selling up his debtor's wife, is a better man than I am. I confess it is beyond me—I am a weakling, my eyes fill with tears. If anybody can save our country it is these Kundus and these Chakravartis and their officials!"

I was shocked beyond words. "If what you say be true," I cried, "I clearly see that it must be the one endeavour of my life to save the country from these same Kundus and Chakravartis and officials. The slavery that has entered into our very bones is breaking out, at this opportunity, as ghastly tyranny. You have been so used to submit to domination through fear, you have come to believe that to make others submit is a kind of religion. My fight shall be against this weakness, this atrocious cruelty!" These things, which are so simple to ordinary folk, get so twisted in the minds of our B.A.'s and M.A.'s, the only purpose of whose historical quibbles seems to be to torture the truth!

XI

I am worried over Panchu's sham aunt. It will be difficult to disprove her, for though witnesses of a real event may be few or even wanting, innumerable proofs of a thing that has not happened can always be marshalled. The object of this move is, evidently, to get the sale of Panchu's holding to me set aside. Being unable to find any other way out of it, I was thinking of allowing Panchu to hold a permanent tenure in my estates and building him a cottage on it. But my master would not have it. I should not give in to these nefarious tactics so easily, he objected, and offered to attend to the matter himself.

"You, sir!" I cried, considerably surprised.

"Yes, I," he repeated.

I could not see, at all clearly, what my master could do to counteract these legal machinations. That evening, at the time he usually came to me, he did not turn up. On my making inquiries, his servant said he had left home with a few things packed in a small trunk, and some bedding, saying he would be back in a few days. I thought he might have sallied forth to hunt for witnesses in Panchu's uncle's village. In that case, however, I was sure that his would be a hopeless quest . . .

During the day I forget myself in my work. As the late autumn afternoon wears on, the colours of the sky become turbid, and so do the feelings of my mind. There are many in this world whose minds dwell in brick-built houses—they can afford to ignore the thing called the outside. But my mind lives under the trees in the open, directly receives upon itself the messages borne by the free winds, and responds from the bottom of its heart to all the musical cadences of light and darkness.

While the day is bright and the world in the pursuit of its numberless tasks crowds around, then it seems as if my life wants nothing else. But when the colours of the sky fade away and the blinds are drawn down over the windows of heaven, then my heart tells me that evening falls just for the purpose of shutting out the world, to mark the time when the darkness must be filled with the One. This is the end to which earth, sky, and waters conspire, and I cannot harden myself against accepting its meaning. So when the gloaming deepens over the world, like the gaze of the dark eyes of the beloved, then my whole being tells me that work alone cannot be the truth of life, that work is not the be-all and the end-all of man, for man is not simply a serf—even though the serfdom be of the True and the Good.

Alas, Nikhil, have you for ever parted company with that self of yours who used to be set free under the starlight, to plunge into the infinite depths of the night's darkness after the day's work was done? How terribly alone is he, who misses companionship in the midst of the multitudinousness of life.

The other day, when the afternoon had reached the meeting-point of day and night, I had no work, nor the mind for work, nor was my master there to keep me company. With my empty, drifting heart longing to anchor on to something, I traced my steps towards the inner gardens. I was very fond of chrysanthemums and had rows of them, of all varieties, banked up in pots against one of the garden walls. When they were in flower, it looked like a wave of green breaking into iridescent foam. It was some time since I had been to this part of the grounds, and I was beguiled into a cheerful expectancy at the thought of meeting my chrysanthemums after our long separation.

As I went in, the full moon had just peeped over the wall, her slanting rays leaving its foot in deep shadow. It seemed as if she had come a-tiptoe from behind, and clasped the darkness over the eyes, smiling mischievously. When I came near the bank of chrysanthemums, I saw a figure stretched on the grass in front. My heart gave a sudden thud. The figure also sat up with a start at my footsteps.

What was to be done next? I was wondering whether it would do to beat a precipitate retreat. Bimala, also, was doubtless casting about for some way of escape. But it was as awkward to go as to stay! Before I could make up my mind, Bimala rose, pulled the end of her sari over her head, and walked off towards the inner apartments.

This brief pause had been enough to make real to me the cruel load of Bimala's misery. The plaint of my own life vanished from me in a moment. I called out: "Bimala!"

She started and stayed her steps, but did not turn back. I went round and stood before her. Her face was in the shade, the moonlight fell on mine. Her eyes were downcast, her hands clenched.

"Bimala," said I, "why should I seek to keep you fast in this closed cage of mine? Do I not know that thus you cannot but pine and droop?"

She stood still, without raising her eyes or uttering a word.

"I know," I continued, "that if I insist on keeping you shackled my whole life will be reduced to nothing but an iron chain. What pleasure can that be to me?"

She was still silent.

"So," I concluded, "I tell you, truly, Bimala, you are free. Whatever I may or may not have been to you, I refuse to be your fetters." With which I came away towards the outer apartments.

No, no, it was not a generous impulse, nor indifference. I had simply come to understand that never would I be free until I could set free. To try to keep Bimala as a garland round my neck, would have meant keeping a weight hanging over my heart. Have I not been praying with all my strength, that if happiness may not be mine, let it go; if grief needs must be my lot, let it come; but let me not be kept in bondage. To clutch hold of that which is untrue as though it were true, is only to throttle oneself. May I be saved from such self-destruction.

When I entered my room, I found my master waiting there. My agitated feelings were still heaving within me. "Freedom, sir," I began unceremoniously, without greeting or inquiry, "freedom is the biggest thing for man. Nothing can be compared to it—nothing at all!"

Surprised at my outburst, my master looked up at me in silence.

"One can understand nothing from books," I went on. "We read in the scriptures that our desires are bonds, fettering us as well as others. But such words, by themselves, are so empty. It is only when we get to the point of letting the bird out of its cage that we can realise how free the bird has set us. Whatever we cage, shackles us with desire whose bonds are stronger than those of iron chains. I tell you, sir, this is just what the world has failed to understand. They all seek to reform something outside themselves. But reform is wanted only in one's own desires, nowhere else, nowhere else!"

"We think," he said, "that we are our own masters when we get in our hands the object of our desire—but we are really our own masters only when we are able to cast out our desires from our minds."

"When we put all this into words, sir," I went on, "it sounds like some bald-headed injunction, but when we realise even a little of it we find it to be *amrita*—which the gods have drunk and become immortal. We cannot see Beauty till we let go our hold of it. It was Buddha who conquered the world, not Alexander—this is untrue when stated in dry prose—oh when shall we be able to sing it? When shall all these most intimate truths of the universe overflow the pages of printed books and leap out in a sacred stream like the Ganges from the Gangotrie?"

I was suddenly reminded of my master's absence during the last few days and of my ignorance as to its reason. I felt somewhat foolish as I asked him: "And where have you been all this while, sir?"

"Staying with Panchu," he replied.

"Indeed!" I exclaimed. "Have you been there all these days?"

"Yes. I wanted to come to an understanding with the woman who calls herself his aunt. She could hardly be induced to believe that there could be such an odd character among the gentlefolk as the one who sought their hospitality. When she found I really meant to stay on, she began to feel rather ashamed of herself. 'Mother,' said I, 'you are not going to get rid of me, even if you abuse me! And so long as I stay, Panchu stays also. For you see, do you not, that I cannot stand by and see his motherless little ones sent out into the streets?'

"She listened to my talks in this strain for a couple of days without saying yes or no. This morning I found her tying up her bundles. 'We are going back to Brindaban,' she said. 'Let us have our expenses for the journey.' I knew she was not going to Brindaban, and also that the cost of her journey would be substantial. So I have come to you."

"The required cost shall be paid," I said.

"The old woman is not a bad sort," my master went on musingly. "Panchu was not sure of her caste, and would not let her touch the water-jar, or anything at all of his. So they were continually bickering. When she found I had no objection to her touch, she looked after me devotedly. She is a splendid cook!

"But all remnants of Panchu's respect for me vanished! To the last he had thought that I was at least a simple sort of person. But here was I, risking my caste without a qualm to win over the old woman for my purpose. Had I tried to steal a march on her by tutoring a witness for the trial, that would have been a different matter. Tactics must be met by tactics. But stratagem at the expense of orthodoxy is more than he can tolerate!

"Anyhow, I must stay on a few days at Panchu's even after the woman leaves, for Harish Kundu may be up to any kind of devilry. He has been telling his satellites that he was content to have furnished Panchu with an aunt, but I have gone the length of supplying him with a father. He would like to see, now, how many fathers of his can save him!"

"We may or may not be able to save him," I said; "but if we should perish in the attempt to save the country from the thousand-and-one snares—of religion, custom and selfishness—which these people are busy spreading, we shall at least die happy."

Bimala's Story

XIV

Who could have thought that so much would happen in this one life? I feel as if I have passed through a whole series of births, time has been flying so fast, I did not feel it move at all, till the shock came the other day.

I knew there would be words between us when I made up my mind to ask my husband to banish foreign goods from our market. But it was my firm belief that I had no need to meet argument by argument, for there was magic in the very air about me. Had not so tremendous a man as Sandip fallen helplessly at my feet, like a wave of the mighty sea breaking on the shore? Had I called him? No, it was the summons of that magic spell of mine. And Amulya, poor dear boy, when he first came to me—how the current of his life flushed with colour, like the river at dawn! Truly have I realised how a goddess feels when she looks upon the radiant face of her devotee.

With the confidence begotten of these proofs of my power, I was ready to meet my husband like a lightning-charged cloud. But what was it that happened? Never in all these nine years have I seen such a faraway, distraught look in his eyes—like the desert sky—with no merciful moisture of its own, no colour reflected, even, from what it looked upon. I should have been so relieved if his anger had flashed out! But I could find nothing in him which I could touch. I felt as unreal as a dream—a dream which would leave only the blackness of night when it was over.

In the old days I used to be jealous of my sister-in-law for her beauty. Then I used to feel that Providence had given me no power of my own, that my whole strength lay in the love which my husband had bestowed on me. Now that I had drained to the dregs the cup of power and could not do without its intoxication, I suddenly found it dashed to pieces at my feet, leaving me nothing to live for.

How feverishly I had sat to do my hair that day. Oh, shame, shame on me, the utter shame of it! My sister-in-law, when passing by, had exclaimed: "Aha, Chota Rani! Your hair seems ready to jump off. Don't let it carry your head with it."

And then, the other day in the garden, how easy my husband found it to tell me that he set me free! But can freedom—empty freedom—be given and taken so easily as all that? It is like setting a fish free in the sky—for how can I move or live outside the atmosphere of loving care which has always sustained me?

When I came to my room today, I saw only furniture—only the bedstead, only the looking-glass, only the clothes-rack—not the all-pervading heart which used to be there, over all. Instead of it there was freedom, only freedom, mere emptiness! A dried-up watercourse with all its rocks and pebbles laid bare. No feeling, only furniture!

When I had arrived at a state of utter bewilderment, wondering whether anything true was left in my life, and whereabouts it could be, I happened to meet Sandip again. Then life struck against life, and the sparks flew in the same old way. Here was truth—impetuous truth—which rushed in and overflowed all bounds, truth which was a thousand times truer than the Bara Rani with her maid, Thako and her silly songs, and all the rest of them who talked and laughed and wandered about . . .

"Fifty thousand!" Sandip had demanded.

"What is fifty thousand?" cried my intoxicated heart. "You shall have it!"

How to get it, where to get it, were minor points not worth troubling over. Look at me. Had I not risen, all in one moment, from my nothingness to a height above everything? So shall all things come at my beck and call. I shall get it, get it, get it—there cannot be any doubt.

Thus had I come away from Sandip the other day. Then as I looked about me, where was it—the tree of plenty? Oh, why does this outer world insult the heart so?

And yet get it I must; how, I do not care; for sin there cannot be. Sin taints only the weak; I with my Shakti am beyond its reach. Only a commoner can be a thief, the king conquers and takes his rightful spoil . . . I must find out where the treasury is; who takes the money in; who guards it.

I spent half the night standing in the outer verandah peering at the row of office buildings. But how to get that fifty thousand rupees out of the clutches of those iron bars? If by some *mantram* I could have made all those guards fall dead in their places, I would not have hesitated—so pitiless did I feel!

But while a whole gang of robbers seemed dancing a war-dance within the whirling brain of its Rani, the great house of the Rajas slept in peace. The gong of the watch sounded hour after hour, and the sky overhead placidly looked on.

At last I sent for Amulya.

"Money is wanted for the Cause," I told him. "Can you not get it out of the treasury?"

"Why not?" said he, with his chest thrown out.

Alas! had I not said "Why not?" to Sandip just in the same way? The poor lad's confidence could rouse no hopes in my mind.

"How will you do it?" I asked.

The wild plans he began to unfold would hardly bear repetition outside the pages of a penny dreadful.

"No, Amulya," I said severely, "you must not be childish."

"Very well, then," he said, "let me bribe those watchmen."

"Where is the money to come from?"

"I can loot the bazar," he burst out, without blenching.

"Leave all that alone. I have my ornaments, they will serve."

"But," said Amulya, "it strikes me that the cashier cannot be bribed. Never mind, there is another and simpler way."

"What is that?"

"Why need you hear it? It is quite simple."

"Still, I should like to know."

Amulya fumbled in the pocket of his tunic and pulled out, first a small edition of the Gita, which he placed on the table—and then a little pistol, which he showed me, but said nothing further.

Horror! It did not take him a moment to make up his mind to kill our good old cashier!* To look at his frank, open face one would

---

* The cashier is the official who is most in touch with the ladies of a zamindar's household, directly taking their requisitions for household stores and doing their shopping for them, and so he becomes more a member of the family than the others.—*Translator* not have thought him capable of hurting a fly, but how different were the words which came from his mouth. It was clear that the cashier's place in the world meant nothing real to him; it was a mere vacancy, lifeless, feelingless, with only stock phrases from the Gita—Who kills the body kills naught!

"Whatever do you mean, Amulya?" I exclaimed at length. "Don't you know that the dear old man has got a wife and children and that he is . . ."

"Where are we to find men who have no wives and children?" he interrupted. "Look here, Maharani, the thing we call pity is, at bottom, only pity for ourselves. We cannot bear to wound our own tender instincts, and so we do not strike at all—pity indeed! The height of cowardice!"

To hear Sandip's phrases in the mouth of this mere boy staggered me. So delightfully, lovably immature was he—of that age when the good may still be believed in as good, of that age when one really lives and grows. The Mother in me awoke.

For myself there was no longer good or bad—only death, beautiful alluring death. But to hear this stripling calmly talk of murdering an inoffensive old man as the right thing to do, made me shudder all over. The more clearly I saw that there was no sin in his heart, the more horrible appeared to me the sin of his words. I seemed to see the sin of the parents visited on the innocent child.

The sight of his great big eyes shining with faith and enthusiasm touched me to the quick. He was going, in his fascination, straight to the jaws of the python, from which, once in, there was no return. How was he to be saved? Why does not my country become, for once, a real Mother—clasp him to her bosom and cry out: "Oh, my child, my child, what profits it that you should save me, if so it be that I should fail to save you?"

I know, I know, that all Power on earth waxes great under compact with Satan. But the Mother is there, alone though she be, to contemn and stand against this devil's progress. The Mother cares not for mere success, however great—she wants to give life, to save life. My very soul, today, stretches out its hands in yearning to save this child.

A while ago I suggested robbery to him. Whatever I may now

say against it will be put down to a woman's weakness. They only love our weakness when it drags the world in its toils!

"You need do nothing at all, Amulya, I will see to the money," I told him finally. When he had almost reached the door, I called him back.

"Amulya," said I, "I am your elder sister. Today is not the Brothers' Day* according to the calendar, but all the days in the year are really Brothers' Days. My blessing be with you: may God keep you always."

These unexpected words from my lips took Amulya by surprise. He stood stock-still for a time. Then, coming to himself, he prostrated himself at my feet in acceptance of the relationship and did me reverence. When he rose his eyes were full of tears . . . O little brother mine! I am fast going to my death—let me take all your sin away with me. May no taint from me ever tarnish your innocence!

I said to him: "Let your offering of reverence be that pistol!"

"What do you want with it, sister?"

"I will practise death."

"Right, sister. Our women, also, must know how to die, to deal death!" with which Amulya handed me the pistol. The radiance of his youthful countenance seemed to tinge my life with the touch of a new dawn. I put away the pistol within my clothes. May this reverence-offering be the last resource in my extremity . . .

The door to the mother's chamber in my woman's heart once opened, I thought it would always remain open. But this pathway to the supreme good was closed when the mistress took the place of the mother and locked it again. The very next day I saw Sandip; and madness, naked and rampant, danced upon my heart.

---

* The daughter of the house occupies a place of specially tender affection in a Bengali household (perhaps in Hindu households all over India) because, by dictate of custom, she must be given away in marriage so early. She thus takes corresponding memories with her to her husband's home, where she has to begin as a stranger before she can get into her place. The resulting feeling, of the mistress of her new home for the one she has left, has taken ceremonial form as the Brothers' Day, on which the brothers are invited to the married sisters' houses. Where the sister is the elder, she offers her blessing and receives the brother's reverence, and vice versa. Presents, called the offerings of reverence (or blessing), are exchanged.—*Translator*

What was this? Was this, then, my truer self? Never! I had never before known this shameless, this cruel one within me. The snake-charmer had come, pretending to draw this snake from within the fold of my garment—but it was never there, it was his all the time. Some demon has gained possession of me, and what I am doing today is the play of his activity—it has nothing to do with me.

This demon, in the guise of a god, had come with his ruddy torch to call me that day, saying: "I am your Country. I am your Sandip. I am more to you than anything else of yours. Bande Mataram!" And with folded hands I had responded: "You are my religion. You are my heaven. Whatever else is mine shall be swept away before my love for you. Bande Mataram!"

Five thousand is it? Five thousand it shall be! You want it tomorrow? Tomorrow you shall have it! In this desperate orgy, that gift of five thousand shall be as the foam of wine—and then for the riotous revel! The immovable world shall sway under our feet, fire shall flash from our eyes, a storm shall roar in our ears, what is or is not in front shall become equally dim. And then with tottering footsteps we shall plunge to our death—in a moment all fire will be extinguished, the ashes will be scattered, and nothing will remain behind.

CHAPTER NINE

Bimala's Story

XV

For a time I was utterly at a loss to think of any way of getting that money. Then, the other day, in the light of intense excitement, suddenly the whole picture stood out clear before me.

Every year my husband makes a reverence-offering of six thousand rupees to my sister-in-law at the time of the Durga Puja. Every year it is deposited in her account at the bank in Calcutta. This year the offering was made as usual, but it has not yet been sent to the bank, being kept meanwhile in an iron safe, in a corner of the little dressing room attached to our bedroom.

Every year my husband takes the money to the bank himself. This year he has not yet had an opportunity of going to town. How could I fail to see the hand of Providence in this? The money has been held up because the country wants it—who could have the power to take it away from her to the bank? And how can I have the power to refuse to take the money? The goddess revelling in destruction holds out her blood-cup crying: "Give me drink. I am thirsty." I will give her my own heart's blood with that five thousand rupees. Mother, the loser of that money will scarcely feel the loss, but me you will utterly ruin!

Many a time, in the old days, have I inwardly called the Senior Rani a thief, for I charged her with wheedling money out of my trusting husband. After her husband's death, she often used to make away with things belonging to the estate for her own use. This I used to point out to my husband, but he remained silent. I would get angry and say: "If you feel generous, make gifts by all means, but why allow yourself to be robbed?" Providence must have smiled, then, at these complaints of mine, for tonight I am on the way to rob my husband's safe of my sister-in-law's money. My husband's custom was to let his keys remain in his pockets when he took off his clothes for the night, leaving them in the dressing room. I picked out the key of the safe and opened it. The slight sound it made seemed to wake the whole world! A sudden chill turned my hands and feet icy cold, and I shivered all over.

There was a drawer inside the safe. On opening this I found the money, not in currency notes, but in gold rolled up in paper. I had no time to count out what I wanted. There were twenty rolls, all of which I took and tied up in a corner of my sari.

What a weight it was. The burden of the theft crushed my heart to the dust. Perhaps notes would have made it seem less like thieving, but this was all gold.

After I had stolen into my room like a thief, it felt like my own room no longer. All the most precious rights which I had over it vanished at the touch of my theft. I began to mutter to myself, as though telling mantrams: Bande Mataram, Bande Mataram, my Country, my golden Country, all this gold is for you, for none else!

But in the night the mind is weak. I came back into the bedroom where my husband was asleep, closing my eyes as I passed through, and went off to the open terrace beyond, on which I lay prone, clasping to my breast the end of the sari tied over the gold. And each one of the rolls gave me a shock of pain.

The silent night stood there with forefinger upraised. I could not think of my house as separate from my country: I had robbed my house, I had robbed my country. For this sin my house had ceased to be mine, my country also was estranged from me. Had I died begging for my country, even unsuccessfully, that would have been worship, acceptable to the gods. But theft is never worship—how then can I offer this gold? Ah me! I am doomed to death myself, must I desecrate my country with my impious touch? The way to put the money back is closed to me. I have not the strength to return to the room, take again that key, open once more that safe—I should swoon on the threshold of my husband's door. The only road left now is the road in front. Neither have I the strength deliberately to sit down and count the coins. Let them remain behind their coverings: I cannot calculate.

There was no mist in the winter sky. The stars were shining brightly. If, thought I to myself, as I lay out there, I had to steal these stars one by one, like golden coins, for my country—these stars so carefully stored up in the bosom of the darkness—then the sky would be blinded, the night widowed for ever, and my theft would rob the whole world. But was not also this very thing I had done a robbing of the whole world—not only of money, but of trust, of righteousness?

I spent the night lying on the terrace. When at last it was morning, and I was sure that my husband had risen and left the room, then only with my shawl pulled over my head, could I retrace my steps towards the bedroom.

My sister-in-law was about, with her brass pot, watering her plants. When she saw me passing in the distance she cried: "Have you heard the news, Chota Rani?"

I stopped in silence, all in a tremor. It seemed to me that the rolls of sovereigns were bulging through the shawl. I feared they would burst and scatter in a ringing shower, exposing to all the servants of the house the thief who had made herself destitute by robbing her own wealth.

"Your band of robbers," she went on, "have sent an anonymous message threatening to loot the treasury."

I remained as silent as a thief.

"I was advising Brother Nikhil to seek your protection," she continued banteringly. "Call off your minions, Robber Queen! We will offer sacrifices to your Bande Mataram if you will but save us. What doings there are these days!—but for the Lord's sake, spare our house at least from burglary."

I hastened into my room without reply. I had put my foot on quicksand, and could not now withdraw it. Struggling would only send me down deeper.

If only the time would arrive when I could hand over the money to Sandip! I could bear it no longer, its weight was breaking through my very ribs.

It was still early when I got word that Sandip was awaiting me. Today I had no thought of adornment. Wrapped as I was in my shawl, I went off to the outer apartments. As I entered the sitting room I saw Sandip and Amulya there, together. All my dignity, all my honour, seemed to run tingling through my body from head to foot and vanish into the ground. I should have to lay bare a woman's uttermost shame in sight of this boy! Could they have been discussing my deed in their meeting place? Had any vestige of a veil of decency been left for me?

We women shall never understand men. When they are bent on making a road for some achievement, they think nothing of breaking the heart of the world into pieces to pave it for the progress of their chariot. When they are mad with the intoxication of creating, they rejoice in destroying the creation of the Creator. This heartbreaking shame of mine will not attract even a glance from their eyes. They have no feeling for life itself—all their eagerness is for their object. What am I to them but a meadow flower in the path of a torrent in flood?

What good will this extinction of me be to Sandip? Only five thousand rupees? Was not I good for something more than only five thousand rupees? Yes, indeed! Did I not learn that from Sandip himself, and was I not able in the light of this knowledge to despise all else in my world? I was the giver of light, of life, of Shakti, of immortality—in that belief, in that joy, I had burst all my bounds and come into the open. Had anyone then fulfilled for me that joy, I should have lived in my death. I should have lost nothing in the loss of my all. Do they want to tell me now that all this was false? The psalm of my praise which was sung so devotedly, did it bring me down from my heaven, not to make heaven of earth, but only to level heaven itself with the dust?

XVI

"The money, Queen?" said Sandip with his keen glance full on my face.

Amulya also fixed his gaze on me. Though not my own mother's child, yet the dear lad is brother to me; for mother is mother all the world over. With his guileless face, his gentle eyes, his innocent youth, he looked at me. And I, a woman—of his mother's sex—how could I hand him poison, just because he asked for it?

"The money, Queen!" Sandip's insolent demand rang in my ears. For very shame and vexation I felt I wanted to fling that gold at Sandip's head. I could hardly undo the knot of my sari, my fingers trembled so. At last the paper rolls dropped on the table.

Sandip's face grew black . . . He must have thought that the rolls were of silver . . . What contempt was in his looks. What utter disgust at incapacity. It was almost as if he could have struck me! He must have suspected that I had come to parley with him, to offer to compound his claim for five thousand rupees with a few hundreds. There was a moment when I thought he would snatch up the rolls and throw them out of the window, declaring that he was no beggar, but a king claiming tribute.

"Is that all?" asked Amulya with such pity welling up in his voice that I wanted to sob out aloud. I kept my heart tightly pressed down, and merely nodded my head. Sandip was speechless. He neither touched the rolls, nor uttered a sound.

My humiliation went straight to the boy's heart. With a sudden, feigned enthusiasm he exclaimed: "It's plenty. It will do splendidly. You have saved us." With which he tore open the covering of one of the rolls.

The sovereigns shone out. And in a moment the black covering seemed to be lifted from Sandip's countenance also. His delight beamed forth from his features. Unable to control his sudden revulsion of feeling, he sprang up from his seat towards me. What he intended I know not. I flashed a lightning glance towards Amulya— the colour had left the boy's face as at the stroke of a whip. Then with all my strength I thrust Sandip from me. As he reeled back his head struck the edge of the marble table and he dropped on the floor. There he lay awhile, motionless. Exhausted with my effort, I sank back on my seat.

Amulya's face lightened with a joyful radiance. He did not even turn towards Sandip, but came straight up, took the dust of my feet, and then remained there, sitting on the floor in front of me. O my little brother, my child! This reverence of yours is the last touch of heaven left in my empty world! I could contain myself no longer, and my tears flowed fast. I covered my eyes with the end of my sari, which I pressed to my face with both my hands, and sobbed and sobbed. And every time that I felt on my feet his tender touch trying to comfort me my tears broke out afresh.

After a little, when I had recovered myself and taken my hands from my face, I saw Sandip back at the table, gathering up the sovereigns in his handkerchief, as if nothing had happened. Amulya rose to his seat, from his place near my feet, his wet eyes shining.

Sandip coolly looked up at my face as he remarked: "It is six thousand."

"What do we want with so much, Sandip Babu?" cried Amulya. "Three thousand five hundred is all we need for our work."

"Our wants are not for this one place only," Sandip replied. "We shall want all we can get."

"That may be," said Amulya. "But in future I undertake to get you all you want. Out of this, Sandip Babu, please return the extra two thousand five hundred to the Maharani."

Sandip glanced enquiringly at me.

"No, no," I exclaimed. "I shall never touch that money again. Do with it as you will."

"Can man ever give as woman can?" said Sandip, looking towards Amulya.

"They are goddesses!" agreed Amulya with enthusiasm.

"We men can at best give of our power," continued Sandip. "But women give themselves. Out of their own life they give birth, out of their own life they give sustenance. Such gifts are the only true gifts." Then turning to me, "Queen!" said he, "if what you have given us had been only money I would not have touched it. But you have given that which is more to you than life itself!"

There must be two different persons inside men. One of these in me can understand that Sandip is trying to delude me; the other is content to be deluded. Sandip has power, but no strength of righteousness. The weapon of his which rouses up life smites it again to death. He has the unfailing quiver of the gods, but the shafts in them are of the demons.

Sandip's handkerchief was not large enough to hold all the coins. "Queen," he asked, "can you give me another?"

When I gave him mine, he reverently touched his forehead with it, and then suddenly kneeling on the floor he made me an obeisance. "Goddess!" he said, "it was to offer my reverence that I had approached you, but you repulsed me, and rolled me in the dust. Be it so, I accept your repulse as your boon to me, I raise it to my head in salutation!" with which he pointed to the place where he had been hurt.

Had I then misunderstood him? Could it be that his outstretched hands had really been directed towards my feet? Yet, surely, even Amulya had seen the passion that flamed out of his eyes, his face. But Sandip is such an adept in setting music to his chant of praise that I cannot argue; I lose my power of seeing truth; my sight is clouded over like an opium-eater's eyes. And so, after all, he gave me back twice as much in return for the blow I had dealt him—the wound on his head ended by making me bleed at heart. When I had received Sandip's obeisance my theft seemed to gain a dignity, and the gold glittering on the table to smile away all fear of disgrace, all stings of conscience.

Like me Amulya also was won back. His devotion to Sandip, which had suffered a momentary check, blazed up anew. The flower vase of his mind filled once more with offerings for the worship of Sandip and me. His simple faith shone out of his eyes with the pure light of the morning star at dawn.

After I had offered worship and received worship my sin became radiant. And as Amulya looked on my face he raised his folded hands in salutation and cried Bande Mataram! I cannot expect to have this adoration surrounding me forever; and yet this has come to be the only means of keeping alive my self-respect.

I can no longer enter my bedroom. The bedstead seems to thrust out a forbidding hand, the iron safe frowns at me. I want to get away from this continual insult to myself which is rankling within me. I want to keep running to Sandip to hear him sing my praises. There is just this one little altar of worship which has kept its head above the all-pervading depths of my dishonour, and so I want to cleave to it night and day; for on whichever side I step away from it, there is only emptiness.

Praise, praise, I want unceasing praise. I cannot live if my wine-cup be left empty for a single moment. So, as the very price of my life, I want Sandip of all the world, today.

XVII

When my husband nowadays comes in for his meals I feel I cannot sit before him; and yet it is such a shame not to be near him that I feel I cannot do that either. So I seat myself where we cannot look at each other's face. That was how I was sitting the other day when the Bara Rani came and joined us.

"It is all very well for you, brother," said she, "to laugh away these threatening letters. But they do frighten me so. Have you sent off that money you gave me to the Calcutta bank?"

"No, I have not yet had the time to get it away," my husband replied.

"You are so careless, brother dear, you had better look out . . ."

"But it is in the iron safe right inside the inner dressing room," said my husband with a reassuring smile.

"What if they get in there? You can never tell!"

"If they go so far, they might as well carry you off too!"

"Don't you fear, no one will come for poor me. The real attraction is in your room! But joking apart, don't run the risk of keeping money in the room like that."

"They will be taking along the Government revenue to Calcutta in a few days now; I will send this money to the bank under the same escort."

"Very well. But see you don't forget all about it, you are so absent-minded."

"Even if that money gets lost, while in my room, the loss cannot be yours, Sister Rani."

"Now, now, brother, you will make me very angry if you talk in that way. Was I making any difference between yours and mine? What if your money is lost, does not that hurt me? If Providence has thought fit to take away my all, it has not left me insensible to the value of the most devoted brother known since the days of Lakshman."*

"Well, Junior Rani, are you turned into a wooden doll? You have not spoken a word yet. Do you know, brother, our Junior Rani thinks I try to flatter you. If things came to that pass I should not hesitate to do so, but I know my dear old brother does not need it!"

Thus the Senior Rani chattered on, not forgetting now and then to draw her brother's attention to this or that special delicacy amongst the dishes that were being served. My head was all the time in a whirl. The crisis was fast coming. Something must be done about replacing that money. And as I kept asking myself what could be done, and how it was to be done, the unceasing patter of my sister-in-law's words seemed more and more intolerable.

What made it all the worse was, that nothing could escape my sister-in-law's keen eyes. Every now and then she was casting side glances towards me. What she could read in my face I do not know, but to me it seemed that everything was written there only too plainly.

Then I did an infinitely rash thing. Affecting an easy, amused laugh I said: "All the Senior Rani's suspicions, I see, are reserved for me—her fears of thieves and robbers are only a feint."

The Senior Rani smiled mischievously. "You are right, sister mine. A woman's theft is the most fatal of all thefts. But how can you elude my watchfulness? Am I a man, that you should hoodwink me?"

"If you fear me so," I retorted, "let me keep in your hands all I have, as security. If I cause you loss, you can then repay yourself."

"Just listen to her, our simple little Junior Rani!" she laughed back, turning to my husband. "Does she not know that there are losses which no security can make good, either in this world or in the next?"

My husband did not join in our exchange of words. When he

---

* Of the Ramayana. The story of his devotion to his elder brother Rama and his brother's wife Sita, has become a byword.

had finished, he went off to the outer apartments, for nowadays he does not take his mid-day rest in our room.

All my more valuable jewels were in deposit in the treasury in charge of the cashier. Still what I kept with me must have been worth thirty or forty thousand. I took my jewel-box to the Bara Rani's room and opened it out before her, saying: "I leave these with you, sister. They will keep you quite safe from all worry."

The Bara Rani made a gesture of mock despair. "You positively astound me, Chota Rani!" she said. "Do you really suppose I spend sleepless nights for fear of being robbed by you?"

"What harm if you did have a wholesome fear of me? Does anybody know anybody else in this world?"

"You want to teach me a lesson by trusting me? No, no! I am bothered enough to know what to do with my own jewels, without keeping watch over yours. Take them away, there's a dear, so many prying servants are about."

I went straight from my sister-in-law's room to the sitting room outside, and sent for Amulya. With him Sandip came along too. I was in a great hurry, and said to Sandip: "If you don't mind, I want to have a word or two with Amulya. Would you . . ."

Sandip smiled a wry smile. "So Amulya and I are separate in your eyes? If you have set about to wean him from me, I must confess I have no power to retain him."

I made no reply, but stood waiting.

"Be it so," Sandip went on. "Finish your special talk with Amulya. But then you must give me a special talk all to myself too, or it will mean a defeat for me. I can stand everything, but not defeat. My share must always be the lion's share. This has been my constant quarrel with Providence. I will defeat the Dispenser of my fate, but not take defeat at his hands." With a crushing look at Amulya, Sandip walked out of the room.

"Amulya, my own little brother, you must do one thing for me," I said.

"I will stake my life for whatever duty you may lay on me, sister."

I brought out my jewel-box from the folds of my shawl and placed it before him. "Sell or pawn these," I said, "and get me six thousand rupees as fast as ever you can."

"No, no, Sister Rani," said Amulya, touched to the quick. "Let these jewels be. I will get you six thousand all the same."

"Oh, don't be silly," I said impatiently. "There is no time for any nonsense. Take this box. Get away to Calcutta by the night train. And bring me the money by the day after tomorrow positively."

Amulya took a diamond necklace out of the box, held it up to the light and put it back gloomily.

"I know," I told him, "that you will never get the proper price for these diamonds, so I am giving you jewels worth about thirty thousand. I don't care if they all go, but I must have that six thousand without fail."

"Do you know, Sister Rani," said Amulya, "I have had a quarrel with Sandip Babu over that six thousand rupees he took from you? I cannot tell you how ashamed I felt. But Sandip Babu would have it that we must give up even our shame for the country. That may be so. But this is somehow different. I do not fear to die for the country, to kill for the country—that much Shakti has been given me. But I cannot forget the shame of having taken money from you. There Sandip Babu is ahead of me. He has no regrets or compunctions. He says we must get rid of the idea that the money belongs to the one in whose box it happens to be—if we cannot, where is the magic of Bande Mataram?"

Amulya gathered enthusiasm as he talked on. He always warms up when he has me for a listener. "The Gita tells us," he continued, "that no one can kill the soul. Killing is a mere word. So also is the taking away of money. Whose is the money? No one has created it. No one can take it away with him when he departs this life, for it is no part of his soul. Today it is mine, tomorrow my son's, the next day his creditor's. Since, in fact, money belongs to no one, why should any blame attach to our patriots if, instead of leaving it for some worthless son, they take it for their own use?"

When I hear Sandip's words uttered by this boy, I tremble all over. Let those who are snake-charmers play with snakes; if harm comes to them, they are prepared for it. But these boys are so innocent, all the world is ready with its blessing to protect them. They play with a snake not knowing its nature, and when we see them smilingly, trustfully, putting their hands within reach of its fangs, then we understand how terribly dangerous the snake is. Sandip is right when he suspects that though I, for myself, may be ready to die at his hands, this boy I shall wean from him and save.

"So the money is wanted for the use of your patriots?" I questioned with a smile.

"Of course it is!" said Amulya proudly. "Are they not our kings? Poverty takes away from their regal power. Do you know, we always insist on Sandip Babu travelling First Class? He never shirks kingly honours—he accepts them not for himself, but for the glory of us all. The greatest weapon of those who rule the world, Sandip Babu has told us, is the hypnotism of their display. To take the vow of poverty would be for them not merely a penance—it would mean suicide."

At this point Sandip noiselessly entered the room. I threw my shawl over the jewel-case with a rapid movement.

"The special-talk business not yet over?" he asked with a sneer in his tone.

"Yes, we've quite finished," said Amulya apologetically. "It was nothing much."

"No, Amulya," I said, "we have not quite finished."

"So exit Sandip for the second time, I suppose?" said Sandip.

"If you please."

"And as to Sandip's re-entry."

"Not today. I have no time."

"I see!" said Sandip as his eyes flashed. "No time to waste, only for special talks!"

Jealousy! Where the strong man shows weakness, there the weaker sex cannot help beating her drums of victory. So I repeated firmly: "I really have no time."

Sandip went away looking black. Amulya was greatly perturbed. "Sister Rani," he pleaded, "Sandip Babu is annoyed."

"He has neither cause nor right to be annoyed," I said with some vehemence. "Let me caution you about one thing, Amulya. Say nothing to Sandip Babu about the sale of my jewels—on your life."

"No, I will not."

"Then you had better not delay any more. You must get away by tonight's train."

Amulya and I left the room together. As we came out on the verandah Sandip was standing there. I could see he was waiting to waylay Amulya. To prevent that I had to engage him. "What is it you wanted to tell me, Sandip Babu?" I asked.

"I have nothing special to say—mere small talk. And since you have not the time . . ."

"I can give you just a little."

By this time Amulya had left. As we entered the room Sandip asked: "What was that box Amulya carried away?"

The box had not escaped his eyes. I remained firm. "If I could have told you, it would have been made over to him in your presence!"

"So you think Amulya will not tell me?"

"No, he will not."

Sandip could not conceal his anger any longer. "You think you will gain the mastery over me?" he blazed out. "That shall never be. Amulya, there, would die a happy death if I deigned to trample him under foot. I will never, so long as I live, allow you to bring him to your feet!"

Oh, the weak! the weak! At last Sandip has realised that he is weak before me! That is why there is this sudden outburst of anger. He has understood that he cannot meet the power that I wield, with mere strength. With a glance I can crumble his strongest fortifications. So he must needs resort to bluster. I simply smiled in contemptuous silence. At last have I come to a level above him. I must never lose this vantage ground; never descend lower again. Amidst all my degradation this bit of dignity must remain to me!

"I know," said Sandip, after a pause, "it was your jewel-case."

"You may guess as you please," said I, "but you will get nothing out of me.

"So you trust Amulya more than you trust me? Do you know that the boy is the shadow of my shadow, the echo of my echo—that he is nothing if I am not at his side?"

"Where he is not your echo, he is himself, Amulya. And that is where I trust him more than I can trust your echo!"

"You must not forget that you are under a promise to render up all your ornaments to me for the worship of the Divine Mother. In fact your offering has already been made."

"Whatever ornaments the gods leave to me will be offered up to the gods. But how can I offer those which have been stolen away from me?"

"Look here, it is no use your trying to give me the slip in that fashion. Now is the time for grim work. Let that work be finished, then you can make a display of your woman's wiles to your heart's content—and I will help you in your game."

The moment I had stolen my husband's money and paid it to Sandip, the music that was in our relations stopped. Not only did I destroy all my own value by making myself cheap, but Sandip's powers, too, lost scope for their full play. You cannot employ your marksmanship against a thing which is right in your grasp. So Sandip has lost his aspect of the hero; a tone of low quarrelsomeness has come into his words.

Sandip kept his brilliant eyes fixed full on my face till they seemed to blaze with all the thirst of the mid-day sky. Once or twice he fidgeted with his feet, as though to leave his seat, as if to spring right on me. My whole body seemed to swim, my veins throbbed, the hot blood surged up to my ears; I felt that if I remained there, I should never get up at all. With a supreme effort I tore myself off the chair, and hastened towards the door.

From Sandip's dry throat there came a muffled cry: "Whither would you flee, Queen?" The next moment he left his seat with a bound to seize hold of me. At the sound of footsteps outside the door, however, he rapidly retreated and fell back into his chair. I checked my steps near the bookshelf, where I stood staring at the names of the books.

As my husband entered the room, Sandip exclaimed: "I say, Nikhil, don't you keep Browning among your books here? I was just telling Queen Bee of our college club. Do you remember that contest of ours over the translation of those lines from Browning? You don't?

> She should never have looked at me,
> If she meant I should not love her,
> There are plenty . . . men you call such,
> I suppose . . . she may discover

All her soul to, if she pleases,
And yet leave much as she found them:
But I'm not so, and she knew it
When she fixed me, glancing round them.

"I managed to get together the words to render it into Bengali,
somehow, but the result was hardly likely to be a 'joy forever' to the
people of Bengal. I really did think at one time that I was on the
verge of becoming a poet, but Providence was kind enough to save
me from that disaster. Do you remember old Dakshina? If he had
not become a Salt Inspector, he would have been a poet. I remember
his rendering to this day . . .

"No, Queen Bee, it is no use rummaging those bookshelves.
Nikhil has ceased to read poetry since his marriage—perhaps he has
no further need for it. But I suppose 'the fever fit of poesy,' as the
Sanskrit has it, is about to attack me again."

"I have come to give you a warning, Sandip," said my husband.

"About the fever fit of poesy?"

My husband took no notice of this attempt at humour. "For
some time," he continued, "Mahomedan preachers have been about
stirring up the local Mussulmans. They are all wild with you, and
may attack you any moment."

"Are you come to advise flight?"

"I have come to give you information, not to offer advice."

"Had these estates been mine, such a warning would have been
necessary for the preachers, not for me. If, instead of trying to
frighten me, you give them a taste of your intimidation, that would
be worthier both of you and me. Do you know that your weakness
is weakening your neighbouring zamindars also?"

"I did not offer you my advice, Sandip. I wish you, too, would
refrain from giving me yours. Besides, it is useless. And there is
another thing I want to tell you. You and your followers have been
secretly worrying and oppressing my tenantry. I cannot allow that
any longer. So I must ask you to leave my territory."

"For fear of the Mussulmans, or is there any other fear you have
to threaten me with?"

"There are fears the want of which is cowardice. In the name of those fears, I tell you, Sandip, you must go. In five days I shall be starting for Calcutta. I want you to accompany me. You may of course stay in my house there—to that there is no objection."

"All right, I have still five day's time then. Meanwhile, Queen Bee, let me hum to you my song of parting from your honey-hive. Ah! you poet of modern Bengal! Throw open your doors and let me plunder your words. The theft is really yours, for it is my song which you have made your own—let the name be yours by all means, but the song is mine." With this Sandip struck up in a deep, husky voice, which threatened to be out of tune, a song in the *Bhairavi* mode:

> *In the springtime of your kingdom, my Queen,*
> *Meetings and partings chase each other in their endless hide and seek,*
> *And flowers blossom in the wake of those that droop and die in the*
> *   shade.*
> *In the springtime of your kingdom, my Queen,*
> *My meeting with you had its own songs,*
> *But has not also my leave-taking any gift to offer you?*
> *That gift is my secret hope, which I keep hidden in the shadows of*
> *   your flower garden,*
> *That the rains of July may sweetly temper your fiery June.*

His boldness was immense—boldness which had no veil, but was naked as fire. One finds no time to stop it: it is like trying to resist a thunderbolt: the lightning flashes: it laughs at all resistance.

I left the room. As I was passing along the verandah towards the inner apartments, Amulya suddenly made his appearance and came and stood before me.

"Fear nothing, Sister Rani," he said. "I am off tonight and shall not return unsuccessful."

"Amulya," said I, looking straight into his earnest, youthful face, "I fear nothing for myself, but may I never cease to fear for you."

Amulya turned to go, but before he was out of sight I called him back and asked: "Have you a mother, Amulya?"

"I have."

"A sister?"

"No, I am the only child of my mother. My father died when I was quite little."

"Then go back to your mother, Amulya."

"But, Sister Rani, I have now both mother and sister."

"Then, Amulya, before you leave tonight, come and have your dinner here."

"There won't be time for that. Let me take some food for the journey, consecrated with your touch."

"What do you specially like, Amulya?" "If I had been with my mother I should have had lots of *Poush* cakes. Make some for me with your own hands, Sister Rani!"

CHAPTER TEN

Nikhil's Story

XII

I learnt from my master that Sandip had joined forces with Harish Kundu, and there was to be a grand celebration of the worship of the demon-destroying Goddess. Harish Kundu was extorting the expenses from his tenantry. Pandits Kaviratna and Vidyavagish had been commissioned to compose a hymn with a double meaning.

My master has just had a passage at arms with Sandip over this. "Evolution is at work amongst the gods as well," says Sandip. "The grandson has to remodel the gods created by the grandfather to suit his own taste, or else he is left an atheist. It is my mission to modernize the ancient deities. I am born the saviour of the gods, to emancipate them from the thraldom of the past."

I have seen from our boyhood what a juggler with ideas is Sandip. He has no interest in discovering truth, but to make a quizzical display of it rejoices his heart. Had he been born in the wilds of Africa he would have spent a glorious time inventing argument after argument to prove that cannibalism is the best means of promoting true communion between man and man. But those who deal in delusion end by deluding themselves, and I fully believe that, each time Sandip creates a new fallacy, he persuades himself that he has found the truth, however contradictory his creations may be to one another.

However, I shall not give a helping hand to establish a liquor distillery in my country. The young men, who are ready to offer their services for their country's cause, must not fall into this habit of getting intoxicated. The people who want to exact work by drugging methods set more value on the excitement than on the minds they intoxicate.

I had to tell Sandip, in Bimala's presence, that he must go. Perhaps both will impute to me the wrong motive. But I must free myself also from all fear of being misunderstood. Let even Bimala misunderstand me . . .

A number of Mahomedan preachers are being sent over from Dacca. The Mussulmans in my territory had come to have almost as much of an aversion to the killing of cows as the Hindus. But now cases of cow-killing are cropping up here and there. I had the news first from some of my Mussulman tenants with expressions of their disapproval. Here was a situation which I could see would be difficult to meet. At the bottom was a pretence of fanaticism, which would cease to be a pretence if obstructed. That is just where the ingenuity of the move came in!

I sent for some of my principal Hindu tenants and tried to get them to see the matter in its proper light. "We can be staunch in our own convictions," I said, "but we have no control over those of others. For all that many of us are Vaishnavas, those of us who are Shaktas go on with their animal sacrifices just the same. That cannot be helped. We must, in the same way, let the Mussulmans do as they think best. So please refrain from all disturbance."

"Maharaja," they replied, "these outrages have been unknown for so long."

"That was so," I said, "because such was their spontaneous desire. Let us behave in such a way that the same may become true, over again. But a breach of the peace is not the way to bring this about."

"No, Maharaja," they insisted, "those good old days are gone. This will never stop unless you put it down with a strong hand."

"Oppression," I replied, "will not only not prevent cow-killing, it may lead to the killing of men as well."

One of them had had an English education. He had learnt to

repeat the phrases of the day. "It is not only a question of orthodoxy," he argued. "Our country is mainly agricultural, and cows are . . ."

"Buffaloes in this country," I interrupted, "likewise give milk and are used for ploughing. And therefore, so long as we dance frantic dances on our temple pavements, smeared with their blood, their severed heads carried on our shoulders, religion will only laugh at us if we quarrel with Mussulmans in her name, and nothing but the quarrel itself will remain true. If the cow alone is to be held sacred from slaughter, and not the buffalo, then that is bigotry, not religion."

"But are you not aware, sir, of what is behind all this?" pursued the English-knowing tenant. "This has only become possible because the Mussulman is assured of safety, even if he breaks the law. Have you not heard of the Pachur case?"

"Why is it possible," I asked, "to use the Mussulmans thus, as tools against us? Is it not because we have fashioned them into such with our own intolerance? That is how Providence punishes us. Our accumulated sins are being visited on our own heads."

"Oh, well, if that be so, let them be visited on us. But we shall have our revenge. We have undermined what was the greatest strength of the authorities, their devotion to their own laws. Once they were truly kings, dispensing justice; now they themselves will become law-breakers, and so no better than robbers. This may not go down to history, but we shall carry it in our hearts for all time . . ."

The evil reports about me which are spreading from paper to paper are making me notorious. News comes that my effigy has been burnt at the riverside burning-ground of the Chakravartis, with due ceremony and enthusiasm; and other insults are in contemplation. The trouble was that they had come to ask me to take shares in a Cotton Mill they wanted to start. I had to tell them that I did not so much mind the loss of my own money, but I would not be a party to causing a loss to so many poor shareholders.

"Are we to understand, Maharaja," said my visitors, "that the prosperity of the country does not interest you?"

"Industry may lead to the country's prosperity," I explained, "but a mere desire for its prosperity will not make for success in industry. Even when our heads were cool, our industries did not flourish. Why should we suppose that they will do so just because we have become frantic?"

"Why not say plainly that you will not risk your money?"

"I will put in my money when I see that it is industry which prompts you. But, because you have lighted a fire, it does not follow that you have the food to cook over it."

XIII

What is this? Our Chakua sub-treasury looted! A remittance of seven thousand five hundred rupees was due from there to headquarters. The local cashier had changed the cash at the Government Treasury into small currency notes for convenience in carrying, and had kept them ready in bundles. In the middle of the night an armed band had raided the room, and wounded Kasim, the man on guard. The curious part of it was that they had taken only six thousand rupees and left the rest scattered on the floor, though it would have been as easy to carry that away also. Anyhow, the raid of the dacoits was over; now the police raid would begin. Peace was out of the question.

When I went inside, I found the news had travelled before me. "What a terrible thing, brother," exclaimed the Bara Rani. "Whatever shall we do?"

I made light of the matter to reassure her. "We still have something left," I said with a smile. "We shall manage to get along somehow."

"Don't joke about it, brother dear. Why are they all so angry with you? Can't you humour them? Why put everybody out?"

"I cannot let the country go to rack and ruin, even if that would please everybody."

"That was a shocking thing they did at the burning-grounds. It's a horrid shame to treat you so. The Chota Rani has got rid of all her fears by dint of the Englishwoman's teaching, but as for me, I had to send for the priest to avert the omen before I could get any peace of mind. For my sake, dear, do get away to Calcutta. I tremble to think what they may do, if you stay on here."

My sister-in-law's genuine anxiety touched me deeply.

"And, brother," she went on, "did I not warn you, it was not well to keep so much money in your room? They might get wind of it any day. It is not the money—but who knows . . ."

To calm her I promised to remove the money to the treasury at once, and then get it away to Calcutta with the first escort going. We went together to my bedroom. The dressing room door was shut. When I knocked, Bimala called out: "I am dressing."

"I wonder at the Chota Rani," exclaimed my sister-in-law, "dressing so early in the day! One of their Bande Mataram meetings, I suppose. Robber Queen!" she called out in jest to Bimala. "Are you counting your spoils inside?"

"I will attend to the money a little later," I said, as I came away to my office room outside.

I found the Police Inspector waiting for me. "Any trace of the dacoits?" I asked.

"I have my suspicions."

"On whom?"

"Kasim, the guard."

"Kasim? But was he not wounded?"

"A mere nothing. A flesh wound on the leg. Probably self-inflicted."

"But I cannot bring myself to believe it. He is such a trusted servant."

"You may have trusted him, but that does not prevent his being a thief. Have I not seen men trusted for twenty years together, suddenly developing . . ."

"Even if it were so, I could not send him to gaol. But why should he have left the rest of the money lying about?"

"To put us off the scent. Whatever you may say, Maharaja, he must be an old hand at the game. He mounts guard during his watch, right enough, but I feel sure he has a finger in all the dacoities going on in the neighbourhood."

With this the Inspector proceeded to recount the various methods by which it was possible to be concerned in a dacoity twenty or thirty miles away, and yet be back in time for duty.

"Have you brought Kasim here?" I asked.

"No," was the reply, "he is in the lock-up. The Magistrate is due for the investigation."

"I want to see him," I said.

When I went to his cell he fell at my feet, weeping. "In God's name," he said, "I swear I did not do this thing."

"I do not doubt you, Kasim," I assured him. "Fear nothing. They can do nothing to you, if you are innocent."

Kasim, however, was unable to give a coherent account of the incident. He was obviously exaggerating. Four or five hundred men, big guns, numberless swords, figured in his narrative. It must have been either his disturbed state of mind or a desire to account for his easy defeat. He would have it that this was Harish Kundu's doing; he was even sure he had heard the voice of Ekram, the head retainer of the Kundus.

"Look here, Kasim," I had to warn him, "don't you be dragging other people in with your stories. You are not called upon to make out a case against Harish Kundu, or anybody else."

XIV

On returning home I asked my master to come over. He shook his head gravely. "I see no good in this," said he—"this setting aside of conscience and putting the country in its place. All the sins of the country will now break out, hideous and unashamed."

"Who do you think could have . . ."

"Don't ask me. But sin is rampant. Send them all away, right away from here."

"I have given them one more day. They will be leaving the day after tomorrow."

"And another thing. Take Bimala away to Calcutta. She is getting too narrow a view of the outside world from here, she cannot see men and things in their true proportions. Let her see the world— men and their work—give her abroad vision."

"That is exactly what I was thinking."

"Well, don't make any delay about it. I tell you, Nikhil, man's history has to be built by the united effort of all the races in the world, and therefore this selling of conscience for political reasons— this making a fetish of one's country, won't do. I know that Europe does not at heart admit this, but there she has not the right to pose as our teacher. Men who die for the truth become immortal: and, if a whole people can die for the truth, it will also achieve immortality in the history of humanity. Here, in this land of India, amid the mocking laughter of Satan piercing the sky, may the feeling for this truth become real! What a terrible epidemic of sin has been brought into our country from foreign lands . . ."

The whole day passed in the turmoil of investigation. I was tired out when I retired for the night. I left over sending my sister-in-law's money to the treasury till next morning.

I woke up from my sleep at dead of night. The room was dark. I thought I heard a moaning somewhere. Somebody must have been crying. Sounds of sobbing came heavy with tears like fitful gusts of wind in the rainy night. It seemed to me that the cry rose from the heart of my room itself. I was alone. For some days Bimala had her bed in another room adjoining mine. I rose up and when I went out I found her in the balcony lying prone upon her face on the bare floor.

This is something that cannot be written in words. He only knows it who sits in the bosom of the world and receives all its pangs in His own heart. The sky is dumb, the stars are mute, the night is still, and in the midst of it all that one sleepless cry!

We give these sufferings names, bad or good, according to the classifications of the books, but this agony which is welling up from a torn heart, pouring into the fathomless dark, has it any name? When in that midnight, standing under the silent stars, I looked upon that figure, my mind was struck with awe, and I said to myself: "Who am I to judge her?" O life, O death, O God of the infinite existence, I bow my head in silence to the mystery which is in you.

Once I thought I should turn back. But I could not. I sat down on the ground near Bimala and placed my hand on her head. At the first touch her whole body seemed to stiffen, but the next moment the hardness gave way, and the tears burst out. I gently passed my fingers over her forehead. Suddenly her hands groping for my feet grasped them and drew them to herself, pressing them against her breast with such force that I thought her heart would break.

Bimala's Story

XVIII

Amulya is due to return from Calcutta this morning. I told the servants to let me know as soon as he arrived, but could not keep still. At last I went outside to await him in the sitting room.

When I sent him off to sell the jewels I must have been thinking only of myself. It never even crossed my mind that so young a boy, trying to sell such valuable jewellery, would at once be suspected. So helpless are we women, we needs must place on others the burden of our danger. When we go to our death we drag down those who are about us.

I had said with pride that I would save Amulya—as if she who was drowning could save others. But instead of saving him, I have sent him to his doom. My little brother, such a sister have I been to you that Death must have smiled on that Brothers' Day when I gave you my blessing—I, who wander distracted with the burden of my own evil-doing.

I feel today that man is at times attacked with evil as with the plague. Some germ finds its way in from somewhere, and then in the space of one night Death stalks in. Why cannot the stricken one be kept far away from the rest of the world? I, at least, have realised how terrible is the contagion—like a fiery torch which burns that it may set the world on fire.

It struck nine. I could not get rid of the idea that Amulya was in trouble, that he had fallen into the clutches of the police. There must be great excitement in the Police Office—whose are the jewels?— where did he get them? And in the end I shall have to furnish the answer, in public, before all the world.

What is that answer to be? Your day has come at last, Bara Rani, you whom I have so long despised. You, in the shape of the public, the world, will have your revenge. O God, save me this time, and I will cast all my pride at my sister-in-law's feet.

I could bear it no longer. I went straight to the Bara Rani. She was in the verandah, spicing her betel leaves, Thako at her side. The sight of Thako made me shrink back for a moment, but I overcame all hesitation, and making a low obeisance I took the dust of my elder sister-in-law's feet.

"Bless my soul, Chota Rani," she exclaimed, "what has come upon you? Why this sudden reverence?"

"It is my birthday, sister," said I. "I have caused you pain. Give me your blessing today that I may never do so again. My mind is so small." I repeated my obeisance and left her hurriedly, but she called me back.

"You never before told me that this was your birthday, Chotie darling! Be sure to come and have lunch with me this afternoon. You positively must."

O God, let it really be my birthday today. Can I not be born over again? Cleanse me, my God, and purify me and give me one more trial!

I went again to the sitting room to find Sandip there. A feeling of disgust seemed to poison my very blood. The face of his, which I saw in the morning light, had nothing of the magic radiance of genius.

"Will you leave the room," I blurted out.

Sandip smiled. "Since Amulya is not here," he remarked, "I should think my turn had come for a special talk."

My fate was coming back upon me. How was I to take away the right I myself had given? "I would be alone," I repeated.

"Queen," he said, "the presence of another person does not prevent your being alone. Do not mistake me for one of the crowd. I, Sandip, am always alone, even when surrounded by thousands."

"Please come some other time. This morning I am . . ."

"Waiting for Amulya?"

I turned to leave the room for sheer vexation, when Sandip drew out from the folds of his cloak that jewel-casket of mine and banged it down on the marble table. I was thoroughly startled. "Has not Amulya gone, then?" I exclaimed.

"Gone where?"

"To Calcutta?"

"No," chuckled Sandip.

Ah, then my blessing had come true, in spite of all. He was saved. Let God's punishment fall on me, the thief, if only Amulya be safe.

The change in my countenance roused Sandip's scorn. "So pleased, Queen!" sneered he. "Are these jewels so very precious? How then did you bring yourself to offer them to the Goddess? Your gift was actually made. Would you now take it back?"

Pride dies hard and raises its fangs to the last. It was clear to me I must show Sandip I did not care a rap about these jewels. "If they have excited your greed," I said, "you may have them."

"My greed today embraces the wealth of all Bengal," replied Sandip. "Is there a greater force than greed? It is the steed of the great ones of the earth, as is the elephant, Airauat, the steed of Indra. So then these jewels are mine?"

As Sandip took up and replaced the casket under his cloak, Amulya rushed in. There were dark rings under his eyes, his lips were dry, his hair tumbled: the freshness of his youth seemed to have withered in a single day. Pangs gripped my heart as I looked on him.

"My box!" he cried, as he went straight up to Sandip without a glance at me. "Have you taken that jewel-box from my trunk?"

"Your jewel-box?" mocked Sandip.

"It was my trunk!" Sandip burst out into a laugh. "Your distinctions between mine and yours are getting rather thin, Amulya," he cried. "You will die a religious preacher yet, I see."

Amulya sank on a chair with his face in his hands. I went up to him and placing my hand on his head asked him: "What is your trouble, Amulya?"

He stood straight up as he replied: "I had set my heart, Sister Rani, on returning your jewels to you with my own hand. Sandip Babu knew this, but he forestalled me."

"What do I care for my jewels?" I said. "Let them go. No harm is done.

"Go? Where?" asked the mystified boy.

"The jewels are mine," said Sandip. "Insignia bestowed on me by my Queen!"

"No, no, no," broke out Amulya wildly. "Never, Sister Rani! I brought them back for you. You shall not give them away to anybody else."

"I accept your gift, my little brother," said I. "But let him, who hankers after them, satisfy his greed."

Amulya glared at Sandip like a beast of prey, as he growled: "Look here, Sandip Babu, you know that even hanging has no terrors for me. If you dare take away that box of jewels . . ."

With an attempt at a sarcastic laugh Sandip said: "You also ought to know by this time, Amulya, that I am not the man to be afraid of you."

"Queen Bee," he went on, turning to me, "I did not come here today to take these jewels, I came to give them to you. You would have done wrong to take my gift at Amulya's hands. In order to prevent it, I had first to make them clearly mine. Now these my jewels are my gift to you. Here they are! Patch up any understanding with this boy you like. I must go. You have been at your special talks all these days together, leaving me out of them. If special happenings now come to pass, don't blame me.

"Amulya," he continued, "I have sent on your trunks and things to your lodgings. Don't you be keeping any belongings of yours in my room any longer." With this parting shot, Sandip flung out of the room.

XIX

"I have had no peace of mind, Amulya," I said to him, "ever since I sent you off to sell my jewels."

"Why, Sister Rani?"

"I was afraid lest you should get into trouble with them, lest they should suspect you for a thief. I would rather go without that six thousand. You must now do another thing for me—go home at once, home to your mother."

Amulya produced a small bundle and said: "But, sister, I have got the six thousand."

"Where from?"

"I tried hard to get gold," he went on, without replying to my question, "but could not. So I had to bring it in notes."

"Tell me truly, Amulya, swear by me, where did you get this money?"

"That I will not tell you."

Everything seemed to grow dark before my eyes. "What terrible thing have you done, Amulya?" I cried. "Is it then . . ."

"I know you will say I got this money wrongly. Very well, I admit it. But I have paid the full price for my wrongdoing. So now the money is mine."

I no longer had any desire to learn more about it. My very blood vessels contracted, making my whole body shrink within itself.

"Take it away, Amulya," I implored. "Put it back where you got it from."

"That would be hard indeed!"

"It is not hard, brother dear. It was an evil moment when you first came to me. Even Sandip has not been able to harm you as I have done."

Sandip's name seemed to stab him.

"Sandip!" he cried. "It was you alone who made me come to know that man for what he is. Do you know, sister, he has not spent a pice out of those sovereigns he took from you? He shut himself into his room, after he left you, and gloated over the gold, pouring it out in a heap on the floor. 'This is not money,' he exclaimed, 'but the petals of the divine lotus of power; crystallized strains of music from the pipes that play in the paradise of wealth! I cannot find it in my heart to change them, for they seem longing to fulfil their destiny of adorning the neck of Beauty. Amulya, my boy, don't you look at these with your fleshly eye, they are Lakshmi's smile, the gracious radiance of Indra's queen. No, no, I can't give them up to that boor of a manager. I am sure, Amulya, he was telling us lies. The police haven't traced the man who sank that boat. It's the manager who wants to make something out of it. We must get those letters back from him.'

"I asked him how we were to do this; he told me to use force or threats. I offered to do so if he would return the gold. That, he said, we could consider later. I will not trouble you, sister, with all I did to frighten the man into giving up those letters and burn them—it is a long story. That very night I came to Sandip and said: 'We are now safe. Let me have the sovereigns to return them tomorrow to my sister, the Maharani.' But he cried, 'What infatuation is this of yours?

Your precious sister's skirt bids fair to hide the whole country from you. Say Bande Mataram and exorcize the evil spirit.'

"You know, Sister Rani, the power of Sandip's magic. The gold remained with him. And I spent the whole dark night on the bathing-steps of the lake muttering Bande Mataram.

"Then when you gave me your jewels to sell, I went again to Sandip. I could see he was angry with me. But he tried not to show it. 'If I still have them hoarded up in any box of mine you may take them,' said he, as he flung me his keys. They were nowhere to be seen. 'Tell me where they are,' I said. 'I will do so,' he replied, 'when I find your infatuation has left you. Not now.'

"When I found I could not move him, I had to employ other methods. Then I tried to get the sovereigns from him in exchange for my currency notes for six thousand rupees. 'You shall have them,' he said, and disappeared into his bedroom, leaving me waiting outside. There he broke open my trunk and came straight to you with your casket through some other passage. He would not let me bring it, and now he dares call it his gift. How can I tell how much he has deprived me of? I shall never forgive him.

"But, oh sister, his power over me has been utterly broken. And it is you who have broken it!"

"Brother dear," said I, "if that is so, then my life is justified. But more remains to be done, Amulya. It is not enough that the spell has been destroyed. Its stains must be washed away. Don't delay any longer, go at once and put back the money where you took it from. Can you not do it, dear?"

"With your blessing everything is possible, Sister Rani."

"Remember, it will not be your expiation alone, but mine also. I am a woman; the outside world is closed to me, else I would have gone myself. My hardest punishment is that I must put on you the burden of my sin."

"Don't say that, sister. The path I was treading was not your path. It attracted me because of its dangers and difficulties. Now that your path calls me, let it be a thousand times more difficult and dangerous, the dust of your feet will help me to win through. Is it then your command that this money be replaced?"

"Not my command, brother mine, but a command from above."

"Of that I know nothing. It is enough for me that this command from above comes from your lips. And, sister, I thought I had an invitation here. I must not lose that. You must give me your *prasad** before I go. Then, if I can possibly manage it, I will finish my duty in the evening."

Tears came to my eyes when I tried to smile as I said: "So be it."

---

* Food consecrated by the touch of a revered person

CHAPTER ELEVEN

Bimala's Story

XX

With Amulya's departure my heart sank within me. On what perilous adventure had I sent this only son of his mother? O God, why need my expiation have such pomp and circumstance? Could I not be allowed to suffer alone without inviting all this multitude to share my punishment? Oh, let not this innocent child fall victim to Your wrath.

I called him back—"Amulya!"

My voice sounded so feebly, it failed to reach him.

I went up to the door and called again: "Amulya!"

He had gone.

"Who is there?"

"Rani Mother!"

"Go and tell Amulya Babu that I want him."

What exactly happened I could not make out—the man, perhaps, was not familiar with Amulya's name—but he returned almost at once followed by Sandip.

"The very moment you sent me away," he said as he came in, "I had a presentiment that you would call me back. The attraction of the same moon causes both ebb and flow. I was so sure of being sent for, that I was actually waiting out in the passage. As soon as I caught sight of your man, coming from your room, I said: 'Yes, yes,

641

I am coming, I am coming at once!'—before he could utter a word. That up-country lout was surprised, I can tell you! He stared at me, open-mouthed, as if he thought I knew magic.

"All the fights in the world, Queen Bee," Sandip rambled on, "are really fights between hypnotic forces. Spell cast against spell—noiseless weapons which reach even invisible targets. At last I have met in you my match. Your quiver is full, I know, you artful warrior Queen! You are the only one in the world who has been able to turn Sandip out and call Sandip back, at your sweet will. Well, your quarry is at your feet. What will you do with him now? Will you give him the *coup de grâce*, or keep him in your cage? Let me warn you beforehand, Queen, you will find the beast as difficult to kill outright as to keep in bondage. Anyway, why lose time in trying your magic weapons?"

Sandip must have felt the shadow of approaching defeat, and this made him try to gain time by chattering away without waiting for a reply. I believe he knew that I had sent the messenger for Amulya, whose name the man must have mentioned. In spite of that he had deliberately played this trick. He was now trying to avoid giving me any opening to tell him that it was Amulya I wanted, not him. But his stratagem was futile, for I could see his weakness through it. I must not yield up a pin's point of the ground I had gained.

"Sandip Babu," I said, "I wonder how you can go on making these endless speeches, without a stop. Do you get them up by heart, beforehand?"

Sandip's face flushed instantly.

"I have heard," I continued, "that our professional reciters keep a book full of all kinds of ready-made discourses, which can be fitted into any subject. Have you also a book?"

Sandip ground out his reply through his teeth. "God has given you women a plentiful supply of coquetry to start with, and on the top of that you have the milliner and the jeweller to help you; but do not think we men are so helpless . . ."

"You had better go back and look up your book, Sandip Babu. You are getting your words all wrong. That's just the trouble with trying to repeat things by rote."

"You!" shouted Sandip, losing all control over himself. "You to insult me thus! What is there left of you that I do not know to the very bottom? What . . ." He became speechless.

Sandip, the wielder of magic spells, is reduced to utter powerlessness, whenever his spell refuses to work. From a king he fell to the level of a boor. Oh, the joy of witnessing his weakness! The harsher he became in his rudeness, the more did this joy well up within me. His snaky coils, with which he used to snare me, are exhausted—I am free. I am saved, saved. Be rude to me, insult me, for that shows you in your truth; but spare me your songs of praise, which were false.

My husband came in at this juncture. Sandip had not the elasticity to recover himself in a moment, as he used to do before. My husband looked at him for a while in surprise. Had this happened some days ago I should have felt ashamed. But today I was pleased—whatever my husband might think. I wanted to have it out to the finish with my weakening adversary.

Finding us both silent and constrained, my husband hesitated a little, and then took a chair. "Sandip," he said, "I have been looking for you, and was told you were here."

"I *am* here," said Sandip with some emphasis. "Queen Bee sent for me early this morning. And I, the humble worker of the hive, left all else to attend her summons."

"I am going to Calcutta tomorrow. You will come with me.

"And why, pray? Do you take me for one of your retinue?"

"Oh, very well, take it that you are going to Calcutta, and that I am your follower."

"I have no business there."

"All the more reason for going. You have too much business here."

"I don't propose to stir."

"Then I propose to shift you."

"Forcibly?"

"Forcibly."

"Very well, then, I will make a move. But the world is not divided between Calcutta and your estates. There are other places on the map."

"From the way you have been going on, one would hardly

have thought that there was any other place in the world except my estates."

Sandip stood up. "It does happen at times," he said, "that a man's whole world is reduced to a single spot. I have realised my universe in this sitting room of yours, that is why I have been a fixture here."

Then he turned to me. "None but you, Queen Bee," he said, "will understand my words—perhaps not even you. I salute you. With worship in my heart I leave you. My watchword has changed since you have come across my vision. It is no longer Bande Mataram (Hail Mother), but Hail Beloved, Hail Enchantress. The mother protects, the mistress leads to destruction—but sweet is that destruction. You have made the anklet sounds of the dance of death tinkle in my heart. You have changed for me, your devotee, the picture I had of this Bengal of ours—'the soft breeze-cooled land of pure water and sweet fruit.'* You have no pity, my beloved. You have come to me with your poison cup and I shall drain it, either to die in agony or live triumphing over death.

"Yes," he continued. "The mother's day is past. O love, my love, you have made as naught for me the truth and right and heaven itself. All duties have become as shadows: all rules and restraints have snapped their bonds. O love, my love, I could set fire to all the world outside this land on which you have set your dainty feet, and dance in mad revel over the ashes . . . These are mild men. These are good men. They would do good to all—as if this all were a reality! No, no! There is no reality in the world save this one real love of mine. I do you reverence. My devotion to you has made me cruel; my worship of you has lighted the raging flame of destruction within me. I am not righteous. I have no beliefs, I only believe in her whom, above all else in the world, I have been able to realise."

Wonderful! It was wonderful, indeed. Only a minute ago I had despised this man with all my heart. But what I had thought to be dead ashes now glowed with living fire. The fire in him is true, that is beyond doubt. Oh why has God made man such a mixed creature? Was it only to show his supernatural sleight of hand? Only a few minutes ago I had thought that Sandip, whom I had once taken to

---

* Quotation from the National song 'Bande Mataram.'

be a hero, was only the stage hero of melodrama. But that is not so, not so. Even behind the trappings of the theatre, a true hero may sometimes be lurking.

There is much in Sandip that is coarse, that is sensuous, that is false, much that is overlaid with layer after layer of fleshly covering. Yet—yet it is best to confess that there is a great deal in the depths of him which we do not, cannot understand—much in ourselves too. A wonderful thing is man. What great mysterious purpose he is working out only the Terrible One* knows—meanwhile we groan under the brunt of it. Shiva is the Lord of Chaos. He is all Joy. He will destroy our bonds.

I cannot but feel, again and again, that there are two persons in me. One recoils from Sandip in his terrible aspect of Chaos—the other feels that very vision to be sweetly alluring. The sinking ship drags down all who are swimming round it. Sandip is just such a force of destruction. His immense attraction gets hold of one before fear can come to the rescue, and then, in the twinkling of an eye, one is drawn away, irresistibly, from all light, all good, all freedom of the sky, all air that can be breathed—from lifelong accumulations, from everyday cares—right to the bottom of dissolution.

From some realm of calamity has Sandip come as its messenger; and as he stalks the land, muttering unholy incantations, to him flock all the boys and youths. The mother, seated in the lotus-heart of the Country, is wailing her heart out; for they have broken open her storeroom, there to hold their drunken revelry. Her vintage of the draught for the immortals they would pour out on the dust; her time-honoured vessels they would smash to pieces. True, I feel with her; but, at the same time, I cannot help being infected with their excitement.

Truth itself has sent us this temptation to test our trustiness in upholding its commandments. Intoxication masquerades in heavenly garb, and dances before the pilgrims saying: "Fools you are that pursue the fruitless path of renunciation. Its way is long, its time passing slow. So the Wielder of the Thunderbolt has sent me to you. Behold, I the beautiful, the passionate, I will accept you—in my embrace you shall find fulfilment."

---

* Rudra, the Terrible, a name of Shiva.—*Translator*

After a pause Sandip addressed me again: "Goddess, the time has come for me to leave you. It is well. The work of your nearness has been done. By lingering longer it would only become undone again, little by little. All is lost, if in our greed we try to cheapen that which is the greatest thing on earth. That which is eternal within the moment only becomes shallow if spread out in time. We were about to spoil our infinite moment, when it was your uplifted thunderbolt which came to the rescue. You intervened to save the purity of your own worship—and in so doing you also saved your worshipper. In my leave-taking today your worship stands out the biggest thing. Goddess, I, also, set you free today. My earthen temple could hold you no longer—every moment it was on the point of breaking apart. Today I depart to worship your larger image in a larger temple. I can gain you more truly only at a distance from yourself. Here I had only your favour, there I shall be vouchsafed your boon."

My jewel-casket was lying on the table. I held it up aloft as I said: "I charge you to convey these my jewels to the object of my worship—to whom I have dedicated them through you."

My husband remained silent. Sandip left the room.

XXI

I had just sat down to make some cakes for Amulya when the Bara Rani came upon the scene. "Oh dear," she exclaimed, "has it come to this that you must make cakes for your own birthday?"

"Is there no one else for whom I could be making them?" I asked.

"But this is not the day when you should think of feasting others. It is for us to feast you. I was just thinking of making something up* when I heard the staggering news which completely upset me. A gang of five or six hundred men, they say, has raided one of our treasuries and made off with six thousand rupees. Our house will be looted next, they expect."

I felt greatly relieved. So it was our own money after all. I wanted

---

* Any dainties to be offered ceremonially should be made by the lady of the house herself.—*Translator*

to send for Amulya at once and tell him that he need only hand over those notes to my husband and leave the explanations to me.

"You are a wonderful creature!" my sister-in-law broke out, at the change in my countenance. "Have you then really no such thing as fear?"

"I cannot believe it," I said. "Why should they loot our house?"

"Not believe it, indeed! Who could have believed that they would attack our treasury, either?"

I made no reply, but bent over my cakes, putting in the coconut stuffing.

"Well, I'm off," said the Bara Rani after a prolonged stare at me. "I must see Brother Nikhil and get something done about sending off my money to Calcutta, before it's too late."

She was no sooner gone than I left the cakes to take care of themselves and rushed to my dressing room, shutting myself inside. My husband's tunic with the keys in its pocket was still hanging there—so forgetful was he. I took the key of the iron safe off the ring and kept it by me, hidden in the folds of my dress.

Then there came a knocking at the door. "I am dressing," I called out. I could hear the Bara Rani saying: "Only a minute ago I saw her making cakes and now she is busy dressing up. What next, I wonder! One of their Bande Mataram meetings is on, I suppose. I say, Robber Queen," she called out to me, "are you taking stock of your loot?"

When they went away I hardly know what made me open the safe. Perhaps there was a lurking hope that it might all be a dream. What if, on pulling out the inside drawer, I should find the rolls of gold there, just as before? . . . Alas, everything was empty as the trust which had been betrayed.

I had to go through the farce of dressing. I had to do my hair up all over again, quite unnecessarily. When I came out my sister-in-law railed at me: "How many times are you going to dress today?"

"My birthday!" I said.

"Oh, any pretext seems good enough," she went on. "Many vain people have I seen in my day, but you beat them all hollow."

I was about to summon a servant to send after Amulya, when one of the men came up with a little note, which he handed to me. It was from Amulya. "Sister," he wrote, "you invited me this afternoon, but I thought I should not wait. Let me first execute your bidding and then come for my prasad. I may be a little late."

To whom could he be going to return that money? Into what fresh entanglement was the poor boy rushing? O miserable woman, you can only send him off like an arrow, but not recall him if you miss your aim.

I should have declared at once that I was at the bottom of this robbery. But women live on the trust of their surroundings—this is their whole world. If once it is out that this trust has been secretly betrayed, their place in their world is lost. They have then to stand upon the fragments of the thing they have broken, and its jagged edges keep on wounding them at every turn. To sin is easy enough, but to make up for it is above all difficult for a woman.

For some time past all easy approaches for communion with my husband have been closed to me. How then could I burst on him with this stupendous news? He was very late in coming for his meal today—nearly two o'clock. He was absent-minded and hardly touched any food. I had lost even the right to press him to take a little more. I had to avert my face to wipe away my tears.

I wanted so badly to say to him: "Do come into our room and rest awhile; you look so tired." I had just cleared my throat with a little cough, when a servant hurried in to say that the Police Inspector had brought Panchu up to the palace. My husband, with the shadow on his face deepened, left his meal unfinished and went out.

A little later the Bara Rani appeared. "Why did you not send me word when Brother Nikhil came in?" she complained. "As he was late I thought I might as well finish my bath in the meantime. However did he manage to get through his meal so soon?"

"Why, did you want him for anything?"

"What is this about both of you going off to Calcutta tomorrow? All I can say is, I am not going to be left here alone. I should get startled out of my life at every sound, with all these dacoits about. Is it quite settled about your going tomorrow?"

"Yes," said I, though I had only just now heard it; and though, moreover, I was not at all sure that before tomorrow our history might not take such a turn as to make it all one whether we went or stayed. After that, what our home, our life would be like, was utterly beyond my ken—it seemed so misty and phantom-like.

In a very few hours now my unseen fate would become visible. Was there no one who could keep on postponing the flight of these hours, from day to day, and so make them long enough for me to set things right, so far as lay in my power? The time during which the seed lies underground is long—so long indeed that one forgets that there is any danger of its sprouting. But once its shoot shows up above the surface, it grows and grows so fast, there is no time to cover it up, neither with skirt, nor body, nor even life itself.

I will try to think of it no more, but sit quiet—passive and callous—let the crash come when it may. By the day after tomorrow all will be over—publicity, laughter, bewailing, questions, explanations—everything.

But I cannot forget the face of Amulya—beautiful, radiant with devotion. He did not wait, despairing, for the blow of fate to fall, but rushed into the thick of danger. In my misery I do him reverence. He is my boy-god. Under the pretext of his playfulness he took from me the weight of my burden. He would save me by taking the punishment meant for me on his own head. But how am I to bear this terrible mercy of my God?

Oh, my child, my child, I do you reverence. Little brother mine, I do you reverence. Pure are you, beautiful are you, I do you reverence. May you come to my arms, in the next birth, as my own child—that is my prayer.

XXII

Rumour became busy on every side. The police were continually in and out. The servants of the house were in a great flurry.

Khema, my maid, came up to me and said: "Oh, Rani Mother! for goodness' sake put away my gold necklace and armlets in your iron safe." To whom was I to explain that the Rani herself had been weaving all this network of trouble, and had got caught in it, too? I had to play the benign protector and take charge of Khema's ornaments and Thako's savings. The milk-woman, in her turn, brought along and kept in my room a box in which were a Benares sari and some other of her valued possessions. "I got these at your wedding," she told me.

When, tomorrow, my iron safe will be opened in the presence of these—Khema, Thako, the milk-woman and all the rest . . . Let me not think of it! Let me rather try to think what it will be like when this third day of Magh comes round again after a year has passed. Will all the wounds of my home life then be still as fresh as ever? . . .

Amulya writes that he will come later in the evening. I cannot remain alone with my thoughts, doing nothing. So I sit down again to make cakes for him. I have finished making quite a quantity, but still I must go on. Who will eat them? I shall distribute them amongst the servants. I must do so this very night. Tonight is my limit. Tomorrow will not be in my hands.

I went on untiringly, frying cake after cake. Every now and then it seemed to me that there was some noise in the direction of my rooms, upstairs. Could it be that my husband had missed the key of the safe, and the Bara Rani had assembled all the servants to help him to hunt for it? No, I must not pay heed to these sounds. Let me shut the door.

I rose to do so, when Thako came panting in: "Rani Mother, oh, Rani Mother!"

"Oh get away!" I snapped out, cutting her short. "Don't come bothering me."

"The Bara Rani Mother wants you," she went on. "Her nephew has brought such a wonderful machine from Calcutta. It talks like a man. Do come and hear it!"

I did not know whether to laugh or to cry. So, of all things, a gramophone needs must come on the scene at such a time, repeating at every winding the nasal twang of its theatrical songs! What a fearsome thing results when a machine apes a man.

The shades of evening began to fall. I knew that Amulya would not delay to announce himself—yet I could not wait. I summoned a servant and said: "Go and tell Amulya Babu to come straight in here." The man came back after a while to say that Amulya was not in—he had not come back since he had gone.

"Gone!" The last word struck my ears like a wail in the gathering darkness. Amulya gone! Had he then come like a streak of light from the setting sun, only to be gone for ever? All kinds of possible and impossible dangers flitted through my mind. It was I who had sent him to his death. What if he was fearless? That only showed his own greatness of heart. But after this how was I to go on living all by myself?

I had no memento of Amulya save that pistol—his reverence-offering. It seemed to me that this was a sign given by Providence. This guilt which had contaminated my life at its very root—my God in the form of a child had left with me the means of wiping it away, and then vanished. Oh the loving gift—the saving grave that lay hidden within it!

I opened my box and took out the pistol, lifting it reverently to my forehead. At that moment the gongs clanged out from the temple attached to our house. I prostrated myself in salutation.

In the evening I feasted the whole household with my cakes. "You have managed a wonderful birthday feast—and all by yourself too!" exclaimed my sister-in-law. "But you must leave something for us to do." With this she turned on her gramophone and let loose the shrill treble of the Calcutta actresses all over the place. It seemed like a stable full of neighing fillies.

It got quite late before the feasting was over. I had a sudden longing to end my birthday celebration by taking the dust of my husband's feet. I went up to the bedroom and found him fast asleep. He had had such a worrying, trying day. I raised the edge of the mosquito curtain very, very gently, and laid my head near his feet. My hair must have touched him, for he moved his legs in his sleep and pushed my head away.

I then went out and sat in the west verandah. A silk-cotton tree, which had shed all its leaves, stood there in the distance, like a skeleton. Behind it the crescent moon was setting. All of a sudden I had the feeling that the very stars in the sky were afraid of me—that the whole of the night world was looking askance at me. Why? Because I was alone.

There is nothing so strange in creation as the man who is alone. Even he whose near ones have all died, one by one, is not alone—companionship comes for him from behind the screen of death. But he, whose kin are there, yet no longer near, who has dropped out of all the varied companionship of a full home—the starry universe itself seems to bristle to look on him in his darkness.

Where I am, I am not. I am far away from those who are around me. I live and move upon a worldwide chasm of separation, unstable as the dew-drop upon the lotus leaf.

Why do not men change wholly when they change? When I look into my heart, I find everything that was there, still there—only they are topsy-turvy. Things that were well-ordered have become jumbled up. The gems that were strung into a necklace are now rolling in the dust. And so my heart is breaking.

I feel I want to die. Yet in my heart everything still lives—nor even in death can I see the end of it all: rather, in death there seems to be ever so much more of repining. What is to be ended must be ended in this life—there is no other way out.

Oh forgive me just once, only this time, Lord! All that you gave into my hands as the wealth of my life, I have made into my burden. I can neither bear it longer, nor give it up. O Lord, sound once again those flute strains which you played for me, long ago, standing at the rosy edge of my morning sky—and let all my complexities become simple and easy. Nothing save the music of your flute can make whole that which has been broken, and pure that which has been sullied. Create my home anew with your music. No other way can I see.

I threw myself prone on the ground and sobbed aloud. It was for mercy that I prayed—some little mercy from somewhere, some shelter, some sign of forgiveness, some hope that might bring about the end. "Lord," I vowed to myself, "I will lie here, waiting and waiting, touching neither food nor drink, so long as your blessing does not reach me."

I heard the sound of footsteps. Who says that the gods do not show themselves to mortal men? I did not raise my face to look up, lest the sight of it should break the spell. Come, oh come, come and let your feet touch my head. Come, Lord, and set your foot upon my throbbing heart, and at that moment let me die.

He came and sat near my head. Who? My husband! At the first touch of his presence I felt that I should swoon. And then the pain at my heart burst its way out in an overwhelming flood of tears, tearing through all my obstructing veins and nerves. I strained his feet to my bosom—oh, why could not their impress remain there for ever?

He tenderly stroked my head. I received his blessing. Now I shall be able to take up the penalty of public humiliation which will be mine tomorrow, and offer it, in all sincerity, at the feet of my God.

But what keeps crushing my heart is the thought that the festive flutes which were played at my wedding, nine years ago, welcoming me to this house, will never sound for me again in this life. What rigour of penance is there which can serve to bring me once more, as a bride adorned for her husband, to my place upon that same bridal seat? How many years, how many ages, aeons, must pass before I can find my way back to that day of nine years ago?

God can create new things, but has even He the power to create afresh that which has been destroyed?

CHAPTER TWELVE

Nikhil's Story

XV

Today we are going to Calcutta. Our joys and sorrows lie heavy on us if we merely go on accumulating them. Keeping them and accumulating them alike are false. As master of the house I am in an artificial position—in reality I am a wayfarer on the path of life. That is why the true Master of the House gets hurt at every step and at last there comes the supreme hurt of death.

My union with you, my love, was only of the wayside; it was well enough so long as we followed the same road; it will only hamper us if we try to preserve it further. We are now leaving its bonds behind. We are started on our journey beyond, and it will be enough if we can throw each other a glance, or feel the touch of each other's hands in passing. After that? After that there is the larger world-path, the endless current of universal life.

How little can you deprive me of, my love, after all? Whenever I set my ear to it, I can hear the flute which is playing, its fountain of melody gushing forth from the flute-stops of separation. The immortal draught of the goddess is never exhausted. She sometimes breaks the bowl from which we drink it, only to smile at seeing us so disconsolate over the trifling loss. I will not stop to pick up my broken bowl. I will march forward, albeit with unsatisfied heart.

The Bara Rani came and asked me: "What is the meaning, brother, of all these books being packed up and sent off in box-loads?"

"It only means," I replied, "that I have not yet been able to get over my fondness for them."

"I only wish you would keep your fondness for some other things as well! Do you mean you are never coming back home?"

"I shall be coming and going, but shall not immure myself here anymore."

"Oh indeed! Then just come along to my room and see how many things *I* have been unable to shake off *my* fondness for." With this she took me by the hand and marched me off.

In my sister-in-law's rooms I found numberless boxes and bundles ready packed. She opened one of the boxes and said: "See, brother, look at all my paan-making things. In this bottle I have catechu powder scented with the pollen of screw-pine blossoms. These little tin boxes are all for different kinds of spices. I have not forgotten my playing cards and draught-board either. If you two are over-busy, I shall manage to make other friends there, who will give me a game. Do you remember this comb? It was one of the Swadeshi combs you brought for me . . ."

"But what is all this for, Sister Rani? Why have you been packing up all these things?"

"Do you think I am not going with you?"

"What an extraordinary idea!"

"Don't you be afraid! I am not going there to flirt with you, nor to quarrel with the Chota Rani! One must die sooner or later, and it is just as well to be on the bank of the holy Ganges before it is too late. It is too horrible to think of being cremated in your wretched burning-ground here, under that stumpy banyan tree—that is why I have been refusing to die, and have plagued you all this time."

At last I could hear the true voice of home. The Bara Rani came into our house as its bride, when I was only six years old. We have played together, through the drowsy afternoons, in a corner of the roof-terrace. I have thrown down to her green *amras* from the tree-top, to be made into deliciously indigestible chutnies by slicing them up with mustard, salt and fragrant herbs. It was my part to gather for her all the forbidden things from the storeroom to be used in the marriage celebration of her doll; for, in the penal code of my grandmother, I alone was exempt from punishment. And I used to be appointed her messenger to my brother, whenever she wanted to coax something special out of him, because he could not resist my importunity. I also remember how, when I suffered under the rigorous régime of the doctors of those days—who would not allow anything except warm water and sugared cardamom seeds during feverish attacks—my sister-in-law could not bear my privation and used to bring me delicacies on the sly. What a scolding she got one day when she was caught!

And then, as we grew up, our mutual joys and sorrows took on deeper tones of intimacy. How we quarrelled! Sometimes conflicts of worldly interests roused suspicions and jealousies, making breaches in our love; and when the Chota Rani came in between us, these breaches seemed as if they would never be mended, but it always turned out that the healing forces at bottom proved more powerful than the wounds on the surface.

So has a true relationship grown up between us, from our childhood up till now, and its branching foliage has spread and broadened over every room and verandah and terrace of this great house. When I saw the Bara Rani make ready, with all her belongings, to depart from this house of ours, all the ties that bound us, to their wide-spreading ends, felt the shock.

The reason was clear to me, why she had made up her mind to drift away towards the unknown, cutting asunder all her lifelong bonds of daily habit, and of the house itself, which she had never left for a day since she first entered it at the age of nine. And yet it was this real reason which she could not allow to escape her lips, preferring rather to put forward any other paltry excuse.

She had only this one relationship left in all the world, and the poor, unfortunate, widowed and childless woman had cherished it with all the tenderness hoarded in her heart. How deeply she had felt our proposed separation I never realised so keenly as when I stood amongst her scattered boxes and bundles.

I could see at once that the little differences she used to have with Bimala, about money matters, did not proceed from any sordid worldliness, but because she felt that her claims in regard to this one relationship of her life had been overridden and its ties weakened for her by the coming in between of this other woman from goodness knows where! She had been hurt at every turn and yet had not the right to complain.

And Bimala? She also had felt that the Senior Rani's claim over me was not based merely on our social connection, but went much deeper; and she was jealous of these ties between us, reaching back to our childhood.

Today my heart knocked heavily against the doors of my breast. I sank down upon one of the boxes as I said: "How I should love, Sister Rani, to go back to the days when we first met in this old house of ours."

"No, brother dear," she replied with a sigh, "I would not live my life again—not as a woman! Let what I have had to bear end with this one birth. I could not bear it over again."

I said to her: "The freedom to which we pass through sorrow is greater than the sorrow."

"That may be so for you men. Freedom is for you. But we women would keep others bound. We would rather be put into bondage ourselves. No, no, brother, you will never get free from our toils. If you needs must spread your wings, you will have to take us with you; we refuse to be left behind. That is why I have gathered together all this weight of luggage. It would never do to allow men to run too light."

"I can feel the weight of your words," I said laughing, "and if we men do not complain of your burdens, it is because women pay us so handsomely for what they make us carry."

"You carry it," she said, "because it is made up of many small things. Whichever one you think of rejecting pleads that it is so light. And so with much lightness we weigh you down . . . When do we start?"

"The train leaves at half past eleven tonight. There will be lots of time."

"Look here, do be good for once and listen to just one word of mine. Take a good nap this afternoon. You know you never get any sleep in the train. You look so pulled down, you might go to pieces any moment. Come along, get through your bath first."

As we went towards my room, Khema, the maid, came up and with an ultra-modest pull at her veil told us, in deprecatingly low tones, that the Police Inspector had arrived with a prisoner and wanted to see the Maharaja.

"Is the Maharaja a thief, or a robber," the Bara Rani flared up, "that he should be set upon so by the police? Go and tell the Inspector that the Maharaja is at his bath."

"Let me just go and see what is the matter," I pleaded. "It may be something urgent."

"No, no," my sister-in-law insisted. "Our Chota Rani was making a heap of cakes last night. I'll send some to the Inspector, to keep him quiet till you're ready." With this she pushed me into my room and shut the door on me.

I had not the power to resist such tyranny—so rare is it in this world. Let the Inspector while away the time eating cakes. What if business is a bit neglected?

The police had been in great form these last few days arresting now this one, now that. Each day some innocent person or other would be brought along to enliven the assembly in my office room. One more such unfortunate, I supposed, must have been brought in that day. But why should the Inspector alone be regaled with cakes? That would not do at all. I thumped vigorously on the door.

"If you are going mad, be quick and pour some water over your head—that will keep you cool," said my sister-in-law from the passage.

"Send down cakes for two," I shouted. "The person who has been brought in as the thief probably deserves them better. Tell the man to give him a good big helping."

I hurried through my bath. When I came out, I found Bimal sitting on the floor outside.* Could this be my Bimal of old, my proud, sensitive Bimal?

---

* Sitting on the bare floor is a sign of mourning, and so, by association of ideas, of an abject attitude of mind.—*Translator*

What favour could she be wanting to beg, seated like this at my door?

As I stopped short, she stood up and said gently with downcast eyes: "I would have a word with you."

"Come inside then," I said.

"But are you going out on any particular business?"

"I was, but let that be. I want to hear . . ."

"No, finish your business first. We will have our talk after you have had your dinner."

I went off to my sitting room, to find the Police Inspector's plate quite empty. The person he had brought with him, however, was still busy eating.

"Hullo!" I ejaculated in surprise. "You, Amulya?"

"It is I, sir," said Amulya with his mouth full of cake. "I've had quite a feast. And if you don't mind, I'll take the rest with me." With this he proceeded to tie up the remaining cakes in his handkerchief.

"What does this mean?" I asked, staring at the Inspector.

The man laughed. "We are no nearer, sir," he said, "to solving the problem of the thief: meanwhile the mystery of the theft deepens." He then produced something tied up in a rag, which when untied disclosed a bundle of currency notes. "This, Maharaja," said the Inspector, "is your six thousand rupees!"

"Where was it found?"

"In Amulya Babu's hands. He went last evening to the manager of your Chakna sub-office to tell him that the money had been found. The manager seemed to be in a greater state of trepidation at the recovery than he had been at the robbery. He was afraid he would be suspected of having made away with the notes and of now making up a cock-and-bull story for fear of being found out. He asked Amulya to wait, on the pretext of getting him some refreshment, and came straight over to the Police Office. I rode off at once, kept Amulya with me, and have been busy with him the whole morning. He refuses to tell us where he got the money from. I warned him he would be kept under restraint till he did so. In that case, he informed me he would have to lie. Very well, I said, he might do so if he pleased. Then he stated that he had found the money under a bush. I pointed out to him that it was not quite so easy to lie as all that. Under what bush? Where was the place? Why was he there?—All this would have to be stated as well. 'Don't you worry,' he said, 'there is plenty of time to invent all that.'"

"But, Inspector," I said, "why are you badgering a respectable young gentleman like Amulya Babu?"

"I have no desire to harass him," said the Inspector. "He is not only a gentleman, but the son of Nibaran Babu, my school-fellow. Let me tell you, Maharaja, exactly what must have happened. Amulya knows the thief, but wants to shield him by drawing suspicion on himself. That is just the sort of bravado he loves to indulge in." The Inspector turned to Amulya. "Look here, young man," he continued, "I also was eighteen once upon a time, and a student in the Ripon College. I nearly got into gaol trying to rescue a hack driver from a police constable. It was a near shave." Then he turned again to me and said: "Maharaja, the real thief will now probably escape, but I think I can tell you who is at the bottom of it all."

"Who is it, then?" I asked.

"The manager, in collusion with the guard, Kasim."

When the Inspector, having argued out his theory to his own satisfaction, at last departed, I said to Amulya: "If you will tell me who took the money, I promise you no one shall be hurt."

"I did," said he.

"But how can that be? What about the gang of armed men? . . ."

"It was I, by myself, alone!"

What Amulya then told me was indeed extraordinary. The manager had just finished his supper and was on the verandah rinsing out his mouth. The place was somewhat dark. Amulya had a revolver in each pocket, one loaded with blank cartridges, the other with ball. He had a mask over his face. He flashed a bull's-eye lantern in the manager's face and fired a blank shot. The man swooned away. Some of the guards, who were off duty, came running up, but when Amulya fired another blank shot at them they lost no time in taking cover. Then Kasim, who was on duty, came up whirling a quarterstaff. This time Amulya aimed a bullet at his legs, and finding himself hit, Kasim collapsed on the floor. Amulya then made the trembling manager, who had come to his senses, open the safe and deliver up six thousand rupees. Finally, he took one of the estate horses and galloped off a few miles, there let the animal loose, and quietly walked up here, to our place.

"What made you do all this, Amulya?" I asked.

"There was a grave reason, Maharaja," he replied.

"But why, then, did you try to return the money?"

"Let her come, at whose command I did so. In her presence I shall make a clean breast of it."

"And who may 'she' be?"

"My sister, the Chota Rani!"

I sent for Bimala. She came hesitatingly, barefoot, with a white shawl over her head. I had never seen my Bimal like this before. She seemed to have wrapped herself in a morning light.

Amulya prostrated himself in salutation and took the dust of her feet. Then, as he rose, he said: "Your command has been executed, sister. The money is returned."

"You have saved me, my little brother," said Bimal.

"With your image in my mind, I have not uttered a single lie," Amulya continued. "My watchword Bande Mataram has been cast away at your feet for good. I have also received my reward, your prasad, as soon as I came to the palace."

Bimal looked at him blankly, unable to follow his last words. Amulya brought out his handkerchief, and untying it showed her the cakes put away inside. "I did not eat them all," he said. "I have kept these to eat after you have helped me with your own hands."

I could see that I was not wanted here. I went out of the room. I could only preach and preach, so I mused, and get my effigy burnt for my pains. I had not yet been able to bring back a single soul from the path of death. They who have the power, can do so by a mere sign. My words have not that ineffable meaning. I am not a flame, only a black coal, which has gone out. I can light no lamp. That is what the story of my life shows—my row of lamps has remained unlit.

XVI

I returned slowly towards the inner apartments. The Bara Rani's room must have been drawing me again. It had become an absolute necessity for me, that day, to feel that this life of mine had been able to strike some real, some responsive chord in some other harp of life. One cannot realise one's own existence by remaining within oneself—it has to be sought outside.

As I passed in front of my sister-in-law's room, she came out saying: "I was afraid you would be late again this afternoon. However, I ordered your dinner as soon as I heard you coming. It will be served in a minute."

"Meanwhile," I said; "let me take out that money of yours and have it kept ready to take with us."

As we walked on towards my room she asked me if the Police Inspector had made any report about the robbery. I somehow did not feel inclined to tell her all the details of how that six thousand had come back. "That's just what all the fuss is about," I said evasively.

When I went into my dressing room and took out my bunch of keys, I did not find the key of the iron safe on the ring. What an absurdly absent-minded fellow I was, to be sure! Only this morning I had been opening so many boxes and things, and never noticed that this key was not there.

"What has happened to your key?" she asked me.

I went on fumbling in this pocket and that, but could give her no answer. I hunted in the same place over and over again. It dawned on both of us that it could not be a case of the key being mislaid. Someone must have taken it off the ring. Who could it be? Who else could have come into this room?

"Don't you worry about it," she said to me. "Get through your dinner first. The Chota Rani must have kept it herself, seeing how absent-minded you are getting."

I was, however, greatly disturbed. It was never Bimal's habit to take any key of mine without telling me about it. Bimal was not present at my meal-time that day: she was busy feasting Amulya in her own room. My sister-in-law wanted to send for her, but I asked her not to do so.

I had just finished my dinner when Bimal came in. I would have preferred not to discuss the matter of the key in the Bara Rani's presence, but as soon as she saw Bimal, she asked her: "Do you know, dear, where the key of the safe is?"

"I have it," was the reply.

"Didn't I say so!" exclaimed my sister-in-law triumphantly. "Our Chota Rani pretends not to care about these robberies, but she takes precautions on the sly, all the same."

The look on Bimal's face made my mind misgive me. "Let the key be, now," I said. "I will take out that money in the evening."

"There you go again, putting it off," said the Bara Rani. "Why not take it out and send it to the treasury while you have it in mind?"

"I have taken it out already," said Bimal.

I was startled.

"Where have you kept it, then?" asked my sister-in-law.

"I have spent it."

"Just listen to her! Whatever did you spend all that money on?"

Bimal made no reply. I asked her nothing further. The Bara Rani seemed about to make some further remark to Bimala, but checked herself. "Well, that is all right, anyway," she said at length, as she looked towards me. "Just what I used to do with my husband's loose cash. I knew it was no use leaving it with him—his hundred and one hangers-on would be sure to get hold of it. You are much the same, dear! What a number of ways you men know of getting through money. We can only save it from you by stealing it ourselves! Come along now. Off with you to bed."

The Bara Rani led me to my room, but I hardly knew where I was going. She sat by my bed after I was stretched on it, and smiled at Bimal as she said: "Give me one of your paans, Chotie darling— what? You have none! You have become a regular mem-sahib. Then send for some from my room."

"But have you had your dinner yet?" I anxiously enquired.

"Oh long ago," she replied—clearly a fib.

She kept on chattering away there at my bedside, on all manner of things. The maid came and told Bimal that her dinner had been served and was getting cold, but she gave no sign of having heard it. "Not had your dinner yet? What nonsense! It's fearfully late." With this the Bara Rani took Bimal away with her.

I could divine that there was some connection between the taking out of this six thousand and the robbing of the other. But I have no curiosity to learn the nature of it. I shall never ask.

Providence leaves our life moulded in the rough—its object being that we ourselves should put the finishing touches, shaping it into its final form to our taste. There has always been the hankering within me to express some great idea in the process of giving shape to my life on the lines suggested by the Creator. In this endeavour I have spent all my days. How severely I have curbed my desires, repressed myself at every step, only the Searcher of the Heart knows.

But the difficulty is, that one's life is not solely one's own. He who would create it must do so with the help of his surroundings, or he will fail. So it was my constant dream to draw Bimal to join me in this work of creating myself. I loved her with all my soul; on the strength of that, I could not but succeed in winning her to my purpose—that was my firm belief.

Then I discovered that those who could simply and naturally draw their environment into the process of their self-creation belonged to one species of the genus 'man,'—and I to another. I had received the vital spark, but could not impart it. Those to whom I have surrendered my all have taken my all, but not myself with it.

My trial is hard indeed. Just when I want a helpmate most, I am thrown back on myself alone. Nevertheless, I record my vow that even in this trial I shall win through. Alone, then, shall I tread my thorny path to the end of this life's journey . . .

I have begun to suspect that there has all along been a vein of tyranny in me. There was a despotism in my desire to mould my relations with Bimala in a hard, clear-cut, perfect form. But man's life was not meant to be cast in a mould. And if we try to shape the good, as so much mere material, it takes a terrible revenge by losing its life.

I did not realise all this while that it must have been this unconscious tyranny of mine which made us gradually drift apart. Bimala's life, not finding its true level by reason of my pressure from above, has had to find an outlet by undermining its banks at the bottom. She has had to steal this six thousand rupees because she could not be open with me, because she felt that, in certain things, I despotically differed from her.

Men, such as I, possessed with one idea, are indeed at one with those who can manage to agree with us; but those who do not, can only get on with us by cheating us. It is our unyielding obstinacy, which drives even the simplest to tortuous ways. In trying to manufacture a helpmate, we spoil a wife.

Could I not go back to the beginning? Then, indeed, I should follow the path of the simple. I should not try to fetter my life's companion with my ideas, but play the joyous pipes of my love and say: "Do you love me? Then may you grow true to yourself in the light of your love. Let my suggestions be suppressed, let God's design, which is in you, triumph, and my ideas retire abashed."

But can even Nature's nursing heal the open wound, into which our accumulated differences have broken out? The covering veil, beneath the privacy of which Nature's silent forces alone can work, has been torn asunder. Wounds must be bandaged—can we not bandage our wound with our love, so that the day may come when its scar will no longer be visible? It is not too late? So much time has been lost in misunderstanding; it has taken right up to now to come to an understanding; how much more time will it take for the correcting? What if the wound does eventually heal?—can the devastation it has wrought ever be made good?

There was a slight sound near the door. As I turned over I saw Bimala's retreating figure through the open doorway. She must have been waiting by the door, hesitating whether to come in or not, and at last have decided to go back. I jumped up and bounded to the door, calling: "Bimala."

She stopped on her way. She had her back to me. I went and took her by the hand and led her into our room. She threw herself face downwards on a pillow, and sobbed and sobbed. I said nothing, but held her hand as I sat by her head.

When her storm of grief had abated she sat up. I tried to draw her to my breast, but she pushed my arms away and knelt at my feet, touching them repeatedly with her head, in obeisance. I hastily drew my feet back, but she clasped them in her arms, saying in a choking voice: "No, no, no, you must not take away your feet. Let me do my worship."

I kept still. Who was I to stop her? Was I the god of her worship that I should have any qualms?

Bimala's Story

XXIII

Come, come! Now is the time to set sail towards that great confluence, where the river of love meets the sea of worship. In that pure blue all the weight of its muddiness sinks and disappears.

I now fear nothing—neither myself, nor anybody else. I have passed through fire. What was inflammable has been burnt to ashes; what is left is deathless. I have dedicated myself to the feet of him, who has received all my sin into the depths of his own pain.

Tonight we go to Calcutta. My inward troubles have so long prevented my looking after my things. Now let me arrange and pack them.

After a while I found my husband had come in and was taking a hand in the packing.

"This won't do," I said. "Did you not promise me you would have a sleep?"

"I might have made the promise," he replied, "but my sleep did not, and it was nowhere to be found."

"No, no," I repeated, "this will never do. Lie down for a while, at least."

"But how can you get through all this alone?"

"Of course I can."

"Well, you may boast of being able to do without me. But frankly I can't do without you. Even sleep refused to come to me, alone, in that room." Then he set to work again.

But there was an interruption, in the shape of a servant, who came and said that Sandip Babu had called and had asked to be announced. I did not dare to ask whom he wanted. The light of the sky seemed suddenly to be shut down, like the leaves of a sensitive plant.

"Come, Bimala," said my husband. "Let us go and hear what Sandip has to tell us. Since he has come back again, after taking his leave, he must have something special to say."

I went, simply because it would have been still more embarrassing to stay. Sandip was staring at a picture on the wall. As we entered he said: "You must be wondering why the fellow has returned. But you know the ghost is never laid till all the rites are complete." With these words he brought out of his pocket something tied in his handkerchief, and laying it on the table, undid the knot. It was those sovereigns.

"Don't you mistake me, Nikhil," he said. "You must not imagine that the contagion of your company has suddenly turned me honest; I am not the man to come back in slobbering repentance to return ill-gotten money. But . . ."

He left his speech unfinished. After a pause he turned towards Nikhil, but said to me: "After all these days, Queen Bee, the ghost of compunction has found an entry into my hitherto untroubled conscience. As I have to wrestle with it every night, after my first sleep is over, I cannot call it a phantom of my imagination. There is no escape even for me till its debt is paid. Into the hands of that spirit, therefore, let me make restitution. Goddess! From you, alone, of all the world, I shall not be able to take away anything. I shall not be rid of you till I am destitute. Take these back!"

He took out at the same time the jewel-casket from under his tunic and put it down, and then left us with hasty steps.

"Listen to me, Sandip," my husband called after him.

"I have not the time, Nikhil," said Sandip as he paused near the door. "The Mussulmans, I am told, have taken me for an invaluable gem, and are conspiring to loot me and hide me away in their graveyard. But I feel that it is necessary that I should live. I have just twenty-five minutes to catch the North-bound train. So, for the present, I must be gone. We shall have our talk out at the next convenient opportunity. If you take my advice, don't you delay in getting away either. I salute you, Queen Bee, Queen of the bleeding hearts, Queen of desolation!"

Sandip then left almost at a run. I stood stock-still; I had never realised in such a manner before, how trivial, how paltry, this gold and these jewels were. Only a short while ago I was so busy thinking what I should take with me, and how I should pack it. Now I felt that there was no need to take anything at all. To set out and go forth was the important thing.

My husband left his seat and came up and took me by the hand. "It is getting late," he said. "There is not much time left to complete our preparations for the journey."

At this point Chandranath Babu suddenly came in. Finding us both together, he fell back for a moment. Then he said, "Forgive me, my little mother, if I intrude. Nikhil, the Mussulmans are out of hand. They are looting Harish Kundu's treasury. That does not so much matter. But what is intolerable is the violence that is being done to the women of their house."

"I am off," said my husband.

"What can you do there?" I pleaded, as I held him by the hand. "Oh, sir," I appealed to his master. "Will you not tell him not to go?"

"My little mother," he replied, "there is no time to do anything else."

"Don't be alarmed, Bimala," said my husband, as he left us.

When I went to the window I saw my husband galloping away on horseback, with not a weapon in his hands.

In another minute the Bara Rani came running in. "What have you done, Chotie darling," she cried. "How could you let him go?"

"Call the Dewan at once," she said, turning to a servant.

The Ranis never appeared before the Dewan, but the Bara Rani had no thought that day for appearances.

"Send a mounted man to bring back the Maharaja at once," she said, as soon as the Dewan came up.

"We have all entreated him to stay, Rani Mother," said the Dewan, "but he refused to turn back."

"Send word to him that the Bara Rani is ill, that she is on her deathbed," cried my sister-in-law wildly.

When the Dewan had left she turned on me with a furious outburst. "Oh, you witch, you ogress, you could not die yourself, but needs must send him to his death! . . ."

The light of the day began to fade. The sun set behind the feathery foliage of the blossoming Sajna tree. I can see every different shade of that sunset even today. Two masses of cloud on either side of the sinking orb made it look like a great bird with fiery-feathered wings outspread. It seemed to me that this fateful day was taking its flight, to cross the ocean of night.

It became darker and darker. Like the flames of a distant village on fire, leaping up every now and then above the horizon, a distant din swelled up in recurring waves into the darkness.

The bells of the evening worship rang out from our temple. I knew the Bara Rani was sitting there, with palms joined in silent prayer. But I could not move a step from the window.

The roads, the village beyond, and the still more distant fringe of trees, grew more and more vague. The lake in our grounds looked up into the sky with a dull lustre, like a blind man's eye. On the left the tower seemed to be craning its neck to catch sight of something that was happening.

The sounds of night take on all manner of disguises. A twig snaps, and one thinks that somebody is running for his life. A door slams, and one feels it to be the sudden heart-thump of a startled world.

Lights would suddenly flicker under the shade of the distant trees, and then go out again. Horses' hoofs would clatter, now and again, only to turn out to be riders leaving the palace gates.

I continually had the feeling that, if only I could die, all this turmoil would come to an end. So long as I was alive my sins would remain rampant, scattering destruction on every side. I remembered the pistol in my box. But my feet refused to leave the window in quest of it. Was I not awaiting my fate?

The gong of the watch solemnly struck ten. A little later, groups of lights appeared in the distance and a great crowd wound its way, like some great serpent, along the roads in the darkness, towards the palace gates.

The Dewan rushed to the gate at the sound. Just then a rider came galloping in. "What's the news, Jata?" asked the Dewan.

"Not good," was the reply.

I could hear these words distinctly from my window. But something was next whispered which I could not catch.

Then came a palanquin, followed by a litter. The doctor was walking alongside the palanquin.

"What do you think, doctor?" asked the Dewan.

"Can't say yet," the doctor replied. "The wound in the head is a serious one."

"And Amulya Babu?"

"He has a bullet through the heart. He is done for."